SOCIAL THOUGHT
IN THE
SOVIET UNION

SOCIAL THOUGHT

IN THE

SOVIET UNION

EDITED WITH AN INTRODUCTION
BY

ALEX SIMIRENKO

CHICAGO

QUADRANGLE BOOKS

Library of Congress Catalog Card Number: 68-26449

Designed by Vincent Torre

Preface

This collection of original essays on Soviet social sciences describes the nature and problems of each of the eleven disciplines: philosophy, political science, law, historiography, economics, education, psychology, psychiatry, linguistics, anthropology, and sociology. An opening chapter on the ideology of the Soviet social sciences is also provided. Since the paths of development and problems of each of the disciplines are quite diverse, it did not seem advisable to impose an artificial uniformity upon the essays. The major leitmotiv of these contributions is the changes undergone by the various social sciences since Stalin's death and their contributions to knowledge of both national and international significance. While the work by the nature of the subject is of particular interest to Sovietologists, it is primarily designed for the general audience of social scientists and intelligent laymen. It is an attempt to familiarize readers with the formal side of current Soviet social thought and the conditions of its development.

The background of authors contributing to the collection corresponds with the major task of the project. Each contributor on a particular social science is first of all a specialist in his own discipline who at the same time follows the development of his chosen field in the Soviet Union. Persons with such qualifications are rare, and I am indebted to many scholars for their kind advice. I would especially like to thank the following persons, in addition to the contributors, for making the book possible: Carl W. Backman, Josef Brozek, Michael Cole, Ethel Dunn, K. Peter Etzkorn, George Feifer, Jan Hajda, Irving L. Horowitz, James Hulse, Peter Juviler, Walter Laqueur, Anatole G. Mazour, Harold J. Noah, Nicholas V. Riasanovsky, Paul F. Secord, H. Gordon Skilling, Dan I. Slobin, and Reginald Zelnik.

An essay on education failed to materialize before the volume went to the printer and had to be replaced by previously published material. Thanks are due to Professor Urie Bronfenbrenner for graciously consenting on short notice to edit and revise two of his papers. The Religious Education Association and the American Psychological Association have given their permission to reprint parts of these articles.

The project could not have been brought to fruition without the aid and encouragement of Ivan R. Dee, whose wise editorial counsel and patience are gratefully acknowledged.

ALEX SIMIRENKO

Reno, Nevada, 1968

Contents

SOCIAL THOUGHT
IN THE
SOVIET UNION

Introduction

The Development of Soviet Social Science

Alex Simirenko

A conscious and continuous development of science in the Russian Empire coincides with the rein of Peter the Great, who in the short span of thirty-six years, from 1689 to 1725, succeeded in establishing science and scientific education as integral parts of Russian life. The establishment of science in Russia followed the peculiarly Russian pattern which was so well described a century later by Madame de Staël:

> A gigantic quality in all things characterizes this nation; ordinary dimensions do not at all apply to it. I do not mean by this that neither true greatness nor stability are to be found in it. But the boldness, the imagination, of the Russians knows no bounds. Among them everything is colossal rather than proportional, audacious rather than thoughtful, and if the target is not hit it is because it is overshot.[1]

What better way is there to characterize Peter's founding of the St. Petersburg Academy of Sciences (1724) in a country which had hardly a single scientist worthy of the name, or the creation of the university attached to the academy in a country which had no students to fill it? Both faculty and students had to be imported from western Europe. This bold venture, however, made it possible for Russian-born and -educated scientists like Michael Lomonosov to make their appearance shortly after the establishment of these institutions. The academy, known today as the Academy of Sciences of the U.S.S.R., has remained to this day the most important institution guiding the development of Russian natural and social sciences.

Continuities in the Development of Russian Science

The history of Russian science can be divided into a number of periods in its 250 years of growth. There are, nevertheless, significant continuities in this development which survived even the cataclysmic events of the Revolution. Throughout the years the principle was established that the support and direction of science are concerns of the state, and that scientists are therefore servants of the state. Alexander Vucinich, the foremost student of Russian science, makes the following evaluation of Peter the Great as the founder of this principle:

His [Peter's] historical significance and his most singular contribution lay in the realm of the control and guidance of scientific pursuits: he made science a "government science," a body of knowledge guided and guarded by the state. This legacy has remained unaltered, if not unchallenged, to the present day. Since Peter's time the state has controlled scientific pursuits by choosing the fields requiring scientific inquiry, by imposing ideological limitations on scientific theory, and by defining the educational policies and the social criteria for selecting the men of science.[2]

Another persisting feature of Russian and Soviet science is an unrestrained willingness to borrow ideas from other countries. The nation that has contributed more than any other to the development of Russian knowledge is Germany. In the words of Walter Laqueur, "there was no nation the Russians admired more; the Germans were the masters, the teachers, the ideal to be imitated by successive generations of young Russian intellectuals." [3] Leibniz was one of Peter's major advisers in the fields of science and education, and Peter's successors staffed the newly formed scientific institutions with predominantly German scientists. Lappo-Danilevsky reported that of 107 members of the academy in the eighteenth century, only 31 members (28.97 percent) were of Slavic origin. The remaining 76 academicians were foreigners, among whom Germans constituted about 65 percent of the total.[4]

During the past fifty years the leaders of Soviet society have also shown a willingness to adopt or adapt Western knowledge to the service of the state. Even in the contest between ideas and ideology there have been many victories on the side of what were considered ideologically dangerous ideas, such as, for example, Heisenberg's principle of indeterminacy, cybernetics, and symbolic logic.[5] In sociology they borrowed many techniques that until recently were considered inappropriate, such as sampling of population and factor analysis. On the more mundane technical level of contemporary borrowing of ideas, the large Soviet organization called *Gostekhnika* (State Committee on New Technology), for example, employs thousands of people processing information on new ideas in the fields of science and technology developed in the West.

The development of science in the Russian Empire and the Soviet Union has also progressed because the state has been able to draw scientific talent from the lower classes of society and from the national minorities as well. Michael Lomonosov, one of the first Russian academicians, a son of a peasant shipbuilder, was given a chance to study at the theological academies of both Moscow and Kiev, and later continued his education at St. Petersburg University, attached to the Academy of Sciences, and in Germany. Toward the turn of the twentieth century, a period that produced many Russian men of genius, many eminent scientists also came from humble situations. Pitirim Sorokin, Russia's greatest sociologist, was born and raised in a northern village, in a family with an alcoholic artisan father. Sorokin's mother died when he was three or four, and at the age of eleven he left his native village to work for a living. The proletarian revolution and subsequent educational policies (at least in the first two decades) broadened the opportunities for able youngsters from peasant and worker homes to achieve scientific careers. Tolerance of lower-class mobility into scientific fields has not been uniform. The reign of Nicholas I, like the present period of Soviet history, was characterized by the raising of barriers against mobility. But even for these periods it is difficult to tell exactly what effect the tightening of controls has had upon the selection of top talent for scientific careers.

While tolerance of minorities had always been pronounced in the field of Russian science, the Revolution did produce a change in the kinds of minorities given access to key scientific positions in the country. In the prerevolutionary period, native minority scholars were primarily either Finns, Latvians, Estonians, Lithuanians, Belorussians, or Ukrainians. The postrevolutionary period has been characterized by the rise of scientists from many of the other nationalities that make up the Soviet Union, particularly among the Jews, who encountered much discrimination in education in the earlier period.

Finally, in any discussion of the dominant continuities in the development of Russian science it is necessary to mention a certain intangible sociopsychological predisposition on the part of Russian students to assimilate ideas alien to them and their culture. Russians studying abroad in prerevolutionary times had always received praise from their professors for their receptivity to ideas and their intellectual curiosity. Nicholas Berdyaev chose to explain this trait of the Russian intelligentsia as a "lack of roots in the soil, a break with all class life and traditions." [6] Whether this receptivity to ideas has been affected by the Revolution and subsequent developments is open to question. The ethnocentrism and dogmatism fostered in the postrevolutionary period testify only to a temporary suspension of receptivity, not necessarily to its elimination. Berdyaev has argued, in fact, that the receptivity of a Russian has always been directed toward a search for a new idol. Even if this questionable thesis should be true, the new Soviet scientist is no longer the same man that Berdyaev knew at the turn of the century, and this new scientist is a man about whom we know practically nothing.

Stages in the Development of Soviet Social Science

Four major periods in the development of Soviet social science are discernible. These periods can be distinguished both according to the scientific accomplishment of the age and according to the economic structure of society at the time. The stages are portrayed in the following table:

Stages in the Development of Soviet Social Science

YEARS	CLASSIFICATION BY ACCOMPLISHMENT	CLASSIFICATION BY THE ECONOMIC STRUCTURE
1689–1861	Pioneering period	Feudal period
1861–1917	Classical period	Capitalist period
1917–1956	Period of decline	Early socialist period
1956–	Period of revival	Modern socialist period

PIONEERING PERIOD

The pioneering period was characterized by the dependence of Russian social science upon the work and ideas of foreigners. This influence was carried into the nineteenth century, and was noted by Madame de Staël, who wrote: "In Moscow I saw the most enlightened men in the field of the sciences and literature. But there, as at Petersburg, almost all the professorial posts are filled by Germans." [7] To this day the work of German scholars remains imprinted on Soviet science. Even the broad definition of science itself in the sense of *Wissenschaft* is still largely accepted by present-day Soviet social scientists. The term "science" is understood to include such studies as philosophy, law, history, and literary criticism.

The newly established St. Petersburg Academy of Sciences had three divisions. The mathematical division consisted of four chairs, of which one was intended for the study of mathematics, one for the study of astronomy, geography, and navigation, and two for the study of mechanics. The division of physical sciences was also alloted four chairs, in the areas of theoretical and experimental physics, anatomy, chemistry, and botany. The division of humanities was limited to three chairs: one chair was alloted for the study of rhetoric and classics, one chair for ancient and modern history, and the remaining chair for the study of law, politics, and ethics. [8]

The first courses taught in the academy and the attached university were in law (including Russian law), moral philosophy, history (including Russian history), and Greek and Roman antiquities. Foreign scholars who laid the foundation for the study of Russian history, law, and institutions were G. S. Bayer, a Königsberg-born professor of classics who arrived in 1725; G. F. Müller, professor of history, who arrived in 1725; J. E. Fischer, professor of history and classics, who arrived in 1732; F. H. Strube de Piedmont, a Piedmont-born professor of law who arrived in 1738; A. L. Schlözer, professor of history, who arrived in 1762; and J. G. Stritter, professor of history, who arrived in 1779. [9]

According to Struve, however, the real development in the social sciences began at the University of Moscow (established in 1755) and not at St. Petersburg. Here the professors were drawn from abroad and from among the newly graduated students of the St. Petersburg Academy, and were divided into the three faculties of law, medicine, and philosophy. The faculty of law taught subjects of natural law, international law, Roman law, public law of the Holy Roman Empire, general and Russian jurisprudence, and politics. The faculty of philosophy taught, in addition to the various philosophical subjects, general and Russian history. It was at the University of Moscow that a disciple of Kant named Schaden lectured, from 1776, on subjects of natural law and politics, and became the teacher of Nicholas Karamzin, the leading Russian historian of the first half of the nineteenth century.[10] It should be noted, however, that Karamzin (1766–1826) was an independent scholar who was not associated with any scholarly institution. There were many such private but generally obscure scholars scattered throughout the Russian Empire during the nineteenth century, men who concerned themselves largely with philosophical and historical subjects.

Perhaps even more important developments in the social sciences occurred outside the academy and the various institutions of learning. From the very beginning of his reign, Peter the Great was intensely interested in the exploration of his empire. He sent surveyors to explore Astrakhan, Kazan, Kamchatka, and many other areas. The exploration of Siberia was undertaken under Peter's direction by Daniel Messerschmidt, who "was assigned by contract to study the area's geography, natural history, medicine, medicinal plants, epidemic diseases, historical documents and antiquities, and 'everything deserving attention.' "[11] Messerschmidt, a learned Danzig physician with a knowledge of Oriental languages, brought back a wealth of valuable data on that yet unknown area of the empire, including maps, rare ores, medicinal herbs, comparative analyses of native languages, and much more. But Peter's greatest contribution to the exploration of the Russian Empire was the so-called Bering expedition, or, as it was officially entitled, the First Kamchatka Expedition (1725–30).[12]

Although Peter was greatly interested in the geographic and ethnographic explorations, he also paid considerable attention to the study of Russian history, particularly the period of his own reign. Perhaps the best of the work in this area is to be found in *The History of the Swedish War*, a book that Peter himself edited, and which contains accounts of the war, official Russian documents, detailed descriptions of the Russian army, and the history of Russian diplomacy.[13]

The development of the social sciences in the pioneering period was further facilitated by the growth of the universities. Four new universities (in addition to that of Moscow) were established: Kazan (1804), Leningrad (1819), Kharkov (1805), and Kiev (1834) Universities. Three more universities were added to the list through the extension of the frontiers of the Russian Empire to include Lithuania, Latvia, and Estonia.[14] Many learned societies and associations also received their start in this period. These included the Free Economic Society in St. Petersburg (1765), the Friendly Society of Learning in Moscow (1782), the Society of Russian History and Antiquity (1805), and the Society of Experimental Science (1805).[15] The efforts of private individuals of wealth and standing, such as Nicholas Rumyantsev (or Rumiantsov), contributed to study and publication in the fields of geography and history.

On the ideological level, the pioneering period represents a struggle between two factions of the newly emerging intelligentsia: Slavophiles and Westernizers. The introduction of western European learning into Russia brought an inevitable stirring among its educated men and weakened the ideological foundations of the Russian Orthodox Church, upon which the tsarist regime rested. Slavophiles were convinced Russian nationalists who condemned Peter's historical role and who tried to save tsarism and feudalism by intellectualizing the stale ideology of the church. The most famous of them in this period were I. V. Kireevsky (1806–56), A. S. Khomiakov (1804–60), the brothers K. S. Aksakov (1817–60) and I. S. Aksakov (1823–86), and Iu. F. Samarin (1819–76). The major antagonists of the Slavophiles were A. I. Herzen (1812–70), T. N. Granovsky (1813–55), N. P. Ogariov (1813–77), V. P. Botkin (1812–69), and V. G. Belinsky (1811–48). Westernizers approved Peter's introduction of Western learning and knowledge into Russia and demanded further changes in the autocratic government of Russia in the direction of constitutionalism and liberalism. Consequently, the major stake in the struggle between Slavophiles and Westernizers was the future of Russia. Nevertheless, both factions joined in their opposition to Western capitalism, which they condemned as inappropriate for Russia. This agreement was not apparent in the heated debates of the 1840's, and was recognized only later by Alexander Herzen in his marvelous memoirs:

> The Slavophiles are to blame for our having so long failed to understand the Russian people and its history; their ikon-painter's ideals and incense smoke hindered us from seeing the realities of the people's existence and the foundations of village life.
> The orthodoxy of the Slavophiles, their historical patriotism and oversensitive, exaggerated feeling of nationality were called forth by the extremes on the other side. The importance of their outlook, what was true and essential in it, lay not in orthodoxy, and not in exclusive nationalism, but in those elements of Russian life which they unearthed from under the manure of civilization.[16]

CLASSICAL PERIOD

The classical period represents the golden age of Russian science, when it was no longer entirely dependent upon the work of foreigners and produced men of international genius. Even a cursory examination of the period would fill many volumes. In the West this period of Russian history is better known for the work of its many brilliant writers, along with some successes in the natural sciences achieved by men like Mendeleev. Nevertheless, the period is also extremely rich in the new ideas produced by the social sciences and the humanities relevant to the social sciences. Outstanding in the fields of physiology and psychology are such distinguished men as Sechenov, Pavlov, and Bekhterev; in statistics, Tchuprov; in history, Rostovtsev, Lappo-Danilevsky, Kliuchevsky, Vinogradoff, and many others; in economics, Tugan-Baranovsky, Struve, Ziber, and Bulgakov; in jurisprudence, Petrazycki, Novgorodtsev, and Korkunov; in political science, Ostrogorski and Lenin; in sociology, Lilienfeld, Novicow, Danilevsky, Mikhailovsky, Kovalevsky, De Roberty, Kropotkin, Lavrov, Plekhanov, Kareev, and Sorokin; in ethnography, Miklukho-Maklai, Anuchin, Schurovsky, Bogdanov, Miller, and hundreds of other ethnographers of many nationalities who gathered folklore material of their own people; in philosophy, Solovyov, Tolstoi, Dostoevsky, Lossky, Berdyaev, Frank, Leontyev, Shestov, Fyodorov, and Chernyshevsky.

Creativity in the social sciences of the classical period was supported by the establishment of five new universities: Odessa University in the Ukraine (1865); Tomsk University, the first Siberian university (1888); Saratov University (1909); Rostov University, established at the evacuated Russian Warsaw University (1915); and Perm University (1916).[17]

In the ideological sphere the period represents a struggle between the Populists and the Marxists. The Populists, descendants of the Westernizers, continued to oppose the introduction of capitalism into Russia, and proposed instead the introduction of socialism organized on the basis of village communes. Under the leadership of, first, P. L. Lavrov (1823–1900) and, later, of N. K. Mikhailovsky (1842–1904), the Populists advocated a peaceful program of education and propaganda among the Russian peasants. A program of "going to the people" envisioned enlightenment not only among the peasants, but also among the members of the intelligentsia, who would become acquainted with the needs and aspirations of the people. Many Populists, including Lavrov, were fond of Marx and his ideas, but they rejected them in their application to the

Russian situation. The Russian Marxists, under the leadership of G. V. Plekhanov (1856–1918), contended that Russia would not be able to escape the world historical movement toward capitalism and the development of an impoverished proletariat. Much of their writing in the 1880's and the 1890's was directed toward documenting the idea that Russia was already a capitalist country, and that therefore Populist ideals were anachronistic. With the further development of capitalism in the Russian Empire, it was inevitable that populism should be transformed, as it was in the program of the Socialist Revolutionary party. With the turn of the century, however, Marxists themselves became divided into a number of groups supporting different positions with respect to the future of the country.

PERIOD OF DECLINE

The Revolution and the first few years following it led to significant departures in the various social science disciplines. For the first time innovations that were only dreamed of before became possible. Perhaps the greatest developments occurred in the various non-Russian areas, in which a free study of native history, institutions, and language became possible. It also became possible to establish many native institutions of learning and national universities. In this period a whole series of new universities became established: Gorky University in Nizhnegorod (1918), Voronezh University (1918), Irkutsk University (1918), Dnepropetrovsk University (1918), Tbilisi University (1918), Azerbaidzhan University (1919), Erevan University (1920), Sredneasiatsky University in Tashkent (1920), Ural University in Sverdlovsk (1920), and Belorussian University in Minsk (1921).[18]

The enthusiasm and hope generated by the social scientists in the early days of the Revolution did not last long. Tsarist censorship and intolerance of contrary opinion were replaced by more dogmatic as well as more efficient thought control by the Communist party and its various agencies, particularly the Cheka. The bourgeois background of a majority of the social scientists, including those sympathetic with the Revolution, and the generally prevailing anti-intellectualism among the masses of the proletariat placed all of the social scientists in jeopardy. As a group, scientists became subjected to an indiscriminate terror which was well expressed in the instructions issued to the Cheka officials by one of Dzerzhinsky's deputies:

Do not look for evidence as to whether an individual has taken up arms or spoken against the Soviets. Your first duty is to interrogate him as to the class to which he belongs, his origin, education, and profession. These are the questions which should determine the fate of the accused. This is the meaning and essence of red terror.[19]

Systematic destruction and persecution of the ablest social scientists in the country began in the 1920's and did not let up until by 1938 most of them had been destroyed.[20]

The extent of the destruction of both people and accumulated knowledge inflicted upon the Soviet social sciences in the period of decline will probably never be established. The old Russian Academy of Sciences was dissolved in 1931, and its officials were indicted on charges of organizing an overthrow of the Soviet government. The NKVD alleged that four of its most prominent academicians were leaders of this underground organization, and a total of one hundred persons were put on trial. The end result of the "Case of the Academy" was that five scholars were shot, fifty-five were sentenced to deportation to Siberia and hard labor for a period of ten years, and the forty remaining were given lighter sentences. Many of those sentenced to Siberian exile were prominent men of science, including Academicians S. Platonov, M. Liubavsky, and L. Likhachev, and Professors V. Beneshevich, A. Borodin, S. Rozhdestvensky, and S. Bakhrushin. Numerically, the greatest suffering was inflicted upon the historians. The attack on the academy was coordinated with the closing of the State Academy for the History of Material Culture. Two directors of the academy were arrested and later disappeared, and nineteen members or associate members were deported and sentenced to hard labor.[21]

Persecution spread to all the corners of the Soviet Union. While in the 1920's the representatives of the social sciences who were particularly singled out for attack were philosophers, political scientists, students of jurisprudence, and sociologists, the repressions of the 1930's were directed against historians, economists, anthropologists, psychologists, and linguists. Particularly extreme suffering was inflicted upon anthropologists, both the older scholars and the young Soviet-trained generation. Almost all of the museum directors, ethnographers, and archeologists were either arrested or dismissed from their positions. Some were shot, others simply disappeared without trial, still others were lucky enough to be able to commit suicide. In a drive against bourgeois nationalism, hundreds of local organizations for the study of native history and culture were dissolved, never to be revived.[22]

Social scientists of all nationalities in all republics and autonomous regions suffered arrests and persecution. The Jewish section in the Communist party organization was dissolved in 1930, and a general attack upon Jewish scientific activities came in 1932–33. Scientific publications in the Yiddish language were discontinued, the Jewish sections in the Ukrainian and the Belorussian Academies of Sciences were closed down, and many of their officials were liquidated. The three daily Yiddish papers published in Moscow, Kiev, and Minsk stopped publication in 1938.[23]

The destruction of the Belorussian intelligentsia, including its most prominent scientists, fell primarily in the years 1929 and 1930. In Minsk alone three hundred leading Belorussians were arrested, among them thirteen full members of the Belorussian Academy of Sciences, seventy-two leading scientists and professors, sixty writers and poets, and a number of other professionals, among whom many were social scientists. Among the victims were also the president of the Belorussian Academy of Sciences and the rector of the Belorussian University. As a consequence of these repressions, much of Belorussia's original contributions to the social sciences was lost. This loss is summarized by Simon Kabysh in the following words:

Simultaneously with the mass murder of their intellectuals the Belorussian people lost a considerable proportion of their national cultural heritage. All scientific works, research studies, literature, music, paintings, ethnographic material, collections, albums, and museum articles produced by those who were arrested or found in libraries and museums were removed or completely destroyed. Among the works which were destroyed were the following: 1) an anthology of Belorussian national art; 2) *Belorussian Archives*, a publication containing reports of the Belorussian academic conferences; 3) the works of the congress of Belorussian archaeologists and geographers; 4) the works of the humanities department of the Belorussian Academy of Sciences (philosophy, history, ethnography, archeology, science, law); 5) all the works of the poet Ales Harun, who died abroad; and 6) Belorussian fairy tales, stories and folklore written down and edited by A. Sierzputouski.[24]

In the Ukraine, three distinct repressive periods of long duration can be noted: (1) the period of war communism and the war with the nationalist Ukrainian forces (1918–21); (2) the period of "socialist reconstruction" (1929–38); and (3) the period following World War II. The number of the intelligentsia destroyed in these periods is staggering and defies any estimation. In one year alone (1932–33) the Ukraine lost some 1,649 of its scientists, or 16.4 percent of the total. From 1930 to 1934 the All-Ukrainian Academy of Sciences lost practically all of its original members, and it was renamed the Academy of Sciences of the Ukrainian S.S.R. Other scientific institutions were also suppressed, in-

cluding the Bagalei Institute for the History of Ukrainian Culture and
the Shevchenko Institute.[25] Among those destroyed are listed such
prominent social scientists as Academician M. Hrushevsky, historian;
Academician S. Efremov, linguist; Academician M. Slabchenko, economist and historian; Academician M. Yavorsky, a Marxist historian; My-
kola Zerov, a poet, linguist, and student of antiquity; Yosip Hermaize,
a Marxist historian; Academician S. Rudnitsky, geographer; V. Babiak,
geographer and student of Rudnitsky; S. Semko, former president of
Kiev University and later chief of the Ukrainian Central Archives; and
M. Rudinsky, archeologist; just to name a few.[26]

This short and extremely incomplete discussion of the destruction of
scientists and scholars will suffice to indicate that it would have been
more to the point to call it the period of disaster and nightmare, not
simply that of decline. The language of prose fails in expressing the full
tragedy of the period. Poets can do this better, and Anna Akhmatova
is the best of them all when she says:

> It seems as if the voice of man
> Will never sound here anymore,
> And only winds from the stone age
> Will knock and knock at the black door.[27]

PERIOD OF REVIVAL

Stalin's death permitted the closing of an exceedingly painful chapter
of Soviet history. The jockeying for power among Stalin's heirs brought
down Beria, and subsequently brought the all-powerful secret police
under the Central Committee's control. The stirrings of the Soviet people were evident in the rebellions of Siberian concentration-camp in-
mates, who in at least one instance were supported by the camp guards.
The most significant change came as a result of Khrushchev's denunciation of Stalin and Stalin's historical role in the speech of February, 1956.
Strong opposition to Khrushchev's de-Stalinization drive was evident in
the fact that the speech was not made public. Despite some outward signs
of change and easing of living conditions of the people in general, many
years went by without any truly significant official shift in the ideological sphere of the social sciences. The standards of scholarship set
in the Stalin days continued to be officially enforced.

The requirement of dogmatism in the social sciences and falsification
of historical records in the name of the "safety and security of the
Soviet people" were altered only in the second half of 1963 and did not
become officially pronounced till the January, 1964, conference of social

scientists organized by the Academy of Sciences of the U.S.S.R. on instructions of the Central Committee of the party. The conference included thirty-six leading social scientists representing different disciplines,
including the newly revived field of sociology.[28] The discussions of the
conference revolved around a paper presented by two leading academicians, P. N. Fedoseev and Iu. P. Frantsev, entitled "On the Study of
Methodological Problems of History." The paper carried an unambigu-
ous stamp of approval from the Central Committee of the party, and
there are indications that it was a collective work of many social scientists
and party ideologists.

The party's new directive to its social scientists, as expressed in the
paper, was that the old-fashioned dogmatism of Stalinist days was to be
replaced by a more flexible policy in which at least a limited objectivity
would be permissible. The paper makes an explicit announcement of the
new era in the work of the social scientists: "The program of the CPSU
indicates that the social sciences are the scientific bases for the direction
of social life. In fact, a new stage has arrived in the century-long development of the Marxist science of society." [29]

Without mentioning the destruction of thousands of social scientists
in the earlier period, Fedoseev and Frantsev nevertheless express themselves sharply on the problems of the Stalinist heritage, which is explicitly recognized as still remaining:

Our task now is to proceed farther and more daringly on the path
laid for historical science by K. Marx, F. Engels, and V. I. Lenin. For
this purpose it is necessary to liquidate once and for all the consequences
of the cult of personality in the area of the social sciences, including historical science. One of the worst consequences of the cult of personality was
the lowering of prestige of the social sciences. This was done by placing
the scientists working in the area of the social sciences in those days into
a situation which limited to the extreme their creative activity. Therefore,
it became widely believed that Soviet social scientists are capable only of
either repeating citations of one and the same man, or restating the contents
of these citations and without end commenting upon the directives these
contained. The works of social scientists were filled with dogmatism alien
to Marxism-Leninism. . . .

In order to facilitate a correct and significant study of the methodological
problems of historical knowledge, it is necessary to ask and answer in a
novel way the question of the relationship between history and sociology.
This problem was badly confused when criticism was directed against the
ideas of M. N. Pokrovsky. In the conditions of Stalin's cult this criticism
turned into the struggle against the so-called sociologism in historical investigations. Broad interpretation and application of the concept of "vulgar

sociologism" contributed to the disappearance from historical investigations
of sociological generalizations and the fear of historians to ask theoretical
questions on the basis of concrete evidence, while it led the philosophers
away from studying the methodological problems of history. Obviously,
the situation is entirely intolerable when a historian or a philosopher
replaces concrete investigation with repetitions of ready-made sociological
formulas. It is also intolerable when historical investigation does not search
for ways of asking the important questions on the regularities of societal
development, without an analysis of which it is impossible to comprehend
the march of historical events.[30]

The changing views of the Central Committee members, reflected in
Fedoseev's paper and in the discussions that ensued during the conference, have led to unprecedented activity and excitement among Soviet
social scientists. Changing editorial policies have permitted publication
of research results that had previously been referred to only in private
conversations. It became officially possible to discuss certain problems
of Soviet society whose existence was denied only a few years earlier.
    The works of the best Soviet scholars to appear since 1964 have an
air of sophistication comparable to that of their colleagues in the West.
They are familiar with Western writings on their subjects, more aware
of their own fallibility, and more balanced in tone. Perhaps most important is the fact that they are also beginning to draw upon the ideas of
their predecessors, even though they cannot reveal their sources. This
rediscovery of their own past has been facilitated by the accidental survival of some prominent social scientists who were already active in the
prerevolutionary period.
    Among such scholars, who are often referred to by the new Soviet
generation as the "Last of the Mohicans," is Academician Stanislav
Gustavovich Strumilin. In 1967 the venerable economist and sociologist,
who is perhaps best known for his pioneering time-budget studies in
the mid-1920's, celebrated his ninetieth birthday and his seventieth anniversary of scholarly work and public service. There is probably no
other man in the Soviet Union who has contributed more to the revival
of sociology and to the rediscovery of its scholarly past. In celebration
of Strumilin's anniversary, Soviet sociologists sent him the following
telegram: "You are not only a noted economist but also the number one
sociologist in the Soviet Union . . . Therefore, the Presidium of the
Soviet Sociological Association has elected you, Stanislav Gustavovich,
our Honorary President and is issuing to you the No. 1 membership
card of our Association." [31] At the same time, the Presidium of the
U.S.S.R. Supreme Soviet conferred upon Academician Strumilin the title

of Hero of Socialist Labor and awarded him the Order of Lenin and the Gold Hammer and Sickle Medal "for his outstanding contributions to the development of the science of economics." [32] All these honors are particularly significant in the light of the bold departures from the prescribed interpretation of Soviet history which have appeared in Strumilin's scholarly work since 1956.[33] Strumilin had already been elected to a full academic position in 1931, and like all the best of Soviet scholars of the period was deprived of his freedom for an unknown period of time.[34]

The Future

The Central Committee's resolution on social sciences issued on the eve of the fiftieth anniversary of the Communist Revolution [35] reinforces the gains made by social scientists since the death of Stalin and particularly since the already mentioned 1964 social science conference sponsored by the Academy of Sciences. The most significant departure is the official recognition of the existence of social problems and the need to deal with them. Social scientists are instructed to work on "concrete social research; elaboration of problems of the social structure of society; the improvement of socialist social relations and their evolution into communist relations . . ."

It is still too early to tell how these directions will be fulfilled in practice and what specific instructions will go out to the Academy of Sciences and other scientific institutions. Nevertheless, at least some consequences can already be discerned from an extremely significant article by Academician A. M. Rumyantsev in *Komsomolskaia pravda*,[36] which is said to have been written before the announcement of the Central Committee's resolution on social sciences. The sociologist Rumyantsev, who is a vice-president of the U.S.S.R. Academy of Sciences and a member of the Central Committee of the party, must have been one of the leading figures in the drafting of the resolution. The basic concern expressed in the article is for attracting talented young people into the social sciences, which are frequently avoided in favor of more attractive and ideologically less threatening positions in the natural sciences and humanities. The article reveals that Rumyantsev and his colleagues are well aware of the fact that ideological security alone is not sufficient to attract able people into certain professions. What is most important is the opportunity to depart from past practices and make innovations. Rumyantsev's job is to persuade the new generation that such innovations are possible now in the social sciences as well:

> Whenever Lenin changed his point of view on questions concerning the strategy and tactics of the Bolsheviks, he was not ashamed to give this wide publicity. That is the attitude which every honest scientist should adopt toward his studies and toward science. . . .
>
> The attitude toward tradition and innovation in science, and also in social life in general, is by no means an artificial question, in my opinion, but a real problem that has been tackled for centuries in various social conditions. If the scientist and science do not strive to explore unknown aspects of social life, the development of our knowledge will stop and society will not be able to move forward through new stages of human civilization.
>
> Today, in the epoch of the search for the most effective social means for building communism, our social studies require, as never before, the development of new ideas, concepts, and theories, and they do indeed originate in our science. . . . Young scientists must remember that conservatism in science is not a symptom of age. In all sciences an innovator may be elderly, while a conservative, on the other hand, may be young.
>
> I should like to emphasize that research nowadays requires the development of creative initiative, search, and heroic enthusiasm, as Giordano Bruno once put it. We are accustomed to speak of creative work and daring in connection with art and in all kinds of exceptional circumstances. Our epoch of the scientific and technical revolution, however, also calls for a dedicated and creative search in the spheres of technology and economics, in the sphere of material production. Social science today offers truly inexhaustible possibilities for impassioned quest.[37]

If Rumyantsev's article is a correct reflection of the party's position on the matter of ideology, the next several years should see a considerable increase in tolerance of alien ideas and a note of cautious irreverence toward the official gods.

Notes

1. Madame de Staël, *Madame de Staël on Politics, Literature and National Character,* ed. and trans. Morroe Berger (Garden City, N.Y.: Anchor Books, 1965), p. 337.

2. Alexander Vucinich, *Science in Russian Culture: A History to 1860* (Stanford, Calif.: Stanford University Press, 1963), p. 73.

3. Walter Laqueur, *Russia and Germany: A Century of Conflict* (Boston: Little, Brown & Co., 1965), p. 13.

4. A. S. Lappo-Danilevsky, "The Development of Science and Learning in Russia," in *Russian Realities and Problems*, ed. J. D. Duff (Cambridge: At the University Press, 1917), pp. 173–74.

5. See Ivan D. London, "A Note on Soviet Science," *Russian Review*, 16, no. 1 (January, 1957): 37–41.

6. Nicholas Berdyaev, *The Origin of Russian Communism* (Ann Arbor: University of Michigan Press, 1962), p. 20.

7. De Staël, *Politics, Literature and National Character*, p. 342.

8. *Istoriia Akademii Nauk SSSR: 1724–1803* (Moscow: Izdatelstvo Akademii Nauk SSSR, 1958), 1: 33–34.

9. See Peter Struve, "Imperial Russia," *Encyclopedia of the Social Sciences*, ed. Edwin Seligman (New York: Macmillan Co., 1930), 1: 280; *Istoriia Akademii Nauk SSSR*, 1: 453–59.

10. See Struve, "Imperial Russia," pp. 280–81; George Vernadsky, *A History of Russia* (New Haven, Conn.: Yale University Press, 1964), pp. 184–85.

11. Vucinich, *Science in Russian Culture*, p. 59.

12. *Ibid.*, pp. 59–60.

13. *Ibid.*, p. 64.

14. A. S. Butiagin and Iu. A. Saltanov, *Universitetskoe obrazovanie v SSSR* (Moscow: Izdatelstvo Moskovskogo Universiteta, 1957).

15. Vernadsky, *History of Russia*, p. 185.

16. Alexander Herzen, *My Past and Thoughts: The Memoirs of Alexander Herzen*, trans. Constance Garnett (London: Chatto & Windus, 1924), 2: 254–55.

17. Butiagin and Saltanov, *Universitetskoe obrazovanie*.

18. *Ibid.*

19. *Pravda*, December 25, 1918; see also Mikhail Zerkalov, "Social Groups," in *Genocide in the USSR*, ed. N. K. Deker and A. Lebed (New York: Scarecrow Press, 1958), p. 234.

20. For a vivid description of the beginning of this destruction, see Pitirim A. Sorokin, *Leaves from a Russian Diary and Thirty Years After* (Boston: Beacon Press, 1950), pp. 217–310.

21. See Leo Dudin and Michel Miller, "The Russians," in *Genocide in the USSR*, pp. 116–17.

22. *Ibid.*, p. 117.

23. See Solomon Goldeman, "The Jews," in *Genocide in the USSR*, pp. 94–110.

24. Simon Kabysh, "The Belorussians," in *Genocide in the USSR*, p. 83.

25. Alexander V. Yurchenko, "The Ukrainians," in *Genocide in the USSR*, pp. 138–47.

26. For a more detailed description of Ukrainian casualties of this period, see S. O. Pidhainy, ed., *The Black Deeds of the Kremlin: A White Book* (Toronto: Basilian Press, 1953).

27. Anna Akhmatova, "Belaya staya" ("The White Flock"), in Leonid I. Strakhovsky, *Craftsmen of the Word: Three Poets of Modern Russia* (Cambridge, Mass.: Harvard University Press, 1949), p. 72.

28. For details, see proceedings of the conference published in *Istoriia i sotsiologiia* (Moscow: Izdatelstvo "Nauka," 1964).

29. *Ibid.*, p. 7.

30. *Ibid.*, pp. 6–7, 13.

31. M. Sonin, "Yubilei Akademika S. G. Strumilina," *Voprosy economiki*, March, 1967, no. 3, pp. 147–49.

32. See *Pravda*, January 29, 1967, p. 3; or *Izvestiia*, January 29, 1967, p. 1.

33. See, for example, his analysis of Soviet population growth in Chapter 12 of this book.

34. The story is credited to a well-informed sociologist of Communist Poland, but is vigorously denied by the Soviet sociologists.

35. See CPSU Central Committee, "On Measures for Further Developing Social Sciences and Heightening Their Role in Communist Construction," *Pravda*, August 22, 1967, pp. 1–2; *Izvestiia*, August 22, 1967, pp. 1, 4.

36. See A. M. Rumyantsev, "The Social Sciences, Marxism-Leninism and the Rising Generation," *Soviet News*, London, October 10, 1967, pp. 20–23.

37. *Ibid.*, p. 22.

I : Social Science Ideology

Soviet Marxism and Social Science

William M. Mandel

Elements of the Soviet World View

A discussion of the basic elements of Soviet ideology is necessary because, first, no objective text on this is available in English. Secondly,
Marxism itself has continued—it would be more accurate to say resumed
—its development, both as ideology and as applied science, in the U.S.S.R.,
in other Communist-led countries, and elsewhere, and historical background is needed to understand the present state of the field. Thirdly,
Soviet ideology—the world view and particularly the picture of development of human society and its present problems that is naturally the
major concern of a volume on social science—has not been presented
even in the U.S.S.R. in any single source which responsible Soviet figures will recommend today. The nearest approach to this, because of the
doctrinal function of the Communist party, is the resolution and the
report of the Central Committee delivered by Mr. Brezhnev at the 23rd

Congress in 1966. Even these have already been modified (not unnaturally) in the Central Committee's "Theses" on the occasion of the fiftieth anniversary of the Revolution in 1967. I shall therefore have occasion to cite the last of these, as well as writings from more customary academic sources. But because the party is today pluralistic and consensual,[1] as well as participatory and disciplined, its statements avoid issues on which agreement has not yet been reached or which could cause unnecessary political difficulties, whether within the Communist camp or elsewhere. Therefore, the presentation here of an integrated statement of the Soviet ideology in its broadest outlines as it stands today does have a certain intrinsic value, despite the fact that the individual component ideas may have been encountered elsewhere.

But before we can even deal with ideology as such, we must face the problem of semantics. For reasons partly philosophical and partly chronological—the fact that Marx wrote a century ago and the commonly understood meaning of certain words at that time was not what it is today—I am compelled to include a glossary of sorts. You really cannot tell the players without a scorecard.

That scorecard incorporates terms, institutions, and individuals. In the U.S.S.R. the makers of ideology are political, academic, and/or cultural figures. Just as Sartre and Camus have vastly affected ideology in the West, certainly among younger academicians and students, so it would be hard to challenge the statement that Yevtushenko, particularly in his very lengthy philosophical and political *Bratsk Station*,[2] and by the stupendous circulation of his work (his last volume of poems had an initial printing of 1,250,000), has done more to influence the actual Soviet ideology of today than any other single individual subsequent to Khrushchev's seismic de-Stalinization speech of 1956.[3] Nor are the contributions of Solzhenitsyn in *For the Good of the Cause* [4] and *One Day in the Life of Ivan Denisovich*,[5] Voznesensky, Ehrenburg, and Tvardovsky (as editor of the free-wheeling *Novy mir*) to be underestimated. Quite naturally, literary criticism also engages in ideological discussion, often quite perceptive and creative.[6] Some argue that there are two ideologies, one official and the other voiced by figures in literature and the arts. I would contend that the latter hold to the former in full, but maintain that this does not necessitate the censorship, rigidity, bureaucracy, logrolling, and nepotism against which they inveigh.

But while those who express themselves in word images or illustrative forms have had the greatest impact, save only for the Khrushchev speech, it is those who employ models with whom we are here more directly concerned. Yevtushenko, for example, wants world peace *and* social revolution in nonsocialist countries (as well as a civil liberties revolution in socialist countries), but spelling out the principles by means of which this excruciatingly difficult combination of goals is to be achieved is the business of the ideologists as such. So is the more important task of finding whether these goals are attainable and wherein they may be, in point of fact, mutually exclusive.

Here we will find academic specialists in all disciplines, from archeologists and ethnographers through historians and philosophers, contributing *directly* to the development of ideology. But we also find a peculiarly Communist institution (whatever partial parallels may be found in other societies) of party ideologists. In earlier years they were identical with the party leaders (Lenin, Stalin, to some degree Khrushchev). But even in Lenin's day, Bukharin, Trotsky, Stalin, Lunacharsky, and others contributed to ideology. Under Khrushchev, it was chiefly Mikoyan who played that role. Today there is a respect for the highly professional academic expert in what were in the past purely political organs. When the most authoritative of such publications, *Kommunist*, the theoretical monthly reaching one-twentieth of the entire 13,000,000 membership of the party—that is, reaching its grass-roots level of leadership—publishes articles containing mathematical formalizations of thought,[7] that is impressive indeed.

To begin with, it must be understood that Soviet social scientists approach any problem, in any field whatever, with a certain mental set. While that set has psychological components of an ethnic and historical nature, it consists chiefly of an integrated view of the world that has been elaborated in very considerable detail: Marxism-Leninism. Courses in its economic theory ("political economy"), its philosophy (dialectical materialism), and its application as a tool for the analysis of history in a single but rather inclusive case (the history of the Communist party of the Soviet Union) are required in all higher education.

It provides a model that, as anyone who has visited the U.S.S.R. and engaged in casual conversation knows, satisfies virtually all Soviet citizens, including those whose education has been merely at the simplified high school or even grade school level. They willingly and aggressively plunge into debate on any subject in the realm of societal affairs on which they have information or on which the visitor provides information that makes any sense at all. By preference (for there are lighter papers available, and magazines as well), they read newspapers whose meat-to-trivia ratio is about the same as that of the *New York Times*, and they do so in numbers twenty times as great (*Pravda* plus *Izvestiia*) as the number of Americans nationally who read the *Times*. Their information is not complete, for there are subjects and points of view that simply are not yet allowed to appear in print, but the average man's interest in and retention of public-affairs data is so great that, as Professor Dale Pontius, a Roosevelt University political scientist, remarked to me after a week of deliberately random conversations in a Leningrad neighborhood park, "We couldn't have had these talks in Chicago. The man in the street wouldn't have been interested in the questions we posed, and if he had been, he wouldn't have had the information with which to pursue the conversation."

I myself am convinced, after four visits to the U.S.S.R., that both the interest and the retentiveness are consequences of the possession of a model that, in the minds of its citizens, makes an intelligible pattern of virtually all information offered to them. Because Soviet citizens believe the world and its events to have meaning, the consequence is a level of curiosity that can be downright embarrassing. I remember, in that series of conversations, a muscular young man in a checked shirt, who turned out to be an engineer, asking me why the foreign minister of Brazil had just resigned. There was no geographic confusion in his mind between the United States and Brazil—geography is a required subject in Soviet elementary schools, as it was in America when I was a boy— but he simply took it for granted that a man who could talk about current developments in the Soviet Union and other places very remote from home would be able to answer his question about a major cabinet change in the largest country but mine in my own hemisphere.

While there is necessarily a gap between the level of thought of the Soviet social scientist and the man in the street, the existence of a model understood and accepted by both, at least in general outline, greatly facilitates communication between them, reduces (without eliminating) academic snobbishness, and increases the pressure upon ideology to face realities. Let us therefore familiarize ourselves with that ideology, beginning with its terminology.

"Ideology" itself is the first term. For while *all* other major terms in use in Soviet social thought carry the meanings that they did for Marx, "ideology" does not. He used it to mean "false consciousness," an erroneous perception of the world. Arne Naess has counted more than thirty meanings in world use today. In Soviet use, it means the overall conception of the world deriving from what are conceived to be the interests of a social class. Thus, "bourgeois ideology" is a world view conditioned by the fundamental assumption that capitalism is right and proper.

"Bourgeois" and "bourgeoisie" are perhaps the Marxist terms most misunderstood by non-Marxists. All Soviet encyclopedias, dictionaries published in the U.S.S.R., and other Soviet reference sources define *burzhuaziia* as "capitalists" or "the capitalist class" and *not* as "middle class," which is the meaning that attaches to "bourgeoisie" in the English language. When the Russians want to say "middle class," they very carefully specify *melkaia burzhuaziia*, that is, petty bourgeoisie. The only exception is in reference to the period before capitalism became dominant; then the prosperous urban people of all sorts, engaged in economic pursuits requiring monetary transactions in a predominantly feudal society, are termed "bourgeoisie" in Russian, as in French and English. Unfortunately, some scholars do not consider the fact that the word does not have the same meaning to their readers as to themselves, and employ it where "capitalist" or "capitalism-oriented" would transmit what the Russians really mean.

Marxism is a self-contained system of thought. It has its own view of economics, of course, for which it employs the term "political economy" to denote basic theory. It has a distinctive view of government, for which it employs the term "the state," except when a particular administration or form of organization is under discussion. It regards history as meaningful and comprehensible, and deduces from history what it regards as laws, with the aid of which current happenings may be understood and the future course of events generally foreshadowed and even shaped. It approaches economics, government, history, and literally everything else in a uniform manner, from the viewpoint of a general philosophy called "dialectical materialism."

In everyday Western usage, the term "materialism" carries the meaning of grossness, selfishness, a concern primarily with things. This is not at all its meaning in Marxism or, for that matter, philosophy in general, where it signifies merely that the world really *is,* and that ideas ultimately, however indirectly, derive from human observation and thought about a world that is a material reality. This is summed up in the notion that matter is primary while ideas are secondary—secondary not in the sense of being unimportant, but simply that they are derivative from actual reality.

"Idealism" in everyday English means devotion to high ideals. Again, this is not its meaning in Soviet usage, where it is applied to the notion of the primacy of an idea, or of ideas. For example, all religions are categorized as idealist philosophies in that they assume either that the world was created by a nonmaterial supreme being who governs our lives from without, or that he gave the universe its initial push and established at least the natural and moral laws by which physical and human existence is guided.

In Soviet writings these notions of materialism and idealism take on exceedingly complicated forms, shadings, and combinations. For example, Marxists—*dialectical* materialists—classify a whole group of philosophies as *mechanical* materialist, and contend that they are actually idealist without being aware of this. A mechanical materialist philosophy is one that does accept matter, reality, as primary, but sees the *laws* governing nature and man as unchanging. To this the dialectical materialist responds that if the laws do not change, then the only logical conclusion is that some outside force, not conceivable within the framework of the material universe, established them. And so one is back to the primary impulse—God, in another name, or idealism.

Idealist philosophy, on the other hand, may be dialectical, as with the German Hegel, to whom Marx and Engels considered themselves deeply indebted, but whom they regarded as wrong in that he stood things on their head, while they, as they saw it, performed the philosophical service of standing them right side up again.

To the reader trained to regard social science as empirical, the usefulness of familiarization with these terms may seem dubious. But, in the first place, Soviet social science denies that anything can be purely empirical and still be science; that is, facts must lead to conclusions. Secondly, even papers describing "concrete" investigations (what would be termed empirical research in the West) are larded with such terms and, more important, presume that the reader thinks in these categories.

"Dialectics" is essentially the notion that everything in the world is interrelated, however remotely, that the waves set in motion by any single happening reach out to intersect others and yet still others, although ultimately their influence may be so eroded by this friction as to have no significant effect beyond a certain point. This point is defined partly by the significance, the force, of the initial happening, and partly by the force of those which it intersects.

Marx and Engels, from observation and study of literally everything on which material was available in their time—their range of knowledge was vast almost beyond belief—derived a series of laws of dialectics, distinctive not so much for their originality (they went to great pains to credit others with all ideas they borrowed), but for the relationship established between dialectics and materialism.

Essentially, dialectics are regularities of change. Perhaps the most striking is the notion of the transition from quantity to quality. The simplest example cited in Marxist texts is that ice remains ice when heat is applied to it until, at a certain temperature for each level of atmospheric pressure, it turns quite suddenly to water. With continuation of the same process, it remains water from 32° F. to 212° F., at which point another sudden change occurs, and it becomes steam. This is highly oversimplified physics, and Soviet philosophers concern themselves with refinements or other changes that have to be made in this law of dialectics in the light of the more elegant knowledge we possess today.

As applied to social science, the transition from quantity to quality is observed in that when a social conflict heats up sufficiently, figuratively speaking, it explodes, exactly as we know that the application of heat to certain chemicals results in explosion beyond a certain point. But while with chemicals this is exact science, reproducible so precisely that mass-scale industrial processes are based upon this and an endless number of other quantity-quality changes of which we know, Soviet social scientists are keenly aware that in society this is by no means the case. No one, for example, has ever been able to predict in what country the next social revolution would break out, or precisely what form it would take. Nor has it been possible to know beforehand whether it would stick or be reversed. The past half century offers examples of successful revolutions, of revolutions canceled by counterrevolution from within as well as from without, and of revolutions headed off by concessions to the social class expected to make them. From this, as well as from examples in the natural sciences in the past quarter century of explosion of knowledge, some Soviet Marxists are beginning to pose the question as to whether each sphere of existence does not have its own dialectics.[8] They often quote Marx's statement that the laws of any sphere of existence cannot be applied to any other, but must be deduced for each sphere from observation of its facts. They are quite clear that the laws of any science cannot be deduced from the generalizations of dialectics, which they regard simply as an approach, a tool for analysis.

The way in which this works may be suggested by another law of dialectics, that of the interpenetration of opposites. It is the basis for the notion of "contradiction," which one is always running into in Soviet writing. To non-Marxists, "contradiction" denotes only words or ideas in conflict. To a Marxist, "contradictions" and their resolution are the normal form of existence of reality, and comprise an endless chicken-and-egg chain constituting the mechanism by which all change occurs. Essentially, the interpenetration of opposites says that nothing can exist without its opposite (in physics one says that every action has its equal and opposite reaction), and that the new develops out of the interaction ("contradiction") between these opposites.

This concept is summarized in the notion of "the unity and struggle of opposites" (sex, marriage, for example). In society, it appears in the

idea that there can be no capitalists without workers, that the class struggle between them (whether contract bargaining* or revolution) is a
permanently observable fact of life occurring with greater or lesser intensity, more or less consciously. The Marxist conclusion, to which Soviet writers uniformly hold, is that the resolution of this contradiction
is revolution by the workers to eliminate another, underlying contradiction: that production under capitalism is a social (joint) endeavor,
while ownership ("appropriation") of the product is private, whether
it goes to one individual or to any number of stockholders.

This simple model was modified by Lenin to account for changes
occurring after the deaths of Marx and Engels. In their time the relationship of manufacturing countries to nonmanufacturing ones was
largely confined to purchase and sale, while capitalism was competitive.
Lenin took note of the development of monopoly, the subordination of
industry to those who finance it, the export of capital in addition to
that of goods, the seizure of colonies to protect that capital or make investment possible (different from the earlier seizure of colonies for
plunder and/or settlement), and wars among great powers because they
had fallen out over these very things. He called these phenomena imperialism, and concluded that revolution would occur not on the basis
of the single contradiction between workers (proletarians) and capitalists, but where the complexity of contradictions reached crisis.[9] In Russia itself, for example, the revolution by a small but highly concentrated
working class was accompanied by and interwoven with a peasant revolution to acquire the land, national liberation revolutions by ethnically
oppressed or colonial peoples of the tsarist empire, and a peace movement taking the extreme form of soldiers shooting their officers and
going home en masse.

One of the most important developments of ideology in the U.S.S.R.,
particularly since World War II, has to do with the change in the
world scene and the potential for revolution caused by the very existence of the U.S.S.R. and the socialist camp, which makes possible anti-
capitalist revolutions under circumstances where they could not previously have occurred, and offers them a chance to survive where they
would have been defeated by armed intervention. The dialectic is re-

---

* This illustrates a distinction highly important in Marxist ideology, but in no
sense unique to it: that between the subjective and the objective. When Walter
Reuther bargains for higher wages, his subjective intention, in the realm of ideology,
does not go beyond employment of the mechanisms of the existing system to improve the living standards of his union members. But in the Marxist view, what
he is doing is engaging in class struggle in the objective sense. Soviet social science
is studded with such references to subjective intent versus objective reality.

garded as vastly more complex now than when imperialism had the world to itself. For example, the dismantling of capitalism in Egypt (nationalization of all large business) by Nasser, not a Marxist, much less a Communist, is believed by Soviet social scientists to represent a pragmatic solution on his part based on observation of the success of the U.S.S.R and other socialist countries in dealing with problems similar to his.

The conversion of Castro to communism after the triumph of his guerrilla war is also seen largely as representing realization on his part of the validity of socialism for Cuba's situation. The revolution in China is regarded not only as the one that was most directly inspired by the observation of the then very recent revolution in Russia, but also as one that could not have survived if there had still been the kind of Russia that participated in crushing the Boxer Rebellion in Peking in company with the other great powers in 1900–1901.[10]

An elaborate structure of thought reaching into such fields as international law has been erected on the notion of the U.S.S.R. and the socialist camp as protectors of revolutions, and the belief that this function is performable only if peace is maintained among nations. Thus the Cuban revolution would have fallen victim to starvation and economic disarray if the U.S.S.R. had not had years of peace in which to become a major maritime power (six times as many ton-miles of cargo moved in 1960 as in 1940) capable of supplying Castro at a distance of five thousand miles, and economically developed enough to absorb or dispose elsewhere of Cuba's entire sugar crop, which the United States now refused to take. Peace is credited with having bought the time to develop the missiles which, carried to Cuba by that new fleet, exacted an American pledge not to repeat the Bay of Pigs as the price for removal of those weapons. Peace made possible the development of industrial capacity enabling Moscow in 1956 to offer to undertake the immense Aswan Dam project, and thus to permit Nasser ultimately to demonstrate, by doubling acreage through irrigation and by industrialization through electric power, that his revolution would produce material benefits. As the protector of revolutions, the U.S.S.R. equipped Chinese industry and trained nuclear engineers for China in the 1950's, supplied Vietnam, and armed Egypt after the Anglo-Franco-Israeli attack on Suez in 1956. Again, because of another decade of peaceful development, the U.S.S.R. was capable of resupplying Egypt after the June war of 1967, this time in part by 250 flights of Soviet transports in a matter of weeks. All these acts are believed to fall within the framework of the long-established principle of international law that a government has the right to assist the recognized government of any other country, and the second principle that established governments are to be recognized, inasmuch as no country has the right to sit in judgment upon the decision of another people as to its government.[11]

The reasoning is pursued into much more tenuous areas. The winning of national independence by numerous Asian and African states without war, contrary to all expectations prior to World War II, is credited to the weakening of imperialism by the Soviet military triumph and the demonstration of the potential of guerrilla warfare by various countries (China, Yugoslavia, Cuba), which, as we have seen, is held to have been possible because of the initial removal of Russia by revolution from the ranks of intervention. In turn, the inspiration given American Negroes by successful struggles for independence, armed and unarmed, in black and other dependent countries, is widely acknowledged in noncommunist circles. So is the influence of foreign policy considerations upon the type of governmental action taken in the United States vis-à-vis Negro movements. Therefore black Americans are helped in their efforts by the success of the Russian revolution and the things its continued existence at peace has made possible. Contrariwise, a feeling on the part of the American white public that war with the U.S.S.R. was a pressing threat would, as during the McCarthy era, create a state of mind justifying the most vigorous repression of dissent and opposition movements.

It need hardly be said that among a people that lost 20,000,000 dead in World War II, there has been virtually no special need for social scientists to validate the desirability of peace for the sake of the Soviet Union itself. A very similar phenomenon has been observed among the Japanese, as a consequence of Hiroshima and Nagasaki. But the concept of international solidarity against imperialism that has been part of Soviet ideology from the very outset, and which was given reality by the advisers and military volunteers sent to Sun Yat-sen in the 1920's, the Soviet volunteers in Spain a dozen years later, and, strangely, even the Soviet action in Hungary in 1956 (which was presented to the Soviet people as defense of the revolution against a CIA-sponsored revolt), has demanded organized thought on the matter of assistance to others abroad. This has been a persistent issue, not confined to the few instances of armed action by Soviet citizens or forces abroad. It is known, for example, that after the serious crop failure of 1963, longshoremen in Odessa struck briefly against the loading of ships with food to be sent abroad when there were shortages in their own stores. It is not only in the U.S.S.R. that social thought on a complex level has been stimulated by thinkers' needs to answer in their own minds, whether for abstract or practical purposes, questions posed by spontaneous social actions at home.*

This illustrative digression on the subject of "contradiction" and "interpenetration and struggle of opposites" (capitalism and socialism; today and tomorrow; peace and war; nationalism and internationalism; colonialism and liberation) was intended to demonstrate that the dialectics of social change are seen as vastly more complex than those of physics, chemistry, or biology. They are also understood to be more complex in each higher form of organization of matter than in the preceding lower one: in chemistry more than in physics, in biology more than in chemistry, in society more than in any of these. In each of these, the laws of each lower level are operative plus those of the level on which one is working. Therefore, Soviet social thought opposes "reductionism" whenever it is aware that it is at work; for example, in the attempt to explain social problems as geographic ones: adequacy or lack of natural resources. But men of affairs in the U.S.S.R. still often behave with respect to domestic matters in a fashion that sustains the Western misapprehension that Marxism as social thought is economic determinism. This misconception is so pervasive, and so important to one's mental set in approaching Soviet social science, as to merit a quotation of some length from Marx's alter ego, Friedrich Engels, co-author of the *Communist Manifesto*, editor of the volumes of *Capital* Marx left unfinished, and the pair's specialist in philosophy (see his *Anti-Dühring* and *Ludwig Feuerbach*) as Marx was in economics. In a letter of 1890, Engels wrote:

The economic situation is the basis, but the various elements of the superstructure—political forms of the class struggle and its consequences, constitutions established by the victorious class after a successful battle, etc.—forms of law—and then even the reflexes of all these actual struggles in the brains of the combatants: political, legal, philosophical theories, religious ideas and their further development into systems of dogma—also exercise their influence upon the course of the historical struggles and in many cases preponderate in determining their *form*. . . .

We make our own history, but . . . the final result always arises from conflicts between many individual wills, of which each again has been made what it is by a host of particular conditions of life. . . . For what each individual wills is obstructed by everyone else, and what emerges is something that no one willed. . . .

Marx and I are ourselves partly to blame for the fact that younger writers sometimes lay more stress on the economic side than is due to it.

---

* Similarly, the Detroit riot of 1967 triggered thought in the U.S. on the relationship between home problems and Vietnam that went much deeper than apologias for preconceived notions in either direction.

We had to emphasize this main principle in opposition to our adversaries, who denied it, and we had not always the time, the place or the opportunity to allow the other elements involved in the interaction to come into their rights.[12]

Those lines are the distilled essence of the ideology of Soviet social science. But attar of roses is not a rose, or even a perfume, and there are still basic terms with which to deal. The third conceived law of dialectics, after the quantity-quality relation and the interpenetration of opposites with its corollary, contradiction, is called "the negation of the negation." The revolutionary replacement of feudalism by capitalism is a negation of feudalism, but the revolutionary replacement of capitalism by socialism negates that negation. Here, too, there are ever new complexities. While the first of these revolutions is understood to replace one exploiting class by another, the second does not, and Marxist economics concludes that the evolution from socialism to communism will abolish classes entirely. Clearly the further qualitative changes to occur in human society subsequent to communism—and they must occur under the basic concept of dialectics that change alone is unending—will have to occur by negations different than those of social revolution in societies having a class structure. So the dialectics of human society will need further development when the outlines of that future change, today beyond the ken of Soviet social science, begin to emerge.

Two definitions remain. "Metaphysics" is a word that is pejorative in both Western and Soviet use, but for entirely different reasons. In the West it means speculative thought, and so non-Marxist philosophy classifies Marxism as metaphysical. Marxism rejects this, holding that it is not speculative, but "scientific"—that is, a series of deductions from observed fact, subject to change as, but only as, the volume and exactness and depth of our observations change. It uses "metaphysics" in a sense that will be readily understood by mathematicians and semanticists: as a form of thought derived from and going beyond Newtonian physics. But Newtonian physics was mechanical in its concepts, and so Marxism employs the term "metaphysical" to denote all thinking of a mechanical nature, in which each category and process is a world unto itself, having its own unchanging laws unrelated to others. Metaphysics is antidialectical. And so Marxism opposes metaphysics.

The last term crying for definition is "methodology." In non-Marxist usage, it is virtually an equivalent for "methods" or "techniques" taken as a body. But Marxists use it as a synonym for "approach," understood in the philosophical sense. So it is the laws of dialectics and materialism that comprise the methodology of Marxism: its way of approaching any problem whatever. For example, the sociological methods and techniques for study of small groups may be employed with a Marxist methodology —that is, a Marxist overview of the entire problem involved, or, let us say, with a neopositivist one.

Ideology of Society

Thus far, but for illustrative digressions, the discussion has been of ideology *qua* ideology: methodology, the approach to all things whatever. But our concern is the application of that ideology to a particular class of things: human society in its various manifestations, and the scientific disciplines that study it. We know from Engels that Marxism holds that man makes his own history. It is not superimposed from without by any god, fundamental principle, prime mover, *or inevitability*, for that would deprive men of their role as makers of history. Marxism holds this to be a reductionist notion, equating men not only with unthinking forms of life, but with inanimate objects governed by inexorable laws of natural science. Both predestination—a frankly and naturally religious concept—and free will are notions long antedating Marxism. It opposes both: "History is not programmed by anything." [13] Predestination failed to explain the varieties of human social experience, as free will could not explain observable similarities which, in mid-twentieth-century terms, would be called statistically significant.

Marxism appeared at a time when the scientific method had proved itself in all fields of nature. Men were able to do things with the laws thus discovered, even change nature itself and predict occurrences in it. As materialists, Marx and Engels regarded mankind as part of nature, subject to its laws but having in addition its own, as does every other level of organization. It followed that application of the scientific method to observation of human society would permit the deduction of laws, but these would be laws differing from those of all lower levels of organization of matter in that mankind is able to comprehend and therefore make use of these regularities to change itself, as it can change lower forms. But human consciousness is operative whether it knows laws or not, and therefore the laws of human society have never been more than broad tendencies, thanks to man's ability to devise differing solutions to the problems with which he is confronted.

The most important of the social laws deduced by Marxism is that men have always been organized (part of the nature of man is that he is a social being), and that the prime purpose of this organization is to wrest a livelihood from nature. The manner in which men are organized for this purpose in any particular place at any particular time in history is called the *mode of production*. This may be a primitive gathering, fishing, and hunting economy in which success is possible only if all cooperate, and in which the results are so meager that they must be shared approximately equally to avoid death by starvation for some, which would endanger the survival of all by making the entire group too small and weak to function and defend itself. This system Marxists call primitive communism.

Another system is one in which these communal groups remain, but chieftains, ruling clans, or priest-kings emerge, who perform trading or military or irrigation-directing functions for the whole, and who obtain the material means of life through taxes exacted more or less voluntarily from the communes. At this stage the members of communes usually no longer share equally in its products, but hold the land more or less jointly, so that the individual on the one hand has the protection of the communal entity and on the other has nothing to gain by seriously improving the parcel he happens to be working for a given season or group of years. This system Marx called the "Asian," because he was aware of it chiefly in ancient Mesopotamia and similar areas. Marxist scholars today, chiefly in France (most Russians have now adopted this as valid),[14] hold this system to be broadly characteristic of all sub-Saharan Africa before the white man came, of southeast Asia, and of pre-Columbian Latin America. Marx regarded the combination of mutual assistance and lack of incentive to individual improvement of farming or cattle raising as making for stagnation in this system, and thus explained its persistence virtually unchanged in many parts of the world for exceedingly long periods. Soviet scholars have done excellent work in archeology and prehistory, from which they have drawn conclusions substantiating this general view and also shedding light on the transition from primitive communism to the Asian mode.[15]

Another mode of production is that which Marx called the ancient, with reference to classical Greece and Rome, and which the Russians denote either by that name or by the term "slaveholding." It is one in which the world's work is done by slaves, and the slave owners may philosophize or fight or whatever at leisure. Some Soviet sources have sought to define the slaveholding order as one in which both slave and free labor were combined in the process of production itself, inasmuch as, in many technically slaveholding societies, there were very few slaves, relatively speaking. However, I believe that this definition was an attempt to avoid the "Asian mode" notion.[16]

Still another mode of production is the feudal, in which the ultimate producer is, in the classical sense, a serf, part of whose time must be given to work for his lord and part of which remains to him to till his own soil. This division of time applies even if it appears in the somewhat concealed form of quitrent in kind or cash or both. This society has all sorts of gradations, toward slavery in the one direction and free yeomanry in the other.

In Europe, commerce developed, chiefly among freemen, some of whom became very wealthy, and riches were later obtained from overseas trade or outright plunder (as of India and South America). The capital thus acquired, plus steps taken to drive the peasants from the land and make them dependent upon finding work for wages, plus the fact that it was learned that products could be made more cheaply if the work were divided into operations of which each participant performed only one or a few, led to the development of capitalism. This is a system in which the members of the proletariat or working *class*, those who possess *no productive property* of their own, work for wages or salaries for those who do, who are defined, by the fact of *ownership*, as the capitalist *class*. (Marxism reserves the notion of social class *solely* to the criterion of ownership and employment, so the middle class consists basically of those who are self-employed.) Those wages or salaries are essentially what is needed to keep the worker or employee and his family going, at the standards *developed by the struggles of that class* through unions, through individual bargaining based on the demand for labor, and through legislation resulting from political organization. But the capitalist class in all its branches (industrialists, bankers, landlords, merchants, etc.) always pockets the difference between what the worker needs to live on, under the conditions thus established, and the actual value produced by the worker's labor. That is profit, and that is what capitalists are in business for. Therefore, in the Marxist understanding, the very highest paid worker, with his home, his car, his boat, and his color TV, is exploited, as otherwise there would be no point to employing him.

Marxism holds that social thought has always *reflected* these various historical realities. But it does not regard "reflection" as an exact image, or as predetermined automatically. (Lenin elaborated the notion of reflection as a philosophical concept at some length, and Soviet philosophers do much work on this.) It is simply that man's mind works with what it observes, and the forms of human society are obviously among the most important stimuli and interests of that thought.

Divine wisdom and divine right, or simple fear of divine wrath for attempts to overthrow stratifications of society or even forms of rule, have dominated one line of thought. This ancient trend was particularly manifest in the U.S.S.R. during the period of secular deification of Stalin.[17] The notion of social law was bowdlerized into that of inevitability, which conflicts with Marxism, and served as a surrogate for predestination. A strong residue remains today in the cult of Lenin, although Khrushchev, as early as 1960, in reasoning the noninevitability of war, performed the service of saying that the world had changed in the forty years since Lenin's day, when imperialism could dictate the course of events, and that attempts to derive all current policy from his writings would not be very productive.

A second traditional mode of thought that has no written support at all in the U.S.S.R. is that which holds that thus things have always been and thus they always will be. It is not entirely absent from the public mind, however, and is heard in such forms as: "Why protest? It won't accomplish anything anyhow." Or, with respect to demonstrative forms of protest: "It isn't our custom" ("*U nas tak ne priniato*"). This is not to be confused with the fear of speaking out in the Stalin period, but it does diminish a social thinker's expectation of public support for radical departures, and helps explain the recourse to literary and particularly poetic forms, which are traditional in Russia as a means of breaking down stereotyped thought, and command vast audiences if there is talent to sustain them. It would be deadly for an American magazine to devote forty pages to a poem, as *Yunost* did for *Bratsk Station*.

A third approach, quite popular in the West today, particularly in historiography, doesn't seek to explain at all, but speaks of fate, accident. In old Russia this was very popular, particularly in the mass mind, but also, along with the two preceding approaches, in conservative social thought. This fact is often ignored today by specialists abroad whose desire to describe the Communist Revolution as a historical aberration causes them to center attention on nonconservative trends that, in their opinion, might have offered alternative solutions.

This view is refuted by the history of Soviet social thought itself. At the time of the Revolution, Russian social scientists were largely liberals and, in Marxist philosophical terms, idealists. Because developments had not followed their ideas, their concepts subsequent to the Revolution were in crisis. The decline in popularity of these ideas was not wholly due to lack of access to them. The very first year after the Communists took power saw, for example, republication of Kliuchevsky's *A Course in Russian History*, which had been out of print,[18] and two volumes of articles by him.[19]

The contest between Marxism-Leninism and its opponents was no mere peaceful competition. From 1922 on there was a constant intimidation of non-Marxist and non-Leninist ideology. Physical force—exile, etc.—was among the techniques employed. The regime largely bypassed the existing ideological establishment and set up a new one in its place, manned by people who owed their opportunities and their positions to the new order. But the same techniques failed to eliminate religion, which in Russia was essentially the ideology of the uneducated. In natural science, they failed to destroy belief in Mendel, Einstein, Wiener, Pauling. If, in contrast to these, liberal, Menshevik, anarchist, and other ideologies actually did disappear in social science, it is difficult to avoid the conclusion that this was because they proved sterile as tools to deal with Russian reality, while Marxism-Leninism did not.

Marxism was able to win the upper hand in university ideology within about a decade after the Revolution. This created a situation without precedent in the social sciences. Until then, Marxism had been simply a tool for social revolution, and its thinkers had directed their energies primarily to the political field. Although, on a world scale, socialist parties had hundreds of thousands of members and millions of votes before World War I, and included very substantial minorities of professional people and some creative intellectuals in certain countries, the number of social scientists who had sought to reexamine their fields of specialization in the light of the Marxist understanding was negligible.

Consider the field of historiography. In Russia, although Lenin himself had written a book on the development of capitalism there that meets the most rigorous standards of historiography, there was actually only one professional historian who was a Communist, M. N. Pokrovsky. He faced a task of many aspects. One was the writing of a history of Russia that would be not merely a chronicle of the doings of tsars, generals, and other big shots, but would offer a rational explanation to the people of the miracle they had wrought in making the Revolution, inasmuch as the mass of the people was absent as a moving force in the existing histories. Another was to persuade the existing historians that they too should reexamine their country's past to understand how the unthinkable had happened. A third was to organize the training of a new generation of historians in the Marxist world view, to organize publishing, and all the rest.

Like everything else in the Soviet Union, this was entirely a pioneering effort. Little wonder that many of its products look, in the eyes of Soviet scholars today, like excessive simplifications. Because the economic had been largely (not entirely) ignored in prior historiography, it was now overemphasized, to fix its significance in people's minds. This was true not only of works written about Russia, but of the new world histories, ancient histories, medieval and modern histories written there. Whereas formerly it was the powerful, the exalted, and the rich who had been the only dramatis personae of history, now the opposite was the case. Spartacus in Rome, the peasants of the jacqueries of France, Wat Tyler's Rebellion, the Peasant War in Germany, the Taiping and Boxer Rebellions in China, the Whiskey Rebellion in the early postrevolutionary United States, those whom Kipling called the fuzzy-wuzzies in Africa, the Sepoy Rebellion in India against British rule a century ago, the Paris Commune, the First International, the so-called Haymarket Riot in Chicago in 1886, and all the strikes of the labor movement everywhere: these were the only good things in history, because they represented the people in motion.

It must be remembered not only that this, along with comparable emphases in other branches of social thought, was righting a wrong in the writing of history, albeit overcorrecting, but also that it arose out of the general mood in Russia at the time, a mood shared as much by historians as anyone else. Everyone was aware that Russia was a terribly backward country—in everything but its people's willingness to pioneer a new order of society. The Revolution was made in the full expectation that the working class of Germany or some other literate and industrial country would also overthrow capitalism in the chaos of defeat in World War I. Lenin firmly expected this, even in England. Revolutions did occur in Germany and Hungary, but they were defeated, and the Russians were overwhelmed by the fact that their country, starving, disease-ridden, unable to read and write, would have to seek, alone, to open a new chapter in history. Thus it was quite natural that, in the chapters mankind had already written, they sought what evidence they could find that their kind of people, the common people, could perform such a feat.

This, plus hatred of those they had ousted, plus the primitive understanding of Marxism they had been able to acquire in this brief period from a tiny handful of competent teachers, also led them to picture all previous rulers and governing classes everywhere in a negative light. This is hardly Marxism. Lenin wrote with the highest esteem of the leaders of the American Revolution, whom he knew perfectly well to be wealthy and often slave owners, because he regarded that revolution as the one step forward *possible in the given time and place*.[20] Marx and Engels had supported Lincoln during the Civil War, for exactly the same reason.[21]

The first generation of Soviet social scientists performed an enormous work, for all its faults and shortcomings, and those of them who are alive today—it should be remembered that the entire period since the Revolution falls within a single working lifetime—are in many cases men and women of distinction by any academic standards.

But it is not merely the normal course of time, or even the hardships of World War II in the U.S.S.R., with its 20,000,000 dead, that account for the small number of the first Marxist generation of Soviet scholars alive today. Stalin sought to make unpersons of Leon Trotsky, Bukharin, and other thinkers over whom he won out in a struggle over policy that became to a substantial degree one for personal power, and he succeeded. Scholars following the lead particularly of these two were, as a consequence, first ousted from the field and then jailed or murdered. Stalin wanted the Communist party's history rewritten to make it the party of Lenin *and* Stalin, with all others absent or mere functionaries executing their ideas. He wished justification of the iron-handed rule he projected, and so favored those who believed Ivan the Terrible to have been a progressive figure in history, and also those who saw only the positive in Peter the Great's modernization of Russia, and not the fact that St. Petersburg was built on the bones of countless numbers of serfs.

During World War II and thereafter until his death, Stalin, who himself was not Russian or a Slav, denigrated the rebels who had held out against Russian conquests in the Caucasus and other places incorporated into the tsarist empire, and glorified their Russian colonialist conquerors.

While Soviet research, writing, and teaching were greatly damaged by this, and in many respects continue to be—for example, there is no biography in the Soviet Union not only of Trotsky, but even of the founding father of Russian Marxism, Plekhanov, whose complete works were reprinted under Lenin despite his opposition to the Revolution—social science did do a vast amount of useful and creative work in fields where no connection could be drawn with Stalin's policies or where honest research happened to coincide with his desires. In anticipation of World War II, Stalin, aware of the terrible sense of inferiority widespread among all sections of Soviet society vis-à-vis the West, wished to strengthen the people's belief that they could successfully withstand Germany or even a combination of anticommunist powers. Original research into early Russian history helped build national pride, and so was permitted and encouraged.

On the other hand, police methods were used to win academic debates even in some spheres having no bearing upon current politics. Earlier I outlined a number of modes of production as Marx believed them to exist. I was careful not to suggest that they were held to have succeeded each other in the precise order listed, or that each of them must necessarily exist at some point in the development of each human society. However, precisely this was insisted upon in a debate among Soviet scholars in 1931. Moreover, what Marx termed the "Asian mode" was ruled out of existence by those who upheld the model of rigid and inevitable sequence. They won out not by historical argument, but by accusing their opponents of being Bukharinite or Trotskyite. Such an accusation became a ticket to a concentration camp, or worse.

That stage is over, but its long-run effects were such that the episode I have just described was not made public to the present Soviet generation until 1965, nearly thirty-five years after the event.

It is in this framework that Soviet social thought has developed: on the one hand, the first situation, in which Marxism had the opportunity to demonstrate what it could produce with the intellectual and material resources of a country's university system at its disposal; on the other hand, the compulsion to function within the confines of what was, for the last twenty years of Stalin's lifetime, an absolute monarchy in the political sense, and is today in some respects still a McCarthyite situation. But a McCarthyite situation is one in which it is perfectly possible to do good work if one agrees with the prevailing ideology, if it is not a priori destructive of one's particular field, or if one's points of difference are not fundamental or do not deal with areas forbidden by the powers that be. Under Stalin, *any* difference was regarded as fundamental, and penalties were fearsome.

I have no reason to believe that any Soviet social scientist supports capitalism, any more than any American supports reinstitution of chattel slavery. Therefore, while it is not yet possible there to write a wholly objective history of the U.S.S.R.—insofar as Trotsky, Molotov, or Khrushchev were major historical figures—it is entirely possible to do objective research, for example, on the changes in the class origins of the people working in factories as the Soviet regime developed: a matter that had a great deal to do with the different political conclusions these men drew. (Were these workers proletarian in ideology, and therefore to be trusted to implement the "proletarian dictatorship," or were they very recent recruits from the peasantry replacing a revolutionary working class decimated in the civil war or recruited into administration, and was it therefore necessary for a dictatorship to be wielded over them?) Likewise, it has been possible, particularly since Stalin's death, to draw highly diverse conclusions about capitalist or underdeveloped countries, and even about theories of social thought.

Let me summarize that situation by quoting an Italian historian after the first bilateral conference of Russians and Italians in that field in 1963. He said that the panorama of Soviet historical work

amazed the majority of members of the Italian delegation with its breadth and riches. . . . Above all, I was struck by the fact that Soviet historiography does not remotely correspond to that picture of uniformity with which persons lacking the necessary knowledge but possessing vast assurance have sought to depict it.[22]

In the literature of Soviet social science we do not find, and should not expect to find, studies of a number of problems which simply do not exist in the Soviet Union, because of differences between its social order and our own. For example, there is no investigation of tuition for higher education, the advisability of free or low-cost medical care, ghettoes, etc. But the Soviet Union does face other problems in accordance with the nature of its system, and these problems are being studied: the degree to which minorities have entered specific fields of employment, patterns of use of medical facilities, the *level* of the universal minimum wage, etc.

The Party and the Social Sciences

In August, 1967, the effective policy-making body of the Soviet Union, the Central Committee of the Communist party, adopted a decision, for the first time in its history, to pour money into the social sciences. Because of its unprecedented nature, and the very real consequences of any such decision in the U.S.S.R., it deserves quotation and analysis at length. It begins by listing that which it claims has already been accomplished: [23]

On the foundation of synthesis of a vast amount of practical experience, the party has developed and enriched Marxist teachings on the socialist revolution, the proletarian dictatorship, and the building of socialism; elaborated theoretical problems with respect to the country's industrialization, the collectivization of agriculture, the cultural revolution, and the development of Soviet democracy, of socialist nations, and of the multinational Soviet state; it has discovered new regularities and motive forces of the development of socialist society, and defined the principal tasks and conditions for the gradual transition from socialism to communism.

In a certain sense, *this is a listing of the contents of the ideology of Soviet social science*, and deserves very careful reading. The document goes on to say that present conditions, including those of "ideological struggle," require "deeper analysis of social development and a new upswing in the level of Marxist-Leninist education" of Soviet personnel. Research in the humanities "does not always yield a deep-going and objective analysis of the real processes in the life of society, and this interferes with proper evaluation of the experience of history and the prospects for the development of our society."

Shortcomings are detailed:

a lag in the study of fundamental problems of theory . . . little attention to the quality and depth of philosophical generalizations derived from the most recent achievements of natural science, and to the study of problems of social psychology, the group, and the individual. . . . Until recently there was not enough concrete social research, and its basis in methods of scholarship remains highly empirical. . . . Many aspects and problems of . . . the national liberation movement still await treatment in depth and interdisciplinary research. . . . Social science personnel . . . have a responsible role in the struggle . . . against the anti-Soviet great-power ideology of Mao Tse-tungism. . . .

The state of scientific information in the social sciences lags seriously behind the needs of the day. The research institutions of the U.S.S.R. Academy of Sciences do not have modern technical means to the required degree. . . .

Further improvement is needed in the teaching of the social sciences in our higher educational institutions. [The responsible ministries and departments] have not yet assured the proper level of teaching of the social sciences. . . . There are shortcomings in the training of personnel for the social sciences. [The administrators and party organizations] are not displaying the required concern for the growth and promotion of young scholars.

The social science disciplines in which special improvement is sought are "philosophy [which formally included sociology in the U.S.S.R. until 1968; sociologists distinguished between the two, as did others], economics, scientific communism, history, law, esthetics, education, psychology." There is a listing of major problems to receive attention in each of these fields. In considering it, and the resolution as a whole, it must be understood that this sort of thing does not come out of the head of the Central Committee full-blown, nor is it imposed from without; it has been arrived at by much discussion between representatives of that body and leading figures in the corresponding disciplines. A very large percentage of social scientists in all spheres are party members, and there are some, as there are natural scientists of distinction, on the Central Committee.

In philosophy-cum-sociology, the list includes: "the relationship of objective and subjective factors in the development of society . . . study of the laws of social consciousness; theoretical treatment of problems of the individual and the group, society and the state, socialist humanism." "Socioeconomic studies in the field of demography" are classified under economics—a consequence of the fact that the resolution still did not recognize sociology as an independent field. Other special emphases in economics were to include study of "new forms of imperialist struggle for redivision of the world; study of the economic, social, and political problems of the developing countries liberated from colonial dependence."

As the present essay is on ideology, I list more fully the subjects to be developed under "scientific communism":

working out of the Leninist theory of socialist revolution as it applies to the present era; identification of the regularities of development of the world revolutionary process, analysis of the class struggle of the international proletariat and problems of the national liberation movement, and the struggle against imperialism; treatment of theoretical problems of the international Communist movement in the present epoch . . . deep-going exploration of the antagonistic contradictions between socialism and capitalism . . . discovery of the social results of the revolution in science and technology . . . elaboration of problems of the development of relationships among nationalities . . . analysis . . . of the directions to be taken in overcoming the residuum of private property, religion, and other traces of the past in the minds and daily lives of the people. . . .

Where differences are known to exist among Soviet scholars over the wisdom of policies the party has pursued in the past, the Central Committee does not surprise us by any departure from conservatism (as in implicitly rejecting the sociologists' demand for recognition of their discipline as independent). Thus, while Soviet scholars are agreed that collectivization of agriculture as it occurred in the U.S.S.R. is not a precedent that must be followed elsewhere, and some raise serious questions as to the way it was pursued there (noting, for example, that kulaks favorable to cooperatives were permitted to join collective farms in the central Asian republics, whereas they were barred beforehand elsewhere in the country), the way in which this problem is listed in the resolution is merely: "demonstration of the heroism of the Soviet people in . . . the collectivization of agriculture."

In law, there is to be "treatment of problems of the organization and activity of the soviets."

The word "sociology" does appear in the resolution, but only in a pejorative context. Yet within one year the Academy of Sciences had founded an institute of "Concrete Social Research," i.e., empirical sociology (*Izvestiia*, June 8, 1968). "Ethnic narrow-mindedness" in theory and politics is one of the manifestations among Communists that are particularly to be fought.

There is specific recognition of the "need for wider practice of the procedure of comradely discussions on disputed matters and those on which there is insufficient clarity."

The resolution contains a striking illustration of the relationship between the party and government:

The Central Committee of the CPSU has assigned the State Planning Commission of the U.S.S.R., the U.S.S.R. Council of Ministers' Committee of State on Science and Technology, the U.S.S.R. Academy of Sciences, and the U.S.S.R. Ministry of Higher and Secondary Education to prepare and submit for examination by the Central Committee of the CPSU, by January 1, 1968, proposals for a fundamental improvement in the organization, planning, and financing of research in the social sciences, with the object of . . . bringing the system of institutes in the humanities into correspondence with the needs of scholarship . . . attaining a proper combination of team and individual forms of work, and of experienced personnel and young scholars, and of strengthening the material position of institutes in the social sciences.

In the light of the continued predominance of old-fashioned individual research, and of entrenched scholars well on in years, the foregoing can only bode well.

The resolution also calls for "comprehensive study of Marxist thought abroad: maintenance of continuing contacts with scholarly institutions of socialist countries and the brother Communist parties, and coordination with them of research in the social sciences."

The party's Institute of Marxism-Leninism and the government's Central Archives Administration are instructed to assure the provision of "modern technical equipment for reproduction and duplication of documentary materials," while the government's Central Statistical Administration, the State Planning Commission, and the Academy of Sciences are commissioned "to develop a scientifically valid system of statistical data essential to social research, and to expand publication of such data, and do so in the various specialties."

Finally, the resolution obligates the party (meaningfully listing all its levels down to the county), the U.S.S.R. Ministry of Higher and Secondary Specialized Education, and the presidium of the Academy of Sciences to "raise their sights with respect to the level of qualification of people professionally employed in the social sciences." It ascribes "enormous importance to the mastery of Marxist-Leninist theory . . . and of scientific forms and methods of work, by party and government personnel."

It must be emphasized that resolutions of the Central Committee of the Soviet Communist party are not statements for the record. They are operative decisions intended to be acted upon, and are not issued until it is believed possible to act upon them, financially, organizationally, and otherwise. Under the concept of discipline obtaining in that organization, the words of such a resolution are supreme authority until another in the same field supersedes it, or until developments over an extended period of time render it moot. Because of that, every phrase quoted has been fought over and argued out before final adoption by the committee. By way of illustration, the previous paragraph reflects judgments as between the entrenched brahmins, who in defense of their own superficiality and quotation-mongering have essentially argued that rote learning of the Marxist Old Testament and Lenin's New are enough, and on the other hand those who hold that Marxism-Leninism is an essential background of approach for any civilized man, but does not make him a social scientist any more than knowledge of Newton and Einstein makes one a physicist. The phrasing shows that the latter have won. Naturally those who emerge with truly original concepts or projects, not envisaged in the discussion preceding adoption of the resolution, will have to fight it out from scratch. But the resolution does provide a more favorable atmosphere for reception of such ideas.

Soviet-Era Additions to Marxism

The Soviet literature is studded with the mysterious words "base" or "basis" (*bazis*) and "superstructure," and often speaks of the relationship between them. "Base" is shorthand for the economic mode of production, but "superstructure" refers, in Marx's words, to "legal, political, religious, esthetic, or philosophic—in short, ideological—forms." As materialists, Soviet thinkers believe that a society best serves its purpose when superstructure harmonizes with base, but as dialecticians they know that the economic system can be changed by the superstructure. As superstructure is, by definition, ideological—that is, the consequence of an effort of thought—proposals to change it must carefully consider whether the results will be a greater harmony with base or a desired modification in the latter. This is why a clear understanding of the rock-bottom character of the economic system or systems existing in the time and place under examination is so insistently sought by Soviet scholars, whatever the discipline of the superstructure an individual may work in, particularly those involved with problems of the present day, whether within the U.S.S.R. or on the world scene.

In recent years, no Soviet social science has witnessed a greater upheaval than economics. Before the needed changes in it could be made, agreement was required on precisely the kind of relations (mode) of production that exist in the U.S.S.R. The answer is not as obvious as it might seem. In a lecture of 1966, the late Isaac Deutscher wrote: "By definition, Socialist Man lives in a . . . stateless society. . . . The society in which he lives has to be so highly developed, so wealthy, educated, and civilized that there is no objective need or necessity for it to allow any recrudescence of inequality or oppression. That is what *all* Marxists before Stalin took for granted." Earlier in the same paper he said: "We maintain that Socialist Man is conceivable only against the background of an unprecedented abundance of material and cultural services. This is the ABC of Marxism." [24]

Soviet economists disagree with this completely. They believe that their society hitherto, and into the future until affluence is achieved, accords with the description provided by Marx in his *Critique of the Gotha Programme:*

What we have to deal with here is a communist society, not as it has *developed* on its own foundations, but, on the contrary, as it *emerges* from capitalist society; which is thus, in every respect, economically, morally and intellectually, still stamped with the birthmarks of the old society from whose womb it emerges. Accordingly the individual producer receives back from society—after the deductions have been made (for amortization, expansion, economic and social insurance, administration and public services)— exactly what he gives to it. . . . The same amount of labor which he has given to society in one form, he receives back in another. . . . On the other hand, nothing can pass into the ownership of individuals except individual means of consumption. . . .

But one man is superior to another physically or mentally and so supplies more labor in the same time, or can labor for a longer time. . . .

This *equal* right [to the proceeds of one's own labor] recognizes no class differences, because everyone is only a worker like everyone else; but it tacitly recognizes unequal individual endowment and thus productive capacity as natural privileges. . . .

But these defects are inevitable in the first phase of communist society as it is when it has just emerged after prolonged birth pangs from capitalist society. Right can never be higher than the economic structure of society and the cultural development thereby determined.

In the higher phase of communist society . . . after the productive forces have also increased with the all-round development of the individual, and all the springs of cooperative wealth flow more abundantly—only then can the narrow horizon of bourgeois right be fully left behind and society inscribe on its banners: from each according to his ability, to each according to his needs.[25]

For semantic convenience, what Marx described in 1875 as "the first phase" later came to be called socialism (not to be confused with socialism as a movement), while "the higher phase" became known as communism. In 1917, just before the Bolsheviks took power, Lenin expanded on this: [26]

Hence, the first phase of communism cannot produce justice and equality; differences, and unjust differences, in wealth will still exist, but the *exploitation* of man by man will have become impossible, because it will be impossible to seize the *means of production*, the factories, machines, land, etc., as private property.

Like Marx, Lenin was keenly aware of problems of psychology, and continued:

If we are not to fall into utopianism, we cannot imagine that, having overthrown capitalism, people will at once learn to work for society *without any standard of right*; indeed, the abolition of capitalism *does not immediately* create the economic prerequisites for such a change. . . .

The state will be able to wither away completely when . . . people become so accustomed to observing the fundamental rules of social life and when their labor is so productive that they will voluntarily work *according to their ability*. "The narrow horizon of bourgeois right," which compels one to calculate with the shrewdness of a Shylock whether he has not worked half an hour more than another, whether he is not getting less pay than another—this narrow horizon will then be left behind.

Lenin did not attempt to play the prophet in terms of dates, writing, two pages on:

By what stages, by what practical measures humanity will proceed to this higher aim—we do not and cannot know.

Soviet economists contend that their "shrewd" calculations of economic incentives in preaffluent socialism flow naturally from these ideological formulations, and that their interest in the techniques of bourgeois society is entirely appropriate so long as "the narrow horizon of bourgeois right" cannot yet be left behind because labor is not yet sufficiently productive. This equally explains, they say, their intense concern both with increasing that productivity and with causing "all the springs of cooperative wealth [to] flow more abundantly."

The interest shown by Soviet political scientists in techniques of government in the West takes its ideological origins from a further notion of Lenin's expressed in the same work:

Hence the interesting phenomenon that communism in its first phase retains "the narrow horizon of *bourgeois* right." Of course, bourgeois right in regard to distribution of articles of *consumption* inevitably presupposes the existence of the *bourgeois state*, for right is nothing without an apparatus capable of *enforcing* the observance of the standards of right. Consequently, for a certain time not only bourgeois right, but even the bourgeois state remains under communism, without the bourgeoisie! [Emphasis throughout in the original.] [27]

Elsewhere, also before the Revolution, Lenin wrote of the duration of persistence of the state:

This truth has been indisputable for socialists and it includes recognition of the fact that the *state* will exist until victorious socialism develops into full communism.[28]

On the other hand, the differences between Soviet and Western economics and political science ultimately rest, in the former discipline, upon Marx's "nothing can pass into the ownership of individuals except individual means of production," and in the latter upon Lenin's "without the bourgeoisie."

The emergence of the Soviet economy from its "command" period, and of government from the period of one-man rule, is certainly related to the improved international position of the U.S.S.R. Social scientists concern themselves, quite naturally, with the maintenance of a tolerable world situation, with improving it, and also with removing the roots, as they see them, of the tensions that exist. The ideological foundation of this work is the by now familiar notion of "peaceful coexistence," words that first appear in Lenin, as far as I have been able to determine, in an interview with a *Manchester Guardian* correspondent in 1922.[29]

The Soviet ideology of coexistence comprises the policies Lenin first enunciated in justifying, against Trotsky and others, the Brest-Litovsk Peace with Germany in 1918, and then developed in interviews and particularly a presentation to William Bullitt, the U. S. ambassador-to-be, in 1919.[30] It includes the principles of the Anglo-Russian trade agreement of 1921, the Rapallo Treaty with Germany of 1922 (in many ways anticipating present Soviet relations with France), and support to the feudal king of Afghanistan in his struggle for independence against England. It draws upon a 1921 treaty with Persia, abandoning old Russia's imperialist privileges but leaving Moscow the right to reenter that country if a third power sought to use Persia as a base for invasion of Soviet Russia. It incorporates the granting of direct aid in arms, money, and military advice to noncommunist nationalists, such as that extended to Mustapha Kemal Pasha (Ataturk) against the British-sustained sultan-caliph in 1920–22. All these facets were developed in Lenin's lifetime and under his direction, and were given generalized form by him as principles governing the existence of a socialist state in a world containing powerful capitalist states as well as nationalist, anti-imperialist movements.[31] That these practices of forty-five years ago, to all of which Lenin, Chicherin, Litvinov, Radek, and others gave theoretical explanation, have crystallized into ideology is indicated both by the quotations from present-day Soviet social scientists that follow shortly and by the practices of the other socialist states. The U.S.S.R., China, and Cuba all pursue very active foreign trade with capitalist western Europe, Japan, and Canada, as well as with underdeveloped countries, and engage in cultural exchange (the Chinese opera, circus, books) with one or more major capitalist lands. Every socialist state engages in diplomatic relations with large numbers of capitalist countries, and every one that has been admitted to the U.N. has accepted admission and participates in its affairs, including Albania and Cuba.

Not only in the literature of international relations, but also in journals of philosophy and law, one finds Soviet social scientists giving serious and extensive treatment to the problem of coexistence and to its relation with revolution. Levintov, a historian, in an article of the highest importance titled "Some Aspects of the Leninist Theory of Revolution," has special reference to Lenin's differentiation among revolution "in general," "in the broad sense," and "in the narrow sense," "the revolutionary role of reactionary periods," his notion of a "crisis of the nation," and the relative roles of objective conditions and conscious leadership.[32] Chinese and Latin-American experiences are used in illustration.

Kovalev, a sociologist, deals with the more overriding question, "War and Revolution." [33] Of the devastating consequences of a world war with today's weapons, he writes: "Entire peoples would be thrown backward by centuries in their development. Under such conditions a world war would not only not accelerate the all-round development of mankind but would seriously complicate the founding and development of a new social order." But "a new war, if the imperialists succeeded in launching it, would inevitably lead to revolution in the countries of the capitalist world." His view on the responsibility of the U.S.S.R. as a revolutionary country is phrased thus: "In this connection both refusal to support struggling peoples against their oppressors, or efforts to change the social system of a given people against its will, from without, would be treason to the principles of proletarian internationalism." * Candid discussion of what occurred in the east European countries after World War II is not yet to be found in Soviet writings. In that zone, direct considerations of the military security of the U.S.S.R. were overriding, but to say this out loud would undermine the legitimacy of these governments. With this exception, Kovalev discusses the question of self-determination quite meaningfully.

Fedoseev, a sociologist who is a vice-president of the U.S.S.R. Academy of Sciences, meets the issue of coexistence versus revolution even more directly: [34]

It is quite clear that to identify peaceful coexistence among states with preservation of the social status quo would be to abandon social progress, would constitute an attempt at theoretical validation of the need to preserve capitalism to eternity, to protect it against revolutionary changes, to place the social, national liberation movements outside the law, and to justify a policy of export of counterrevolution.

He takes issue with P. Gallois and Raymond Aron on the matter of nuclear stalemate:

It seems to us that they sound contemptuous of the human race as a whole. . . . When dealing with *homo sapiens* . . . it is necessary to have recourse not to the sense of terror but to human reason. . . . A peace erected on the basis of oversaturation with thermonuclear weapons is a bivouac at the crater of a volcano which may start erupting at any moment. Never mind the instability of any such "equilibrium," we note only that the economic and material costs associated with a competition in

---

* Che Guevara's attempt to launch a guerrilla movement in Bolivia from without is regarded as having been predoomed to failure by Soviet people to whom I have broached the matter, although his gallantry and ideals were admired. This view has not found its way into print because that would have a negative impact on relations with Castro.

intimidation is an excessive luxury under conditions in which millions are starving or on the edge of starvation. Moreover, terror has its own internal "logic," the logic of irrationality not subject to control by reason.

In a world of sovereign states, reason must take on organized form:

The very fact of the existence of the U.N. for a period of over 20 years, for all the great shortcomings of its work, testifies to the possibility of unifying in a world organization the forces directed to maintaining peace.

This is the point of departure for an article by Tunkin, president of the Soviet International Law Association: "The United Nations: 1945–65 (Problems of International Law)." [35]

While "ideological coexistence" is denounced, that attitude is difficult to reconcile either with the Soviet notion that coexistence is in any case a unity involving struggle as its dialectical opposite or with the actual practice of participation in international academic discussion. Perhaps the characteristic Soviet tone is best suggested in Velikovich's "Catholicism's Dialogue with the Contemporary World." [36] This review of the ecumenical councils and current Catholic affairs takes as point of departure the idea that the dialogue arises out of the Church's need "to abandon those political and ideological concepts that cannot influence the masses of the people today and, in certain instances, damage the authority of the Church." Velikovich conducts his side of the dialogue itself, however, in highly civilized fashion. This style is beginning to penetrate back into discussion of religion within the U.S.S.R. For a Soviet Ukrainian atheist journal, *Liudnya i svit*, to have published, as it did in April, 1966, a defense of the ethical values contributed by Judaism, including Christianity itself, at that stage in history when all moral thought appeared in religious form, was probably without precedent in such a magazine. It also carried a rejoinder, of course. Even more remarkable was the publication in the 6,000,000-daily-circulation youth newspaper *Komsomolskaia pravda*, in 1967, of an article by a reader in defense of religion as the only source of morality. This, too, was responded to by the editors. But the atheist nature of Marxism as a materialist philosophy continues generally to be the basis for a militant ideology of "antireligion," contrary to the situation in other Communist-governed countries, and this has a negative effect on the attempts to set up a real sociology of religion by people like Klibanov [37] and Mitrokhin. [38]

Just as international relations provide the stimulus and the need for an ideological base not only in the discipline of that name, but also in philosophy, branches of sociology, and the like, so has the recent anticolonial revolution created a similar need among anthropologists and others. In point of fact, the very first ideological principle worked out in the U.S.S.R. subsequent to Lenin's death (although he certainly foreshadowed it) was that industrialization is a prerequisite to the building of socialism in any country underdeveloped at the time of a revolution having socialism as its goal. In a nonindustrialized country, production is essentially individual (except in societies still communal), and no class exists whose interests can be served, in the Marxist view, only by a socialist organization of society consequent upon the fact that it produces in social fashion, through division of labor. Soviet ideology recognizes that industrialization in the U.S.S.R. proceeded under conditions that subsequent states have not had to face: capitalist encirclement, the isolation of the U.S.S.R. as the one Communist country of that period, and the consequent need for a forced pace of development with utmost mobilization of resources in the absence of availability of outside loans, requiring very rigid economies. Therefore it is industrialization per se, not its high rate and accompanying political strains in the Soviet Union, that is regarded as having the validity of social law in backward lands.

Ultimate collectivization of agriculture is another principle taken as a universal point of departure by Soviet social scientists dealing with societies moving toward socialism. Collectivization is understood to represent a compromise between social and private interest: cooperative work side by side with retention of a personal household patch and minimal individual livestock ownership. It raises to the level of ideology the recognition that the need to undermine spontaneous growth of capitalism in the countryside by bringing the peasant into cooperative *production* (as distinct from distributive and consumer cooperatives) must recognize the deeply ingrained proprietor psychology.

In addition to the concepts of industrialization and collectivization, the immediate post-civil-war period produced certain other ideas which, although initially conceived of as temporary practical expedients in a devastated and disorganized country, have proved applicable with the force of regularities wherever social revolutions have occurred, and are now treated as such by Soviet social scientists concerned with these problems. One such ideological *sine qua non* is that while government should take basic industry, large-scale light industry, banking, foreign and wholesale trade, communications, railroads, health, education, and science entirely into its own hands, it is permissible and helpful for a greater or lesser period of time to allow private initiative to discover and meet consumer needs through small manufacturing, crafts, entertainment, local stores, and family farming, including seasonal employment of hired hands.[39] A second is that fundamentally nonexploiting (that is, family-scale) producers in town and country should be brought to socialism not through nationalization, as with all large enterprise depending upon numerous hired personnel, but by persuasion to join or convert into co-operatives.[40] The consequences of violation of the voluntary approach in the U.S.S.R. and elsewhere to the productivity of agriculture have been so clear that the importance of conviction is now stressed by Soviet students of this problem.

Another concept, extraordinarily important to anthropologists and political scientists today, is the idea of a multinational state, with frontiers redelineated to correspond with ethnic realities, with each component assured its own language and culture. The basic notions were originally developed by Bolshevik political figures: the Georgian Stalin in 1913, the Armenian Stepan Shaumian, the Russian Bukharin. World War I brought the problem into sharper focus, and so Lenin wrote in 1916:

> There is every sign that imperialism will leave its successor, socialism, a heritage of *less* democratic frontiers, a number of annexations in Europe and in other parts of the world. . . . Will victorious socialism . . . reject the *democratic* delineation of state frontiers? . . . In actual fact the frontiers will be delineated . . . in accordance with the will and "sympathies" of the population. . . . Socialism . . . gives *full play* to the "sympathies" of the population and thereby promotes and greatly accelerates the fusion of the nations.[41]

After the Revolution, such delineations took place very widely in the U.S.S.R. The best-known case is central Asia,[42] but the Caucasus and the Slavic Ukraine, Belorussia, and Russia proper witnessed similar developments. Because border areas are usually places of ethnic mixture, and because historical frontiers come into being more often than not through violence and forcible shifting and extermination of populations, emigrant nationalists of all these origins continue to debate the justice of the internal (and external) Soviet borders. But Soviet scholars argue the validity of this solution on the basis of the pragmatic fact that while no use of force has been able to bring an end to ethnic violence over territory or other issues in Belgium (Walloon-Fleming), Italy (the Tyrol), India, Nigeria, Canada, the United States, and elsewhere, violence or even hostile demonstrations are absent today in countries with such histories of mutual mass murder as the Russian Empire, and Yugoslavia through World War II. Expressions of ethnic prejudice have been reduced to the level of acts by individuals.

The full depth of the problem was not understood until the Soviet government had to deal with it in practice after the Revolution. In writ-

ings of 1922, Lenin formulated the matter in terms cited as basic ideology
by social scientists today:

A distinction must necessarily be made between the nationalism of an
oppressor nation and that of an oppressed nation . . . nationals of a big
nation have nearly always been guilty . . . of an infinite number of cases
of violence . . . we commit violence and insult an infinite number of times
without noticing it. . . .

Internationalism on the part of . . . "great" nations . . . (they are great
only in their violence . . .) must consist . . . even in an inequality for the
oppressor nation, the great nation, that must make up for the inequality
which obtains in actual practice. . . . In one way or another, by one's
attitude or by concessions, it is necessary to compensate the non-Russians
for the lack of trust, suspicion and insults . . . "offended" nations are not
sensitive to anything so much as to the feeling of equality and the violation
of this sentiment, if only through negligence or as a joke . . . it is better
to overdo rather than underdo concessions and leniency toward the national
minorities. . . .

The strictest rules must be introduced on the use of the national language
in the non-Russian republics of our union. . . . Special ingenuity is necessary
. . . not to mention special sincerity on the part of those who undertake
that struggle. A detailed code will be required, and only the nationals
living in the republic in question can draw it up at all successfully.[43]

In insisting that these are no mere matters of practical politics, but concepts that must be considered by social scientists advising governments
today as well as by those seeking to derive regularities of interethnic
relations, Soviet scholars point to the fact that India came, in 1967, to
the official conclusion that ultimate unity will be possible only if first
its great language groups are permitted to pursue education in their own
tongues instead of having a foreign lingua franca (English, Hindi) imposed upon them. To an American audience, the matter acquires greater
pertinence in light of the fact that California also legalized education in
languages other than English in 1967, in recognition of the pervasive
persistence of its Mexican heritage.

The post-Lenin period brought forth an additional principle in the
realm of ethnic problems, and one that has very wide importance and
discussion today in a broad range of disciplines: international relations,
economics, political science, anthropology. This is the ideological notion
of noncapitalist development in precapitalist areas. Just as the U.S.S.R.
itself represents the building of socialism in a country not answering to
the original Marx-Engels notion of revolution where industry was most
advanced, so did it confront the problem of what to do with respect to

peoples within its frontiers who had not progressed to industry at all. The ideological model which its scholars had at hand simply assumed that capitalism would have to do that job, for that was how it had always happened. The problem was solved by devising an unprecedented approach, today designated "development program" by the West, although there are fundamental differences between the Western and the Soviet concepts.

The Soviet approach was to build industry in the indigenous areas—publicly owned, of course—by a flow of investment that to this day continues deliberately to be higher per capita in each year's U.S.S.R. budget than for Russia proper. This brought with it the formation of a wage-earning proletariat to which socialism had concrete meaning. Whereas the first significant application of the "noncapitalist path" was in Soviet central Asia, the first such attempt outside Soviet boundaries was in the Mongolian People's Republic, with respect to which the U.S.S.R. served as source of capital and where socialism in agriculture was developed very cautiously, requiring forty years to become predominant. From these examples, social scientists have derived the postulate that states emerging from colonial or semicolonial status would not have the single recourse of modernization by the capitalist route.

A rich literature has developed on this subject, dealing with the U.S.S.R. itself, with the young nations, and even with ethnic problems in advanced countries such as the United States. Thus Bogina, reviewing Glazer and Moynihan's *Beyond the Melting Pot*,[44] challenges, with specific reference to Negroes, the authors' "capitalism-oriented notion that business people alone are destined to be the natural leaders of each nationality group." A similar ideological motivation underlies the sociologist Zakharov's painstaking analysis of "The Make-up and Structure of the Syrian Working Class," with its clearly stated concern for determining whether it is yet significant enough to provide leadership to the nation.[45] As early as April, 1964, Saltanov expressed the view that

There are still strong capitalist elements in the Egyptian countryside, but at the same time the working peasantry is uniting into producing cooperatives. The development of other anti-capitalist forms is also possible. Therefore . . . for countries such as the UAR, Algeria, and Burma . . . we may speak of the preparation of conditions for transition to a course of noncapitalist development.[46]

The entire subject is a major concern of the U.S.S.R. Academy of Sciences' Institute of the Peoples of Asia, the Institute of African Studies, the chair of Near and Middle Eastern history at Moscow University, the

newly founded Far Eastern Institute of the Academy of Sciences, and
the Institute of World Economy and International Relations. Investigations have reached a high level of sophistication, and views are neither
unanimous nor stereotyped. The best article I have seen is Landa's
"Once Again on the Non-capitalist Path of Development." Landa sum-
marizes his excellently documented and closely reasoned presentation as
follows:

> Under the present conditions existing in Asia and Africa, non-capitalist
> development: 1) usually proceeds as a continuation of the anti-imperialist
> and anti-feudal national-liberation revolution; 2) in different countries, at
> different stages of social development, the problems demanding first-priority
> solution are not identical; 3) it is an uninterrupted process of exacerbated
> class struggle, in the course of which the choice of direction for future
> development becomes more and more clearly defined; and 4) it may not
> coincide, necessarily, with a socialist course of development.[47]

Particularly interesting is his disagreement with another Soviet scholar
who seeks to elevate the present concern for economic profitability in
the U.S.S.R. to the status of an ideological criterion in the study of the
noncapitalist states.

Discussion continues of the principles underlying conclusions in the
realm of political science with respect to Soviet nationalities themselves.
Dzhunusov informs us that there are those who would simply abolish the
autonomous republics (not the constituent [union] republics) and vigorously assails such "great-power chauvinists." [48] Perevedentsev discovers
that economic policies sometimes work counter to "nationality policy"
as defined in our quotations from Lenin, and offers sociological solutions:
wage differentials to tailor migration to desired ends, job quotas in favor
of indigenous nationalities (something pioneered by the U.S.S.R. forty-
five years ago but permitted to lapse, except for educational-institution
admissions policy, because of war-enforced industrial relocation during
World War II), and further study of the matter with the participation
of ethnographers, particularly of indigenous nationalities.[49]

Looking Forward

In September, 1967, three leading social scientists, Academician A. Rumyantsev, and Dr. F. Burlatsky, and Dr. I. Bestuzhev, published an article

in *Pravda* directing attention to the need to organize studies for forecasting the course of social development. They pointed out that "in capitalist countries . . . research teams, departments and whole institutes are organized for this purpose." While stating that "scores" of teams of like nature have recently come into being in the U.S.S.R., they stress the need for "a scientific center or possibly several, to act as pilot organizations . . . and to coordinate work in this field." [50] They regard economic forecasting as relatively well developed, but say that "political forecasting, especially as regards future international developments, deserves special attention." Their greatest emphasis, however, is on "sociological forecasting, i.e., forecasts concerning demographic and ethnic processes, urban development, the social effects of scientific and technical progress, changes in the social pattern of society and developments in public education, health and culture. Nearly all these trends are much less well developed."

They speak of techniques: "mathematical modeling, experiments, surveys . . . the application of probability theory, game theory, limits theory . . ." All this sounds thoroughly empirical, until they speak of the need to "rely on scientific methodology and methods." "Methods" here is "methodology" in the Western sense, while "methodology" is ideological underlying principle in the Marxist understanding, as we discussed it early in this article. In that connection it is fascinating and hopeful that they want "a special center dealing with . . . the methodology of social forecasting, since pertinent research is so far mostly in the embryonic state."

But this embryonic methodology differs fundamentally from that obtaining in the West in the realm of social forecasting. The basic ideological postulate of the latter generally encountered is that existing social orders resting on private property should persist, and that where forecasting is directed to resolution of social problems, its function is to assist in the maintenance of the present organization of society in its underlying principles. The ideology of Soviet social science, on the contrary, presumes that its function is to change the world, away from capitalism outside the present socialist camp, and from socialism to communism within it, specifically in the U.S.S.R. The former problem has had ample discussion in these pages. It is the latter that remains to be treated.

Earlier, in quoting Marx's *Critique of the Gotha Programme* and Lenin's interpretation and development of those notions, I presented, so to speak, the skeleton of the embryo. At that point, however, it was necessary to turn to the relevance of those ideological principles to

Soviet social science in the first stage of the development of that society, from capitalism to socialism. With respect to what the present stage in the U.S.S.R. is understood to be, "from socialism to communism," let us recall that the difference between the two is that while both rest on public ownership of the means of production, socialism requires differentiated payment in accordance with work performed, due to society's inability as yet to meet virtually all needs for goods and services. Under communism, it is envisaged that material problems will have been solved and distribution can be free of payment, as none will suffer want of any material kind if only all have by then developed the awareness that "work is the first necessity of life."

In this connection, the most recent authoritative statement of Soviet ideology, the *Theses of the Central Committee of the Communist Party on the 50th Anniversary of the Revolution*, formulated in 1967, says that

communism . . . does not arise spontaneously but is the result of conscious efforts on the part of the whole people and a ceaseless quest for correct solutions to the problems posed by life. . . . The building of communism is a complex process. It embraces the sphere of material production, social relations and social consciousness, and entails the overcoming of difficulties and the resolving of contradictions, the conquest of nature, the continuing search for effective solutions to new problems, and the struggle against imperialism.[51]

Since the Stalin period, in which the notion of "contradiction," basic to Marxist thought, was an "unthought" as far as Soviet social science was concerned in its examination of its own society, that concept has come back into its own, and the problem of defining the contradictions of socialism that must be resolved for attainment of communism is intensively discussed. Some of them are known from Marx: the contradiction between town and country life, one aspect of which is that between worker and peasant, and another that between mental and manual labor. Lenin spoke of "the idiocy of rural life." The material changes involved in resolving that contradiction are largely clear: the planting of greenery, pollution control, and development of small, human neighborhoods in the cities; urbanization, television, consolidated schools, telephones, and roads in the countryside.

For the U.S.S.R. to develop from socialism to communism, it is accepted, as a fundamental principle, that there must be further progress in man's ability to relate to the world on the conscious level. This means education. The notion of universal educability is a basic premise without which communism as a society of equals would be unthinkable. Erected on this postulate as substrata are the ideas of mobilization of the country's resources, based in the immediate postrevolutionary years upon volunteer involvement of all persons with education, to make social mobility and intelligent citizenship possible by elimination of absolute and functional illiteracy, institution of universal education, abolition of fees, and institution of compulsory education requirements. Today and for the future, educational research serves to implement the principle of rapid increase in compulsory education requirements and to make the best possible use of the constantly rising fund allocations so as to disseminate and assure creative assimilation of the accumulated storehouse of worldwide cultural achievement and scientific knowledge. It is this complex of measures that is meant when the term "cultural revolution" is employed in Soviet ideology.

Attainment of full communism involves development of the measures required to bring about elimination of the difference between the workers of hand and brain. This ideological principle gives direction, in the broadest sense, to industrial, educational, and other research in psychology. The significant difference between the narrowly educated engineer and the well-rounded individual is a complication of the "embryonic" contradiction of mental versus manual labor, which has only recently made its appearance in life, particularly in the U.S.S.R., and poses a problem of which its social scientists are just now becoming aware. With recognition of the fact that the need for specialization of professional skills is still rising as technology progresses, there is a reexamination of the realism of Marx's notion that in a communist society a man can be a hunter in the morning, a fisherman in the afternoon, and an artist in the evening.

To deal with such ideological problems, scholars in the humanities must first of all abandon the thought that Marx is sacrosanct. Theoretically, that should have presented no problem, because the essence of dialectics is that there is nothing eternal but change, in human thought as in everything else. In practice, the fundamentalist religious tradition of thought of the Russian masses has been an obstacle to this. Although the precedent of revision of Marx by Lenin exists, there is a difference between what has been allowed to authority and what has been permitted to ordinary mortals. In that sense, it is a step forward when, for example, Lifshits, a literary critic (and it must be remembered that literary criticism is specifically listed among the social sciences in the U.S.S.R.) [52] writes: "Yes, two contemporaries—Marx and [the Russian] Herzen— failed to understand each other" [53] with respect to Herzen's *political* views, thus making clear (as does Lifshits' entire argument) that Marx was capable of human error.

As for Engels, who was the Marx-Engels team's specialist in natural science, the geneticist V. M. Zhdanov, in a discussion of the relationship between philosophy and biology, spelled out the form taken by worship of the founders:

> In Engels' well-known formulation, life is associated with protein bodies. . . . To hold that after the passage of a hundred years everything said by Engels is utterly true means to respect neither science nor Engels. Nevertheless all encyclopedias and textbooks repeat this definition of his.[54]

Georgiev and Khrustov, dealing with experimental data on the making and use of simple tools by higher anthropoids, challenge Engels' definition of man as *the* tool-making animal and Marx's oft-quoted remark that the difference between the poorest human architect and the best bee is that only a human builder sees his planned structure in his mind's eye beforehand. They conclude that what truly differentiates man is that human goal setting develops in a labor process that is *"societally-mediated* and therefore *communicative."* [55]

It is a very much bigger step when Soviet social scientists treat Lenin as less than perfect. In philosophy, one reads of the "Leninist stage" in dialectical materialism, inferring not that that stage was wrong, but that it has been surpassed. In history, Gukovsky writes: "one must take a critical approach even to Lenin—and there's nothing to be afraid of in that 'awful' idea." [56]

Once fundamentalism is abandoned, thought is essentially unchained and moves rapidly. But even the fundamentalists can play a useful role. None deserves the designation more than the editor of the leading philosophy journal and member of the party's Central Committee since 1939, M. B. Mitin. In the past, probably no one did more to discredit dialectical materialism by "disproving," in its name, every major scientific advance in the West. Now he lists quite neatly the opposites in Soviet life comprising contradictions to the solution of which social science must contribute: "the personal and the public, centralization and decentralization, planning and the manifestation of local initiative, balanced development of the economy and the priority development of its most important branches." [57]

Later he speaks of "the contradiction between the development of the joint farming operation of a collective farm and retention of personal farming plots by its members. . . . This is a real contradiction in our life."

And on nationalities: "ignoring the common interests of our country leads to recurrences of local nationalism, while to ignore the distinctive features of a nation may lead and does lead to recurrences of great-power chauvinism."

While it is possible for socialism, the lower stage, to have been conceived of as a purely economic problem, particularly when faced in a country that was highly underdeveloped and alone in a frankly hostile world, communism cannot be imagined without a fundamental psychological change, because of its assumption that human beings will work without measuring reward, and that individual good will be understood to be attainable only by work for the common good. In that sense, Soviet scholars are deeply indebted—although they do not yet acknowledge that debt—to Western scholars for having rediscovered and pressed the themes of alienation and humanism in Marx. What is important for the present paper is that both notions are by this date accepted parts of the ideological heritage in the U.S.S.R. Social scientists are grappling with them creatively and in controversy with each other. Murray Yanowitch has provided a stimulating survey of the decade of Soviet work on these concepts, 1956–66, and has also called our attention to the fact that writings from 1925 to 1936 indicate that this is yet another area in which the triumph of Stalinism cut off work well begun.[58] His bibliography should perhaps be supplemented by reference to a brilliant survey of world history by a Soviet scholar of Toynbeean erudition, Nikolai Konrad,[59] who finds the entire meaning of history to rest in man's increasing consciousness of his own humanity, with implementation of humanism as the sole worthy target. But what is most impressive is to find such notions expressed in the writings of men whose decisions directly affect human lives. Thus Chief Justice Anashkin of the U.S.S.R. Supreme Court Criminal Cases Bench took that ideological concept as point of departure in seeking to draw a scientific generalization from the very sharp decline in long sentences since 1958:

"Force," said Marx, "is the midwife of every old society pregnant with the new." Yet we know that socialism seeks to abolish all use of violence against human beings. . . . Socialist humanism is love not only for the individual person but above all for all members of society. . . . A distinctive feature of socialism is the fact that, the farther it develops along the road to communism, the less it makes use of compulsion.[60]

In the context of Russian and Soviet history, that last sentence is true despite the outrageous conviction and jailing of the editors of *Phoenix 66*. Bullets have nowhere been used in the U.S.S.R. against a protest by its citizens since the Novocherkassk incident of 1962. Regrettably, an American cannot write that of his own country, where the trend is unmistakably in the opposite direction.

Conclusions

The U.S.S.R. can today claim to be the first major socialist state to have emerged from the stage of internal terror * (dictatorship of the proletariat plus the unneeded massacres in its name). And although the time since Khrushchev is still short, it has already persuaded the world that it is also the first to emerge from the stage of one-man-ism that has existed, grossly or subtly, wherever an indigenous revolution has occurred: Stalin, Mao, Tito, Castro.

With the stability that the U.S.S.R. today enjoys, and the fact that as long ago as World War II Harvard University's interviewers of refugees from the Soviet Union found that even such people accepted its basic value of public ownership, there remains no ideological excuse for the censorship of social science (as of literature and the arts). Nor is there any for the selective barring of dissenting opinion on certain topics in learned publications and the mass media: foreign policy, Trotsky, Freud, the Jews in the U.S.S.R., sexual deviation, whether government would benefit by public discussion of shortcomings of members of the Political Bureau before replacement behind closed doors and by open debate between them of their own natural and human differences of opinion. This pertains also to the barring of scholarly discussion of the refusal to permit the organization of any other parties citizens may desire (minority parties were represented in the soviets until 1923; that is, so long as Lenin was effectively in charge), the failure to rehabilitate (outrageous notion and term!) certain scientific, cultural, and political figures to this day, and the internal-passport system, which even Khrushchev once described as a tsarist police device reintroduced by Stalin.

These unfreedoms truly fall into a category the Russians are fond of describing as "vestiges in men's minds." They are in part vestiges of the prerevolutionary past, not the capitalist past (most Western capitalist

---

* The disappearance of the mood that engendered is nowhere so well documented as in William Taubman's account of a year as exchange student at Moscow University, *The View from Lenin Hills* (New York: Coward McCann, Inc., 1967), with his eyewitness reports of Soviet students asking speakers from the party's Central Committee as well as its Moscow Committee, at public meetings, the very questions that would have meant expulsion only a couple of years earlier, and concentration camp a dozen years before that.

countries are superior to the U.S.S.R. in most of these matters), but the Russian absolute-monarchist past. In part, they are vestiges of the very recent Stalinist past.

They exist in the world of ideology, which Soviet social scientists recognize to have an existence of its own by no means in one-to-one relationship to the material circumstances from which it once originated. But to the *degree* that these vestiges are Communist rather than Russian (everything in a genuine indigenous revolution is stamped by national character and tradition), they represent the elevation to ideology of practices of the period of dictatorship of the proletariat that were unjustified by any standard. (How otherwise would a Soviet scholar explain the greater freedom under Lenin?) At this writing, it is six years since the Soviet Communists have officially recognized that stage to be past, and they make clear that that transition occurred sometime prior to the formal acceptance of its reality.

The job of bringing men's minds to the level at which they will make the institutional changes necessary to get rid of these vestiges in practice and in law (many are unconstitutional and have no foundation in Soviet law right now) * is precisely the function of Soviet social scientists. But this cannot be done by empiricism in the U.S.S.R. any more than the empirical documentation of the damage done by racism and poverty, and by such "minor" matters as discrimination against women, tuition for higher education, glorification of war and individual violence in the mass media, unequal access to legal defense and to medicine by rich and poor, etc., has been able to solve America's problems in these aspects of life. Soviet scholars have a fundamental commitment to the notion that a correct ideology is an indispensable social science tool for developing a better and more human society. As the material and social base develops, the next decades will demonstrate whether they are capable of employing and developing their ideology toward that end.

There is a familiar argument that the problem lies precisely in a basic incapacity of that ideology to meet real needs, and that what progress there has been in Soviet social science is in direct proportion to its willingness to abandon it. Were that the case, Soviet thought would truly be in a quandary. Its criterion of validity lies in what a philosophy can do for man. It asks what other criterion human beings can possibly accept,

* It speaks well for the *kind* of changes sought by dissidents in the U.S.S.R. that their expressed demands now indicate that they regard constitution and law as desirable values. Thus Alexander Solzhenitsyn demanded an end to censorship on the stated grounds that it is nowhere provided for in the Soviet constitution. Bukovsky of *Phoenix 66* organized a peaceful demonstration specifically for repeal of Article 70 of the Criminal Code, the Soviet "McCarran Act."

and in forming self-judgments it weighs world opinion more carefully than ever before.

For their issues analyzing the first half century of Soviet rule, the world press of all levels subjected the U.S.S.R. to the most massive and microscopic scrutiny in its history. One really cannot seriously contend that the American commercial mass media approached that task with a pro-Communist bias, and the reputation of its top-level editors for hard-boiled cynicism is well earned. What, then, is the reaction of Soviet thinkers when they find the European editor of *Look*, after three weeks in a raw (eleven-year-old) Siberian industrial town of 155,000, writing:

I had come so empty, and I was leaving so full. I had gone full circle, trying at first to set aside my own ideas, leaping at each glimmer of critical faculty, then finally seeing the answer, the Communist man: happy— happy *here*, that is so important—confident, fulfilled.[61]

Or when they read the utterly worldly Alexander Werth, who was for many years a British correspondent in Moscow, a man of Russian émigré origin, now resident in Paris, concluding after yet another two-month visit:

Russia today gives the impression of being about the best-educated, most literate nation in the world. . . . What is developing is something rather different . . . the very civilized human being, mad on culture and education . . . with a remarkably non-sectarian view of the world.[62]

Or, finally, when the author of the containment policy himself, Ambassador George F. Kennan, concludes twenty years later:

For the fact that . . . the experiment has gone on so long, and for the fact that it has yielded a stable civilization, capable of providing adequate outlets for many if not all of the positive human impulses—for this, credit must be given, even by those who constitute its ideological opponents, to the Russian Communist Party. In creating a new order out of the chaos of 1918–1919; in clinging to power successfully for half a century in a great and variegated country where the exertion of political power has never been easy; in retaining its own discipline and vitality as a political instrument in the face of the corrupting influence that the exercise of power invariably exerts; in realizing many of its far-reaching social objectives; in carrying to the present level the industrialization of the country and the development of new technology; in giving firm, determined and in many ways inspired leadership in the struggle against the armies of German fascism; in providing political inspiration and guidance to many of the radical-socialist forces of the world over most of this period, and to some of them over all of this period; in these achievements the Communist Party of the Soviet Union has not only stamped itself as the greatest political organization of the century in vigor and in will, but has remained faithful to the quality of the Russian Revolution as the century's greatest political event.[63]

When the Soviet thinker, with his Marxist premise that the test of theory lies in practice, finds such endorsement for the results produced by his ideology, including even its very special notion of the role of the Communist party, what is there to cause him either to abandon his ideology or to look for another? And where can he find one of which even its own proponents will make such claims to accomplishment?

It is a very great error to regard his new willingness to try to see his own shortcomings through the eyes of others—a willingness born of the confidence of success—and to borrow what is useful in other philosophers' works as an abandonment of his own philosophy. Does one take his borrowing of planning techniques to mean that he has forgotten that the world tries to plan only because the U.S.S.R. planned first, and that no nonsocialist country has yet managed to hold its own economy nearly as close to course as the Soviet Union?

His self-criticism (and we shall read more of it) does not mean a defensive attitude. We have seen the sociologist Fedoseev, the historian Levintov, the political anthropologist Saltanov thrust with confidence into new areas: peace in a thermonuclear time, revolution, the third world. In a recent article Professor T. I. Oizerman, head of Moscow University's respected Department of the History of Bourgeois ("Foreign") Philosophy, comes to grips with another very contemporary problem, the population explosion. Responding in *Literaturnaia gazeta* to an article by Sir Julian Huxley reprinted there, Oizerman agrees that in developing countries "where the growth of population is considerably outstripping the growth of material wealth," population control is desirable. But he sees the reasons for the problem very differently:

A scientist who attempts, from the standpoint of abstract humanism, to rise above the differences between the exploiter and the exploited and between the socialist and capitalist systems, deprives himself of any real possibility of understanding the true causes of the "threatening catastrophe" and the means of averting it.

The geography of hunger is determined by the economics of capitalism, an insufficiently high level of production and other historically transitory conditions. . . .

The spread of culture and medical knowledge and the comprehensive development of human capabilities and requirements will lead to a check in the unrestrained growth of population. This trend is already making itself felt in all the highly developed industrial countries.[64]

He blames Huxley's interpretation of a problem of human social organization as one of a united mankind versus nature upon "sociological naturalism," and says:

> The only thing he proposes, apart from an improvement and spread of birth-control devices, is a *change in consciousness*, a *change in attitudes* which, according to the logic of an idealist understanding of history, should lead to a change in the life of society. The whole thing, according to Huxley, boils down to creating a new and dominant organization of thought and belief that will stimulate our research and promote our advance.
>
> However, as Marx and Engels explained more than 100 years ago, a change of consciousness in itself merely signifies a change in interpretations of the existing state of affairs. . . . But is this what Huxley is striving for? His entire article speaks of something else—the need to change social existence as well as social consciousness.

In earlier times, a Soviet philosopher would have confined himself merely to putting down a bourgeois opponent. But now, not only does Oizerman express respect for the intent of Huxley's "abstract" "evolutionary humanism," which has to be replaced by "revolutionary humanism," but he then turns to admonish his own readers:

> It seems to me, however, that when we are arguing with people like Huxley we ought not to adopt a stance of arrogant omniscience—something that often happens. We have our own difficulties and our own unsolved problems, many of them big problems. . . . Huxley's thesis that man must not confine himself to aspiring to material values but should seek paths toward growth of the spirit, a thesis to which Marxists have always subscribed, is something we accept in theory but often do not practice.

There is a self-deluding habit in Sovietology, reaching into all the special disciplines, of regarding the portion of an article such as this, in which a Westerner is criticized, as "cover" so that the writer may also express his "real" thoughts, which the Sovietologist always identifies with the self-critical portion of the article. It seems to me that a rereading of the Kennan quote might suggest that it is time to realize that there is no earthly reason for such self-denigration by Soviet thinkers, and that a procedure more in accord with the record the U.S.S.R. has made in the world would be to assume that the writer believes both aspects of what he has stated, unless there is specific evidence to the contrary.

Perhaps a more striking example of this is presented by another recent article, by Bogomolov, Melvil, and Narsky, in that it deals with philosophy as such, at home and abroad, while Oizerman simply applies it. While Western scholars see dialectical materialism in decay because of its unprecedented willingness to accept philosophical advances outside its system, these three writers advocate acceptance of what is useful in the course of a critique of the eclecticism, dressed up in the less revealing term "pluralism," of Western philosophy today. They say:

The epistemological pluralism of contemporary bourgeois philosophical systems is primarily due to the exceptional complication and differentiation of the most modern knowledge in science, which has propounded many new problems of methodology. . . . The pluralism of philosophical trends is becoming, essentially, that single possible mode of existence for bourgeois philosophy which permits it to retain its influence. In offering to virtually every group in the population and to every individual a broad choice of solutions of the problems of world-view and a theory of knowledge, it retains the ability to influence people's minds to what is still a very substantial degree. This pluralism leads to diverse and highly contradictory consequences. On the one hand, it results in an increasing scattering of opinions and to eclecticism.[65]

Later they deal with the integration that is the opposite trend simultaneously occurring in Western philosophy, but state that it is an irreconcilable hash of disparate elements—neopositivism, irrationalism, and religion—and that it is this inability to find a unified view of the world that has led to the burgeoning revival of Western interest in dialectical materialism in the sixties. But for the purposes of our discussion, what is most striking is that the quotation above is followed *immediately* by an explanation of why this eclecticism, helpless to provide a satisfactory overview, leads creative minds to do *particularized* work from which Marxists can learn:

But on the other hand, the variety of philosophical ideas leads to a sharpening of the attention paid to special and highly specific problems. . . . In some cases . . . one finds a treatment of theoretical problems with a care and profundity that is by no means always encountered in the works of theorizers taking a dialectical materialist position.

Such cases are then pointed out in analytical detail. I must repeat that most Soviet thinkers see this as in the same category as planning: Marxist political economy demonstrated theoretically and then in practice that planning was possible, while the West provided the advanced techniques. Specifically, a Soviet economist offers a closely reasoned argument [66] that macroanalysis is simply an applied business economics for the total economy to meet the demands of a time when state capitalism and monopoly are dominant, that this discipline accepts as immutable the fundamental capital-labor relationships of capitalism, and that it therefore is limited to making things-as-they-are work as well as can be expected, and avoids the basic questions of economic science: what next, and why? But he agrees that techniques for the total economy are useful to the U.S.S.R., except for those, such as business-cycle treatments, that have meaning only for an economy whose fundamentally unplanned nature is demonstrated by the very fact that business cycles exist.

Many Western scholars find it comforting, but it is truly not very useful, to reject all consideration of broad and long-range problems as "metaphysical," and to look down their noses at the competition for lack of "professionalism." Since when does technical professionalism rank higher than the scientific approach? But contentions that Soviet social science does not deal in matters of technical interest are no longer true, although the lag in many fields is granted. In sociology, economics, education, etc., there is no longer an argument. Therefore let us look, for a moment, at philosophy.

When the leading philosophical journal publishes an article, "On the Equal Standing of Positive and Negative Numbers," [67] involving no debate of any kind with Western philosophers, is this of technical interest or not? Or isn't anyone who is not a very specialized philosopher or mathematician justified in asking whether it is of any interest other than technical? And incidentally, the article offers itself as an original contribution to thought, a matter that none but specialists can possibly decide.

On the opposite end of the spectrum of scale is an article, "On the Problem of Infinity," [68] in the same journal, postulating "that infinity exists in reality, and not merely as an abstract idea." The contention is not original, but the argument is. One finds not metaphysical hairsplitting versus the finitists, but employment of the language of geometry to classify infinities: practical infinity, infinity as boundlessness, metric infinity, afine and projective infinities, topological infinity, set-theory infinity, metamathematical infinity (the author's term). The origins of each, the relationships to progressively more complex concepts in modern science and mathematics, and the role of infinity in cosmology are discussed, culminating in comments on the philosophical status of infinity.

The author approaches his conclusion with a very neat formulation of the difference between *particular* Marxist conclusions and the Marxist *method:*

The *definition* of infinity offered by Engels and cited above is now hopelessly obsolete. Nor could a century of headlong development of science have had any other result. But Engels' *approach* to the question of infinity is not obsolete (the need to examine infinity as a process, as the embodiment of a contradiction, as a concept of not only quantitative but internal, qualitative specificity).

His closing paragraph does not contain the words "dialectical materialism," but to my mind it is an elegant application of stated principles of that mode of thought, and leaves the nonphilosopher with the notion that perhaps philosophy is something more than argument over how many angels can dance on the point of a needle:

The problem of infinity does not lie in determining whether the universe corresponds to any one of our standards (concepts) of infinity, but in the degree to which our constantly improving model of infinity corresponds to the various aspects of the real infinity of the universe. In other words, we know that the universe is infinite, but do not know in what exact sense this is so. However, with each step forward in scientific knowledge we know this better. The inexhaustibility of nature does not permit us to rest content in self-satisfied routine; and as for the bruises we suffer on the road to knowledge, nature rewards us over and over again with the fascination of the new.

Our writer approaches his problem in a spirit of modesty, confidence that mysteries can be unraveled, and expectation that he will not always find himself in the right. An approach to Soviet ideology in that light would be of benefit to all.

There is no trace of superciliousness or condescension in Arnold Toynbee's letter to historian Nikolai Konrad in *Novy mir* (July, 1967),[69] no veiled digs at Soviet ideology, no disingenuous questions, no suggestion that the man to whom the letter is addressed is somehow a "different" Russian. Toynbee poses what is essentially his view of the philosophy of society to an equal, and asks for comment. Konrad offers that comment, at one point defending Toynbee against Western criticism that the latter had himself accepted, at others disagreeing. His response constitutes, in my view, an original contribution to the philosophy of society. And his view, which space prevents us from dealing with, is entirely Marxist. Commenting on Toynbee's statement that he had abandoned the notion of the self-contained uniqueness of each civilization, Konrad writes:

And so you developed the notion of a different monad of the historical process. Your thought could be carried further. Examining the course of the world process, we see that a point was reached when the world cleaved into two camps, as the phrase has it—the capitalist and the socialist. And each of these also functions in some measure as an historic monad of sorts. This means that it is also possible that the criterion for the monad in this instance is what we term the socio-economic system. Isn't that so?

In our time the so-called "developing countries" also comprise an historic monad in some measure, and this means that it is possible to see criteria for monadicity in the general level of socio-economic and cultural development as well.

Thus Konrad, who is fundamentally a historian of culture, makes clear that he is a materialist. And in posing for his discipline the task of "discovering system in the culture of each epoch" he discusses seventeenth-century German literature. In it he describes conflicting lines, on which he comments:

Does this not comprise a system? And one purely dialectical in construction? And it is precisely in this dialectic that there lies the historical and sociological unity of the entity—the whole system.

So although Nikolai Konrad, who is a man of ultimate urbanity, is clearly a dialectical materialist, Arnold Toynbee regards him unreservedly as a colleague. The Toynbee-Konrad exchange might well serve as a model for discussion and debate of problems in the realm of ideology. Accepting it as such will be easier if one is aware of the degree to which Soviet scholars are abandoning their stereotypes of the West and of their colleagues in the capitalist world. At the very beginning of this essay we noted the traditional importance of the creative writer and of literary journals in Russian and Soviet social thought. In December, 1967, *Novy mir* carried an article, "Sociology and Literature," informing its readers, on the basis of a Gallup study:

Money is not the sole criterion of status in the United States. A professor ranks higher than the average banker, and a pilot or scientist higher than the average factory owner. Members of many of the free professions came out ahead even of directors of large corporations.[70]

The author has no patience with hackneyed Soviet views of the academic world in the West:

Things aren't helped in the slightest by blanket put-downs of capitalism-oriented scholarship, or by polemics conducted on anything but a serious plane. . . . The empirical research done in the West is not nearly all done by apologists for capitalism. Such major scholars as Fromm, Adorno, Mills, Balandier, and others are known for their criticism of capitalism and even reverence for the heritage of Marx (particularly his "theory of alienation"). To proclaim all of them apologists for capitalism and agents of imperialism is just as absurd as to place Kafka, Hemingway, Faulkner, and Böll in the same category as the authors of things like the James Bond books. . . . The contempt for the entire vast range of scientifically processed information contained in progressive sociology abroad, which some authors of articles on sociology have inspired, damages precisely our own, Soviet, scholarship.

Alexander Lvovich Mongait, one of the few Soviet social scientists sufficiently respected in the West to have had a translated book of his published in England at the beginning of this decade,[71] exposes the fact that it had been perfectly all right to import from the West ideas supporting the supernationalism cultivated in the U.S.S.R. during the Cold War years on behalf of the Slavs in general and Russians in particular, even when such ideas were specifically Nazi in concept. In an article, "Archeological Cultures and Ethnic Communities," [72] he writes:

> The negative influence of Kossinna's views [German archeologist, 1858–1931—W.M.] . . . lies . . . in the assertion that we are allegedly always in a position . . . to find the forebears of a modern people as early as in the Stone Age and that, moreover, this is the sole or principal ancestor of the given people.
> This notion, taken together with the assertion that the more ancient the people, the greater its rights to a special role in the modern world, became the foundation of the nationalist constructs that won Kossinna's theory glory among the fascists, and that continue to have a negative influence upon archeology to this day. In the 1940's and 1950's that thesis strangely penetrated into Soviet scholarship, despite the fact that it was in conflict with its fundamental principles, the principle of internationalism above all. . . .
> Our duty in treatment of theoretical problems of ethnogenesis in particular is great because various nationalist and racist constructs are associated with it, and in our time Asian and African racisms have come into existence, in addition to European. It must be stated that, in the past as well, many scientists were not consistent and, in fighting against Aryan racism, were unable to find anything better than to counterpose to it their own non-Aryan racism.

As it is impossible to de-Stalinize by barring proponents of his views (the result would only be Stalinism in reverse: a dictatorship of an opposing set of views), the uprooting of the kind of notion to which Mongait objects can only occur in a process of scholarly discussion. Before the Mongait article was published, it was subjected to two sessions of debate by historians, archeologists, ethnographers, and linguists, organized by the Academy of Sciences. It is pleasant to report that not only was Mongait upheld, but others refused to permit whitewashing of the prior practice:

> Entering into debate with Rybakov, Pomerants observed that it is false to speak of the errors of the pre- and postwar period as merely insignificant digressions due to the struggle against fascist ideology. The very framing of the problem as one of priority for one race or nation is meaningless from the standpoint of science and cannot be justified in any way, because it transfers the polemic to the methodological level of the enemy.

The same sort of merciless criticism of weaknesses in Soviet social science—even more impressive, in fact, because we now encounter self-criticism of the entire field rather than demolition of the mistakes of others—was presented to the entire Soviet public, the eight million readers of *Izvestiia*, in a three-quarter-page article on June 8, 1968, announcing the founding of the Institute of Concrete Social Research under the Academy of Sciences. The authors, Academician Rumyantsev and ranking sociologists Burlatsky and Osipov, wrote:

The first publications of work devoted to concrete social investigations have made their appearance. . . . Neither the scale nor, particularly, the depth of the social research in progress meets current needs. . . . Regrettably, until very recently virtually no work has been done to study the life of the spirit of socio-demographic groups in our society, or problems of the development and functioning of public opinion. . . . Marked expansion of information in social statistics, and skilled processing of that information, is a most important prerequisite for deeper social research. . . . The present system of social information suffers from a lack of coordination in the programs for observation and processing and from divergence in the principles and systems of classification. . . . The vast quantities of social information accumulated in cultural-and-educational and other organizations at places of employment have thus far hardly been touched for the purposes of generalization and study from them. The teams of sociologists working at various [government] committees, ministries, and bureaus are only just beginning to function. . . . The very first steps have been taken to make use of mathematical methods, accompanied by the processing of statistical data by computers. But such mathematical methods as linear programming, factor analysis, latent analysis, information theory, and game theory have not yet been seriously applied at all in sociological research.

In earlier years admissions of this order from authoritative Soviet sources would have been welcomed with a virtually audible rubbing of hands in certain scholarly circles in the West. More than one Ph.D. thesis and a great many articles in academic journals have consisted of little more than compilations of just such quotations. To which the best response is an admonition from the authors of that article to Soviet scholars who had done the same thing:

Mere descriptiveness for the purpose of piling up positive or negative facts should be inherently foreign to . . . social research.

I hope my attempt in these pages to analyze the state of, and changes in, the ideology of Soviet social science, its contributions as well as its sins of commission and omission, will stimulate objective study and dialogue rather than serve to reinforce any set of preconceived notions whatever. Certainly, the Soviet intervention in Czechoslovakia indicates that some years will elapse before the more open thinking of social scientists in the U.S.S.R. percolates to the level of governmental policy-making.

Notes

1. William M. Mandel, "Reflections on the Soviet System," in *The USSR After 50 Years*, ed. Samuel Hendel and Randolph Braham (New York: Alfred A. Knopf, Inc., 1967), pp. 159–203.

2. Yevgeny Yevtushenko, *Bratsk Station and Other New Poems* (Garden City, N.Y.: Anchor Books, 1967).

3. Nikita S. Khrushchev, "The Cult of the Individual," in Russian Institute of Columbia University, *The Anti-Stalin Campaign and International Communism* (New York: Columbia University Press, 1956), p. 1–89.

4. Alexander Solzhenitsyn, *For the Good of the Cause* (New York: Frederick A. Praeger, Inc., 1964).

5. Solzhenitsyn, *One Day in the Life of Ivan Denisovich* (New York: E. P. Dutton & Co., 1963).

6. Iu. Kariakin, "An Episode in the Current Battle of Ideas," *Soviet Review*, 6 (Fall, 1965): 21–31.

7. A. Postyshev, "The Labor Theory of Value and Optimal Planning," *Kommunist*, 1967, no. 3.

8. M. N. Rutkevich, "Evolution, Progress, and the Laws of Dialectics," *Soviet Studies in Philosophy*, 4 (Winter, 1965–66): 34–43; M. N. Gretsky, "Does Dialectics Exist in Nature?" *ibid.*, 4 (Spring, 1966): 56–62.

9. V. I. Lenin, *Imperialism, the Highest Stage of Capitalism*, in *Collected Works* (English edition) (Moscow: Izdatelstvo Progress, 1964), 22: 185–304.

10. "Open Letter from the CPSU Central Committee to Party Organizations and All Communists of the Soviet Union," *Pravda*, July 14, 1963, trans. in *Soviet Weekly*, London, week of July 14, 1963.

11. G. I. Tunkin, "The 22nd Congress of the CPSU and the Tasks of the Soviet Science of International Law," *Soviet Law and Government*, 1 (Winter, 1962–63): 18–28; V. Nilin, "6th Annual Meeting of the Soviet International Law Assn.," *ibid.*, 2 (Winter, 1963–64): 43–47.

12. Friedrich Engels, "Letter to Joseph Bloch," in *Reader in Marxist Philosophy*, ed. Howard Selsam and Harry Martel (New York: International Publishers, 1963), pp. 204–206.

13. A. Ia. Gurevich, "Universal Law and Special Regularity in History," *Soviet Review*, 7 (Fall, 1966): 3–18; also see M. Ia. Gefter and V. L. Malikov, "A Reply to an American Scholar," *Voprosy istorii*, 1966, no. 10, trans. in *Soviet Studies in History*, 5 (Winter, 1966–67): 3–23, and in *Soviet Review*, 8 (Summer, 1967): 3–23. The Gurevich article is the best single presentation of Soviet ideology by a Soviet author of which I am aware.

14. L. S. Vasiliev and I. A. Stuchevsky, "Three Models for the Origin and Evolution of Precapitalist Societies," *Voprosy istorii*, 1966, no. 5, trans. in *Soviet Studies in History*, 5 (Winter, 1966–67): 24–37.

15. "Discussion on the Problem of the Clan and Rural Communes in the Ancient East," *Vestnik drevnei istorii*, 1963, no. 1, trans. in *Soviet Anthropology and Archeology*, 2 (Spring, 1964): 61–65; 2 (Summer, 1964): 37–53.

16. K. K. Zelin, "Principles of Morphological Classification of Forms of Dependence," *Vestnik drevnei istorii*, 1967, no. 2, pp. 7–31.

17. The most important step forward in treating this problem, subsequent to the Khrushchev speech, is a thorough, devastating, and creative article by Stepan Shaumian, "Cult of an Individual," *Filosofskaia entsiklopediia* (1964), vol. 3, trans. in *Soviet Studies in Philosophy*, 5 (Summer, 1966): 24–36.

18. Arthur Ransome, *Russia in 1919* (New York: Huebsch, 1919), p. 186. See my note in *Slavic Review*, 27, no. 2 (June, 1968). A new edition of N. P. Pavlov-Sil'vansky's prerevolutionary *Feudalism in Ancient Rus'* was published in 1924, and a new edition of M. A. D'iakonov's *Essays on the Social and Governmental Structure in Ancient Rus'* in 1926. At least one living non-Marxist historian, S. B. Veselovsky, published up to 1926 (*The Question of the Origin of the Appanage System*) and again in 1947 (*Feudal Landholding in Northeastern Rus'*).

19. *Malaia Sovetskaia entsiklopediia* (Moscow, 1959), 4: 891.

20. Lenin, "Letter to American Workers," in *Collected Works*, 28: 62–78.

21. Marx and Engels, *The Civil War in the United States* (New York: International Publishers, 1937).

22. S. D. Skazkin *et al.*, "The Soviet-Italian Historiographic Conference," *Voprosy istorii*, 1965, no. 8, trans. in *Soviet Studies in History*, 4 (Winter, 1965–66): 42.

23. *Izvestiia*, August 22, 1967.

24. *National Guardian*, September 24, 1966.

25. Marx, *Critique of the Gotha Programme* (New York: International Publishers, 1938), pp. 8–10.

26. Lenin, "The State and Revolution," *Selected Works* (New York: International Publishers, n.d.) 7: 85–88, *passim*.

27. *Ibid.*, p. 80.

28. Lenin, *Questions of National Policy and Proletarian Internationalism* (Moscow: Foreign Languages Publishing House, n.d.), p. 155.

29. Lenin, *Collected Works*, 33: 387.

30. William Bullitt, *The Bullitt Mission to Russia* (New York: Huebsch, 1919), pp. 123–24; Lenin, *Collected Works*, 30: 39, 50–51, 365–67, 491–93; 33: 387.

31. Louis Fischer, *The Soviets in World Affairs*, 2 vols. (New York: Jonathan Cape and Harrison Smith, 1930).

32. N. G. Levintov, "Some Aspects of the Leninist Theory of Revolution," *Voprosy filosofii*, 1966, no. 4, trans. in *Soviet Studies in Philosophy*, 5 (Fall, 1966): 35–45.

33. A. M. Kovalev, "War and Revolution," *Filosofskie nauki*, 1965, no. 2, trans. in *Soviet Studies in Philosophy*, 4 (Fall, 1965): 43–49.

34. P. N. Fedoseev, "The Peace Problem in Contemporary Social Thought," *Voprosy filosofii*, 1967, no. 1.

35. Tunkin, "The United Nations: 1945–65 (Problems of International Law)," *Sovetskoe gosudarstvo i pravo*, 1965, no. 10, trans. in *Soviet Law and Government*, 4 (Spring, 1966): 3–12.

36. L. N. Velikovich, "Catholicism's Dialogue with the Contemporary World," *Soviet Review*, 7 (Spring, 1966): 22–31.

37. A. I. Klibanov, "The Dissident Denominations in the Past and Today," *Voprosy istorii religii ateizma*, 1961, no. 9, "Sovremennoe sektantstvo," trans. in *Soviet Sociology*, 3 (Spring, 1965): 44–60.

38. L. N. Mitrokhin and E. Ia. Liagushina, "Some Characteristics of the Modern Baptist Movement," *Voprosy filosofii*, 1964, no. 2, trans. in *Soviet Sociology*, 3 (Fall, 1964): 44–55.

39. Lenin, *New Economic Policy*, in *Selected Works* (1937), 9: 83–401.

40. Lenin, "On Co-operation," *ibid.*, pp. 402–12.

41. Lenin, *Questions of National Policy*, pp. 156–57.

42. Mandel, *The Soviet Far East and Central Asia* (New York: Institute of Pacific Relations, 1944), pp. 89–129.

43. Lenin, *Questions of National Policy*, pp. 201–204.

44. Sh. Bogina, "Review of Glazer and Moynihan, *Beyond the Melting Pot*," *Sovetskaia etnografiia*, 1966, no. 1.

45. A. M. Zakharov, "The Make-up and Structure of the Syrian Working Class," *Narody Azii i Afriki*, 1967, no. 2, trans. in *Soviet Sociology*, vol. 6 (Winter, 1967–68).

46. In Iu. G. Aleksandrov, "The Agrarian and Peasant Question in the Developing Countries of Asia and Africa at the Present Stage," *Narody Azii i Afriki*, 1964, no. 5, trans. in *Soviet Anthropology and Archeology*, 4 (Summer, 1965): 56.

47. R. G. Landa, "Once Again on the Non-capitalist Path of Development," *Narody Azii i Afriki*, 1966, no. 6, trans. in *Soviet Sociology*, vol. 6 (Winter, 1967–68).

48. M. S. Dzhunusov, "Soviet Autonomy and the Vestiges of Nationalism," *Istoriia SSSR*, 1963, no. 1, trans. in *Soviet Sociology*, 2 (Summer, 1963): 11–25.

49. V. I. Perevedentsev, "On the Influence of Ethnic Factors upon Geographical Population Shifts," *Izvestiia Akademii Nauk SSSR, Seriia geograficheskaia*, 1965, no. 4.

50. A. Rumyantsev, F. Burlatsky, and I. Bestuzhev, *Soviet News*, London, September 19, 1967.

51. *Ibid.*, July 4 and July 11, 1967.

52. M. B. Mitin, "Problems of Philosophy and Sociology in Light of Decisions of the 23rd Congress of the CPSU," *Voprosy filosofii*, 1966, no. 8.

53. M. A. Lifshits, "On Reading Herzen," *Voprosy filosofii*, 1967, no. 1, trans. in *Soviet Studies in Philosophy*, 6 (Summer, 1967): 28–39.

54. V. M. Zhdanov, "The Present Situation in Biology and Genetics: Report of a Discussion," *Voprosy filosofii*, 1965, no. 7, trans. in *Soviet Studies in Philosophy*, 4 (Fall, 1965): 25–42.

55. F. I. Georgiev and G. F. Khrustov, "On the Preconditions and Essential Elements of Consciousness," *Voprosy filosofii*, 1965, no. 10, trans. in *Soviet Studies in Philosophy*, 4 (Spring, 1966): 42–48.

56. A. I. Gukovsky, "How I Became a Historian," *Istoriia SSSR*, 1965, no. 6, trans. in *Soviet Studies in History*, 5 (Fall, 1966): 3–26.

57. Mitin, "Problems of Philosophy."

58. Murray Yanowitch, "Alienation and the Young Marx in Soviet Thought," *Slavic Review*, 26 (March, 1967): 29–53.

59. N. Y. Konrad, "Notes on the Meaning of History," *Soviet Review*, 3 (October, 1962): 44–63; 3 (November, 1962): 21–45.

60. G. Z. Anashkin, "Tasks and Trends in the Development of Socialist Justice," *Vestnik Moskovskogo Universiteta, Seriia pravo*, 1966, no. 4, trans. in *Soviet Law and Government*, 5 (Winter, 1966–67): 29–40, and in *Soviet Review*, 8 (Summer, 1967): 46–57.

61. Leonard Gross, "Three Weeks in a Russian Town," *Look*, October 3, 1967, p. 92.

62. Alexander Werth, "A Portrait of the Soviet Union in Jubilee Year 1967," *New Statesman*, September 29, 1967, pp. 390, 392.

63. George F. Kennan, "The Russian Revolution—50 Years After: Its Nature and Consequences," *Foreign Affairs*, October, 1967.

64. *Soviet News*, London, January 9, 1968.

65. A. S. Bogomolov, Iu. K. Melvil, and I. S. Narsky, "Concerning Certain Aspects of the Critical Analysis of Contemporary Bourgeois Philosophy," *Voprosy filosofii*, 1967, no. 9, trans. in *Soviet Studies in Philosophy*, vol. 6 (Spring, 1968), 45–55.

66. V. Afanasev, "Marx' *Capital* and the Crisis of Capitalism-Oriented Political Economy," *Voprosy ekonomiki*, 1967, no. 7, trans. in *Problems of Economics*.

67. A. V. Shubnikov, "On the Equal Standing of Positive and Negative Numbers," *Voprosy filosofii*, 1966, no. 6, trans. in *Soviet Studies in Philosophy*, 5 (Winter, 1966–67): 33–36.

68. G. I. Naan, "On the Problem of Infinity," *Voprosy filosofii*, 1965, no. 12, trans. in *Soviet Studies in Philosophy*, 4 (Spring, 1966): 30–41.

69. "Historians' Dialogue. Correspondence between A. Toynbee and N. Konrad," *Novy mir*, July, 1967, pp. 174-85.

70. Vl. Kantorovich, "Sociology and Literature," *Novy mir*, December, 1967, trans. in *Soviet Sociology*, in press.

71. A. L. Mongait, *Archaeology in the U.S.S.R.* (Baltimore, Md.: Penguin Books, 1961).

72. A. L. Mongait, "Archeological Cultures and Ethnic Communities," *Narody Azii i Afriki*, January, 1967, trans. in *Soviet Anthropology and Archeology*, in press.

II : Philosophy

Soviet Philosophy 1917-67

Eugene Kamenka

I

Sensitive, educated Russians have long recognized the tragic inadequacies of Russia's past and present, inadequacies only underscored by the vastness of her territory and the pretensions of her rulers. The window that Peter the Great hacked through to Europe brought in the icy chill of realized inferiority; the increasing contact with Europe during and after the Napoleonic Wars exacerbated it.

We are among those nations [Peter Chaadaev wrote between 1829 and 1831] that do not fit into the structure of humanity, but are here to serve as a lesson to the world—in the present time, no matter what one says, we constitute a gap in human understanding. . . . In our homes we live as though in bivouacs: we are strangers in our own families; in our cities we are like nomads—worse than the tribes wandering in our steppes, because those tribes are more attached to their steppes than we are to our towns. . . . In the beginning savage barbarism, then crude superstition, then that brutal and humiliating [Tatar] domination the spirit of which was later inherited by our national rulers—that is the sad story of our youth. We have never known an age of uninterrupted activity and the natural play of moral forces. . . . Our memory does not harbor any

This paper, presented to the Sixth World Politics Conference, Berlin, September, 1967, draws heavily on my article "Philosophy: The Bolshevik Period," enchanting reminiscences, and our tradition knows of no edifying examples. If you look back at the centuries of our history and at the enormous territory we occupy on this planet, you will not find a single memory which would make you stop, or a moment which would speak of our past in a powerful, lively, and colorful manner. One has to hammer into our heads the things which in other nations are a matter of instinct and habit.[1]

Philosophical reasoning, in the sense of close argument and careful logical analysis, has not been in the history of Russia a matter of instinct and of habit. The Eastern Slavs had no doctors of theology or of canon law, no medieval disputations, no Reformation or Counterreformation. The Byzantine Church was antirational enough; the Russian cut itself off even from Byzantine neo-Platonism. Logic might have begun to flourish in the academies of Kiev; to the military autocrats of Muscovy it stood for foreign (Polish) cunning. "The Russians are philosophers not in words, but in deeds," the Croatian Catholic priest Iuri Krizhanich, librarian and archivist in the Kremlin between 1659 and 1661, wrote sadly after his unsuccessful attempt to bring the philosophic ideas of the Counterreformation into Russia.[2] The Orthodox Church, in his time and later, saw philosophy as irrelevant to salvation and subversive of faith: to the Orthodox and to the sectarians, Western rationality produced Catholicism and its logical consequences—Protestantism and atheism. Russia's temporal rulers were no doubt suspicious of Krizhanich's proselytizing aims and activities, but more often than not in the centuries that followed they too were to regard philosophy as a dangerous import, leading men to contemplate the overthrow of kingdoms and the abolition of all authority. The Catherine who admired Voltaire and translated Beccaria took fright at the events of 1789, sentenced Radishchev to exile, and allowed a follower of Hume to be forced out of the newly founded Moscow University and a dissertation on natural religion to be publicly burned. As professors of philosophy, mostly German, came to the new universities being founded in Alexander's reign, the censorship of philosophy lectures began in earnest until, in response to the revolutions of 1848, Nicholas I excluded philosophy (except for psychology and logic) from the university curriculum altogether. The total ban was lifted in 1863, but crippling restrictions excluding post-classical philosophy from the curriculum remained in force until 1889. For more than three hundred years police and ecclesiastical censorship,

---

Survey, no. 64 (July, 1967), pp. 80–98, and on my "Communism, Philosophy under," in *The Encyclopedia of Philosophy*, ed. Paul Edwards (New York and London, 1967), 2:163–68.

backed by capital punishment, exile, monastic imprisonment, and the knout, had combined to make impossible the frank discussion of anything affecting religion and authority and difficult the dissemination of secular learning. In such a society, without foreign havens, philosophy was hardly likely to flourish.

Conditions of religious and political oppression amid general backwardness tend to produce an indirect threat to philosophy and rational thinking that is often even more subversive of these than the direct impediments. The conditions of nineteenth-century Russia produced an intelligentsia more readily than they produced intellectuals: philosophy became ideology, more often the object of uncritical enthusiasm than of careful and critical study. Fichte and Schelling in the first decades of the century, Hegel and Feuerbach in the succeeding ones, had an appeal that Descartes, Leibniz, Hume, and Kant had not—anthropology triumphed over analysis, the Promethean over the Socratic. Russians wanted solutions, not problems.

As we move closer toward the twentieth century, through the growing movement of the revolutionary groups for union with "the people" and the development of Russian Marxism, the consciously and unconsciously anti-intellectual trends in the radical Russian intelligentsia become even more marked. "The Russian *intelligent*, in the literal meaning of the word, lives *outside himself* . . . recognizing as the only object worthy of his interest and concern something that lies beyond his personality—the people, society, government," M. O. Gershenzon wrote in the collection *Vekhi* (1909), in which the liberal intelligentsia strove to take stock after the 1905 uprising. The philosopher N. A. Berdyaev complained in the same volume that "love of egalitarian justice, public good, the well-being of the people has all but destroyed the concern for truth." The attitude of the intelligentsia, he said, could be formulated as "may truth vanish without a trace, if through its destruction people's lives will become happier." Four years later, indeed, that fierce prerevolutionary defender of *partiinost* (party spirit), Maxim Gorky, was to attack the Moscow Art Theater for staging *The Brothers Karamazov* and *The Possessed:*

Dostoevsky deeply understood and presents with relish two diseases bred in the Russian by his monstrous history, his dreary and humiliating life: the sadistic cruelty of a thoroughly disillusioned nihilist and its opposite, the masochism of a beaten, frightened creature . . . Dostoevsky is great and Tolstoy is a genius, and all of you, gentlemen, are gifted and clever; but Russia and her people are more important than Tolstoy, Dostoevsky and even Pushkin, to say nothing of ourselves.[3]

Not only Lenin, but even the comparatively detached and scholarly Plek-hanov appealed primarily to these extraintellectual longings. The revo-lutionary Angelica Balabanoff, here typical, found in Plekhanov's *The Development of the Monistic View of History* "exactly what I needed at the time, a philosophy of method that gave continuity and logic to the process of history and endowed my own ethical aspirations, as well as the revolutionary movement itself, with the force and dignity of an historical imperative." [4]

The great split between Westernizers and Slavophiles that dominated so much of the intellectual life of Russia in the nineteenth century was not productive of subtle and important philosophical argument. To the Westernizers, philosophy was primarily a means of overcoming Russia's stagnation and barbarism, her "Asiatic" or "medieval" past and her servile present. Cut off from full participation in Western intellectual life by language and by censorship, the Westernizers readily became translators and popularizers of Western conceptions, conceptions they were more concerned to propagate and adapt to Russian conditions than to examine and discuss for their own sake. Their contribution to the appreciation and working out of genuine philosophic problems was of the same order as the contribution of German "social democracy" or of George Bernard Shaw and the Fabian Society.* The Slavophiles, recognizing just as clearly that Russia stood outside the European *oikoumene,* that its religion and its "philosophy," its domestic life and its political traditions made it an object of scorn and incomprehension to Western man, reacted with a passionate defense of mystical together-ness and nonrational faith. "Russia cannot be measured with a yardstick"; "Western cunning"—individualism, rationalism, capitalism—are not for the Slav soul. Of course, both sides were able to make points, and often perceptive points; but they were more interested in life than in logic, in the history of Russia than in the history of philosophy, in material or spiritual salvation than in analysis and argument. Taken together with the comparative absence of an advanced division of labor and specialized professional traditions in Russian society, all this tended to produce what have been regarded as the main characteristics of the Russian "philo-sophical" tradition: the ideal of *integral* knowledge, blending into a single harmony the nature of the cosmos and the aspirations of man; the tend-

---

* Professor G. L. Kline seems to me to exaggerate a little the philosophical content in the Russian tradition of criticism, or to underrate the philosophical content in Nietzsche, J. S. Mill, Sartre, etc., when he says of the major Russian thinkers that "their Western counterparts are thinkers like Kierkegaard, John Stuart Mill, Nietzsche, and Sartre" (see the entry "Russian Philosophy" in *The Encyclopedia of Philosophy,* ed. Paul Edwards [New York and London, 1967], 7: 258).

ency to fuse truth as righteousness and theoretical truth; the placing of ethical personalism at the very center of philosophy. While these characteristics are at their most obvious in the work of the Slavophiles and Christians, they are as important in the work of the positivists and naturalists and in the revolutionary tradition that finally turned to Marxism as the union of theory and practice, of science and morality. "Fearlessly to face reality and its reflection—the theoretical, objective truth," the Populist Mikhailovsky wrote in the preface to the third edition of his *Collected Works*, "and at the same time to defend truth as justice, the subjective truth—this is my life's purpose." The result was both a failure to appreciate the critical, analytical content of the Western philosophic tradition and a fantastic dissipation of energy into social and political writing of a popular character, writing that in itself reinforced moralizing and popularizing habits of mind.

Nevertheless, the restoration of philosophy courses to the university curriculum after 1863 and especially the comparative relaxation of censorship in the 1890's did a great deal to lay the foundations for the development of a professional philosophic tradition in Russia. What Professor Zenkovsky calls "the period of systems" in Russian philosophy, beginning with Vladimir Solovyov, is a period of academic philosophy taking seriously the professional traditions of (primarily German) philosophy—Hegelianism, neo-Leibnizianism (including Lotze), neo-Kantianism, and, more in psychology and the natural sciences, positivism. It is common among traditional Russians to regard the birth of this more professional and systematic kind of philosophizing as being due to the first of the Russian system builders, Solovyov himself. But it seems to me that it has much more to do with the fact that philosophy was allowed back into the classroom, where it had to be taught seriously and systematically, and with the growing contacts with European intellectual life as censorship became looser and travel easier. The German Leibnizian and follower of Lotze, Gustav Teichmüller, professor of philosophy in the University of Yurev (Dorpat, now Tartu) in Estonia, where lectures were given in German, had an important influence, especially on A. A. Kozlov (1831–1900), translator of Hartmann's *Philosophy of the Unconscious*, who as professor in Kiev published the first philosophical journal in the Russian language, and later, from St. Petersburg, issued irregularly his *A Personal Word (Svoyo slovo)*, devoted to philosophical questions, published between 1888 and 1898. By the latter time, the journal *Voprosy filosofii i psikhologii*, supported by the Moscow Philosophical Society, was coming out in Moscow with professional articles on philosophical questions. More serious study in the history of philosophy, in logic, ethics, and epistemology began to appear; Sofia Tseretelli at Yurev published her translations of Hume; the work of Husserl, of the Marburg school, of Rickert and Windelband became more widely known and published. Men like the Princes S. N. and E. N. Trubetskoi, A. I. Vvedensky, I. I. Lapshin, S. N. Bulgakov, L. M. Lopatin, S. L. Frank, and V. F. Ern—to take a random sample of the professional philosophers of the time—were unquestionably as unimportant and as undistinguished by international standards as the run-of-the-mill professors of philosophy who dominated German universities between the collapse of Hegelianism and the neo-Kantian revival. Nevertheless, they were just as unquestionably men promoting the tradition and some of the values of philosophical inquiry in the technical sense and laying the foundations for its further development. Apart from Solovyov—who had a vogue among foreign theologians and other uncritical thinkers, and whom I am usually accused of underrating—only two Russian philosophers proper, N. O. Lossky for his doctrine of direct knowledge (intuitionism) and N. A. Berdyaev as an early existentialist, have attracted any attention outside Russia, and then not a great deal. To be sure, it was the misfortune of Russian philosophy to become professional and more directly linked to European university life at a period of philosophic confusion and decline and to be cut off from Europe again just as important new movements—logical positivism and epistemological realism, mathematical logic and the philosophy of science—were getting under way. Just as no one today is likely to read Eucken and the personal idealists and feel that they are still important fifty years later, so few thinkers are likely to return to Russian professional philosophy on the eve of the Revolution for its own sake.* Its importance is only that it serves to remind us how much less than thirty years of comparative professionalism and still circumscribed freedom could accomplish and how much more might have been accomplished if Lenin's October Revolution had not once again cut Russia off from Europe and soon made philosophy subservient again to a "materialist" version of the ideas of Karamzin and Arakcheev.

---

* There is, however, some semiclandestine revival of interest in technical pre-revolutionary philosophy among some younger Soviet philosophers—especially in Lossky, Berdyaev, Lapshin, and Vvedensky—primarily, I think, for the freshness of their style and their nondogmatic form of argument. There are also, I think, traces of their neo-Kantian education in older Soviet philosophers like Asmus and Bakradze.

II

Prerevolutionary Russian philosophy (except, perhaps, for the philosophy of law, where Petrazycky's psychological theory of law and legal norms had deserved, if brief, international standing) attracted no attention and acquired no standing above the remote provincial; Bolshevik philosophy in the period 1919 to 1956 earned nothing but contempt from serious philosophers of all nationalities. Bolshevik theory and Bolshevik practice openly proclaimed goals that amounted to the complete politicalization, dogmatization, and vulgarization of philosophy. Dialectical materialism became the official philosophy of the Communist party and the Bolshevik state, consistently invoked as the ultimate ideological foundation of all Communist political activity and as the only correct foundation for all science, whether social or natural. The repression of non-Marxist philosophy became a necessary consequence of the dictatorship of the proletariat; Lenin's principle of *partiinost* was taken to require of the philosopher complete identification with both the general theoretical and specific practical aims of the Communist party. This view of philosophy as total (though allegedly scientific) ideological *Weltanschauung* quickly led to the blurring of all serious distinctions between the philosophical, the ideological, and the political. Bolshevism, insisting on the unity of theory and practice, made all the problems that arose in the building up of a Communist society philosophical questions, whether they concerned military strategy, the nature of a "Marxist" biology, or the raising of agricultural production. "Philosophical" questions were discussed at meetings of factory workers and in popular publications; not only philosophers, but leading party administrators, not only philosophical publications, but the party press and the newspaper of the Red Navy played decisive roles at certain stages of "philosophic" discussion.

The attempt to make philosophy a mass ideology—Soviet primers of dialectical materialism were published in editions of 250,000 or 500,000 copies and yet quoted as serious contributions to a difficult and technical subject—led (not unnaturally in these conditions) to a philosophical dogmatism organized along religious lines. Philosophy was seen as having its sacred texts (Marx and Engels, and then Lenin and Stalin), its unchallengeable ecclesiastical authority (the Communist party), its officially recognized teachers (the approved party ideologists, strictly censored and promptly removed for deviation or independence), and its innumerable heresies suppressed and persecuted as such.* Consummated under Stalin, this dogmatic organization of philosophy as a state ideology resulted in thinking which, as N. A. Berdyaev once put it, "is purely anonymous." Communist philosophers showered with praise any platitude or absurdity coming from their leaders; they attacked the disgraced or the unpopular in utterly unprincipled fashion; they confessed and recanted and attacked views they had themselves held a little earlier in the style made familiar by the Inquisition and heresy hunts.

The adoption of Lenin's political style into philosophy—by men of infinitely less ability than Lenin—led to a *reductio ad absurdum* of all his worst intellectual traits. His abusive style, his impatience with complexity, his readiness to ascribe unworthy political motives to any opponent, his insistence on bringing everything down to a single issue, and his unprincipled readiness to distort the positions he was criticizing, all became pervasive features of Soviet philosophy, features that these philosophers defended in the most philistine way. Amid this dogmatism and cynicism, it was constantly proclaimed that dialectical materialism was the only scientific world view. The suppression of all other philosophies and the failure to teach seriously even the history of philosophy were defended as being analogous to the suppression of medical quacks and the failure to teach the phlogiston theory to modern classes in chemistry. Yet to non-Marxist philosophers of the most divergent views, the scientific and intellectual content of dialectical materialism as a philosophy seemed remarkably slight and its basic propositions uninteresting in the light of contemporary philosophical developments. Substituting abuse for argument, constantly writing for a low-level audience, not subjected to intellectual criticism that counted in their eyes, Soviet philosophers seemed to their Western counterparts to have regressed far behind the standards of criticism and analysis achieved by professional philosophers in Russia before the Revolution, let alone by contemporary Western philosophers. The attempt to reduce all philosophical conflicts to the conflict between idealism and materialism obscured more than it illuminated philosophical problems; difficulties both in the Soviet conception of materialism and in their exposition and criticism of other philosophers

---

* This trend paralleled the bureaucratization of the party, and, like that bureaucratization, had its roots in Leninism, but flourished most obviously from the 10th Congress onward. The details of the process of dogmatization have been insufficiently studied.

were constantly ignored, often by downright falsification of opponents who caused or brought out these difficulties. The concept of contradiction, so fundamental to Soviet philosophy, was never carefully examined, and technical criticism of Hegel's logic was never taken into account. The Leninist theory of "reflection"—accompanied by an inability to grasp the force of Berkeley's criticisms—made Soviet epistemology remarkably naïve. For all the bombast and self-congratulation with which Soviet ideologists accompanied their work, the "philosophy" of dialectical materialism in their hands became a system of platitudes, half-truths, and lies designed by unprincipled bureaucrats for semi-educated peasants.

Western critics have been rightly conscious of the crude political control that has determined the character of Soviet philosophy and made it a parody both of philosophy generally and of the thought of Karl Marx in particular. They have been somewhat less conscious of the less direct effects of the general social crudity that Bolshevism produced and elevated in Russia. The rejection of elegance, wit, and learning as characteristic of "bourgeois" culture can still be felt among Soviet philosophers; the boorishness and simpleminded bluntness that have so long been exalted in Soviet social relations carry over into philosophical work. Enormous emphasis is put on classification: a study must begin by defining its subject matter *per genus et differentiam* and then proceed to the relevant subdefinitions. Not only does this encourage the Soviet belief in essential characteristics; by insisting on "basic definitions" it enables such definitions to act as media of political control. With the constant changes of political line and the consequent constant rewriting of textbooks, with the lack of serious monographic literature and of serious specialist courses, Soviet philosophical writing was indeed mostly devoted to such pedestrian classification and definition and the abuse of opponents, and not to the examination of problems of detail in specific areas. The enormous publicity given to dialectical materialism often makes the outsider forget that the study of philosophy in detail was long not encouraged in the Soviet Union, and that students and teachers of philosophy are still today underprivileged in relation to admission to study, exemption from productive work, funds, and travel. As an ideology, it has seemed to Soviet administrators, philosophy ought to be simple; in so far as it becomes complex, it is a luxury.

We should also not forget that the October Revolution, unlike the February Revolution, did not represent the consummation of the revolutionary strivings and traditions of the Russian intelligentsia, even in its most radical form. The emigration from Russia in the years of the civil war included not only merchants and aristocrats, unpolitical poets and the liberal (Kadet) intellectuals, but much of the Menshevik and Social Revolutionary intelligentsia as well. To the majority of Marxist intellectuals even it seemed clear from July, 1917, onward (as it had been clear to Martov since 1903) that Lenin was appealing to the anti-intellectual forces in Russian life and that his victory would mean an age of barbarism. (Non-Russian Marxists, Kautsky, Luxemburg, and the later Otto Bauer, held much the same view.) The Menshevik Internationalist N. N. Sukhanov, one of the few revolutionary intellectuals present in St. Petersburg from the first days of the February to the last days of the October Revolution, brings this out graphically by contrasting the people present at the Second Congress of Soviets summoned by the Bolsheviks on October 25, 1917, with the membership of the First Congress, which had met a few months earlier:

The hall was filled with a crowd of a completely different order. Out of tunnels and obscure holes and corners had crept utterly crude and ignorant people whose devotion to the Revolution was spite and despair, while their socialism was hunger and an unendurable longing for rest. Not bad material for experiments, but—those experiments would be risky.[5]

This was the crowd with whose aid Lenin was able to disband the Constituent Assembly and to end parliamentary democracy before it had properly begun; this was the gallery to which Soviet philosophers were ordered to play. In a famous passage of the *Economico-Philosophical Manuscripts* Karl Marx describes the first form of communism, a crude and primitive communism, in which the concept of property is hated but not overcome:

The domination of material property looms so large that it aims to destroy everything which is incapable of being possessed by everyone as private property. It wishes to eliminate talent etc. by *force*. . . . The role of *worker* is not abolished, but is extended to all men. . . . This Communism, which negates the *personality* of men in every sphere, is only the logical expression of private property, which is this negation. Universal *envy* setting itself up as a power is only a camouflaged form of cupidity, which re-establishes itself and satisfies itself in a different way. The thoughts of every individual private property are *at the least* directed against any wealthier private property, in the form of envy and the desire to reduce everything to a common level. . . . Crude Communism is only the culmination of such envy and levelling-down on the basis of its *preconceived* minimum. How little this abolition of private property represents a genuine appropriation is shown by the abstract negation of the whole world of culture and civilization. . . .[6]

When studying the philosophy of the Bolshevik period, we should not—
in our preoccupation with its antecedents in Marxism and the traditions
of the Russian intelligentsia, and in our concern with political direction—
neglect the extent to which it reflected that crude communism, that
universal envy and leveling, which Sukhanov sensed and Lenin used.

III

Bolshevism may have aimed at a monolithic philosophy, steadfast and
unchanging in its fundamental principles, progressing steadily in one
direction in its continued working out of details and its absorption of new
developments. (The model, no doubt, was the workers' movement, surg-
ing on to victory.) In fact, of course, Soviet philosophy, like the Soviet
state (and, for that matter, the "workers' movement") already has a
history—a history of conflicts and changes, of survivals and revivals—
some of which mark the changes in the political organization and spirit
of Soviet communism, and some of which—ultimately, perhaps, more
important—mark more pervasive changes in social climate. Let us now
turn, briefly, to the details of that history.

The men who made the October Revolution quickly proclaimed the
pervasive nature of Communist political control, but the reality took
some time to achieve. The academic teachers of philosophy in Russian
universities were for the most part religious philosophers, Hegelians and
neo-Kantians, with a strong tendency toward ethical personalism; during
the disorganization of the period of wartime communism (1917–21) they
were permitted to go on teaching, though under difficult conditions.
"Free philosophical societies," concerned to maintain traditions of non-
Marxist philosophical discussion, were organized in St. Petersburg,
Moscow, Kostroma, Saratov, and other towns; non-Marxist publications
still appeared. The Institute of Red Professors and the Communist Academy formed during this period were still seen as not controlling all intellectual life, but as minority cells meant to aid the spreading of Marxism
in intellectual circles. When, in 1921, a serious campaign against religion
and "idealism" was inaugurated, non-Marxist professors in the ideological
subjects were removed from their posts, intellectuals were arrested, and
the leading academic philosophers (Lossky, Berdyaev, Frank, Bulgakov,
Lapshin, Vvedensky, Karsavin, Ilyin) were banished. From that time on,

anti-Marxist philosophical activity, such as that of the religious philosopher S. A. Askoldov (the son of the philosopher A. A. Kozlov, mentioned above), had to be carried on as an illegal, "counterrevolutionary" act.*

Within the materialist camp, however, an official dogma and complete authoritarian control were not to be established until the consolidation of the Stalinist dictatorship in the years 1929 to 1931. Among Communist writers, there were basic disagreements about the status of philosophy and about the respective roles of dialectic and of materialism in dialectical materialism. There was genuine excitement about new developments not directly arising out of Marxism; e.g., the work of Freud, which influenced such Marxist writers as A. I. Varyash and the legal theories and philosophy of religion of M. Reisner, and the work of Meinong and the New Realists, which provided a stimulus for the collection *Puti realizma* published by Babynin, Berezhkov, Ognev, and Popov in 1926. Several non-Marxist philosophers who had remained in the Soviet Union were able to issue books, until the eary 1930's, under the imprint "published by the author." These included B. Ia. Rudaev, whose "materialism" derived from Aristotle and Husserl as much as from Marx; V. N. Ivanovsky (the translator of Mill), a "positivist" who showed the influence of Vaihinger and Rickert; M. M. Rubenstein, another pupil of Rickert's, who saw philosophy as not primarily methodology of science, but as the exposition of values and the search for the meaning of life; A. F. Losev, whose books on the philosophy of art, music, and language and on ancient conceptions of the cosmos show the influence of early phenomenology, especially in his analysis of the philosophical significance of naming; A. Shpet, another phenomenologist; the historian of Greek philosophy A. O. Makovelsky; and a few others, such as the historian of philosophy P. P. Blonsky and Lopatin's pupil Ognev.

Part of the difficulty was that communism in this period took very seriously its claim to be creating new material foundations on which a new proletarian culture would arise. Yet what this culture was, or would be, was still far from clear. Marx had written little—virtually nothing— on philosophy proper; Engels' later philosophical works were fairly general in character, and Lenin, too, had hardly been a systematic philosopher. In Russia itself Marxist philosophy of a more technical kind

---

* Askoldov, apparently, organized a religious philosophical society which met secretly until 1928, when all its members were arrested and Askoldov himself was exiled to the northern Urals. A well-known philosopher before the Revolution, when he had written on ontology and theory of knowledge, he returned from exile in 1935 and was allowed to settle in Novgorod, whence he escaped to Germany after the German occupation of 1941. He died in 1945, after publishing some works critical of Marxism which pleased the Nazi authorities.

had been represented primarily by Plekhanov (who died in 1918 and who had deserted Lenin to become a Menshevik and a supporter of the "Imperialist war effort"), L. I. Akselrod, N. I. Bukharin, and Plekhanov's pupil the Menshevik A. M. Deborin, who certainly disagreed among themselves. There was a feeling that the whole history of philosophy should be rewritten from the Communist point of view; yet this task certainly had barely been begun. There was a very great dearth of people with competent philosophical training and background; for a long period the standards required of people training to become teachers of philosophy or professional ideologists were abysmally low. As late as 1926, according to Professor Wetter, all that was required of persons wishing to study for the candidate's degree in the Philosophical Institute of the Academy of Red Professors was a knowledge of the first volume of Lange's *History of Materialism*, Harald Höffding's *History of Modern Philosophy*, Gomperz' *Greek Thinkers*, and Wundt's *Introduction to Philosophy* (presumably because, although a non-Marxist, Wundt treats philosophy in an "empirical" fashion as the inductive summation of the theses of particular sciences), and of dialectical materialist writers such as Engels, Plekhanov, Lenin, L. I. Akselrod, Bukharin, and Deborin.

At the same time a major conflict was going on within the Communist camp over the very existence of a Communist philosophy. While the tradition established by Plekhanov and supported by Lenin insisted that philosophy was a crucial part of Marxism and rested on a creative, materialist development of Hegelian dialectic, another group, consisting largely of natural scientists, claimed that Marxism meant the overcoming of all philosophy and its supercession by science. This group of "mechanists" consisted of S. K. Minin, I. I. Skvortsov-Stepanov, Varyash, A. K. Timiryazev (son of the famous Russian biologist K. A. Timiryazev and himself a physicist as well as a philosopher), V. N. Sarabyanov, and others, including in some respects Bukharin. The most extreme of the antiphilosophical views held by members of this group was expressed in S. K. Minin's article *"Filosofiia za bort"* ("Overboard with Philosophy"). Skvorstov-Stepanov, in a more substantial work, wrote: "The Marxist recognises no special field of 'philosophical activity' distinct from that of science; for the Marxist, materialist philosophy consists in the latest and most general findings of modern science. To understand any organic phenomenon is to trace it back to relatively simple chemical and physical processes." [7] In general terms, as Professor Wetter has reminded us, the mechanists argued that dialectic was merely a method and not present in reality. They agreed with Bukharin that the language of Hegelian dialectics could be transcribed into the language of modern mechanics and treated as a special case of the theory of equilibrium, being here applied to material systems in motion. The mechanists thus attributed all motions to impulses from without; "contradictions" were the conflict of separate forces within each relevant system. There was no emphasis on dialectical self-propulsion or on the two sides of a contradiction presupposing each other. The mechanists argued that quality could be completely deduced from and reduced to quantity; "quality," from the standpoint of logic, was a category of evaluation by consciousness. They denied that there were basic "leaps" from the inorganic to the organic and from the organic to consciousness. In the social field the mechanists relied on an ultimate economic determinism (*stikhinost'*) by which socialism is simply fated and comes about by gradual quantitative changes in social forces. "Freedom," they argued, was not a true dialectical counterpart to "necessity," but an illusory concept expressing the fact that we did not know all the causes operative.

Though mechanist conceptions were perhaps dominant in Communist intellectual life between 1922 and 1925–26, the mechanists were strongly opposed by a number of Soviet philosophers later characterized as "Menshevizing idealists." These were led by the most learned of the (new) Bolshevik philosophers, the pupil and admirer of Plekhanov, A. M. Deborin (he finally joined the Communist party in 1929), and included Milonov, Perelmann, B. Hessen, G. S. Pymiansky, N. A. Karev, I. K. Luppol, I. A. Sten, and others. The Deborinist view, developed mainly in controversy with the mechanists, amounted to a strong emphasis on the importance and integrity of philosophy (as dialectical materialism) and was based to a considerable extent on the philosophical work of Plekhanov. "Materialism rose again enriched by all the acquisitions of idealism," Plekhanov had written in his *Defense of Materialism*. "The most important of these acquisitions was the dialectical method." The Deborinists argued that dialectical materialism exists as an independent discipline alongside the positive sciences and is the methodology and theory of scientific knowledge in general. The Marxist *Weltanschauung*, Deborin argued in his *Dialektika i estestvoznanie*, had three components: the materialist dialectic as a general scientific methodology and theory of knowledge, the dialectic of nature as the methodology of the natural sciences or scientific materialism, and the dialectic of history or historical materialism. Marx and Engels had established the guidelines for all of these, but had elaborated only the third; the task of Soviet philosophers was to elaborate the first.[8] In doing so, Deborin treated seriously the history of philosophy, especially Hegel's *Science of Logic*, and he brought out an edition of Hegel with an elaborate introduction. (He also conducted a specialist seminar on Kant, attacked for "scholasticism" by those of its younger participants—Mitin and Yudin—who were to replace Deborin.) The Deborinists rejected both the a priori "philosophy of nature" and the empirical conception of natural science as the mere unphilosophical collection of facts and building of inductive conclusions. Only dialectic can weld facts into a significant whole. The Deborinists emphasized the internal contradiction of the Hegelian dialectic proper, in which the antithesis is presupposed by the thesis, brought into being by it, and held in a single system with it. The Deborinists also put great stress on the law of the transformation of quantity into quality and therefore on the "leaps" and the emergence of new forms. Mechanism, they said, left out of account the specific character of the specific levels or stages of the development of matter (being, life, consciousness); it left out of account the existence of these as particular "nodes" or categories of being. The *origin* of the organic could be derived from the inorganic, but not its *form*.

Although the initial "scientism" of the Bolsheviks gave aid and comfort to the mechanists, Communist ideological tradition and doctrinal authority were on the whole on the side of the Deborinists. In 1922 Lenin had written to the journal *Under the Banner of Marxism* advising Bolshevik philosophers to regard themselves as a society of materialist friends of the dialectic of Hegel; the first publication, in 1925, of Engels' *Dialectics of Nature* (written 1872–86) lent the support of Engels to the proposition that higher forms cannot be reduced, without residue, to lower forms. Further support came from the publication in 1929 of Lenin's *Philosophical Notebooks*, treating philosophy as a central and creative field of Marxist endeavor. The Deborinists had already been winning an organizational struggle: Deborin himself had been appointed director of the Institute of Philosophy of the Communist Academy, and he had been responsible editor of *Under the Banner of Marxism* since 1926 and editor of the philosophical section of the first *Soviet Encyclopedia* since the same year. In 1929, at the Second All-Union Conference of Marxist-Leninist Scientific Institutions, the Deborinists achieved a decisive condemnation of mechanism.*

* The victory, of course, had been preceded by fairly unscrupulous denunciations of opponents which bore little evidence of Deborin's comparative philosophical culture. Thus, in a predominantly illiterate article in the Ukrainian *Bolshevik* in 1928, P. Demchuk denounced the director of the Institute of Marxism-Leninism in Kharkov, Professor S. Iu. Semkovsky, for liquidating dialectical materialism and thus taking a line which meant "the ideological disarming of the proletariat, its capitulation to the mercies of bourgeois positive science." The same article, for good measure, accuses Semkovsky of keeping anti-Marxist idealists in their jobs.

The victory of the Deborinists over the mechanists was aided by the impact of Einstein's theory of relativity and the electron theory generally upon scientific thought in the 1920's, but was probably at least partly conditioned by a recognition of the social usefulness of ideology as a means of control and of the incompatibility of "scientism" with authoritarianism. Mechanism was condemned both as a departure from the Marx-Engels-Plekhanov-Lenin tradition of Marxism and as being out of step with the developments of contemporary science. The Deborinist victory, however, was short-lived. On September 27, 1929, a speech of Stalin's had condemned the mechanists but at the same time complained that theoreticians generally had not kept pace with practical developments in the Soviet Union. The speech became the signal for an attack on two fronts, spearheaded by two new figures on the scene, M. B. Mitin and P. F. Yudin, directors of the Communist cell in the Moscow Institute of Red Philosophers, then young men who were, and have remained, philosophically illiterate. Mechanism was accused of being a right-wing deviation and the theoretical foundation of the kulak agents within the party (Bukharin had opposed Stalin's plans for forced collectivization on the ground that the larger peasant would in any case "inevitably" be drawn into socialism), of leading to economism and to such revisionist doctrines as the neo-Kantian supplementations of Marxism. The Deborinists, on the other hand, were accused of overemphasizing leaps (just as the mechanists had overemphasized evolutionary continuity) and of thus giving ideological support to Trotsky's "left-wing deviation" or Menshevizing idealism. They had taken over the Hegelian dialectic without transforming it into a materialist dialectic, they had separated form and content, they had taken from Plekhanov his "erroneous" discounting of Lenin's copy-theory of knowledge and his Feuerbachian attempt to solve the subject-object relation in epistemology in purely metaphysical terms without regard for historical and revolutionary reality. Above all, the Deborinists were accused of being "abstract," of divorcing theory from practice, philosophy from politics. In May, 1930, while Yudin was attacking Deborin for holding aloof from the great problems of socialist construction, an article "By Ten Authors" in *Under the Banner of Marxism* still insisted that "the working out of the materialist dialectic is, in fact, the chief service called for *from philosophy* by the class struggle and the construction of socialism." On January 25, 1931, after a speech by Stalin, the Central Committee of the Communist party condemned both mechanism and "the idealist distortion of Marxism on the part of Comrades Deborin, Karev, Sten, and others." Deborin recanted, admitting in the subsequent discussion before the Communist Academy that he had fallen into the errors of Menshevizing idealism and of separating theory and practice, and publicly thanked the Central Committee of the Communist party and especially Comrade Stalin for having "restrained him just in time." *

IV

The decision of January, 1931, is acknowledged by all serious historians of Soviet philosophy as forming a crucial dividing line. Professor Bochensky correctly characterizes the preceding years (1917–1930) as a period of discussion; Soviet writers, since the decisions of the 20th Congress and the repudiation of the cult of personality, attempt to present it as a period of creative philosophic endeavor amid conditions of democratic discussion, in which the foundations for a Marxist philosophy were laid by means of the critical consideration of various Communist views and the intellectual exposure of errors, without recourse to unjustified "administrative measures" as a means of philosophical criticism. These latter claims are simply not true: what have seemed to many of us the appalling qualities of Soviet philosophical style and organization were evolving in this "period of discussion" as the characteristic Bolshevik contribution to philosophy. The struggle between mechanists and Deborinists had all the features of an organizational struggle for hegemony,

* Surprisingly, Deborin did not fall victim to the subsequent purges, but remained in Moscow until his death in 1963. After Stalin's death in 1953, he was again able to write occasional uncontroversial articles on minor philosophical themes, and a collection of his essays has recently been republished in the Soviet Union. The final volume of the new Soviet six-volume *History of Philosophy* now deals with the dispute in an interesting and still dishonest way. Deborin's condemnation is presented as primarily the result of democratic discussions in the Communist Academy and the Institute of Red Professors, in which Deborin was generally held to be guilty of a "formalistic bent" and in which he himself admitted holding aloof from the practical problems of socialist construction. In December, 1930, the account continues, Stalin substituted for the phrase "formalistic bent" the phrase "Menshevizing idealist," and the discussions then went on to charge Deborin and his followers with formulating the political methodology of Trotskyism. For this, "although N. Karev was a Trotskyist, and although some other followers of Deborin admitted left opportunist mistakes," there was no foundation. But "in the conditions of the cult of personality," Deborin and some other comrades were unjustly removed from philosophical activity. (See *Istoriia filosofii*, 6, no. 1 (1965): 143–45.) The sufferings of Marxist philosophers who fell out of favor under Stalin (many of whom have since returned to university appointments) are often discussed privately, but are still not acknowledged in anything like full measure in Soviet histories or public discussions.

in which philosophical argument alone was never decisive. The huge Russian editions of the works of Marx, Engels, and Lenin begun early in the 1920's were increasingly appealed to as unchallengeable doctrinal authority; the dictatorship of the proletariat, the greatness and relevance of Marx, and the possibility and superiority of a Marxist materialist science or philosophy, supporting the proletarian revolution and the upbuilding of communism, simply could not be questioned. What constitutes the difference between the "period of discussion" and the Stalinist philistinism that followed it is simply that the last vestiges of prerevolutionary traditions and culture had not yet been entirely destroyed by denunciation and terror and by the coming forward of new cadres "who knew not Joseph." Deborin and Akselrod had been raised in an atmosphere where criticism and learning still counted; they had brought with them a certain intellectual baggage they could not discard. Mitin and Yudin had no such baggage, and knew that, in the conditions of a party dictatorship, neither learning nor critical acumen counted in comparison with political unscrupulousness and cynical willingness to provide what the party wanted. In the work of Deborin in the 1920's one can still feel the creative sweep and confidence of a man expressing his own views and working out his own position, as well as a comparative richness of language and subtlety of argument shaped in conditions in which discussion was still serious and intelligent. In the succeeding period, these qualities were to disappear entirely from Soviet philosophical writing, which took on the style and mentality of the petty bureaucrat with a streak of viciousness.*

After the decree of January 25, 1931, the course of Soviet philosophy, as Gustav Wetter puts it, "flows in the narrow channel of official prescribed opinion." Stalin is quickly elevated to the fountainhead of all wisdom; controversy is now directed solely against bourgeois ideology; internal discussions quickly degenerate into the "routing out" of heresies or errors.

---

* Even the comparative liberalizations since the death of Stalin have not been able to restore so far the intellectual liveliness that lingered on from prerevolutionary intellectual conditions into the 1920's. One has only to compare the only substantial monographs on Ludwig Feuerbach (regarded by Marxists as a figure of major importance) published in fifty years of Soviet philosophic activity: Deborin's *Ludwig Feierbakh* (Moscow, 1923; reprinted 1929) and A. I. Ardabev's *Ateizm Ludwiga Feierbakha* (Moscow, 1963). The latter is a cliché-ridden, pedestrian "study" rigidly adhering to simple and naïve Soviet conventions of writing, inflated, repetitive, and unoriginal, always using the standard Soviet phrase, and simply elaborating the standard, safe view given in the textbooks. The difference between the two authors is not simply one of ability, but marks a complete break in cultural traditions. The positive aspects of the new tone in post-1956 Soviet philosophy are scientific rather than literary, professional rather than cultured.

The leading official philosopher of the 1930's, still active as an official spokesman of Soviet philosophy at recent international congresses, but now in the process of retiring and deprived of all respect from his colleagues, was Mark Borisovich Mitin. On specifically philosophical questions, the new official philosophy headed by him remained close to the positions that had been preached by Deborin against the mechanists. The status and importance of philosophy as a discipline continued to be upheld. Soviet philosophers continued to insist that phenomena of higher orders could not be reduced to those of lower orders. The law of the conflict and interpenetration of opposites was maintained as a fundamental law of dialectics distinguishing "true" Marxist philosophy from vulgar mechanistic materialism, but in practice it was interpreted in a less Hegelian spirit. (Even today, Deborin's main error is given as lying in his "formalism" and his undervaluing of Lenin as a philosopher, rather than in any concrete philosophical doctrine.)

The main difference between the new movement and Deborinism was one of spirit rather than of dogma. The new Stalinist philosophers made themselves entirely subservient to the day-to-day requirements of party policies; they gave the impression that there was only one creative philosopher in the Soviet Union, Joseph Stalin. Wetter cites a characteristic example: In his book *Dialectical Materialism* (Moscow, 1933), Mitin wrote, "The further advancement of Marxist-Leninist theory, in every department, including that of the Philosophy of Marxism, is associated with the name of Comrade Stalin. In all Comrade Stalin's practical achievements, and in all his writings, there is set forth the whole experience of the worldwide struggle of the proletariat, the whole rich storehouse of Marxist-Leninist theory." The main effort went into making up for the lack of official textbooks and into revising textbooks that had been made out of date by new denunciations and shifts in the party line. Mitin and Razumovsky published their two-volume textbook on dialectical and historical materialism and other textbooks and monographs started coming off the presses laying down the "correct" Marxist view on various philosophical questions.

In 1936 there was another about-turn. The new Stalin constitution, adopted in 1936, was claimed to mark the end of the period of the construction of socialism. Socialism had now been achieved; there was much talk of socialist legality, of the creative role of socialist law, of the rights and importance of human personality, etc. The philosophical works published by Mitin and his colleagues between 1931 and 1935 were suddenly accused of abstract and scholastic presentation and political illiteracy; i.e., in part of mentioning the writings of Trotsky and Zinoviev, about to be finally exposed at the great purge trials. Mitin hastened to acknowledge his errors and to promise to follow the party line "on the philosophical front." No action was taken against him. But the effect of the enormous purges of 1936–38, of the atmosphere of terror that swept over the Soviet Union (followed by the terrible, incredibly destructive defense against the German invasion), was to cut down enormously the volume of philosophical production and to remove almost completely any incentive for independent or original work even within the narrow confines of the new Stalinist philosophy. As part of entering upon the era of socialism the Communist Academy was incorporated into the Academy of Sciences of the U.S.S.R., and the Institute of Philosophy was considerably enlarged and placed under the direction of V. V. Adoratsky and Mitin, the far more serious Marx scholar D. Riazanov having been arrested and removed from his post. A collectively written three-volume history of philosophy and a so-called dictionary of philosophy were issued, but generally there was little work and virtually no original work of even small significance done after 1936.* In 1944, at the height of the war effort, the Central Committee complained of shortcomings in the work done by philosophers, but in the same breath criticized "serious errors" in the just published third volume of the *History of Philosophy*, errors which consisted of passing over in silence the reactionary attitudes of Hegel, his nationalism, and his deification of the Germans as a chosen people. Generally, however, the treatment of German philosophers by Soviet writers during World War II was at best reminiscent of George Santayana's *Egoism in German Philosophy*.

The criticism of bourgeois philosophy and the building up of the native "democratic" philosophical traditions of the Russian people—both increasingly emphasized during the war and especially soon after it— were at a similar crude level. In the treatment of Russian philosophy great stress was put on the "progressive attitudes" of Russian "Democrat-enlighteners," literary critics, and scientists; where possible their religious commitments were passed over in silence, and belief in the people or in the importance of economic and social conditions was treated as a most acceptable substitute for genuine philosophic discussion. On this almost fraudulent basis it was proclaimed that pre-Marxist philosophical materialism had reached its highest point of development in the Soviet Union. The criticisms of bourgeois philosophy were similarly on an extremely low level of abuse, while both contemporary philosophers and the classics of philosophy were forced into the rigid and unilluminating

---

* G. F. Aleksandrov, however, published his Stalin Prize–winning work on Aristotle in 1940, and—perhaps largely through his influence—the three-volume history of philosophy is not significantly more philistine than many productions issued after Stalin's death. Students still use it.

schematism of being either materialists (good) or idealists (bad). Typical of this sort of work is an article in *Bolshevik* of May, 1951 (no. 9), reviewing Maurice Cornforth's *In Defense of Philosophy*, in which the author writes:

The philosophy of the contemporary imperialist bourgeoisie is degraded and emaciated. It vegetates today by leading a repugnantly dirty existence which reflects the whole depth of the vileness of the degenerated bourgeoisie. Stultifying human conscience with the poison of hatred of mankind, of racialism and cosmopolitanism, exciting war psychosis and the anti-Communist hysteria, propagating mysticism and irrationalism, justifying the most brutal examples of the oppression of everything that is leading and progressive—these are the most typical symptoms of that philosophy. . . . The contemporary positivist philosophy, whatever may be its verbal form, is thoroughly reactionary and continues to swallow the two-hundred-year-old narrow ideas of the English priest Berkeley. This is particularly evident, for instance, in the "theory of logical analysis" propagandized by one of the contemporary philosophical obscurantists, Bertrand Russell. . . . It is not difficult to discover that Russell's "logical analysis" is nothing but a new variation of the subjective idealism, which was long ago thrown away in the dustbin of history, of the priestly preaching, a re-edition of Berkeleyism, of empirio-criticism which was routed by V. I. Lenin in his writing of genius: *Materialism and Empirio-Criticism.* . . But it is not accidental that this antiquated junk is again brought to light and proclaimed to be the "newest" philosophy. Using his "logical analysis" Russell tries to justify certain definite political conclusions necessary for his masters.

These attitudes continued into and were even intensified in the early post-1948 period, especially in more popular or official writing. The *Short Philosophical Dictionary*, issued under the editorship of M. M. Rozental and P. F. Yudin in 1951, devoted fifteen columns to Stalin and three columns each to Lenin, Marx, Hegel, and Aristotle, against two columns on Plato and one on Socrates; it had eight columns on Mao Tsetung and six columns on the Stalinist cultural commissar A. A. Zhdanov. It described Bertrand Russell as "The English reactionary philosopher . . . militant ideologue of Anglo-American imperialism . . . one of the inciters toward a new world war," and John Dewey as "a reactionary bourgeois American pedagogue, confirmed idealist; ideological sword-bearer for American imperialism seeking world hegemony, participant in dirty campaigns of calumny against the Soviet Union." The dictionary had no entries for such figures as Thales, Anaximenes, and Anaximander, for Zeno, Protagoras, Leucippus, William of Occam, Thomas Aquinas, or Machiavelli.

Stalin himself was, of course, exempt from pressures and criticism and the fear of terror. His works had to be treated as authoritative by Soviet philosophers and also as displaying, on every occasion, unexampled signs of incredible genius. His short pamphlet on *Dialectical and Historical Materialism*, initially published as part of *The History of the CPSU (B). Short Course*, was hailed by Mitin as a "creation . . . marking an epoch in the development of Marxist-Leninist philosophy, and of world-historical significance." His earlier, rather inept *The Foundations of Leninism* had similar status, though it was quoted in philosophical contexts somewhat less frequently. More important perhaps was his intervention to condemn the linguistic school of Marr, published as *Marxism and Problems of Linguistics* (1950), which made an important common-sense rather than philosophical emendation to the theory of basis and superstructure and set the intellectual tone of the closing years of the Stalin era. But to the philosopher there is not one sentence of Stalin's work that displays any philosophical competence or insight or directly raises questions of philosophical interest. Even to the political theorist Stalin is a specimen rather than a colleague.

In 1946 it was decreed that philosophy should be taught in all higher educational institutions and that a sufficient number of specialists should be trained for this purpose by the universities by 1948. (This did not happen until more than ten years later.) At the same time, however, the stress on partisanship was reemphasized. *The History of Western European Philosophy*, by one of the most important of Soviet philosophers, G. F. Aleksandrov, was suddenly denounced, through the personal intervention of Zhdanov, as displaying the vice of "bourgeois objectivism." Before a large audience of leading "workers in philosophical science" from all over the Soviet Union, brought together on the initiative of the Central Committee of the CPSU in June, 1947, Zhdanov criticized Aleksandrov's work for the abstract neutrality of its style, for its failure to show Marxism as a revolutionary and qualitative leap in the history of philosophy, for not linking philosophical ideas with the material conditions of life, and especially for omitting Russian philosophy and thus giving tacit support to the "bourgeois" belittlement of Russian philosophy and the "bourgeois" distinction between Western and Eastern culture. Zhdanov went on to say that generally Stalin was dissatisfied with the timidity, abstractness, and laziness of Soviet philosophers. The time for more serious expansion of philosophical work had come. The philosophers agreed. Aleksandrov recanted and promised to try to do better work.*

---

* He atoned with the highly propagandist, crudely adulatory work *Trudy I. V. Stalina o iazykoznanii i voprosy istoricheskogo materializma* (Moscow, 1952). But his fate was to be denounced in 1955 for having passed from the "bourgeois objectiv-

V

In the postwar development of Soviet philosophy two dates compete for a significance analogous to that which we have ascribed to 1931. June, 1947, the date of Zhdanov's intervention into philosophy, heralds an extremely significant increase in quantitative production by Soviet philosophers; from 1948 onward there is a steady, unchecked expansion of philosophical teaching and publication. There is no marked change in quality, however, until 1955–56, when Krushchev's secret speech to the 20th Congress dramatically symbolizes an important change in attitude leading to marked qualitative improvement in philosophical teaching and philosophical work.

The quantitative growth which unquestionably dates from the last years of Stalin's regime issued from the combined effect of his growing concern with ideology as a means of stabilization and of the growth in technical and general education leading to increased specialization and more postgraduate studies. The ideology of "the one thing needful," so prominent in the period of revolutionary struggle and of the five-year plans, had been officially abandoned in 1936, but the purges and the war naturally enough gave it a great residual strength. Thus the 1920's and even the early 1930's had been periods to stress the dependence of everything on economic change and economic progress. From 1936 onward, however, Stalin had turned toward converting the dialectic into the basis for a stable ideology of Soviet rule. Its task now was not to sharpen class struggle, but to help create consensus. The economic reductionism implicit in the materialist interpretation of history was therefore further modified. In 1938, in his *On Dialectical and Historical Materialism*, Stalin had stressed the capacity of the ideological superstructure for reacting back on the base; in 1950, in his *Marxism and Questions of Linguistics*, he went further and stressed the comparative independence of the ide-

---

ism" of his *History of Western European Philosophy* in 1946 to a "nihilistic denial of the value of bourgeois philosophers" in the volume *Dialectical Materialism*, published under his editorship in 1953. In this volume, the editors of *Voprosy filosofii* complained, the creators of the great philosophical systems of the past are presented simply as ideologists of the exploiting classes occupied solely with defending the existing order. The collectively written *History of Philosophy*, which Aleksandrov edited until 1953, is accused of similar errors, and of giving the false impression that dialectical materialism had simply dropped from heaven.

ological superstructure, its "creative role" in "aiding the base," and insisted that some cultural phenomena, such as language, transcended class
divisions and were therefore ideologically neutral. The pamphlet not only
opened up the way for a study of formal logic as the ideologically
neutral—though abstract and static—laws of thought, but symbolized
generally the new stress on ideology.

The stress on ideology was accompanied by, and also reflected, a general growth in education and specialization. The 1920's had been a period
of educational "crash programs," designed to maximize literacy and basic
skills. By the late 1930's, a more stable educational system producing
more seriously trained people had emerged, but its impact on Soviet society was interrupted by purges and total and destructive war. The early
postwar period had to undertake once again an enormous expansion of
education, but this time at a (comparatively) much higher level. The
demand now was not for literacy, but for more jurists, more teachers,
more scientists, more administrators. The sophistication of Soviet society
had enormously increased; so had the absolute numbers of people capable
of reading serious work. In 1916 there were some 90 institutions of higher
learning in all Russia; by 1959 there were 770, including 40 universities.
There are now well over 2,000,000 full-time or correspondence students
of tertiary institutions, compared with some 200,000 in any year of the
1920's.

In line with all this, then, the discussions of 1947 marked the beginning of a period of renewed philosophical activity. The Soviet Union's
only continuous philosophical journal, *Under the Banner of Marxism*,
had ceased publication in 1944. In 1947, the journal *Voprosy filosofii*
(*Problems of Philosophy*) was launched as a biannual; by 1957 it was a
monthly. A second philosophical journal, *Filosofskie nauky* (*Philosophical Sciences*), published from the philosophy faculty in Moscow State
University, has appeared since 1958, and has tended to become increasingly technical. The series comprising the *Bulletin* of Moscow State
University has been gradually expanded and made more specialist; philosophy, formerly put together with economics and law, is now (1967)
about to issue its special bulletin. The bibliographies and reports compiled by Professor Bochensky's Institute of East European Studies in the
University of Fribourg, Switzerland, show a similar marked increase in
the publication of philosophical books (from an average of 33 books a
year in the period 1947 to 1956 to 112 in the academic year 1957–58
alone). The number of candidates' theses in philosophy submitted in three
leading Moscow institutions rose from 53 in 1947 to 228 in 1954, and the
number of postgraduate students of philosophy from 1,000 in 1951 to
2,000 in 1954. Together with this expansion in numbers has come an ex-

pansion in area. In 1951 the editors of *Voprosy filosofii* complained that outlying philosophical institutions, such as those in the Ukraine, White Russia, and Georgia, "confine themselves exclusively to the history of philosophy in their respective countries and are content to leave the working out of contemporary problems of Marxist philosophy as a monopoly to the Philosophical Institute of the Academy of Sciences of the U.S.S.R." in Moscow. Since then, the number of serious philosophy departments has been increased (though the majority of Soviet universities still have none, but only a department of Marxism-Leninism), philosophical work outside Moscow and Leningrad has been greatly intensified, and such universities as those of Tbilisi, Erevan, and Kiev have become significant philosophical centers.

During the final years of Stalin's rule, when this buildup of philosophical teaching, discussion, and publication began, the party was nevertheless extremely anxious to keep philosophers to a strictly partisan line, with the party as active arbiter on the most philosophical and scientific questions. This was the point of the denunciation of Aleksandrov's *History*, followed by a campaign against "objectivism." The criticism of contemporary "bourgeois" philosophy was encouraged, but carried on in the crudest and most vindictive terms; prerevolutionary materialist philosophy in the territories making up the Soviet Union was grossly overvalued. In 1948 the Central Committee of the Communist party organized a conference for the purpose of condemning orthodox genetics and announcing that the Michurin-Lysenko school of biology, with its rejection of genes and its belief in the heritability of acquired characteristics, was the correct Marxist-Leninist view of biology. The Central Administration of the Statistical Institute had to recant the heresy that statistics was based on the mathematical relationships of large numbers and to concede that statistical relations had meaning only in the context of Marxist-Leninist social science. A. A. Maksimov and a group of philosophers of science attacked the physicists for using and defending the subjective-idealist theory of relativity, but were in this case successfully repelled. Then in 1950 came Stalin's shattering blow to Marxist linguistics, in which the theories of N. Ia. Marr (1864–1934) and his Marxist disciples—that languages unfolded by qualitative leaps—was proclaimed as nonsense, and his followers were accused of stifling Soviet linguistics. This pamphlet led to two years of hasty philosophical activities in which everything was brought into line with Stalin's new pronouncements on the relation between base and superstructure and the character of language and formal logic.

The year 1948, like the year 1931, did not produce any major revolution in the Soviet philosophical line; the dominant (Deborinist) trend in Soviet philosophy has never been repudiated wholesale in the way in which the Stuchka-Pashukanis-Reisner position on law was repudiated in 1936. There were differences in emphasis, a growing national chauvinism, increasing cold-war bitterness in writing on contemporary bourgeois philosophy, less tendency toward economic reductionism, and increasing stress on ethics and moral education and on the administrator's delusion that policies can shape society.

The death of Stalin, however, saw the beginnings of a new tone in Soviet philosophy, presaging the qualitative leap that became possible after 1955–56. Within a year laudatory references to Stalin as a great philosophical genius had disappeared from the journals and demands for a certain respect for professional competence and integrity began to be heard. While lawyers were publicly much more forthright than philosophers in demanding a certain professional standing and respect for their professional integrity, a certain section of leading philosophers—apparently with full party approval—began calling for more "objective" and creative philosophical work. In 1955, the journal *Kommunist* complained that of the 1,000 or more graduate philosophers then supposedly active in the Soviet Union, only about 100 published with any degree of regularity; the remaining 900 preferred to rest on their laurels. "Their philosophical swords are covered with rust . . . bleak 'quotology' has become their stock in trade. . . . They are capable of making a deal with their conscience, they praise a book to the skies today and readily tear it to pieces tomorrow. . . . We must put an end to such depravity." In 1956, at the 20th Congress of the CPSU, N. S. Khrushchev in his secret speech inaugurated the campaign for liquidating the cult of personality in Soviet cultural life, and in 1961, at the 22nd Congress, Stalin's errors, including the error of dogmatically laying down positions in fields in which he was not competent, were exposed to the world. In general terms, this was an extremely important trend—of course, within the limits of ultimate party control—toward declassifying the specific details of professional disciplines and permitting professional discussion without the threat of political punishment for taking the wrong side. By 1958, the leading Soviet philosopher P. N. Fedoseev was emphasizing the importance of concrete analysis in philosophy and the impropriety of importing methods appropriate to the struggle against hostile ideology into scientific discussions.

The trend toward professionalization and professional integrity becoming more evident in Soviet philosophical discussion has been accompanied by some important surrenders by dogma coming in contact with life. In 1955 discussions on the philosophy of science led to the acceptance of the theory of relativity (both the general and the special) as fully compatible, in its physical formulations, with the doctrines of dialectical materialism; it was taken to confirm the *diamat* view that geometry is a branch of physics, that space and time cannot be abstracted from matter, and that matter is not inert material but can also be energy. In these discussions the leading Soviet philosophers identified with the attack on relativity, A. A. Maksimov and R. Ia. Steinman, together with the antirelativity physicist I. V. Kuznetsov, were branded as reactionary. The following year, cybernetics, previously condemned as a bourgeois pseudoscience, was fully accepted as the science of computers, bringing out certain important analogies with human thinking. In connection with this the development of mathematical logic and the truth-table technique were accepted by an increasing number of Soviet philosophers as an important expansion of formal logic—a development culminating in the decision by the Moscow University philosophy faculty in 1966 to accept Professor I. S. Narsky's recommendation that the department of logic in the faculty confine itself to teaching formal and mathematical (symbolic) logic and that the teaching of dialectical logic be split off from it. At the same time, the regime of Lysenko in biology was overthrown in favor of orthodox genetics.

All these developments have produced very significant signs of a new atmosphere in considerable areas of Soviet philosophy. There is now a great deal of emphasis on problems within dialectical materialism—the relation of formal and dialectical logic, the philosophy of physics, the relationship and coordination of the categories of dialectical materialism, and so on. An increasing amount of publication on these questions is being done by university presses and marketed in small editions of seven to ten thousand copies, thus enabling would-be authors to address a more technical audience. The standard argument in such works is mostly still by way of deduction from unquestioned fundamental principles of dialectical materialism, or from Lenin, whose philosophical writings have taken on a specially canonical character since the rejection of Stalin and the alleged return to Leninist norms. There is now a great deal of new nonsense in low-level Soviet philosophical teaching about the "Leninist stage" in the history of philosophy, the philosophical critique of religion, epistemology, etc., but even the use of doctrinal authorities is now comparatively intelligent and increasingly looks to the context and spirit in which the cited pronouncements were made. Nevertheless, the need to be orthodox still encourages concentration on issues that fit in with doctrinal pronouncements.

The renewed emphasis on Lenin's contribution to philosophy fortunately, however, has been accompanied by a switch of attention from his *Materialism and Empirio-Criticism* to his subtler, more interesting, and more philosophical *Philosophical Notebooks*. This has provided useful authority, and perhaps stimulus, for a certain renewed Hegelianizing trend within contemporary Soviet philosophy, evident in some of the discussions concerning the relation between theory of knowledge, dialectical logic, and formal logic, in some studies of the logical structure of Marx's *Capital*, and in discussion of various metaphysical problems, including the categories. Within limits, this Hegelianizing has led, as it did in Deborin's work, to a somewhat subtler appreciation of philosophical problems, and it has led to genuine, if still crude and uncritical, philosophical disputes between what Professor Bochensky has called the "Hegelians" and the "Aristotelians" in Soviet philosophy.

In the history of philosophy and the criticism of contemporary bourgeois philosophy there have been similar important changes in style and seriousness of content. The journal *Voprosy filosofii* already in 1955 objected to the nihilistic denial of the value of the history of philosophy, to improper attacks on "objectivism," to the incorrect overevaluation of the role of Russian philosophy, and to false conceptions that the philosophy of Marxism did not build on previous achievements. The history of Russian philosophy has been enriched by a new willingness to look at technical philosophers in Russia before the Revolution and to distinguish more subtly in dealing with nonmaterialist or anti-Marxist writers. The Department of the History of the Philosophy of People of the U.S.S.R. has lost its organizational power in Moscow University and remains (together with the Department of Scientific Communism) an outlet for the dumber careerist. Respect now goes to the Department of the History of Foreign Philosophy, which undergraduate and postgraduate students see as dealing with true philosophy, and the spread of philosophical knowledge in Moscow University is to a significant extent the spread of this department's influence on other departments. In general, the less a department concerns itself with the elaboration of Marxism-Leninism for its own sake and the more its members show their knowledge of traditional and contemporary Western philosophers, the higher the regard in which it is held. There has been increasing interest in philosophers who do not fall into either of the simple classifications materialist and idealist—Aristotle, Kant, Hegel. The projected five- to six-volume *Encyclopedia of Philosophy*, issued since 1960 under the editorship of F. V. Konstantinov, presents a complete break from earlier dictionaries and encyclopedias by giving fair and reasonably accurate accounts of the work of present-day "bourgeois philosophers" and of some of the condemned philosophers of the 1920's, whose works are even included in bibliographies on Kant and Hegel. (This applies to such philosophers as L. I. Akselrod and the early Deborin; it does not apply to Trotsky and Bukharin, who are simply left out.) The new *Philosophical Dictionary* edited by Rozental and Yudin in 1963, replacing their earlier *Short Philosophical Dictionary*, displays an enormous improvement in range, technicality, and fairness of the entries. It is no longer a handbook of dogmatic instruction and denunciation; it contains several hundred new entries (previously thought unworthy of mention) ranging from antinomies in Kant and approbative ethics in Barth, Brunner, and Tillich to combinatory logic and quantification of the predicate.

The six-volume *History of Philosophy* completed in 1965, though smothering the truly philosophical with material on social thought among Bulgarians and Buryat-Mongols, gives reasonably fair accounts and bibliographies in its discussion of contemporary non-Marxist philosophy, and recognizes, for the first time, the internal history of Soviet philosophy as something more than the routing out of heresies. The serious unabusive tone of K. S. Bakradze's book on contemporary "bourgeois" philosophy, of I. S. Narsky's work on Hume and "positivism," of A. S. Bogomolov's studies in "bourgeois" theories of evolution (leading him to his recent plea in *Voprosy filosofii* that Soviet philosophers should take account of the contributions to dialectic made by non-Marxists since Hegel's time), and of B. V. Biriukov's studies on Frege are not uncharacteristic of a new and ever growing trend in Soviet professional philosophy and have no parallel in Soviet philosophy under Stalin.

Extremely important in this connection have been the growth of contacts with the West through scholarly exchanges, somewhat less restricted travel opportunities for Russians, and a general rise in the sophistication of criticism that now demands some genuine acquaintance with the object of that criticism. Access to non-Marxist sources has been made much easier for senior students and postgraduate students, and there seems to be consistent pressure from members of the Institute of Philosophy and of the philosophy faculty at Moscow State University for the publication, in Russian, of nonmaterialist philosophers, of Marxist revisionist work, and of contemporary Western philosophical work. Students are increasingly referred to original sources in non-Marxist philosophy; Plato, Hume, and Kant have been published in Russian for the first time since the Revolution; several Western texts in mathematical logic have been translated; there is even a Russian translation, published in 1966 but available only on restricted order, of the American compilation *Sociology Today*, edited by Robert K. Merton. Some Marxist revisionist work, including Adam Schaff's critical study of the significance of alienation under communism, is being translated and circulated semiofficially to select groups within the Institute of Philosophy and the philosophy faculty.

Together with increasing professionalization and partial de-ideologization and slightly liberalized contact with the West has come an increasing stress on having dogma take more genuine account of most recent scientific and social developments. Rather important in this connection has been the ever increasing stress placed by the party on the role of ideology as an educator for the conditions of the new life. Since 1951 there has been a growing concern with the problems of Marxist-Leninist ethics, a field in which A. F. Shishkin has become a leading representative of the official view. The tendency here has been to soft-pedal or reject altogether the end-directedness of Marxist (especially Lenin's) ethics (good is what helps the Revolution and the coming of communism) and to emphasize the specific categories of ethical living as expressions of the commonly accepted rules of social life. The reaction against Stalinism among Soviet intellectuals has produced a climate in which the integrity of aesthetic and ethical qualities is being stressed. This was reflected in the 1960 work by the Leningrad professor V. P. Tugarinov *On the Values of Life and Culture*. He argues there that in aesthetics, and to a lesser extent in ethics, there are categories of beauty and the good, logically independent of the categories of historical materialism, though they interact with the categories of historical materialism. Since then, the Department of Ethics at Moscow has begun to turn its attention to axiology and to the *criteria* of progress. While Soviet theorists must still completely reject "revisionism," and include in this the Marxist humanism that emphasizes alienation as a fundamental category going deeper than mere economic exploitation, recent Soviet writing has put more emphasis on the early works of Marx and has attempted to take over, within the officially approved dogma, some of the humanist points. In public, of course, they still criticize Schaff and Garaudy, let alone Havemann or Kolakowsky.

In law, where there is a trend toward treating more seriously the rights of the accused, there have been studies on truth and the judicial process, and attempts to ask as a theoretical question how truth is best established. Further, sociology, previously rejected as a bourgeois substitute for Marxism, has now been accepted as a genuine science in the Soviet Union, and research into absenteeism, adaptation of workers from rural districts, and so on is being undertaken in Soviet universities and reported in philosophical journals. There is, indeed, considerable enthusiasm among undergraduate and postgraduate students about sociology, both as a radical critique of the shortcomings of Soviet society and as a means of providing some sort of empirical control over dialectical materialism, as a way of bridging the shocking gap that used to exist between the fantasy world of Soviet philosophy and the realities of Soviet life. This gap, it should be said, is being significantly narrowed. At recent conferences discussing sociology, held in Minsk and Leningrad in 1966, a group of younger people made determined attempts to suggest that sociology and sociological inquiry made necessary a reconsideration of the applicability of the traditional Marxist-Leninist definition of such concepts as "class" to Soviet society. In private, I found younger men very ready to argue that U. S. stratification theory was a better tool for the sociological study of Soviet society than the traditional concept of classes.

Less philosophically valuable has been the marked trend in Soviet philosophical journals and publications toward avoiding a European-centered treatment of philosophy. There is an increasing number of articles on Indian, classical Chinese, Latin-American, Korean, etc. philosophy. The six-volume *History of Philosophy* mentioned earlier dutifully deals with philosophy in European countries, in India, in China, in Russia, in Central Asia, in Latin America, in North America, and in the Middle East, as though these were all of equal significance, and in one volume devotes as much space to the development of philosophic and sociological thought in Central Asia, Azerbaidzhan, Armenia, and Kazakhstan as it had devoted in an earlier volume to philosophic and sociological thought in England betwen 1800 and 1850. The result is to strengthen the blurring of the distinction between technical philosophy and mere proclamation of outlooks. But this trend is seen as "political" by most Soviet philosophers today.

The general position reached in the Soviet Union, then, is this: Since 1953, and especially since 1956, there has been an enormous improvement in the quantity, style, and professional competence of philosophical writing on technical philosophical questions and on the history of philosophy. In public, the fundamental principles of dialectical materialism are still treated as given and attested assumptions that cannot be challenged, but they are being interpreted and reinterpreted with specific problems in mind. In ontology and logic there is a serious awareness of problems; there is a steady and not unintelligent concern with the philosophy of physics. In all these fields, however, problems can still be dealt with only in the framework of a dialectical materialist view, which often involves the shirking or glossing over of problems, and Soviet philosophers have not developed the precision of language, the skepticism about large-scale metaphysical answers, and the habit of examining limited problems, utterances, and concepts in depth. In the fields that come closer to social questions—in ethics, aesthetics, and the historical aspects of the history of philosophy—work is still rather poor and uncritical, vacillating between conventionalism and crude ideologizing, but seems to be improving. The philosophy of society in any serious sense does not yet exist.

VI

Philosophers, especially professional philosophers, know themselves to be regarded as the most dispensable of men. They build no rockets and deliver no consumer goods; their writing is generally too technical to inspire demonstrations or create mass adoration. Yet their discipline is one that does bring them into touch consistently with sharp and critical minds and trains them to distinguish ranting from thinking. It is the tension between these aspects of the Soviet philosopher's position that accounts for the very strong strain of cynicism in Soviet philosophical life. The philosopher, whose only outlet is in a university career, is particularly vulnerable to the careerist pressures that have been substituted for Stalin's technique of terror; the philosopher's books can be and are more easily censored and the line that he is supposed to follow is in many ways more concretely laid down. In consequence, there is a much greater disparity between what people write and what people believe in philosophy than in any other academic subject in the Soviet Union, and there is a constant vacillation, on the part of sensitive Soviet philosophers, between optimism and despair, between cynicism, modest self-congratulation, and bitter self-contempt.

When we view the progress of Soviet philosophy in the last fifty years, we are not, I think, exposed to any surprises, to any phase where the development of philosophy seems markedly out of step with other Soviet social developments. The 1920's saw the gradual triumph of crude political ideology over culture; the 1930's and 1940's saw its elaboration into a crude dogmatic theology; the 1950's saw a gradual and limited growth of sophistication, rationality, and responsiveness.

Primarily, I should argue, the changes are to be explained in terms of the relaxation of revolutionary struggle, of the changeover from the crude Messianic ideology suitable to a society requiring the mobilization of labor for vast industrial projects based on preindustrial techniques to a society that has become industrialized and comparatively sophisticated and requires stability, professional competence, and the creative imagination of the teacher, the administrator, and the engineer. Philosophy itself is related to these primarily as a by-product, though it has both suffered and gained from the lip service paid to it by a totalitarian party. In specific terms, philosophy in the Soviet Union today is returning to somewhere near (but still well below) the level of the 1890's; its improvement can be traced almost entirely to its professionalization within the universities and to increasing contact with Europe; its difficulties are censorship, administrative surveillance, and a government afraid of criticism. The machinery of control is still very much more efficient than it was under the tsars, though the methods are no longer outstandingly more brutal.

The striking thing is that just as the professionalization of philosophy in Russia at the turn of the century consisted of the spread of Western philosophical movements to Russia, and not of the development of some important native tradition, so all the improvements in Soviet philosophy in the last twelve years have depended on the assimilation of non-Marxist philosophy, and have produced no significant creative contributions of dialectical materialism itself. I myself share with Soviet philosophy atheism, empiricism, and—in at least one of the senses in which Soviet philosophers use the word—materialism; yet I can think of no Soviet philosophical production over the past fifty years that seems to me to illuminate any philosophical problem that worries me or that makes a creative contribution to the development of a significant Marxist tradition in philosophy. The striking thing to any Western reader is that Soviet dialectical materialism, like Soviet interior decoration, is incredibly old-fashioned; an observer from the English-speaking countries would also note its heavy dependence on continental conceptions and what seem to the Englishman continental vices. In retrospect, the Bolshevik period in philosophy will seem to us a crude and naïve mixture of idealist logic and "materialist" pseudo-metaphysics, heavily politicized and vulgarized in tone, and making no independent contribution to any area of philosophy. The improvement of Soviet philosophy that I believe is taking place consists entirely in the gradual disintegration of dialectical materialism as a specific and distinct philosophical view, and in the abandonment of the Bolshevik style. The creation of the genus "industrial society" in the Soviet Union not only fatally undermines the relevance of Marxism; it may put the Russian intelligentsia more firmly into Europe than they were under the tsars. It still does not provide the intellectual liberation promised by the February Revolution.

Notes

1. Peter Chaadaev, "First Philosophic Letter," in *Sochineniia i pisma*, ed. M. Gershenzon (Moscow, 1913–14), 2:111–14. The letter, first published in Russian in Nadezhdin's periodical, *The Telescope*, in 1836, caused an understandable sensation. For a recent Soviet view of Chaadayev, attacking "bourgeois" interpretations and stressing his role as a radical critic of tsarist society, see P. S. Shkurinov, *P. Ya. Chaadayev* (Moscow: U.P., 1960).

2. Iuri Krizhanich, *Dialogues de Calumnis*, cited from *Istoricheski arkhiv*, 1958, no. 1, p. 162, in James H. Billington, *The Icon and the Axe* (London, 1966), p. 309.

3. Cited in Helen Muchnic, *From Gorky to Pasternak* (London, 1963), p. 89. Compare Belinsky's letter to Gogol: "The Russian public can forgive a bad book, but not a harmful one."

4. Angelica Balabanoff, *My Life as a Rebel* (London and New York, 1938), p. 18.

5. N. N. Sukhanov, *Zapiski o revoliutsii*, here cited from Joel Carmichael, *A Short History of the Russian Revolution* (London, 1966), p. 199.

6. I cite the translation by T. B. Bottomore in his *Karl Marx—Early Writings* (London, 1963), p. 153.

7. I. I. Stepanov, *Istoricheski materializm i sovremennoe estestvoznanie* (Moscow and Leningrad, 1927), p. 57, cited in Gustav A. Wetter, *Dialectical Materialism*, trans. Peter Heath (London, 1958), p. 138.

8. Cf. Wetter, *Dialectical Materialism*, pp. 160–61.

III : Political Science

The Study of Politics
in the U.S.S.R.: Birth Throes
of a Soviet Political Science

Bohdan R. Bociurkiw

I

Among the effects of the post-Stalin "thaw" on Soviet legal and social sciences has been a growing tendency toward the differentiation within the "established" divisions of Soviet scholarship, on the one hand, and the integration of related or overlapping branches of knowledge, with the resulting emergence of new autonomous disciplines struggling for recognition from the Academy of Sciences and the party-state agencies responsible for science and higher education. One of the manifestations of this tendency has been a slow but discernible movement of Soviet "state scientists" (*gosudarstvovedy*) toward the emancipation from the confines of legal sciences and the crystallization out of the bordering

This is a revised and updated version of a paper that was first published under the title "The Post-Stalin 'Thaw' and Soviet Political Science," in *Canadian Journal of Economics and Political Science*, 30, no. 1 (February, 1964): 22–48.

branches of law, philosophy, history, sociology, and economics of a new discipline dedicated to a comprehensive study of Soviet and foreign politics. Encountering opposition both within and outside the scholarly community, this movement has not yet succeeded in attaining its goals, though it has already made a significant imprint on the scope, interests, and methods of the Soviet "science of the state and law."

Although the term "Soviet political science(s)" has been occasionally used in Soviet literature of the last decade, and though in 1960 a Soviet Association of Political (State) Sciences was formed, the Academy of Sciences and the institutions of higher learning in the U.S.S.R. have until recently viewed political science as a somewhat alien concept, ideologically ambiguous and academically suspect.[1] While the conservatism,[2] academic background, and vested interests of Soviet scholars might be partly responsible for this attitude, the chief objections to the official recognition of political science as a bona fide academic discipline appear to derive from the theoretical premises of Marxism-Leninism, which has viewed the state and law as inseparably bound up with each other, and denied that either could be studied separately. Hence the official concept of science of the state and law has, at least since 1938, led to the absorption of the study of government and politics by juridical sciences and to a formal, legalistic treatment of political problems. To quote from a 1957 statement appearing in the principal Soviet legal journal:

the law is formed by the state and represents the objectively necessary expression of the state will elevated into a law. While determined by economics, the law is not directly created by it. An objective quality [zakonomernost] of the law is also its guaranteed character, the ensurance of the observance of legal norms by the coercive force of the state power. On the other hand, the state structure, the forms of rule, the organization of the [state] mechanism, and the activity of the state themselves need reinforcement by the norms of law. . . . the law and the state are the two necessarily and directly connected sides of one and the same historical phenomenon, namely, the political rule of a class in society. . . . Such is the objective basis determining the necessity of uniting the study of these social phenomena in a single juridical discipline.[3]

In contrast to the situation in Western scholarship, the science of the state and law, as indeed all other branches of learning in the U.S.S.R., is restricted to a single theoretical framework, that of dialectical materialism as authoritatively interpreted and "creatively developed" by the Communist party. From the assumption that Marxism-Leninism is a "true" science of objective laws of social development, Soviet study of politics derives a number of important methodological notions which, in the words of Soviet writers, make it "truly scientific" and "qualitatively different" from its Western counterparts.[4] These notions, referring to the relationship between politics and science, partisanship and objectivity, facts and values, provide a set of rationalizations for the most important and most lasting characteristics of Soviet state science—its apologetic and subservient role in relation to Soviet political leadership.

Thus, in a 1962 text on the theory of the state and law, a senior Soviet legal scholar, M. S. Strogovich, rejects the possibility of a "nonpartisan" science and sees the superiority of a "Communist partisanship" over its "bourgeois" counterpart both in the former's honest admission by the Soviet scholars and in its "objectively true" nature:

Communist partisanship guarantees the most profound, most objective and all-encompasing knowledge [*poznanie*] of reality, including the political and juridical superstructure of a class society. The interests of the working class coincide with the objective course of historical development. The proletariat represents a consistently revolutionary class, and aiming at a revolutionary transformation of society, it is interested in an objective, i.e. true, knowledge.[5]

According to a Leningrad legal journal, no contradiction arises between political and legal questions, "because politics itself in a socialist state rests on a scientific base, on the assessment of objective regularities, which science is called upon to study." [6]

In the words of another Soviet legal theorist, A. A. Piontkovsky:

Soviet theory of the state and law shows the complete failure of the Kantian dualism of "ought" and "is." Categories of materialistic dialectic—"potentiality" and "actuality"—explain how the legal notion of "ought" [*dolzhenstvovanie*] is born out of social existence and how it transforms itself into real actuality in the social relations of men. . . .[7]

Arguing against the "amoralism" and "bourgeois relativism" of Western political science, I. D. Levin opposes to them the teleological orientation of the Soviet social science, which employs an objective, scientific criterion of mankind's "progress" toward communism for the evaluation of political phenomena.[8]

The Soviet science of the state and law as "stabilized" by the 1938 Conference of Legal Scholars includes such disciplines as the theory of the state and law, the history of the state and law, the history of political doctrines, state (constitutional) law, and administrative law,[9] as well as the recently revitalized discipline of the "Soviet [state] construction" (*sovetskoe stroitelstvo*).[10] These disciplines, known in the U.S.S.R. under the joint designation of state science (*gosudarstvovedenie*), had by 1960 attained something akin to an autonomous status within the juridical sciences, despite the continued official insistence of the inseparability of the state and law. For a variety of reasons, above all its "heterogeneous" ideological character and the impossibility of its deriving from a single economic base, international law occupies a distinct and somewhat isolated position within the Soviet legal sciences.[11]

Were we to view political science as a systematic study of the nature, justification, distribution, and use of political power "in connection with the formulation and execution of authoritative policy for a society," [12] our synthetic image of the Soviet counterpart would also have to include elements of several disciplines which are formally placed outside the "state and law" pattern in the U.S.S.R. In addition to the "generalizing science" of historical materialism, such overlapping disciplines include the partially revitalized sociology, political economy, diplomatic and modern history, and, especially, the history of the Communist party and the so-called party construction. Needless to say, a Western student of political science in the U.S.S.R. will notice that the latter's treatment of some of the most crucial aspects of the Soviet political system displays a number of blind spots arising from an uncritical acceptance of the ruling dogmas and from the secretiveness surrounding much of the party's decision making and policy enforcement.

In what follows, I shall restrict my discussion of the Soviet study of politics to the state science in the sense described above, and shall touch only marginally upon the related social sciences. Throughout the paper, the terms "political science" and "state science" will be used interchangeably. As a comprehensive survey of the post-Stalin developments in this branch of Soviet scholarship escapes the confines of a single paper, I propose to dwell merely on three aspects of the problem: (1) the post-Stalin criticism and self-criticism of the Soviet state science; (2) the opening of contacts with political science abroad as epitomized by the establishment of a Soviet Association of Political (State) Sciences; and (3) the changes in scope, content, methodology, and organization that have taken place in the Soviet state science since 1953.

II

The Soviet science of the state and law did not really experience the thaw until the 1956 party congress, at which the official exposures of

Stalin's violations of "socialist legality" were combined with criticism of the role performed by the legal sciences during the Stalin era.[13] Called upon by the party leadership to purge themselves of "the consequences of the personality cult," the Soviet *gosudarstvovedy* were launched into a prolonged process of revaluation of their past performance, a process that has continued with some ups and downs until the present.[14] It appears that the regime's motive for this soul-searching in the field of the state and law was a desire to revitalize the latter through a sort of collective catharsis, to bring this branch of learning closer to Soviet practice, and to transform it into a more effective instrument of social engineering. The criticism and self-criticism that followed the 20th Congress provided a remarkable insight into the predicament of a captive science suffocating in a straitjacket of dogmatic formulas, reduced to a handmaiden of politics—an image that could not but haunt post-Stalin state science with the larger questions which could be neither asked nor answered aloud without eroding the basic theoretical assumptions of the party dictatorship.[15]

The principal obstacle to the development of the state science under Stalin was, in the words of Professor Strogovich:

. . . the thesis that J. V. Stalin created a "comprehensive and definitive teaching on the socialist state." Such treatment of the problem left no room for a further development of science. All that remained to be done was to produce commentaries on the "comprehensive and definitive teaching"; at the same time, any attempt to change or to add anything to the formulations of the aspects of the proletarian dictatorship, the phases and functions of the socialist state, etc., resulted in serious accusations against the scholars. In reality, Stalin's teaching on the socialist state was neither comprehensive nor definitive, and contained serious errors.[16]

From the late 1930's, in the reflected light of the Stalin cult, another, more immediate personality cult developed in the realm of the state and law—that of Andrei Vyshinsky, Stalin's mouthpiece and grand inquisitor in Soviet political science and law. Since some of Vyshinsky's past victims—the prominent Soviet jurists Stuchka, Krylenko, and Pashukanis [17] —were granted a qualified rehabilitation after the 20th Congress,[18] Vyshinsky's record in the realm of the state and law was subjected to an increasing criticism that culminated in his posthumous purge at the 1961 party congress.[19]

The freezing of creative thought within the dogmatic framework of pronouncements by Stalin and Vyshinsky extended beyond the matters of principles and affected the scope, the style, and even the vocabulary of scholarly writing.[20] Scholars were fettered, moreover, by the suppression of statistical data and even of information about current internal legislation, by severely limited opportunity to observe the actual operation of the Soviet government organs, by the proscription of most of the earlier Soviet works in the field, and by an almost complete isolation from relevant foreign scientific literature.[21]

Surrounded by an atmosphere of institutionalized suspicion, those Soviet scholars who risked publication sought security in a scholastic, quotation-ridden approach and in the politically least controversial problems; on the whole they limited themselves to dogmatic analyses of the Soviet laws, commentaries on "Stalin's constitution," or simply the restatement of well-known, officially certified truths. With Stalin being personally credited with creating the Soviet system of laws, legal fetishism flourished: "All laws were recognized as fully expedient and their criticism was not allowed. The task of the science was reduced exclusively to that of proving their expedience." [22]

In the "most neglected area of the juridical sciences"—the history of the Soviet state and law—historical evidence was distorted to "glorify Stalin in every possible way," the unpleasant facts were "varnished," and "any references to the contradictions of the development, the difficulties of growth, the shortcomings and errors" were "almost completely" eliminated from works on this subject.[23]

With no scope for bona fide scholarly research, "the main attention was centered on the search for errors in the works of other jurists." [24] Intellectual dishonesty and "legal nihilism" poisoned the atmosphere in the Soviet science of the state and law. In the words of the Leningrad *Pravovedenie:*

It is not a secret that during the years of the cult of personality, individual legal scholars appeared among us whose basic task appeared to be "intuitively" to comprehend the tendencies prevailing "at the top" on this or that question, so as to "explain" in the corresponding manner the existing law.[25]

As will be seen from our examination of the post-Stalin developments in the Soviet science of the state and law, the latter has still not fully recovered from the maladies of intellectual dishonesty and opportunism, and their symptoms—"dogmatism," "scholasticism," "quotation method," and "the isolation from practice"—continue to be scored by party spokesmen.[26]

III

One of the most significant developments in Soviet scholarship during the past decade has been a broadening of the external contacts of Soviet specialists in the state and law. Previously restricted to participation in the so-called progressive international organizations, Soviet scholars were now permitted to join the bona fide international learned societies. As far as the Soviet authorities were concerned, this "opening to the West" appears to have been motivated primarily by political considerations, such as the desire to influence foreign scholars, to advertise the current Soviet policy objectives, and in particular to counter the unfavorable political effects of the burgeoning field of Sovietology in the West. The memory of the once formidable risks involved in such foreign contacts subsided with the relaxation of internal police controls since 1953, and Soviet scholars have been showing increasing interest in the work of their Western counterparts, an interest extending beyond the officially required function of unmasking the bourgeois science.[27] It was above all the combination of these two considerations—political and scholastic—that ultimately led to the establishment in 1957 of the Soviet International Law Association, and some three years later of the Soviet Association of Political (State) Sciences.[28]

The genesis of the Soviet Association of Political Sciences can be traced back to the Law Section of the All-Union Society for Cultural Contacts with Foreign Countries (*VOKS*). *VOKS* was founded in 1925 as an important channel for external propaganda and cultural diplomacy. The Law Section of *VOKS* became a member of the International Association of Democratic Jurists in 1946, and in August, 1955, it joined the International Political Science Association.[29]

The obvious disadvantage of having to represent an official propaganda organization at international meetings might have led Soviet scholars to argue for the less objectionable alternative of a professional organization. In any event, in June, 1959, the Section of the Economic, Philosophical, and Legal Sciences of the former *VOKS* was incorporated into the structure of the Soviet Academy of Sciences, and subsequently was given the form of an interdisciplinary Soviet Association of Political (State) Sciences.[30] Selected to head the new association was Dr. V. S.

Tadevosian of the Institute of the State and Law of the Academy of Sciences.[31]

The association held its first meeting in September, 1960, to discuss its future activities. Soviet scholars were called upon to prepare for the next year's meeting of the IPSA papers "illuminating the superiority of the Soviet state institutions" over their bourgeois counterparts, and the gathering resolved in favor of the publication of a Soviet political science yearbook and "articles devoted to the different problems of political science." [32]

The annual meeting of the association in March, 1961, which was attended by some one hundred state scientists, economists, and philosophers, brought about some clarification in the nature and tasks of the organization. The purposes of the association, as outlined by Dr. Tadevosian, combined the advancement of political science in the U.S.S.R. and contacts with foreign political scientists, through international meetings and the exchange of visits, publications, and scientific information, with a number of political objectives, including the "realization of peaceful coexistence" and the "unmasking of the reactionary essence of contemporary 'anticommunism' . . . [and of] the revisionist and reformist tendencies in political science." [33]

The 1961 meeting devoted a great deal of attention to the nature and tendencies of Western political science. One speaker saw the reasons for the emergence of this "so-called 'political science' " in "the ever growing role of the state at the contemporary stage of the development of human society, the growth of the political activity of millions of men . . . in the rapid development of the Soviet state system, and . . . in the establishment of national statehood in the countries which freed themselves of colonial dependence." [34] Another speaker, Dr. Levin—the principal Soviet critic of Western political science—took a somewhat less charitable view, stressing the "defensive, apologetic character of" Western political science "with regard to the bourgeois system." "Political science," in his assessment, "develops to the detriment of juridical science, politicizes the latter, and this indicates a profound crisis of bourgeois legality." [35]

Only about sixty people attended the 1962 meeting of the association, which reflected the sharpened emphasis of the recently adopted party program on ideological struggle. Members were urged to "more widely propagandize Soviet state science, to unmask the slanderous concoctions of the bourgeois state scientists, and carry on an active struggle against anticommunism." Voices were raised in favor of a greater coordination of the association's activities with the regime's cultural propaganda apparatus and for a more aggressive proselytism abroad, including the dispatch of "specialized tourist groups of state scientists." [36] Once again, for the third time, the association resolved to approach the "proper authorities" (*instantsii*) for permission to publish its yearbook, "because the absence of a published organ considerably limits the possibilities of the propaganda of Soviet political science." The bafflement of the members about the exact role the association was expected to perform was reflected in the remarks of Dr. Zivs of the Institute of State and Law, who observed that

it would be of certain importance for the future fruitful activity of the association to clarify the range of questions that should guide its scholarly activities within the country and those on which it is necessary for her to act in the international arena.

It would be advisable to establish a commission which should clearly define the direction of the association's activities in the immediate future. . . . [This] would help to activate the work of the association's groups in the union republics, would facilitate a clear definition of the profile of the association, and would serve the cause of coordination of its activities with other analogous institutions.[37]

The third annual meeting of the Soviet Association of Political Sciences, which was held in January, 1963, reflected some reinvigoration of this organization, both in view of a relatively large number of participants (some 120 jurists, philosophers, sociologists, and historians) and in terms of a more positive approach to the tasks of the association. In his presidential report, Dr. Tadevosian significantly underplayed the external propaganda functions of the association, stressing instead its "practical," "domestic" objectives:

The science of the state should study the practical implementation of political ideas contained in the party program and the new laws adopted in accordance with it, assist the party and the state along the line of improving the ways and methods of building communism, pay special attention to questions of economics—the administration of national economy—[and] promote a further democratization of Soviet society [and] the upbringing of a new man.[38]

Dr. Tadevosian and other speakers stressed the interdependence of the individual branches of social science, arguing for "complex" methodological approaches and "concrete sociological investigations" (empirical case studies) in the study of the Soviet state. Reportedly, "a series of organizational questions" was decided at the 1963 meeting of the association, yet only one of these was found fit for publication—the long-delayed sanction was given to the formation of "groups" (branches) of the association in union republics and major university centers.[39]

Strangely enough, no report was published on the 1964 meeting of the association (if it was held at all). Following the removal of Khrushchev, the more empirical, "scientist" mood of the new leadership evidently encouraged the advocates of a Soviet political science to press their demands for its official recognition. On January 10, 1965, *Pravda* carried an article entitled "Science and Politics" signed by Dr. F. M. Burlatsky of the academy's Institute of State and Law, in which he stressed the "necessity of elaborating the problems of *political science*." This, he argued, "should provide answers to the basic questions of the forms and methods of social leadership, a clear distribution of functions, rights, and duties among all the links of the administrative apparatus, [and to] the problems of elevating and educating the cadres." Soviet political science should combine elements of "scientific communism, theory of state and law, sociology, as well as economics," focusing its attention on the dynamics and mechanism of "social leadership," i.e., on such questions as "how it functions, [and] what is necessary for its improvement and development." Specifically, as outlined by Burlatsky, it should concern itself with such problems as "the constitution [*ustroistvo*] and activities of the state, political parties, social [public] organizations, mass movements, international unions and organizations, forms and methods of diplomatic activities, the study of public opinion, propaganda methods, etc." To facilitate the development of this new discipline in the U.S.S.R., Burlatsky proposed that problems of political science be incorporated into the programs of the already existing institutes and that special scientific institutions be established for this branch of learning, which would elaborate its theoretical questions, "fulfill direct assignments from the party and state organs, and also train the cadres of specialists" in this new field.[40]

Burlatsky's article and his paper "On Political Science" presented to the next annual meeting of the Soviet Association of Political Sciences, in February, 1965, set the stage for the most elaborate discussion to date of the problems and prospects of this discipline in the U.S.S.R.[41] Though all discussants at this gathering "unanimously supported Burlatsky's thesis concerning the special relevance [*aktualnost*] of studying the contemporary political problems," the gathering divided on the question of whether it was necessary to develop an independent political science or whether it would suffice simply to expand the scope of the existing "political sciences" [42] to include the study of political phenomena. A number of speakers (V. A. Tumanov, M. A. Krutogolov, F. F. Petrenko, Iu. A.

Arbatov, A. A. Galkin, G. Kh. Shakhnazarov, and others) supported Burlatsky's plea for a separate discipline of political science dedicated to a comprehensive and predominantly empirical investigation of the "totality of political relations [and] of political activities in all their manifestations." No single branch of social science can encompass all of these problems, nor can they be adequately studied with the methodological tools employed by the existing "political" disciplines. A number of crucial problems of Soviet politics are left out from the purview of the established social sciences, including those of political communication, political planning and policy making, mass activities, and, in particular, the mechanics of the party leadership. In the words of F. F. Petrenko:

One could hardly name a more powerful, by its influence, force than the party. And yet, paradoxically, the questions of the party's role [and the] forms and methods of the party leadership are being elaborated least of all. So far, the place and the role of the party in the construction of communism are not adequately studied, [and] no research has been done on the specific regularities [*zakonomernosti*] of its influence on science, politics, ideology, [or] the questions concerning the tendencies revealed in the interrelationship of different forms of leadership.[43]

Some speakers pointed out that none of the existing branches of social science devotes adequate attention to international politics or to comparative study of socialist regimes or revolutionary movements. The new political science, argued Shakhnazarov, should have a "complex," interdisciplinary character, and therefore cannot be confined to the framework of the purely legal sciences.

While all the discussants agreed that "political sciences" ought to be based on the general methodology of Marxism-Leninism and employ "concrete sociological" (empirical) research approaches, several speakers, especially V. M. Chkhikvadze, S. F. Kechekian, and V. E. Guliev, spoke against the need for or even the possibility of an independent political science, and favored the retention of the study of political problems within the established disciplines, in particular legal sciences. V. M. Chkhikvadze argued:

Among political sciences, an exceptionally important place is occupied by the juridical, state sciences. . . . Juridical science should deal more than heretofore with politics [and] the study of political institutions. Legal scholars can and should produce profound studies of politics in general, of political relationships [and] power. The jurists must not avoid a deeper elaboration of the questions connected with the role of the party. . . . In the broad sense of the term . . . political science embraces all sciences which investigate political relations. At the same time, one could speak of political science in a narrow sense as a study of society's political organization. These studies should occupy above all the state scientists.[44]

It seems that the 1965 meeting of the SAPS failed to reach a consensus on the question of the emancipation of political science, and indeed "considered it premature to widely introduce the teaching of new political disciplines in educational institutions." Nevertheless, a number of proposals were made at the meeting with regard to the further development of Soviet political studies: the Institute of State and Law of the Academy of Sciences was called upon to take the "initiative in coordinating political research" and to form a "commission for the elaboration of the problems of political sciences"; higher institutions of learning, scholarly journals, and the association were asked to offer "organizational assistance to political sciences"; and at least one of the discussants proposed the establishment of advanced academic degrees in this new discipline. Once again, requests were made that the association launch the publication of a Soviet yearbook of political science.

The meeting changed the name of the association by dropping the parenthetical term "State" (*Gosudarstvovedcheskikh*) from its title and elected an enlarged executive of the SAPS, with V. M. Chkhikvadze (director of the Institute of State and Law) as president and M. A. Krutogolov as secretary general.[45]

During the following months the discussion on the scope and methodology of Soviet "political sciences" and their relationship to the established disciplines continued in Soviet legal journals. Several positions crystallized in the process. The case for the conservatives was restated by M. S. Strogovich, who, having cited with relish a "bourgeois scholar's" 1945 criticism of political science and other social sciences as lacking a truly scientific nature,[46] argued that "from the viewpoint of Marxism-Leninism, law cannot be considered in separation from the state . . . just as the state cannot be considered apart from law"; [47] accordingly, political problems can and should remain within the realm of juridical sciences. A. I. Lepeshkin, the editor-in-chief of *Sovetskoe gosudarstvo i pravo*, called for the broadening of the framework of the "science of Soviet state law" to combine the study of *actual* operation of the government with the adoption of sociological, survey, and statistical methods of research.[48] Similar attempts to bypass the still unsolved problem of a comprehensive political science appeared in the proposal of several Soviet scholars to develop a broadly conceived, "complex" "science of administration" (*nauka upravleniia*). The latter, argued V. M. Manokhin, while overlapping with administrative law, and especially with the new discipline of "Soviet construction," should concentrate on the study of organization, function, and methods of operation of state and social administration.[49]

The position taken in the discussion by the jurists S. S. Alekseev and V. E. Chirkin came much closer to Burlatsky's notion of a Soviet political science. While considering the latter too broad in its attempt to integrate elements of several established disciplines, the two writers proposed to develop within the juridical sciences a "complex" new branch, "the theory of the political organization of society," which they felt should be offered as a course to senior law students. The scope of this course was to be limited to such problems as (1) the social-economic foundations of the political organization of society; (2) relationships among society, the state, and the individual; (3) forms and methods of popular participation in political activities; (4) methods of political activities; (5) types and activities of social organizations, including the party; (6) the state apparatus; and (7) forms and methods of economic administration.[50]

The follow-up editorial surveying responses to Burlatsky's January article appeared in *Pravda* on June 13, 1965.[51] The reactions cited in the article on the whole endorsed Burlatsky's case for the emancipation of political science into an independent scholarly discipline. Thus the article quoted several members of the academy's Institute of Latin American Studies who complained that though "political sciences already exist, they lack however the formal citizenship rights, and this hampers their development." Members of the Institute of World Economics and International Relations pointed out that while there are scholars already working in some of the areas listed by Burlatsky (contemporary international relations, international workers' movements, the study of socialist and capitalist societies, etc.), the level and scope of their works are not satisfactory, largely because these areas of research are still officially treated as stepchildren. This also affects dissertations that are being written on contemporary foreign politics and international relations and movements, which have to be arbitrarily fitted into the framework of historical, philosophical, or juridical disciplines. A writer from the Lenin Library in Moscow reported on the predicament of Soviet bibliographers who have been compelled to classify artificially foreign works in political science under the traditional categories of social history, state and law, or philosophy.

Summing up the responses from its readers to Burlatsky's article, *Pravda* significantly departed from the latter in listing a narrower and more conventional set of problems to be studied by Soviet political sciences. In *Pravda's* version, political sciences were to include: (1) the study of political systems, leadership, organization, and administration in socialist countries; (2) the study of political power in capitalist and developing nations; (3) international relations and theoretical problems of foreign policy; (4) basic problems of the Communist workers' and national liberation movements; and (5) the study of contemporary political ideologies and theories. The *Pravda* editors concluded with a warning against diverting the discussion of political science toward the problem of a "correct" designation for this new discipline, and urged the scholars, without waiting for the establishment of special scientific institutes in this field, to "considerably broaden their study of political problems in the existing institutions" of higher learning and research.

The promising start made by Burlatsky's *Pravda* article and the 1965 meeting of the SAPS in carrying into the open the discussion of the problem of a Soviet political science and its relationship to the established branches of learning did not bring about any official recognition of this discipline and the corresponding reorganization of Soviet social sciences and their institutional equivalents in the Academy of Sciences. Indeed, by the second half of 1965 the discussion of this problem had largely disappeared from Soviet legal journals. The meager report on the 1966 annual meeting of the association—the last one reported so far—showed that it dealt only with the question of Soviet participation in international political science conferences; in this connection only it was observed at the meeting that "the preparation of papers on the general problems [of politics for international meetings] required a profound elaboration of the problems of political science" in the U.S.S.R.[52]

Surveying the seven-year record of the Soviet Association of Political Sciences, one is left with a distinct feeling of improvisation and uncertainty, if not frustration. There seems to be little doubt that the party and state authorities ultimately responsible for Soviet social sciences—a realm of ideology where no coexistence is permitted—conceived originally of a Soviet political science association as a façade organization, a means of projecting a favorable image of the Soviet political system abroad and of combating anticommunism in Western political science. The anemic state of the Soviet Association of Political Sciences, its repeated failure to secure authorization for the publication of at least a yearbook devoted to the problems of "political sciences," as well as the continued lack of recognition for this new discipline in the Academy of Sciences (despite the fact that the association is dominated by the academy's Institute of State and Law) and the higher institutions of learning

—all attest to powerful influences blocking progress in this field. This state of affairs may be explained not only in terms of the party's ideological inhibitions, but also in terms of the opposition of at least some important members of the Soviet academic establishment to the emancipation of political science from law and several other related disciplines, an opposition deriving from habit, tradition, and possibly bias about "imports from the bourgeois West." [53]

Yet there is ample evidence that despite the still considerable obstacles, there are growing tendencies among Soviet social scientists and jurists working in the direction of the crystallization of political studies into a separate, comprehensive scholarly discipline. At least four factors seem to favor these tendencies: (1) the admitted need for a framework within which—in line with the current emphasis on "complex," interdisciplinary research methods—legal scholars could communicate and pool resources with sociologists, historians, philosophers, economists, and other specialists in exploring the operation of the Soviet political system; (2) the regime's increasing impatience with the failure of the science of state and law both to supply the policy makers with reliable and useful data about the effectiveness of their domestic and foreign policies and to produce qualified cadres of party-state executives; (3) the obvious inadequacy of the purely juridical treatment of Western politics and hence the recognized need for retraining Soviet critics of the "bourgeois state and law" to enable them to cope with Western political science; and (4) the realization that unfavorable foreign analyses of the Soviet political system must be countered abroad with more than just outbursts of righteous indignation or glossy propaganda depictions of the Soviet constitutional wonderland. At the same time one should not minimize the effect of the increasing exposure of Soviet scholars to Western political science on their investigation of domestic political phenomena, even if such exposure is said to be motivated by the legitimate desire to get to know the opponents better in order to combat them more successfully.

Of an even greater immediate significance in encouraging the development of political science in the U.S.S.R. has been the influence of scholars in other socialist countries, especially Czechoslovakia,[54] Hungary,[55] Poland,[56] and Yugoslavia,[57] where more advance has been made in recent years in the integration and "sociologization" of domestic political studies.[58]

The state of political studies in the U.S.S.R. cannot, however, be adequately assessed if we limit our insights to the case of the Soviet Association of Political Sciences. A more meaningful and somewhat more promising picture of the prospects for Soviet political science emerges

when we turn to the consideration of changes that have taken place since
the mid-1950's in the scope, content, and methodology of Soviet state
science (*gosudarstvovedenie*) as reflected in scholarly publications and
research activities in the U.S.S.R.

IV

During the last decade, scholars in the field of Soviet state science have
tended increasingly to combine analysis of legal norms and formal institutions with inquiry into political *practice*, deriving their insights from
other social sciences and, much less openly, from Western political science. Among the established branches of Soviet state science, the theory
of the state underwent the greatest substantive changes, which not only
eliminated or modified a number of Stalin's pronouncements on the state,
but led to the revision of some hitherto hallowed tenets of Marxism-
Leninism.[59] Perhaps the most striking of these revisions was introduced
by the 1961 party program, which ended the identification of the socialist state with the dictatorship of the proletariat.[60] Superimposed upon
the latter was a "new" and "final stage" of a socialist state—"the state of
the entire people," which the Soviet Union has allegedly become with the
complete victory of socialism and the beginning of a "full-scale construction of communism." [61] Similarly, the CPSU has now evolved into the
"party of the entire people," and the Soviet law into "the expression of
the will of the entire people." [62] While dedogmatizing certain of Stalin's
teachings, the party ideologists erected the theoretical pronouncements of
the 1961 program into another dogma whose sudden appearance caught
the uninitiated Soviet scholars completely unawares.[63] The immediate
effect of the new program—which, incidentally, elevated the status of the
social sciences to that of a "scientific basis for guiding the development
of society" [64]—was the obsolescence of the earlier studies of the theory
of the state and law, which only in 1962 were replaced by a collective
work produced by the academy's Institute of State and Law.[65] Another consequence of the adoption of the 1961 program was a new set of
the rather vaguely defined tasks on which the Soviet specialists in theory
and constitutional law were told henceforth to concentrate their efforts:

the investigation of the basic, objective laws of development of the Soviet state of the entire people [and] of the process of transformation of socialist statehood into a communist social self-government; the elaboration of the questions of the ways and means of the further development and improvement of socialist democracy . . . [and] of the growing role of the Communist party in the state and social life . . .[66]

The scholars' response to the new directives disappointed the Central Committee, which pointed out, in July, 1964, the continuing shortcomings in the "elaboration of the theory of the socialist state and law of the entire people." [67] Within the Institute of State and Law, specialists in this field were attacked by other jurists for their conservatism, intellectual timidity, and the predominantly "descriptive," "commentary-like" treatment of the theoretical innovations of the 1961 party program.[68] After the fall of Khrushchev, however, specialists in the theory of state and law came to share the blame for some of his "harebrained" schemes.[69] Now they were officially castigated for "running ahead" of objective development and charting "remote perspectives" of a stateless Communist society rather than concerning themselves with the "objective necessity of constantly improving the mechanism of the socialist state." [70]

With the party's directives shifting the emphasis from legal to sociopolitical questions, the nature of the theory of the state, hitherto classified under legal sciences, came to be questioned by some Soviet writers. Thus, writing in a 1962 issue of the Leningrad legal journal, Dr. Alekseev observed that

the theory of the state and law has a general sociological and not specifically juridical character, for it is utterly impossible to classify as juridical such problems as, for example, the nature of the state, its functions, mechanism, and other specific problems of the state science. . . . It is necessary to verify, to rethink theoretically some juridical categories which so firmly acquired currency among scholars that they are in all cases applied as axioms.[71]

In line with this approach, some state scientists have proposed to develop the "theory of the socialist state" into an independent discipline, separate from the general theory of law.[72] Though such a de facto separation was acknowledged by the party's theoretical journal in November, 1963,[73] and though some recent Soviet works have dispensed with the integrated treatment of state and law, little has been done so far to institutionalize the emancipation of the theory of the state within the Academy of Sciences and the higher institutions of learning. The ambitious four-volume *Course of the Theory of State and Law* planned by the academy's Institute of State and Law for 1970 provides, however, for a separate volume on the socialist state, and the entire outline of the course attempts to combine the juridical approach with those of sociology, economics, and philosophy.[74]

By virtue of its intimate dependence on the current ideological line, the realm of the theory of the state has remained under the closest scrutiny of the party ideologists. The successive theoretical problems submitted by the party to the state scientists invariably carry implications as to what conclusions the latter are to arrive at. To be sure, much of the detail of the ways and means is being left to further elaboration, and, in contrast to the pre-1953 practices, the party ideologists appear prepared to have the scholars fill the void through "concrete sociological," empirical research.[75] However, the prevailing tendency of the "workers on the theoretical front" has been, to the evident dissatisfaction of the party leaders, to take the line of least resistance and smallest risks, by relapsing into the familiar chore of lining up quotations and "examples" to prove "objective necessities." [76]

Turning to the "specialized" branches of the Soviet state science, we are bound to note some advancement over the standards of the Stalin era, especially marked in the quality of criticism addressed to Soviet scholarly works. Thus, while the appearance in 1959 of a new text in the history of political doctrines represented a modest improvement over the earlier works, both in scope and in approach,[77] the Soviet reviewers severely attacked the authors for the surviving elements of "vulgarized sociologism" and distortion in this book:

> The history of political doctrines . . . from the Marxist point of view must not be reduced merely to the explanation whose class interests the given theory expresses. Such a vulgarized sociological approach impoverishes our science very much and is extremely harmful in an educational sense, for, instead of showing how the best minds sought the social truth, it claims that they all consciously or subconsciously pursued only the egoistic interests of their class. . . .[78]

In the related field of the history of the state and law—most thoroughly Stalinized in the past—no satisfactory text has yet appeared.[79] To meet the needs of law students, a posthumously "revised" edition of the old textbook on the pre-1917 history of the Russian state and law by S. V. Iushkov was published in 1961.[80] A year later it was supplemented by a collective work on the history of the Soviet state and law—a descriptive survey of the principal legislation and changes in the state structure, with no attempt at critical analysis.[81] Little has been done so far to fill in the gap created in the history of Soviet science of state and law since 1938 by the eradication of the contribution of early Soviet scholars.[82]

So far, perhaps the greatest contribution to this field has been made by the non-Russian scholars in the form of comprehensive constitutional histories of the Ukrainian, Kazakh, Uzbek, Moldavian, and the three Baltic republics.[83] A number of specialized monographs, especially on the Leninist period of the Soviet state, appeared during the past decade, some of them based on painstaking documentary research.[84] Another noteworthy development in this area has been the publication of hitherto classified or long-withdrawn documents, including the acts of the Congresses of Soviets,[85] the collections of laws and decrees, and select archive documents.[86] Parallel developments have taken place in the closely related and crucially important discipline of the party history in the form of the first publication or republication of the proceedings and documents of the party congresses, conferences, and plenary sessions of the Central Committee, some internal correspondence of the party administrative organs, and select documents from the party archives.[87] A six-volume history of the CPSU is being published with the three editions of the new one-volume party history, and a growing number of specialized studies in party history significantly, though "selectively," illuminate the once secret recesses of the ruling elite's past.[88]

While restricted to the theoretical framework of the current theory of the state and detrimentally affected by the fluidity of Soviet institutional forms and legal norms, the study of the state (constitutional) law has also experienced a marked recovery from the procrustean bed of Vyshinsky's "system." Though Vyshinsky's dogmatized commentator's approach still survives—as, for example, in the text by Denisov and Kirichenko (which, surprisingly, was selected in 1960 for publication in the English language) [89]—the 1961 text for the Higher Party School and Zlatopolsky's concise *State System of the USSR* (also translated into English) [90] stand out for their antonomous approach, the amount of factual material they contain, and their attention to the actual practices of Soviet government.

By far the best work in this special field, if not the most significant achievement of the post-Stalin Soviet political science, is Professor Lepeshkin's two-volume text published in 1961–62.[91] It surpasses previous works on a number of counts: its scope extends to the "not legally regulated" practices and conventions; it introduces a large body of hitherto unavailable information on the operation of the Soviet government; it relies on a wide variety of literature, including Western and

prerevolutionary Russian works; and in the analysis of the Soviet institutions it adapts a number of constructs and classifications evolved in
modern political science. Its two weakest features appear to be the in-
escapable glossing over of the centrally important questions of party
decision making and controls, and the book's "comparative" sections,
where biased treatment of Western governmental counterparts com-
bines with occasional falsification of the views of Western political
scientists. In 1964 Lepeshkin supplemented his text with a badly needed
anthology of state and party documents on Soviet government.[92] Among
other works on state law one should mention the first selected bibliography of works in this field covering the period from 1917 to 1957,[93] and
A. I. Kim's 1965 monograph on the Soviet electoral law, based on a
broad analysis of both normative acts and electoral practices in the
U.S.S.R.[94]

While "comparative government" has not yet been recognized as a
separate branch of political studies in the U.S.S.R., three autonomous
subdivisions emerged within the constitutional law: (1) a "science of
state law of the countries of people's democracy," which is likely to
develop into a "comparative socialist government" seeking to derive generalizations applicable to all countries of the Communist bloc, including
the U.S.S.R.;[95] (2) the "state law of the countries which have liberated
themselves from colonial dependence";[96] and (3) the "state law of the
bourgeois countries."[97] The Soviet study of politics in the "capitalist
countries" has been conceived by the party's ideological spokesmen as
an ideological battleground in which Soviet scholars should "militantly
unmask the reactionary essence of the bourgeois state law"; traditionally
it has been the most "politicized" area of study, in which a combination
of heavy bias and ignorance has blurred the boundary between deception
and self-deception. In the past decade, however, Soviet students of the
problem have shown a somewhat greater appreciation of the complexities of Western politics and more willingness to consult the now more
readily available literature from abroad.[98] Closely attuned to the shifting
emphases of the party ideological line and foreign policy, this branch of
Soviet political science remains extremely uneven in quality, with rep-
utable scholars sharing the stage with party hacks. While some of Lenin's
and Stalin's theses on "imperialist capitalism" have been dropped or
modified, the current assessment of the basic tendencies in the Western
world is still conceived within the eschatological framework of a "general and deepening crisis."[99]

During the 1960's a series of symposia and monographs on "bourgeois"
politics have appeared in the Soviet Union, some of them based on a

wide spectrum of Western political science literature.[100] The most important event in this field has been the preparation of a five-volume series entitled *The Contemporary Imperialist State*, a major comparative study undertaken by the Academy of Science scholars under the editorship of V. A. Tumanov and I. D. Levin. The already published volumes have dealt with the relationship between "imperialist state and capitalist economy," the constitutional "mechanism," and the parties and pressure groups in major Western states, respectively.[101]

Of considerable significance to our inquiry has been the appearance of Soviet studies of Western political science, the most important of which was a 1960 monograph by I. D. Levin of the Institute of State and Law, investigating the postwar trends in Western constitutional theory.[102] While highly colored by the author's ideological assumptions, this study at least attempts to restate the views of such writers as Jennings, Duverger, Gosnell, Finer, Friedrich, and others, before subjecting them to criticism that is not always malicious. A number of articles on various aspects of Western political science have appeared in recent years in Soviet legal journals, some of which reveal remarkably little partisanship and attest to an intimate knowledge of the newest trends and schools of thought of political science in the United States and western Europe.[103] Despite repeated warnings from the party watchdogs over Soviet social sciences against any "borrowings" from their "bourgeois" counterparts,[104] the study of Western political science literature has evidently been the principal channel for the absorption by the Soviet state scientists of new concepts, methodology, and research techniques in this field. Not unconnected with this development have been cautious attempts in recent Soviet legal literature to break down the arbitrary ideological barriers blocking the development of comparative politics and law in the U.S.S.R.[105]

V

In the field of Soviet administrative law, a relatively small number of scholarly works have appeared since 1953. Though outdated by successive reorganizations of Soviet government and administration, the 1959 text on Soviet administrative law by Vlasov and Studenikin still remains the best general work in the field.[106] Three monographs deserve to be singled out: Ananov's 1960 study of the formal structure and functioning of the Soviet ministries at the federal, union republic, and autonomous republic levels—the first study of this kind in twenty years; [107] the revised edition of Vlasov's *Soviet State Apparatus* (1959), a formal but useful study of the little investigated Soviet bureaucratic structure; [108] and *The Soviet State [Civil] Service* (1966) by V. M. Manokhin, probing into an important area of public personnel management.[109]

While the limitations of space necessitate the omission of specific references to such related areas as Soviet financial law, the judiciary, and the procuracy, in which a number of useful studies have appeared in the past few years,[110] we must dwell for a while on the revived discipline of the "Soviet [state] construction" (*sovetskoe stroitelstvo*).[111] Concerned with the *practical* organization and operation of the system of soviets, their executive apparatus, and the mechanism of the "mass organizations" —rather than with the constitutional or administrative laws [112]—this discipline has combined elements of local government and "administrative science." In a significant reversal, it has again been fostered by the party authorities since 1946 as a "practical" adjunct to the legal sciences, necessary for the training of "practical workers" for the Soviet apparatus.[113] Most of the representatives of the established legal disciplines have tended to take a rather dim view of the new discipline as potentially "subversive" of the juridical nature of the state science, and there is still no consensus in the Soviet literature as to the subject matter of the "Soviet construction." [114] Nevertheless, with the support of the pragmatically oriented party leaders, from a "teaching discipline" in the party schools the "Soviet construction" has in recent years graduated to a "scientific discipline" taught in a number of Soviet universities and institutes and recognized as a legitimate area of scholarly research by the Academy of Sciences.[115] During the past decade, in addition to a number of specialized studies, several texts have appeared in this discipline, the best being *Sovetskoe stroitelstvo* (1965) by Barabashev and Sheremet.[116]

Beginning in the fall of 1964, voices began to appear in Soviet legal journals in favor of reviving yet another "complex" discipline—"the science of administration" (*nauka upravleniia*)—which had been eliminated in the 1930's. In an article opening the discussion of this discipline, the writers broadly defined it as

a science [investigating] the nature and content of the process of administration of governmental and social affairs, organization of administration of individual branches of economy and culture, enterprises, institutions, and organizations . . . [seeking] the ways of rationalizing the systems and structures and improving the forms and methods of activity of the administrative apparatus on the basis of the newest achievements of science and technology, and of its [the apparatus'] further democratization.[117]

In the discussion that followed, some advocates of this discipline proposed that it should absorb administrative law and most of "Soviet construction," as well as certain aspects of the theory of the state, constitutional law, and other branches of juridical science, thus extending the scope of the new discipline far beyond that reserved in the West for the field of public administration.[118] Writing in *Kommunist*, in January, 1965, the director of the Institute of State and Law, V. M. Chkhikvadze, reported that the institute had been authorized to develop the theoretical study of the "administration of the state and social affairs" in order "to more actively assist the party in the struggle for the increased effectiveness of the administrative apparatus." [119] A theoretical conference on the legal problems of "administrative science" was held at the Institute of State and Law in December, 1965, to discuss the problems of improving the structure and functioning of the Soviet governmental and economic administration; it also produced proposals to introduce the teaching of the "scientific foundations of administration" at the higher institutions of learning and to establish specialized institutes and schools in this field.[120] Though the prospect of an applied "science of administration" has evidently been welcomed by some elements in the Soviet government, it has not found much support among either the "conservative" legal scholars or the advocates of a Soviet political science.[121] The reformist zeal shown by the participants in the 1965 conference on administrative science [122] may also be responsible for the fact that the subject has not yet been introduced in the curricula of the higher institutions of learning.

Of equal if not greater importance to the study of the actual operation of the Soviet political system has been the growing volume of studies within the area vaguely described as "party construction" and, occasionally, "party science," including commentaries of the party rules, case studies of individual party organizations, and studies of party work in various areas of Soviet life.[123]

Both symptomatic of and contributing to the general revitalization of Soviet political studies has been the increase in the number of legal journals devoted in varying degrees also to the state science. Until recently the only journal in the field, *Sovetskoe gosudarstvo i pravo*, published by the Institute of State and Law of the Academy of Sciences, has been joined since 1958 by seven more journals, two of which—the Leningrad *Pravovedenie* and the Ukrainian *Radianske pravo*—devote considerable space to the state science. Increasing space had also been allocated to the study of political problems in the *Vestnik Moskovskogo Universiteta, Vestnik Leningradskogo Universiteta,* and the proceedings and papers of other Soviet universities.[124] On the other hand, the pleas of the state scientists for more specialized journals, for example in the fields of constitutional history and "Soviet construction," not to mention the repeated requests for a Soviet political science yearbook, have not been granted so far by the higher authorities. The increase in the number of periodicals in the field was only to a limited degree accompanied by an improvement in quality. The journals have remained extremely uneven in this respect, with scholarly articles appearing side by side with run-of-the-mill propaganda pieces.

VI

Paralleling these developments of the last decade has been the resurgence of advanced studies, research, and publications in the field of the state and law in the academies of science and the universities of the non-Russian republics, where this field had turned almost completely sterile following the great purges of the 1930's.[125] This revival, however, enhanced at first by the broadening of jurisdiction of the republican governments, might be losing some of its spontaneity with the reversal in the 1960's toward governmental centralization, as evidenced already by the growing subordination of the republican scholarly institutions to the Academy of Sciences in Moscow.[126]

The latter—more specifically, its Institute of Law (later, of State and Law)—has traditionally taken the lead in graduate study and research in the Soviet science of the state and law. A significant role in this field has also been played by the law faculties of Moscow, Leningrad, and Kiev Universities, the All-Union Scientific Institute for the Study of Soviet Legislation, and the Academy of Social Sciences—a party institution for advanced study and research established in 1946.

The Institute of Law, dominated at first by the holdouts of the Vyshinsky era, appeared during the first post-Stalin years to have taken a conservative line on a number of problems, including the questions of the system of legal sciences, the discipline of Soviet construction, and the autonomization of the state science. The repeated party criticism of the "lagging" of the institute "behind the demands of the time" finally led to its reorganization into the Institute of State and Law in the summer of 1960.[127] While the ultimate rationale behind the reorganization might have been the party's desire to put the scholars to work on the practical problems connected with the announced "full-scale construction of Communist society," the immediate significance of the changes involved was described by the institute spokesmen as a shift toward a comprehensive and "more profound elaboration of the problems of the state and its organization." [128]

As a result of the reorganization, the sector of the theory of the state was separated from the theory of law and merged with that of constitutional law, and a new sector of the "state administration and Soviet construction" was established.[129] Among the several other new or modified sectors, a separate subdivision was set up for "the study of international-legal relations among the socialist countries." [130]

The official expectations that were associated with the 1960 reorganization have evidently fallen short of realization in the face of scholars' inertia, timidity, and confusion, which were only reinforced by the theoretical innovations of the 22nd Party Congress. Following the congress, at which the state of "juridical science" came under party criticism,[131] the presidium of the academy admitted early in 1962 that

the reorganization of the Institute [of State and Law] in 1960 has to a considerable degree had a formal character and did not result in a substantial intensification of the elaboration of the problems of the theory of the state, and especially the theory of the socialist state and the problems of Soviet construction. The structure of the Institute does not sufficiently facilitate the concentration of its resources on the elaboration of the most important problems of the science of the state and law. . . . The press organ of the Institute, the journal *Soviet State and Law,* has not yet become the center of scientific and theoretical thought on the questions of the state and law . . . There are shortcomings in the coordination and the planning of scholarly research.[132]

Accordingly, the presidium decreed a series of new organizational measures that, while striving to overcome the tight interdisciplinary boundaries, had the effect of centralizing and regimenting research activities in line with the ideological formulations and priorities determined by the party-state leadership. A thematic learned council was set up within the academy on the "regularities [*zakonomernosti*] of development of socialism and the transition to communism," chaired by the party ideological secretary, Academician L. F. Il'ichev. The new council was entrusted, under the government-approved "two-year plan of scientific work" (1963–64), with the coordination of research on this grand theme, whose several aspects were allocated to the departments and institutes of social science and humanities within the Academy of Sciences, to which *all* republican research institutions were now subordinated.[133] Within the council a separate section on the "political organization of society" was set up, under the chairmanship of the director of the Institute of State and Law, Professor Romashkin. The section was in turn assigned corresponding coordinating functions vis-à-vis the republican institutions in the field of state and law.[134]

Steps have also been taken since 1961 toward some coordination of activities of the academy's Institute of State and Law with those of similar institutes in the "people's democracies" through a system of regular conferences of the institute directors, designed to combine the joint elaboration of the common problems with a measure of division of labor.[135]

Beginning in the fall of 1962, the regime began to place greater emphasis on the ideological indoctrination of the Soviet population and a sharpened struggle against "foreign ideas" penetrating the U.S.S.R. and undermining the foundations of Communist orthodoxy and party dictatorship. At the inevitable risk of mixing scholarship with propaganda, Soviet social scientists were now to give priority to the "unmasking of all forms of ideological diversions of imperialism, in order to paralyze them in time." [136]

Accordingly, a separate "complex" sector of contemporary bourgeois state and law was formed within the Institute of the State and Law.[137] At a 1963 session of the learned council of the institute, V. A. Tumanov, the head of the new sector, admitted a serious lag in Soviet studies of *modern* Western political institutions and processes, and severely criticized the still prevalent dogmatic schemes and constructs which either dwelled on the long-obsolete aspects of "bourgeois" political and socioeconomic systems or substituted for a critical study of these systems sweeping generalizations about the "complete bankruptcy of bourgeois law." [138]

Following the removal of Khrushchev and his ideological watchdog over social sciences, L. F. Il'ichev, Soviet state scientists found some respite from the frequent "mobilization" campaigns, fundamentalist pressures, and calls for immediate "practical" results of their activities. In the more pragmatic atmosphere characteristic of the post-Khrushchev regime, the Institute of State and Law has been centering its scholarly activities around the political and social problems of an interdisciplinary rather than a purely legal nature, with a growing emphasis on collective research projects. The learned council on the "regularities of development of socialism and transition to communism" was dissolved in 1966.[139] Among several new bodies created in its place, a "learned council on the regularities of the development of state, administration, and law" was formed within the academy's division of philosophy and law, with V. M. Chkhikvadze as chairman. It was entrusted with the coordination of research on such problems as

the theory and history of the socialist state and law; socialist legality and organization of the struggle against crime; Soviet construction and the improvement of the activities of the state apparatus; the administration of national economy; the regulation of civil and labor relations; questions of international law; problems of the bourgeois state and law; and legal problems of the countries which liberated themselves from colonial dependence.[140]

During the last two years, the Institute of State and Law produced a series of important studies, including a three-volume history of the Soviet state and law—the first major monograph in the field, a collective work on the methodological problems of juridical science, studies on the Soviet constitution and the central state organs of the U.S.S.R., and a symposium on the problems of state and law in the developing countries (the first such Soviet study)—and the fourth volume in the series, *Contemporary Imperialist State* (on its "mechanism of direct coercion").[141]

Reflecting the current trend in the Soviet social sciences, legal scholars at the institute, some republican academies, and the universities [142] have been increasingly employing the techniques of "concrete" sociological research, joining their efforts with those of specialists in various social sciences and "exact sciences"; recently, the first Soviet conference on "quantitative methods in social research" was held in Sukhumi, featuring some papers on political behavior in the U.S.S.R.[143] In 1965–66, the Institute of State and Law sponsored jointly with other academic institutions and governmental agencies several "complex" (multidisciplinary) "scientific expeditions" to study the operation of the government apparatus and the local soviets in the Kazakh and Estonian republics,[144] as well as a case study of an autonomous republic based on the Tatar A.S.S.R.[145]

To provide overall guidance and support for this new area, the presidium of the Academy of Sciences created in 1966 a learned council on "the problems of concrete sociological research," with a specialized "laboratory for concrete social and legal research" established in the Institute of State and Law.[146] The recent Central Committee resolution on the social sciences reiterated the party's support for the increased employment of "complex research" techniques, and indeed instructed the Academy of Sciences "to take into account the emergence of new branches of social sciences and the necessity of a complex elaboration of problems arising at the boundaries of various social sciences, as well as social and physical sciences." [147]

VII

It may still be premature to advance the thesis that a political science in the Western sense is emerging in the Soviet Union,[148] despite some apparent analogies that could be drawn between recent Soviet developments and the familiar process of the emancipation of the study of politics from that of law in a number of Western countries. To be sure, a number of tendencies in the U.S.S.R. seem to be working in that direction: the pragmatic orientation of the present Soviet leadership, evidently shared by a number of the younger state scientists; the greater willingness on the part of the Soviet leadership to give publicity to some hitherto secret operations of the party and government, and to take into their confidence the embryonic public opinion in the U.S.S.R.; the greater readiness to admit *past* errors and difficulties and to submit some previously dogmatized questions of means and organization to the test of practice and a well-meaning criticism; the recognition of the practical need of training more knowledgeable and efficient party and government personnel; and the tendency toward a somewhat more realistic assessment of the "bourgeois" world, coupled with the desire to counter Western political science at the latter's level by assimilating some of its concepts, approaches, and techniques.

Yet our evaluation of the state of Soviet state science would be unduly optimistic and one-sided were we to concentrate our attention only on change and to ignore the strong elements of continuity with the Stalinist past. For, at least as far as Soviet leadership is concerned, the search for rationality must not be carried too far, lest it subvert the utopian core of the ruling world view that supplies the party dictatorship with its rationale, its claim to legitimacy, and its dynamic momentum. The gap between the theory and practice of the regime must thus not be narrowed to the point of destroying the useful myths of "socialist democracy," "nonantagonistic" social structure, "friendship of peoples," and the "unbreakable unity of the party and people." The "facts" that Soviet political scientists may state have social and political consequences, and hence only such aspects of the truth may be brought to light as will strengthen, and not weaken, the present party leadership; and if necessary, some facts must be suppressed or distorted and new ones created to eradicate or slander the memories of men and events that challenge the integrity and wisdom of the current guardians of absolute truth. In the final analysis, the "dogmatism," "quotationism," and "personality cult" of the Stalin and Khrushchev eras were wrong not in the absolute sense, but because, from later political perspective, the scholars relied on the wrong dogmas and wrong quotations, and cultivated the wrong kind of personality. There is a preciously thin line separating the condemned "intellectual opportunism" of the Stalin era from the prescribed *ideinost* and *partiinost* of the post-1953 or post-1964 era.[149]

From the regime's point of view, Soviet state science must thus restrict its freedom of intellectual speculation to the scope bound by the shifting extremes of "dogmatism" and "revisionism." Admittedly, with the party "creatively" revising some of the established "truths" and increasingly experimenting with new methods, this scope has noticeably widened during the past decade. Yet surrounding the Soviet students of politics there is still a charged wire of "definitively solved questions," "objective necessities," and "regularities of development," which may be touched only at a risk that few scholars would be prepared to take. The price of nonconformity, however, has become somewhat less than the fearful penalties of the Stalin era, and the younger generation of Soviet state scientists, less visited by memories of the past, appears to be probing the confining walls of the dogma, groping for a more rational conception of their own system and of the surrounding world.

Notes

1. See, e.g., I. D. Levin, *Sovremennaia burzhuaznaia nauka gosudarstvennogo prava* (Moscow, 1960), p. 135. For recent assessments of the Soviet scholars' views on political science and of the status of political studies in Soviet institutions of higher learning and research, see Gordon Skilling, "In Search of Political Science in the USSR," *Canadian Journal of Economics and Political Science*, 29, no. 4 (November, 1963): 519-29; and L. G. Churchward, "Towards a Soviet Political

Science," *Australian Journal of Politics and History*, 12, no. 1 (May, 1966):
66–75.

2. There is a striking continuity between the post-1938 Soviet concept of the "science of the state and law" and the prerevolutionary academic treatment of the "state science(s)" as juridical in nature. The latter's development in tsarist Russia had been strongly influenced by German *Staatslehre*, especially Jellinek's school (see M. I. Sveshnikov, *Ocherk obshchei teorii gosudarstvennogo prava* [St. Petersburg, 1865], 13: 106–14; and N. M. Korkunov, *Russkoe gosudarstvennoe pravo* [St. Petersburg, 1909], 1: 48–52, 72–74).

3. D. A. Kerimov and B. V. Sheidlin, "O predmete obshchei teorii gosudarstva i prava," *Sovetskoe gosudarstvo i pravo* (cited hereafter as *SGP*), 1957, no. 12, pp. 6–7. For a more elaborate though slightly outdated treatment of the problem of the state-law relationship, see M. A. Arzhanov, *Gosudarstvo i pravo v ikh sootnoshenii* (Moscow, 1960), pp. 6–78.

4. F. Konstantinov, "Politicheskie teorii i politicheskaia praktika," *Kommunist*, 1958, no. 16, p. 86. Cf. Levin, *Sovremennaia burzhuaznaia nauka*, pp. 27–28.

5. P. S. Romashkin, M. S. Strogovich, and V. A. Tumanov, eds., *Teoriia gosudarstva i prava* (Moscow: Izdatelstvo Akademii Nauk, 1962), p. 14.

6. "Iuridicheskaia nauka i kodifikatsiia," *Pravovedenie*, 1958, no. 1, p. 11.

7. A. A. Piontkovsky, "Nekotorye voprosy obshchei teorii gosudarstva i prava," *SGP*, 1956, no. 1, p. 18. See also Piontkovsky, "Iuridicheskaia nauka, ee priroda i metod," *SGP*, 1965, no. 1, pp. 75–76.

8. Levin, *Sovremennaia burzhuaznaia nauka*, p. 191.

9. See Akademiia Nauk SSSR, *Osnovnye zadachi nauki sovetskogo sotsialisticheskogo prava* (Moscow, 1938), pp. 176–91; and V. F. Meshera, "O delenii sovetskogo prava na otrasli," *SGP*, 1967, no. 3, pp. 93–99.

10. For a discussion of this discipline, see p. 132.

11. In the words of Arzhanov, illustrating the difficulties of fitting the notion of international law into the Soviet ideological framework, "it is impossible to view international law as an ordinary 'branch of law.' By its nature it cannot enter into any system of law of a separate country, as it is called upon to regulate relations among countries, including those with dissimilar social-economic systems . . ." (*Gosudarstvo i pravo v ikh sootnoshenii*, pp. 79–81, 96, 97).

12. David Easton, "Problems of Method in American Political Science," *International Social Science Bulletin*, Spring, 1952, no. 1, p. 108.

13. Speaking of the 20th Party Congress in February, 1956, A. I. Mikoyan pointed out that "during the first period of the Soviet regime, in Lenin's time and a few years after his death, [Soviet juridical science] developed faster in accord with the ideas of Marxism-Leninism [and] the principles of socialist legality. . . . This cannot be said about the later period and this evoked a legitimate concern within the C.C. [Central Committee] of the CPSU, which felt that it must intervene without delay in these affairs to correct the situation . . ." (A. I. Mikoyan, *Promova na X z'izdi KPRS* [Kiev, 1956], p. 37).

14. The latest wave of "self-criticism" in the Soviet legal journals followed the Central Committee resolution of June, 1964, "On the Measures Concerning a Further Development of Juridical Science and the Improvement of Juridical Education in the Country." See, in particular, P. P. Gureev and V. V. Klochkov, "Za dalneishii pod'em sovetskogo pravovedeniia i uluchshenie iuridicheskogo obrazovaniia," *SGP*, 1964, no. 8, pp. 3–13.

15. The question, never adequately answered by the post-Stalin leadership, was eloquently posed in Togliatti's June, 1956, interview for *Nuovi argomenti*: ". . . as long as we confine ourselves, in substance, to denouncing the personal faults of Stalin as the cause of everything we remain within the realm of the 'personality cult.' First, all that was good was attributed to the superhuman, positive qualities of one man; now all that is evil is attributed to his equally exceptional and even

astonishing faults. . . . The true problems are evaded, which are why and how Soviet society could reach and did reach certain forms alien to the democratic way and to the legality which it had set for itself, even to the point of degeneration" (cited in *The Anti-Stalin Campaign and International Communism* [New York, 1956], pp. 120–21, 128).

16. Romashkin, Strogovich, and Tumanov, eds., *Teoriia gosudarstva i prava*, p. 20.

17. P. I. Stuchka (1865–1932), M. V. Krylenko (1885–1938), and E. B. Pashukanis (1891–1937) represented a sociological school of legal thought which dominated Soviet jurisprudence until the early 1930's. See Kazimierz Grzybowski, *Soviet Legal Institutions: Doctrines and Social Functions* (Ann Arbor, Mich., 1962), pp. 2–3; John N. Hazard, *Settling Disputes in Soviet Society: The Formative Years of Legal Institutions* (New York, 1960), pp. 477–91; Andrei Y. Vyshinsky, *The Law of the Soviet State* (New York, 1954), pp. 36–38, 53–59); and J. N. Hazard's introduction to *Soviet Legal Philosophy* (Cambridge, Mass., 1951), pp. xxi–xxvi. See also N. Ia. Kuprits, "Iz istorii nauki sovetskogo gosudarstvennogo prava," *Vestnik Moskovskogo Universiteta: Seriia XII, pravo*, 1966, no. 2, pp. 37–50; no. 3, pp. 24–35; no. 5, pp. 14–22.

18. See the editorial "Za podlinno nauchnuiu razrabotku korennykh voprosov nauki istorii sovetskogo gosudarstva i prava," *SGP*, 1956, no. 6, pp. 3–11; I. V. Pavlov, "O razvitii sovetskoi pravovoi nauki za sorok let," *SGP*, 1957, no. 11, pp. 30–49; and M. S. Strogovich, "Kov prosu o postanovke otdelnykh problem prava v rabotakh P. I. Stuchka, M. V. Krylenko, E. B. Pashukanis," in Vsesoiuznyi institut iuridicheskikh nauk, *Voprosy obshchei teorii sovetskogo prava* (Moscow, 1960), pp. 384–405.

19. The official attack on Vyshinsky opened shortly after the 20th Congress with the editorial "XX sezd KPSS i zadachi sovetskoi pravovoi nauki," *SGP*, 1956, no. 2, pp. 3–14. A more elaborate list of Vyshinsky's errors was soon supplied in the editorial "Ukreplenie sotsialisticheskoi zakonnosti i iuridicheskaia nauka," *Kommunist*, July, 1956, no. 11, pp. 21–22. The purge of Vyshinsky became official with Shelepin's speech at the 22nd Congress (see *Pravda*, October 27, 1961). For a much more comprehensive recent criticism of Vyshinsky's influence on the science of the state and law, see the editorial "Za polnuiu likvidatsiiu posledstvii kulta lichnosti v iuridicheskoi nauke," *Pravovedenie*, 1962, no. 3, pp. 3–14; P. Nedbailo and E. N. Nazarenko, "Ostatochno podolaty naslidky kultu osoby v radianskii iurydychnii nauki," *Radianske pravo*, 1962, no. 3, pp. 3–12; and Romashkin, Strogovich, and Tumanov, eds., *Teoriia gosudarstva i prava*, pp. 358–59.

20. See M. P. Kim, "O zadachakh izucheniia istoricheskogo opyta sotsialisticheskogo stroitelstva v SSSR v svetle reshenii XII sezda KPSS," *Voprosy istorii*, 1962, no. 2, p. 14; "Vsesoiuznoe soveshchanie istorikov," *ibid.*, 1963, no. 2, pp. 7–9; and V. M. Chkhikvadze, "Problemy sovetskoi iuridicheskoi nauki v sovremennyi period kommunisticheskogo stroitelstva," *SGP*, 1964, no. 9, p. 5.

21. See *Vestnik Moskovskogo Universiteta: Seriia ekonomiki, filosofii, prava*, 1957, no. 2, p. 156.

22. Nedbailo and Nazarenko, "Ostatochno podolaty naslidky kultu," p. 8. See also G. S. Gurvich, "Nekotorye voprosy sovetskogo gosudarstvennogo prava," *SGP*, 1957, no. 12, pp. 106–12.

23. "Za podlinno nauchnuiu razrabotku korennykh voprosov," p. 3.

24. S. S. Alekseev, "Tendentsii razvitiia iuridicheskoi nauki v period razvernutogo stroitelstva kommunizma," *Pravovedenie*, 1962, no. 2, p. 9.

25. "Za polnuiu likvidatsiiu posledstvii kulta lichnosti," p. 10.

26. *Ibid.*, pp. 8–9, 12; see also L. F. Il'ichev's speech at the December, 1961, All-Union Conference on the Problems of Ideological Work, in *XXII sezd KPSS i voprosy ideologicheskoi raboty* (Moscow, 1962), pp. 37–44; the editorial based on the (yet unpublished) resolution of the Central Committee on the CPSU (July, 1964) "On the Measures Concerning the Further Development of Juridical

Science and the Improvement of Juridical Education in the Country," "Nasu-shchnye zadachi iuridicheskoi nauki," *Kommunist*, August, 1964, no. 12, pp. 70–74; and the August, 1967, resolution of the Central Committee "On the Measures Concerning the Further Development of Social Sciences and the Raising of Their Role in the Communist Construction," reproduced in *Voprosy istorii KPSS*, 1967, no. 9, pp. 3–11.

27. Until the mid-fifties, participation of Soviet legal scholars in international organizations was largely limited to the International Association of Democratic Lawyers, a front organization that was established in 1946 and was made up of the official representatives of the Communist-bloc jurists (in the case of the U.S.S.R., representatives of the Law Section of *VOKS*) and "progressive" groups of jurists in other countries. After the death of Stalin, Soviet jurists began to participate in such international learned societies as the International Association of Legal Sciences, the International Association for the Study of Comparative Law, the International Institute of Administrative Sciences, and the International Political Science Association. See *SGP*, 1959, no. 8, pp. 138–39; 1959, no. 10, pp. 60–69; 1960, no. 6, pp. 126–27; 1960, no. 8, pp. 73–82; 1961, no. 2, pp. 9–17; 1961, no. 7, pp. 128–35; 1962, no. 5, pp. 132–34; 1962, no. 8, pp. 126–27; and 1963, no. 1, pp. 136–38. Illustrative of the Soviet attitude toward international learned societies is the criticism of the International Association of Legal Sciences appearing in P. S. Romashkin and S. L. Zivs, "MAIUN dolzhna sluzhit ideiam mira i progressa," *SGP*, 1959, no. 10, pp. 60–69. The writers argue against the notion of an "apolitical" learned society, admitting at the same time that "the broadening of the scientific contacts between Soviet and foreign jurists should become a serious obstacle to the people spreading misinformation and slanderous concoctions about Soviet law." In another article Dr. Romashkin, the director of the Institute of Law, observed: ". . . participating together with the bourgeois jurists in the work of the organizations dealing with comparative legal science, Soviet jurists should express and defend Soviet conceptions, show the superiority of Soviet law as a law of a higher historical type, and not find the common [denominator] in socialist and bourgeois law (which, unfortunately, has sometimes been the case with us)" (*SGP*, 1959, no. 7, p. 144).

28. The exact date on which the Soviet Association of Political (State) Sciences was created could not be established from the available Soviet sources. The first reported meeting of the SAPS took place in September, 1960, at which time Dr. V. S. Tadevosian, its president, stated that "one can observe some weakening of the association's activities in recent times [*za poslednee vremia*]" (*SGP*, 1961, no. 1, p. 143). While it is possible that the association was formed as early as the summer of 1959 (see the ambiguous footnote 1, *ibid.*), the indirect evidence rather points to the first half of 1960 as the most likely date of the founding of the SAPS.

29. See Frederick C. Barghoorn, *The Soviet Cultural Offensive* (Princeton, N.J., 1960), pp. 17, 31, 39, 43, 48–50, 161–66. In February, 1958, *VOKS* was renamed the Union of Soviet Societies for Friendship and Cultural Contacts with Foreign Countries. "For all practical purposes the new alliance represented the continuation of *VOKS* under a new name . . . [However] *VOKS*' conspicuous association with foreign Communist parties and the crudity and obstructionism of its past policies, one inferred, were to be modified and its activities brought into better coordination with the foreign policy of coexistence" (*ibid.*, pp. 160–61). To direct and coordinate Soviet cultural and scientific relations with foreign countries, a ministerial-status body, the State Committee for Cultural Relations with Foreign Countries, was established in May, 1957. See also Konstantinov, "Politicheskie teorii i politicheskaia praktika," p. 86; and *SGP*, 1961, no. 1, p. 143.

30. Another motive for the establishment of a Soviet political science organiza-tion appears in the first authoritative critique of Western political science, published

in the January, 1960, issue of *Kommunist*: "In the conditions of the contemporary ideological struggle, the study and critical analysis of the new phenomena and processes in bourgeois social science and propaganda assume an especially great importance. . . . Since political questions of social development are at the root [*vo glave ugla*] of the present ideological struggle, it is natural that they have found a corresponding reflection also in bourgeois sociology, within which, as its separate branch, there [emerged] a special [discipline], [the] so-called 'political science,' [which] spread widely a long time ago. . . ." (B. Shabad, "Apologiia politicheskoi sistemy kapitalizma [O tak nazyvaemoi 'politicheskoi nauke' v burzhauznoi sotsiologii]," *Kommunist*, January, 1960, no. 2, p. 87). It is significant that Soviet authorities turned down the conception of a broad union of Soviet jurists proposed in 1958–59 by a number of Soviet legal scholars and "practical workers" (see Iu. M. Aristakov, M. I. Piskotin, Kh. S. Suleimanova, and L. I. Urakov, "O neobkhodimosti sozdaniia Soiuza sovetskikh iuristov," *SGP*, 1958, no. 10, pp. 32–35; and the summary of the letters to the editors supporting this proposal appearing under the same title, *SGP*, 1959, no. 7, pp. 125–27).

31. *Vestnik Akademii Nauk SSSR*, February 1961, no. 2, p. 101. The undated item in *Vestnik* announces the confirmation by the presidium of the academy of Dr. V. S. Tadevosian as president of the association, stating that Dr. Tadevosian is attached to the division (*otdelenie*) of economic, philosophical, and legal sciences of the academy. The "basic tasks" of the Soviet Association of Political (State) Sciences are described in *Vestnik* as "the assistance in the development of these sciences in the spirit of the strengthening of mutual understanding and international cooperation of scholars—specialists in this branch of learning—[and] in the name of the strengthening of peace in the entire world and peaceful coexistence of states with different social-political systems; the acquainting of the public in the Soviet Union with political sciences; the acquainting of foreign scholarly circles with the achievements of Soviet political science; the participation of Soviet scholars in international meetings and conferences along the line of the International Political Science Association; as well as the establishment of personal contacts with foreign scholars." Significantly, similar language was used in 1958 to describe the tasks of the newly formed Soviet Sociological Association (see *Vestnik Akademii Nauk SSSR*, 1958, no. 6, p. 100).

32. V. P. Shatrov, "V Sovetskoi Assotsiatsii Politicheskikh (Gosudarstvovedcheskikh) Nauk," *SGP*, 1962, no. 8, pp. 143–44.

33. V. Slavin, "Pervoe ezhegodnoe sobranie Sovetskoi Assotsiatsii Politicheskikh (Gosudarstvovedcheskikh) Nauk," *SGP*, 1961, no. 7, pp. 131–35.

34. The speaker was V. A. Tumanov, a candidate of juridical sciences (*ibid.*, p. 133).

35. *Ibid.*, p. 134.

36. Shatrov, "V Sovetskoi Assotsiatsii Politicheskikh (Gosudarstvovedcheskikh) Nauk," pp. 126–27.

37. *Ibid.*, p. 127. Dr. Zivs's suggestion apparently remained unheeded.

38. Shatrov, "Tretie ezhegodnoe sobranie Sovetskoi Assotsiatsii Politicheskikh (Gosudarstvovedcheskikh) Nauk," *SGP*, 1963, no. 5, p. 161. About half of the participants in the 1963 meeting came from Leningrad and the academies and university centers in the union republics.

39. *Ibid.*, pp. 162–63.

40. F. M. Burlatsky, "Nauka i politika," *Pravda*, January 10, 1965.

41. G. S. Ostroumov, "Nauchnye osnovy politiki—v tsentre vnimaniia Sovetskoi Assotsiatsii Politicheskikh (Gosudarstvovedcheskikh) Nauk (Obsuzhdenie problem politicheskikh nauk na ezhegodnom sobranii assotsiatsii)," *SGP*, 1965, no. 7, pp. 148–51.

42. *Ibid.*, p. 148.

43. *Ibid.*, pp. 149–50.

44. *Ibid.*, p. 149.

45. *Ibid.*, p. 151; Churchward, "Towards a Soviet Political Science," p. 69, n. 11.

46. The citation was from D. Frank, *Fate and Freedom, A Philosophy for Free Americans* (New York, 1945), pp. 40–41.

47. M. S. Strogovich, "Filosofiia i pravovedenie," *SGP*, 1965, no. 6, pp. 77–78.

48. A. I. Lepeshkin, "Nazrevshie voprosy razvitiia nauki sovetskogo gosudarstvennogo prava," *SGP*, 1965, no 2, pp. 5–15.

49. V. M. Manokhin, "O predmete i zadachakh nauki upravleniia v sovremennyi period," *SGP*, 1965, no. 2, pp. 85–91. See also M. I. Piskotin *et al.*, "O nauke upravleniia," *SGP*, 1964, no. 9, pp. 15–27; Ts. A. Iampolskaia, "Nekotorye cherty metoda nauki upravleniia," *Pravavovedenie*, 1966, no. 3, pp. 3–10; P. N. Lebedev, "Ob upravlenii obshchestvennymi protsessami," *ibid.*, pp. 11–18; and V. Tsvetkov, "Dali rozvyvaty nauku upravlinnia," *Radianske pravo*, 1965, no. 8, pp. 15–21.

50. S. S. Alekseev and V. E. Chirkin, "O sisteme nauk, izuchaiushchikh problemy politicheskoi organizatsii obshchestva, gosudarstva i prava," *SGP*, 1965, no. 5, pp. 45–52; and V. E. Chirkin, "Ob osnovnykh problemakh teorii politicheskoi organizatsii obshchestva," *Pravovedenie*, 1965, no. 2, pp. 3–14.

51. 'O razrabotke problem politicheskoi nauki," *Pravda*, June 13, 1965.

52. *SGP*, 1966, no. 6, p. 135.

53. See, for example, the editorials "Za vysokuiu partiinost v sovetskoi iuridicheskoi nauke," *SGP*, 1964, no. 1, pp. 3–11, directed against "borrowings" from "bourgeois social science," and "Nasushchnye zadachi iuridicheskoi nauki," *Kommunist*, August, 1964, no. 12, pp. 70–74, attacking "some scholars" for "tolerance and neutrality with regard to hostile attacks by bourgeois jurists."

54. See F. Samalik in *Právnik*, 1963, no. 3, pp. 179, 183; and J. Fibich, *ibid.*, 1964, no. 9, pp. 785 ff. See also Churchward, "Towards a Soviet Political Science," p. 74, n. 27, 28.

55. See Z. Peteri, "La science politique bourgeoise et la théorie marxiste-leniniste de l'état," *Acta juridica*, 6 (1964): 3–4.

56. See J. Wiatr, "Uwagi o metodzie integracji nauk politycznych." *Panstwo i prawo*, 1965, no. 1, p. 107.

57. See Chirkin, "Ob osnovnykh problemakh teorii," p. 11.

58. *Ibid.*, pp. 9–12.

59. The catalogue of Stalin's theoretical "errors" includes, among others, his "mistaken and harmful" thesis about the sharpening of the class struggle *after* the victory of socialism (officially interpreted now as Stalin's theoretical justification of the "crudest violations of socialist legality"); his 1939 thesis that the "economic-organizational" and "cultural-educational" functions of the Soviet state did not "seriously develop" during the "first stage," i.e., the period of transition from capitalism to socialism; his 1936 thesis that the dictatorship of the proletariat not only should be left intact (despite the "broadening" of its social basis), but also should be intensified, with emphasis on its punitive, coercive functions; and his limited interpretation of "socialist legality" as merely limited to the "protection of socialist property." See Romashkin, Strogovich, and Tumanov, eds., *Teoriia gosudarstva i prava*, pp. 20–21, 216, 222. Among the Leninist theses "creatively" abandoned by the post-Stalin Soviet leaders are Lenin's rejection of a parliamentary means of transition to socialism under the conditions of "imperialism"; his identification of the socialist state with the dictatorship of the proletariat (the view also shared by Marx and Engels); and his thesis on the inevitability of wars.

60. The working class, according to the 1961 program, nevertheless remains a "leader of society," as "the foremost and best organized force of Soviet society" (*Program of the Communist Party of the Soviet Union* [New York, 1961], pp. 103–104).

61. *Ibid.* Several possible explanations could be advanced for this essentially semantic change in the Soviet theory of the state: (1) propaganda considerations

aiming at removing the stigma of dictatorship—a universally unpopular concept—from the Soviet system (according to *Izvestiia*, August 18, 1961, the replacement of the formula of the dictatorship of the proletariat with that of the "state of the entire people" "strikes a crushing blow at bourgeois and reformist ideologists who spread cock-and-bull stories about the egoism of the working class and the adherence of Communists to totalitarianism and violent methods of dictatorship"); (2) a symbolic concession to the popular desire for the strengthening of the rule of law and of the guarantees of individual rights; (3) an implicit recognition of the actual leading class in Soviet society, the intelligentsia; and (4) a rationalization further postponing the "withering away" of the state in the U.S.S.R.

62. *Program of the CPSU*, pp. 137–38; S. A. Golunsky, "Osnovnye napravleniia razvitiia obshchenarodnogo prava," *SGP*, 1962, no. 11, pp. 3–14.

63. See, e.g., the editorial "Proekt novoi programmy KPSS i nekotorye voprosy teorii gosudarstva i prava," *Pravovedenie*, 1961, no. 3, pp. 3–14. *Voprosy istorii KPSS*, 1961, no. 4, compiled *before* the publication of the draft program but published *after* it, still quoted Marx and Lenin in support of the thesis that "the dictatorship of the proletariat is essential throughout the period of transition from capitalism to communism" (p. 42). The subsequent manipulation and distortion of "quotations" from Lenin to "prove" the orthodoxy of the new concept of the Soviet state is exemplified by Farberov's and Romashkin's article in Romashkin, Strogovich, and Tumanov, eds., *Teoriia gosudarstva i prava*, pp. 226–27.

64. *Program of the CPSU*, p. 129.

65. Romashkin, Strogovich, and Tumanov, eds., *Teoriia gosudarstva i prava*.

66. *Vestnik Akademii Nauk SSSR*, April, 1962, no. 4, p. 112.

67. "Nasushchnye zadachi iuridicheskoi nauki," p. 71.

68. *SGP*, 1965, no. 2, p. 144.

69. See Alekseev, "Iuridicheskaia nauka v sovremennyi period," *SGP*, 1965, no. 1, pp. 13–14.

70. "XXIII sezd KPSS i voprosy sovetskogo sotsialisticheskogo gosudarstva i prava," *SGP*, 1966, no. 5, pp. 5–6.

71. Alekseev, "Tendentsii razvitiia iuridicheskoi nauki v period razvernutogo stroitelstva kommunizma," *Pravovedenie*, 1962, no. 2, p. 9. Cf. *SGP*, 1962, no. 10, pp. 134–36.

72. In addition to Alekseev, who again raised this issue early in 1965 (see his "Iuridicheskaia nauka v sovremennii period," p. 18), this position had been taken by Chirkin in "Ob osnovnykh problemakh teorii," p. 5.

73. See the editorial "Iuridicheskaia nauka v usloviiakh kommunisticheskogo stroitelstva," *Kommunist*, November, 1963, no. 16, p. 28.

74. "O kurse teorii gosudarstva i prava," *SGP*, 1966, no. 2, pp. 135–50.

75. See, in particular, Il'ichev's speech at the general meeting of the Academy of Sciences in October, 1962, setting out "concrete" problems for the elaboration by legal scholars, especially their assistance in the preparation of the new Soviet constitution (*Vestnik Akademii Nauk SSSR*, 1962, no. 11, p. 25); the summary of the July, 1964, resolution of the Central Committee on legal sciences ("Nasushchnye zadachi iuridicheskoi nauki," pp. 72–73); the editorial "XXIII sezd KPSS i voprosy sovetskogo sotsialisticheskogo gosudarstva i prava," pp. 5–8; and the August, 1967, resolution of the Central Committee, "O merakh po dalneishemu razvitiu obshchestvennykh nauk i povysheniiu ikh roli v kommunisticheskom stroitelstve," *Voprosy istorii KPSS*, 1967, no. 9, pp. 7–8.

76. See S. S. Alekseev, D. A. Kerimov, and P. E. Nedbailo, "Metodologicheskie problemy pravovedeniia," *Pravovedenie*, 1964, no. 4, pp. 16–18, 21; Alekseev, "Iuridicheskaia nauka v sovremennyi period," p. 19; and "XXIII sezd KPSS i voprosy sovetskogo sotsialisticheskogo gosudarstva i prava," pp. 5–8.

77. The previous text was S. F. Kachekian and G. I. Fedkin, eds., *Istoriia politicheskikh uchenii* (Moscow, 1955). The 1959 text of the same name was edited by K. A. Mokichev.

78. Professor Ladyzhensky in *Radianske pravo*, 1960, no. 5, p. 148. Cf. the review of Mokichev's book in *SGP*, 1960, no. 3, p. 150–54.

79. See *SGP*, 1963, no. 2, p. 146–49 and A. M. Davidovich, "Vazhnye problemy istorii gosudarstva i prava SSSR," *Pravovedenie*, 1965, no. 4, pp. 163–68.

80. S. V. Iushkov, *Istoriia gosudarstva i prava SSSR*, 4th ed. rev. (Moscow, 1961), pt. 1.

81. K. A. Sofronenko, ed., *Istoriia gosudarstva i prava SSSR* (Moscow, 1962), pt. 2: *Istoriia sovetskogo gosudarstva i prava*. A highly critical review of both volumes appeared in *Pravovedenie*, 1965, no. 4, pp. 163–68.

82. A colorless two-volume symposium, *Sorok let sovetskogo prava*, was published by the Leningrad University scholars in 1957. In 1964 selected works of Stuchka were published in Latvia. Perhaps of greatest interest in reconstructing the history of this discipline in the U.S.S.R. are the articles by N. Ia. Kuprits and K. A. Sofronenko in *Vestnik Moskovskogo Universiteta, Seriia XII, pravo*, 1965, no. 4, and 1966, nos, 2, 3, 5, 6.

83. Akademiia Nauk URSR, *Istoriia derzhavy i prava Ukrainskoi RSR (1917–1960)* (Kiev, 1961); Akademiia Nauk KSSR, *Istoriia gosudarstva i prava Sovetskogo Kazakhstana*, 3 vols. (Alma-Ata, 1961–65); Akademiia Nauk UzSSR, *Istoriia sovetskogo gosudarstva i prava Uzbekistana*, 2 vols. (Tashkent, 1960, 1963); A. V. Surilov, *Istoriia gosudarstva i prava Moldavskoi SSR (1917–1959 gg.)* (Kishinev, 1963); *Ocherki razvitiia gosudarstvennosti sovetskikh Pribaltiiskikh respublik (1940–1965 gg.)* (Tallin, 1965). One of the difficulties encountered by Soviet scholars in this field has been the lack of any officially approved periodization of the constitutional history of the U.S.S.R. and the republics, after the Stalinist periodization (identical with the now withdrawn *Short Course*) was found to be "subjective" and "scientifically incorrect." See Iu. P. Titov and O. I. Chistiakov, "Nekotorye voprosy istorii gosudarstva i prava SSSR," *SGP*, 1961, no. 3, pp. 30–39, and especially the section "Voprosy istorii sovetskogo gosudarstva i prava v svetle programmy KPSS," *SGP*, 1962, no. 10, pp. 25–46. The obvious and, indeed, most formidable factor hindering scholarly research in this field has been the rapidly changing "historical perspective" of the party, which exposes the historians of the Soviet state to charges of "dogmatism," "distortions," and "errors" with every official revaluation of the past.

84. See, e.g., S. P. Margunsky, *Sozdanie i uprochenie Belorusskoi gosudarstvennosti, 1917–1922* (Minsk, 1958); A. A. Gordienko, *Sozdanie sovetskoi natsionalnoi gosudarstvennosti v Srednei Azii* (Moscow, 1959); and, especially, M. B. Babiy, *Ukrainska radianska derzhava v period vidbudovy narodnioho hospodarstva (1921–1925)* (Kiev, 1961), based to a large degree on the hitherto classified archive documents. On the other hand, the more recent the period of investigation, the more "dogmatized" and the less factual the relevant studies tend to be. The history of the R.S.F.S.R. and of the Russian state and law during the half century before the 1917 Revolution have been perhaps the most sadly neglected periods of study. Two valuable recent studies in this field are N. P. Eroshkin, *Ocherki istorii gosudarstvennykh uchrezhdenii dorevoliutsionnoi Rossii* (Moscow, 1960), and E. Gorodetsky, *Rozhdenie sovetskogo gosudarstva (1917–1918 gg.)* (Moscow, 1965).

85. *Sezdy Sovetov Soiuza SSR, Soiuznykhi avtonomnykh sotsialisticheskikh respublik. Sbornik dokumentov v semi tomakh, 1917–1937*, 7 vols. (Moscow, 1959–65). The collection is limited, however, to the resolutions of the Congresses and lacks adequate references and commentaries.

86. *Dekrety Sovetskoi vlasti*, 3 vols. (Moscow, 1957, 1959, 1964). In addition, a number of specialized collections of government and party documents have appeared during the past few years, dealing with such areas as foreign affairs, the army, "cultural construction," religion, economy, youth, etc.

87. In particular, the republication of the stenographic records of the party congresses and conferences; the publication of the early correspondence of the secretariat of the Central Committee and of "new" articles, letters, and other

materials by Lenin; and the appearance of specialized collections of party documents and of memoirs of the "old Bolsheviks." Some of the most important documents in these categories have appeared in the party journal, *Voprosy istorii KPSS,* launched in 1956.

88. The most important publications in this area are the histories of the republican and local party organizations, as well as those of party organizations in the individual functional branches of the Soviet system.

89. A. Denisov and M. Kirichenko, *Soviet State Law* (Moscow, 1960).

90. Vysshaia partiinaia shkola pri TsK KPSS, *Osnovy sovetskogo gosudarstvennogo stroitelstva i prava* (Moscow, 1961), and D. Zlatopolsky, *State System of the U.S.S.R.* (Moscow, 1962), dealing largely with the origin, nature and tendencies of development of Soviet federalism.

91. A. I. Lepeshkin, *Kurs sovetskogo gosudarstvennogo prava,* 2 vols. (Moscow, 1961, 1962). The first volume was produced by Lepeshkin alone, the second (under his editorship) jointly with A. I. Kim, N. G. Mishin, and P. I. Romanov.

92. A. I. Lepeshkin, ed., *Sbornik ofitsialnykh dokumentov primenitelno k kursu sovetskogo gosudarstvennogo prava* (Moscow, 1964).

93. Akademiia Nauk SSSR, *Sovetskoe gosudarstvennoe pravo. Bibliografiia, 1917–1957* (Moscow, 1958). In 1960 the Institute of the State and Law produced a rather selective English-language guide to bibliographies of Soviet law, including also state science and international law (*Literature on Soviet Law. Index of Bibliography* [Moscow, 1960]).

94. A. I. Kim, *Sovetskoe izbiratelnoe pravo* (Moscow, 1965).

95. Constitutional law of the "countries of people's democracy" has been introduced into the curriculum of the Soviet juridical institutes and faculties since 1946 and has subsequently developed into a specialized area of research. Until recently, no satisfactory (from the Soviet point of view) text had been produced for this discipline, which has suffered not only from the fluidity of laws and institutions in the "people's democracies," but also from the attempts mechanically to apply in the study of their constitutional laws the scheme of the Soviet Constitution and the familiar "dogmatic," "commentary" style (see Chirkin, "O sisteme uchebnogo kursa gosudarstvennogo prava stran narodnoi demokratii," *Pravovedenie,* 1961, no. 2, pp. 143–52). A slight recovery from these tendencies appears in the two recent texts in the field: I. P. Il'insky and B. V. Shchetinin, *Gosudarstvennoe pravo stran narodnoi demokratii* (Moscow, 1964), and, especially, A. Kh. Makhnenko, *Osnovnye instituty gosudarstvennogo prava stran narodnoi demokratii* (Moscow, 1964). The first attempt at a joint research project by the Soviet and satellite scholars resulted in the publication of a 1960 symposium (V. F. Kotok and N. P. Farberov, eds., *Voprosy gosudarstva i prava stran narodnoi demokratii* [Moscow, 1960]).

96. Two publications in the field had been completed in the Institute of State and Law in 1964: a collective work on the "Noncapitalist Road of Development of the African Countries: Problems of the State and Law," and a collection of documents, "The Constitutions of the States of Africa" (see *Vestnik Akademii Nauk SSSR,* 1967, no. 3, p. 154).

97. See the editorial "Glubzhe izuchat i kritikirovat burzhuaznuiu iurisprudentsiiu," *SGP,* 1956, no. 4, pp. 3–14. The article attacks such shortcomings as the almost complete ignoring by Soviet critics of "the so-called 'political science'" in the West, "the substitution of shouting and loose language for a substantive critique," the failure to read *contemporary* Western works in the field, and the obsolete nature of sources used, combined with sweeping generalizations about the "epigonism" of Western scholars, factual errors and careless documentation, "declarative and unproved general phrases," and vulgarization of the process of the subordination of the capitalist state to monopolies, which "many researchers even now reduce to the enumeration of the representatives of big firms who occupy responsible posts in the government." With greater ambivalence evident in the

official Soviet view of the West and the opening of access to relevant Western literature, some improvement could be observed in Soviet studies of Western politics. See, for example, a recent text in this field, I. D. Levin and B. S. Krylov, eds., *Gosudarstvennoe pravo burzhuaznykh stran* (Moscow, 1962), and *Uchenye zapiski* of the Department of State Law of the Institute of International Relations, a series started in 1960 under the title *Voprosy gosudarstva i prava zarubezhnykh stran*. Among the recent works in the field, see Guliev, *Imperialisticheskoe gosudarstvo (Ocherk kritiki burzhuaznykh teorii)* (Moscow, 1965), and Levin and Krylov, *Burzhuaznie konstitutsii v period obshchego krizisa kapitalizma* (Moscow, 1966). A recent article on Western political science by V. G. Kalensky, "O predmete i metode burzhuaznoi politicheskoi nauki," *SGP*, 1966, no. 9, pp. 33–41, is illustrative of a highly sophisticated approach that can occasionally be found in Soviet legal journals. In February, 1966, Moscow University sponsored a theoretical conference on "The Problems of the Critical Study of the Contemporary Bourgeois State and Law," with the participation of scholars from the Institute of State and Law and other academic institutions (see *Vestnik Moskovskogo Universiteta, Seriia XII, pravo*, 1966, no. 4, pp. 94–95). In the same year a special learned council, under Academician M. B. Mitin, was formed in the Academy of Sciences to coordinate research "on the problems of foreign ideological currents," including the study of Western "Sovietology" (*Vestnik Akademii Nauk SSSR*, 1967, no. 1, p. 144).

98. See L. G. Churchward's account of his meetings and discussions with younger Soviet scholars at the Institute of State and Law ("Towards a Soviet Political Science," pp. 67–68).

99. See Levin, *Sovremennaia burzhuaznaia nauka*, pp. 81–95, 239–56, 290–300, and 390–94; Lepeshkin *et al.*, *Kurs sovetskogo gosudarstvennogo prava*, 2: 251–54, 571–86; and the prospectus "O kurse teorii gosudarstva i prava," p. 142.

100. However, during the period from 1946 to 1963 only two doctoral dissertations were devoted to the "bourgeois" theory of state and law (S. N. Bratus, A. A. Piontkovsky, and I. F. Pobezhimov, "Problematika dissertatsionnykh rabot i razvitie iuridicheskoi nauki," *SGP*, 1965, no. 3, p. 34).

101. Tumanov and Levin, eds., *Imperialisticheskoe gosudarstvo i kapitalisticheskaia ekonomika* (Moscow, 1963); *Konstitutsionnyi mekhanizm diktatury monopolii* (Moscow, 1964); and *Partii v sisteme diktatury monopolii* (Moscow, 1964).

102. Levin, *Sovremennaia burzhuaznaia nauka gosudarstvennogo prava* (Moscow, 1960).

103. For example, Kalensky's article "O predmete i metode burzhuaznoi politicheskoi nauki."

104. See, in particular, the editorial "Za vysokuiu partiinost v sovetskoi iuridicheskoi nauke," pp. 10–11.

105. See the articles on the problem of the comparative study of socialist and Western state and law: Zivs, "O metode sravnitelnogo issledovaniia v nauke o gosudarstve i prave," *SGP*, 1964, no. 3, pp. 23–35 (arguing against comparative study of *similarities* between the two systems); Alekseev *et al.*, "Metodologicheskie problemy pravovedeniia," p. 27; and A. I. Kosarev, "Ob ispolzovanii sravnitelnogo metoda v istoriko-pravovom issledovanii," *SGP*, 1965, no. 3, pp. 78–86 (stressing the need for the study of both *similarities and contrasts*, since the latter can be established only on the basis of the common features of the systems compared).

106. V. A. Vlasov and S. S. Studenikin, *Sovetskoe administrativnoe pravo* (Moscow, 1959).

107. I. N. Ananov, *Ministerstva v SSSR* (Moscow, 1960).

108. Vlasov, *Sovetskii gosudarstvennyi apparat* (Moscow, 1959). See also his *Osnovy gosudarstvennogo upravleniia* (Moscow, 1960).

109. Manokhin, *Sovetskaia gosudarstvennaia sluzhba* (Moscow, 1966).

110. See, for example, E. A. Rovinsky, ed., *Sovetskoe finansovoe pravo* (Moscow, 1961); the series of monographs by T. N. Dobrovolskaia: *Narodnyi sud— osnovnoe zveno sudebnoi sistemy SSSR* (Moscow, 1956); *Oblastnoi (kraevoi) sud*

(Moscow, 1958);*Verkhovnyi sud Soiuznoi respubliki* (Moscow, 1960); and *Verkhovnyi sud SSSR* (Moscow, 1964); and M. P. Maliarov, ed., *Prokurorskii nadzor v SSSR* (Moscow, 1966)—the first text for the course in this field.

111. During the early 1930's, the discipline of "Soviet construction" embraced, however, elements of all other branches of state science, which, it was later charged, was representative of the orientation of Krylenko and Pashukanis toward the "withering away" of law.

112. See G. V. Barabashev and K. F. Sheremet, "O prepodavanii sovetskogo stroitelstva v iuridicheskikh vuzakh," *Vestnik Moskovskogo Universiteta*, 1960, no. 1, pp. 41–48; a much broader scope was claimed for this new discipline by L. S. Galesnik, "O predmete sovetskogo stroitelstva," *Pravovedenie*, 1964, no. 2, pp. 121–29.

113. See the October 5, 1946, resolution of the Central Committee "On Extending and Improving Legal Training in the Country."

114. Barabashev and Sheremet, *Sovetskoe stroitelstvo* (Moscow, 1965), pp. 16–18. Cf. V. Barakhtian and P. Pavlovsky, "Vykladannia kursu radianskoho budivnytstva u vuzakh," *Radianske pravo*, 1966, no. 5, pp. 13–14.

115. See *ibid.*, pp. 13–18. Since 1960, chairs of the state (constitutional) law in the faculties of law and at the juridical institutes have been transformed into chairs of "state law and Soviet construction."

116. Barabashev and Sheremet, *Sovetskoe stroitelstvo.*

117. M. I. Piskotin *et al.*, "O nauke upravleniia," *SGP*, 1964, no. 9, p. 20.

118. See E. Starostsiak, "Predmet i zadachi nauki upravleniia v sotsialisticheskom gosudarstve," *SGP*, 1965, no. 5, pp. 77–80; V. M. Manokhin, "O predmete i zadachakh nauki upravleniia v sovremennyi period," *SGP*, 1965, no. 2, pp. 85–91; Ts. A. Iampolskaia, "Nekotorye cherty metoda nauki upravleniia," *Pravovedenie*, 1966, no. 3, pp. 3–10; and P. N. Lebedev, "Ob upravlenii obshchestvennymi protsessami," *ibid.*, pp. 11–18.

119. V. M. Chkhikvadze, "Pravovaia nauka i obshchestvennaia praktika," *Kommunist*, 1965, no. 1, p. 28. In this connection the sector of administrative law was transformed into the sector "for the problems of improving the state apparatus and administrative law" (*SGP*, 1966, no. 4, p. 113).

120. See "Teoreticheskaia konferentsiia po pravovym problemam nauki upravleniia," *SGP*, 1966, no. 4, p. 116.

121. Several discussants at the meeting challenged the "complex" (interdisciplinary) nature of "administrative science" (*ibid.*, p. 114). None of the leading exponents of a Soviet political science or the "Soviet construction" was reported among the discussants.

122. Some speakers at the conference called for greater rights for the union republics and a substantial decentralization of Soviet administration, for the introduction of the merit system in the Soviet public service, and for less party interference with local government administration (*ibid.*, pp. 115–18).

123. Several years ago the discipline of the "party construction" (*partiinoe stroitelstvo*) was authoritatively described as "a component part of the Leninist teaching on the Communist party; a science of regularities of the emergence, development, and strengthening of the Marxist-Leninist party, [dealing with] the Leninist principles of the party's organizational structure, its historical experience, the principles of party leadership, the Leninist style, forms, and methods of party work, the political and organizational direction of the state, economic and cultural construction, and the Communist education of the toilers. The party construction includes the practice of the organizational work of the party organizations and the leading party organs" (*Ukrainska radianska entsyklopediia* [1962], 10: 548). Among the available publications in this field, the most useful have been collections of lectures offered at the Central Committee's Academy of Social Sciences and the leading higher party schools. The semimonthly journal *Partiinaia zhizn*, which resumed publication in April, 1954, is devoted primarily to the theoretical and practical questions of "party construction."

124. The other five journals, more concerned with the "practical questions" of the judiciary, procuracy, arbitration, and lawyers' and notaries' practice, are *Sotsialisticheskaia zakonnost* (Moscow), the organ of the procuracy and the Supreme Court of the U.S.S.R.; *Sovetskaia iustitsiia* (Moscow), published by the Ministry of Justice (now the Juridical Commission of the Council of Ministers) and the Supreme Court of the R.S.F.S.R.; the Georgian-language *Soviet Law* (Tbilisi); the Estonian legal bulletin of the same name (Tallin); and the Lithuanian *Soviet Legality* (Vilnius). By 1961, twenty-two Soviet juridical institutes and law faculties were publishing their "proceedings" or "papers," the most recent addition to this field being the Ukrainian *Problemy pravoznavstva*, published by Kiev University.

125. See "Iuridicheskaia nauka i pravovye uchrezhdeniia v soiuznykh respublikakh," *SGP*, 1962, no. 12, pp. 96–101.

126. See P. S. Romashkin, "Koordinatsiia issledovanii—neobkhodimoe uslovie razvitiia sovetskoi iuridicheskoi nauki," *SGP*, 1963, no. 3, pp. 3–5.

127. "O reorganizatsii Instituta prava v Institut gosudarstva i prava," *Vestnik Akademii Nauk SSSR*, 1960, no. 8, p. 116.

128. Romashkin, "O zadachakh Instituta gosudarstva i prava," pp. 13–15; cf. E. A. Rakhmaninova, "Obsuzhdenie voprosa o zadachakh Instituta gosudarstva i prava," *SGP*, 1961, no. 1, p. 141.

129. Romashkin, "O zadachakh Instituta gosudarstva i prava," pp. 15, 17.

130. *Ibid.*, p. 17.

131. See *Pravda*, October 27, 1961.

132. "O rabote Instituta gosudarstva i prava," *Vestnik Akademii Nauk SSSR*, 1962, no. 4, p. 112.

133. *Ibid.*, 1962, no. 12, pp. 6–8, 19–62; Romashkin, "Koordinatsiia issledovanii," p. 6.

134. For the research program to be supervised by the new section, see *ibid.*, pp. 6–15. See also the report of the December, 1962, meeting of the section on the "Political Organization of Society," *SGP*, 1963, no. 3, p. 130, and the subsequent official criticism of the scholars' performance in this area, *ibid.*, 1963, no. 8, pp. 3–14.

135. See the report "Soveshchanie direktorov institutov gosudarstva i prava sotsialisticheskikh stran," *SGP*, 1962, no. 12, pp. 148–49; and V. P. Shatrov, "O mezhdunarodnykh nauchnykh sviaziakh Instituta gosudarstva i prava Akademii Nauk SSSR v 1962 g.," *ibid.*, 1963, no. 4, p. 144. The first such conference met at the initiative of Hungarian jurists, in Budapest, in November, 1961; the second meeting took place in Warsaw in September, 1962; after a pause of nearly four years, the third conference was held in Moscow in June, 1966. The last conference adopted proposals listing "themes suitable for joint elaboration," and stating "the desirability of holding multilateral and bilateral symposia and conferences . . . the usefulness of a greater exchange of scholarly publications, [and] information on the development of juridical science in the socialist countries . . . the necessity of further coordination and alignment of efforts of legal scholars from socialist countries in the international scientific organizations, and the importance of improving cooperation among juridical journals" (I. T. Pomerantsev, "Tretye soveshchanie direktorov institutov gosudarstva i prava i glavnykh redaktorov zhurnalov evropeiskikh sotsialisticheskikh stran," *SGP*, 1966, no. 9, pp. 118–21. In the early sixties, two joint works were produced by Soviet, Polish, Czechoslovak, and East German jurists dealing with "Legal Cooperation among Socialist Countries" and "The Representative System of the U.S.S.R. and the Countries of People's Democracy" (Shatrov, "O mezhdunarodnykh nauchnykh sviaziakh," p. 144).

136. See Il'ichev, "Nauchnaia osnova rukovodstva razvitiem obshchestva: Nekotorye problemy razvitiia obshchestvennykh nauk," *Kommunist*, 1962, no. 16, p. 37.

137. E. F. Leoniuk, "Ob osnovnykh napravleniiakh kriticheskogo izucheniia sovremennogo imperialisticheskogo gosudarstva i prava i borby s vrazhdebnoi ideologiei," *SGP*, 1963, no. 6, p. 136. Previously this field of study was under the

sector of state (constitutional) law and was largely confined to this branch of "bourgeois" law.

138. *Ibid.*, pp. 136–37. It is noteworthy that in trying to cope with Western political systems, Soviet scholars have admittedly found their legalistic conceptual framework too narrow. Thus, commenting on the experience of the new sector, Dr. I. D. Levin pointed out that "the study of bourgeois political institutions cannot be carried on exclusively in the framework of the science of state and law. There emerges the problem of creating a broader scientific discipline which conditionally could be designated as state science [*gosudarstvovedenie*]" (*ibid.*, p. 137).

139. *Vestnik Akademii Nauk SSSR*, 1966, no. 4, p. 158.

140. *Ibid.*, 1966, no. 7, p. 119.

141. See *ibid.*, 1966, no. 3, pp. 114–15, 139–42; and 1967, no. 3, pp. 152–54. See also *Sovetskaia iustitsiia*, August, 1967, no. 16, p. 7. At the 1966 general meeting of the Academy of Sciences, Dr. Chkhikvadze, director of the Institute of State and Law, called for greater autonomy for his institute (*Vestnik Akademii Nauk SSSR*, 1966, no. 3, p. 140).

142. In 1963 a group of the Leningrad University scholars established an "Association for Complex Social Research," to guide and coordinate interdisciplinary empirical research on society and the problems of the individual. In 1965 it was transformed into a regular university institute (*Pravovedenie*, 1964, no. 2, pp. 157–59; D. A. Kerimov, "O perspektivakh razvitiia obshchestvennykh nauk v universitete," *Vestnik Leningradskogo Universiteta. Seriia ekonomiki, filosofii i prava*, 1965, no. 23, pp. 3–24).

143. *SGP*, 1967, no. 8, p. 143.

144. See the editorials "Obshchestvennye problemy i iuridicheskaia nauka (Nekotorye itogi kompleksnogo pravovogo issledovaniia, provedennogo v Kazakhskoi SSR)," *SGP*, 1965, no. 7, pp. 3–12; and "O rezultatakh izucheniia gosudarstvennogo stroitelstva Estonskoi SSR," *SGP*, 1966, no. 9, pp. 3–14.

145. "O rezultatakh izucheniia gosudarstvennogo stroitelstva Tatarskoi ASSR," *SGP*, 1967, no. 5, pp. 3–11. The published summaries of findings and recommendations of these three major "field expeditions" attest to the marked improvement in Soviet research techniques and contain many interesting critical observations about the constitutional and legal framework of these republics, union-republican relations, and the structure and practices of the governmental apparatus.

146. *Vestnik Akademii Nauk SSSR*, 1966, no. 5, p. 16. Among the tasks of the new learned council are the study of social psychology and public opinion in the U.S.S.R. and research on relations among Soviet nationalities.

147. "O merakh po dalneishemu razvitiiu obshchestvennykh nauk," p. 8.

148. Cf. Churchward, "Towards a Soviet Political Science," pp. 71–74; and J. Frankel, "Theory of State, Cybernetics and Political Science in the Soviet Union," *Political Studies*, 15, no. 1 (February, 1967): 59–61; both writers appear to be somewhat more optimistic about the prospects of a Soviet political science, though Churchward suggests that it will differ in several important respects from its Western counterpart.

149. In his December, 1962, address, one of the principal party spokesmen in social sciences, Academician B. Ponomarev, elaborated on the principle of *partiinost* ("party spirit") in scholarship: "In determining the topic, selecting the object of research, choosing the form of generalization from the [source] material, presenting and illuminating this or that event, a scholar must always realize the social significance of each of the elements of his work, strictly control what and how he announces to the masses, to what extent his evaluations are permeated by the spirit of Marxism-Leninism, [and] what will be the real contribution of his work to the cause of the people's movement toward communism" (B. Ponomarev, "Istoricheskuiu nauku i obrazovanie—na uroven zadach kommunisticheskogo stroitelstva," *Kommunist*, 1963, no. 1, p. 35). Cf. the most recent definition of the

tasks of the Soviet social sciences supplied in the August, 1967, resolution of the
party Central Committee: "The efforts of scholars must, above all, be subordinated
to the fulfillment of the tasks presented by the program of the CPSU and
the 23rd Party Congress—active participation in the work on the further development of the country's economy, the strengthening of its defense, the raising of
the level of the people's welfare and culture, the Communist education of the
people—[and] to the tasks of the struggle against bourgeois ideology" (*Voprosy
istorii KPSS*, 1967, no. 9, p. 6).

IV : Law

Law and Social Science: Recent Developments

I

The law doesn't fit very well among the ranks of the social sciences. It is neither a purely academic discipline populated by scholars nor a profession made up strictly of practitioners. It is this dichotomy that most sets it apart from the other social sciences. While no one would question the propriety of including anthropology, history, political science, or sociology among the social sciences, neither Western [1] nor Soviet [2] commentators are in agreement that law clearly belongs in this category.

The fact that "the law" as a profession of practitioners preceded the development of law as an academic discipline; that much work connected with the law in any country involves the handling of day-to-day, practical matters; the consequent predominance of practitioners of one sort or another over those primarily engaged in teaching or research:

The author wishes to acknowledge the aid of the Institute of Research, Lehigh University, and of the Russian Research Center, Harvard University, in the preparation of this manuscript.

all of these factors make law a somewhat different animal from the other disciplines of the humanistic tradition.

Yet the potential relevance of law to social science is unquestionable. The purpose of any corpus of rules and practices which comes to be known as "the law" is the regularization of modes of social control and interaction. This ought to be of great interest to anyone seeking to draw conclusions about how a social system operates. And many lawyers (and, particularly in the United States, scholars whose basic training has not been in the law) have pursued and continue to pursue studies in the field of law which have a clear claim to being called social science research.

Ideally, then, one would want, for the purposes of a symposium such as this, to concentrate on the work being done in Soviet law which is of a truly social-scientific character, and to omit that which is done purely for the practitioner, be he the *advokat* (lawyer for individual parties) handling a divorce or tort case, the procurator prosecuting an individual accused of theft, or the staff lawyer of the industrial enterprise seeking to protect his firm's interests. If one does not attempt to be overly precise as to metes and bounds, legal literature can be looked at in this way.

A further caveat necessary at this point is that virtually all legal research (and this applies to the United States as well as to the Soviet Union) is likely to have a more avowedly practical orientation than the other social sciences. The factors cited above bring to the field of law a technical, problem-solving inclination which extends to those doing legal research and writing. Because legal education is aimed largely at producing practitioners,[3] the mode of training and the research interests of teaching personnel reinforce the technical bent of the discipline.[4] While these generalizations can be said to characterize both Soviet and American law, the gap between law and the other social sciences appears to be less extreme in the Soviet Union than in the United States. In the main this is due to the fact that all of the Soviet social sciences, under far greater central direction and control than comparable disciplines in the United States, have a relatively strong practical and problem-centered orientation.[5]

Such control explains much about the nature of law as a social science in the Soviet Union, and no realistic examination of the subject can omit a consideration of this factor. With this in mind, this essay will proceed by the following stages: a brief commentary on legal scholarship in the pre-Stalin and Stalinist periods; an analysis of the implications of de-Stalinization for legal scholarship, concentrating on recent planning and coordination of legal research; an examination of the major approaches and techniques used in legal research, with emphasis on areas or problems in which some of the more systematic techniques of analysis are being attempted. No attempt has been made in this essay at a comprehensive analysis of all branches of Soviet law. The topics selected for consideration were those which seemed to bear most directly on the development of law as a social science.

II

How free must inquiry be in the legal field for significant work to be produced? There are those who have argued that a social science can operate effectively only when it is unfettered by political interference.[6] Experience indicates that one must approach such generalizations with caution, for it was not so long ago that responsible Western analysts were declaring that Soviet natural science could not produce viable results because of a stifling ideological and political atmosphere.[7]

One's conclusion as to results depends, of course, upon the kind of objectives one designates. If the aim of scholarly analysis is simply truth unattended by practical considerations or by politics, then, of course, a maximization of freedom of inquiry is desirable. But for more limited ends, such as research on specific social problems assigned by the political authorities, complete latitude in the range of inquiry may not be necessary. It is undoubtedly true, however, that even such limited objectives become impossible at some point as the level of political interference increases. A brief sketch of the climate for legal research during the Soviet period will show how this point was reached during the 1930's.

Before Stalin's death, the most significant period of legal scholarship was the NEP period (1921–29). Between 1922 and 1926 the basic R.S.F.S.R. codes were adopted. They remained in force throughout the whole of the Stalinist period, and began to be replaced by new legal documents only in the late 1950's and early 1960's.[8]

The period was characterized not only by significant accomplishments on such pressing matters as codification, but also by a relatively high level of practical and theoretical discussion. There were a number of legal periodicals publishing a great many judicial decisions and interpretive articles, the latter surprisingly free from ritualistic references to the wisdom of Soviet leaders and the superiority of Soviet law, with which Soviet legal writing of later years has been laden. Another mark of the writing of the time was the willingness of writers to acknowledge their considerable debt to Western "bourgeois" law, especially in the field of code writing. In later years any favorable or even neutral reference to bourgeois law would be condemned. This is not to say that the writing of this period amounted to a free exchange of ideas. Those who were allowed to take part did not represent antisocialist points of view, and this alone prevented fundamental differences of opinion. Even on issues which seemed to be neutral politically, differences with the established line were expressed cautiously. But by comparison with both earlier and later periods of Soviet history, this was, as Fainsod put it, a "liberal interlude." [9]

In this atmosphere particularly significant strides in several areas of legal research were made. Work in judicial statistics was carried on for a time at the high level established in prerevolutionary years, and considerable attention was directed at modern techniques of criminology. In 1921 the Institute for the Study of the Personality of the Offender was established in Petrograd, followed by the creation of similar institutes in several other cities. There was considerable research applying sociological methods in criminology.[10]

By the end of the decade, however, the situation was beginning to change. The increase in totalitarian controls that accompanied the demise of the NEP quickly engulfed the legal sphere. Empirical data in the form of statistics and judicial decisions gradually declined or disappeared. Most of the institutes of criminology were abolished, and criminological work was reoriented from sociological analysis to sterile exegetical discussion. Some of the law journals went out of existence, and legal scholars, like other intellectuals, faced an era of criticism and self-criticism. By the late 1930's the proponents of a separate body of "economic law" and of a withering away of the law had been purged,[11] in spite of their willingness to admit their errors, and a number of legal scholars, to use the Soviet phrase, "met a tragic end." The advocates of "stability of laws" (Stalin's phrase), as opposed to withering of law, had won the day.

This atmosphere produced results that might be expected: wariness, unwillingness to experiment, retreat into the analysis of less controversial or unimportant subjects, and writings laden with slavish praise of Stalin. Another clear effect was a decline in published legal writing. Vyshinsky, who had emerged by the late 1930's as the authoritative interpreter of all matters relating to law, complained in 1938 that several of the law institutes were grossly underfulfilling their plans for legal writing.[12] This silence was to characterize a number of legal scholars throughout the Stalin period, a fact which Soviet publications did not fail to note.[13]

Other scholars found it possible to fulfill their publishing plans by writings which amounted largely to compilations of approved quotations. As Vyshinsky noted in 1948:

It must be said that the method of "scientific work" which might be called "citology" is fairly widespread among us. Until this very moment the method of stringing together as much as possible on the thread, the very slender thread of a writer's thought, of quotations from the works of the great thinkers, is widespread.[14]

The level of control over Soviet legal scholarship established in the 1930's continued, with minor vacillations, until after the death of Stalin. Soviet lawyers, who spoke up when they got their chance, were unanimous in attesting to the harm that had been done during this twenty-five-year period. One of the best short summaries of the effects of the Stalin period on Soviet law is that of the director of the Institute of State and Law of the U.S.S.R. Academy of Sciences, V. M. Chkhikvadze, who wrote in 1964:

Being a political science, juridical science found itself in a grave position under the conditions of the cult of the personality. It was forged into "the integrated and finished teaching" of Stalin on the socialist state. This brought about the stagnation of legal science. Questions of the completion of legislation in essence stood still. It was because of this that scholastic arguments and discussions having no practical significance were carried on by jurists. In legal science there existed an atmosphere of inertness and spiritual conservatism which encouraged time serving and a dread of concrete and broad sociological generalizations. Juridical science in general found itself in the shadows. Moreover, it often found itself the object of malevolent, ignorant "criticism." Suggestions of legal scholars were either ignored or rejected. At the head of the legal front was installed Vyshinsky, who, to please Stalin, created "theoretical conceptions" which justified arbitrariness and illegality. . . . [15]

The break which allowed such statements as this one to be made was, of course, the 20th Party Congress. A significant portion of Khrushchev's "secret speech" was devoted to criticism of the "brutal acts in violation of socialist legality" by the Stalinist regime. The congress produced the atmosphere which not only permitted discussion of breaches of socialist legality, but paved the way for many positive accomplishments on the legal front.[16] This is not to say that the post-Stalin period has amounted to an uninterrupted era of continued liberalization and progress. As has been the case in other spheres, law has been marked by alternating periods of progress and regression.[17] But in general, conditions since 1956 have been far more favorable than at any time during the Stalin period, and this has enhanced the research opportunities of the legal scholar.

Scholarship has particularly benefited from several more or less logical consequences of the relaxed atmosphere: the more secure personal position of the scholar, the greater availability of legal literature, and the renewed interest in codification. The tendency toward the elimination of terror after Stalin and the rehabilitation or release from incarceration of a number of formerly prominent jurists encouraged legal writers to begin directing their attention to important legal problems. Coincidentally, the wherewithal for more efficient research and writing was provided. Published judicial decisions, which in the later Stalinist years were very limited in circulation, became readily available again to scholars and to the public.[18] Some writers even called for the publication of all decisions of Soviet higher courts, but to date this has not been done.[19] Legal periodicals, which had also been distributed to a limited audience, resumed their wide circulation, and several new periodicals were started.[20]

The post-Stalin emphasis on law reform and codification created the need for legal experts to give workable form to the policies adopted. This role of juristic technician had been played by the lawyer to a limited extent in the Stalin period. But during that time almost no significant accomplishments in codification had taken place, and the state of Soviet legislation was "appallingly chaotic."[21] In this situation the need for jurists, who "hold a monopoly over the technique which alone is able to produce the advantages of orderly government,"[22] naturally increased. This alteration in circumstances provided the opportunity for lawyers to do more than simply offer expert advice, and they began to push for substantive and procedural changes on their own initiative. The main avenue for this activity was the public discussion prior to the adoption of new laws which took place in the press, in periodical literature, and at legal conferences. This participation, as limited as it has been, has shown the influence that the Soviet lawyer can have on policy-making.[23]

Thus the security and influence of the legal scholar have definitely been increased and his opportunities for serious research undoubtedly enhanced. Factors remain, however, which prevent him from being an autonomous social scientist and profoundly affect the character of social science research in law. Before we discuss contemporary legal research, these factors should be examined. For purposes of discussion, they will be taken up under the following headings: the impact of Marxism-Leninism on current legal scholarship, influences on the selection of research projects by legal scholars, and influences on the content of research and writing.

III

MARXISM-LENINISM AND LEGAL SCHOLARSHIP

Of the three subjects to be considered in this section, the first, the impact of Marxism-Leninism on current legal scholarship, can be dealt with most quickly. It is the view of the author that Marxism-Leninism is now largely considered by the average Soviet jurist to be a part of the ritualistic baggage that he must carry around with him, but that it must not be permitted to interfere in his serious research any more than is absolutely necessary. The comprehensiveness of the doctrine and the authoritative insistence that it be preserved inviolate and unprofaned (at least in theory) have practically guaranteed this development.[24]

While all Soviet jurists strongly affirm the theoretical centrality of dialectical materialism to current legal research, at least one of their number has acknowledged a different state of affairs in practice:

[T]he method of jurisprudence consists of an entire system of inter-related and mutually determined techniques and tools for cognition, including the materialist dialectic and many methods of research special to the field. It must be borne in mind that the dialectical method is not an "appendage" of some kind to the special techniques of research in the field, but organically permeates all the other techniques and methods applied by the given science. . . . In developing its methodology, Soviet jurisprudence did not pay sufficient attention to this aspect of the matter [the relationship between the materialistic dialectic and specific techniques of research], with the consequence that, not uncommonly, the special techniques of the field and the methods of study of law were mechanically detached from the dialectical method, and questions were posed that bore no relationship to the methodology of law whatever.[25]

Thus, while Soviet legal writers assiduously continue to seek, in Hollander's apt phrase, "secure ideological vindication of their work," [26] it is hard to attribute any concrete impact on the development of legal research to this practice.

If considerations of Marxism-Leninism can be looked upon as having little influence on the development of legal science, the same cannot be said of the more current authoritative statements and actions aimed at the legal community. What Raymond Bauer refers to as a "pragmatic approach to scientific truth" and a "highly instrumental attitude toward ideas" [27] requires that the regime attempt to influence both the research subjects which Soviet legal scholars work on and the content (particularly in certain areas) of the work they produce.

INFLUENCES ON THE SELECTION OF RESEARCH PROJECTS

At the highest level this influence is exercised through pronouncements by high party or political authorities. Such pronouncements are of two basic types. One is the statement concerning some specific legal matter or problem of law enforcement, such as the 1966 Central Committee action on increasing the struggle against hooligans. This is generally followed by some formal kind of governmental action, such as the adoption of a law on the subject or a Supreme Court decree.[28] Such an action does not have the immediate and direct effect on legal scholars that it has on workers in governmental organs, but the indirect effect, in the form of pressure to do research and writing on the problem pinpointed by the authorities, is unquestionable.

The second form of pronouncement is the generalized one about law as an academic discipline. These statements are less frequent than the first kind, but there is no doubting their greater and more permanent impact when they come. In recent years there have been two such statements, one in 1963 and the other in 1964. Because of their influence on the lines of research and writing in law, they merit detailed consideration. The first of these was an unsigned editorial in the theoretical party journal *Kommunist*, entitled "Jurisprudence under the Conditions of the Building of Communism," and the second was a Central Committee decree entitled "Concerning Measures for the Further Development of Legal Science and Improvement of Legal Education in the Country." [29]

Although the *Kommunist* editorial was not directly attributed to the party, there can be no doubt as to its authoritativeness. The editorial was occasioned by the June, 1963, meeting of the party Central Committee, which discussed ideological work and the role of the social sciences. The tone of the editorial was set in the early paragraphs, which made clear the highly practical, problem-solving aim the party has for legal scholarship: "[T]he principal task of jurisprudence is to develop, on the basis of a deep and systematic study of social processes, scientifically valid recommendations to aid in the improvement of the state and legal structure of Soviet society."

The editorial dealt with several matters of indirect importance for legal scholarship, such as the need for further popular understanding of Soviet law and the inefficient management practices of the legal publishing house (which was shortly thereafter reorganized). Also, there were the well-worn criticisms focusing on the legal scholar's lack of practical experience, aversion to hard data and statistics, inadequate criticism of bourgeois law, and weaknesses in criminological research. More important were the points made regarding new kinds of research recommended. Emphasis was placed on the scientific study of public administration and a more interdisciplinary research approach by Soviet lawyers (with special stress on greater use of economics). Official sanction was given for the use of so-called concrete sociological investigations in the field of law. Some such research had already been going on for a short time, but the purpose of its being mentioned in the editorial was clearly that of encouraging further development. The caveat was included that the use of this new type of research "is possible only on the basis of a Marxist-Leninist ideology." The practical lines such research was to follow were indicated by the conclusion that research results were not to "gather dust on the shelves," but to be "sent by the most direct route to the agencies engaged in drafting legislation and applying the norms of law."

Other subjects discussed in the editorial were the recent reorganizations of research institutes, the need for a higher degree of planning in legal research, and defects of legal training. The first two of these matters will be examined below. That this editorial discussed so many important matters in so authoritative a way is one sign of its significance. Another indicator, the response to it from the legal community, is harder to measure. Frequent references to it immediately began to make their appearance in the literature, and certainly many meetings of legal specialists were convened to discuss it. Even the research format of the theoretical journal *Sovetskoe gosudarstvo i pravo* seemed to change to accommodate it: a regular section entitled "Problems of Methodology in Soviet Legal Science" began to appear in 1964. Frequently issues also contained other groups of articles under headings such as "Sociology and Law," "Problems of Administration in the All-People's State," and "Economics and Law."

The impact of the *Kommunist* editorial was relatively short-term, however, as it was in effect superseded by the Central Committee decree of mid-1964. The conditions surrounding the issuance of the decree are unclear. It was not published, nor was the date of its issuance made known,[30] but writings on legal subjects began to make references to this "recently adopted decree" as early as August, 1964. The two most authoritative statements on the decree were articles in *Kommunist* and *Pravda*.[31] These sources will be used in the following discussion of the decree.

One of the interesting features of the decree is the degree to which it was similar to the *Kommunist* editorial of a year earlier. Many of the same points were made concerning the weaknesses of legal science: the gap between legal research and practical matters, the insufficient struggle against bourgeois legal ideology, the poor planning and coordination of research, the weaknesses in legal education and in criminological research. Several points stand out, however, distinguishing the decree from the earlier statement: (1) The decree gave increased attention to the weakness of research on state and law on the administration of economic matters. There was, of course, good reason for this increased attention, since the party was in the midst of a discussion about reorienting economic operations on the basis of new principles of management. (2) To bring legal science closer to life, some specific recommendations were made for increasing interaction between legal research and practical legal matters. The decree called for greater participation of scholars and legal institutes in the drafting of laws; more work experience in the state apparatus and judicial organs for law teachers and researchers; increased use of governmental lawyers in the discussion and carrying out of legal research by scholars; and greater cooperation between the organs of state and the legal research institutes in putting to practical use the research results and recommendations of the latter. (3) Concrete sociological investigations, as such, were not mentioned, but it was noted that there were serious shortcomings in methodology and that legal research was not marked by "creative searching, scientific daring, fresh original thoughts." Certainly this omission was not meant to curb the use of concrete sociological investigations. This approach continues to be widely used and discussed (although not as frequently, it would seem, as during 1964 or early 1965), and the lack of specific reference to it probably was an indication that the primary thrust of the decree was in the direction of pressing practical problems to be solved rather than the methods to be used. Undoubtedly many of the party criticisms of legal scholarship made at this time were sound. Research in law was not particularly advanced or exciting, nor was it providing solutions to the practical problems the authorities wanted solved. Much of the explanation for the lag in legal science, however, as everyone admitted after 1956, was due to excessive political interference. Now the political authorities were at it again, attempting to influence the development of legal research. Typically, the thrust of their message was aimed at the solution of their own relatively short-term problems, not at the development of legal science.

The signs of the impact of the decree were those one would expect: immediate and respectful references to it in the literature and the calling of meetings at legal research institutions for special discussions of the decree.[32] Beyond these superficial manifestations, the real influence of the decree is difficult to measure. It is clear, however, that an effort was made to exert influence on the type of research done by the scholar, and the following discussion takes up some of the specific ways in which this effort has been carried out.

Legal scholars, like other workers in the Soviet labor force, operate on the basis of plans which they are expected to fulfill. This also applies to the organizations for which they work. There are five-year plans of research, as well as yearly plans.[33] As part of this arrangement there is a certain amount of pressure on the scholar to pursue work on something which the higher authorities consider worthy. This pressure is transmitted both through the teaching and research institutes and by means of specialized legal publications.

A primary salient factor is simply the nature of the research institutions themselves. Leaving to the side the university-level law schools, there are three so-called leading scientific research institutions.[34] In 1963 a reorganization of the work of these institutes, which included some name changing and redistribution of research tasks, was carried out. As a short description of these changes will show, one of the main objectives was to give an even more pronounced emphasis to the study of practical problems than before.[35] The All-Union Institute of Criminalistics was reorganized into the All-Union Institute on the Causes and Prevention of Crime [36] under the jurisdiction of the U.S.S.R. Procuracy. At the same time, the sections associated with criminological research of the All-Union Institute of Legal Science and the Institute of State and Law were incorporated into the All-Union Institute on the Causes and Prevention of Crime, making it the main research organ on criminological problems. The All-Union Institute of Legal Sciences was transformed into the All-Union Research Institute on Soviet Legislation (under the jurisdiction of the Law Committee of the U.S.S.R. and the Council of Ministers) and became the main research organ for codification and the drafting of laws. The Institute of State and Law of the U.S.S.R. Academy of Sciences was thus left as the main organ of theoretical research, as well as of research on problems of civil law, labor law, constitutional law, administrative law, and several other branches of law. In 1964 another institute, the Research Institute of the Militia (police), was transformed into the All-Union Research Institute for the Preservation of Public Order (under the jurisdiction of the Ministry for the Preservation of Public Order of the U.S.S.R.) in order to bring about "the correct organization and carrying out of scientific research on problems of the correction and reeducation of lawbreakers." [37]

As for the legal publications, the fact that they are all run and controlled by governmental agencies makes it natural for them to seek to publish materials which will measure up to party aims. Moreover, the legal scholar seeking to have an article or book published knows that his chances will be better with an approved theme. But more positive efforts are exerted on and at this level to control the subject matter of published materials. The main publisher of lawbooks in the country is the publishing house Legal Literature, which was called the State Publishing House of Legal Literature—*Gosiurizdat*—until it was reorganized in 1964. One the main reasons for the reorganization was to achieve greater control over the kind of research published in book form in the U.S.S.R.[38] The legal periodicals give wide attention to all party and governmental pronouncements on law and attempt to publish materials related to problems raised by these pronouncements. They also seek to point out the relevance for legal science of party statements or meetings which have no direct or obvious connection with law [39]—a task which the editors sometimes must strain to accomplish. Another important matter is the general publishing orientation of legal periodicals. The main law journals (those of the U.S.S.R. and those of the R.S.F.S.R. which have national importance) all have characteristic orientations. The organs of the Supreme Courts of the U.S.S.R. and R.S.F.S.R.[40] are largely given over to publishing judicial decisions or Supreme Court decrees, with occasional articles by high judicial officials or professors. The practitioner, be he procurator, advocate, or judge, is the focus of attention of *Sotsialisticheskaia zakonnost'* (the journal of the U.S.S.R. Procuracy and the U.S.S.R. Supreme Court) and *Sovetskaia iustitsiia* (the journal of the R.S.F.S.R. Supreme Court and the Law Committee of the R.S.F.S.R. Council of Ministers). A new journal, *Problemy preduprezhdeniia prestupnosti*, also has a clearly pragmatic inclination. That leaves only the Institute of State and Law's *Sovetskoe gosudarstvo i pravo* and the U.S.S.R. Ministry of Higher and Intermediate Special Education's *Pravovedenie*. Both of these can be called theoretical journals, although there is constant pressure on the editors to publish articles dealing with important current problems.[41]

A related subject, which is also pertinent to the types of investigation conducted by scholars, is what the Soviets refer to as coordination of

legal research. Coordination is attempted at two stages, theme selection
and publication. Regarding theme selection, considerable concern has
been shown in recent years about overlapping and duplication in legal
research, that is, when a number of authors or more than one research
facility concentrate on a single legal issue. Both the 1963 *Kommunist* editorial and the 1964 Central Committee decree noted this problem, and
several jurists have discussed it at considerable length.[42]

In a country without a planning mentality, particularly in the area of
scholarly endeavors, the fact that a number of scholars or legal institutions were studying a problem like liability for automobile accidents, as
has been the case recently in the United States, would probably be
looked upon as a sign of widespread concern about a serious problem.
In the Soviet Union, however, this goes against the precepts of a planned
society and is considered wasteful.[43] Several steps have been taken so far
to improve coordination.[44] In 1962 the Section on Political Organization
of Society was established as a component part of the Research Council
of Laws of Development of Socialism and the Transition to Communism
of the U.S.S.R. Academy of Sciences. The section began creating commissions to coordinate research for the various branches of law, and by
1965 all of the branches were covered. The methods of coordination and
the powers of the coordinating bodies are still points of controversy
among jurists. Some favor giving the coordinators a virtual veto power
over research plans, while others propose that their powers be limited
to recommending. As matters now stand, the latter view still prevails in
practice. The coordinating organs collect and disperse information on
research taking place in the various institutions, make recommendations
as to the types of research that need most attention, attempt to eliminate
duplication and research on unimportant themes, and encourage collective as opposed to individual undertakings. Perhaps as a result of the fact
that the recommendations of the coordinating organs do not carry obligatory force, there has been a problem with institutions which do not
submit their research plans in time for effective action to be taken. This
may lend decisive weight to the arguments of those favoring "imperative
planning."

Coordination in the field of lawbook publishing constitutes, if anything, a more serious problem for the Soviets. Although the Legal Literature Publishing House is the main publisher of legal books, until 1963
more than two hundred other organizations in the country also had been
publishing legal materials.[45] What this meant in practice, to quote the
director of the Legal Literature Publishing House, E. M. Vorozheikin,
was that "manuscripts which had not been accepted for publication be-

cause of their low quality by one publisher were constantly being accepted in another publishing house." [46]

Just as serious, however, this lack of control resulted in considerable duplication of effort. To cite examples offered by Vorozheikin, in 1959 about eighty books and brochures on the participation of "the public" in governmental administration and in the works of the soviets were brought out by various publishers. In 1961 and 1962 there were forty titles aimed at acquainting the reader with the participation of the public in the struggle against crime. As a result of these practices, great numbers of unsellable books were piling up on warehouse and bookstore shelves. A large percentage of titles were failing to break even in sales. All of these factors contributed to the 1964 reorganization, which was aimed at achieving far greater centralization and control in lawbook publishing. In the reorganization the State Publishing House of Legal Literature was transformed into the specialized central publishing house Legal Literature under the jurisdiction of the State Committee on Publishing of the U.S.S.R. Council of Ministers. Under this new arrangement Legal Literature received preferential rights over all other publishers in the publication of books in most of the major areas of law. Republic-level publishers were to limit their lawbook publications to books about legal problems on the republic level, and local-level publishing houses to matters of a strictly local nature. Publishing by universities and other educational institutions was to embrace only technical teaching materials such as course syllabi and occasional individual lectures.

It is too early to tell how well this publishing reform has succeeded. For our purposes, however, it is enough to know that this level of coordination is being attempted. One might argue that the need for the reform was created by the success of the Soviet authorities in getting the legal writers to work on subjects the authorities were pushing. That is, the egregious examples of publishing saturation cited above surely must be attributed to the fact that political leaders had placed such great emphasis on the role of the *obshchestvennost'* (public) in the late 1950's and early 1960's.

In many areas of activity the Soviet system is characterized by a series of campaigns initiated by the political leadership and carried on at a high level of activity for a comparatively short period of time. Others have noted that this campaign mentality marks the legal sphere,[47] and, as has been shown above, it extends both to law enforcement and application and to legal scholarship. Those interested in succeeding in the system are careful to take note of these campaigns and do their part.[48]

As long as this process continues to have an effect on the legal sphere, the high level of coordination in publishing that the Soviets are moving toward will probably be necessary.

THE CONTENT OF RESEARCH AND WRITING

Without going into a full discussion of this matter, examination of a few points will make clear the considerable efforts made to observe and exercise influence over the content of scholarly endeavors.[49] The attempt to encourage more collective as opposed to individual research and writing has already been mentioned. Another important collective influence is, literally, the *kollektiv*, or peer group, to which the scholar is attached in a working relationship. All important research efforts (including books, articles, and dissertations) are reviewed and criticized by the kollektiv (the usual administrative unit is the *kafedra*, or sector), and a decision to recommend or not to recommend for publication is rendered.[50] Although these recommendations certainly carry strong force, authors are not obligated to follow them. Some proponents of increased coordination urge that the recommendations be made binding.[51]

The scholar's kollektiv, then, can help keep the content of research within the bounds of the permissible. Another device which aids in achieving this objective is the designation of what might be termed authoritatively settled issues. It is not always clear when issues fall into this category, and this is the reason scholars sometimes get into trouble. But except for borderline cases, it is generally possible to pick up the cues and signals which allow one to determine when an issue is still open to debate. Thus, there was no public debate on the extensions of the death penalty or the adoption of the parasite laws in the early 1960's. But other important issues have been opened up to long-standing discussion and controversy. Examples are the presumption of innocence in criminal procedure and the participation of defense counsel in preliminary investigation. Debate is usually cut off when an authoritative statement on a subject, often in the form of a new law, is issued. Thus the controversy in the late 1950's and early 1960's over whether there should be a body of "economic law" separate from civil law abruptly stopped when a new law answered this question in the negative.[52]

It is in the sphere of political issues (broadly defined) that the reins on the scholar's freedom of discussion will be drawn most tightly. In such areas the completeness of official proscriptions is likely to be irrational and to work in a way contrary to the objectives of the control. A good example is that of Vyshinsky. His association with the cult of personality has meant that everything connected with Vyshinsky, including the legal precepts he advocated, must be rejected. One who finds anything positive in the contributions of Vyshinsky is subjected to severe criticism.[53] A remarkable *Pravovedenie* editorial of several years ago noted and criticized this practice of "doubting the correctness of several basic principles of Soviet legal science only because they are found in the works of Vyshinsky in addition to the writings of other authors." [54] But this practice still continues. Yesterday's dogma is read out of existence, not just discarded, and the new dogma that replaces it brooks no criticism.

Another example is Soviet criticism of Western law and legal writers. Carrying on the "struggle against bourgeois ideology" is not, of course, limited to Soviet lawyers. Nor, in all probability, is the pressure to participate any stronger now than it has been in other stages of Soviet history, although it may be that it is more institutionalized.[55] Because it has been authoritatively declared that there can be no peaceful coexistence in the ideological sphere, positive conclusions concerning bourgeois law are not permissible. This puts a strain on the credibility of Soviet scholarly writing, no matter how elegantly it may be phrased. But so far the opportunity to depart from the extremity of this enforced position has not been accorded to Soviet jurists. This is well illustrated by the case of Professor M. D. Shargorodsky of the law faculty of Leningrad University.

At a conference on criminal law in Leningrad in May, 1963, Shargorodsky read a paper in which he committed "gross theoretical and political errors." [56] No very complete details of his paper have been published, but, among other things, it was said to have been marked by "a nihilistic attitude toward practice," and to have "propounded a theory contrary to the practical realization of Soviet legislation," "incorrectly defined the perspective of the liquidation of crime on the road to the construction of communism," and "overestimated the possibility of the use of the means of bourgeois science in the struggle with crime in our country." [57] Only the last of these points is at all specific, and in the context in which the criticisms of Shargorodsky are found,[58] it is clear that this is the main charge against him.

Shargorodsky was removed from membership on the editorial board of *Pravovedenie* and since the criticism his writings have not appeared in print, but as far as is known he has retained his teaching position. Apparently, because of Shargorodsky's excesses, the whole conference came under fire for violating established procedures. The criticisms which were made identify some devices for influencing and controlling scholars' statements. Among the necessary things to be done in planning such a conference are "to define precisely the circle of questions suitable for discussion" and "to plan a reasonable number of papers so that the participants have the time for deep and comprehensive discussion of them." At this conference there were so many papers that such discussion was impossible and Shargorodsky's "obviously incorrect propositions were not subjected to critical analysis." Moreover, no minutes or stenographic records were made, so that accurate *post hoc* criticisms could not be rendered. Further prerequisites for such conferences are several forms of prior clearance, which were also not observed. First, an organizational committee, which would be ultimately responsible for the conferences, was not named. Second, *tezisy,* or brief summaries of the main points of a paper, are supposed to be circulated beforehand and formally discussed by the author's kollektiv. For some papers tezisy simply weren't prepared, while for others they were "reviewed secretly without a suitable convening of specialists." One source suggested that Shargorodsky's paper, not just its tezis, should have been reviewed beforehand either by the learned council of the law faculty or by the kafedra of criminal law. In conclusion, then, the fact that "gross ideological and theoretical errors were committed in the course of the conference" was attributed in large measure to "organizational errors," that is, the breakdown in the exercise of the controls which normally operate at conferences of legal scholars.[59]

It should be made clear that much of what has been discussed in this section has been not the *actual* control over legal scholarship, but the devices by which the authorities *attempt* such control. Soviet scholars do not always follow plans assigned to them and they are sometimes adept at circumventing formal controls.[60] Enough has been said, however, to indicate that these efforts at control do have considerable impact, and that the researcher in the field of law must at least appear to accommodate himself to the ground rules.

It is also clear that in spite of all the talk of planning and coordination of legal research, what planning there is generally operates only on a short-term basis. Official impatience with studies having no immediate practical use plus officially inspired campaigns aimed at the most imminent problems add up to a bias against long-term planning. As a result, Soviet lawyers have not been particularly successful thus far in providing a body of research findings and recommendations which can be brought out and applied when practical tasks need to be solved. While the party pronouncements of 1963 and 1964 were in part aimed at long-term scientific considerations, this was overshadowed by the predominant emphasis on current problems. One must look to the statements of the lawyers themselves for a fuller awareness of more basic needs of legal scholarship. It is undoubtedly this awareness which explains in large part the emphasis on new research techniques which has come to the fore among Soviet lawyers in recent years.

IV

TRADITIONAL RESEARCH APPROACHES AND TECHNIQUES

Until recently Soviet lawyers have not devoted much attention to legal methodology. In 1963 a Soviet jurist was able to say that "our literature does not contain one monograph specially devoted to the methodology of Soviet jurisprudence." [61] This statement was made at the beginning of a period which has seen considerable concentration on methodology (including at least one book) and during which a number of new techniques have been applied or suggested for application. One of the elements of this new concentration on methodology has been the increasing dissatisfaction with traditional research methods expressed implicitly and explicitly both by Soviet jurists and in official statements. Before examining this criticism, we shall make a few comments about the main lines of the traditional research.

The Historical Approach. By means of the historical approach the scholar examines the development of a legal problem or aspect of the law through a given period of time. The purpose is not only description, but the better understanding of the law of the present day. Although the historical approach has been widely used by Soviet scholars, there are several problems with its use. First, the Soviets have sought to play down the importance of the influence of prerevolutionary law on the law of the Soviet period. While Soviet jurists have done a fair amount of work on law during the prerevolutionary years (particularly on periods other than that just prior to the Revolution), little attention has been given to the continuity between the prerevolutionary and post-revolutionary periods.[62]

The same thing is true to some extent of the 1920's. Although these years saw the creation of basic codes of law which are still in force or have been only recently replaced, the 1920's was also the time of the

NEP and the writings of a number of "bourgeois" jurists. Moreover, the unsettled nature of the official attitude toward other periods of Soviet history (the most obvious example is the difference in the treatment of the Stalin period before and after 1956) has probably made Soviet lawyers somewhat reluctant to examine even the Soviet period from a historical viewpoint. Nevertheless, some of this work continues to be done,[63] and particular emphasis is given to the historical approach at times of significant anniversaries of the Revolution.[64]

The Analytical Approach. This heading is used for convenience to bring together a group of methods or tools, often used in conjunction with one another, which have traditionally formed "the stuff of legal scholarship" [65] both in the West and in Russia and the Soviet Union. The basic mode of operation is "close verbal analysis of judicial decisions, statutes and similar materials" [66] in order to clarify the basic precepts of the legal system and to indicate the relationship between "law in books and law in action." This approach relies heavily on logic and analogy. Its reasoning tends to proceed deductively, which is to be expected (particularly in a system based on codes, rather than common law), since so much research of this kind examines the relation between a given law and a case or set of cases decided thereunder. Analytical legal research also is based on "the artificial reason of law," that is, the technical legal vocabulary and the system of legal distinctions which both Russia and the West inherited from Roman law.[67] Thus the analytical approach often separates laws into various divisions (contract law, torts, etc.) in order to illuminate the logical interrelationship within fields.

The research and writing produced in the U.S.S.R. by the use of these tools may be placed in several categories, which can be distinguished on the basis of purpose, approach, and style of analysis. One of the most important of these is so-called dogmatic analysis. This is a term which is rarely used by Soviet jurists today, although it was in wide use in the prerevolutionary and early Soviet periods. Dogmatic analysis involves the systematic and detailed exposition of the positive law on a given question or in a given branch of law. Dogmatic analysis normally takes one of two general forms: the treatise which makes a general but systematic examination of an area of law,[68] and the "commentary," or article-by-article exposition of a code of laws or other basic statute.[69]

Strictly speaking, dogmatic analysis should not include an evaluation of the rightness or effectiveness of a law, but should be limited to exposition.[70] This has led to some criticism of the method for being "superficial." [71] Still, dogmatic analysis is looked upon by some jurists as a useful and necessary undertaking. As *Pravovedenie* has put it, "The strengthening of socialist legality demands the ability to analyze the norm, to establish the will of the legislator, which means that dogmatic analysis (in the legal sense) in jurisprudence is unavoidable for the correct application of the law." [72]

Another category of analytical research, which involves the added dimension of isolating shortcomings in the law and recommending changes, may be referred to as "critical analysis." [73] As one might suspect, conditions in the Soviet system have created a certain ambivalence toward this approach. On the one hand, there is the instrumental attitude toward research which demands practical recommendations on legal problems. On the other hand, there is the "command" nature of control over the legal sphere, which means that certain developments will take place regardless of the informed expertise of the legal scholars. The latter tendency has had the effect of putting certain subjects at least temporarily beyond the sphere of critical analysis. Still, this is by far the most prevalent research approach used by Soviet scholars. Some critical analysis degenerates into review and criticism of one's colleagues' comments on the law rather than examination of the law itself, and this tends to be the least useful type of writing in this category.

Another designation for the category just discussed is "doctrinal interpretation." The term admittedly derives from the "bourgeois science of law." [74] As with the French *doctrine*, or the opinions of the text writers, some Soviet scholars attribute considerable influence on the development of the law to some of the better doctrinal interpretations.

As Pound has pointed out,[75] it is logical that legal research carried on by means of any approach should eventually move in the direction of comparison, because comparison increases analytical power. This generalization holds whether or not one sees the need for a formally designated subfield of "comparative law." While Soviet jurists have become increasingly interested in comparative legal analysis in recent years, they acknowledge the fact that little of a truly comparative nature has yet been done in the Soviet Union.[76] Most of their work on foreign law has involved the analysis of individual legal systems in developing countries, the "bourgeois" nations, or the people's democracies. However, serious research efforts in comparative law appear to be under way, and more writing in this area by Soviet jurists should begin to appear in the near future.

Although judicial decisions may be used in the types of analysis discussed above, they also form the subject matter for a separate kind of examination by legal scholars. In Soviet law a judicial decision does not carry the force of precedent. Generally, it is held that a body of pertinent judicial decisions (Soviet law uses the term *sudebnaia praktika*, judicial practice) is not formally considered a source of law.[77] The case law, therefore, is not as vital to the Soviet lawyer as it is to his American counterpart. But there are numerous examples in Soviet law of accepted legal principles which have developed through the accretion of similar judicial decisions,[78] and there is no doubt that those judicial decisions of the higher Soviet courts which are published are meant to serve a guidance function. Judicial practice, therefore, is an important source of data for the scholar. Articles on judicial practice in the problem areas of Soviet law appear from time to time in the periodicals, and collections of articles on judicial practice in several segments of a single branch of law, such as civil law, are also common.

The roots of the Soviet legal system are in the civil law system of continental Europe. One of the characteristics of major countries identified with that system (France and Germany) is selective rather than complete reporting of cases decided by the higher courts. As already mentioned, this is also the practice in the U.S.S.R. A further way in which the Soviet system operates basically like the French and German is that there is no designation of the judges participating in a case, and differences of opinions within the court, if any, are not indicated.[79] This, of course, makes the judicial decision in the Soviet Union a more limited source of research data than is the case in the United States. For one thing, one cannot assess the whole of the U.S.S.R. Supreme Court's work during a given term, as American scholars are wont to do with regard to the U. S. Supreme Court. Also, the anonymous character of the Soviet judicial decision prevents the use of both of the major types of case-law research which have become the common fare of lawyers, political scientists, and others in the United States: the traditional, basically impressionistic examination of majority and dissenting opinions and the more recent, highly systematic, and often mathematical studies of judicial behavior.

Until recently, the Soviet scholar who included an analysis of judicial decisions in his research pretty well established his claim to examining "life itself," as he is constantly urged to do. He was, after all, dealing with actual instances of law in action. It was pointed out in 1964, however, as a part of the recent emphasis on concrete sociological investigations, that to examine judicial decisions is really to look at the exceptional, rather than the typical, in the sense that most human actions in regard to legal regulations do not reach the stage of judicial consideration.[80] This is only one rather minor example of the increasing criticism in recent years of the traditional research and the results obtained by it.

Undoubtedly this criticism has been in large part inspired by the party pronouncements discussed above. But clearly the soundest and most pointed commentary on traditional legal research has come not from party spokesmen, but from the jurists themselves. Given the opportunity for more straightforward analysis of the successes of legal research, some lawyers have been able to combine criticism of the traditional approaches with the implication that the degree of political control has led to sterility in research output. Legal writers have acknowledged how relatively little they know about criminal punishment and how useful to policy making a systematic study of the effects of punishment would be. They have commented upon numerous examples of an absence of needed research findings during the recent period of code writing. They have discussed valuable pieces of "basic research" in law which have been criticized for allegedly not being directly applicable to concrete problems, but which later turned out to be of considerable practical significance.[81]

At times scholarly commentary has carried strongly implied criticism of Soviet officialdom for initiating ill-advised and unplanned campaigns in the legal sphere. A good example is the case of *otdacha na poruki*. This term designates the issuing by the courts of suspended sentences to those who have committed less serious crimes and entrusting them to their kollektiv rather than incarcerating them. Increased use of this device was strongly recommended at the 21st Party Congress in 1959. Shortly thereafter decrees were issued by the U.S.S.R. Supreme Court and the U.S.S.R. Procuracy ordering the wider use of suspended sentences.[82] The courts complied with these orders and in the following years the percentage of suspended sentences rose markedly.[83] As a reaction to a reported rise in the crime rate which was apparently attributed in part to the increased use of suspended sentences,[84] the latter were again deemphasized, and some writers even advocated abolishing their use completely.[85]

The party leaders who ordered this increase could not foresee its effects. But the result of this lack of foresight was to make the application of Soviet law more erratic, and the journal *Pravovedenie* took this as an example of a practice that needed to be corrected. The problem, an editorial stated, is with legal norms that "have not been sufficiently checked out in theory prior to their introduction but are checked out in practice, and which betray their practical unsoundness sometimes after a long period of time and are substituted for by the direct opposite tendency, even though this, too, has no theoretical basis but ensues from the disappointment with and practical unsoundness of the previous normative regulation." This, continued the editorial, "was the case with the tendency toward extensive practice of *otdacha na poruki* and the following tendency of a sharp limitation on the same *otdacha na poruki*.

Meanwhile, a preliminary, scientifically based study of the problem could, of course, have prevented this vacillation in practice." The solution, in this and other cases, the editorial concluded, was "the use of extensive sociological material in scientifically worked-out studies of the influence of legal norms." [86]

This particular piece of writing preceded by several months the inauguration of "concrete sociological investigations" in law. But it shows a readiness to accept the new approach when official sanction was received. And perhaps it indicates (and this speculation is all that the evidence allows at this point) that the scholars themselves had more to do with bringing about this new direction in legal research than has heretofore been suggested.[87]

CONCRETE SOCIOLOGICAL INVESTIGATIONS

The term "concrete sociological investigation" had been in use in the 1920's and was revived in the early 1960's. It appears to have been launched as an officially sanctioned research approach for the social sciences at a general meeting of the U.S.S.R. Academy of Sciences in 1962.[88] The expression quickly began to find currency in legal writings, and was, as indicated earlier, encouraged as a research approach in the 1963 *Kommunist* editorial on law. As a matter of fact, the official encouragement created a situation tantamount to the officially inspired campaigns discussed above, which have a natural influence on the modes of research and subjects chosen by scholars (one Soviet writer referred to a "rush to sociological methods of research" [89] by Soviet lawyers in recent years). One wonders whether, like some other campaigns, the emphasis on concrete sociological investigations will have a relatively short life. This is doubtful, given the considerable institutionalization which has already taken place through the establishment of "laboratories of concrete sociological investigation" within a number of university legal faculties and law institutes. In any case, the basically instrumental objective of this new approach is unquestioned. As one writer put it, concrete sociological investigation "is carried out with the aim of working out suggestions and recommendations for the practice of Communist construction." [90]

There appears to be some difference of opinion as to what the expression "concrete sociological investigation" implies. Apparently some Soviet jurists have looked upon the term as a rough equivalent of survey research or the use of questionnaires. But the majority of writers seem to reject this narrow conception, holding that, unlike bourgeois scholars, who carry out research by means of only one method at a time, the

Soviet approach is to apply a number of methods concurrently. Out of this type of reasoning has come another talismanic expression which is finding increasing currency among jurists interested in the new methodology. This expression is "complex research" (*kompleksnoe issledovanie*), which emphasizes an interdisciplinary research approach and a multifaceted assault on the problem under study. Complex research is often undertaken by means of a "scientific expedition" (*nauchnaia ekspeditsiia*) by a number of scholars to the research site, where data are gathered by such means as analysis of official documents and announcements, planning and accounting materials, correspondence, and statistics; "the method of observation"; and the use of interviews and questionnaires.[91] As one can see, with the exception of the use of survey research, and perhaps the emphasis on getting into the field, complex research relies largely upon the materials and methods that the legal scholar has traditionally used. Moreover, in the literature on complex research to date, little has been seen of an interdisciplinary approach, either in the methods used or in the professional orientations of the participating personnel.

Critical evaluation of the research techniques used in complex research is difficult, since published discussions of methodology are rare and references to methods used are quite guarded. This in itself leads one to suspect a certain casualness of approach, and this feeling is heightened by the degree of emphasis one finds on "combining theory and life" in the studies—in other words, on using the study as a means of correcting shortcomings in the object of study. This practice is well illustrated by the use in one study of "seminars" attended by the researchers and local government officials in the Kazakh Republic, in which the researchers told the officials how to improve governmental administration.[92]

In spite of the assertion that concrete sociological investigation implies the application of a number of methods, the best single effort published under that heading with which this author is acquainted is a study based strictly on questionnaire data.[93] The research was aimed at examining the time spent by local soviet deputies in the performance of their public duties. Nearly a thousand deputies from the Estonian Republic were queried to determine the effects of education, age, experience, occupation, sex, party affiliation, and other factors on the amount and efficiency of official work. The use of background data makes this research reminiscent of the "elite studies" recently popular in the West. Careful attention was given in the study to methodology, including a frank discussion of the weaknesses of the questionnaire and an explanation of the formulae used for significance tests in the computer processing of the data. In all of these respects this study stands out in comparison with both the complex studies and most of the other attempts at concrete sociological investigation so far reported. Another way in which this study favorably distinguishes itself from others is the reluctance to make premature conclusions and recommendations. Whereas some of the other studies mentioned definite and specific recommendations based on (as far as one could tell) a limited amount of factual data, the authors of this study limited themselves to turning over the computer data to the presidium of the Supreme Soviet of the Estonian Republic. Two other characteristics of this study may be pertinent. First is the fact that it was performed by personnel from the Estonian Republic rather than from Moscow or Leningrad. It may be that there is less pressure for concrete recommendations and therefore a greater opportunity for more scientifically based and methodologically sophisticated work in the provincial research centers than in the central ones.[94] Second, a genuine attempt at an interdisciplinary approach is indicated by the fact that the authors of this work are a historian, a computer specialist, and a lawyer. This kind of cooperation is still the exception, and in the other complex studies referred to above the research staffs were made up strictly of lawyers.

One way in which this study follows the mainstream, however, is in the research subject. By far the most popular single object of concrete sociological investigation thus far has been the local soviets. Among the other more frequent objects of analysis by lawyers using this method are: the Soviet worker, with particular attention to leisure time, problems of labor mobility, and labor discipline; overcoming religious vestiges; and criminological studies.[95] It is proper to ask why lawyers are concentrating on these problems. Other than criminology, which will be discussed separately below and which is considered a special preserve of the lawyer in the Soviet Union, these subjects would seem to belong more clearly within the realm of sociology or political science than law. As a matter of fact, very similar studies of religion and of the Soviet worker have already been carried out by Soviet sociologists and others.[96] Aside, again, from criminology, there is a marked absence of research on strictly legal or judicial subjects such as courts, judges, people's assessors, the procuracy, and the *advokatura*. Subjects such as these would seem to constitute proper subject matter for the Soviet legal scholar.[97]

The study of local soviets, which, from the American viewpoint, would be most logically performed by political scientists, falls to the lawyer because of the absence of a separately trained and distinct group of scholars known as political scientists. Interestingly, although there are no political scientists as such, there is a burgeoning field of political science in the Soviet Union, which is the subject of another of the essays in this volume. Because of the importance of lawyers in this growing discipline, a few words are in order concerning political science. Since its inception in 1960, the Soviet Association of Political (State) Sciences (which, incidentally, dropped the "State" from its name recently) has been dominated by lawyers. The Institute of State and Law has taken the lead in sponsoring and hosting activities of the association, and of the association's officers elected in 1965, the president, the general secretary, five of the six vice-presidents, and all twelve members of the executive committee are lawyers.[98] A controversy is under way as to whether there should be a distinctly separate scholarly discipline of political science, including provisions for training and awarding advanced degrees.[99] But whether this comes to pass or not, it seems clear that an increasing amount of political-science-type research will be done by persons with legal training, and that in this work great emphasis will be given to the newer methodology. This, in turn, ought to improve the methodological perspective of legal scholarship as a whole. In a sense, Soviet scholars are being pushed in this direction as a result of increased contacts with work in political science in foreign countries. Attendance at international political science meetings and acquaintance with the sophisticated work being done in some of the east European socialist countries has definitely influenced Soviet scholars.[100]

Bordering on political science and also within the ken of the Soviet legal scholar is public administration—"the science of administration" in the Soviet parlance. As with political science, the recent impact of international contacts on Soviet public administration has been significant.[101] In September, 1964, in line with the party's recent decree on legal work, *Sovetskoe gosudarstvo i pravo* began a series on "Problems of Administration in the All-People's State" and asked representatives of various branches of knowledge to contribute.[102] Research in this field took on even greater significance the next year in connection with the new system of planning and material incentives for enterprises outlined at the September, 1965, Central Committee plenum. There has been some talk about the science of administration being a "new social science."[103] Although it is doubtful that it will be accorded this separate status, the continuing significance of public administration, in the light of its potential for practical application, seems assured, and it appears that the science of administration may eclipse administrative law as a relevant area of study.

In terms of the work carried out under the name of administration, most of it has tended to be theoretical rather than applied or empirical.[104] Some attention has been devoted to defining and indicating the boundaries of the field, but significant consideration has also been given to methodology. The best of the theoretical discussions thus far have tended to follow several lines. First, there is a clear management science orientation, emphasizing a systematic, functional approach to administration, economic or governmental. Second, extensive use of cybernetics, both in administration itself and in the study of administration, is foreseen. At this point its *actual* use in studying administration has been limited, but researchers have explored its potentialities, particularly for studying communication within administrative systems, and have high hopes for its effective application.[105]

Another form of concrete sociological investigation which has been the subject of some discussion in legal writing is the so-called social experiment (*sotsialnyi eksperiment,* or simply *eksperiment*). Soviet authors are fond of saying that such experiments were used in the early years of Soviet power on the recommendation of Lenin,[106] and such statements constitute a key to the Soviet conception of a social experiment. Lenin used the term in the "try it and see if it works" sense. The examples cited from the Lenin period by present-day authors [107] are clearly of this variety and appear to pay scant attention to methodology or observational rigor.

As is the case in other forms of research, the real aim of the experiment is not knowledge in the abstract, but practical immediacy; the experiment "is a preliminary practical check of a valuable public policy measure to clarify its advisability and effectiveness and the possibility of wide applications in practice in the future." [108] An interesting and suggestive exercise in impressionistic comparison of Soviet and American legal research is trying to imagine a research undertaking such as the University of Chicago jury studies, which its authors refer to as "controlled legal experiments," [109] taking place in the Soviet milieu. The purpose of these studies admittedly "was not to evaluate [let alone recommend] but only to find out as carefully as we could how the jury actually performs." [110] Surely neither the research itself nor the product of research such as this would be acceptable in the Soviet setting. It is frequently noted by Soviet jurists that the people's assessor, the closest Soviet counterpart of the jury, is far from perfected as an institution, and one could without difficulty think of a number of enlightening experiments that might be performed on it. As mentioned earlier, however, the judicial system has so far been overlooked by the new legal methodology in favor of subjects of study which have been authoritatively declared more important. It is safe to say that the people's assessors will remain far down the list of research topics, at least for the present.

Soviet writers have said that the legal experiment actually has been used during recent years for legal research, but this does not yet appear to be the case. Cited as examples of "experiments" are trial-and-error types of governmental or party actions similar to those of the Lenin period. In these experiments there is no indication of participation by scholars in any stage of the proceedings, and no apparent attention is devoted to control or methodological rigor. In an otherwise sound theoretical article by a young Soviet scholar, a certain governmental action is identified by the author as a legal experiment. But he then as much as admits that this is not the case by saying: "However, strict scientific controls in the course of the experiment and an effective, systematic accounting of its results would be necessary. Also special persons should be chosen who will be responsible for carrying out the experiment and so forth." [111] This author and others have written very clearly about the scientific requirements of a real experiment in law: that it must be limited in time, space, and the circle of subjects to whom it applies; that it should test a precisely stated hypothesis; that in general it should be methodologically sound and responsibly controlled. At the same time, however, these writers seem to feel compelled to indicate that Soviet law has already had considerable experience in this area and that it does not lag behind bourgeois or east European social science in this respect. It is clear, however, that the actual application of experimental technique in law lies largely in the future.[112]

COMPUTER APPLICATIONS IN LEGAL RESEARCH *

As already indicated, the writing on concrete sociological investigations often includes a discussion of the use of computers for processing research results. There is also a substantial and growing body of literature the central theme of which is computer applications in law. Thus far this literature has tended to concentrate on discussing the potential contributions of the computer to legal science and law enforcement, but some actual studies based on computer applications are also beginning to appear.[113] It is clear that the application of cybernetics is regarded as a new frontier of legal research, and appropriate research facilities have been developing quickly. The Cybernetics and Law Section of the Learned Council on Cybernetics of the U.S.S.R. Academy of Sciences, which was created in 1959, was reorganized in 1964 and now attempts to coordinate the activities of the various centers engaged in pertinent research. These include, in addition to the leading law institutes, a number of university law faculties and union-republic research organs.[114] No

---

* The intention of this section is not to deal with technical matters connected with the use of computers in legal work, but to describe briefly the kinds of legal research being done with computers, and the possible future applications Soviet jurists see for computers.

doubt because of the technical nature of the research, there appears to be more cooperation between lawyers and other specialists, particularly computer experts and mathematicians, in this field than in other areas of the new legal methodology. This applies both to the determination of tasks which can be facilitated by using computers and to actual empirical studies based on computer processing of data.

Among the aspects of legal research considered by jurists writing on the subject to be most amenable to computer applications are the following: storage and retrieval of existing law as well as judicial practice, uses in police work for such tasks as handwriting analysis and the keeping of data on criminals, programmed instruction in law, and law drafting and codification. The last subject requires a further word of explanation. As mentioned earlier, one of the characteristics of the post-Stalin era in law has been public discussion of major legal documents prior to their adoption. This is a process ideally involving mass participation, and it is thought that computer organization and storage of recommendations made in the course of public discussion would considerably facilitate this process.[115]

STATISTICS AND CRIMINOLOGY *

The emphasis on the use of statistics in legal research far predates the rise of either concrete sociological investigations or computer applications. As mentioned early in this essay, excellent work on judicial statistics was done in the 1920's, and although most of this had ceased by the early 1930's, the need for reviving statistical work was recognized early in the post-Stalin period.

In the past decade the Soviet authorities have paid considerable attention to improving the system of reporting legal statistics, and judicial statistics has long been a regular part of the law school curriculum.[116] Still, Soviet scholars themselves assert that so far, work with judicial statistics has not been very satisfactory, and anyone acquainted with the field must agree. The reasons are to be found in the adequateness of statistical reporting and the availability of such data for scholarly use.

In spite of attempted improvements in the gathering and organization

---

* Normally in Soviet law and particularly in criminology, references to statistics have to do with descriptive statistics and the statistical reporting system rather than with inferential or probability statistics. The latter are more often discussed under the heading of mathematical methods or cybernetics, although lately the word "statistics" is beginning to be used in this context, too (compare, for instance, the use of the term in two conferences on statistics described in *Sotsialisticheskaia zakonnost'*, 1965, no. 6, p. 70, and 1966, no. 7, p. 89). In line with the more traditional Soviet usage, this section will discuss descriptive statistics.

of judicial statistics, many shortcomings remain.[117] For instance, although a single system of statistical reporting applies to all of the investigatory organs, the same system does not extend to the courts or the correctional institutions. It has been suggested that statistical reporting be unified for all organs connected with criminal administration, from the stage of investigation through imprisonment.[118] Statistics on cases reviewed by comrades' courts and by commissions for cases involving minors are not compiled, and this is seen as another shortcoming of the reporting system.[119] It is complained that those statistics that are collected do not get at the crucial issues or do not probe deeply enough.[120] A further problem is with indexes of statistical measurement. To give one example, for statistical purposes in the investigatory agencies a crime is considered solved when a formal charge is brought against a person. This, declares the eminent criminologist G. S. Ostroumov, creates a "race for a high percentage of solutions" which works "to the detriment of objectivity" and which sometimes "essentially violates legality." [121]

There are, then, several areas of needed improvement in statistical reporting, and the governmental organs look to the scholars for help on this problem. Ostroumov believes that it makes little sense to try to put judicial statistics to more sophisticated uses when there are shortcomings in the basic data. He states that the great amount of attention devoted recently to the application of cybernetics and mathematical statistics in criminology is "superfluous" at this stage, and that "something of a fetish" is being made of these methods. He deplores this because "it distracts the power of scientific workers from the really necessary research for practice and theory." Ostroumov sees some of the recent concrete sociological research as a waste of effort, since, he contends, it simply duplicates data already in existence through the routine collection of judicial statistics.[122] This brings up the second point mentioned above: the availability of such data to the scholar. It is safe to assume that the judicial statistics collected by governmental organs serve a useful internal purpose in governmental operations. For instance, by indicating the relative growth in certain types of crime, they probably play a part in determining the types of law-enforcement campaigns that will be initiated by the political and governmental leadership. But as data to be used by legal scholars and to be included in published studies, the situation is considerably different. Publication of judicial statistics has been severely restricted since the late 1920's, although the situation has improved somewhat in recent years. Ostroumov, who is certainly the most prolific Soviet writer on judicial statistics at present, published the third edition of his textbook, *Soviet Judicial Statistics*, in 1962.[123] Of the literally dozens of illustrative tables in this volume, not one utilized contemporary

Soviet judicial statistics. A kind of index of changes since that time is a more recent work by Ostroumov involving statistics.[124] In this article a considerable amount of statistical data is used. These data, all of which are expressed only in percentages, may be characterized as follows: Some are given with no indication as to source, pertinent time period, or geographical area to which the data apply; some figures are based on earlier published sources but omit designations of either time period or geographical area or both. Some of the most intriguing of the statistics come from what is identified as "selective observation" [125] (or, in some cases, a "complete survey") of the Black Earth Economic Region. Although a fairly large amount of data for this region is presented, none of it is identified as to time period, and there is no discussion of the methodology or any other aspect of the study.

In short, it not only takes a greater than usual leap of faith to accept such statistics as these, but the very incompleteness of the data presented makes the percentages of extremely limited usefulness to the reader. Still, this article raises some questions which Soviet criminological writings of a decade ago would not have dared to raise (concerning the personality of the criminal and factors involving the material status of criminals, such as housing conditions, etc.), and it shows a considerably greater use of statistical data than earlier. A number of writers are urging that this modest advance in the study and publication of judicial statistics by scholars be continued.[126] Given the strongly expressed desire of the Soviet authorities that legal researchers take part in solving important practical problems, it seems likely that this development will continue.

Although the importance of statistics in the legal field has not been limited to criminology, this field has always been the area of its greatest application. So far criminology has remained a subject studied only by lawyers. It has been designated as an area of research amenable to concrete sociological investigations, however, and with the recent emphasis on interdisciplinary study it may be that sociologists and specialists of other fields will begin to participate in criminological work.

Recently the question of whether criminology should be an autonomous subject or should continue to be basically a subfield within criminal law has been vigorously debated by Soviet jurists.[127] The proponents of autonomy argue that research on the causes of crime, crime prevention, and other basically sociological questions lie beyond the bounds of criminal law. The 1963 reformation of the so-called leading institutes discussed above might aid in the development of an autonomous discipline of criminology by grouping virtually all criminological study in the All-Union Institute on the Causes and Prevention of Crime. In any case, it does now appear that a separate field of criminology is beginning to emerge. For instance, a textbook on criminology published in 1966 is referred to as "the first Soviet textbook on criminology." [128]

This developing autonomy seems also to be related to the public acknowledgment of the inadequacy of the study of crime from the Stalin period to about 1960. Once Soviet lawyers could go beyond the outworn dogmas about the causes of crime being due to survivals of the past and nothing else, the door began to open for true sociological studies of the phenomenon of crime. As others have indicated, this development began somewhat before the recent emphasis on concrete sociological investigations in the social sciences.[129] Further impetus for the trend did come from this period,[130] however, and a new type of research emphasizing empirical examination of the personality of the criminal adds another dimension to criminological studies in the Soviet Union.

V

CONCLUSION

The picture of Soviet legal science which emerges from this essay is one that, one suspects, would be familiar to Western analysts of some of the other Soviet social sciences: the attempt at a high level of coordination and control of research by the authorities; a consequent research orientation best described as "practical empiricism" (in the words of Merton and Riecken),[131] designed to aid in the solution of practical problems; a relatively low level of respect for research having no direct and obvious connection with such problems; a dissatisfaction with traditional research methods; and an emphasis in recent years on new methodological approaches, primarily on the method designated as concrete sociological investigation. This method is only in the early stages of development in the legal sphere. Proposals for research and promising beginnings far outnumber completed studies. The extent to which the new methodology will contribute to making law an autonomous social science, or, alternatively, to the absorption of much of what is now considered legal research into the infant discipline of political science, remains to be seen.

Notes

1. Among recent Western writings which fail to include law among the social sciences are Bert Hoselitz, ed., *A Reader's Guide to the Social Sciences* (Glencoe, Ill.: Free Press, 1959); Mirra Komarovsky, ed., *Common Frontiers of the Social Sciences* (Glencoe, Ill.: Free Press, 1956); Leonard D. White, ed., *The State of the Social Sciences* (Chicago: University of Chicago Press, 1956); Edwin W. Patterson, *Jurisprudence* (Brooklyn: Foundation Press, 1953), p. 50. Maurice Duverger includes the "sociology of law" among the "special disciplines" of the social sciences (*An Introduction to the Social Sciences* [New York: Frederick A. Praeger, Inc., 1964], p. 21). Peter R. Lewis, in *The Literature of the Social Sciences* (London: Library Association, 1960), includes law in his consideration, although he notes (p. 142) that "the specialized language of the law, the enormous volume of its literature and the inaccessibility of the great law libraries to any but legal practitioners, have all given weight to the suspicion that it is a subject that stands apart from the social sciences . . ." Some Western writers, of course, simply assume that law occupies a place among the social sciences. See, for instance, Roscoe Pound, *Law Finding through Experience and Reason* (Athens: University of Georgia Press, 1960), especially p. 17.

2. An authoritative volume by the U.S.S.R. Academy of Sciences includes law among the social sciences: *Social Sciences in the USSR* (Paris and The Hague: Mouton & Co., 1965). An article published about the same time by a well-known Soviet social scientist does not include law: A. A. Zvorykin, "The Social Sciences in the USSR: Achievements and Trends," *International Social Science Journal*, 16 (1964): 588–602. A recent collection of readings on "methodological problems of the social sciences" implicitly includes law, but the book's lead article makes clear the ambiguous position of law: *Metodologicheskie voprosy obshchestvennykh nauk* (Moscow, 1966); see especially p. 4 and pp. 11–17. Many recent legal writings simply assume the link between law and the social sciences. See, for example, V. P. Kazimirchuk, *Pravo i metody ego izucheniia* (Moscow, 1965).

3. Or, in the Soviet case, "practical workers," meaning not only lawyers who represent private individuals, but employees of judicial and other governmental organs and legal advisors to enterprises.

4. See the comments of David Riesman, a lawyer by training and a sociologist by profession, on the differences between legal scholars and academic sociologists in the United States with regard to this matter: "Law and Sociology: Recruitment, Training and Colleagueship," in *Law and Sociology*, ed. William M. Evan (New York: Free Press, Macmillan Co., 1962), especially pp. 26–31.

5. For confirmation of this generalization with regard to Soviet sociology, see Alex Simirenko, ed., *Soviet Sociology* (Chicago: Quadrangle Books, Inc., 1965), pts. 4 and 5.

6. With regard to sociology, see Alex Inkeles, *What is Sociology?* (Englewood Cliffs, N.J.: Prentice-Hall, Inc., 1964), p. 117. A critique of Inkeles' point of view is made by Paul Hollander in Simirenko, ed., *Soviet Sociology*, pp. 307 and 313.

7. This is not, of course, to argue that Soviet science would not have made greater progress in a more congenial atmosphere. Nor is it to suggest that all

Western analysts underestimated the strength of Soviet science in the late 1940's and early 1950's. Still, the following characterization of the situation during that period by John Turkevich does seem sound: "A number of studies were published on the subject of Stalinism and freedom of scientific research. Some of our scientific and educational leaders concluded that a country that indulged in such an inquisition of science as in the Lysenko case could not have an effective science. The public readily accepted the verdict that all science was dead in the Soviet Union" ("Science," in *American Research on Russia*, ed. Harold H. Fisher [Bloomington: Indiana University Press, 1959], p. 106).

8. On codification, both during the 1920's and in recent years, see Harold J. Berman, *Justice in the USSR* (Cambridge, Mass.: Harvard University Press, 1963), pp. 34 and 74–77.

9. Merle Fainsod, *How Russia Is Ruled*, rev. ed. (Cambridge, Mass.: Harvard University Press, 1963), p. 429.

10. See Kazimierz Grzybowski, *Soviet Legal Institutions* (Ann Arbor: University of Michigan Press, 1962), pp. 53 and 205.

11. On this subject see the following sources: Vladimir Gsovski, *Soviet Civil Law* (Ann Arbor: University of Michigan Law School, 1948), 1: 169–75 and 195–99; John N. Hazard, "The Function of Law," *Survey*, no. 38 (October, 1961), pp. 74–75.

12. As cited in Zigurds L. Zile, *Ideas and Forces in Soviet Legal History* (Madison, Wis.: College Printing and Typing Co., 1967), p. 253.

13. See, for instance, "Certain Questions of the Scholarly Work of the Law Institutes," *Kultura i zhizn*, September 21, 1950, p. 3, as published in *Current Digest of the Soviet Press* (hereafter cited as *CDSP*), 2, no. 41 (November 25, 1950): p. 4.

14. Andrei Vyshinsky, *Voprosy teorii gosudarstva i prava*, 2nd ed. (Moscow, 1949), p. 406.

15. V. M. Chkhikvadze, "Problemy sovetskoi iuridicheskoi nauki v sovremennyi period kommunisticheskogo stroitelstva," *Sovetskoe gosudarstvo i pravo* (hereafter cited as *SGP*), 1964, no. 9, p. 5.

16. The progress of Soviet law reform in the post-Stalin period has been described by many writers. Probably the best single article is Harold J. Berman, "The Dilemma of Soviet Law Reform," *Harvard Law Review*, 76 (March, 1963): 929.

17. Western specialists have catalogued this ebb and flow. See, for instance, on the late 1950's, Leon Lipson, "The New Face of Socialist Legality," *Problems of Communism*, 7 (July-August, 1958): 22, and John Hazard, "Laws and Men in Soviet Society," *Foreign Affairs*, January, 1958, p. 267. Harold Berman has noted other signs of regression evident in the early 1960's; see above, n. 16.

18. See Berman, "Soviet Law Reform—Dateline Moscow 1957," *Yale Law Journal*, 66 (July, 1957): 1209; Berman, *Justice in the USSR*, pp. 235–36.

19. R. A. Rudenko, procurator general of the U.S.S.R., recommended in 1956 that all judicial decisions of the U.S.S.R. Supreme Court be published. He stated that the practice of selective publication meant that "the choice of published materials often has an accidental character and hence cannot serve as a reliable guide for the work of the judicial and procuratorial organs" ("Zadachi dalneishego ukrepleniia sotsialisticheskoi zakonnosti v svete reshenii XX s'ezda KPSS," *SGP*, 1956, no. 3, p. 20).

20. See L. I. Ratner, "Novye iuridicheskie zhurnaly v SSSR," *SGP*, 1958, no. 8, p. 133.

21. Berman, *Justice in Russia* (Cambridge, Mass.: Harvard University Press, 1950), p. 166.

22. Grzybowski, *Soviet Legal Institutions*, p. 178.

23. See Berman, "The Role of Soviet Jurists in the Struggle to Prevent a Return to Stalinist Terror," *Harvard Law School Bulletin*, 14 (December, 1962):

3; Donald D. Barry, "The Specialist in Soviet Policy-Making: The Adoption of a Law," *Soviet Studies*, 14 (October, 1964): 152.

24. On this point Maurice Duverger's discussion of Marxist contributions to social science is particularly pertinent. Duverger points out that Marx provided "the first general theory of the social sciences," but adds that the influence of "Marxist cosmogony" is "probably more fruitful for non-Marxists than for Marxists. The comprehensiveness of the doctrine has encouraged Marxists to use deductive reasoning rather than experimental research, thus developing a new scholasticism within a dogmatic framework: the disciples of one of the greatest among the founding fathers of social science have thus, paradoxically, returned to the primitive confusion between science and philosophy" (*Introduction to the Social Sciences*, pp. 19–20).

25. L. S. Iavich, "K voprosu o metodologii iuridicheskoi nauki," *SGP*, 1963, no. 5, p. 71, trans. in *Soviet Law and Government* (hereafter cited as *SLG*), 2, no. 2: 13 (page references to specific quotations or passages in writings which are listed both in their original source and in *SLG* will be to the latter).

26. In Simirenko, ed., *Soviet Sociology*, p. 312. Three eminent Soviet jurists have noted the limitations which may be imposed on creative legal research by hewing too closely to "a prepared formula of the dialectic." They are able to make such a statement by claiming that the use of such prepared formulae characterized the period of the cult of the personality and that "such an a priori approach to the study of legal phenomena has nothing in common with the true dialectic" (S. S. Alekseev, D. A. Kerimov, and P. E. Nedbailo, "Metodologicheskie problemy pravovedeniia," *Pravovedenie*, 1964, no. 4, p. 23).

27. Raymond Bauer, "The Bolshevik Attitude toward Science," in *Totalitarianism*, ed. Carl J. Friedrich (Cambridge, Mass.: Harvard University Press, 1954), p. 143.

28. Regarding hooliganism, the CPSU Central Committee, the presidium of the U.S.S.R. Supreme Soviet, and the U.S.S.R. Council of Ministers issued a joint statement on June 26, 1966. At the same time the presidium of the U.S.S.R. Supreme Soviet issued a decree "On Increasing the Responsibility for Hooliganism." The texts of these documents are published in *Biulleten' Verkhovnogo Suda SSSR*, 1966, no. 4, pp. 3–10, and are translated in *SLG*, 5, no. 2: 13–24. A month later the U.S.S.R. Supreme Court also issued a decree on increasing the struggle against hooliganism. This is published in *Biulleten' Verkhovnogo Suda SSSR*, 1966, no. 5, p. 13.

29. The editorial is "Iuridicheskaia nauka v usloviakh kommunisticheskogo stroitelstva" (hereafter cited as "Iuridicheskaia nauka"), *Kommunist*, 1963, no. 16, pp. 26–33; trans. in *SLG*, 2, no. 4: 3–12. Documentation of the Central Committee decree may be found below, n. 31.

20. No footnote references were given in discussions of the decree in the legal literature. Discussions of the decree dating from 1964 usually referred to it as having been "recently adopted." Later, the month was given as June, 1964, although no specific day has been indicated to date. A further indication that the decree's text was not widely circulated is that a report on a meeting of the law faculty of Moscow State University devoted to discussing the decree noted that "those present were familiarized with the contents of this decree" (see *Pravovedenie*, 1964, no. 4, p. 150). One possible reason for the ambiguity surrounding the decree was that no plenary meeting of the Central Committee had been held in June, 1964, or for several months before or after that time, which might lead one to speculate on the regularity of the circumstances of the adoption of the decree.

31. "Nasushchnye zadachi iuridicheskoi nauki" (hereafter cited as "Nasushchnye zadachi"), *Kommunist*, 1964, no. 12, pp. 70–74; "Iuridicheskuiu nauku na uroven' novykh zadach," *Pravda*, August 4, 1964, pp. 2–3. Other discussions of the decree are P. P. Gureev and V. V. Klochkov, "Za dalneishii pod'em sovetskogo pravovedeniia i ulushchenie iuridicheskogo obrazovaniia," *SGP*, 1964, no. 8, p. 3, and

"K novomu pode'mu iuridicheskoi nauki i iuridicheskogo obrazovaniia v SSSR," *Pravovedenie*, 1964, no. 4, p. 3.

32. For descriptions of such meetings, see *Pravovedenie*, 1964, no. 4, p. 150; 1965, no. 1, p. 188; 1965, no. 2, p. 197; 1965, no. 3, p. 3.

33. Among other sources which discuss these plans is V. F. Maslov, "Kharkhovskii Iuridicheskii Institut v borbe za osushchestvlenie postanovleniia TsK KPSS 'O merakh po dalneishemu razvitiiu iuridicheskoi nauki i ulushcheniiu iuridicheskogo obrazovaniia v strane,'" *Pravovedenie*, 1965, no. 3, pp. 3 ff., especially pp. 5–6.

34. "Nasushchnye zadachi," p. 73. A number of establishments on the union-republic level also carry on legal research. They will not be taken up as such in this article, although some of the legal research done at them will be referred to in Section IV.

35. As the *Kommunist* editorial of 1963 put it, the reorganization was aimed at "strengthening the connection between jurisprudence and practical life" and improving "the organization of scientific investigations in the field of Soviet law and legislation, and also on problems of combatting crime" ("Iuridicheskaia nauka," p. 10).

36. The Russian *kriminalistika* is often translated as "criminology," but this is misleading, since *kriminalistika* is roughly equivalent to what we would call "police science," that is, the technical methods of criminal investigation. The change in the name of this institute, then, clearly implies a broadening of the scope of the institute's work and an increased criminological orientation. Incidentally, the translation of the new name of the institute given in the text is an abbreviation. A more literal translation would be "The All-Union Institute for the Study of the Causes and the Working Out of the Means of Preventing Crime."

37. "Nasushchnye zadachi," p. 73.

38. A more detailed description of the reorganization will be made below in connection with the coordination of legal research.

39. See, for instance, "XXIII sezd KPSS i voprosy sovetskogo sotsialisticheskogo gosudarstva i prava," *SGP*, 1966, no. 5, p. 3; O. A. Kichatova, "Resheniia fevralskogo (1964) g.) plenuma TsK KPSS i nekotorye voprosy kolkhoznogo zakonodatelstva," *Pravovedenie*, 1964, no. 2, p. 3. The various juridical institutions often call special convocations for the discussion of these party statements or meetings.

40. *Biulleten' Verkhovnogo Suda SSSR* and *Biulleten' Verkhovnogo Suda RSFSR*.

41. The editors of *Pravovedenie*, in taking note recently of the completion of ten years of the journal's publication, declared that the present stage of Communist construction had created new tasks for legal science, and that in this connection *Pravovedenie* "must devote basic attention to the most important questions raised by the practice of Communist construction" ("Za dalneishee sovershenstvovanie nashei raboty," *Pravovedenie*, 1967, no. 1, p. 8).

42. See P. S. Romashkin, "Koordinatsiia issledovanii—Neobkhodimoe uslovie razvitiia sovetskoi iuridicheskoi nauki," *SGP*, 1963, no. 3, p. 3, trans. in *SLG*, 2, no. 1: 49; S. N. Bratus and I. S. Samoshchenko, "O nauchno-organizatsionnikh formakh sovershenstvovaniia sovetskogo zakonodatelstva," *SGP*, 1964, no. 4, p. 57, trans. in *SLG*, 3, no. 3: 26; Gureev and Klochkov, "Za dalneishii pod'em sovetskogo pravovedeniia," op. cit.; V. N. Kudriavtsev, "Effektivnaia koordinatsiia issledovanii—Vazhnoe uslovie nauchnoi raboty," *Pravovedenie*, 1965, no. 3, p. 12. Except as otherwise indicated, the following discussion is based on these sources.

43. Authors who have complained about duplication of research efforts on the subject of automobile accidents are Gureev and Klochkov, "Za dalneishii pod'em sovetskogo pravovedeniia," p. 10, and N. Zhogin, "Vrovenso vremenem," *Izvestiia*, January 22, 1964, p. 3; also "Nasushchnie zadachi," p. 71.

44. Seeking greater coordination in legal research is no small task, given the number and location of research facilities and the multiplicity of jurisdictions to which the various facilities are subordinate. In addition to the leading research

institutions already mentioned, there are 29 institutions of higher legal education (25 university law faculties and 4 legal institutions) and a section or division of law in each union-republic academy of sciences. All of these facilities carry on some kind of research program. See A. F. Shebanov, *Iuridicheskie vysshie uchebnye zavedeniia*, (Moscow, 1963), p. 103; Romashkin, "Koordinatsiia issledovanii," p. 51.

45. E. M. Vorozheikin, "Nasushchnye voprosy podgotovki i izdaniia iuridi-cheskikh knig," *SGP*, 1964, no. 3, p. 5. Except as otherwise indicated, the discussion of coordination in book publishing is based on this source. Another good source on this subject and on the subject of illegal payment of the authors' honoraria is "Raskoshelivaites' iz svoego karmana," *Izvestiia*, November 2, 1963, p. 4.

46. *Ibid.*, p. 4.

47. A discussion of such campaigns may be found in George Feifer, *Justice in Moscow* (New York: Simon & Schuster, 1964), pp. 246–52.

48. That this kind of pressure creates opportunism has been recognized. A *Pravovedenie* editorial of several years ago discussed "some legal scholars whose basic job involved the ability 'intuitively' to catch the tendencies holding sway 'at the top' on this or that question and to 'elucidate' the existing law in the same spirit." Although this passage attributes this practice to the time of the personality cult, the fact that the subject of the editorial is liquidating the consequences of the personality cult suggests that such practice is seen as still continuing ("Za polnuiu likvidatsiiu posledstvii kulta lichnosti v iuridicheskoi nauke," *Pravovedenie*, 1962, no. 3, p. 10).

49. The discussion will not touch on regular censorship activities carried on at the publishing houses.

50. Most articles in the journal *Pravovedenie* include the notation that they were recommended by the kafedra to which the author is attached. The "Form Rules for Manuscripts" submitted to *Pravovedenie* require such recommendations for legal scholars but not for practitioners. See "Pravila oformleniia rukopisei," *Pravovedenie*, 1966, no. 2, p. 168.

51. Kudriavtsev, "Effektivnaia koordinatsiia issledovanii, p. 17.

52. See a short discussion of and references to this controversy in Barry, "Specialist in Soviet Policy-Making," p. 160, n. 30.

53. See the selection of materials on this point translated in Zile, *Ideas and Forces*, pp. 309–11.

54. "Za polnuiu likvidatsiiu posledstvii kulta lichnosti v iuridicheskoi nauke," *Pravovedenie*, 1962, no. 3, p. 5.

55. Several of the journals carry fairly regular sections on criticism of Western law ("Za rubezhom" in *SGP* and *Sovetskaia iustitsiia*, "V mire burzhuaznoi iustitsii" in *Sotsialisticheskaia zakonnost*). A "Sector on Bourgeois State and Law" of the Institute of State and Law was created in 1963, "the aim of which is the comprehensive study of contemporary bourgeois state and law and the struggle with bourgeois and reformist ideology and anticommunism" (E. F. Leoniuk, "Ob osnovnykh napravleniakh kriticheskogo izucheniia sovremennogo imperialisticheskogo gosudarstva i prava i borby s vrazhdebnoi ideologie," *SGP*, 1963, no. 6, p. 136). In a statement of aims in the initial issue of *Pravovedenie*, the editors promised an "active struggle against all reactionary legal literature in the world" ("Nashi zadachi," *Pravovedenie*, 1957, no. 1, p. 17).

56. "Za vysokuiu partiinost v sovetskoi iuridicheskoi nauke," *SGP*, 1964, no. 1, p. 9.

57. "Iuridicheskuiu nauku—Na uroven trebovanii sovremennogo etapa kom-munisticheskogo stroitelstva," *Pravovedenie*, 1963, no. 4, p. 13.

58. Invariably the context was a discussion of the ideological struggle and the fact that in this struggle there can be no compromises. In addition to the sources already cited, see "Nauchno-prepodavatelskie kadri i vospitanie nauchnoi molodezhi v iuridicheskikh vuzakh SSSR," *Pravovedenie*, 1963, no. 3, p. 13. A source which

is more detailed in criticizing some of the other errors in Shargorodsky's paper is "Za vysokuiu ideinost, printsipalnost i deistvennost pravovoi nauki," *Sotsialisticheskaia zakonnost*, 1963, no. 11, p. 6.

59. The material for this summary paragraph, including the quotations, is from the sources cited above in nn. 56 and 57, at pp. 8–9 and 12–13 respectively.

60. This point is well expressed by D. A. Senior, "The Organization of Scientific Research," *Survey*, no. 52 (July, 1964), p. 147.

61. Iavich, "K voprosu o metodologii," p. 14.

62. That continuity is discussed in Berman, *Justice in the USSR*, pt. 2, "Russian Law." See particularly chap. 8, "The Russian Character of Soviet Law."

63. Among several recent notable books which take a largely historical approach is one by M. S. Strogovich on the concept of socialist legality: *Osnovnye voprosy sovetskoi sotsialisticheskoi zakonnosti* (Moscow, 1966).

64. See, for instance, *Sorok let sovetskogo prava 1917–1957*, 2 vols. (Leningrad, 1957); M. V. Kozhevnikov, *Istoriia sovetskogo suda* (Moscow, 1957). Leading up to the fiftieth anniversary of the Bolshevik Revolution, several legal periodicals featured sections containing historical studies. See, for instance, the series "To the Fiftieth Anniversary of the Soviet State" in various issues of *SGP* in 1967.

65. Ralph S. Brown, "Legal Research: The Resource Base and Traditional Approaches," *American Behavioral Scientist*, 7 (December, 1963): 6.

66. *Ibid.*

67. Berman, *Justice in the USSR*, p. 189.

68. For instance, N. Lazerevsky's classic prerevolutionary study of civil wrongs by governmental officers was identified by him as a "dogmatic study" (*Otvetstvennost za ubytki prichinennii dolzhnostnymi litsami (dogmaticheskoe issledovanie)* [St. Petersburg, 1905]).

69. Such commentaries have been extensively used throughout most of the Soviet period and have been especially numerous in the years following the adoption of basic codes of law. An example of this genre based on the R.S.F.S.R. Civil Code of 1964 is E. A. Fleishits, ed., *Nauchno-prakticheskii kommentarii k GK RSFSR* (Moscow, 1966). A slight variation on the commentary is the publication of the texts of basic laws together with pertinent court decisions, governmental decrees, etc., arranged by article. An example of this type of publication is *Grazhdanskii kodeks RSFSR—Grazhdanskii protsessualnyi kodeks RSFSR* (Moscow, 1965).

70. Gsovski quotes a Soviet jurist writing in the 1920's as terming this approach "an instrumentality without a face," or, as Gsovski puts it, "a mere device for systematization and explanation" (*Soviet Civil Law*, p. 194).

71. As the *Kommunist* article summarizing the 1964 Central Committee decree on law put it, "many jurists limit themselves to a dogmatic analysis of concepts, to superficial commentary" ("Nasushchnye zadachi," p. 71). In a discussion of one of the dogmatic commentaries on the 1964 Civil Code of the R.S.F.S.R. (Fleishits, ed., *Nauchno-prakticheskii kommentarii*), one Soviet critic complained that the commentary amounted only to a "simple reiteration of the basic articles of the code" ("Obsuzhdenie nauchno-prakticheskogo kommentariia k GK RSFSR," *Pravovedenie*, 1967, no. 1, p. 139).

72. "Za polnuiu likvidatsiiu posledstvii kulta lichnosti v iuridicheskoi nauke," *Pravovedenie*, 1962, no. 3, p. 12.

73. Roscoe Pound states that the mode of treatment of various approaches to the study of law may be "dogmatic" or "critical" (*Jurisprudence* [St. Paul, Minn.: West Publishing Company, 1959], 1: 23). Two of the four methods of research which the eminent prerevolutionary Russian jurist G. F. Shershenevich lists are the "dogmatic" and the "critical" method (*Uchebnik russkago grazhdanskago prava* [Moscow, 1912], pp. 10–15).

74. A. S. Pigolkin, *Tolkovanie normativnykh aktov v SSSR* (Moscow, 1962), p. 161.

75. Pound, *Jurisprudence*, p. 21.

76. Kazimirchuk in 1965 noted that "not one monographical study" of the comparative method had been written (*Pravo i metody*, p. 91).

77. *Iuridicheskii slovar*, 2nd ed., 2 vols. (Moscow, 1956), 1: 412.

78. See, for instance, Professor John Hazard's discussion of a "common law of divorce" in Soviet law: *The Soviet System of Government* (Chicago: University of Chicago Press, 1960), p. 136.

79. On France and Germany with respect to these matters, see Arthur Taylor Von Mehren, *The Civil Law System* (Englewood Cliffs, N. J.: Prentice-Hall, Inc., 1957), pp. 833 and 835.

80. Alekseev, Kerimov, and Nedbailo, "Metodologicheskie problemy pravovedeniia," *Pravovedenie*, 1964, no. 4, p. 26.

81. On these points see V. N. Kudriavtsev, "Iunskii plenum TsK KPSS i nekotorye voprosy nauchnoi organizatsii borby s prestupnostiu," *SGP*, 1963, no. 9, p. 15, trans. in *SLG*, 2, no. 4: 13. See also Alekseev, Kerimov, and Nedbailo, "Metodologicheskie problemy pravovedeniia."

82. See the texts of these decrees in *CDSP*, 11, no. 41: 14–16.

83. See A. F. Gorkin, "Zadachi sotsialisticheskogo pravosudiia v sovremennykh usloviakh," *SGP*, 1962, no. 8, p. 8, trans. in *SGL*, 1, no. 3: 3; see especially p. 5.

84. See "XXIIII sez'd KPSS i voprosy sovetskogo sotsialisticheskogo gosudarstva i prava," *SGP*, 1966, no. 5, p. 8.

85. See "Ob effektivnost' ugolovnogo nakazaniia," *Sotsialisticheskaia zakonnost*, 1965, no. 8, p. 6, trans. in *SLG*, 4, no. 3: 35.

86. "Za polnuiu likvidatsiiu posledstvii kulta lichnosti v iuridicheskoi nauke," *Pravovedenie*, 1962, no. 3, pp. 13–14.

87. Janos Toth appears to suggest that the advocacy of new research methods, particularly sociological and comparative methods, is being used by Soviet purists to strengthen the relative independence of law from Marxist ideology ("Comparative Law in Eastern Europe," *Journal of the International Commission of Jurists*, 6 [Winter, 1965]: 269–71). See the comment by two leading Soviet jurists on this point: V. M. Chkhikvadze and S. L. Zivs, "Novye tendentsii v iuridicheskoi sovetologii i nashi zadachi," *SGP*, 1967, no. 3, pp. 63–64.

88. See Kazimirchuk, *Pravo i metody*, p. 145, and sources cited therein.

89. O. I. Gatsikho, "O Planirovanii sotsialogicheskogo issledovaniia v prave," *Pravovedenie*, 1967, no. 2, p. 109. The word translated above as "rush" is *pribegat'*, which can connote "have resort to" as well as "come running." From the context it seems fairly clear that the author chose the word because of its double meaning.

90. Kazimirchuk, *Pravo i metody*, p. 125.

97. Most complex research designs also include the processing of data by computers. Among descriptions of studies based on complex research are: "Obshchestvennye problemy i iuridicheskaia nauka" (hereafter "Obshchestvennye problemy"), *SGP*, 1965, no. 7, p. 3; "O rezultatakh izucheniia gosudarstvennogo stroitelstva Estonskoi SSR," *SGP*, 1966, no. 9, p. 3; "O rezultatakh izucheniia gosudarstvennogo stroitelstva Tatarskoi ASSR," *SGP*, 1967, no. 5, p. 3; S. Zimanov, "Opyt vnedreniia metoda konkretno-sotsiologicheskogo issledovaniia v pravovuiu nauku," *SGP*, 1964, no. 12, p. 14, trans. in *SLG*, 4, no. 2: 42.

92. "Obshchestvennye problemy," p. 4.

93. I. Kalits, A. A. Laumets, and Kh. Kh. Shneider, "Izuchenie deiatelnost deputatov s pomoshchiu konkretno-sotsiologicheskogo metoda," *SGP*, 1965, no. 9, p. 65, trans. in *SLG*, 4, no. 3: 47.

94. On the basis of the concrete sociological investigations published so far, it is the author's opinion that the work done by scholars outside of Moscow and Leningrad constitutes, on the whole, the more important research contribution. In addition to the study discussed above, see G. A. Prudensky and I. V. Chernov, "O pravovykh aspektakh svobodnogo vremeni trudiashchikhsia v SSSR," *SGP*,

1964, no. 12, p. 3 (work carried out by the Institution of Economics and the Organization of Industrial Production of the Siberian Branch of the U.S.S.R. Academy of Sciences); V. A. Pertsik, "Puti sovershenstvovaniia deiatelnosti deputatov mestnykh sovetov," SGP, 1967, no. 7, p. 16 (work carried out at Irkutsk State University).

95. This listing is based on Kazimirchuk, Pravo i metody, p. 124. But the author considers it an accurate summarization of the subjects of sociological investigations reported thus far.

96. One of the studies of labor mobility by lawyers acknowledges that the research methodology is based on earlier studies by sociologists and others (E. M. Akopova, "Izuchenie prichin tekuchesti rabochei sily konkretno-sotsiologicheskim metodom," SGP, 1965, no. 7, p. 83).

97. With regard to the courts, this point is made by V. V. Lazerev, a Soviet graduate student in law, who advocates, among other things, a much more extensive system of statistical reporting of judicial work and polling of judges and other judicial workers, including the collection of personal background data. See "O roli konkretno-sotsiologicheskikh issledovanii organizatsii i deiatelnosti sovetskogo suda," Sovetskaia iustitsiia, 1966, no. 18, p. 10.

89. See G. S. Ostroumov, "Nauchnye osnovy politiki—v tsentre vnimaniia Sovetskoi Assotsiatsiia Politicheskikh (Gosudarstvovedcheskikh) Nauk," SGP, 1965. no. 7, p. 148.

99. See generally the discussion in ibid. Also F. Burlatsky, "Politika i nauka," Pravda, January 10, 1965, p. 4, trans. in SLG, 4, no. 1: 52. For the views of an eminent Soviet jurist who opposes a separate political science, see M. S. Strogovich, "Metodologicheskie voprosy iuridicheskoi nauki," Voprosy filosofii, 1965, no. 12, p. 3, trans. in SLG, 4, no. 4: 13.

100. See Ostroumov, "Nauchnye osnovy politiki"; Pomerantsev, "V. Sovetskoi Assotsiatsii Politicheskikh Nauk," SGP, 1966, no. 6, p. 135; Alekseev and Chirkin, "O sisteme nauk, izuchaiushchikh problemy politicheskoi organizatsii obshchestva, gosudarstva i prava," SGP, 1965, no. 5, p. 49.

101. See "XII mezhdunarodnyi kongress administrativnykh nauk," SGP, 1963, no. 1, p. 136; Ts. S. "XIII mezhdunarodnyi kongress po problemam administrativnykh nauk," SGP, 1965, no. 11, p. 146; see also the report on the meeting at the Institute of State and Law to discuss the work on public administration by the Polish scholar E. Starostsiak, "Obsuzhdenie problem nauki upravleniia," SGP, 1966, no. 1, p. 142.

102. See SGP, 1964, no. 9, p. 15.

103. Ts. A. Iampolskaia, "Nekotorye cherty metoda nauki upravleniia," Pravovedenie, 1966, no. 3, p. 3.

104. Some of the concrete sociological investigations have had at least peripheral significance for administration, of course.

105. This paragraph is based particularly on the following sources: Iampolskaia, "Nekotorye cherty metoda"; Iampolskaia, "K metodologii nauki upravleniia," SGP, 1965, no. 8, p. 12, trans. in SLG, 4, no. 3: 37; G. S. Iakovlev, "O metodakh, soderzhanii i strukture nauchnogo znaniia v oblasti upravleniia," SGP, 1965, no. 4, p. 91.

106. R. A. Safarov, "Sotsialnyi eksperiment i problemy gosudarstva i prava," SPG, 1964, no. 10, p. 15; V. I. Nikitinsky, "Znachenie eksperimenta v normotvorcheskoi deiatelnosti," SGP, 1967, no. 6, p. 26.

107. Among those cited by Safarov in "Sotsialnyi eksperiment" were the introduction of a few new administrative-territorial subdivisions and a decree allowing industrial workers to keep a part of the goods they produce to trade for agricultural products. From Safarov's description, the second of these seems not to satisfy the requirements of an experiment established by other writers (see, for instance, Nikitinsky, "Znachenie eksperimenta," p. 28) in not being limited in terms of the sphere of persons to whom it applies.

108. Safarov, "Sotsialnyi eksperiment," p. 14.

109. See Hans Zeisel, "Social Research on the Law," in *Law and Sociology*, ed. William M. Evan, p. 124.

110. Harry Kalven, Jr., and Hans Zeisel, *The American Jury* (Boston: Little, Brown & Co., 1966), p. 498.

111. Lazerev, "K voprosu o poniatii i predelakh eksperimenta v oblasti gosudarstva i prava," *Pravovedenie*, 1966, no. 1, p. 22.

112. The same can be said about the method of "modeling," which has been the subject of some discussion but little or no practical application in legal research so far. See the discussion in Kazimirchuk, *Pravo i metody*, chap. 5.

113. The best of several recent studies in this category known to the author is A. F. Deev, G. M. Galperin, and Iu. T. Ivanov, "Kibernetika i opyt resheniia nekotorykh pravovykh zadach," *SGP*, 1964, no. 10, p. 81. The first author is a mathematician, the other two are lawyers. This study examines the legal aspects of labor turnover. It does not concentrate on the use of real data, but rather spells out in detail the computer methodology.

114. See A. R. Shliakov and L. G. Edzhubov, "Sovremennoe sostoianie i nekotorye problemy ispolzovaniia kibernetiki v prave," *SGP*, 1965, no. 6, p. 83.

115. In addition to the sources already mentioned, the following are the writings mainly relied on in this section: D. A. Kerimov, "Kibernetika i pravo," *SGP*, 1962, no. 11, p. 98, trans. in *SLG*, 1, no. 4: 54; Kerimov, "Pravo i kibernetika," *SGP*, 1964, no. 9, p. 86; R. M. Lautsman, "Primenenie kompleksnogo kiberneticheskogo metoda pri issledovanii pocherka," *SGP*, 1964, no. 9, p. 95; V. E. Chugunov, "Ispolzovanie kiberneticheskikh i schetno-analiticheskikh mashin v konkretnosotsiologicheskikh issledovaniiakh," *SGP*, 1964, no. 11, p. 98; O. A. Gavrilov, "O vozmozhnosti ispolzovaniia metodov kibernetiki v normotvorcheskoi deiatelnosti," *SGP*, 1965, no. 10, p. 119; Kh. A. Randalu, "Organizatsiia pravovoi informatsionnoi sluzhby," *SGP*, 1967, no. 3, p. 124.

116. On both of these points see the author's "Soviet Legal Statistics," *Soviet Studies*, 14 (April, 1963): 433.

117. See *ibid.*, pp. 437-41. A more recent discussion of this problem is Ostroumov, "Statisticheskie metody v kriminologii," *SGP*, 1967, no. 7, p. 68.

118. Ostroumov, "Statisticheskie metody," p. 70.

119. V. N. Kudriavtsev, "Analiz plius tekhnika," *Izvestiia*, September 30, 1966, p. 3.

120. See "Ukrepliat sviazi iuridicheskoi nauki s praktikoi," *Sovetskaia iustitsiia*, 1965, no. 18, p. 2, and Lazerev, "O Roli . . ." pp. 10-11; this discussion has been limited to criminal statistics.

121. Ostroumov, "Statisticheskie metody," p. 74.

122. *Ibid.*, pp. 74-75.

123. See the discussion of this book in Barry, "Soviet Judicial Statistics." As indicated there, one new chapter not found in the first two editions did contain some contemporary statistics. In general they were of the nature and quality of those described in this essay in the text accompanying n. 124.

124. Ostroumov and V. E. Chugunov, "Izuchenie lichnosti prestupnika po materialam kriminologicheskikh issledovanii," *SGP*, 1965, no. 9, p. 93, trans. in *SLG*, 4, no. 3: 21.

125. The Russian term is *vyborochnoe nabliudenie*, which, in the translation in *SLG* (n. 124, above), is translated as "sampling survey."

126. In this way they have pointed to the restrictions placed on the publication of statistics by scholars. For example, Ostroumov has stated recently that "the existing rich statistical material is still little known, and at times it is simply not accessible to legal scholars. It is time to resolve the question of accessibility (within reasonable limits) to this material and its partial publication" ("Statisticheskie metody," p. 75). Two eminent Soviet jurists have indicated that it is necessary to "resolve the problem of the procedure to be followed in their [i.e., judicial statistics'] employment by scholarly institutions" (Bratus and Samoshchenko, "O

nauchno-organizatsionnykh," p. 32). Two other scholars have argued forcefully that "legal science must have the chance to use the data of judicial statistics. Judicial statistics should be at last accessible, verifiable and, what is most important, open. In this they should be distinguished in no way from other kinds of statistics." These writers recommend the publication of a "Monthly of Judicial Statistics." (See A. S. Pashkov and D. M. Chechot, "Effektivnost pravovogo regulirovaniia i metody ee vyavleniia," *SGP*, 1965, no. 1, p. 8.)

127. See the description of the views of various Soviet jurists on the subject of an autonomous criminology in V. A. Sergievsky, "O sovetskoi kriminologii," *Pravovedenie*, 1963, no. 2, p. 94.

128. See a review of this book: P. P. Mikhailenko and I. A. Gelfand, "Pervyi uchebnik po sovetskoi kriminologii," *SGP*, 1967, no. 6, p. 149.

129. See R. Beerman, "Study of the Soviet Criminal," *Soviet Studies*, 14 (July, 1962): 85.

130. In this regard *Pravovedenie's* editorial on the 1964 party decree on law is enlightening: "In the analysis of the causes of crime the science of criminal law until recently has not gone further than the general sociological judgments about the influence of capitalist survivals and the bourgeois world juxtaposed on the socialist system. Of themselves these propositions cannot be doubted in their corrections. But they are far from satisfactory for explaining such phenomena as a drop in crime in one place and its growth in another, the almost complete elimination of crime of some kinds and the relatively great incidence of crime of other kinds, the episodic 'waves' or, on the contrary, the disappearance of some forms of crime, etc." The editorial then goes on to suggest other possible causes of crime, including shortcomings in education and training, bureaucracy and red tape, and others. ("K novomu pod'emu iuridicheskoi nauki i iuridicheskogo obrazovaniia v SSSR," 1964, no. 4, p. 7.)

131. Robert K. Merton and Henry W. Riecken, "Notes on Sociology in the U.S.S.R.," in *Current Problems in Social-Behavioral Research*, Symposia Studies Series No. 10 (Washington, D.C.: National Institute of Social and Behavioral Science, March, 1962), p. 10.

V : Historiography

Current Soviet Theory of History: New Trends or Old?

Arthur P. Mendel

Over the past few years, Soviet historians and philosophers have been carrying on a curious discussion about the nature and methods of historical inquiry. It is too early to say with any confidence what the outcome will be. Taken by itself or set in the context of the "thaw," the discussion encourages cautious optimism. Still, historical publications look much the same as they did in Joseph Stalin's time, and many of the concepts and arguments I will be reviewing seem more like further developments of revisions in historical theory introduced under Stalin in the 1930's than reactions against them. It is also reasonable, although not necessarily correct, to claim party-political interests behind everything written in this field. But, however interpreted, the current discussion is remarkably fresh and interesting compared with customary Soviet publications on historical theory, the sacred domain, after all, of the *istmatchiky*, the historical materialists.

To judge from official party pronouncements, the aims and methods of Soviet history remain what they were under Stalin. "A historian is

This is a revised version of a paper that appeared in the *American Historical Review*, vol. 72, no. 1 (October, 1966).

not a dispassionate reporter who identifies facts or even places them in a scientifically valid pattern," declared Central Committee Secretary and Academician B. N. Ponomarev in his opening address to the all-union conference of historians in December, 1962. "He is a fighter who sees his goal in placing the history of the past at the service of the struggle for communism," and whose purpose it is to promote "a firm conviction of the inevitability of the triumph of communism." Similarly, we learn from a party Central Committee decree of October, 1959, that secondary-school history courses should develop in students "a scholarly understanding of the laws of development of society, implant in them the conviction that the doom of capitalism and the victory of communism are inevitable. . . ." Since this is the task to be met by historians, the "obsolete, sterile problems and overly narrow, insufficiently topical, private, and incidental themes, which here and there still divert historians from the treatment of the pressing problems of historiography, must be resolutely swept aside." [1]

The dominant character and central concerns of the official declarations are represented by the above quotations, and only rarely does one encounter a hint of less doctrinaire judgments. In the current discussion on historical theory and methods by the historians themselves the proportion is reversed: the prevailing tone, the specific topics, and the quality of thought and argument are, relative to the official statements, refreshingly undoctrinaire; only occasionally do we find ourselves back in the dark age, usually at the beginning or end of an analysis or when some protection is required to cover too flagrantly "bourgeois" ideas.

Consider, for example, one of several less doctrinaire points made in Ponomarev's speech. As part of the general anti-Stalin campaign that was given an added thrust at the 22nd Party Congress in 1961, the party has continued to attack Stalin's "arbitrary," "subjective" distortions of history and has encouraged a limited return to the archives. Ponomarev, accordingly, decried the time when "as a rule, material in the archives was employed only to illustrate commonly known propositions," and when "respect for facts, without which history as a science is unthinkable, was lost." Also, at the close of his speech, he quoted Lenin's exhortation to scholars "to take not individual facts, but the *entire totality* of the facts bearing upon the problem under consideration, *without a single exception.* . . ." [2] These admirably liberal comments stand out in glaring contrast to the rest of Ponomarev's speech. When they appear in the recent publications on historical theory, however, the contrast, while still there, is far less extreme.

First of all, the historians have naturally welcomed with enthusiasm the opportunity to attack Stalinist repression and intellectual corruption.

At a conference on historical method arranged by the U.S.S.R. Academy of Sciences in early 1964, for example, participants repeatedly denounced Stalinist historiography for its "arbitrary attitude toward the facts." Under Stalin "the most fundamental norms of scientific ethics were violated," one historian recalled, going on to remind the conference that "the value, the authority of historical investigation lies in its objectivity, in the truthfulness of the description of events and phenomena." History teachers were similarly criticized for confining their lectures within the "framework of a special set of ideas, quotations and propositions" and were urged to expose students to "doubts and unsolved problems" and to "the controversial ideas that promote independent thought." [3]

This concern for more scholarly objectivity (or perhaps only for works that appear to be more objective) is reflected in a number of recent tendencies familiar to students of Russian history, particularly the campaign against doctrinaire "quotism," that is, "proving" arguments by quotations from Marxist classics, and the related insistence on the careful study of primary sources. Both tendencies have received considerable attention in the West and need not concern us here, other than to mention that they continue to be prominent.[4] Another less familiar but perhaps more important expression of what seems to be a growing respect for scholarly objectivity is the current treatment of opposing views. Those who have not read recent Soviet reviews of Western thought, even anti-Marxist "idealistic" historical theory, would be surprised at both the completeness and the fairness of summaries and excerpts.[5]

Next to this apparently enhanced regard for professional integrity,[6] the most persistent theme in the current discussion is the "respect for facts," the criticism of historians who use facts "only to illustrate commonly known propositions." Both quotations, it will be recalled, are from Ponomarev's official party declaration. In making these statements, however, he was careful to associate them specifically with the attack against Stalin's abuses, and he avoided any inference that might undermine the "laws" and "commonly known propositions," which, as we have seen, are still the *sine qua non* of the ideologists. In the analyses by the historians themselves, on the contrary, inferences drawn from the admonition to "respect the facts" are having precisely this effect.

A. V. Gulyga, of the Institute of Philosophy, touched the essential point when he maintained at the 1964 conference that "the fact in historical science is not supplanted by the generalization; it is an end in itself [*samodovleiushchaia tsenost*]." [7] In a field such as history, he wrote elsewhere, "which, along with generalization, also aims at description, factual material plays a special role, one that is different from that

played in purely theoretical disciplines. The latter use factual data only
to support generalizations. . . . For the historian," he continued, "the
fact is not only material for generalization, not simply an example illustrating the action of a general law which can be left out or replaced by
others." [8] The director of the Institute of History, Academician V. M.
Khvostov, referred approvingly to Gulyga's statement about facts being
ends in themselves in order to justify the historians' right to study facts
simply for the sake of "enriching our factual knowledge." [9] The subjects
historians study might seem petty and unrelated to specific problems,
B. F. Porshnev, also of the Institute of History, added, but such themes
are similar to the "preparatory experiments" in natural science necessary
before more general studies are undertaken.[10] The main point, restated
endlessly, is that the familiar, sweeping Marxist generalizations will no
longer do: "History is concreteness at its maximum." [11] A lead article in
Voprosy istorii on the treatment of historical subjects by Karl Marx and
Friedrich Engels referred to their concern with specific, concrete facts,
and praised this attitude as "the categorical imperative of scientific
ethics" and "the methodological requirement for scientific knowledge of
the historical process." [12] The current attitude toward Pokrovsky is
relevant here also. Although rehabilitated with praise and honors, he
continues to be criticized for his "naked" or "abstract" "sociologizing,"
and the dominant role he played in the twenties and early thirties is attributed to "the inadequate scientific preparation" of young historians at
the time.[13]

The most explicit and elaborate example that I have found illustrating
this attempt to liberate the study of concrete historical facts from sub-
mission to Marxist laws and generalizations is contained in a prominently
placed article by A. Ia. Gurevich, one of the most thoughtful contributors to the discussions. The general laws of historical materialism regarding the transition from one social system, or "formation," to another
are true, Gurevich readily acknowledged, but they are simply not immediately relevant to the historian's inquiry.

Most often, a scholar is necessarily concerned with a geographically
limited and relatively brief phase of the historical process during which
a general law may be only partly expressed by merely a few of its aspects
or even a single one or it may not appear at all. . . . Does the scholar
search his empirical data only for manifestations of the general law discussed
above [that of transition from one system to another]? It is obvious that
History requires concrete explanations of occurrences, and mere references
to sociological laws do not solve the problem.

As a specific example, Gurevich discussed the historical materialist
interpretation of the fall of the Roman Empire. After summarizing the

familiar Marxist picture of socioeconomic development, class struggle, and revolution, he went on to write: "It is well known that for a long time this was how Soviet historiography explained the fall of the Roman Empire. However, this kind of approach failed every time one took into account concrete facts and processes of history." Above all, Gurevich insisted, the historian must regard categories of historical materialism simply as epistemological guides to research and not a priori, ontological descriptions of reality, which they are for philosophers. He rejected, furthermore, the "proposition long dominant in our intellectual life that there are no other laws of history besides the laws of historical material-ism, interpreted and edited, moreover, subjectively." On the contrary, he argued, there is a great variety of causal patterns (which he considers synonymous with laws) besides those associated with production, the focus of historical materialism. Whatever the general sociological law might say about the economic base of historical developments, "the con-crete historical actions of people depend on the most diverse causes, among which, besides production, one must find a place for natural en-vironment, national characteristics, psychology, ideology, external influ-ences, all sorts of traditions, the level of cultural development, biological and demographic factors, and many others." As to the problem of de-ciding which are the most important: "It is hardly possible to establish a scale of factors a priori, to determine degrees of significance apart from a concrete empirical analysis of the interrelationships of these factors in a particular period and particular country." The historian must also realize, he noted, that different factors play dominant roles at dif-ferent times.

Concerning the question of "accidents" and unpredictable, alternative paths of historical development, Gurevich was particularly frank. After indignantly denouncing attempts to portray Marxism as a "materialistic interpretation of Biblical eschatology," a secularized faith in "providen-tial history," he analyzed at length the category of "possibility" in his-tory. There is nothing at all predetermined in history, he insisted, and simply because something actually happened does not mean that nothing else could have happened. For example, neither Hitler's rise to power nor World War II was inevitable, and merely because the "basic conditions" for revolution were present did not mean that revolution must occur. Without specific reference to Engels, Gurevich criticized his contention that "historical law cuts a way for itself through the chaos of accidents." As with the general law on transitions, Gurevich considered this theory correct, "but only on the level of sociology!" Such "macrolaws" are not the immediate concern of historians, who study specific events and for whom "the possible varieties of historical process are extremely diverse and pregnant with the most serious consequences for its later development." [14]

Every historical event is the result of a convergence of many contributing conditions. A different convergence might result in a different event, which, influenced by all the remaining factors, would in turn lead to consequences different from those that in fact occurred, and thus there would begin an entire chain of events and phenomena—a different variant of development. . . . The historian who regards the historical process as something ineluctable, and begins with the conviction that what in fact occurred was the only possible result of all that came before, incorrectly ignores other, unrealized possibilities, does not study different and perhaps mutually contradictory tendencies of development.[15]

Thus, once interest focuses on specific facts, their individual attributes and kaleidoscopic conjunctions cannot so easily be encompassed by general laws. Reality becomes complex and elusive. And, indeed, the words "complex" and "diverse" appear as frequently in recent Soviet historiography as do "concrete" and "specific," and usually in association with them. The good Marxist historian presents history "in all its immense diversity," while the bourgeois scholar is accused of squeezing complex reality into narrow schemata. Even the great social transformations that used to unfold, at least in theory, so neatly and orderly are now set in a context of "the most variegated assortment of different economic systems, social systems, unprecedented diversity of traditions, customs, and living conditions." Consequently, the author of this statement continued, a major task facing Soviet historians is "the reconsideration of the theory of knowledge and the problems of its application in analyzing the particularly complex and variable phenomena of social life." [16] The following statement by Gulyga represents an adequate summary of this part of the current discussions:

[The historians'] task is to re-create historical reality through a unity of necessity and contingency, to reconstruct the course that humanity has actually traversed, with all its zigzags, all the diversity and unique individuality of the events that have occurred. A pattern of the historical process is not yet history, just as the subject and the concept do not yet make a work of art. Each historical event possesses individual attributes characteristic of it alone, and to disclose these and preserve them for posterity is just as much the responsibility of the historian as is the generalization of materials studied by him.[17]

Is this what Ponomarev had in mind when he talked about "respect for facts"? It would seem to be one thing to use this line as part of the campaign against Stalin, but quite another to use it as part of an argument that is increasingly separating historical research from the Marxist laws and predictions that have from the beginning provided the principal source of legitimacy for party rule.

The sad state of *zakonomernost,* the term used to denote historical and social "laws," is a revealing indication of the demise of rigorous determinism. It would be worth a separate study to show the different ways the term is used, since each new usage increases the ambiguity and undermines the essential purpose of the concept, which is, to recall Ponomarev's injunction, to inspire "a firm conviction of the inevitability of the triumph of communism." It is now used to refer to constants persisting through history, to typical or repeated social relations, or to the core attribute of a society reflected in its various facets. Most often, "laws" are mentioned briefly as the "essence" "hidden" somewhere within the complex fabric of events, then dismissed as the historian turns to the serious business of working with the factual events themselves. Perhaps its most general usage is as a synonym for a causal relation of any kind, permitting the statement, for example, that realism in art is the "lawful [*zakonomernii*] result of an artistic comprehension of life." In fact, there seems now to be little that distinguishes the term from its common meaning of reasonable or intelligible, as in the phrases "We consider this completely reasonable [*zakonomerno*] for the progress of social science," or "It is entirely reasonable [*zakonomerno*] to put the question: What is historical methodology?" In short, we have come a long way from the time when Plekhanov proclaimed euphorically that history à la Marx was "going to its logical conclusion with the ineluctable character of astronomical phenomena."

At several places in Ponomarev's speech he also commented on another theme that has become a leitmotiv for the methodologists: the historians' return to "the richness of colors and gradations that one finds in real life." He urged historians to show more concern for style, and he warmly recommended "prerevolutionary Russian" and foreign historical works as "first-class models." [18] In his response to the principal paper delivered at the 1964 conference, the editor of *Voprosy istorii,* V. G. Trukhanovsy, echoed these views when he said that he was "most pleased by the appeal of the speakers to historians to write living history, with flesh and blood, emotions and passions." Explicitly associating the "living" quality of history as it should be written with the emphasis on the "concrete facts," Iu. S. Borisov asserted that "authentic historical scholarship excludes stilted schematism and illustrationism: it is always factual in the best sense of the word, because it reconstructs the past in all its full-bodied, many-colored, living clarity." [19]

L. V. Cherepnin, long a leading Soviet medievalist, used an article on

N. V. Gogol as a historian to argue the need for historians to capture the unique, vital, personal aspects of their subjects: "Gogol was interested in everything, the people's customs, ceremonies, holidays, superstitions, clothing and the like." He avoided "bare abstractions," wanted to know " 'the true existence, the essential characteristics, all the shifts and shades of feeling, excitement, suffering and joys' " of his subjects, and gave special attention to such things as music, art, and fashions as sources for what was worth knowing about people.[20] In Cherepnin's words, Gogol believed "that the work of a historian should not merely provide material for the literary writer but should itself, without losing its own specific character, represent an artistic production affecting the feeling and imagination of the reader as well as his mind." How wonderfully different Soviet historical works would become if Soviet scholars took heed of Cherepnin's implicit prompting here, through the medium of Gogol, to involve themselves in "the expressiveness, color, diversity of the unfolding pictures of the past, whose incessant change provides such a fascinating study. . . ." [21]

Both here and to a lesser extent in the concern for more factual and less dogmatic history one can easily appreciate the party's motives for promoting these arguments. History books written in the familiar Soviet manner are simply not read. Compared to the citizen of the thirties and forties, there is indeed a "new Soviet man," and the change affects the consumption of literature and history no less than shoes: the shoddy and crude stay on the shelves.[22] But here again, as in the preceding theme, the historians seem to go further than necessary in supporting the party's interests. And, after all, party interests or not, historical works that are closer to the facts and that are written in a way that brings alive the events of the past are better history than those written in the Stalinist manner. The question becomes who is using whom. Are the party ideologists using the historians to make their propaganda more effective, or are the historians taking advantage of a fortunate conjunction of interests to improve the quality of Soviet historical research and publication?

The same question can be raised with regard to another major theme in these recent publications on historical theory: the emphasis on the role of human will and goals in determining the course of historical development. "History is *nothing but* the activity of man pursuing his aims"—such is the classic quotation from Marx most often brought in to legitimize this voluntarist position. There has always been, of course, a tension in Marxism between an emphasis on objective, ineluctable economic laws necessary to guarantee victory and the large role of political initiative demanded for revolutionary leadership and self-sacrifice. Leninism and Stalinism represent successive heightening of the tension, with the advantage steadily increasing on the side of voluntarism. Essentially the reverse side of the attack on abstract, "sociological" generalization, this voluntaristic theory of history (as well as of politics, economics, and psychology) was a fundamental part of Stalin's "great retreat," and it is important for an understanding of the main trends of Soviet life and thought to appreciate the persistence of this theme. Party leadership, the vanguard of the proletariat, consciousness over spontaneity, the primacy of politics over economics in socialist revolution and "Communist construction," the socialist hero in literature, the high rewards for achievers in all spheres of Soviet life—these and many other characteristic aspects of Stalin's Russia were associated with such voluntarism or, better, idealism.[23]

What are the theorists doing with it now? The theme itself appears constantly. Such statements as the following, expressed at the 1964 conference, are common: "Gifted with consciousness and will, people make their own history and in this sense come forth not as the passive objects of history, but as its subjects, as its active, creative force, transforming reality in the course of historical practice." [24]

This emphasis on will as a determinant force in history obviously continues to have great political value. In his outspoken article directed against those exaggerating the place of objective social laws or alleged inevitabilities in history, Gurevich repeatedly stressed the importance of "energy and enterprise of leaders, parties, and classes." With such activism, Hitler and World War II could have been stopped, and without it revolutions do not occur, even if the "basic" objective conditions are present.[25] The Bolshevik victory in 1917 provides a fine example, for it was due above all to Lenin's ability to appreciate the role of the "subjective" political factor, in decisive contrast to the "turgid dogmatism" of the Mensheviks, who thought only about the "insufficient development of productive forces and the small number of proletariat," and the "metaphysical approach" of the "right opportunists," like Lev Kamenev and Alexei Rykov, who were against moving from the "democratic" to the "socialist" phase of revolution after the February upheaval.[26]

Understandably it is with reference to the "liberation movement" that such voluntarism now finds its most frequent and unmistakable expression. There is no longer any doubt about skipping the "stage of capitalism" or, with regard to Africa, both feudalism and capitalism, of advancing directly from feudalism or tribalism to socialism.[27] The theory holding that "the whole world follows one and the same series of stages" must be rejected, according to K. A. Antonova, because "before our very eyes the industrial development of new Asiatic and African nations is occurring in a manner so very unlike that of the classical European model. . . ." [28] It is frankly acknowledged, moreover, that the key factor allowing this extraordinary violation of objective Marxist "laws" is the contribution of external influences.

M. I. Braginsky, of the Academy of Sciences' African Institute, argued the case quite reasonably. The Marxists were right and the Populists wrong in their debate over the chances of Russia's skipping the stage of capitalism, he writes, because such a leap could occur only if Russia had the support of an advanced society that had already moved on to socialism. Sadly, this had not happened. But things were different now: socialist Russia could provide the helping hand to underdeveloped economies lacking just about all the necessary objective conditions for a Marxist socialist revolution. Braginsky brings out clearly the relationship between this argument and idealistic voluntarism: "When we speak of a noncapitalist path of development, we must keep in mind not only the objective factors, but also the subjective." [29] Gurevich gave historical examples to illustrate this view when, in connection with his emphasis on the importance of "accidents" in history, he referred to the impact of foreign colonial powers on the development of native societies. Similarly, he considered the decisive factor in the fall of the Roman Empire (the factor neglected by the customary Marxist picture of transitions generated from within a given society) to be the barbarian invasions.[30]

Besides this relationship between theoretical voluntarism and the practical politics of "national liberation," one might argue a similar connection between the latter and the shift by historians from the "general" to the "concrete" discussed above. The paramount concern of Russian Marxists before and immediately after the October Revolution was to prove both the universality of Marx's historical patterns and the orthodoxy of the Bolshevik victory. The result of this was to exaggerate to absurd degrees the "capitalist" development of prerevolutionary Russia. Today the main political concern is to present Russia as a model for the underdeveloped economies, an example of rapid progress from an underdeveloped economy to a highly advanced one. Consequently, one finds historians criticized for underestimating the persisting feudal elements in prerevolutionary Russia as well as a new emphasis on the similarities between Russia on the eve of the Bolshevik Revolution and present-day underdeveloped societies. For example: "While linked through its monopolies with the imperialist West, Russian capitalism as an object of study is far more relevant and instructive for contemporary developing countries because of its contradictions, its social complexity, the immense gentry latifundia, the adaptation of the wealthy bourgeoisie to fit the remnants of serfdom, the union between the landed class and the wealthy capitalists, with political predominance for the landowners and economic predominance for the capitalists." [31] To illustrate his point, the author went on to note the remarkable similarities between conditions of Russian life as described in the works of L. N. Tolstoi and A. P. Chekhov and those prevalent today in the underdeveloped societies.

Still, here as in the case of the preceding topics, theorists seem to go beyond the point necessary for meeting political interests, in the direction, that is, of serious methodological reflection. In the article just discussed, for example, Gurevich suggested that objective tendencies, where they did obtain, were the resultants, or the "statistical average," of different individual "wills, emotions, ideas, predispositions, and personal, social, and class interests." Also, he continued, while such individual actions are based on conditions, that is, determined in the sense of being caused, "this determinism can never be complete, totally reducible to the influence of sociological laws: to one degree or another human action is autonomous, with regard both to its causes and to the results it achieves." History, he wrote toward the end of the article—and I am uncertain of the level of insight involved—is not the memory of humanity and society so much as it is their "self-consciousness." [32]

As noted earlier, Soviet historians are finding a fundamental difference between history and natural science in their contrasting approaches to individual events. In the "colossal degree," as Gurevich put it, to which events and conditions in history depend on human will and aims,[33] they now see another distinction between these two realms of being and inquiry. Whereas forces in nature "are blind and unconscious," Gulyga wrote, "society consists of people endowed with consciousness and will who set for themselves specific aims and strive to realize them." Consequently, he continued, in virtually the same phrases that Gurevich used, "regularity emerges as a kind of resultant of millions of individual actions. A social law, therefore, is realized only in an approximate way." [34] G. E. Glezerman seems to go a step further by spelling out the separation between historical study and dialectical materialism implicit in these definitions:

Dialectical materialism regards as materialistic those objects, phenomena, and relationships that exist apart from and independent of human consciousness. But social life is different from that in nature, since social phenomena and relationships are the result of human actions, and people are conscious beings.[35]

Making explicit the question begged by all this, M. T. Iovchuk declared: "It is now necessary to concern ourselves with creating—if it can be so expressed—a Marxist, scientific phenomenology of the spirit. . . ." [36]

In what is perhaps his most important article, Gurevich boldly pressed on toward precisely such a "phenomenology of the spirit" by urging Soviet historians to pay more attention to psychology. Since individuals and masses "are the subjects of historical actions, their authors and executors," he wrote, the historian

must consider in each concrete case how the social life he studies is reflected in the minds of people, articulated into concepts, images, and feelings, and how, after undergoing an appropriate subjective transformation, these factors determine people's actions, moving separate individuals as well as social groups and masses to one or another activity.[37]

The central theme of Gurevich's argument lies in the phrase "subjective transformation," found near the end of the last quotation. It is not enough to study such "objective factors" as the "economic, social, political, and ideological," since these do not act "mechanically and directly," but rather through the minds of people, through the prism of a particular social psychology. As an illustration, Gurevich described at considerable length the way economic aims and activities in ancient and medieval societies were "linked with a complex of images and instincts unrelated to economics." "For the member of such a society, ceremonies and magic were as essential as (and perhaps even more important than) production itself in agriculture, cattle breeding, and handicrafts," and economic activity was closely interwoven with religion, both directly through morality and indirectly through law. It may be more than a coincidence that Gurevich chose for this exercise in psychological reductionism those very economic activities that had for so long reigned in the realm of "the final analysis," the irreducible, ultimate motivating force of all social and historical processes.[38]

As recommended examples of historians who made use of psychology in historical analysis, he noted Georges Lefebvre and his "Marxist" students Albert Soboul and Georges Rudé. But he urged as well the study of Western bourgeois scholars, including Max Weber, Georg Simmel, Werner Sombart, Lucien Febvre, and Johan Huizinga.[39] Of these, he gave particular attention to Huizinga and his psychological analysis of the waning of the Middle Ages. From Gurevich's excellent summaries of Huizinga's argument one sees a willingness to give fair treatment to non-Marxist, even idealistic and Freudian, interpretations, and, when considered along with the rest of his article, perhaps also Gurevich's own inclination toward the same approach.

A fear of hell and a naïve joy of life were so close in the minds of the people of the time that they sometimes merged. Cruelty and kindness, vengeance and indulgence, love and hate, greed and generosity—these abruptly interchanged. Emotional tension was extraordinarily great. . . . Man swayed between extremes of behavior, between the ideal and the base. On the lower, unconscious level of the psyche were all shades of desire and inclination, repressed by a conformist society and its severe ethics. On the higher level of conscious aims, only the most elevated motivations, the Christian virtues, approved by society and morality, were permitted. The split between the two levels of the psyche, the intense strain arising between them, was the source of the intense emotionality and the fluctuations from one extreme to the other.[40]

It has been a long time since this sort of thing appeared in a Soviet publication.

If the emphasis on will and emotions and the consequent search for a "phenomenology of the spirit" help undermine oversimplified categories of historical materialism by directing attention to complex personal motivations, they also do so by encouraging an awareness of ethical and intellectual themes that have accompanied the evolution of the human spirit throughout its history, disregarding "class" divisions, contrasting socioeconomic "formations," and Marxist "periodization." A fascinating article by the Orientalist N. I. Konrad provides a fine illustration.[41]

Konrad's concern is to find the meaning of history. As one might expect, he finds the meaning in progress. But throughout the essay both the content and the dynamics of progress are described in a remarkably unmaterialistic manner. Only midway in the article do we find as a sign of progress the theme with which one would expect a Soviet article like this to begin: economic advance. And even this is treated in a strangely un-Marxian manner. We are told that from the beginning man had to assure his material conditions, but the supporting quotations come not from Marx or Lenin, but from ancient Chinese proverbs. The criterion recommended for economic periodization is, moreover, totally unrelated to the usual Marxian categories of class theory: Konrad suggests the division of history into the era of natural materials and the "polymer age" of synthetics.[42] Moreover, Konrad's discussion of economic exploitation, when it does come, could be interpreted as much an attack on the Soviet system as on any other: "Exploitation results in various forms of social relations, of which two are the most clearly defined—exploitation by noneconomic compulsion, i.e., outright force, and exploitation by economic compulsion. *Both forms include variants determined by different relationships of the exploited to the tools and means of pro-*

duction and, in conjunction therewith, different situations relative to the exploiter." [43] Whether intended or not, there is present in this abstract formulation the system of economic and/or political compulsion *without* private property which has always been a central theme in the revisionists' contest with Soviet Marxists.

The major index of progress, to which virtually the entire article is devoted, is the gradual extension of culture and especially the growth in man's knowledge of nature, society, and man himself. We meet little from Marx, Engels, or Lenin in all this. By way of introduction to each area of progress in knowledge (nature, society, man himself), we find instead quotations from ancient Chinese wisdom, and throughout this section the reader passes through a fine array of illustrative references to mythology, religious symbolism, and classical philosophy. [44]

The most striking theme of the article comes in the final section. Man's conquest of nature and his rational achievements in general are judged inadequate in themselves as evidence of progress. The advance of rational knowledge can be considered truly progressive only when united to "the social principle in man's nature." To show that for him this is more than the usual propaganda slogan, Konrad again surveyed the sweep of history and related his "social principle" to the Confucian pictogram for "sympathy," Buddhist "compassion," the teachings of Jesus, and the ideals of the Renaissance. [45] Toward the end of the article, the ethical factor emerges as the essential and distinguishing one in human history: "the truly great achievement of mankind and perhaps the highest manifestation of progress is the fact that people . . . called evil, evil; coercion, coercion; crime, crime. The very appearance of the concepts denoted by these terms is proof of progress, for these words did not merely describe phenomena and actions, but evaluated and drastically condemned them." [46] Thus, notwithstanding his explicit emphasis on "progress," Konrad's splendid essay surveys and honors the fundamental human values that have persisted through the course of history. At the end of the article he offered elaborate homage to the concept that represents for him a unity of the two values that pervade the essay as its central themes: reason and charity. The concept is humanism, and in his lengthy praise of it, it seems to me, one finds a meeting of Soviet idealism and the heritage cherished by the West.

The above themes concern current Soviet theories on the proper subject matter for historical inquiry. But theories of the known and theories of knowledge go together. When the selection and treatment of subjects are guided by preestablished patterns, abstracted from individual events, historians can easily claim the attainment of objective, "scientific" laws. Indeed, the entire process is notoriously circular. A host of epistemological problems arises, however, when the concrete facts are brought back in, when an effort is made to grasp and communicate the dynamic complexities and the "living," elusive quality of reality, and when the ideological "superstructure," including even unconscious motivations, not only gains autonomy, but becomes increasingly a major "moving force" in history.

First of all, to "respect the facts" means to raise that essential problem of all historical study, the problem of selection. As Gulyga wrote, "the historian must select facts and interpret them. He faces a problem in logic. What criteria should be used in the selection of factual material?" [47] Others as well are raising this fundamental question, which in Western historiography fostered relativism, subjectivism, and skepticism. The phrasing of a similar statement by Glezerman is even more reminiscent of the early years of relativist thought in the West.

I would like first of all to say something about the theory of knowledge in historical science. There is much here that still remains meagerly studied, particularly concerning the epistemological analysis of the nature of the historical fact. The special character of history as a science consists in the fact that it is mainly concerned with the past, with that which has left its imprint on contemporary conditions of society, but which no longer exists. In contrast to the natural scientist, who has immediately before him the object of his investigation, and in contrast with the sociologist, whose subject is society after it has attained a certain level of development, the historian is concerned with historical facts belonging mainly to the past. Consequently we face here the task of re-creating the historical fact. What should be the criteria for selection from the endless diversity of phenomena those that are most characteristic, those we call historical fact? [48]

In an article on Lenin as a historian, G. M. Ivanov attempted to reconcile objectivity and subjectivity by proposing an approach that he called "retrospective knowledge," by which the historian is to use insights and concepts reflecting the later development of a particular phenomenon in order to understand its earlier phases, taking care, however, not to read back present meanings into the past. As one might imagine, it is no simple matter for Ivanov to prove that this is entirely different from the presentist position. Ivanov here also expresses another of the difficulties that fostered historical relativism in the West. "Of course, since man is both the subject of historical development and, at the same time, the subject of historical knowledge, he is learning his own history when studying the past, and, in this sense, historical reality and historical consciousness coincide. . . . Since the object of investigation is the history of human society and not the history of nature, it is significantly more difficult in historical science than it is in natural science to solve the problem of the relationship between the object and the subject." [49] In his usually frank manner, Gulyga dots the *i* when he states simply that "history makes no claims to the laurels of natural science; it has other possibilities and problems." [50] Since it is common knowledge that much of Soviet ideology and political practice rests ultimately on the assumed affinity between history and natural science, the significance of this line of thought should be self-evident.

An acceptance of part of the relativist argument seems implicit also in V. F. Asmus' statement that ideas "are never simply selected, but undergo a certain change, a reevaluation," that besides being chosen because they "are suitable for supporting present-day views about reality," they are "brought nearer the present by means of a particular kind of revision, of alteration." [51] We have already met the same view in Gurevich's article on social psychology. In an article on French archival studies, O. M. Medushevskaia offered still another example when she wrote that "before either serving as the cornerstone of investigation or being thrown out as insignificant, the fact must pass through the prism of the historian's consciousness, become known to him and evaluated by him." [52]

One may suggest a variety of factors contributing to the emergence of such subjectivism. There is, first of all, the strong tendencies in that direction in Marx's relativistic sociology of knowledge. In connection with the current emphasis on greater objectivity, Soviet scholars like to recall Marx's attack on those "base" persons who "subordinate facts to predetermined aims" drawn from other than scholarly considerations, or Engels' similar judgment that "any scholar who subordinates science to his ideal 'cannot be considered a man of science since he begins with preconceived ideas.' " But how can the Soviet historian heed these commendable exhortations when he is so often reminded that "one of the particular characteristics of the reflection of reality in historical science consists in the fact that it always takes place, consciously or unconsciously, through the prism of class interests; since it is not people in general, not some general subject, but a completely concrete subject, the bearer of the interests of a particular class, who apprehends historical reality and the struggle of social classes, in regard to which he cannot be impartial"? [53]

Subjectivism also results from the problems of selection, once guiding "laws" are abandoned in favor of a "respect for facts," and from the subtle demands of empathy, once the historian turns his attention to human will and to the "richness of color and gradations" in human experience. Such, at any rate, was the case in Western historiography. It may also be that the impact of the "new physics" on social and historical thought that has been so long familiar in the West is beginning to be felt by Soviet theorists. Since the victory of Soviet scientists over the "philosophers" and the consequent acceptance of relativity theory, indeterminateness, and so forth, this would seem a likely development. "As one of the most distinguished Soviet physicists informed me," writes the Polish physicist Leopold Infeld, "physicists no longer read the Soviet philosophical journals and they don't care a damn what the philosophers [i.e., dialectical materialists] have to say." [54] The Russian physicist P. L. Kapitsa is no less explicit. "If, then, our scientists had listened to the philosophers in 1954 and had accepted this definition [of cybernetics as 'a reactionary pseudoscience'] as a guide for the further development of this science, it can safely be said that the conquest of cosmic space, of which we are all legitimately proud and for which the entire world respects us, could not have taken place, because it is impossible to direct spaceships without cybernetic machines." Or again: "It is still fresh in many people's minds how a number of our philosophers, dogmatically applying the method of dialectics, demonstrated that the theory of relativity was without foundation. . . . And so the physicists carried out a number of nuclear reactions and verified Einstein's law, not with individual atoms, but on the scale of the atom bomb." [55] In this connection one should keep in mind, finally, the monistic character of Marxist and Soviet epistemology, according to which the science of nature and the "science of society" share common assumptions, "categories," and methods.

Here, too, politics may be served. If, as discussed above, the stress on "energy and enterprise" and other subjective factors in history has political value, so, clearly, does the emphasis on epistemological subjectivism. In listing criteria for selecting data, Gulyga included the "criterion of value" and went on to explain this by saying that "the historian frequently turns his attention to facts that play no role in the causal chain of past events, but that are of interest to contemporaries." In a later article, after restating this theme, he likened historical displays of military heroism to artistic productions, since such heroism was valued not for its place in a past causal pattern, but for its effect on people today. This calls to mind a laudatory reference by Ponomarev to earlier Russian military battles with Germany which "alert the people to vigilance against the revival of aggressive forces in West Germany." [56] Is the criterion for selecting facts and events still to be, and now admittedly, only propaganda potency?

But whatever the reason for this emerging subjectivism, it cannot but be helped by the remarkably full and fair summaries and quotations of Western "idealistic" historiography in works designed to "unmask" such theories. As long as Soviet students and scholars knew little or nothing about Benedetto Croce, R. G. Collingwood, Heinrich Rickert, Charles Beard, Carl Becker, and the like, the dogmatists could more easily get away with ritualistic pronouncements and *ad hominem* denunciations. But the contrast between such primitivism and the sophisticated Western thought and argument now openly displayed in extended paraphrases and quotations is too crudely glaring. Having presented these Western views,[57] Soviet theorists seem to feel the need to work out more imaginative responses.

In Gurevich's discussion of general laws, multiple causation, accidents, statistical "resultants," and alternative possibilities in history, we see one such approach toward a more sophisticated analysis of the individual-general problem. But some theorists have recently become particularly attracted by another approach: the concept of "ideal type." Since the central concern that pervades virtually all that is written in this field by Soviet theorists is the need to reconcile the historians' focus on concrete events with the ideological and methodological interest in generalization, the appeal of this approach is understandable. With reference to Goethe, Rickert, and, most of all, Weber, Gulyga devoted an entire article to this theme. It is important to add that it was the lead article in *Voprosy istorii*, a place usually reserved for authoritative party editorials. Weber's essential and valuable contribution, according to Gulyga, was his distinction between the ideal type or form of some phenomenon and its actual existence. Since the ideal type was essentially a "protoimage" permitting wide deviations from it in reality, Gulyga urged historians to remember that the ideal type was only a useful guide, an epistemologically valuable construction and not a picture of actual patterns and processes in historical reality. (Gurevich, it may be recalled, advanced the same warning.) Marx's logical analysis of capitalism, for instance, "while for sociology a concrete picture of the structure and functions of this society, is for the historian only an abstract point of departure for the reconstruction of the concrete origins of capitalist relations in one or another country, in one or another epoch." [58]

Here, it would seem, we might have a meeting point between at least some Soviet theorists and one school of thought among our own historians. Ironically, what might stand in the way of such cooperation, assuming this optimism warranted, is the reorientation of those Soviet historians who write about concepts like "ideal type" away from scientific models of knowledge toward aesthetic ones.

As in the case of other themes discussed in this study, Gulyga expressed this reorientation with particular clarity. History, he wrote, represents "a special kind of synthesis between the theoretical and the artistic apprehension of the world. It is dualistic by nature. There coexist here the abstract and the sensitively concrete, the conceptual and the visual picture of the past." In its characteristic use of "ideation in the form of imagery and emotions" he saw one more way in which history differed from "the majority of the sciences," and he went on to attribute this difference to the special subject matter of history, the "unique lives of individuals, their intentions and achievements." [59]

S. O. Schmidt had some still more intriguing thoughts along these lines. Because of the vast accumulation of facts, he said, it was becoming increasingly necessary to "crystallize" in our minds some stable historical types, and he advised historians to look to creative literature for help in this. In addition, he noted that historical types, "freed from the narrow framework of specific time and place, and turned into something like timeless symbols, have an effect similar to that of literary-artistic images." Examples from history, he went on, provide people with types by which they classify real life experiences, in the same way that literary characterizations often provide the historian with types around which he crystallizes his historical data. What the historian and writer have most in common, however, is their desire "to convince the reader of the authenticity of their characterizations." [60]

In Cherepnin's article on Gogol, we have already seen a full treatment of this theme, associating artistic and historical creativity. Only by following such methods as Gogol adopted in creating concrete, living individuality can the historian fulfill his proper task:

The task of the historian-artist, according to N. V. Gogol, was to draw from his multicolored palette, and to make use of, the most suitable colors for depicting one or another national image on the historical canvas. One should not "accumulate a great number of features, but only those that would reveal much, the most original characteristics, the most distinctive, those possessed only by the people described." To reproduce past phenomena, N. V. Gogol considered necessary a fusion of "historical" truth and artistic, "poetic" truth. The study of past facts and the penetration into the depths of the past with the artist's eye—here were the two sides of the creative process, the two paths to historical knowledge.[61]

But the next question immediately arises: How is the historian to apprehend the "typical"? What is there to replace the at least allegedly objective analysis, the dispassionate rationalism that the historian could claim as his guide when he looked to natural science for his method and chose the general as his subject? There are hints of the kind of answers that lie ahead for Soviet historians and philosophers who pursue this line of thought. It is no easy task to "feel about for [*nashchupat*]" the regularities in the complexity of individual events, Academician P. N. Fedo-

seev said at the 1964 conference. He then went on to quote V. G.
Belinsky's description of the proper historical method:

The difficulty in the prerequisites for a good historian consists in the
necessity of joining a rigorous study of historical facts and materials, a
critical, cold, dispassionate analysis, with poetic inspiration and a creative
capacity to combine events, forming from them a living picture, in which
all the principles of perspective and chiaroscuro are observed.[62]

In all this we have left far behind the traditional Marxist picture of
both natural and social "science" and have entered the realm of aesthetics. Gulyga does not balk even here:

Speaking of the particularities of historical science, one must stress the
special role played in it by imaginative thought. The questions of imaginative
thought, the aesthetic apprehension of reality in the work of the historian
is a theme for thought and investigation. Categories of aesthetics belong
to reality and consequently to history. They are concerned not only with
art, but with the knowledge of reality in general, with the knowledge of
the historical process.[63]

In a later article, Gulyga nicely merged together the various approaches with which he has been closely associated. The "typical" in
history, the image that permits a fusion between the specific and the
general (which is, in turn, the historians' main concern), is identified by
him as an "aesthetic category," as a means for expressing the "essence" of
a phenomenon "in its most complete and clearest form." The processes
of apprehending the "typical," of "finding material and giving it meaning," he refers to as an "intuitive act." [64] Thus, from an admonition to
"respect the facts," through an appeal for a "phenomenology of the
spirit," we arrive at an appreciation of the need for "an aesthetics of
history." [65] Again, one can reasonably ask, is this what Ponomarev had
in mind?

Were Soviet historians to heed these promptings from the "methodologists," there would open to them a wide range of immensely fruitful
sources of knowledge and insight so long blocked by dogmatic conservatism and obscurantism. From the manner of his presentation, there can
be little doubt that Gurevich thoroughly approves of the way Huizinga
and Febvre made use of "works of art and literature for discovering,
through analysis of a society's aesthetic values, a people's psychology,
their forms of perceiving life and nature, and their normative systems.
. . . In the works of creative writers, poets, intellectuals, theologians,
historians, and scientists of the later Middle Ages," Gurevich continued,
"both Febvre and Huizinga are concerned not only, and perhaps not so

much, with what people intentionally express, as with what they express unconsciously, without intent." [66]

How much of this is new and how much old? Does current Soviet historical theory deserve a place in the "thaw," or does it continue to fulfill the familiar political and ideological functions, those so clearly laid down in Ponomarev's speech? Do the apparently novel themes indicate a serious reorientation on the part of some Soviet historians and philosophers, or do they merely indicate efforts to provide a cloak of sophistication for official doctrines, and thereby more subtly and effectively to satisfy party directives?

Certainly caution is the first principle to be followed when interpreting seemingly novel and hopeful trends in Soviet thought, and throughout this article I have suggested arguments favoring the cloak-of-sophistication theory. But the second principle is to be aware that such caution may be unsound as well as deeply unjust to Soviet scholars, trying courageously, perhaps, to inch their way out of still vastly powerful ideological controls. One can, of course, find all manner of tediously orthodox statements in even the most revisionist of Soviet publications, but this has always been a form of political insurance, and, moreover, none of the already numerous changes in Soviet theory and practice have ever lacked supporting quotations from the classics. The orthodox comments are also at times so flagrantly inconsistent, either logically or in style and quality of thought, with the rest of the publication (as they are not in such pronouncements as Ponomarev's) that it is hard to take them seriously. Finally, it is less weighty an argument than it might seem to note that some of the liberal statements are expressed by highly placed and long-familiar party functionaries in the historical profession whose major achievements lie well within the Stalin era. For one thing, there is something encouraging in the fact that the liberal bandwagon is considered the profitable one to jump on. In any case, anyone sensitive to the endless combinations of personal motivation and rationalization as well as to the character and intensity of Stalinist oppression would hesitate to pass judgment here or hurl abusive epithets.[67]

My own bent, therefore, is toward a qualified optimism. All potential or actual service to the party notwithstanding, both the tone and the quality of the current discussion lead me to take much of it at face value. But besides the impression made by the publications on historical theory themselves, I am encouraged in this judgment by parallels between them and current developments elsewhere in Soviet life and thought. The exigencies of national defense and economic growth have forced the liberation of the natural sciences from the control of dogma and also a significant and increasingly broader tolerance for experimentation in economic theory and practice. It is hardly likely that professionals in other fields, including history, who have equivalent training, background, and aspirations are unaffected by the return to reason in these favored disciplines.

Still more indicative of the tendency involved, however, since it is less clearly attached to practical gains, is the veritable obsession with "truth" that pervades the "thaw" literature. That the trends toward professional integrity in history are part of this massive reaction against Stalinist mendacity seems to me very likely. I have referred already to a related pressure in this same direction: change in the reading public. To inculcate desired attitudes and ideas in the minds of Soviet readers, the books have to be read, but to get them read, the style and content of the message must be radically altered to suit far more critical, self-confident, and sensitive readers.

There is, finally, another way, less obvious but more basic, in which the achievements in Soviet science and economy may be contributing to the present state of Soviet historiography. Historical and economic determinism, with all their derivative categories, patterns, and laws, provided together an encouraging crutch for powerless Russian Marxists in the last decades of the nineteenth century. Having nothing, they looked to inevitable historical and social processes to guarantee them all. Soviet society is now more than strong enough to throw the crutch away. Present achievements are providing realistic grounds for the hope and expectation that the first Russian Marxists could derive only from Marxist historical mythology.[68] With tangible scientific and economic success winning allegiance for the regime from those who matter politically, the authorities may feel secure enough to lessen their dependence on Marxist eschatology. Consequently, if this is correct, the historian can begin to withdraw from service on the "historical front" and to return, at least partly, to his traditional pursuit of historical truth.

The hesitant reemergence of sociology as an acceptable field may be the other side of the coin of history's return to its customary enterprise. Boundaries seem in the process of being drawn: historians study specific events; sociologists focus on general trends, patterns, and laws. As for historical materialism, it is quite possible that under the combined blows of rational history and rational sociology its fate will be the same as that suffered by its mate, dialectical materialism, under the blows of demythologized science. Perhaps the coffin for historical materialism is already being prepared under the title "scientific communism," to which the familiar propaganda slogans and clichés are now being consigned, leaving history and sociology somewhat freer to engage in, or at least to search for, their proper concerns.

Notes

1. B. N. Ponomarev, "The Tasks Facing Historical Scholarship and the Training of History Teachers and Researchers," trans. from *Voprosy istorii*, 1963, no. 1, in *Soviet Studies in History*, 2, no. 1 (1963): 5, 6; "Soviet Historiography at a New Stage of Development," trans. from *Voprosy istorii*, 1960, no. 8, in *Current Digest of the Soviet Press*, 12 (November 2, 1960): 11; "The Party Central Committee Resolution 'On the Tasks of Party Propaganda in Present-Day Conditions' and Historical Science," trans. from *Voprosy istorii*, 1960, no. 6, in *ibid.*, August 31, 1960, p. 8. In 1957 Soviet historians were sharply reprimanded for moving too near "bourgeois objectivity" during those hopeful months surrounding the 20th Party Congress. For an account of this repression, see Merle Fainsod, "Soviet Russian Historians, or the Lessons of Burdzhalov," *Encounter*, 18 (March, 1962): 82–89, and Alexander Dallin, "Recent Soviet Historiography," in *Russia under Khrushchev*, ed. Abraham Brumberg (New York, 1962), pp. 470–88.

2. Ponomarev, "Tasks," pp. 8, 26.

3. Excerpts and summaries from the discussions at the 1964 conference were published in "O metodologicheskikh voprosakh istoricheskoi nauki," *Voprosy istorii*, 1964, no. 3, pp. 3–68. Later that year, a much fuller compilation was published as a separate volume, *Istoriia i sotsiologiia* (Moscow, 1964). For these and similar "anti-Stalin" declarations, see the conference coverage in *Voprosy istorii*, 1964, no. 3, pp. 4, 6, 8, 26, 33, 34, 38, 39, 44, 51, 53, 55, 57–59; and in *Istoriia i sotsiologiia*, pp. 230, 234–35, 244–45.

4. For a discussion of the return to the archives, see the relevant articles, particularly S. V. Utechin, "Soviet Historiography after Stalin," and George Katkov, "Soviet Historical Sources in the Post-Stalin Era," in *Contemporary History in the Soviet Mirror*, ed. John Keep and Lilianna Brisby (New York, 1964); see also translations in *Current Digest of the Soviet Press*, e.g., 7, no. 15 (1955): 20–21, and 14, no. 8 (1962): 18–21. Here are two samples of current Soviet criticism of "quotism," both drawn from the 1964 conference: "Naturally, historians are no longer satisfied with stock formulas, based on nothing but a clever selection of quotations and often having nothing at all to do with the circumstances, country, or period about which a particular historian is writing"; and "Can one really limit oneself when explaining one or another set of historical phenomena to a few statements from the classics of Marxism that were relevant to concrete situations, and that were, moreover, based on a study of sources and literature accessible to them at that time, before the appearance of a great deal of new factual data?" (*Istoriia i sotsiologiia*, pp. 274, 292).

5. One of the most remarkable illustrations of this tendency is a study very frequently cited by Soviet historians: I. S. Kon, *Filosofskii idealizm i krizis burzhuaznoi istoricheskoi mysli* (Moscow, 1959).

6. It may well be this concern that makes Soviet historians now so uncomfortable with the slogan, attributed to M. N. Pokrovsky, according to which "history is

politics projected back into the past." See their rejection of this view of history and their denial of Pokrovsky's ever having expressed it in "Obsuzhdenie staty S. M. Dubrovskogo 'Akademik M. N. Pokrovsky i ego rol v razvitii sovetskoi istoricheskoi nauki,'" *Voprosy istorii*, 1962, no. 3, pp. 34, 35, 37; and A. V. Gulyga, "O kharaktere istoricheskogo znaniia," *Voprosy filosofii*, 16, no. 9, (1962): 33.

7. "O metodologicheskikh voprosakh," p. 37.

8. Gulyga, "O kharaktere," pp. 32–33.

9. *Istoriia i sotsiologiia*, p. 101.

10. "O metodologicheskikh voprosakh," p. 48.

11. *Istoriia i sotsiologiia*, p. 313.

12. N. E. Zastenker, "Problemy istoricheskoi nauki v trudakh K. Marksa i F. Engelsa," *Voprosy istorii*, 1964, no. 6, p. 19.

13. "Obsuzhdenie staty S. M. Dubrovskogo," pp. 34–35; "O metodologicheskikh voprosakh," p. 53.

14. A. Ia. Gurevich, "Obshchii zakon i konkretnaia zakonomernost v istorii," *Voprosy istorii*, 1965, no. 8, pp. 15, 16, 19, 22, 23, 26. Gurevich, a professor at Kalinin Pedagogic Institute, is a specialist in medieval English and Norwegian history.

15. *Ibid.*, pp. 26–27. Gurevich is hardly alone in this shift away from determinism and inevitability. The same point is argued by M. Ia. Gefter, "O metodologicheskikh voprosakh," p. 48; Zastenker, "Problemy," p. 20; E. N. Gorodetsky, "Voprosy metodologii istoricheskogo issledovaniia v posleoktiabrskikh trudakh V. I. Lenina," *Voprosy istorii*, 1963, no. 6, p. 32. Near the close of a lengthy survey of the evolution of Soviet historiography published in the leading party journal, *Kommunist*, we find the authors lamenting the absence of "a scholarly work containing a comprehensive answer to the question of why it should have been Russia that became the birthplace of Leninism and that was the first to throw off the domination of the exploiters" (*Current Digest of the Soviet Press*, 13 [August 23, 1961]: 17–18). Even more surprising is G. E. Glezerman's complaint that "the particular characteristics of causal relations in history have been very little studied," that "there is not a single work" on this theme by a Soviet author ("O metodologicheskikh voprosakh," p. 43).

16. "O metodologicheskikh voprosakh," pp. 5, 8, 47–48.

17. Gulyga, "O kharaktere," p. 32.

18. Ponomarev, "Tasks," pp. 15, 26.

19. "O metodologicheskikh voprosakh," p. 44; *Istoriia i sotsiologiia*, p. 322.

20. L. V. Cherepnin, "Istoricheskie vzgliady Gogolia," *Voprosy istorii*, 1964, no. 1, pp. 77–78, 82, 90–91.

21. *Ibid.*, p. 78.

22. For references to the poor response of Soviet readers to Soviet history books, see "O metodologicheskikh voprosakh," pp. 21, 57, 59, and *Istoriia i sotsiologiia*, p. 285. For a Madison Avenue approach to this problem, see *Istoriia i sotsiologiia*, p. 248, where we find one enterprising participant in the 1964 conference urging history publications "on good paper, illustrated with colorful pictorial reproductions and at an inexpensive price."

23. Still the best analysis of Stalin's radical "idealization" of Soviet historiography is Klaus Mehnert, *Stalin versus Marx* (London, 1952). For the complete account of this transformation through its several stages, see Konstantin F. Shteppa, *Russian Historians and the Soviet State* (New Brunswick, N.J., 1962).

24. G. M. Ivanov, "Svoeobrazie protsessa otrazheniia deistvitelnosti v istoricheskoi nauke," *Voprosy istorii*, 1962, no. 2, p. 21.

25. Gurevich, "Obshchii zakon," pp. 24–26.

26. "O metodologicheskikh voprosakh," pp. 31–32; Gorodetsky, "Voprosy metodologii," pp. 23, 30; *Istoriia i sotsiologiia*, pp. 271, 307, 317.

27. "O metodologicheskikh voprosakh," p. 27; *Istoriia i sotsiologiia*, p. 273.

28. *Ibid.*, p. 282. An interesting expression of this more flexible approach to social development is the revival of Marx's "Asiatic mode of production" theory, repressed by Stalin (*ibid.*, p. 275; Gulyga, "O kharaktere," p. 30; Zastenker, "Problemy," p. 5).

29. *Istoriia i sotsiologiia*, pp. 265–74. See also Glezerman, "K voprosu o predmete istoricheskogo materializma," *Voprosy filosofii*, 14, no. 3 (1960): 12.

30. Gurevich, "Obshchii zakon," pp. 15, 26.

31. A. Ia. Avrekh, "K voprosu o metodakh istoricheskogo issledovaniia," *Voprosy istorii*, 1963, no. 10, pp. 110–20; *Istoriia i sotsiologiia*, pp. 308–10. Politically motivated or not, this return to "concrete" Russian realities can only be welcomed by Western scholars.

32. Gurevich, "Obshchii zakon," pp. 17–18, 29. In a footnote, Gurevich makes it explicitly clear that by autonomy here he means more than the familiar Marxist "reciprocal relationship" between the substructure and the superstructure. Existence does determine consciousness, he agreed, in the sense that the "spiritual life of society" is influenced constantly by "economic, social, biological, and natural-geographical" factors. (Even this listing is remarkable.) Nevertheless, he continues, this spiritual life is "to a certain extent self-determined, possessing its own laws," and the historian should keep this self-determination of the spiritual life in mind and not only its "interrelationship with the base" (*ibid.*, p. 18, no. 14).

33. *Ibid.*, p. 27.

34. Gulyga, "O kharaktere," p. 31.

35. Glezerman, "K voprosu," p. 9.

36. "O metodologicheskikh voprosakh," p. 58. The way toward such a "phenomenology" was paved by Stalin's long and emphatic stress on the ideological and political superstructure. Although Stalin's last party congress, the 19th, and his last ex cathedra pronouncement, *Economic Problems of Socialism in the USSR* (New York, 1952), gave evidence of a return toward the "objective" and "lawful," the subjective idealistic position has become increasingly bold since his death. In addition to publications already cited, particularly Gurevich's, see, for example, the attack by philosophers V. F. Asmus and M. M. Rozental against those who try to derive philosophy from class or other economic categories (V. F. Asmus, "Nekotorye voprosy dialektiki istoriko-filosofskogo protessa i evo poznaniia," *Voprosy filosofii*, 15, no. 4 [1961], pp. 111–12, 115–17, 121–23; M. M. Rozental, "O sviazi filosofskikh teorii s ekonomicheskim bazisom," *Voprosy filosofii*, 4, no. 3 [1960], pp. 146–47). A. M. Deborin similarly warns against considering philosophy exclusively from the point of view of its relationship to extraneous factors and giving too little attention to the "relatively independent, inner, logical development, the historical continuity of universal scientific thought" ("Ob istorizme vozzrenii V. G. Belinskogo," *Voprosy istorii*, 1962, no. 3, p. 53).

37. Gurevich, "Nekotorye aspekty izucheniia sotsialnoi istorii," *Voprosy istorii*, 1964, no. 10, p. 55. This article appeared approximately a year before the article by Gurevich discussed above. The articles are obviously two aspects of a single and dramatically idealistic argument. Unless the themes in this 1964 article had the complete approval of party authorities, it is hardly likely that Gurevich's 1965 article would have been published at all, much less honored with first mention on the cover list of contents.

38. *Ibid.*, p. 59.

39. *Ibid.*, pp. 54, 66.

40. *Ibid.*, p. 66.

41. N. I. Konrad, "Notes on the Meaning of History," trans. from *Vestnik istorii mirovoi kultury*, 1961, no. 2, in *Soviet Studies in History*, 1, no. 1 (1962).

42. *Ibid.*, p. 13.

43. *Ibid.* (Italics mine.)

44. *Ibid.*, pp. 14–17.

45. *Ibid.*, pp. 20–21.

46. *Ibid.*, p. 21.

47. "O metodologicheskikh voprosakh," pp. 36–37. Elsewhere, Gulyga elaborated on this view somewhat: "One can determine the actual facts but present a distorted picture of the events, because all facts are not equivalent. There are important, determining facts and there are facts of secondary importance. . . . What criteria are there for selecting facts? How can one avoid here subjectivism and arbitrariness?" (Gulyga, "O kharaktere," p. 34).

48. "O metodologicheskikh voprosakh," p. 43.

49. Ivanov, "Svoeobrazie protsessa otrazheniia," pp. 21, 22, 31–35.

50. Gulyga, "O kharaktere," p. 31.

51. Asmus, "Nekotorye voprosy," p. 112.

52. O. M. Medushevskaia, "Voprosy teorii istochnikovedeniia v sovremennoi frantsuzskoi burzhuaznoi istoriografii," *Voprosy istorii*, 1964, no. 8, pp. 81–82.

53. Ivanov, "Svoeobrazie protsessa otrazheniia," pp. 24, 31; Medushevskaia, "Teorii istochnikovedeniia," p. 81; Zastenker, "Problemy," p. 23; *Istoriia i sotsiologiia*, p. 244.

54. Leopold Infeld, "As I See It," *Bulletin of the Atomic Scientists*, 21 (February, 1965): 14.

55. P. L. Kapitsa, "Theory, Experiment, Practice," trans. from *Ekonomicheskaia gazeta*, March 26, 1962, in *Current Digest of the Soviet Press*, 14, no. 19 (1962): 14–15.

56. "O metodologicheskikh voprosakh," p. 37; Gulyga, "Poniatie i obraz v istoricheskoi nauke," *Voprosy istorii*, 1965, no. 9, pp. 10, 14; see also Gurevich, "Obshchii zakon," p. 29.

57. Unfortunately, space does not permit a discussion of this welcome tolerance of Western thought. For examples, see Asmus, "Nekotorye voprosy," p. 123; Deborin, "Ob istorizme," pp. 62–63; *Istoriia i sotsiologiia*, p. 275; "Obsuzhdenie staty S. M. Dubrovskogo," p. 38; Medushevskaia, "Teorii istochnikovedeniia," p. 88; Zastenker, "Problemy," pp. 21–22. During the first, tense weeks of the Vietnam crisis, in February, 1965, a group of about fifty books on American history written mainly by American "bourgeois" historians was on display in one of the most conspicuous sections of the Lenin Library in Moscow, visible to everyone passing from the main catalogue halls to the central reading room. The revival in Soviet dialectics of the "negation of the negation" concept, suppressed by Stalin, seems at least in part due to this willingness to accept the emergence of bourgeois tendencies in Soviet life and thought. "The 'second negation' represents a surmounting of the limitations of the 'first,' a particular kind of necessary 'historical corrective' to it," correcting the excesses committed by the first negation in its too thorough destruction of the "thesis" (O. O. Yakhot, "Otritsanie i preemstvennost v istoricheskom razvitii," *Voprosy filosofii*, 15, no. 3 [1961]: 147–48, 151).

58. Gulyga, "Poniatie i obraz," pp. 5, 7–8.

59. Gulyga, "O kharaktere," pp. 36–38, and "The Subject Matter of Historical Scholarship," trans. from *Voprosy istorii*, 1964, no. 4, in *Soviet Studies in History*, 3, no. 4 (1965): 54. As an example of such artistic history, Gulyga referred to the works of the great prerevolutionary "bourgeois" historian Vasily Kliuchevsky ("O kharaktere," p. 38). In his most recent article on the subject, Gulyga goes on at some length illustrating how "tragedy" and other literary categories are applicable to historical interpretation, and why "universal history is a superb poetess" ("Poniatie i obraz," pp. 11–14). He even draws some support from H. Stuart Hughes, *History as Art and as Science* (New York, 1964).

60. *Istoriia i sotsiologiia*, pp. 294–95. Another member of the Academy of Sciences' Institute of History attending the 1964 conference supported this view of history by reminding the conference "that 'history' is a translation from the Greek word for 'story'" (*ibid.*, p. 320).

61. Cherepnin, "Istoricheskie vzgliady Gogolia," p. 83. And from whom did Gogol in turn learn "the art of re-creating the historical past"? From the great

works of world literature beginning with Homer, we find from a letter from Gogol to the poet A. N. Zhukovsky, quoted by Cherepnin (*ibid.*, p. 79).

62. "O metodologicheskikh voprosakh," pp. 10–11. Much the same terms are used by Cherepnin in describing the faculties employed by Gogol, who "apprehended the past not simply through the eyes of a historian, but through the inspired sensitivity of the artist" ("Istoricheskie vzgliady Gogolia," p. 81).

63. "O metodologicheskikh voprosakh," p. 37.

64. Gulyga, "Poniatie i obraz," pp. 13–14.

65. Gulyga, "O kharaktere," p. 38.

66. Gurevich, "Nekotorye aspekty," pp. 60–61, 63, 66.

67. After all, it was Ilya Ehrenburg who gave the name to the "thaw," and who by his public statements, fascinating memoirs, and personal interventions did as much as anyone to keep it going. And speaking of literature, who would have expected that Stalin's "engineers of the soul" would be carrying on as they have been since Stalin's death? For brief biographical sketches of the more prominent historians and philosophers mentioned in this article, see, among other such works, *Who's Who in the USSR*, published by the Munich Institute for the Study of the USSR, a second edition of which was published in New York and London in 1966.

68. In the light of all that has been said here about voluntarism and subjectivism in Soviet historical theory, it might be more accurate to say that the myths have changed, that the symbol of Prometheus, representing the transformation of nature, society, and man himself through endless conquests of conscious human will and reason, has replaced the myth of that weird, impersonal, animistic material force that somehow guaranteed the realization of the good society. The current development of Soviet historical theory may therefore be viewed as one more phase, following quite consistently the Lenin and Stalin phases, in a process that is bringing Soviet theory in line with Soviet practice, which from the beginning so dramatically demonstrated the determining power of ideas and ideals in history.

VI : Economics

The "Revolution" in Soviet Economics

Howard J. Sherman

In the theories of economic planning and economic organization under socialism, Soviet economics has made ten times as much advance in the last decade as in all the dreary years of Stalin's dictatorship. This "revolution" is fully as great as the Keynesian revolution in Western economics, and has suddenly removed Soviet economists from the stagnant backwaters of dogma to the most advanced and exciting pioneering research and debate. Here we shall begin by looking at the three interrelated debates on planning: (1) growth strategies, (2) achieving balance and full employment, and (3) optimal planning or programming. The first two controversies will be discussed somewhat briefly, since they are necessary to understand the whole planning debate, but do not constitute the area of the theoretical revolution, which is limited mainly to the third issue. Finally, we shall examine the recent debates on reorganization and decentralization of the Soviet economy.

Growth Strategy

The means to the most rapid economic growth were debated extensively in the Soviet Union in the 1920's.[1] These debates have been thoroughly and critically reported in many places,[2] so we need not discuss them in detail here. They dealt with how to transform the backward agrarian Soviet economy most rapidly into a modern industrialized economy. For our purposes, it is enough to say that the debates were very intensive, with a wide spectrum of differing opinions presented and vigorously defended (until Stalin exiled or imprisoned the opposition by 1928; he executed some of them in the mid-thirties). We may add that in the 1920's several sophisticated and highly original mathematical growth models were published by Soviet economists. All of these—and their authors—were condemned by Stalin as "bourgeois mathematical formalism." They did not come to light again in the Soviet Union until after Stalin died and was himself criticized in 1956 (at the 20th Congress of the Communist party, which launched the Soviet renaissance in economics).

The best of these early models actually was the same in essence as the famous Harrod-Domar model, discovered decades later in Western economics. It was finally Domar who unearthed this gem in the long-neglected works of the Soviet economist G. A. Feldman.[3] Feldman's model was explicitly based on Volume 2 of Marx's *Capital*. Although it was cruder mathematically, Marx's model showed all the essentials. It stated (1) the conditions for a steady growth at full capacity, and (2) that the growth rate of output will be higher if there is a higher ratio of producers' goods to consumers' goods (or of investment to consumption). All of these models revolve around the arithmetic truism that:

$$\frac{\text{Change in output}}{\text{Output}} = \frac{\text{Change in output}}{\text{Investment}} \cdot \frac{\text{Investment}}{\text{Output}}$$

In other words, if it is impossible to increase the *productivity* of investment, then the only means to more rapid growth is *more* investment out of output.

Of course, these models also show that the economy with the higher ratio will *eventually* also have a larger amount of consumption—but the question is how many years we wish to wait for consumption; that is, at what date do we want the optimum consumption? (Of course, this date is a political and ethical decision to be made by the whole community, not something for an economist to decide, as we shall see below.) We should also note that it is possible to go too far in reducing consumption, even from the cold and calculating viewpoint of economic growth. Lower consumption opportunities below some point will lower labor productivity, and after some length of time may even cause strikes (or revolutions). Thus a certain percentage of consumption remains necessary if we are not to cancel out the gains made by more saving and investing of capital.

Finally, on the ideological front, we may note a strange and false notion which Stalin raised to the level of an unassailable dogma. This is the idea that steady growth cannot be achieved unless the investment sector grows faster than the consumption sector.[4] Actually, Marx merely showed that this is sometimes the case in a "capitalist" economy, and that in its extreme form it is a disproportion that usually leads to a depression. The Soviets don't claim to have a capitalist economy, and they don't desire a depression, so it is hard to see the relevance of this notion of Marx to their forced conclusion. The real reason for Stalin's doctrine that investment goods *must* grow faster was merely to reinforce the arguments for even more investment. In reality, steady growth may be achieved with any constant positive amount of net investment; the investment sector would have to grow more rapidly than the consumption sector only if one wished not steady, but constantly accelerating growth.

It would seem that a Marxist, who based himself on a socialist type of humanist ethics, would decide to maintain (in an industrially developed country) an *equal* percentage increase of consumption and investment. There is no reason to value the consumption of future humanity above that of present humanity. At any rate, the economist can only calculate the different growth rates to be gained by alternative ratios of investment to consumption. The question of which alternative ratio of investment to consumption should be picked is a political one, to be decided by democratic choice based on our collective ethical evaluations of present versus future consumers. (A somewhat similar view has now been expressed by several contemporary Soviet economists,[5] though we may differ on how and by whom the "democratic" choice is to be made.)

Most political disputes in the Soviet Union have had this issue as one of the underlying bones of contention. In the thirties it was, of course, vitally necessary to raise the level and percentage of investment by a drastic amount if industrialization were to be seriously begun. This took the concrete form of collectivization of agriculture and the removal of large amounts of agricultural goods for use as exports to buy machinery, or as cheap raw materials for industry, or as food for industrial workers.

The application of growth economics is quite different in content in the industrially developed Soviet Union of today. There are still violent political disputes over the percentage of investment to consumption, but the debate is over a small percentage either way. Now that industry is established, no one would argue that it is necessary to again double or triple the investment percentage in a few years' time. Moreover, agriculture is relatively much smaller and industry relatively much larger now. So the debate no longer centers on shifting a large product from agriculture to industry, but rather on how much of the total product is to go for wages of workers (mostly in industry) and how much should go into government profits and taxes for more investment.

Full Employment and Inflation

Soviet economists recognize today that the question of aggregate balance in the Soviet economy is mostly a reflection of the growth problem already discussed. Basically, the resources supplied for investment must just equal the amount required or demanded for investment; while the amount supplied to consumers must just equal the amount they will demand at present prices. Soviet economists must assume that the politicians have already told the planners what percentage of national output is to be put into investment. Now the planners must calculate what amounts of consumer goods with what wages and prices will be consistent with the given investment decision.

In contrast to the Soviet Union, the economy of the United States has been frequently plagued by lack of adequate demand for the products of private enterprise. In the planned economy of the U.S.S.R. there has *always* been sufficient aggregate demand (at least, since the planning period began in 1928), and there has never been general or aggregate unemployment. The reason is that a lack of aggregate demand is very easy to correct in such an economy through the device of additional government investment (or by higher real wages to consumers). In reality, the problem has usually been that the government has demanded for investment much more than could be supplied.

Since aggregate demand has always more than equaled the amount of resources and men available, aggregate unemployment has been non-existent (since 1929). Of course, the Soviet Union does have some frictional unemployment. This occurs when the structure of industry and technology changes, so that millions of workers must change jobs from one place to another or from one industry to another or from one skill to another. These millions may require retraining, and some may have little desire (or even ability) to move to distant and very different locations. The Soviet Union may also have some seasonal unemployment. This occurs because there are times of the year in certain industries, and especially in agriculture, when much labor is needed and times when very little is needed. It may not always be profitable for society to transfer these workers to other jobs for only a few months of the year, though the problem may be corrected to some extent by establishing new industries with opposite seasonal variations.

As we have implied, the main problem of aggregate balance in the Soviet economy has not been lack of demand and unemployment, but rather an excessive demand and inflation. The main reason for the inflation is that a great deal of money goes into wages for workers producing investment goods, military supplies, and free welfare goods. Yet workers can spend their wages only on consumer goods, so these goods have faced an excess demand and have risen in price. Historically, we must add that the inflation problem was very severe in the civil war, the period of initial industrialization, and World War II. Since that time, however, it has mostly been brought under control, as expressed in the facts of largely falling or constant prices (free market as well as official).

Only in the drastic circumstances of the First Five-Year Plan (and World War II) was there an actual lowering of consumption associated with higher investment (and military production). In most years, however, wages climbed much faster than the slowed growth of consumer goods, so inflationary pressures did result.

We may note some additional complicating factors. First, in addition to their basic prices, all Soviet consumer goods have a large sales or turnover tax placed upon them. Obviously, an imbalance might be corrected by raising the turnover tax rather than the before-tax price. On the other side, wages available for spending may be reduced by many other kinds of personal taxes or licenses, of which the income tax has been the most important to date. Lastly, if workers increase their personal savings, by bank deposits or purchase of government bonds, then they obviously have less money left to spend for consumption. In other words, there will be balance in the consumer-goods sector only if the turnover tax on consumer goods plus the before-tax price times the amount of consumer goods is just equal to the wages paid out in consumer, invest-ment, military, and welfare goods, less the amounts of personal saving and personal taxes. Otherwise, there will be imbalance and deflationary or inflationary pressures.

Relations Between Industries: Microbalances

The Soviet planners have till recently (compared with the latest pro-posed mathematical methods) used a fairly simple approach, called the "method of balances." For example, we might portray the balance for the iron industry as follows:

Iron Industry

1. Imports	1. Exports
2. Initial inventory	2. Closing inventory
3. Production listed by plants or regions	3. Uses by other industries, usually listed by region
Total sources	Total uses

Of course, it is only the totals that must balance.

An important economic question is the units in which these balances are stated. It turns out that the plan may be calculated in physical units because each balance deals with just one commodity, and may use that as its unit of account (or common denominator or *numéraire*). The balances may be and are also presented in terms of arbitrary rubles, which is necessary because in practice each "industry" is an aggregate of several "products"; for example, the steel industry produces several kinds of steel (which must be added together by a ruble measure).

Nevertheless, if we ignore the practical need for some aggregation of different things, it is only necessary (and sufficient) that the price be constant per unit during the time covered by the plan. It will cause no problem to the balancers that each particular price may be arbitrary in relation to all other prices, because only one price enters into each bal-ance. For this reason, the question of the "value" of a good (discussed in a later section), or the effects of consumer preference or the different labor of supplying one good as opposed to others, does not affect the balance problem. Hence, although Marxist and non-Marxist writers disagree on how to "value" or price goods, they agree in practice on how to balance industries and sectors. In fact, the Soviet method of balances is a close relative of the Western "input-output" method (a system which calculates the input requirements of each output as a set of ratios or coefficients).

This doctrinal situation (the less crucial role of valuation in balance problems) helps to explain why Soviet economists have spent so much effort on this particular problem, and have encountered many fewer difficulties in balancing than in optimizing problems.[6] Of course, it is also true that this problem, especially in the area of achieving a *full* employment of workers and resources, is of overwhelming practical importance. Furthermore, this was an area in which Marx did make a contribution.[7] Marx's scheme of balanced economic growth has been translated with some difficulty by several Marxist economists as a simplified type of Keynesian scheme of national income accounting.[8] Marx's scheme has also been translated by Lange, using a great deal of verbal skill and ingenuity, into a simple input-output model.[9] In spite of their advanced work on input-output analysis, Soviet economists apparently still use the "method of balances" in actual national planning (but are experimenting with input-output in some local and regional planning).

It should be noted to their credit that the Soviet economists of the 1920's grappled with most of the problems of balance in a very sophisticated manner. In fact, Wassily Leontief,[10] the creator of the input-output method, first began his work on this method while connected with the Soviet planning apparatus, and undoubtedly benefited from the Soviet experience and debates before he emigrated to the United States. Aside from Leontief, several other Soviet economists constructed models that might have led to a full-blown input-output analysis. Unfortunately, most of these economists were on the most conservative side of the debate on development. When Stalin attacked and even imprisoned some of them in the early thirties, he condemned *all* of their theories and related theories (including early growth models as well as balance models) as "bourgeois" or "mathematical formalism." Given the dogmatic and repressive atmosphere, it was unhealthy to pursue such models any further. Dobb[11] comments further that:

> In the second half of the '30's a half-hearted attempt was, indeed, made (prompted, it has been said, by Stalin) to revive a discussion about a synthetic "balance of the national economy." . . . The discussion scarcely got beyond questions of classification (i.e. a listing of the actual relationships of which account must be taken); it was soon to be dismissed by authority as unsatisfactory and was rather abruptly adjourned. After that for two decades silence reigned.

The intensive analysis of input-output relationships was revived only after the anti-Stalinist 20th Congress of the Communist party in 1956.

One of the great difficulties with the Soviet method of balances has been that it does not take into account the secondary effects on other industries of a change in the output of any one industry. For example, an increase in Soviet auto production means a need for more rubber tires, but that implies that the rubber-tire industry will need more rubber as well as more tire-making machinery and other supplies. By contrast, the input-output method automatically takes into account all secondary and further removed effects.

Thus, by the method of balances, it would be necessary to go through several approximations and changes affecting each balance (because all are interrelated) before getting all the different industries to balance. This takes so long, even with Soviet shortcuts, that the balancing process not only takes a great deal of energy, but also is usually completed late. Thus the final plan arrives at the enterprise *after* the period covered has already begun. Furthermore, an increasing labor force is being wastefully used in the planning process. Theoretically, the input-output method would remedy the main defect of the balance method, since it does take into account all of the indirect adjustments to any change in one item. It is also more suitable for use with electronic computers.[12]

Optimal Planning

Now we come to the question of an *optimal* balance; there are many possible balances, but only a correct theory of valuation can find the one possible optimal balance (as we shall define "optimality"). The revolutionary impact of the modern Soviet debates on optimal efficiency can be understood only in the light of their ideological history, especially the long debate over the "law of value." The Marxist law of value states that the value of any commodity is equal to the amount of average socially necessary labor embodied in it;[13] that is, the labor time usually necessary with present equipment and present technology.

HISTORY OF THE DEBATE

During the period of war communism, from 1917 to 1921, the Soviet Union did not in practice make much use of prices or of money. This lack of prices and money was idealized in theory as a true state of communism, so during this period it was held very dogmatically (but with some truth as to the actual state of affairs) that the law of value had no application under socialism, but was only a description of the situation under competitive capitalism. Then, in the period of the New Economic Policy of the 1920's, trade and exchange became general and the use of money permeated the economy. In this period there ensued a great deal of debate over the uses of prices in socialism and over the methodology of planning, but without much, if any, clarification of the use of the Marxist law of value. It was in this environment of intense discussion in 1925 that Leontief first sketched the input-output method of planning.

Unfortunately, we have noted that Stalin killed off this promising discussion (and some of the discussants as well), and attacked all model building as "bourgeois, mathematical formalism." As a result, the years of Stalin's dictatorship, from 1928 to 1953, were uncreative and terribly dull in economics. The tasks of Soviet economists in these years were characterized by one harsh critic as "perpetual propagation of Marxism, peremptory assessment of the processes of disintegration in capitalism, and exorbitant praise for the success of Soviet industrialization." [14] At any rate, it is a fact that in all those years there were no translations and few discussions of Western economics. It is a more damning fact that in all those years there was published *no* new textbook of economics and planning; the first weak effort toward a new Soviet textbook was published in 1954. Available statistical data were greatly reduced in the thirties, and their publication almost ceased after 1937; Soviet statistical yearbooks began to appear again only in 1957.

During the five-year plans of the 1930's Stalin stressed that there were no limits to what could be done—there was no need or possibility for the operation of an authentic law of value, but room only for the law of the plan. Thus Soviet economics in this period reverted to a loose Marxist formulation that "value" would disappear in socialism, which was taken to mean that the planners could do anything that Stalin desired. In fact, the official Soviet view urged planners "not to study, but to change economics, to disregard economic laws." [15] Stalinist planning was mostly empirical, using little theory and no attempt at optimal efficiency, but simply pushing as much investment as possible (with the rule of thumb in basic industry that it was wisest to follow the output mix of the United States at that period).

One Western Marxist economist who took this view was Paul Sweezy in 1942.[16] Sweezy quotes Marx on the capitalist marketplace, where Marx states that "Only as an internal law, and from the point of view of the individual agents as a blind law, does the law of value exert its influence here and maintain the social equilibrium of producton in the turmoil of the accidental fluctuations." [17]

We may note that Marx here is merely describing the way that the law of value operates under capitalism, but of course he has not said that it may not operate—although in a very different fashion—under socialism. Yet that is Sweezy's interpretation, for he writes on the basis of this quote from Marx that:

It follows that in so far as the allocation of production activity is brought under conscious control, the law of value loses its relevance and importance; its place is taken by the principle of planning. In the economics of a socialist society the theory of planning should hold the same basic position as the theory of value in the economics of a capitalist society. Value and planning are as much opposed, and for the same reasons, as capitalism and socialism. [18]

If anything is clear in this debate, it would seem to be that Sweezy and the Soviet economists of that period used the term "law of value" in a very particular fashion. For them the law of value means that prices are formed by the unconscious and automatic working of the competition of independent units. It is obviously true that in this sense the law of value does not exist in pure centrally planned socialism. Yet by the operation of a law of value in socialism most economists would mean merely that prices *should* exist and that these prices *should* somehow reflect reality. We say "should" here to express a normative (or policy) judgment that such use of prices and values will be a necessary aid to optimal planning. Obviously, in the latter sense the law of value not only exists in socialism, but is absolutely necessary and compatible with planning. (Incidentally, Sweezy does not explain the "planning principle," and one might ask what determines the optimal plan itself if there is no value calculation. Is it determined by free will?)

We might also note that while Stalin was rejecting any but purely empirical methods of planning, various important theoretical advances were beginning to poke their heads up from the practical operational fields of Soviet engineering and project making. For example, it was in 1939 that the Soviet mathematician Kantorovich, employed by an engineering firm to advise on the optimal use of their machinery, discovered what has become the most famous of all planning methods, the method of linear programming. Yet this discovery, too, was buried under the heap of ideological trash exuded by the Stalinist dictatorship. It is true that U.S. economists took several years to realize the importance of linear programming after its first appearance here, but in the Stalinist atmosphere any general utilization of such a radically new economic concept was simply inconceivable. Not only was an official dogma promulgated in scholastic detail, but Stalin's crimes included the execution or imprisonment of several of the most brilliant and daring economists of the thirties. For a feeling of the rapid change a difference in atmosphere can make, compare the drivel in the *Political Economy* text (1954) written collectively by several members of the U.S.S.R. Academy of Sciences under Stalin's personal supervision with the very sophisticated book published by the liberal Nemchinov, *The Uses of Mathematics in Economics*, in 1959, just five years later (cited in full and discussed below).

In 1943 came the first official breakthrough and recognition of value problems in the Soviet Union. At that time, in a famous article first appearing in a Soviet journal,[19] there appeared a vague but definite statement that the law of value does apply under socialism. Nothing more concrete evolved in the Soviet discussions for some time, however; in fact, not until Stalin himself took a hand in the discussion. In 1952 Stalin made his last authoritative pronouncement on the subject,[20] leading to a major debate throughout the socialist countries and the ranks of Western Marxists.

Stalin argues that "wherever commodities and commodity production exist, there the law of value must also exist." [21] He implies, and later shows that he really means to say, that wherever commodity production does *not* exist, the law of value also does not exist. By "commodity production" he means production for sale in the competitive marketplace, just as Marx and Sweezy described it in connection with the marketplace of capitalism. Stalin saw commodity production in the Soviet Union existing exclusively in the exchange of goods between the collective farm and the government-owned factories. Thus, one sympathetic Western Marxist writes, in agreement with Stalin, that "Under socialism in a country like the U.S.S.R. where a semi-private agricultural sector continues to exist alongside the state sector, commodity production (and therefore the law of value) will also continue to exist, although in a relatively restricted sphere." [22] On the other hand, and this is the crux of the question, it is quite clear that under (complete) centrally planned socialism there is no free competitive market exchange of goods between state-owned firms, and therefore there is no "commodity production" in that sphere in the peculiar sense used by Stalin. Thus, the same Western Marxist writer continues, again in agreement with Stalin, that:

> So far as manufactured goods are concerned, their situation is somewhat anomalous, since although they are technically "commodities" the

concept of a supply price is not really applicable to them, and I can not see that there is much point in attempting to analyze their prices in terms of our conceptual apparatus.[23]

In other words, Stalinist theology could admit only that some manufactured goods are "commodities" because they exchange on the market with some agricultural goods (a very thin reed on which to hang a theory), but argued that there is no possibility—or need?—to plan manufactured prices in accordance with value. This very limited recognition of value did not improve the quality of the Soviet debate by very much, if anything.

It was not until Stalin's death, and especially after the criticism of Stalin in 1956, that Soviet economists felt once again really free to discuss the importance of money and prices (as they had before Stalin took full power in the late twenties). After 1956, almost all Soviet economists did come to agree that the law of value has great importance in socialism, that is, that planning must be based on the objective facts of social needs and costs. And it was only at this time that official Soviet recognition was given to Leontief's input-output discovery and Kantorovich's linear programming discovery, indeed, claiming both as purely Soviet achievements (although both had returned to the Soviet Union only via the extensive research and writings of Western economists).

After it was admitted that the law of value does apply to a socialist economy, three different views of the value of manufactured means of production (which are the things whose values are really at issue) arose in the Soviet Union.[24] The first view is that of Ostrovitianov,[25] who assumes, like Stalin, that the law of value operates under socialism only where there is market exchange. But means of production are owned and exchanged only between government firms and the collective farms, so "value" exists only in the market exchange between manufacturing and these agricultural units, nowhere else. This is naturally a very limited view of the role of value, and does not allow the rational circulation of values or prices of the manufactured means of production exchanged by government firms.

The second view of value, that of Kronrod,[26] assumes that "value" operates wherever there is "exchange," but he argues that government enterprises (*a*) do exchange goods, (*b*) are autonomous units and may not be treated as one big firm, and (*c*) must exchange equivalent value products in order to provide material incentives for the workers of each enterprise. Therefore, he concludes that the law of value does operate in the government sector of the economy.

By contrast, the third and most radical view, that of Malyshev,[27] argues that value does *not* arise from exchange in socialism at all, nor from any automatic market process. Rather, in socialism value, or the need for valuation, arises from the necessity in the planning process of measuring the amount of labor expended on each product and in the aggregate. This view obviously sees the need for a rational calculation of value on all products coming within the plan.

We might ask why in more recent years not only the liberals, but even Stalin and his followers, began to talk about the need for rational valuation and calculation in the Soviet economy. The increased need seems to grow out of the increased complexity of the Soviet economy. For one thing, it has many more enterprise units than it did in the early days, perhaps as many as 200,000 important units at the present time. Second, there are many more technological possibilities and variants open to the Soviet planners in each industry. Third, there is a much wider variety of consumer goods to choose among, and the average income puts the Soviet consumer now far above the absolute biological-need level. Other reasons for more efficiency include the shortage of labor (from the terrible losses of World War II) and the increase on international trade.

Still further reasons for increased Soviet interest in optimal efficiency may be found in the relationship with the Western economies. On the one hand, there is the race to grow more rapidly than the United States, for which maximum efficiency is essential, or at least extremely helpful. On the other hand, there is the fact that great advances in practical methods of planning have been made in the Western countries, and that these are available for imitation. Of course, the new planning methods have been used in the United States only for planning at the micro or enterprise level, since the United States has no national economic planning. In the U.S.S.R., on the other hand, not only have the new planning methods been applied at the enterprise level, but they also have been applied—or the attempt is being made to apply them—at the macroeconomic level of national economic planning.

MARXIST ECONOMIC LAWS AND PLANNING MODELS

Is there a conflict between the Marxist economic law of value and the modern theories and methods of rational economic planning? Specifically, can the Soviet Union continue to promote Marxist economics while using the latest planning devices? There are three opposing views. First, most Anglo-American experts, such as Campbell,[28] believe that there is indeed a conflict between Marxism and modern planning theory. An extreme view is expressed by Zauberman, who claims

that the price arrived at in the calculus [of the new Soviet mathematical models] . . . turns out to be in unmistakable conflict with that derived from Marx. Marx's price is a cost price, while the conservative Soviet critics of the . . . mathematical scheme . . . correctly identified . . . [its] value-weights as scarcity prices, typically marginalist in their nature. Many of these critics . . . have rightly pointed to the deep roots of the mathematicians' price in the subjective value concept, and to its incompatability with Marx's objective value, reducible to "congealed" socially necessary labor.[29]

It follows, according to this argument, that Marxian value economics must be eliminated if the Soviet Union is to plan rationally.

Strangely enough, the major premise of this argument is accepted among the second group, the more dogmatic (orthodox?) Soviet Marxist economists, such as Boyarsky.[30] Boyarsky agrees that there *is* a conflict between Marxist economics and certain modern theories of planning. Since he believes in the absolute truth of Marxism, however, his conclusion is directly opposite to that reached by Campbell. He concludes that these planning theories must not be followed in the Soviet Union. Particular devices, such as input-output or linear programming, may be used if they are first completely purged of their marginal-utility taint.

A third position is that of the less dogmatic (liberal? creative? revisionist?) Marxists in the Soviet Union, such as Novozhilov or Kantorovich.[31] They hold that modern theories of economic planning are quite compatible with Marxism, and that the modern instruments of rational planning should be used to the fullest extent. For these views, Novozhilov and others have been labeled as revisionists of Marx both by their own dogmatic Soviet colleagues and by most Anglo-American experts. On the other hand, a more perceptive critic, Alec Nove, writes:

One should not assume, as some Western critics do, that Marxian economics is inherently inconsistent with reality, that the "vulgar Marxist" simplifications of the late-Stalin period are the essence of the theory. Novozhilov, for instance, would certainly argue that his theories are consistent with Marxism; are indeed the correct application of Marxist theory to the circumstances of the Soviet Union.[32]

In fact, Novozhilov himself admits that some of his categories of calculation under socialism, such as profits, are semantically similar to those used under capitalism, but argues strongly that this is due only to the mathematical similarities in all optimization problems.[33]

Coming now to the specifics of the argument, Campbell's criticism [34] argues that the Marxist labor theory is completely opposed to the late-nineteenth-century "reduction of all explanations to the common denominator of utility." It follows that, if all rational planning must be based on neoclassical marginal-utility economics, then the Marxist labor theory is completely opposed to any rational planning (even though Marx was the most emphatic advocate of the socially planned economy). The liberal Marxists, from Lange to Novozhilov, tend to oppose this argument on two levels. First, writers such as Lange and Sweezy in the thirties argued that Marxist economics does not conflict directly with neoclassical economics, but merely uses a different approach appropriate to different problems. As a second line of defense, Soviet writers like Novozhilov allege that it is possible to present all of the specific methods of rational planning within a Marxist framework, regardless of whether or not neoclassical economics reaches the same conclusions.

In fact, a great many of the Soviet writers now argue that there is no conflict between Marxism and the modern neoclassical theories of rational allocation of resources.[35] Specifically, the more liberal Soviet writers point out that to advocate a mathematical device (like a rate of interest) for rationally allocating capital in a planned economy is quite different from advocating that any profit (or interest) be given as individual income. If the neoclassical theory of allocation, which has largely been concerned with the allocation of scarce resources in capitalist firms, also happens to meet the similar problems of socialist firms, there is no reason not to use it.

The liberal Marxists of the West, like the early Lange, argue that there is a qualitative difference between the technical problems of planned allocation of resources and the political-ethical problems of class ownership and distribution. They agree that the technical problems of socialist planning may be best discussed in terms of "bourgeois" neoclassical economics. Yet they still believe that the political-ethical questions of income distribution by classes, as well as the macroeconomic problems of capitalism, are to be understood in terms of Marxist political economy. Of course, these tendencies are only vaguely discernible even in the boldest of the Soviet economists. Thus Novozhilov speaks of the "essential difference between Marxist-Leninist political-economy and bourgeois economic science." [36] He emphasizes the difference of principle, yet the language he uses in this article indicates that he may rather view the pertinent difference as being mainly in approach and subject matter.

Perhaps the more liberal Soviet economists will apply in economics the distinction made by Stalin in linguistics: the difference between what is in the economic base of society and what is in the ideological super-structure.[37] Stalin argued that the components of the technological-eco-nomic base, such as the science of engineering, are not partisan and are not limited to one class or society. It is only the elements of the ideolog-ical superstructure, such as political institutions or laws of property or ethical philosophies, that are necessarily partisan in nature and class-biased. The components of the economic base, on the other hand, may pass directly from use in bourgeois society to use in socialist society. Stalin characterized language as part of this technical economic base. The same argument has been extended by the Soviets to cover formal logic and relativity physics, which are now accepted as valuable tools (though their accompanying philosophies are still attacked as part of the ideolog-ical superstructure).

Similarly, in Marxist terms the economists might claim that the range of issues covered by Marxist political economy is part of the ideological superstructure of socialism, and should be opposed to "bourgeois political economy" on the same range of issues. *But* the technical-economic theory of allocation of resources advanced by neoclassical economics (in either its marginal or its linear-programming form) might be safely consigned to the economic base. Then it might be considered nonpartisan (*when separated from its political and ethical connotations*), and a val-uable analytic tool as applicable to planning in socialism as to planning within a capitalist firm.[38]

If the above attitude were accepted, then a fortiori there would be no conflict between Marxism and any prospective tool of Soviet economic planning. Since it is far from fully accepted, each action of Soviet planners is still gauged by the politicians in terms of a very dogmatic interpretation of Marxism.

PRICING IN THE SOVIET ECONOMY

The Importance of Prices. Prices enter the problem of interindustry balance only in a very simple way, not necessarily involving a theory of value (unless we want an *optimum* balance, as we shall see below).[39] In other words, balances among industries might theoretically be done in wholly physical terms (and are to some degree in the Soviet Union). Where prices are used, they may be any arbitrary or randomly chosen prices, just so long as they remain constant for each item everywhere it appears during the entire planning period. This is because prices are used in the balancing procedure only for aggregate purposes (even in a particular industry), merely to ensure that the flow of money in one direction equals the value (in arbitrary prices) of goods or services flowing in the other direction. For example, assuming no changes in taxes and saving, whatever amount of wages is paid out in rubles, the aggregate problem of preventing inflation is merely to ensure that these wages are a certain number of rubles less than the value of consumer goods on the market (also in some ruble prices).

Notice that *if* we are allowed to vary the amounts of final outputs required, then there are an infinite number of solutions of balanced input mixes and corresponding output mixes (hereafter called simply input-output solutions) possible, corresponding to the infinite number of output mixtures possible with the transfer of the given inputs to different industries. Furthermore, there is another infinite set of balanced input-output solutions possible, even with set outputs, *if* we are allowed to vary the technological processes (reflected in the input-output ratios).

The situation is quite different when we turn to the other problem of planning, the optimization of economic efficiency. There is only *one optimal* balance, and what it is depends on how we "value" or price each of the inputs and outputs. The optimization problem has two aspects: (1) the choice of a most preferred output mixture to give us a maximum output, and (2) the choice of most efficient technology to give us a minimum cost or maximum output.

To obtain the optimum balance, or most outputs for our inputs, we need to do things in the way that produces the *most* valuable output with the least costs. Either to calculate costs or to evaluate output, we must therefore have prices that rationally reflect social costs and social needs. The problem may actually be solved exclusively *either* by minimizing costs *or* by maximizing the value of output. We do not need to do both, and indeed will have too many fixed and inconsistent goals if we try to work from both ends at once.

As a concrete example, suppose the Soviet economy produces only two kinds of outputs: apples and oranges. With the given amount of labor and capital inputs available, the economy can produce either (*a*) five apples and ten oranges *or* (*b*) ten apples and five oranges. Those are the only possibilities. Which output mixture should be produced to maximize output? That obviously depends on the value or price of each output, relative to the price of the other output. If the relative prices are two rubles an apple and one ruble an orange, then we maximize by choosing mixture *b*, ten apples and five oranges. But if the prices were one ruble an apple and two rubles an orange, then we would maximize by choosing mixture *a*, five apples and ten oranges.

The case is exactly analogous if we wish to minimize the cost of inputs. Suppose the only inputs available are capital and labor. To produce a certain required amount of output (for example, a given number of apples and oranges), there are two technological processes available, involving either (*a*) the use of five units of labor and ten units of capital *or* (*b*) the use of ten units of labor and five units of capital. Each "unit" is a physical measure such as hours of labor expended or numbers of machines used. Processes *a* and *b* are the only ways of producing the required output. Which process will minimize the cost of inputs? Again, this depends on the relative prices of the inputs. We will choose *a* if a unit of labor costs two rubles and a unit of capital one ruble. But we will choose *b* if a unit of labor costs one ruble and a unit of capital costs two rubles.

Soviet Price Policies. The Soviet views on price policy follow fairly clearly from their different views on value. One view, which has been labeled "voluntarist," is simply to have the planners set prices as they desire. This view derives from the notion that the law of value has no application to the socialist economy, and that prices need have no effect on planning. Needless to say, this view has no explicit defenders anymore in the Soviet Union. On the other hand, the Soviet price structure still bears an unfortunate resemblance to what might be expected of it under such a view. That is to say, in practice Soviet prices do not seem clearly correlated with any particular value theory, though a major reform is now being carried through.

If the present Soviet prices do resemble the results expected under some value theory, it would be those value and pricing theories deriving from a legalistic interpretation of the application of Marxist theory in a socialist economy. Thus all of these theories begin with the notion that price must equal the value in labor terms, which must represent the total of the wage cost (Marx's variable capital) plus the cost of materials and capital depreciation (Marx's constant capital) plus a profit margin (Marx's surplus value). Assuming that it is possible to calculate the wage and other current costs (variable plus constant capital), there still remains the problem of calculating the profit margin or surplus value in a socialist economy. The Soviet economists call this portion of the value the amount of "surplus for society," indicating it is that amount of the product which does not go to the individual worker, but which is used for social purposes, such as investment in expanded facilities. There is considerable disagreement among Soviet economists (cited below) as to exactly how the calculations should be made.

One group would calculate the surplus value as equal to the wage cost times the rate of surplus value (the rate being the ratio of surplus to wage cost).[40] A second group would calculate the surplus as equal to the total cost of production times the ratio of surplus to the total cost of production.[41] The first notion seems to derive more closely from Marx's first volume of *Capital*, though the second seems to give a more comprehensive meaning to the profit margin, which its advocates argue will help make socialist enterprises aware of the need to economize on materials as well as labor. A third group, still apparently the smallest of the three, advocates a formula similar to Marx's "price of production." [42] They would have the surplus calculated as equal to the total amount of capital times the ratio of surplus to capital. Advocates of the third view would argue that this pricing procedure might also encourage socialist enterprises to economize on capital goods (which were provided free of charge to the individual enterprises until the 1965 reforms). We might note that all three seem to assume a knowledge of the aggregate social surplus, and are merely stating formulas for the calculation of individual prices on the basis of that knowledge.

The small group advocating price of production as the basis of price setting shade over into an even smaller group that reaches similar conclusions, not on the basis of any authoritative theological text (such as *Capital* has come to be in the Soviet Union), but on the basis of imputing prices from the objective facts of either social costs or social needs. One widely known approach, which falls within the imputationist group, is that of the Soviet economist Novozhilov,[43] who wishes to impute all the prices of inputs from the objective conditions of the cost of production to society; that is, he wishes to minimize the cost of production in terms of the total expenditure of labor. He wishes to calculate that alternative of the plan which has the minimum costs, estimated in terms of labor expenditure as the common denominator or *numéraire*. Novozhilov still claims that all cost "consists of labor cost," but this remains a somewhat abstract statement. The key operational point is that these methods include in their calculations not only the cost of the direct expenditure of living labor, *plus* the labor embodied in the used-up plant, equipment, and materials, but *also* certain so-called indirect labor costs.

The indirect labor costs are the costs of using natural resources and capital in this project rather than elsewhere (in non-Marxist terms, the opportunity costs of using scarce resources). Why must central planners consider these indirect costs? The most precise or concrete answer is this: If capital and natural resources are used in certain projects in large amounts, then there may not be sufficient capital and natural resources remaining to use them as desired in all other projects. In that case, the other projects will have to switch to the use of more labor-intensive methods, thus indirectly causing an increase of labor costs. Of course, this problem would not arise if there were an infinite amount of capital and natural resources readily available, but according to Novozhilov, *"some means of production cannot be reproduced and are in short supply as compared to the demand for them."* [44] Natural resources can hardly be replaced at all when they are depleted; and there is a given stock of capital goods at a given time, which can be expanded only in the future and within limits.

Since these goods are limited (or "scarce"), they must be rationed; and that is the function of the calculation of the indirect labor costs. In choosing the plan alternative with the minimum cost (for *given* projects), the planner compares not only current labor costs and the using up of capital and materials, but also the indirect labor costs of directing scarce resources here rather than elsewhere. In this sense the indirect costs play a similar role to the rate of profit (and rent) in private enterprise, which rations capital (and natural resources) to different industries so that the marginal return is uniform for all industries. If we imagine Soviet enterprises borrowing all capital from the government, then this calculation acts like a rate of interest which ensures that (1) investment funds are used where most profitable to the society, and (2) investment goes to just that point where aggregate supply and demand are equal. Novozhilov notes the fact that his scheme is similar in form, *not* to the simple labor-value picture (with profits related only to costs of living labor), but to the "prices of production" of Marx's Volume 3 of *Capital* (with profits related to total use of capital).[45]

Novozhilov does emphasize that all of the calculations are in terms of labor expended (directly or indirectly). Yet the indirect labor costs do allow a rate of return on capital (similar to profit or interest) and a rate of return on natural resources (similar to rent); thus the scheme might appear to raise certain ideological problems for Marxists. Campbell argues that these methods "necessarily implied the productivity of capital, a proposition in conflict with the labor theory of value." [46] We have seen in discussing Marx's theories of surplus value that he admits that the use of capital may greatly increase the product per worker. Indeed, he emphasizes in discussing growth and innovation that new and better capital vastly reduces the *total* labor expenditure on the product, even including the labor necessary to produce the machines; this is Marx's definition of technological advance. Moreover, his theory of profit is based on the idea that it is the capitalists' private (and monopoly) ownership of capital that allows them to make a profit. In these senses, Marx admits the "produc-

tivity" of *capital*, but he does not admit that the capitalist is "productive";
which is to say that he makes an ethical judgment that the capitalist does
nothing to "justify" his receiving the profit.

In any event, whether the loan of capital justifies the private making
of profit in a private-enterprise economy is irrelevant to the discussion of
a centrally planned economy, since no one (certainly not Novozhilov) is
proposing to give the "profit" to any private individual. The point is only
that the planners must take into consideration the necessary rate of profit
or uniform return on capital (and natural resources) in order to determine whether it is worthwhile for the society to use it here rather
than elsewhere, and in order to bring an equality between the aggregate
supply and demand for capital (and natural resources). In both societies
the rates of profit or interest (and rent) function as devices to allocate
scarce resources, but only in a private-enterprise economy do these rates
also affect the distribution of income among individuals (the latter being
the only aspect that interested Marx). It follows that the objections by
the Soviet dogmatists to words such as "profit" and "productivity of
capital" in this context are formal and purely semantic, and have no
foundation either in Marxist value theory or in real issues.

Campbell writes that "it is disquieting to good Marxists to see such
concepts as rent, returns for capital, and opportunity costs emerge as
implications of assumptions with which they cannot quarrel, but this
unpleasantness is no refutation." [47] But, of course, we have seen that a
good Marxist should not attempt to refute the use of these concepts in
socialism, since Marx himself said nothing against the technical economic
concept of profit (or rent or interest) as an allocator of a limited amount
of capital to different industries. What Marx clearly argued against was
the political-economic notion of private profit as a justifiable return to
private capitalists. It seems to be only the confused thinking of some
Western economists [48] and dogmatic Soviet economists that finds anything un-Marxist in the use of profitability as a criterion of planning or
as an indication of enterprise performance, especially since the advocates
of the profit criterion have emphasized that they would not allocate the
profit to any private individual.

We may note one practical objection to any set of centrally planned
prices based on labor time, regardless of how the indirect or capital costs
are converted into labor-hours. It is certainly not easy, if it is possible,
to estimate consistently the long-run cost in labor-hours of all the
hundreds of thousands of commodities produced. Moreover, with every
change in technology, all of the labor costs must be recalculated. Even
a technological change in one small area will effect many other areas in

widening ripples; and we are in an era of vast technological changes occurring quite often. Thus, whatever formula is agreed upon, the actual calculation will obviously be difficult at any one time, and extremely difficult in keeping abreast of necessary changes.

CALCULATIONS OF MAXIMUM OUTPUT

Western economists have for some time been planning (by the method of linear programming) how exactly to maximize the value of output of a given enterprise by choice of the optimal mixture of outputs. The same procedure can theoretically be used to calculate a maximum solution for the whole economy.[49]

This solution will give us those particular outputs that will be the maximum possible production (if valued in terms of their prices) in the given circumstances. We must know, in order to set up and solve the problem, three kinds of facts. First, we must know the total amounts of each available input, such as the number of workers in the labor force, which constitute the constraints or limitations to the possible amounts of production. Secondly, we must know the prices of each output, which constitute our valuation of the outputs based upon social preferences and social costs of production. Finally, the third item that we must know is the technical coefficient relating each output to its inputs (with the assumption that there is only *one* technically feasible method of production). Given these ingredients, we can find that combination of final outputs that will give us the maximum value of (a balanced) output with these inputs.

Western economists have also used linear programming methods to calculate the minimum cost of technological process for a firm with a given output goal. This requires merely a knowledge of (1) the total required output, (2) the available technological variants (expressed as linear equations), and (3) the price of each input.

When faced with the theoretical problem of choosing minimum-cost technologies for a whole economy at once, however, Western economists have usually set up the (linear) programming problem in terms of which choice of technology (*and* choice of output mixture) will maximize the value of output produced. In other words, for the whole economy they assume a given amount of resources (natural, labor, and capital) rather than given production targets. We shall see later that they consider it more useful to planners to calculate how to produce the greatest possible output within the limits of their resources, rather than to calculate the cheapest way to produce for particular goals (because the latter may leave some labor and other resources unemployed in the initial calculation).

CALCULATIONS OF MINIMUM COSTS

The problem presents itself quite differently to Soviet economic planners, who are *given* a set of production targets (chosen by God or by Stalin, though they might be chosen on the basis of questionnaires to all consumers or a referendum to all voters, or by some mixture of political leadership and consumer desire). To meet fixed production targets, the planners' task is to minimize production costs by choosing the best possible technology (and not by interfering in the political choice of output mixture).

More specifically, in the Soviet context, what we are talking about here when we mention the choice of technology is the choices of investment projects. New investments, after all, involve most of our technological choice, simply because already established facilities for current output must be using certain fixed kinds of capital goods and technological procedures which may not be varied. It is only with new investment, or the addition of new capital goods, that we may choose between old and new types of technology. Thus in the Soviet Union the problems of cost minimization in the choice of new technology have been much debated under the heading of the "choice of the best investment."

One ideological problem which arises—and which we have mentioned briefly in the discussion of prices—is the determination of the price of capital, or the interest rate in Western terminology. This interest rate is necessary as a rationing device in both capitalism and socialism, though in socialism it does not become a private income as it does under capitalism.

Capital was provided freely to each Soviet firm until the 1965 reforms, but it is clearly not a free good to the Soviet economy. The Soviet writer Novozhilov [50] speaks of the extremely limited amount of capital in the Soviet Union compared with its possible uses. In other words, previous labor has produced only so much capital at the present time, and it is this present supply that must be matched with the demand. Thus we shall see that we cannot choose all of the possible investment opportunities for capital, or at least not all of the most intensive capital-using variants, but only those that are more effective within the limits of the total supply. Novozhilov explains a method for choosing the more effective uses for the limited supply of capital, in order to minimize the cost of inputs, utilizing a device that closely resembles the interest rate and profit calculation. We may note that physical capital in this sense includes not only the present supply of factories and equipment (which may be increased in the future), but also the amounts of natural resources which we desire to add to inventories (which are limited by nature).

Novozhilov [51] assumes as given (1) the number of units of output of each good, (2) the input-output coefficients for each possible technological variant of production for each good, and (3) the price of each input. He also includes one more item, the total investment funds available for the economy. This last is really a substitute for the rate of interest, which is not given beforehand, but which is to be determined so that the total amount of available investment funds are just exactly used up in new investment projects. In fact, he looks at the whole problem only in terms of the need to distribute effectively capital rather than all inputs. Although somewhat cruder than the method suggested above, it will reach the same results under most circumstances.

In Novozhilov's method we measure the "effectiveness" of each investment according to how much labor is saved by that investment. The term "effectiveness" might be translated into Western economics approximately as "opportunity cost," or in plain English as "benefit" or "gain." It appears that he assumes the amount of labor itself to be sufficient for all of the uses determined for the limited amount of capital. Notice also that, since the output plan must be made in any case, there is no question but that we must use some variant that will produce that amount of output. The question is only whether it would be more effective to use additional investment (beyond the necessary minimum) in this industry or in some other industry—up to the point where we have used up the entire available investment fund.

The Coefficient of Relative Effectiveness. Novozhilov specifically calls for the following method of application of investment choice to the economy: first, each technological variant is to be listed according to the economic effectiveness of the additional or marginal investment, which listing is generally called the coefficient of relative effectiveness (CRE). Secondly, he would sum up the minimum necessary investment in each industry, that is, the variant which uses the least amount of capital in order to produce the required output. Thirdly, he would sum up the additional investment in each industry necessary for the most efficient variant—those with the highest coefficients of relative effectiveness —and would continue to add investment for further projects up to the level where the sum of all these projects equals the supply of investment funds. By this method, he would ensure that the required output is not only produced, but produced in the most efficient manner.

Now we must examine more carefully exactly what is the coefficient of relative effectiveness and, more generally, what is the appropriate criterion of the most effective or efficient investment. In its most abstract form, we can easily say that the criteria for the best investment should be the social gain, that is, the social benefit minus the social cost from the additional project, as a ratio to the amount of additional capital required for the project. Thus we should always use those projects with the greatest social gain per unit of investment. We may note that one emphasizes the word "social" here as opposed to the gain to a single enterprise. Soviet planning in the past has often examined the gain from a single project in isolation from both the secondary cost and benefits to the rest of the economy. Clearly in a socialist economy one should emphasize, as Novozhilov does, that both the direct and the indirect costs and benefits are of importance.

Earlier Soviet planners would always have been tempted to use the variant which is more efficient in their particular enterprise or project, and which usually uses the most capital as a consequence. Novozhilov, however, is careful to point out that the limited amount of capital means that an increase in efficiency in one project with the use of much capital must mean a loss of efficiency and productivity elsewhere, in those projects that are deprived of the additional capital. Thus he constructs his coefficient of relative effectiveness in this way: Suppose we have two projects called 1 and 2, each of which is designed to produce exactly the same amount of output. In project 1 we use less capital, but more labor and higher current cost per year; whereas in project 2 we use more capital, but less annual labor and other current cost. Novozhilov's coefficient of relative effectiveness is designed to compare not only these two projects, but also any other project which might have used the additional capital required in project 2.[52]

We have already seen that Novozhilov calculates the price of capital —that is, its "effectiveness"—in terms of the saving of labor by the use of that capital. Since the CRE also measures the need for greater expenditure of labor elsewhere, it is very similar to the Western concept of "opportunity cost." It may now be clear that his CRE amounts to the same thing as an interest or profit rate on capital. The object of his calculations may be restated as the listing of all possible new investment projects according to their rate of profit, and the choosing of those which have a higher rate of profit than the socially given rate of interest, where this rate of interest should be chosen so as to just equate the supply and demand for new investment.

Where the single U.S. firm looks at the rate of interest simply as the price it must pay for money capital, the Soviet planner thinks of the same rationing instrument as simply that physical rate of return which will allow the economy to recoup its investment in a given number of years. Thus, if the interest rate or CRE, set so as to equalize aggregate supply and demand, is 5 percent, Soviet planners used to speak of a twenty-year "period of recoupment." Actually, the CRE criterion is considerably more crude than the efficiency models of U.S. economists, but it is quite similar to the break-even points and other rules of thumb actually used in practice by many U.S. managers and managerial economists.

Obviously, which of the terms we use does not matter so long as the calculations are the same.[53] This coefficient of relative effectiveness or profit rate would then be compared with the socially required "normal" coefficient of relative effectiveness or minimum interest rate to see if the project is worth doing. For example, if the socially required coefficient of relative effectiveness were 5 percent (or a twenty-year recoupment period), then a project with a mere 4 percent coefficient of relative effectiveness would not be chosen. We would then be forced to choose project 1, since the planned quantity of output must be produced in any case.

Ideology and Criticism. Novozhilov here emphasizes that, in order to compare all projects in the economy that might have made use of the capital to save labor, it is obviously necessary to use the same normal coefficient of relative effectiveness or interest rate as a requirement for approval *in all projects* of the economy. This would represent a considerable improvement on present Soviet practice, which uses different coefficients for different parts of the economy. Of course, it may be that Soviet planners believe that a distorted price structure would otherwise lead to choice of the wrong distribution of investments among different industries, so that they use the coefficient of relative effectiveness only to choose among projects within an industry (assuming a given volume of investment going to that industry).

In fact, when the argument is made against Novozhilov that "profitability" or "effectiveness" should not rule over the *planned* development of heavy industry, this can only mean that the conservatives do not trust the price weights given to different items; or it may even mean that they want further to increase the planned output of heavy industry. This is the case because Novozhilov is only comparing costs for all *approved* planned outputs, and would reject a project only if it were not the most effective way of producing the desired output mixture within the limits of the available capital. It sometimes appears that the conservative critics really mean in practice to approve even more capital-using projects in the heavy industries and to increase the output of these industries beyond what is originally given. They should then admit this and set either higher output quotas *or* a higher social minimum coefficient of relative effectiveness, which would mean allocating more of total national income to investment than has previously been given. Since Novozhilov is willing to assume that the politicians have already made the decision on how far to restrict consumption for a maximum growth rate, his method does *not* affect that decision.

Western economists still attack Novozhilov (and his comrade in arms, Kantorovich) on the basis that

. . . Kantorovich's and Novozhilov's theories are cost theories of value. In terms of Alfred Marshall's famous metaphor, they still imply that since one blade of the scissors is stationary (that is, that demand is given) it is the action of the other blade (cost or supply) that cuts the paper. They represent an advance over the more primitive labor-cost theory of value that Marx employed, but still fall short of complete generality.[54]

But in the first place this would seem to accord with Marx's special case of the Marshallian model, so that Novozhilov could certainly maintain that he is exactly within the Marxist tradition. In the second place, we have seen that Novozhilov's theory is sufficient to cover the choice of more effective investment when outputs are given, so that he does actually present a sufficient theory to cover the actual special circumstances met by the Soviet planners under the present institutional setup.

A more vital objection to the method so far proposed by Novozhilov is the assumption that the total output of each commodity is fixed in the plan independently of any value calculation. This has to be the case when the problem is approached in terms of minimizing costs. But the problem was set in this fashion only for ideological convenience, so as to make it sound genuinely Marxist by reducing everything to labor costs (and so as not to disturb the politicians, who like to set the planned outputs). In Soviet reality the problem faced by the planners is most usefully approached as the maximization of output, provided, of course, that we also use as little labor as possible so as also to maximize leisure. It makes far more sense to consider how to maximize the value of all outputs with given amounts of land, labor, and capital.

This means, however, that one would have to attach a price tag reflecting the marginal utility of each output. That would indeed be even more heretical in terms of the semantics involved. We have already observed, however, that there is no real analytic conflict between marginal-utility analysis and the labor theory of value. And whether we minimize cost (which sounds most Marxist) or maximize output (which sounds most neoclassical), we shall arrive at the same mathematical results if we begin with the same technical coefficients and constraints. Moreover, many of the liberal Marxists see in technical economic schemes for the recognition of use-value in allocation of resources *no* substantive conflict with Marx's "political economy." [55] Finally, we can even quote a very orthodox Marxist authority to the effect that maximization of satisfaction is exactly the task of socialist economics; Stalin writes:

The essential features and requirements of the basic law of socialism might be formulated roughly in this way: the securing of the maximum satisfaction of the constantly rising material and cultural requirements of the whole of society through the continuous expansion and perfection of socialist production on the basis of higher techniques.[56]

LIMITATIONS OF OPTIMAL PROGRAMMING

Optimal kinds of programming, such as linear programming, can solve any planning problem in theory. In practice, however, they are not a panacea for Soviet planning. In the first place, a huge amount of accurate information is necessary.

The extent of this problem is recognized by many economists in the Soviet Union today. Soviet central planners would not only need more information, but would also need it in different forms and categories than are presently available. Moreover, they would somehow have to prevent the systematic distortion of information which is now practiced by many self-seeking individuals at various levels of reporting, from the directors right up to the ministers.

Secondly, once the millions of pieces of information are gathered, it is still an enormous job in terms of time as well as labor actually to perform the necessary calculations. If every detail of the economy's technology and output mixture is to be planned, the problem will even tax the capacity of the total number of available modern electronic computers. Finally, even if the information is obtained and all the equations are calculated, it is no simple task to get managers and workers to follow the plan exactly as directed.

When we look at Soviet reality, we find some careful macroplanning for growth, some crude but fairly successful planning for balance among industries, but very little consideration of optimum technology and output mixes. This shortcoming in optimization is reflected in—and made inevitable by—the helter-skelter and irrational structure of Soviet prices (to be corrected to some extent, it is hoped, by the recent extensive price reforms).

The fullest defense of actual Soviet practices, as well as criticism of other, more decentralized market-exchange practices of socialism, is to be found in the works of the British Marxist Maurice Dobb.[57] He argues, first, that the optimum plan is not so difficult as it seems in the abstract, because planning is not done from scratch, but always starts with an existent technology and output mix. Secondly, he stresses that in many cases there are only a few technologies available, or even just one, so physical planning of technology without rational prices is not so difficult as it might seem in theory. Thirdly, he is very suspicious of basing all prices on consumer desires, since they are irrational or antisocial even in some of their own individual decisions, not to speak of the relative weight they might give to defense or investment (presumably, politicians elected by these same consumers will somehow have a longer-run viewpoint). Fourthly, he of course emphasizes the difficulties of the nonplanned competitive alternative, whether capitalist or market socialist; specifically, the problems of price and income distortion by monopoly and production restriction by depressions.

The last two points point the direction of Dobb's overall view, which is that centrally planned socialism successfully provides rapid economic growth, even though it is at the expense of a certain degree of economic inefficiency or nonoptimality at any given time. This view has also been expressed pointedly in the witty remarks of Wiles, who writes:

There is substance in the charge that "scarcity" economics is finicky and academic. . . . The loss of "welfare" or "efficiency" through an incorrect micro-economic allocation of resources is surely less than that brought about by unemployment, restrictive labor practices, the refusal to share trade secrets or the suppression of workable patents, could any of these losses ever be measured. Thus in the Soviet economy there are, as it were, always too few hairbrushes and too many nailbrushes in view of the resources available, while in a "capitalist" economy this proportion is always more nearly right. But the production of both these articles is growing at about 10 percent per annum in the U.S.S.R. and at about 2 percent per annum in "capitalist" countries. In the end the Soviet citizen will be better supplied even with hairbrushes.[58]

The Debate on Decentralization

Soviet reformers have not only tried to evolve a more rational economics in order to achieve more perfect central calculation, but have also advocated the decentralization of much decision making down to the level of the enterprise. In addition to some of the writing and experience with the decentralized New Economic Policy system of the 1920's,[59] we may briefly note one theoretical source and one practical source of the recent Soviet (and east European) controversy on central planning versus decentralized market socialism. These two sources are the prolific and influential writings of the Polish economist Oskar Lange and the experience of market socialism in Yugoslavia.

Lange's Model. Lange's scheme [60] is in the minds of each of the participants in the present debate on decentralization in eastern Europe, and is probably known to most or all of the Soviet writers. Although Lange mentioned the possibility of price and output decisions by completely independent socialist firms, the more interesting variant today is his somewhat more centralized proposal. In brief, he proposed (1) that the central planners set some arbitrary prices, but (2) that they change them if at those prices there is excess demand (shown by long lines of unsatisfied consumers) or excess supply (shown by goods left on the shelves). Then (3) the managers would choose output so that the given price equals their actual marginal cost. In long-run decisions, (4) industries would invest so as to maximize profit (up to the point where interest equals expected profit), and (5) central planners would loan capital (from taxes?) to firms at the rate of interest which would equalize firm demand and the supply determined at the center. Households would have freedom of choice as to where to work and as to what consumer goods to buy with their wages.

Yugoslav Experience. After Yugoslavia broke away from Stalin's control in 1948, it instituted within a few years a radically decentralized version of socialism. In theory, the workers in each enterprise could (1) elect the manager, (2) determine the production plan and the prices of outputs (in competition with other firms), and (3) split the profits in any way desired. Although Yugoslav practice was never anywhere near so extreme, the Yugoslav experiment nevertheless shook eastern Europe

and the Soviet Union. At first it was declared pure anathema and condemned as mere reversion to capitalism, but it has come more and more
to be considered a fruitful experience for study and partial imitation. It
is attractive because it has achieved a high rate of growth, but Soviet
economists emphasize that Yugoslav success is partly built on a large
volume of U.S. aid and on the relatively large earnings sent home by
Yugoslavs working in western Europe.

HISTORY OF THE LIBERMAN PROPOSALS

The "Great Debate" on decentralization ostensibly emanated from a
1962 article in *Pravda* by Kharkov economist Evsei G. Liberman,[61] proposing to revamp the existing incentive system for Soviet enterprises.
The editorial board of *Pravda* footnoted the article with a request for
written responses to the proposals; reactions were immediate. The discussion which followed was extended to include nearly every aspect of
Soviet economic life, essential for evaluating the implications as well as
the specifics of Liberman's plan. In the press, in technical discussion
groups, in the U.S.S.R. Academy of Sciences, and in a plenary meeting
of the Central Committee of the Communist party, notables and new-
comers among economists, planners, and politicians participated in a
search for truths about the present and proposed systems, and often
disagreed.

There followed a year of relative slack in open debate (1963–64),
during which important experiments with reform ideas were implemented on a limited basis. Then, in 1964, a second round began, again
with a *Pravda* article inviting responses.[62] The winds of change gained
further momentum during this 1964–65 phase of the controversy, and
the government responded with what some regard as a major alteration
of state-enterprise relations: the September, 1965, Kosygin reform. Each
phase of the debate as well as of the reforms is worth examining in some
detail.

Within the atmosphere of increased freedom for scientific inquiry
after 1956, there arose—in addition to the theorists of more perfect
calculation, whom we have already discussed—a faction of economists
whose approach was more pragmatic. They analyzed concrete matters,
seeking experiments and solutions to deal with limited problems. Criticism of malfunctions of the enterprise incentive system during the fifties
flowed largely from their evidence and conclusions. Kharkov Professor
E. G. Liberman was one of these pragmatists. Liberman published three
papers in Soviet journals during the fifties,[63] arguing that specific prob-

lems created by existing success indicators could be overcome by appropriate changes in the operational constraints of enterprises. By the 1959 paper the scheme of reforms he advocated was essentially of the same kind as that which kicked off the 1962 controversy. However, until 1962 neither this man nor his recommendations were the subjects of public focus or the attentions of other writers.

The debate was given urgency when the Soviet political leadership became alarmed over the retardation in growth rates apparent in the early 1960's. The thesis has been advanced that the difficulties and the need for reform are both due to the growing complexity and interdependence of Soviet allocations, which make it increasingly difficult to devise priority ranking and balance the plan. Yet we may note the opposite argument by one U.S. economist:

that Rumania, which has experienced the highest consistent rate of growth in the postwar years, is blithely retaining the old planning methods for the next five years, anticipating annual increases in national income (8%), industrial production (11.6%), and real wages (4 to 5%)—all of which are higher than those expected in other socialist regimes. It may be argued that it is only a question of time before the Rumanians will run into difficulties and be forced to emulate the Bulgarians and Hungarians—both of whom have opted for the reforms. Perhaps this is so, but until this happens, we may emphasize the more tangible explanations for the generally recognized slowdown in socialist growth rates outside Rumania, and possibly Bulgaria. These factors are: (1) the slowdown in birthrates during World War II; (2) the increase in military and space expenditures; and (3) the overextension of economic assistance. The importance and impact of these factors varies from country to country, but they least affect the Rumanians and Bulgarians.[64]

Of course, one could also speak of unique success factors, such as the special advantage of Rumania in sitting on a very remarkable pool of oil (which may simplify the planners' problems). On the ideological side, in the U.S.S.R. by 1962 the theoretical reformers and the pragmatists had begun to converge on agreed general directions in institutional reform. Thus in 1962 it was economic theorist V. S. Nemchinov who gave pragmatist Liberman a first chance to influence important academic personnae, persuading the Scientific Council of the Academy of Sciences to hear the then obscure Kharkov professor. Despite the strong support of Chairman Nemchinov, the proposals were rejected by the council. By September, however, the initiation of a public discussion of them had apparently been decided upon, and the discussion was begun on the ninth of that month.

THE ESSENTIALS OF THE LIBERMAN PLAN [65]

The Kharkov incentive system (as Liberman calls his plan) overtly calls for structural changes in the planning process only at the level of the firm. Planning down to that level is to proceed as before; that is, "the basic levers of centralized planning—prices, finances, budget accounting, large capital investments . . . all the value, labor and natural indices of rates and proportions of production, distribution and consumption will be determined entirely at the center." [66] The relationship of the planning apparatus to the individual enterprise, however, is to be fundamentally changed.

To encourage greater "economic maneuverability" and initiative, the large number of indicator targets presently passed down to the firms is to be steamlined to "key indices" only. Analyzing the "principal demands that society makes of socialist enterprises," Liberman recommends assigning enterprises just those targets which exclusively pertain to their final output mix: quantity and assortment of production, product destinations, and delivery dates. The input mix is to be determined by each individual firm (though he leaves unclear what is to be the status of the centrally planned system of material allocations).

How well an enterprise fulfills society's demand for maximum efficiency is to be assessed solely on the basis of "ultimate efficiency." Profitability—profits expressed as a percentage of productive capital—is to serve as this inclusive evaluator, being estimated in yearly plans submitted by all firms. Provided that the stated output goals are attained, the level of profitability achieved will become the sole determinant of the size of bonus funds awarded to the firm and its employees. Liberman depicts the central planners as "relieved from petty tutelage over enterprises" and from "costly efforts to influence production through administrative measures rather than economic ones." [67]

Bonus payments to enterprises will be computed by comparing the profitability rate of a particular firm with a "profitability norm" established for the "branch of industry" or "group of enterprises" within which each firm is to be included. The attempt is to set a "single standard of profitability for enterprises in roughly the same natural and technical conditions." Norms also will vary with the proportion of new products in a firm's production program—being raised, for example, when no new products are being introduced. Different incentive payment scales will then be set up for the different branches of industry. The bonus premiums earned by the firm under this system will be utilized, as the manager directs, to (1) pay salary bonuses to management and workers, (2) provide new housing, nurseries, kindergartens, and recreation facilities for worker families, and (3) finance decentralized investments.

To motivate directors to draft as ambitious plans as their productive potential allows, Liberman advances three proposals. First, incentive premiums per ruble of capital invested are to rise as the rate of profit increases. Second, the firm is to benefit more from fulfilling its own profitability plan than from overfulfilling it. Third, the norms of profitability are to be established "for an extended period of time" (from two to five years or more), so that firm directors can count on reaping benefits from successful innovations or particularly effective cost-saving programs, for example, without worrying that targets will be quickly ratcheted upward. The concern for profitability is also supposed to stimulate the manager to search for cost reductions and to produce the output mix demanded by his consumers.

ANALYSIS AND CONTROVERSY: 1962–63

Both moderate and active supporters of the Kharkov system in the Soviet Union agree that a "rational" price system is a necessary precondition for a profit-based index to serve as an effective evaluator of enterprise efficiency. Although Liberman himself has been somewhat indefinite about what changes in pricing methodology would be necessary to achieve this "rationality," others (such as V. S. Nemchinov) have been taking a strong stand for many years. Since profits derive from revenues, which derive from prices, profitability will be a measure of real and not merely of paper efficiency only if prices reflect the relative values of all inputs into production. Consequently, as L. Gatovsky asserts, substantial price deviations "above or below the socially necessary outlays result, regardless of the operation of the enterprise, either in an unjustifiably low profitability, and even loss, or in excessive profitability." [68] Furthermore, the most rigorous advocates openly recognize capital goods (at least fixed capital) as a scarce factor of production, representing "socially necessary outlays of labor." [69]

Among the evaluations of the most active supporters of the Kharkov system, a few have strongly criticized another of their country's major economic institutions: the system of administrative allocation of materials by central planners (and there are now some actual moves to switch to freely contracted wholesale trade). Although Liberman was extremely vague as to how firm directors would be able to get the input mix they desire when the production and physical distribution of basic materials is controlled by central planners, Nemchinov, Vaag, and Zakharov stated their opinions clearly. They concluded that the existing material supply system was too complex and inflexible to give enterprises the freedom of input determination envisioned in Liberman's incentive scheme (in fact, Novozhilov estimated that the rigid supply system costs Soviet industry each year roughly 25 percent of its potential output). Therefore, they advocated replacing administrative allocation with a system of "state trade," in which enterprises would negotiate independently agreements with suppliers and customers.[70] Economist Nemchinov, their chief spokesman and powerful figure in the U.S.S.R. Academy of Sciences, boldly argued that planning intermediate goods should cease; the state should decide only what final products it needs. "The conversion to state trade . . . will doubtless make possible the rapid liquidation of the state of constant scarcity of supplies." [71]

Commentators who were for the most part sympathetic to Liberman's general approach were, however, in a minority. The majority of responses to *Pravda's* initial request were characterized by either total hostility or considerable criticism. Representative of the most vigorous attacks on Liberman's plan are the views of A. Zverev, former Minister of Finance, and K. Plotnikov, director of the Institute of Economics of the Academy of Sciences.

First, Zverev denounces the theory he sees lurking behind Libermanism: that profit is created not only by the worker's labor, but also by fixed and current assets. "It is hardly necessary to prove the erroneousness of such a theory." [72] Second, he argues against the premise that the central planners are less informed as to the capabilities of enterprises than the enterprise itself. They "are obligated to know, and actually do know, the production capacities of enterprises." [73] Third, Zverev, Plotnikov, and I. Kasitsky declare that no need for major reform exists, and condemn the Kharkov system as a grave threat to national economic planning: "The proposals of Professor Liberman would lead to utter unbalancing of the national economy. Planning is a great achievement of the October revolution." [74]

Turning more directly to the actual operation of a national Liberman incentive scheme, Zverev and Bor maintain that "broad economic maneuverability," supposedly gained under the proposed system, in fact "is not possible when the enterprise must meet an obligatory production volume with specified assortment of goods . . . specified delivery dates and consumers." [75] Next Zverev points to the profitability norms to be established for branches of industry, asserts that they would not be objective for all firms in a grouping, and predicts that constantly changing technical conditions among firms would cause persistent pressure on any norm-setting government agency to revise the norm. The only way to keep the norms "fair," he concludes, would be continuously to revise them.[76]

Finally, a full measure of hostility is unleashed to attack the increase in decentralized investment likely to occur with the adoption of a Liberman scheme. Convinced that existing defects in "capital construction" are due to insufficient centralization, Plotnikov, Zverev, and Kasitsky emphatically decry leaving investment decisions with enterprises, which are "ignorant of the various national economic interrelations," thereby increasing "parochialism" and multiplying "disproportions in the national economy." [77]

A second group of Soviet critics offered substantial criticism of Liberman's program but were considerably more receptive to the prospect of reform. This school of thought recognizes the need for major changes in the existing system and praises Liberman for suggesting the use of long-term standards for material incentives and greater rewards for planned achievements than for overfulfillment. They affix no stigma to assigning the profitability criterion a more important role. To those who would confuse the use of profits under capitalism with their use in a socialist economy, Gatovsky explains that the national effort of the socialist country "is not to produce for profit, but to satisfy the needs of society"; at the level of the individual firm, however, profit can be "of great importance as an economic index of the efficiency of its operation." [78]

Yet in the moderates' judgment, profitability should not be adopted as the sole criterion for all firms. Different criteria should be adopted for different industries, profitability being but one of several basic indices which can be used.[79] Gatovsky argues that existing price imperfections and frequent divergence between costs and benefits to the enterprise and to the community would prevent profitability from being the accurate measure of "ultimate efficiency" it is intended to be. Sukharevsky adds that using profitability as the single source of bonuses would allow firms to continue receiving substantial premiums from previous increases in efficiency, while currently in a stagnant state with no improvements being made.

Weighing approaches taken by extremists on both sides of the Liberman debate, B. Alter concludes that two unhealthy tendencies must be overcome: the first is treating planning as an act of pure central administration; the second is attempting to convert all the basic economic levers into an automatically functioning mechanism. He asserts both are incompatible with the principle of "democratic centralism." [80] He emphasizes that the country cannot be directed toward planned goals if the enterprise is in "isolation . . . from the common targets of the national economy." [81]

Finally, let us note Professor Liberman's reply in 1962 to his critics. First, Liberman attempts to clear away the confused notion some hold that he proposes a single index to regulate automatically enterprise behavior: production goals society demands of enterprises (quantity and assortment of output) are still to be centrally planned and individually assigned to firms. Second, he counters the charge that enterprises will be able to rest on past efficiency achievements: "even a small increase in incentive payments is of some interest" and "every manufacturing enterprise must constantly introduce new production . . . or its incentive scale will drop." [82] Next, he argues the center will not lose control over capital investments, as large projects "will be fixed and set by assignment." True, current investments will be handled by the enterprise, but Liberman maintains that with the firm's concern for profitability, a more intensive use of internal reserves for these projects will result. Fourth, he points out that intraplant incentives for individual shops can of course use any single or multiple indices on which to base rewards to workers. The enterprise fund is to be the "collective result" of a firm's ultimate efficiency, as measured by its profitability, but the fund shall "be distributed to the departments individually and separately in the light of the achievements of each shop, sector, and worker." [83]

Because public discussion of Liberman's proposals was initiated two months prior to a plenary session of the Central Committee, and had created much commotion by then, many believed the political leadership might be preparing to introduce some real changes. Also pointing to this possibility was *Pravda's* release during October, 1962, of a previously unpublished document dictated by Lenin in 1918 which argued that socialism could learn much from the organizers of capitalism.[84] But by the end of the November plenum the ruling party had not been won over to reform. In his final words to the session, Khrushchev announced the proposals were premature; the issue was turned over to the Scientific Council on Accountability and Material Stimulation for further consideration. On the other hand, the party program for 1962 emphasized the need for

the formation of a system for planning and assessing the work of enterprises so that they have a vital interest in higher plan assignments, in the introduction of new technology, and in improving the quality of output, in a word, achieving the greatest production efficiency.

By May, 1963, however, controversy had died down considerably. The government gave no further indication of its readiness to alter the basics of the given system of minutely detailed planning and supervision of enterprises; yet during the lull in public debate which lingered through mid-1964, problems with unbought consumer goods became critical, precipating the first Soviet experiments with profit incentives and direct ties to customers.

The allegedly drastic situation of soaring inventories of textile and clothing goods stirred the government in early 1964 to place two large garment-manufacturing associations—the Bolshevoika in Moscow and the Mayak in Gorky—under the constraints of essentially an isolated Liberman system. The two producers were to work out their own output plans on the basis of orders from retail outlets; their performance was to be judged by sales and profits; they were to negotiate their own contracts with principal suppliers; and financial penalties were to be levied for failure to make deliveries according to contract. In spite of a number of predictable difficulties (especially difficulties with surrounding bureaucracy), both associations overfulfilled output and profit plans for the year. The U.S.S.R. Council of National Economy decided to extend the experiment to 400 associations in the textile, clothing, leather, and footwear industries during 1965. Trials of the new system even among producer-goods factories, in the Lvov region, were reported early in that year.

THE RESUMPTION OF DEBATE: 1964–65

Shortly after this initial experimentation with the Liberman form of incentives got under way, public discussion was again requested by the editors of *Pravda*.[85] The inference is that desires for economic reform from within the party had significantly grown during the interim from the November plenum to mid-1964. The party was probably influenced by the intensification of the Soviet economy's problems in 1962–64—the mounting inventories of consumer goods and the trauma of grain-crop failures in 1963—but also by the virtual stagnation of the Czech economy in 1963, the inception in 1964 of profit sharing and a charge on capital in Hungary, and the continued success of the decentralized Yugoslav system.

Six months after Trapeznikov reiterated Liberman's demands and additionally advocated a charge on capital, *Pravda* could report having received 600 articles and letters in response. The bulk of public communication at this time showed a substantial shift in mood from the

1962–63 controversy. The author of "Survey of Readers' Letters," *Pravda*, February 17, 1965, concluded that the overwhelming majority of writers felt it necessary to "intensify sharply the role of economic levers in the management of the national economy to expand the rights of enterprises, to enhance the importance of profit . . . and to put price formation in order." Expressions of total hostility were practically non-existent, and an expanded, vocal group of economists, research workers, and enterprise managers became increasingly insistent in their demands for the adoption of widespread, intensive change.

At the same time, Liberman's incentive scheme, the system of "state trade" among firms, and reform of both the methodology of price calculation and the locus of price decision making were all brought together in an extraordinary paper presented by Nemchinov.[86] Special features were proposals to adhere strictly to prices that covered the "full factory costs of production," including charges on fixed and circulating assets placed at the disposal of enterprises by society; or even to let these prices be fixed by the enterprises themselves on condition they adhere to the approved pricing calculus. Further, Nemchinov recommended compulsory charges on fixed capital, differentiated "according to material composition of the assets and economic effectiveness of their utilization in different branches of production," as well as introduction of automated regulation systems for collecting, processing, and transforming economic information.

The degree of enterprise autonomy urged by V. Belkin and I. Birman also went considerably beyond the Liberman plan and its 1962–63 extensions. Arguing that output plans should be based on orders from customers, they asserted, first, that enterprises "should be given the right to amend the output plan with the consent of the customer," and second, that when an enterprise is producing a product "with higher consumer properties than are stipulated by the standards, it should be given the right to fix the price with the agreement of the customer." [87]

The goals of most hopeful reformers, however, did not at first include changes which would decentralize price setting. The introduction of direct links with suppliers to supplant the unwieldy system of central supply allocations had become more popular, as had a price calculus with capital charges, but complete central control over national parameters (including prices) was still regarded as integral to preserving economic balances and a high rate of accumulation.[88] Only after reforms actually began, in 1966 and 1967, was there voiced considerable sentiment for price decentralization as well as output decentralization.

Critics of what by 1964 could be construed as varying degrees of

Libermanism directed their attacks against any attempt at automatic regulation of enterprise activity through "economic levers" alone. Introduction of the originally outlined Kharkov incentive system, they feared, would only necessitate further relegation of national planning controls, making it impossible to ensure an identity between the interests of enterprises and those of society. Arguments advanced were essentially the same as those which dominated the 1962–63 controversy; but the tone of criticism was closer to the moderate position than to that of the more doctrinaire critics.[89]

OFFICIAL REFORMS

Although "economic experiments" were extended and given more varied trials during 1965, it was not until September of that year that the government responded with a major organizational reform in industry (in the direction of the Liberman proposals). Adopted as law by the Supreme Soviet on October 2,[90] the stipulations of the Kosygin reform were a conservative and tentative but promising result of the three-year-old controversy. The section pertaining to the individual enterprise contained measures to (1) replace the "gross value of output" indicator with "output sold"; (2) eliminate target directives for labor productivity, number of workers and employees, and average wages; (3) permit a large proportion of profits to be retained and utilized by the enterprise for bonuses, welfare purposes, and decentralized investment, and allow a portion of the enterprise depreciation charges likewise to be channeled into decentralized investments; (4) finance half of centralized investment by repayable and interest-bearing loans from banks, and levy interest charges (in the form of a tax) [91] on fixed and working capital put at the enterprise's disposal; (5) pay bonuses for fulfillment of sales, profit or profitability, and physical output indicators, with scales being designed so as to provide higher bonuses for fulfillment of planned profits than for overfulfillment of targets; and (6) have contracts more strictly enforced, prohibiting superiors from changing enterprise plans at will during the plan period.

Attention to what has been left out of the Kosygin system, however, gives us a more pessimistic view of the possibility that the reform will implement the kind of changes Liberman sympathizers have been proposing. Thus, for example, it has been pointed out ad infinitum and ad nauseam that any attempt at greater reliance on value relations, on profits or credit, would be "unoperational without a rational price system." Yet the wholesale price reform originally set for 1962 was postponed several times, and not completed till 1967. Moreover, the new system continues to maintain the system of materials allocation. This will certainly not result in the Liberman objective of enterprise freedom to vary inputs in producing a centrally given output schedule. At the same time, the apparent intent to allow more decentralized investments may result in a decrease in central control over the determination of future output. Indeed, the allowance of a large amount of decentralized investment may turn out to be one of the most important practical features of the reform.

The undoubted difficulties of the new system will be resolved eventually by retrogression or by further reform. Which direction is taken will depend on many factors, including external ones such as peace in Vietnam, but the pressure and prestige of reform are now very strong. It seems that we may expect the winds of progress and change to keep blowing strongly in the Soviet economy.

Convergence of Central Planning and Market Socialism

We noted the attempts of Soviet reformers to arrive at a more perfect method of calculation for central planning. We have also seen the attempts of Liberman and other Soviet and east European economists to decentralize planning so that the decision making would focus primarily on the enterprise manager, who would make his decisions on the basis of the market supply and demand. The question of the relationship between these two sets of reforms arises. The vision of Liberman is a picture of the invisible hand of the market operating so that each socialist firm must act out of its own self-interest so as to bring about the best interests of socialist society. The vision of Novozhilov and Kantorovich is one of information pouring into central calculating machines, which have been programmed so that they will turn out a plan which gives an optimal choice on technological variants of production as well as the mixture of outputs. If it is true that optimal programming can determine all of the best methods of production and allocation of resources, then why not merely do this and give the results as direct orders to each enterprise? Why should the market mechanism play any further role once we have perfected optimal programming?

In fact, in the Soviet Union today the conservatives, in so far as they accept Novozhilov's vision of more perfect calculation, argue that better computational methods and more sophisticated electronic calculators make continued central planning the best road to follow, and make it unnecessary to decentralize.[92] On the other hand, Novozhilov himself and many others believe that rational prices are merely the necessary basis for decentralization. These Soviet writers insist that rational prices for use by managers in decentralized decision making must stem from an optimal output plan (based in turn on demand preferences and the objectively existing supply conditions of labor and resources).[93] On the basis of centrally calculated rational prices, managers at the enterprise level could then make all output and input decisions more efficiently, with more detailed information and with a more "democratic" content (based on workers' and consumers' preferences), than could the central planners.[94]

Specifically, modern methods of optimal programming do theoretically allow us to calculate the correct inputs and outputs for each enterprise. But the staggering amount of data and calculation work required to accomplish this job make it somewhat unfeasible in practice. A contrary suggestion is emerging from Soviet and east European practice as well as from their newer economic theory. This is to have the central planners calculate rational prices from a more limited amount of data, which can be done with modern methods just as easily as the calculation of all inputs and outputs. These centrally calculated prices, usually called "shadow prices," would then be given to the enterprise managers as the facts upon which they must operate. The managers would then go ahead on the basis of these prices to reach their own decisions on input and output mixtures. We might note, in addition, that the proposals of the central planners to charge interest and rent as the prices of fixed capital and internal resources will then complete the necessary factual price information upon which managers must act.

The managers will thus act upon the basis of their own knowledge of the technical conditions in the firm, as well as the price given them by the central planners. As we have noted, the tendency does exist for central planners to continue to set prices (though even price setting is being increasingly decentralized in Czechoslovakia and some other east European countries), while managers are receiving more freedom in decisions of technological methods and output mixtures. The end result would be a mixed system wherein the enterprise managers would make all of the current and short-run decisions concerning the use of available labor, raw materials, and capacity. The central planners would be free of this day-to-day detail, so they could concentrate on long-run macroeconomic investment planning for the expansion of capacity and the introduction of new technology. While we discern some such converging trend between central planning and market socialism in the Soviet Union and eastern Europe, it is still not clear where on the socialist planning spectrum these countries will finally alight.

Notes

1. See, e.g., the translated articles in Nicholas Spulber, ed., *Foundations of Soviet Strategy for Economic Growth: Selected Soviet Essays, 1924–1930* (Bloomington: Indiana University Press, 1964).

2. See, e.g., Maurice Dobb, *Soviet Economic Development since 1917* (London: Routledge & Kegan Paul, Ltd., 1948), especially chap. 8, or Alexander Erlich, *Soviet Industrialization Controversy* (Cambridge, Mass.: Harvard University Press, 1960).

3. See Evsey D. Domar, "A Soviet Model of Growth," *Essays in the Theory of Economic Growth* (London: Oxford University Press, 1957).

4. An extended critique of this doctrine may be found in P. J. D. Wiles, *The Political Economy of Communism* (Cambridge, Mass.: Harvard University Press, 1964), pp. 272–300.

5. See, e.g., V. Volkonsky, "Methods of Mathematical Economics and the Theory of Planning and Administering the Economy," trans. in *Problems of Economics* (forthcoming).

6. For a sophisticated discussion by a Soviet writer, see A. A. Konus, "Dynamic Intersector Balances in Perspective Planning," *Economics of Planning*, 4 (1964): 1–15.

7. See Karl Marx, "The Reproduction and Circulation of the Aggregate Social Capital," *Capital* (Chicago: Charles H. Kerr, 1909), vol. 2, pt. 3.

8. See, e.g., the confused discussion by Shigeto Tsuru, "On Reproduction Schemes," in Paul Sweezy, *The Theory of Capitalist Development* (New York: Oxford University Press, 1942), app. A, pp. 365–74.

9. See Oskar Lange, *Introduction to Econometrics* (New York: Pergamon Press, 1959), pp. 218–28.

10. See, e.g., his simplified explanation in Wassily Leontief, "Input-Output Economics," *Scientific American*, October, 1951, pp. 3–9.

11. Maurice Dobb, *Soviet Economic Development since 1917*, rev. ed. (New York: International Publishers, 1966), p. 361.

12. This is the view of the more liberal Soviet economists. See, e.g., V. S. Nemchinov, "Mathematical Methods in Economics," in V. S. Nemchinov, ed., *The Use of Mathematics in Economics*, trans. under editorship of Alec Nove (London: Oliver & Boyd, 1964), p. 24.

13. See Marx, *Capital*, vol. 1, chap. 1.

14. Vladimir Treml, "Revival of Soviet Economics and the New Generation of Soviet Economists," *Studies on the Soviet Union*, 5 (1965): 4.

15. Stanislav G. Strumilin, quoted in *ibid.*, p. 3.

16. See Sweezy, *Theory of Capitalist Development*, pp. 52–54.

17. Marx, *Capital* (Kerr ed.), 3: 1026.

18. Sweezy, *Theory of Capitalist Development*, pp. 53–54.

19. Anon., "Some Problems in the Teaching of Political Economy," *Pod znamenem marksizma*, 1943, trans. in *American Economic Review*, September, 1944.

20. Joseph Stalin, *Economic Problems of Socialism in the U.S.S.R.* (New York: International Publishers, 1952).

21. *Ibid.*, p. 18.

22. Ronald Meek, *Studies in the Labour Theory of Value* (New York: International Publishers, 1956), p. 293.

23. *Ibid.*

24. These three views are discussed in detail in Gregory Grossman, "Gold and the Sword: Money in the Soviet Command Economy," in H. Rosovsky, ed., *Industrialization in Two Systems* (New York: John Wiley & Sons, 1966).

25. K. B. Ostrovitianov, *Stroitelstvo kommunizma i tovarno—Denezhnie otnosheniia* (Moscow, Gosudarstvenoe Izdatelstvo Politicheskoi Literaturi, 1962).

26. I. A. Kronrod, *Dengi v sotsialisticheskom obshchestve* (Moscow Gosudarstvenoe Izdatelstvo Politicheskoi Literaturi, 1960).

27. I. S. Malyshev, *Obshchestvennii uchet truda i tsena pri sotsializme* (Moscow, Gosudarstvenoe Izdatelstvo Politicheskoi Literaturi, 1960).

28. Robert W. Campbell, "Marx, Kantorovich, and Novozhilov," *Review*, 20 (October, 1961): 402–18. A discussion of more general conflicts is given by Joseph Berliner, "Marxism and the Soviet Economy," *Problems of Communism*, 13 (September–October, 1964): 1–10.

29. Alfred Zauberman, "Revisionism in Soviet Economics," in Leopold Labedz, ed., *Revisionism* (New York: Frederick A. Praeger, Inc., 1962), p. 276.

30. See, e.g., A. Y. Boyarsky, "On the Proper Relationship between Mathematics and Economics in a Socialist Society," trans. in *Problems of Economics*, January, 1962, pp. 12–24. Also see the similar views in A. I. Kats, "Concerning a Fallacious Concept of Economic Calculations," trans. in *Problems of Economics*, November, 1960, pp. 42–52. A history of the various viewpoints in the Stalin era is available in Gregory Grossman, "Scarce Capital and Soviet Doctrine," *Quarterly Journal of Economics*, 67 (August, 1953): 311–43.

31. See, e.g., L. V. Kantorovich, "On the Calculation of Production Inputs," trans. in *Problems of Economics*, May, 1960, pp. 3–10. Also see Benjamin Ward, "Kantorovich on Economic Calculation," *Journal of Political Economy*, 68 (December, 1960): 545–56. Further see V. V. Novozhilov, "On Choosing between Investment Projects," trans. in *International Economic Papers*, 1956, no. 6, pp. 66–87. Also see Novozhilov, "Calculation of Outlays in a Socialist Economy," trans. in *Problems of Economics*, December, 1961, pp. 18–28. Finally, his fullest presentation is "Investment Decisions in the Socialist Economy," in Nemchinov, ed., *Use of Mathematics*.

32. Nove, ed., *Use of Mathematics*, ed. Nemchinov, Introduction, p. x.

33. Novozhilov, "Investment Decisions," p. 189.

34. Campbell, *Marx, Kantorovich, and Novozhilov*, p. 403.

35. See, e.g., A. Postyshev, "The Labor Theory of Value and Optimal Planning," trans. in *Problems of Economics*, forthcoming. He identifies the "shadow prices" obtained from the modern linear programming method as the reflection of the Marxist labor theory of value.

36. Novozhilov, "Spornie voprosy primeniia metoda uspomogatelnykh mnozhitelei v sotsialisticheskoi ekonomiki," *Narodokhoziastvennie modeli teoreticheskie voprosy potrebleniia* (Moscow: Izdatelstvo Akademii Nauk SSSR, 1964).

37. See Stalin, *Marxism and Linguistics* (Moscow, 1952).

38. This view of the distinction between Marxist political economy and technical bourgeois economics is presented by the Marxist writers Paul Baran and Paul Sweezy in "Economics of Two Worlds," in *On Political Economy and*

Econometrics: Essays in Honour of Oskar Lange (New York: Pergamon Press, 1965), pp. 15–29.

39. An excellent Soviet statement of the importance of rational prices to planning appears in N. Fedorenko, "Price and Optimal Planning," trans. in *Problems of Economics,* 1967.

40. See, e.g., Ostrovitianov, *Stroitelstvo kommunizma.*

41. See, e.g., Kronrod, *Dengi v sotsialisticheskom obshchestve.*

42. See, e.g., Malyshev, *Obshchestvennii uchet truda.*

43. Novozhilov, "Investment Decisions."

44. *Ibid.,* p. 19.

45. See Novozhilov, "On Choosing between Investment Projects," p. 87 n.

46. Campbell, *Marx, Kantorovich, and Novozhilov,* p. 410.

47. *Ibid.,* p. 414.

48. See, e.g., P. J. D. Wiles, *The Political Economy of Communism* (Cambridge, Mass: Harvard University Press, 1964), who says at p. 129 that "rent is . . . condemned by Marx," and adds that Marx implies that there would be no rent in socialism.

49. See, e.g., Hollis B. Chenery and Paul G. Clark, *Interindustry Economics* (New York: John Wiley & Sons, 1959), chap. 4.

50. See Novozhilov, "Investment Decisions," p. 77.

51. See *ibid.,* pp. 77–84.

52. The coefficient of relative effectiveness of project 2 in comparison with project 1 may then be represented in the following manner:

$$CRE_{2/1} = \frac{C_1 - C_2}{K_2 - K_1}$$

where K_1 and K_2 represent the capital used in projects 1 and 2 respectively, and C_1 and C_2 represent the labor and other current cost in projects 1 and 2 respectively.

53. Let us examine an example of these calculations. Suppose that we wish to produce 100 million rubles' worth of shoes per year. Suppose the two possible technological ways of doing it involve in one variant an investment of 50 million rubles and an annual cost of production of another 50 million rubles, but in the second variant an investment of 75 million rubles and an annual cost of production of only 49 million rubles. Then the coefficient of relative effectiveness of project 2 as compared with project 1 can be calculated as:

$$CRE_{2/1} = \frac{50 - 49}{75 - 50} = .04$$

54. Campbell, *Marx, Kantorovich, and Novozhilov,* pp. 415–16.

55. Another liberal Soviet writer, Kantorovich, has actually formulated a full solution for output maximization based on final demands; see Ward, "Kantorovich on Economic Calculation," pp. 553–54.

56. Stalin, *Economic Problems,* p. 33.

57. See, e.g., Dobb, *Economic Theory and Socialism* (New York: International Publishers, 1965).

58. Wiles, "Scarcity, Marxism, and Gosplan," *Oxford Economic Papers,* October, 1953, pp. 315–16.

59. For a view of the NEP as a successful experiment in market socialism, see V. N. Bendera, "The NEP as an Economic System," *Journal of Political Economy,* 71, no. 3.

60. See Lange, *On the Economic Theory of Socialism* (New York: McGraw-Hill Book Co., 1964; first published 1938).

61. Evsei G. Liberman, "The Plan, Profits, and Bonuses," *Pravda*, September 9, 1962. This and almost all the other Soviet contributions to this debate have been translated and collected in M. E. Sharpe, ed., *The Liberman Discussion: A New Phase in Soviet Economic Thought* (White Plains, N.Y.: International Arts and Science Press, 1965).

62. V. Trapeznikov, "For Flexible Economic Management of Enterprises," *Pravda*, August 17, 1964, trans. in Sharpe, *Liberman Discussion*, pp. 193–201.

63. Liberman, "Cost Accounting and Material Encouragement of Industrial Personnel," *Voprosy ekonomiki*, 1955, no. 6; "Planning Industrial Production and Material Stimuli for Its Development," *Kommunist*, 1956, no. 10; and "Economic Levers for Fulfilling the Plan for Soviet Industry," *Kommunist*, 1959, no. 1; all trans. in Sharpe, *Liberman Discussion*, pp. 3–64.

64. Lynn Turgeon, "Comments on Papers Concerning 'Libermanism,'" unpublished speech at Socialist Scholars' Conference in New York City, September 10, 1966.

65. Derived from the three 1962 Liberman articles: "Plan, Profits, and Bonuses," trans. in Sharpe, *Liberman Discussion*, pp. 65–78; "Planning Production and Standards of Long-Term Production," *Voprosy ekonomiki*, 1962, no. 8, trans. in Sharpe, *Liberman Discussion*, pp. 77–87; and "Reply to Critics of the Profit Proposal," *Ekonomicheskaia gazeta*, November 10, 1962, trans. in *Current Digest of the Soviet Press*, 1962, no. 45, p. 18.

66. Liberman, "Plan, Profits, and Bonuses," in Sharpe, *Liberman Discussion*, p. 79.

67. *Ibid.*

68. L. Gatovsky, "The Role of Profit in a Socialist Economy," *Kommunist*, 1962, trans. in *Soviet Review*, Summer, 1963, p. 20.

69. For instance, see Nemchinov, "The Plan Target and Material Incentive," *Pravda*, September 21, 1962, trans. in Sharpe, *Liberman Discussion*, pp. 107–113.

70. See, e.g., L. Vaag and S. Zakharov, "State Trading," *Voprosy ekonomiki*, 1963.

71. Nemchinov, "Plan Target and Material Incentive," p. 5.

72. A. Zverev, "Against Oversimplification in Solving Complex Problems," *Problems of Economics*, *Voprosy ekonomiki*, 1962, no. 11, trans. in Sharpe, *Liberman Discussion*, pp. 141–48.

73. *Ibid.*, *Voprosy ekonomiki*, p. 16.

74. *Ibid.*, p. 17.

75. M. Bor, "For Broad Economic Maneuverability," *Ekonomicheskaia gazeta*, November 10, 1962, trans. in *Current Digest of the Soviet Press*, 14, no. 46 (1962): 23.

76. Zverev, "Against Oversimplification," *Voprosy ekonomiki*, p. 18.

77. K. Plotnikov, "E. G. Liberman: Right or Wrong," *Voprosy ekonomiki*, 1962, no. 11; Zverev, "Against Oversimplification"; and I. Kasitsky, "The Main Question: Criteria for Premiums and Indices Planned for Enterprises," *Voprosy ekonomiki*, 1962, no. 11; all trans. in Sharpe, *Liberman Discussion*.

78. Gatovsky, "Role of Profit," p. 16.

79. Sukharevsky suggests four—volume of output, labor productivity, production costs, and profitability—in "On Improving the Forms and Methods of Material Incentives," *Voprosy ekonomiki* (November, 1962), tranlated in Sharpe, *Liberman Discussion*, pp. 114–34.

80. B. Alter, "Incentives Must Be Linked with the Long-Term Planning of an Enterprise," *Problems of Economics*, April, 1963, p. 26.

81. *Ibid.*, p. 27.

82. Liberman, "Reply to Critics of the Profit Proposal," *Ekonomicheskaia gazeta*, November 10, 1962, pp. 10–11, trans. in *Current Digest of the Soviet Press*, 14, no. 45 (1962): 18.

83. *Ibid.*, p. 19.

84. B. J. McFarlane and I. Gordijew, "Profitability and the Soviet Firm," *Economic Record*, 40 (December, 1964): 568.

85. In a footnote to Trapeznikov, "Flexible Economic Management."

86. Nemchinov, "Socialist Economic Management and Production Planning," *Kommunist*, 1964, no. 5, trans. in Sharpe, *Liberman Discussion*, pp. 173–92.

87. V. Belkin and I. Birman, "Independence of the Enterprise and Economic Stimuli," *Izvestiia*, December 4, 1964, trans. in Sharpe, *Liberman Discussion*, pp. 225–30.

88. See, e.g., Trapeznikov, "Flexible Economic Management."

89. Some Western views of the decentralization debate may be found in the following articles: Campbell, "Economics: Roads and Inroads," *Problems of Communism*, November–December, 1965, pp. 23–33; Nove, "The Liberman Proposals," *Survey*, April, 1963; Harry G. Shaffer, "Ills and Remedies," *Problems of Communism*, May–June, 1963, pp. 27–32; and Marshall Goldman, "Economic Controversy in the Soviet Union," *Foreign Affairs*, April, 1963, pp. 498–512.

90. See text of laws in *Pravda* (October 3, 1965). See also the official discussion by Kosygin and Brezhnev in English in *New Methods of Economic Management in the U.S.S.R.* (Moscow: Novosty Press Agency, 1965).

91. See I. Liberman, "Payments on Assets: Their Budgetary and Cost Accounting Functions," trans. in *Problems of Economics*, forthcoming.

92. See, e.g., the dogmatic defense of central planning in I. Rusinov, "Prospects in the Planning of Agricultural Production," trans. in *Problems of Economics*, September, 1967, pp. 25–32.

93. See, e.g., the quite clear exposition in N. Fedorenko, "Price and Optimal Planning," trans. in *Problems of Economics*, forthcoming.

94. For an extensive discussion of the new developments and some of their relationships, see Egon Neuberger, "Libermanism, Computopia, and Visible Hand: The Question of Informational Efficiency," *American Economic Review*, 56 (May, 1966): 131–44. Also see Jere L. Felker, *Soviet Economic Controversies: The Emerging Concept and Changes in Planning, 1960–1965* (Cambridge, Mass.: MIT Press, 1966).

VII : Education

Theory and Research in Soviet Character Education

Urie Bronfenbrenner

Every society faces the problem of the moral training of its youth. This is no less true of Communist society than of our own. Indeed, Communist authorities view as the primary objective of education not the learning of subject matter, but the development of what they call "socialist morality." It is instructive for us in the West to examine the nature of this "socialist morality" and the manner in which it is inculcated, for to do so brings to light important differences in the ends and means of character education in the two cultures. For research workers in the field of personality development, such an examination is especially valuable, since it lays bare unrecognized assumptions and variations in approach. Accordingly, it is the purpose of this paper to provide a much-condensed account of Soviet methods of character education and to examine some of the provocative research questions that emerge from the contrast between the Soviet approach and our own.

This chapter is based upon two previously published articles: "Soviet Methods of Character Education: Some Implications for Research," *Religious Education*, 57, no. 4 (1962): S45–S61; "Soviet Studies of Personality Development and Socialization," in *Some Views on Soviet Psychology* (American Psychological Association, Inc., 1962). Parts of these articles are reproduced by permission of the Religious Education Association and the American Psychological Association. Footnotes have been provided.

The Work and Ideas of A. S. Makarenko

To examine Soviet methods of character training is to become acquainted
with the thinking and technology developed primarily by one man—
Anton Semyonovich Makarenko. Makarenko's name is virtually a household word in the Soviet Union. His popularity and influence are roughly
comparable to those of Dr. Spock in the United States, but his primary
concern is not with the child's physical health but with his moral upbringing. Makarenko's influence extends far beyond his own voluminous
writings, since there is scarcely a manual for the guidance of Communist
parents, teachers, or youth workers that does not draw heavily on his
methods and ideas. His works have been translated into many languages
and are apparently widely read not only in the Soviet Union, but
throughout the Communist-bloc countries, notably East Germany and
Communist China. Excellent English translations of a number of his works
have been published in Moscow,[1] but they are not readily available in
this country.

Makarenko developed his ideas and methods over the course of a lifetime of practical work with young people. In the early 1920's, as a young
schoolteacher and devout Communist, Makarenko was handed the assignment of setting up a rehabilitation program for some of the hundreds
of homeless children who were roaming the Soviet Union after the civil
wars. The first group of such children assigned to Makarenko's school,
a ramshackle building far out of town, turned out to be a group of
boys about eighteen years of age with extensive court records of house-
breaking, armed robbery, and manslaughter. For the first few months,
Makarenko's school served simply as the headquarters for the band of
highwaymen who were his legal wards. But gradually, through the development of his group-oriented discipline techniques, and through what
can only be called the compelling power of his own moral convictions,
Makarenko was able to develop a sense of group responsibility and commitment to the work program and code of conduct that he had laid out
for the collective. In the end, the Gorky Commune became known
throughout the Soviet Union for its high morale, for its discipline, and
for the productivity of its fields, farms, and shops. Indeed, Makarenko's
methods proved so successful that he was selected to head a new com-

mune set up by the Ministry of Internal Affairs (then the Cheka, later to become the GPU and NKVD). In the years that followed, Makarenko's theories and techniques became widely adopted throughout the U.S.S.R. and they now constitute the central core of Soviet educational practice.

To turn to the ideas themselves, we may begin with an excerpt from what is possibly the most widely read of Makarenko's works, *A Book for Parents.*

But our [Soviet] family is not an accidental combination of members of society. The family is a natural collective body and, like everything natural, healthy, and normal, it can only blossom forth in socialist society, freed of those very curses from which both mankind as a whole and the individual are freeing themselves.

The family becomes the natural primary cell of society, the place where the delight of human life is realized, where the triumphant forces of man are refreshed, where children—the chief joy of life—live and grow.

Our parents are not without authority either, but this authority is only the reflection of societal authority. The duty of a father in our country towards his children is a particular form of his duty towards society. It is as if our society says to parents:

You have joined together in good will and love, rejoice in your children and expect to go on rejoicing in them. That is your personal affair and concerns your own personal happiness. Within the course of this happy process you have given birth to new human beings. A time will come when these beings will cease to be solely the instruments of your happiness, and will step forth as independent members of society. For society, it is by no means a matter of indifference what kind of people they will become. In delegating to you a certain measure of societal authority the Soviet State demands from you the correct upbringing of its future citizens. Particularly it relies on you to provide certain conditions arising naturally out of your union; namely, your parental love.

If you wish to give birth to a citizen while dispensing with parental love, then be so kind as to warn society that you intend to do such a rotten thing. Human beings who are brought up without parental love are often deformed human beings.[2]

Characteristic of Makarenko's thought is the view that the parent's authority over the child is delegated to him by the state and that duty to one's children is merely a particular instance of one's broader duty toward society. A little later in his book for parents, the author makes this point even more emphatically. After telling the story of a boy who ran away from home after some differences with his mother, he concludes by affirming: "I am a great admirer of optimism and I like very much young lads who have so much faith in the Soviet State that they are carried away and will not trust even their own mothers." [3] In other words, when the needs and values of the family conflict with those of society, there is no question about who gets priority. And society receives its concrete manifestation and embodiment in the *kollectiv*, which is an organized group engaged in some socially useful enterprise.

This brings us to Makarenko's basic thesis that optimal personality development can occur only through productive activity in a social collective. The first collective is the family, but this must be supplemented early in life by other collectives specially organized in schools, neighborhoods, and other community settings. The primary function of the collective is to develop socialist morality. This aim is accomplished through an explicit regimen of activity mediated by group criticism, self-criticism, and group-oriented punishments and rewards.

Makarenko's ideas are elaborated at length in his semibiographical, semifictional accounts of life in the collective. [4] It is in these works that he describes the principles and procedures to be employed for building the collective and using it as an instrument of character education. More relevant to our purposes, however, is the manner in which these methods are applied in school settings, for it is in this form that they have become most systematized and widely used.

Socialization in the School Collective

The account which follows is taken from a manual [5] for the training and guidance of "school directors, supervisors, teachers, and Young Pioneer leaders." The manual was written by staff members of the Institute of the Theory and History of Pedagogy at the Academy of Pedagogical Sciences and is typical of several others prepared under the same auspices and widely distributed throughout the U.S.S.R.

This particular volume carries the instructive title: *Socialist Competition in the School*. The same theme is echoed in the titles of individual chapters: "Competition in the Classroom," "Competition between Classrooms," "Competition between Schools," and so on. It is not difficult to see how Russians arrive at the notion, with which they have made us so familiar, of competition between nations and between social systems. Moreover, in the chapter titles we see already reflected the influence of dialectical materialism: conflict at one level is resolved through synthesis at the next higher level, always in the service of the Communist collective.

Let us examine the process of collective socialization as it is initiated in the very first grade. Conveniently enough, the manual starts us off on the first day of school with the teacher standing before the newly assembled class. What should her first words be? Our text tells us:

> It is not difficult to see that a direct approach to the class with the command "All sit straight" often doesn't bring the desired effect since a demand in this form does not reach the sensibilities of the pupils and does not activate them.

How does one "reach the sensibilities of the pupils" and "activate them"? According to the manual, here is what the teacher should say: "Let's see which row can sit the straightest." This approach, we are told, has certain important psychological advantages. In response,

> The children not only try to do everything as well as possible themselves, but also take an evaluative attitude toward those who are undermining the achievement of the row. If similar measures arousing the spirit of competition in the children are systematically applied by experienced teachers in the primary classes, then gradually the children themselves begin to monitor the behavior of their comrades and remind those of them who forget about the rules set by the teacher, who forget what needs to be done and what should not be done. The teacher soon has helpers.

The manual then goes on to describe how records are kept for each row from day to day for different types of tasks so that the young children can develop a concept of group excellence over time and over a variety of activities, including personal cleanliness, condition of notebooks, conduct in passing from one room to another, quality of recitations in each subject matter, and so on. In these activities considerable emphasis is placed on the externals of behavior in dress, manner, and speech. There must be no spots on shirt or collar, shoes must be shined, pupils must never pass by a teacher without stopping to give greeting, there must be no talking without permission, and the like. Great charts are kept in all the schools showing the performance of each row unit in every type of activity together with their total overall standing. "Who is best?" the charts ask, but the entries are not individuals, but social units—rows, and later the "cells" of the Communist youth organization which reaches down to the primary grades.

At first it is the teacher who sets the standards. But soon, still in the first grade, a new wrinkle is introduced: responsible monitors are designated in each row for each activity. In the beginning their job is only to keep track of the merits and demerits assigned each row by the teacher. Different children act as monitors for different activities, and, if one is to believe what the manual says, the monitors become very involved in the progress of their row. Then, too, group achievement is not without its rewards. From time to time the winning row gets to be photographed "in parade uniforms" (all Soviet children must wear uniforms in school), and this photograph is published in that pervasive Soviet institution, the wall newspaper. The significance of the achievement is still further enhanced, however, by the introduction of competition between *classes* so that the winning class and the winning row are visited by delegates from other classrooms in order to learn how to attain the same standard of excellence.

Now let us look more closely at this teacher-mediated monitoring process. In the beginning, we are told, the teacher attempts to focus the attention of children on the achievements of the group; that is, in our familiar phrase, she accentuates the positive. But gradually, "it becomes necessary to take account of negative facts which interfere with the activity of the class." As an example we are given the instance of a child who despite warnings continues to enter the classroom a few minutes after the bell has rung. The teacher decides that the time has come to evoke the group process in correcting such behavior. Accordingly, the next time that Serezha is late, the teacher stops him at the door and turns to the class with this question: "Children, is it helpful or not helpful to us to have Serezha come in late?" The answers are quick in coming. "It interferes, one shouldn't be late, he ought to come on time." "Well," says the teacher, "how can we help Serezha with this problem?" There are many suggestions: get together to buy him a watch, exile him from the classroom, send him to the director's office, or even exile him from the school. But apparently these suggestions are either not appropriate or too extreme. The teacher, our text tells us, "helps the children find the right answer." She asks for a volunteer to stop by and pick Serezha up on the way to school. Many children offer to help in this mission.

But tragedy stalks. The next day it turns out that not only Serezha is late, but also the boy who promised to pick him up. Since they are both from the same group, their unit receives two sets of demerits and falls to lowest place. Group members are keenly disappointed. "Serezha especially suffered much and felt himself responsible, but equal blame was felt by his companion, who had forgotten to stop in for him."

In this way, through both concrete action and explanation, the teacher seeks to forge a spirit of group unity and responsibility. From time to time, she explains to the children the significance of what they are doing, the fact "that they have to learn to live together as one friendly family, since they will have to be learning together for all of the next ten years, and that for this reason one must learn how to help one's companions and to treat them decently."

By the time the children are in the second grade, the responsibilities expected of them are increased in complexity. For example, instead of simply recording the evaluations made by the teacher, the monitors are taught how to make the evaluations themselves. Since this is rather difficult, especially in judging homework assignments, in the beginning two monitors are assigned to every task. In this way, our text tells us, they can help each other in doing a good job of evaluation.

Here is a third-grade classroom:

Class 3-B is just an ordinary class; it's not especially well disciplined nor is it outstandingly industrious. It has its lazy members and its responsible ones, quiet ones and active ones, daring, shy, and immodest ones.

The teacher has led this class now for three years, and she has earned the affection, respect, and acceptance as an authority from her pupils. Her word is law for them.

The bell has rung, but the teacher has not yet arrived. She has delayed deliberately in order to check how the class will conduct itself.

In the class all is quiet. After the noisy class break, it isn't so easy to mobilize yourself and to quell the restlessness within you! Two monitors at the desk silently observe the class. On their faces is reflected the full importance and seriousness of the job they are performing. But there is no need for them to make any reprimands: the youngsters with pleasure and pride maintain scrupulous discipline; they are proud of the fact that their class conducts itself in a manner that merits the confidence of the teacher. And when the teacher enters and quietly says be seated, all understand that she deliberately refrains from praising them for the quiet and order, since in their class it could not be otherwise.

During the lesson, the teacher gives an exceptional amount of attention to collective competition between "links." (The links are the smallest unit of the Communist youth organization at this age level.) Throughout the entire lesson the youngsters are constantly hearing which link has best prepared its lesson, which link has done the best at numbers, which is the most disciplined, which has turned in the best work.

The best link not only gets a verbal positive evaluation, but receives the right to leave the classroom first during the break and to have its notebooks checked before the others. As a result the links receive the benefit of collective education, common responsibility, and mutual aid.

"What are you fooling around for? You're holding up the whole link," whispers Kolya to his neighbor during the preparation period for the lesson. And during the break he teaches her how better to organize her books and pads in her knapsack.

"Count more carefully," says Olya to her girl friend. "See, on account of you our link got behind today. You come to me and we'll count together at home."

In the third grade still another innovation is introduced. The monitors are taught not only to evaluate, but to state their criticisms publicly.

Here is a typical picture. It is the beginning of the lesson. In the first row the link leader reports basing his comments on information submitted by the sanitarian and other responsible monitors: "Today Valadya did the wrong problem. Masha didn't write neatly and forgot to underline the right words in her lesson. Alyoshi had a dirty shirt collar."

The other link leaders make similar reports (the Pioneers are sitting by rows).

The youngsters are not offended by this procedure: they understand that the link leaders are not just tattle-telling but simply fulfilling their duty. It doesn't even occur to the monitors and sanitarians to conceal the shortcomings of their comrades. They feel that they are doing their job well precisely when they notice one or another defect.

Also in the third grade, the teacher introduces still another procedure. She now proposes that the children enter into competition with the monitors, and see if they can beat the monitor at his own game by criticizing themselves. "The results were spectacular: if the monitor was able to talk only about four or five members of the row, there would be supplementary reports about their own shortcomings from as many as eight or ten pupils."

To what extent is this picture overdrawn? Although I have no direct evidence, the accounts I heard from participants in the process lend credence to the descriptions in the manual. For example, I recall a conversation with three elementary schoolteachers, all men, whom I had met by chance in a restaurant. They were curious about discipline techniques used in American schools. After I had given several examples, I was interrupted: "But how do you use the collective?" When I replied that we really did not use the classroom group in any systematic way, my three companions were puzzled. "But how do you keep discipline?"

Now it was my turn to ask for examples. "All right," came the answer. "Let us suppose that ten-year-old Vanya is pulling Anya's curls. If he doesn't stop the first time I speak to him, all I need do is mention it again in the group's presence; then I can be reasonably sure that before the class meets again the boy will be talked to by the officers of his Pioneer link. They will remind him that his behavior reflects on the reputation of the link."

"And what if he persists?"

"Then he may have to appear before his link—or even the entire collective—who will explain his misbehavior to him and determine his punishment."

"What punishment?"

"Various measures. He may be censured, or if his conduct is regarded as serious, he may be expelled from membership. Very often he himself will acknowledge his faults before the group."

Nor does the process of social criticism and control stop with the school. Our manual tells us, for example, that parents submit periodic reports to the school collective on the behavior of the child at home. One may wonder how parents can be depended on to turn in truthful accounts. Part of the answer was supplied to me in a conversation with a Soviet agricultural expert. In response to my questions, he explained that, no matter what a person's job, the collective at his place of work always took an active interest in his family life. Thus a representative would come to the worker's home to observe and talk with his wife and children. And if any undesirable features were noted, these would be reported back to the collective.

I asked for an example.

"Well, suppose the representative were to notice that my wife and I quarreled in front of the children [my companion shook his head]. That would be bad. They would speak to me about it and remind me of my responsibilities for training my children to be good citizens."

I pointed out how different the situation was in America, where a man's home was considered a private sanctuary, so that, for example, psychologists like myself often had a great deal of difficulty in getting into homes to talk with parents or to observe children.

"Yes," my companion responded. "That's one of the strange things about your system in the West. The family is separated from the rest of society. That's not good. It's bad for the family and bad for society." He paused for a moment, lost in thought. "I suppose," he went on, "if my wife didn't want to let the representative in, she could ask him to leave. But then at work, I should feel ashamed." (He hung his head to emphasize the point.) "Ivanov," they would say, "has an uncultured wife."

But it would be a mistake to conclude that Soviet methods of character education and social control are based primarily on negative criticism. On the contrary, in their approach there is as much of the carrot as the stick. But the carrot is given not merely as a reward for individual performance, but explicitly for the child's contribution to group achievement. The great charts emblazoned "Who Is Best?" which bedeck the halls and walls of every classroom have as entries the names not of individual pupils, but of rows and links (the link is the smallest unit of the Communist youth organization, which of course reaches into every classroom, from the first grade on). It is the winning unit that gets rewarded by a pennant, a special privilege, or having their picture taken in "parade uniforms." And when praise is given, as it frequently is, to an individual child, the group referent is always there: "Today Peter helped Kate and as a result his unit did not get behind the rest."

Helping other members of one's collective and appreciating their contributions—themes that are much stressed in Soviet character training—become matters of enlightened self-interest, since the grade that each person receives depends on the overall performance of his unit. Thus the good student finds it to his advantage to help the poor one. The same principle is carried over to the group level with champion rows and classes being made responsible for the performance of poorer ones.

Here, then, are the procedures employed in Soviet character education. As a result of Khrushchev's educational reforms, they may be expected to receive even wider application in the years to come, for, in connection with these reforms, several new types of educational institutions are to be developed on a massive scale. The most important of these is the *internat*, or boarding school, in which youngsters are to be entered as early as three months of age with parents visiting only on weekends. The internat is described in the theses announcing the reforms as the kind of school which "creates the most favorable conditions for the education and Communist upbringing of the rising generation." [6] The number of boarding schools in the U.S.S.R. is to be increased during the current seven-year plan from a 1958 level of 180,000 to 2,500,000 in 1965,[7] and according to I. A. Kairov, head of the Academy of Pedagogical Sciences, "No one can doubt that, as material conditions are created, the usual general educational school will be supplanted by the boarding school." [8]

If this prophecy is fulfilled, we may expect that in the years to come the great majority of Soviet children (and children in some other countries of the Communist bloc as well) will from the first year of life onward be spending their formative period in collective settings and will be exposed daily to the techniques of collective socialization we have been describing. It is therefore a matter of considerable practical and scientific interest to identify the salient features of these techniques and subject them to research study, in so far as this becomes possible within the framework of our own society.

Guiding Principles of the Soviet Approach to Character Training

As a first approximation, we may list the following as distinguishing characteristics or guiding principles of Communist methods of character education:

1. The peer collective (under adult leadership) rivals and early surpasses the family as the principal agent of socialization.

2. Competition between groups is utilized as the principal mechanism for motivating achievement of behavior norms.

3. The behavior of the individual is evaluated primarily in terms of its relevance to the goals and achievements of the collective.

4. Rewards and punishments are frequently given on a group basis; that is to say, the entire group benefits or suffers as a consequence of the conduct of individual members.

5. As soon as possible, the tasks of evaluating the behavior of individuals and of dispensing rewards and sanctions is delegated to the members of the collective.

6. The principal methods of social control are public recognition and public criticism, with explicit training and practice being given in these activities. Specifically, each member of the collective is encouraged to observe deviant behavior by his fellows and is given opportunity to report his observations to the group. Reporting on one's peers is esteemed and rewarded as a civic duty.

7. Group criticism becomes the vehicle for training in self-criticism in the presence of one's peers. Such public self-criticism is regarded as a powerful mechanism for maintaining and enhancing commitment to approved standards of behavior, as well as the method of choice for bringing deviants back into line.

There are of course many other important features of the Soviet approach to socialization, but the seven listed above are those which present the greatest contrast to the patterns we employ in the West. It is for this reason that they are selected for special consideration here. We shall now proceed to examine each feature in greater detail with particular attention to the research ideas which it may generate.

The Family versus the Collective

American theory and research on moral development have given almost exclusive emphasis to the family as the principal context and agent of socialization. The Soviet pattern, with its predominant emphasis on the collective, therefore raises the question of how these two socializing agents may differ in the nature and effect of the techniques they employ. To put the problem in another way: What type of socialization process and character structure emerge under the predominant influence of one or the other agent, or a combination of the two?

Stated in this form, the question seems an obvious and important one. Yet, to the writer's knowledge, research to date has little to offer in reply. True, there have been studies of personality development in several diverse types of children who, for one reason or another, have grown up outside the context of the nuclear family. But for several reasons these studies do not shed much light on the problem at hand. The limitation springs in part from the highly specialized character of the groups investigated: youngsters removed to residential nurseries during wartime,[9] children rescued from Nazi concentration camps,[10] delinquent gangs,[11] and kibbutz children.[12]

Second, by and large these investigations take the form of clinical or case studies focusing on the particular problem at hand; they lack the structured design and comparative frame of reference which enhance the possibility of recognizing important differences, distinguishing characteristics, functional relationships. The advantages of these strategic devices are evidenced in the researches which employ them. Thus in a comparative ethnographic study, Eisenstadt[13] demonstrated that peer collectives are most likely to develop in a society when there is marked discontinuity between values and role allocations in the family and in the adult world. Exploiting another kind of naturalistic experiment, two investigations[14] have studied situations in which parental values conflict with those of the peer group, and have found in each instance that although both sources are influential, the peer group tends to outweigh the parent in the age range studied (twelve to eighteen). The research bearing most directly on the problem at hand is Boehm's comparative study [15] of conscience development in Swiss and American children. She finds that the latter transfer parent dependence to peer dependence at an earlier age, and that

One result of this earlier transferring appears to be that the American child's conscience becomes less egocentric and interiorizes earlier than does that of the Swiss child. There is, however, some indication that the content of conscience differs in these two types of societies. Whereas the American child's conscience is turned, primarily, toward social adjustment, the Swiss child's is geared toward character improvement.[16]

The principal shortcoming of all these studies for the issue at hand, however, is their failure to examine and analyze their data from the point of view of the group processes of socialization that may be occurring in the collective setting outside the family. To the extent that socialization is dealt with at all in these investigations, it is treated in conventional fashion with attention accorded primarily to the behavior of a parent or a parent surrogate toward the child. Such a restricted focus is of course understandable, given the traditional emphasis in Western culture, reflected in scientific work, on the centrality of the parent-child relationship in the process of upbringing. It is this circumscribed conception which probably accounts for the fact that Western personality theory and research, highly developed as they are in comparison with their Russian counterparts,[17] offer little basis for ready-made hypotheses bearing on processes and effects of socialization in collective settings.

Nevertheless, despite their limitations, the existing researches have considerable potential value. To begin with, many of them, especially the clinical and case studies, contain excellent descriptive data that could be reexamined from our new perspective to discover whether they might not shed some light on phenomena of collective socialization. Second, the more structured investigations suggest research designs that might profitably be employed in future work. The first research paradigm, exemplified by both the Eisenstadt and Boehm studies, makes use of groups with contrasting degrees of exposure to socialization in family versus collective settings. Such contrasts are understandably found most readily in different cultures, but under these circumstances interpretation is complicated by the presence of other factors associated with each culture that might account for the observed differences in character development. Eisenstadt endeavors to circumvent this difficulty by using data from a large number of societies in which other factors besides those under immediate investigation may be expected to vary widely. While highly useful, particularly in the exploratory stages of research, this approach has its serious limitations. Either one must make do with only partially adequate data gathered by other investigators with other objectives in mind, or one must carry out new, specially designed cross-cultural studies in a substantial number of different settings.

But there is an alternative strategy which, to the writer's knowledge, has hardly been exploited to date. It involves finding groups exposed to different agents of socialization within the same or closely comparable cultural contexts. Such comparable groups may be difficult to discover, but once identified they offer rich opportunities for research on differential processes and outcomes of character training in familial versus peer-group settings. The ideal contrast in this regard would be two groups of children from the same social milieu, one group having attended boarding school from an early age, the other raised at home with minimal and relatively late exposure to group influences in school or peer group. Obviously this ideal would be almost impossible to achieve, but it can certainly be approximated, especially in such countries as England, Switzerland, or, should the opportunity arise, the Soviet Union, where boarding schools are relatively common; or in Israel, with a focus on the comparison between children raised in the kibbutz, where the young are reared primarily outside the family in collective settings, and the *moshav*, where adult life is collectively organized but children are brought up in the nuclear family. The last contrast should be particularly instructive, since collective ideology would be present in both settings but the principal agent of socialization would differ.

Another research opportunity found more easily outside the United States is that provided by families living in relative geographic isolation. An extreme example in a modern Western country occurs in Norway, where some families live in mountainous areas that remain isolated during a large part of the year. A current study of this group by Aubert, Tiller, and their associates at the Oslo Institute for Social Research should shed light on the character development of children raised in a nuclear family under conditions of minimal contact with others outside the home.

The American scene is of course not without its possibilities for research along the same lines, even if over a somewhat more restricted range. Thus we, too, have our boarding schools, and although their enrollment tends to be limited to children who are highly selected on socioeconomic, religious, or psychological characteristics, an appropriately matched sample of controls not attending boarding school can usually be found. Indeed, to minimize differences in family values and background one could make use of those private schools which enroll both boarding and day pupils. Similarly, instances of families living in geographic isolation can still be found, especially in the receding remnants of the American frontier in mountains, deserts, and the north country; moreover, with the occasional influx of skilled technicians to such areas, the possibility arises of studying families who are living in an isolation which is primarily physical and not cultural as well. Finally, among the run-of-the-mill families in any American community there is likely to be an appreciable range of variation in the amount of socialization children experience outside the nuclear family. Some youngsters participate from an early age in nursery schools, camps, clubs, gangs, and other peer-group settings both with and without adult supervision. Others remain relatively isolated from peers until they enter kindergarten or first grade, and even then extrafamilial associations may be minimal. A study of differences in character development in children exposed to varying degrees of familial versus extrafamilial socialization could be illuminating.

The last proposal highlights a difficulty plaguing all of the research designs outlined above. It is obvious that families in which contact with peers is postponed and minimized are likely to exhibit different value systems and techniques of socialization from those in which children are permitted or encouraged to have early associations outside the home. Such differences will be found also even in the "cleanest" and most closely matched comparisons. Thus day and boarding pupils in the same school will still differ in family background, values, and child-rearing practices. The fact that particular values and techniques may be functionally linked to the setting in which they occur does not remove the necessity of identifying them and taking them into account in the interpretation of results and in the design of subsequent studies.

Comparing groups with differing socialization experience is not the only strategy available for studying the differential influences of the family versus the peer collective. The researches of Rosen and Haire mentioned above suggest still another gambit, that of comparing the relative effects of both types of influence on the same children. The strategy here involves finding instances in which familial and peer-group standards conflict in varying degrees and observing which influence prevails under what circumstances.

The last strategy focuses even more sharply the question of what dependent variables should be investigated in studies of this kind. Quite naturally one thinks first of the variables that have been emphasized in American studies of moral development; namely, projective measures of conscience and guilt of the type employed by Allinsmith,[18] Aron-

freed,[19] Hoffman,[20] and Miller and Swanson,[21] or the behavioral measures
of similar variables growing out of the work of Whiting and Sears and
their colleagues at the Harvard Laboratory of Human Development [22]
and implemented most recently in a study of antecedents of resistance
to temptation conducted by Burton, Maccoby, and Allinsmith.[23]

It would clearly be a matter of considerable theoretical and practical
interest whether children experiencing different ratios of exposure to socialization within the family versus within the peer group exhibit differences in types and degrees of self-blame, tendency to blame others,
resistance to temptation, or any of the other patterns of moral judgment
commonly examined in current research on this topic. The psychoanalytic theories on which most of these instruments are based would lead
one to expect stronger internalization and self-blame among children raised
primarily within the nuclear family, and this prediction receives at least
indirect support from the one study we have found [24] that comes near to
dealing with the problem. But much depends on the particular socialization processes employed in one or another collective setting. In the absence of adequate data or theory dealing directly with this issue, we can
only resort to speculation on the basis of what knowledge we do have
about socialization processes in general. And since this knowledge is based
almost entirely on studies of the family, we are forced into the risky
expedient of arguing by analogy. Accordingly, in order to try to become
aware of both the possibilities and the pitfalls of this approach, we shall
begin by assuming isomorphism and then call the assumption into
question.

What are the principal generalizations, then, to be drawn from existing
studies of factors in the nuclear family affecting the moral development
of the child? A growing number of independent researches [25] point to
the conclusion that the internalization of moral standards is a function
of the degree and ratio of parental affection and discipline. Specifically,
internalization appears to be maximized when both affection and discipline are high. When parents rely primarily on the assertion of power
in a relatively nonaffectionate context, the child is likely to be responsive only to external controls (i.e., fear of punishment). When both
affection and discipline are low, or when the former appreciably out-
weighs the latter, moral standards tend to be weak or ineffective and the
child resorts to distortive mechanisms such as denial or displacement
(for example, unjustly blaming others). But internalization can also take
nonadaptive forms characterized by inflexibility or excessive self-blame.
Such rigid or self-deprecatory standards are especially likely to arise
when parents are generally affectionate but rely on discipline techniques
which "involve ego attack and depreciation of the child." [26] In contrast,

parents of children whose moral standards are more realistic and responsive to extenuating circumstances tend to "appeal more to approach motives." Hoffman, in the most recent and extensive study of this problem, elaborates on the differences between the two groups of parents as follows:

> The two groups are similar in that their parental discipline relies primarily on the frequent use of inductive techniques within an affectionate context, and the infrequent use of power assertion. What mainly characterizes and differentiates [that adaptive group] is that they report their parents as more frequently using techniques that communicate disappointment in the child for not living up to the parent's expectations and less frequently as using ego attack and love withdrawal techniques. It seems to us that the expression of disappointment, while it indicates that the parent has in a sense hurt the child, also conveys the feeling that the child is capable of living up to an ideal.[27]

Pursuing our argument by analogy and shifting the context from the family to the school collective, we may ask whether any of these patterns of socialization apply to the Soviet case and, if so, what kinds of consequences in moral development we might expect. With due regard to the tentative and largely impressionistic character of this initial comparison, it is nevertheless striking to note the correspondence between the techniques recommended in our Soviet manual and Hoffman's description of the pattern of socialization most likely to lead to the internalization of realistic and appropriately flexible moral standards. Both situations involve high levels of discipline and support with the primary emphasis on an appeal to motives of approach rather than of avoidance. (E.g., "How can we help Serezha with his problem?") Also in both instances there is infrequent use of power assertion. Finally, the many examples of group criticism appearing in the Soviet manual are surely more appropriately described, in Hoffman's terminology, not as an "ego attack and depreciation of the child," but precisely as statements "that communicate disappointment in the child for not living up to expectations," which "convey the feeling that the child is capable of living up to an ideal."

If the analogy is a valid one, and *if* the Russians actually practice what they preach, we should therefore expect that the pattern of socialization in the peer collective would lead to the development of the same quality of moral standards achieved by an optimal balance of support and control in the American nuclear family. The two "if's," however, can hardly be allowed to stand unquestioned. To consider the purely empirical question first, it seems likely that, as in every society, actual practice in Soviet society falls somewhat short of the ideal, or at least deviates from it. The nature of this deviation must await the results of systematic objective observations in Soviet schoolrooms. And it may be some time before such data are made available by either Soviet or Western behavioral scientists. In the meanwhile, however, there is nothing to prevent American workers from initiating a systematic program of research on group atmospheres in the classroom or other peer-collective settings and observing, through naturalistic or contrived experiments, the differential effects of various ratios of support and control on the development of moral standards and behavior. Indeed, the prototype of such research already exists in the classic experiment of Lewin, Lippitt, and White,[28] and it is both regrettable and surprising that this study has not been followed up by others in a systematic program of research on socialization processes in peer-group settings. Perhaps White and Lippitt's recently published reanalysis [29] of their data will help stimulate a renewed interest in this neglected area.

Our second "if" gives rise to even more questions and complexities. It seems hardly likely that generalizations derived from studies of the American family could be applied directly to the analysis of socialization processes in the classroom, and a Soviet classroom at that. To begin with, such an analogy assumes that the teacher and the classroom group have reinforcement power equivalent to that of the parent. This assumption can be challenged from both directions. On the one hand, psychoanalytic theory, and probably common belief as well, discounts the possibility that any other social group could approach the family in the strength of its affectional and controlling influences. Yet a growing body of research stemming from the work of Asch [30] demonstrates that the group is capable of exerting tremendously powerful forces toward conformity, even to the extent of inducing distortions in reality perception. The question of the relative potential of the family and the peer group as agents of socialization therefore remains an open one, resolvable only through empirical research.

The issue is complicated further by the fact that, to a greater or lesser degree, the child is usually exposed to some measure of socialization within the family before he enters the collective. In fact, the responsiveness of the child to socialization in a group setting may even depend on prior experience in the family. It is noteworthy in this connection that, up until now, most of the children who have been exposed to Soviet methods of character education in school have spent the first seven years of their lives in the bosom of the family. Should the preceding speculations be valid, the Russians may experience some difficulty with their methods once they begin, as they propose, to place children in collectives during the first year of life.

Apart from questions about the relative socializing power of the family and the collective, there are of course important differences in the social structure of the two systems. Yet, while influential theorists like S. Freud [31] and Parsons and Bales [32] have stressed the analogy between parent and children on the one hand and group leader and group members on the other, to this writer's knowledge little attention has been given to the theoretical implications for the process of socialization of such obvious differences as group size, range of role differentiation, specificity of function, duration through time, and their psychological consequences in degree of ego involvement. At the same time, so far as Soviet society is concerned, we must take note of the two-way theme constantly reiterated in Russian writings on character education that the family must become a collective and the collective must take on the characteristics of a family. As a result, it is conceivable that over time the differences between these two types of social structure in Soviet society will become attenuated and the similarities maximized. This possibility highlights the value of comparative longitudinal studies of the changing character of Western and Communist family and peer-group structures. Such studies would of course have special significance as necessary background for research on character development.

The preceding consideration points directly to the most important difference between American and Soviet socialization practice, whether in the family or out. This is the matter of ideological content and the special procedures which this content inspires. It is this content and these procedures that are the burden of the remaining six of the guiding principles we have listed earlier.

Group Incentives

Principles 2–4 emphasize the importance of the collective over the individual as the frame of reference for evaluating behavior and distributing punishments and rewards. As the principles indicate, there are three elements to the pattern: desired behavior is motivated through competition between groups rather than between individuals; behavior is judged in terms of its implication for the achievement and reputation of the group; and rewards and punishments are given on a group basis so that all members of the group stand to gain or lose from the actions of each individual.

The arousal of motivation through competition between groups is certainly not an unfamiliar phenomenon in American society or in the American schoolroom. But even without the support of systematic evidence, one could confidently assert that this motivating device used to be employed far more frequently three or more decades ago than it is today. This same trend is dramatically reflected in the character of research studies carried out in the late twenties and thirties as compared with the present time. Thus Murphy, Murphy, and Newcomb, in the 1937 revision of their *Experimental Social Psychology*,[33] tabulate as many as twenty-five studies dealing with competition in children's groups, many of them focusing directly on the issue of group versus individual incentive. In contrast, a contemporary survey of group research [34] scarcely mentions the topic. Even though the earlier studies of group incentives focus almost entirely on motor and intellectual tasks rather than attitude formation, the results are instructive. Group competition generally increases output but is less effective as an incentive than self-oriented or individual competition. As Murphy, Murphy, and Newcomb properly caution, however, "Any discussion of . . . studies of the effects of incentives must be seen in relation to the cultural background which has set so much store by individual achievement, and has nourished this movement to find ways of stimulating the greatest achievement in the individual." [35]

This caveat carries implications for a potentially fruitful research design in which children with contrasting individualistic versus collectivist backgrounds would be exposed to both types of competitive situations and their performance observed. Although one's first impulse is to discount such a proposal on the practical ground that it would be virtually impossible to find children with such diverse backgrounds in the same culture, further consideration suggests that good research opportunities do exist. The most obvious example is Israel, where both types of orientation are common even within the same ethnic and socioeconomic subgroups. Furthermore, the contrast can be approximated in our own society, since many private schools differ widely precisely along this continuum. For example, many progressive schools are ultraindividualistic in their philosophy and practice, whereas others would probably be shocked to learn that their emphasis on subgroup solidarity and competition is properly described as collectivistic.

But in view of the dearth of research studies of the phenomenon over the last twenty-five years, there would be much to learn from research on the effects of group incentives even with children coming from the predominantly individualistic background characteristic of American society. On the independent side, these researches should give attention to such specific variables as the motivating power of intergroup versus interindividual competition, evaluation of individual behavior in terms of its contribution to the status of the group as a whole, and the giving of punishments and rewards on a group basis. On the dependent side, the spectrum of variables should be broadened beyond problem solving to include personality measures, such as the indices of moral standards employed in much current research, as well as other relevant social attitudes and behaviors. These important additions are more appropriately discussed after we have completed examination of the last three of the distinguishing characteristics of Soviet methods of character education—those having to do with group criticism and self-criticism.

Group Criticism and Self-Criticism

The feature of Soviet socialization practices that clashes most sharply with the American pattern is the Russians' widespread resort to the procedure of criticizing others and oneself in public. The practice is common throughout all levels of Soviet society, from school, farm, and factory to the highest echelons of the party. Thus by being taught these techniques in early childhood, Soviet youths are being prepared in patterns of response that will be expected and even required of them throughout their life-span. Since such practices are uncommon in American society, it is not surprising that they have not been subjected to research study in any direct way. As already noted, however, the work of Asch and others [36] testifies to the power of an overwhelming majority to force the deviant subject to conform to majority views. In these experiments members of the majority do not engage in criticism, but simply give responses which conflict with the reality perceptions of the experimental subject. The effect on the subject is to lead him, in an appreciable number of instances, to change his own response in the direction of that of the majority. In a sense, such alteration represents a confession of his own previous "error." Obviously, the experiments cannot be said to reproduce explicit features of Soviet group criticism and self-criticism, but the fit could be made much closer by instructing confederates to engage in criticism and by asking the subject to admit that his previous responses had not been correct. Such variations would of course make even more salient questions of scientific ethics that invariably arise when experiments of this kind are viewed from the perspective of the Western Judeo-Christian moral tradition. (It is doubtful, incidentally, that such questions would ever be raised in a Communist society.) Still, ways can probably be found to conduct experiments on the processes of group criticism and self-criticism without doing serious violence to our own ethical traditions.

The fact remains, however, that such socialization procedures as group criticism and self-criticism have moral implications and hence may be expected to have moral consequences; that is to say, they are likely to influence the moral attitudes, actions, and character structure of the individuals on whom they are employed. Moreover, it is doubtful whether such consequences are fully or even adequately reflected by the measures of conscience and guilt currently employed in research on moral development. Certainly it would be important to know about the nature of conscience and guilt in the "new Soviet men" who have been exposed to a lifetime of experience in group criticism and self-criticism. But in building "socialist morality," Soviet educators are less concerned with such questions as whether the individual tends to blame others or himself than with his sense of commitment to the collective, especially in the face of competing individualistic values and preferences.

Accordingly, perhaps the most important research implication to be drawn from our examination of Soviet methods of character education is the necessity of expanding the spectrum of what we conceive as moral development beyond the characteristically Judeo-Christian concern with personal responsibility and guilt to a consideration of the broader moral issues inherent in the relation of man to man and of the individual to his society.

Examples of Soviet Research

Unlike their American colleagues, Soviet psychologists are little interested in studying individual differences in motives and interpersonal relationships, and are primarily concerned with the development of group skills. In many instances the skills are those for developing common motives for the group and the optimal translation of these motives into effective group performance.

To illustrate the last point, as well as the methods typically employed in Soviet research in this sphere, I shall describe an experiment recently completed by N. F. Prokina at the Laboratory on the Psychology of

Upbringing, Institute of Psychology, Moscow. Her study is one of a series of investigations at the laboratory, based on and supporting the general thesis that "personality characteristics develop as a result of the incorporation by the child of certain aspects of his social activity." Prokina's study was described as involving four stages: (1) defining a specific desirable mode of behavior for children; (2) arousing the motive to behave in the appropriate manner; (3) providing for systematic practice in the desired behavior; (4) determining whether the behavior persists after special measures for evoking it are discontinued.

The particular "desirable behavior" selected as the focus of investigation was that of orderly forming of ranks prior to leaving the classroom. This behavior was chosen for both methodological and substantive reasons. On the former grounds it had the advantages of being readily observable, lasting a short time, and recurring several times each day. But the primary basis of choice was "practical importance." According to the investigator, before the experimental procedures were instituted, children spent as much as eight to ten minutes lining up after every class, so that in the course of a single day they could lose as much as an hour and a half on this single routine.

The subjects in the experiment were the entire class (thirty children) in the first grade at a Moscow boarding school. The class had been chosen because it had the reputation of being one of the most difficult and disorganized. In the first experiment the children were simply told about the specific behaviors that necessarily entered into orderly lining up (e.g., rise when the bell rings, stand quietly, etc.). Upon then being asked to perform these actions, the pupils did so quickly and well. The investigator viewed this phase of the experiment as essential in demonstrating that the pupils had the ability to engage in the desired behavior, even though they might not make use of this ability on particular occasions.

The aim of the second experiment was to translate the "latent capacity into an active and enduring form." For this purpose the children were divided into six groups of five persons each. A chart was made showing six stairways with series of steps equaling the number of lineups required each day. Successful performance was recognized immediately afterward by allowing the team's representative to move a little red flag up the steps. The "competitive motive" aroused by this procedure proved highly effective, but not enduring. At the first lining up, time was reduced to one minute, but by the end of the day it had lengthened to the customary interval of seven minutes.

Accordingly, in a series of further experiments, the investigator sought to increase the duration of improved performance by evoking additional motives. The most effective of these proved to be the "motive of play," aroused by designating competing teams as pilots, soldiers, or sailors, and asking each group to line up quickly and well, "the way real sailors do." Although performance improved with this additional incentive, there was still marked retrogression over the course of the day. Further observation revealed that, despite being able and motivated to form straight lines quickly, as the day wore on pupils became easily prone to distractions (casual conversation, looking out the window, fiddling with objects, etc.). To meet this problem the investigator employed a three-minute sand timer that was started as soon as the bell sounded. As a result children continued to line up promptly throughout the day.

As a final step in perfecting performance, times were taken at successive phases of the lining-up process and teams given points for the most rapid completion of each phase (standing, walking, sitting, etc.). In consequence, the entire procedure was completed in an average duration of one to one and a half minutes. This level of performance was maintained to the end of the academic year, three months after the "game" had been discontinued.

In the investigator's view, the series of experiments establishes three major conditions as facilitating enduring changes in behavior: (1) there must be arousal of a strong motive (competitive play) ensuring positive orientation toward acquisition of the desired behavior; (2) the behavior to be learned should be broken up into component elements; and (3) the child should be instructed to relate the corresponding behavioral elements to the time intervals allotted to them.

SOVIET METHODOLOGY FOR THE
STUDY OF PERSONALITY DEVELOPMENT

The foregoing investigation is typical, both in method and in substance, of Soviet work in this area. Indeed, so far as research design is concerned, the study is more structured than the average: the number of subjects is specified (although age and sex are not), and some results are expressed in numerical form. But, viewed in the framework of American psychology, this is not, strictly speaking, an experiment, but an observational study of an experimental program. As such, it exemplifies Soviet preference and practice. Especially in the study of personality and social process, Russian psychology eschews the analytic, quantitative approach so characteristic of the American scene in favor of an almost anecdotal, holistic orientation. This view, expressed in virtually every center visited, has recently been stated systematically in a definitive paper by V. A. Krutetski.[37] Writing on problems of method in the study of personality, Krutetski asserts:

Soviet psychology categorically rejects the possibility of building personality study on the basis of different types of tests and questionnaires. The mechanistic approach to man, the subjective interpretation of results, the attempt by primitive, standardized methods to "analyze" a most complex and ever-changing object, giving quantitative form to personality characteristics and manifestations—all this, which is organically inherent to tests and questionnaires, has prompted Soviet psychologists once and for all to repudiate this antiquated method.

Soviet psychology has established a set of principles for the scientific study of personality: (1) personality should be investigated in an analytic-synthetic manner with proper regard for its wholeness; (2) personality can be studied only on the basis of objective material; i.e., in investigating character one must proceed from concrete behavior, man's actions, and the motives they reveal; (3) personality can be studied only with due regard to the determining influences of external and internal conditions (conditions of life and upbringing, the state of the organism and its life activity); (4) personality characteristics must be examined in their genetic development and change; (5) individual personalities can be studied only in the collective, through the collective, and against the background of the collective, in which character forms and develops . . . ; (6) personality must be studied in the perspective of its development . . . that is, personality must be viewed not only as an object of investigation, but also as an object of training; (7) investigation must have an activistic character, have the goal of controlling the process of personality formation. . . .

The specific methods for the study of personality accepted in Soviet psychology conform to the foregoing principles. These methods include observation, naturalistic experimentation, laboratory experimentation, as well as the biographical method, interviews, the analysis of products of activity, techniques which are ordinarily applied together, thus supplementing, correcting, and controlling one another.[38]

Although Soviet psychologists, by and large, agree in their condemnation of the statistical, variable-oriented approach of much American research, they differ among themselves in the degree to which they prefer one or another of the approved methods listed above. For example, the psychologists at the University of Leningrad are suspicious of the validity of experimental methods for the study of personality. Indeed, Professor Kovalev has stated flatly, "It is entirely clear that the laboratory experiment cannot serve as a means for studying the essential characteristics of the school-age child." [39] A contrary position is taken by Moscow University psychologists, who look to the laboratory as the most hopeful source of progress in child psychology. But even though their researches are conducted in the laboratory, their methods have more in common with those employed in Leningrad than with those in use in any leading research center in the United States.

In observing and training schoolchildren under conditions of social competition and control, Soviet psychologists are studying and teaching skills that have enduring relevance to life in the Soviet society.

Moreover, psychologists represent but a small segment of the many professional groups engaged in what is in effect applied social psychology on a massive scale. It is in this sense that one of my informants was substantially correct in stating that what we call social psychology is primarily carried on in the Soviet Union not by psychologists, but by educators and party workers. For this reason, future Western students of social psychology in the U.S.S.R. should not confine their attention to work in psychological departments and institutes, but should also give careful attention to applied social psychology as it is practiced in schools, youth organizations, farms, factories, and governmental bodies.

New Perspectives in Soviet Psychology

The implications of these developments for psychology are spelled out in an address by Kairov in the official Soviet educational journal, *Sovetskaia pedagogika*, in which he criticizes psychologists and others for failing to give adequate attention in research to problems of "society and the school." Such recommendations are reflected at the operational level in the direction of developing research in three of the centers I visited (the Department of Psychology at Leningrad, and the Institutes of Psychology at Moscow and Kiev) and in programmatic statements published recently by leading Soviet psychologists.[40]

Especially noteworthy in this connection is the call, on the part of several of these psychologists, for guarded reconsideration of one or another approach characteristic of psychology in the West and regarded over the past quarter century as reactionary. Kairov, for instance, criticizes Soviet psychologists for too narrow an interpretation of the 1936 Decree of the Central Committee on "pedological distortions," with resultant neglect of the important problem of individual differences.

. . . Certain of our workers in the pedagogical sciences, having failed to examine this decree as they properly should have, adopted an incorrect attitude. Contrary to common sense, they began simply to deny the need and the orthodoxy of any research whatsoever into differences between children, to be used for pedagogical purposes. . . . They attacked as "pedological" all methods involving research into age and individual differences of school children which went beyond the bounds of simple observation and the common methods of checking their knowledge.

Despite the fact that over 20 years have elapsed since that decree, this incorrect and one-sided attitude has yet to be subjected to criticism, and continues to interfere seriously with the development of true Marxist teachings on children. Meanwhile, there is no doubt that, without studying the personality of the youngster, it is impossible for a teacher to carry on his practical educational activity on a scientifically sound basis. The most important thing here is the careful compilation of materials giving the specific developmental history of the child's individuality, the history of the development of children's collectives, and the history of the inter-relations formed within those collectives. But, having cut out research on the age and individual differences of children, pedagogy became essentially "childless." [41]

In another sphere, Bozhovich reopens the possibility of conducting research on unconscious processes.

Soviet psychologists have shown a fully understandable tendency to oppose with the supremacy of the conscious the "unconscious" of Freud and other representatives of "depth psychology," to demonstrate that man is by no means a mere marionette dancing at the whim of certain dark powers, but instead is the master of his own behavior, capable of governing his actions and deeds on the basis of consciously posed tasks and consciously taken decisions.

However, in the course of battle against its domination the "unconscious" came to be viewed as the demiurge of personality. It was thought that one had only to convince a child, to develop his conscious awareness, and his total personality would be developed. One cannot agree with such an overestimation of the role of conscious processes. In our investigations, we constantly encounter phenomena that do not lie within the child's conscious awareness, but which nevertheless cannot be overlooked either by the psychologist or the pedagogue. For example, in the course of investigating motives for academic performance in schoolchildren, we have established on the basis of obtained data that the main motives of learning, those which express the social needs most significant for the child and which thereby constitute the principal instigators of academic performance, are, as a rule, not recognized by the child himself.

In the investigation of the development of the affective aspects of personality, we likewise constantly come face to face with the fact that moral feelings and habits which arise in the course of social activity determine the behavior of the child often quite independently of his consciousness and even in direct contradiction to it. . . .

In the light of these considerations, it seems to us of the utmost importance in further studies of problems in the psychology of personality to give special attention to the investigation of psychological phenomena which arise in the course of the child's life and activity but of which he remains unaware. It is necessary to study the characteristics of such phenomena, their origins, and their role in the behavior of the child as well as in the formation of his personality.[42]

But perhaps the most revolutionary change urged by a leading Soviet psychologist is Kovalev's proposal to redeem social psychology from its purgatorial status and reinstate it as a legitimate sphere of investigation for Soviet science. Acknowledging as entirely proper and justified the severe criticisms of bourgeois social psychology which appear in the definitive article on that subject in the *Great Soviet Encyclopedia*, Kovalev nevertheless challenges the official view, as expounded most recently by the late dean of Soviet psychology, S. L. Rubinstein, that to express interest in social psychology is to "defend that which is so dear to the hearts of the reactionaries, that which, in the last analysis, is an attempt to psychologize sociology; that is, to drag idealism into the scientific study of social phenomena." [43]

Such a position, Kovalev suggests, forces one to question the legitimacy of studying "philosophy, political economy, sociology, and psychology," since these subjects too might be "dear to the hearts of reactionaries." The real question, the author argues, is whether or not an objective social reality exists; if it does exist, then it is necessary to find methods appropriate for its study. He then cites Soviet philosophers in support of the thesis that "social psychology is a real phenomenon made manifest in the psychology of a given society, a given class, and in the psychological character of national groups; social psychology is the sum total of social feelings, attitudes, experiences, habits, illusions, etc." Citing the work of the "great Soviet educator, A. S. Makarenko," Kovalev asks:

Are not Soviet pedagogues and psychologists investigating questions of the psychology of upbringing in essence working on one of the most important problems of social psychology? The question of the formation of the collective (and for that matter of public opinion) and of the development of personality in the collective, through the collective, and for the collective constitutes precisely such a problem. It follows that in actuality social psychology is already being investigated in Soviet pedagogical science. . . .

The majestic program of developing socialist construction approved after all-union discussion at the 21st Congress of the Communist Party of the Soviet Union poses great and responsible tasks, not only for the natural, but also for the social sciences.

The program laid down for the Communist upbringing of the Soviet peoples, at the center of which stand the problems of developing a Communist orientation toward work and collectivism as hallmarks of the personality of the new man, makes imperative the investigation of social psychology, which must make its contribution to the solution of these most vital problems.[44]

American social scientists will be watching with interest the future of this "new look" in Soviet psychology.

Notes

1. A. S. Makarenko, *Pedagogicheskaia poema* (Leningrad: Leningradskoie gazetno-zhurnalnoie i knizhnoie izdatelstvo, 1949), available in English under the title *The Road to Life*, trans. Ivy and Tatiana Litvinov (Moscow: Foreign Languages Publishing House, 1951); Makarenko, *Learn to Live* (Moscow: Foreign Languages Publishing House, 1953); Makarenko, *Kniga dlya roditelei* (Petrozavodsk: Gosudarstvennoie Izdatelstvo Karelskoi ASSR, 1959), trans. as *A Book for Parents* (Moscow: Foreign Languages Publishing House, n.d.).

2. Makarenko, *Book for Parents*, p. 29.

3. *Ibid.*, pp. 37-38.

4. Makarenko, *Road to Life* and *Learn to Live*.

5. L. E. Novika, ed., *Sotsialisticheskoie sorevnovanie v shkole* (Moscow: Uchpedgiz, 1950).

6. Communist Party of the Soviet Union, *Ob ukreplenii svyazi shkoly s zhiznyu i o dalneishem razvitii sistemy naraodnogo obrazovaniia v strane* (theses of the Central Comittee of the CPSU) (Moscow: Gospolitizdat, 1958).

7. *Pravda*, November 18, 1958.

8. I. A. Kairov, "Long-Range Plans for the Development of Pedagogical Sciences and Coordination of the Work of the Academy and Chairs of Pedagogy of Pedagogical Institutes, U.S.S.R.," translation of an article in *Sovetskaia pedagogika*, 24, no. 2 (1960): 16-44 (New York: United States Joint Publications Research Service, 1960).

9. D. Burlingham and A. Freud, *Infants without Families* (London: George Allen & Unwin, 1944).

10. A. Freud and S. Dann, "An Experiment in Group Upbringing," in *Readings in Child Development*, ed. W. E. Martin and C. B. Stendler (New York: Harcourt, Brace & Co., 1954).

11. A. K. Cohen, *Delinquent Boys—The Culture of the Gang* (Glencoe, Ill.: The Free Press, 1955); A. K. Cohen and J. F. Short, Jr., "Research in Delinquent Subcultures," *Journal of Social Issues*, 1958, no. 14, pp. 23-37; W. Miller, "Lower-

Class Culture as a Generating Milieu of Gang Delinquency," *Journal of Social Issues*, 1958, no. 24, pp. 5–19; F. M. Thrasher, *The Gang* (Chicago: University of Chicago Press, 1936); W. F. Whyte, *Street Corner Society* (Chicago: University of Chicago Press, 1943).

12. G. Caplan, "Clinical Observations on the Emotional Life of Children in the Communal Settlements in Israel," in *Transactions of the Seventh Conference on Problems of Infancy and Childhood*, ed. M. J. Senn (New York: Josiah Macy, Jr., Foundation, 1953); H. Faigin, "Case Report: Social Behavior of Young Children in the Kibbutz," *Journal of Abnormal and Social Psychology*, 56 (1958): 117–29; E. E. Irvine, "Observations on the Aims and Methods of Child-Rearing in Communal Settlements in Israel," *Human Relations*, 5 (1952): 247–75; A. I. Rabin, "Kibbutz Children—Research Findings to Date," *Children*, 5 (1958): 179–84; M. E. Spiro, *Children of the Kibbutz* (Cambridge, Mass.: Harvard University Press, 1958).

13. S. N. Eisenstadt, *From Generation to Generation* (Glencoe, Ill.: The Free Press, 1956).

14. M. Haire and F. Morrison, "School Children's Perceptions of Labor and Management," *Journal of Social Psychology*, 46 (1957): 179–97; B. C. Rosen, "Conflicting Group Membership: A Study of Parent–Peer Group Cross Pressures," *American Sociological Review*, 20 (1955): 155–61.

15. L. Boehm, "The Development of Independence: A Comparative Study," *Child Development*, 28 (1957): 85–92.

16. *Ibid.*, pp. 91–92.

17. U. Bronfenbrenner, "Soviet Studies in Personality Development and Socialization," dittoed (Ithaca, N.Y.: Cornell University, Department of Child Development and Family Relationships, 1961).

18. W. Allinsmith, "Conscience and Conflict: The Moral Force in Personality," *Child Development*, 28 (1957): 469–76, and "The Learning of Moral Standards," in D. R. Miller and G. E. Swanson, *Inner Conflict and Defense* (New York: Henry Holt & Co., 1960), pp. 141–76.

19. J. Aronfreed, "Internal and External Orientation in the Moral Behavior of Children" (paper read before the American Psychological Association, Cincinnati, September, 1959), and "Moral Behavior and Sex Identity," in Miller and Swanson, *Inner Conflict and Defense*, pp. 177–93.

20. M. L. Hoffman, "Techniques and Processes in Moral Development," mimeographed (Detroit: Merrill-Palmer Institute, 1961).

21. Miller and Swanson, *Inner Conflict and Defense*.

22. R. R. Sears, E. E. Maccoby, and H. Levin, *Patterns of Child Rearing* (Evanston, Ill.: Row, Peterson & Co., 1957); J. W. M. Whiting and I. L. Child, *Child Training and Personality* (New Haven: Yale University Press, 1953); Whiting, "Fourth Presentation," in *Discussions on Child Development*, ed. J. M. Tanner and B. Inhelder (London: Tavistock Publications, 1954), vol. 2.

23. R. V. Burton, E. E. Maccoby, and W. Allinsmith, "Antecedents of Resistance to Temptation," mimeographed (Washington: National Institute of Mental Health, U.S. Department of Health, Education, and Welfare, n.d.).

24. Boehm, "Development of Independence."

25. Bronfenbrenner, "The Changing American Child," in *Values and Ideals of American Youth*, ed. E. Ginsberg (New York: Columbia University Press, 1961), pp. 71–84 (also in *Merrill-Palmer Quarterly*, 7 [1961]: 73–84); Bronfenbrenner, "Some Familial Antecedents of Responsibility and Leadership in Adolescents," in *Leadership and Interpersonal Behavior*, ed. L. Petrullo and B. M. Bass (New York: Holt, Rinehart & Winston, 1961), pp. 239–72; Bronfenbrenner, "Toward a Theoretical Model for the Analysis of Parent-Child Relationships in a Social Context," in *Parental Attitudes and Child Behavior*, ed. J. C. Glidewell (Springfield, Ill.: Charles C Thomas, 1961), pp. 90–109; Hoffman, "Techniques and Processes"; Miller and Swanson, *The Changing American Child* (New York:

John Wiley & Sons, Inc., 1958), and *Inner Conflict and Defense;* Sears, Maccoby, and Levin, *Patterns of Child Rearing.*

26. Hoffman, "Techniques and Processes," p. 5.

27. *Ibid.,* pp. 37-38.

28. K. Lewin, R. O. Lippitt, and R. K. White, "Patterns of Aggressive Behavior in Experimentally Created 'Social Climates,'" *Journal of Social Psychology,* 10 (1939): 271-99.

29. R. K. White and R. O. Lippitt, *Autocracy and Democracy* (New York: Harper & Row, 1960).

30. S. E. Asch, "Studies of Independence and Conformity: A Minority of One against a Unanimous Majority," *Psychological Monographs,* 70, no. 9 (1965) (whole no. 416).

31. S. Freud, *Group Psychology and the Analysis of the Ego* (London: Hogarth Press, 1948).

32. T. Parsons and R. F. Bales, *Family, Socialization and Interaction Process* (Glencoe, Ill.: The Free Press, 1955).

33. G. Murphy, L. B. Murphy, and T. M. Newcomb, *Experimental Social Psychology,* rev. ed. (New York: Harper & Bros., 1937), pp. 476-93.

34. J. W. Thibaut and H. H. Kelley, *The Social Psychology of Groups* (New York: John Wiley & Sons, 1959).

35. Murphy, Murphy, and Newcomb, *Experimental Social Psychology,* p. 501.

36. Asch, "Independence and Conformity"; R. W. Berenda, *The Influence of the Group on the Judgments of Children* (New York: King's Crown Press, 1950).

37. V. A. Krutetski, 1960.

38. *Ibid.,* pp. 67-68.

39. Bozhovich, 1960, p. 225.

40. *Ibid.*; Kovalev, 1959; Krutetski; Smirnov, 1959.

41. Kairov, "Long-Range Plans," p. 12.

42. Bozhovich, p. 223.

43. Kovalev, p. 70.

44. *Ibid.,* pp. 79-81.

VIII : Psychology

Is There a New Soviet Psychology?

John A. Molino

Until the death of Stalin in 1953, Soviet psychological sciences were dominated by two principles: the concept of the conditioned reflex as developed by Pavlov and the Marxist-Leninist philosophical doctrines relating consciousness and reality. The students of Pavlov pursued a robust program of experimental research. But it was a program which, even after his death in 1936, seemed always to look toward the theories of Pavlov for its direction, and which was almost invariably reported by his students replete with reverential statements as to the wisdom of their mentor. At the same time the philosophical underpinnings of the science of psychology were carefully being constructed by such men as S. L. Rubinstein to ensure their firm foundation in the principles of dialectical

This paper is the result of study at Moscow State University during the academic year 1965–66. While an exchange student under the auspices of the Inter-University Committee on Travel Grants, the author had an opportunity to become acquainted with some aspects of Soviet research in the field of experimental psychology. For guidance in filling in the details of this general picture he is indebted to his research advisors, A. N. Leontiev and A. R. Luria. But to a larger extent the author is even more indebted to these two leaders of Soviet psychology for forcing the realization that one year was totally inadequate for the task. Thus the present paper does not pretend to be either an analysis in depth or a complete coverage of the vast domain of Soviet psychology. For these kinds of treatment the reader is referred to the excellent reviews of Soviet research listed among the notes.

materialism. Many of these philosophical excursions were not, however, within the strict framework of an experimental, scientific investigation of the brain and of behavior, and assumed more the character of a distinctly Marxist armchair psychology.

This is not to say that there were no dissenters to these two dominant themes in Soviet psychology. Even in the 1920's and 1930's L. S. Vygotsky, P. K. Anokhin, I. S. Beritov (in his native Georgian, Beritashvili), and others sometimes disagreed with the prevailing ideas or at other times proposed their own original substitutes. In many cases these new departures met with little support and were rarely published; the studies that did manage to appear in print were either poorly received and forgotten or their authors suffered harsh criticism from the scientific community and beyond.[1] Thus the picture of Soviet psychology before the death of Stalin was rather close to what the Western observer had been led to believe: psychology in the Soviet Union was synonymous with Pavlov and Marx, in that order. Since this conception still persists in the minds of those who have not followed recent developments closely, and since it is reinforced by years of scientific and extrascientific propaganda, there is no need for further amplification here.

Indeed, it is the purpose of this paper to counteract the influences which have led to the belief that present Soviet psychology is still limited by the teachings of Pavlov and Marx. Today psychological research in the Soviet Union has developed far beyond this stage. Most of the progress has been made in the last ten years, and many recent advances are relatively unknown in the West. This paper will be concerned with contemporary Russian research in four basic areas of psychology: conditioned reflexes, cognitive processes, developmental parameters, and orienting reactions. At the same time, the work of present-day scientists will be repeatedly compared with the Pavlov-Marx dyad that prevailed before the death of Stalin in an attempt to answer the question: Is there a new Soviet psychology?

Conditioned Reflexes

In the Russian scientific literature, conditioning is synonymous with learning. In fact, the highly specific term "conditioned reflex" is a mistranslation of the more general Russian term "conditional reflex" (*uslovny refleks*) first used by Pavlov. Thus in the Russian context conditioning may refer to a classical Pavlovian conditioned response or an instrumental response such as pressing a bar for food. For this reason various theories of instrumental learning are subsumed under the topic of conditioned reflexes. As a result of yet another difference between Western and Russian scientific jargon, the topic of conditioned reflexes includes many physiological aspects of psychology as well. The Russians make a rather sharp distinction between physiologists (sometimes called physiologists of higher nervous activity), who investigate conditioned reflexes, and psychologists, who study higher psychological processes such as perception and thought. Since in the Soviet Union most of the scientists working with conditioned reflexes are formally trained as physiologists, it is not surprising that much of the research and theorizing is of a physiological nature.

Adopting just such a physiological point of departure, E. A. Asratian [2] recalls that modern reflex theory regards the simple inborn reflex arc not as a stereotyped form, but as a dynamic and mobile one. It is well known that the simplest inborn reflexes vary greatly depending upon the intensity and duration of stimulation and the internal condition of the organism. Asratian argues that if the phenomenon of lability is a characteristic and biologically important feature of inborn reflexes, then lability must be even more significant in conditioned reflexes, which regulate the more delicate adaptation of the organism to the external environment.

In an attempt to verify this hypothesis, Asratian performed an experiment where one conditioned stimulus (CS) acquired two different signal meanings, eliciting one or the other response depending upon the initial state of the reflex apparatus. The experiment was conducted on dogs and consisted of reinforcing the CS with food in the morning in the presence of experimenter A and reinforcing the *same* CS with shock in the afternoon in the presence of experimenter B. Soon the dogs learned to respond with salivation to the CS in the morning and with paw withdrawal in the afternoon. Special experiments later demonstrated that the experimenters themselves were the agents for switching the conditioned reflexes in the dogs. For when experimenter B presented the CS in the morning, the dogs immediately demonstrated the defensive paw withdrawal response, although the morning sessions had previously consisted of CS-food pairings. This experiment launched Asratian into an entire program of research on the "switching reflex."

As a result of these studies, Asratian believes that the constant experimental conditions that can be designated as the "switching agents" (for example, the presence of experimenter A) are in effect conditioned stimuli themselves, but of a different type. The ordinary CS acts for only a short time and produces the repeated phasic conditioned reflex of salivation or paw withdrawal. The switching agents act for a long period and evoke a long-term tonic conditioned reflex which determines the particular signal meaning of the CS. Moreover, Asratian has elaborated a physiological model incorporating these phasic and tonic reflexes. The cortical projection system that receives the single CS is linked to two cortical response areas (consummatory and defensive in this case) by means of two mediating cortical loci representing the two tonic reflexes to experimenter A or B.[3] The fact that his discovery of tonic and phasic components in acquired external reflexes corroborates one of the fundamental principles of modern physiology—the tonic-phasic distinction in inborn internal reflexes—is taken as confirmation of Pavlov's principle of the "natural community of basic relationships." However, when looked at another way, Asratian's discovery adds a new dimension to the Pavlovian concept of the conditioned reflex.

The prominent Georgian psychophysiologist I. S. Beritov proposed [4] that in addition to the conditioned reflex form of central nervous system activity there exists an entirely different form called "psychoneural activity," which accounts for the behavior of animals in instrumental, place-learning situations. Beritov believes that the conditioned reflex applies only to short-term automatic behavior. For example, a delayed reaction with a delay of one day is not a conditioned reflex. If a dog returns to the place where food was found the day before, this behavior is the result of an image of the location of the food; if the location is changed, the dog searches for the food on the basis of this image. In the opinion of Beritov, images resulting from a complex of processes in the stellate neurons of cortical layers III and IV are projected into the environment by visual and labyrinth perception. In other words, there is spatial organization. Stimulation of any one part of the complex revives the whole image (the old concept of redintegration), which then directs the animal toward the location of the food.[5]

The role of the muscle receptors in the formation of these images was discounted by an ingenious experiment. A blindfolded dog was led around a room containing several food dishes, each hidden from view by a small screen. As he was led through the room by the collar, the dog was permitted to sniff each dish briefly in order to determine which one of them contained the food. The dog was then returned to the starting position and the blindfold was removed, whence he proceeded to scamper directly to the dish containing the food. Since all the dishes were hidden behind screens and since scent cues had been controlled for, Beritov con-

cluded that either labyrinth or muscle receptors or both were involved
in forming the place image. The muscle-receptor hypothesis was rejected, however, by repeating the experiment, only this time the blindfolded dog was carried about the room in a small cage so that no motor
movements were needed to sample the dishes. Nevertheless, when returned to the starting position, the dog ran unerringly to the dish containing the food. These results were used not only to prove the existence
of place images, but also to show the limitations on the kinds of stimuli
that are effective in defining the spatial representation of external objects.
Visual and labyrinth receptors alone are responsible for "psychoneural
activity." The muscle receptors, while of utmost importance in regulating automatic Pavlovian reflexes, play no part in this form of central
nervous system activity.[6] In its rejection of simple stimulus-response
motor chains, as well as in its adoption of images to explain instrumental place learning, the "psychoneural" theory of Beritov resembles
quite closely the "cognitive map" theory of Tolman, which represents
a position about as far from Pavlov as any reflexologist can take.

L. V. Krushinsky has investigated what he has called "extrapolation
reflexes." [7] These reflexes are exhibited in situations where an organism
must foresee the future course of a developing stimulus pattern and behave accordingly. The prototype experiment involves a long barrier with
a small vertical slit in the middle through which the animal can observe
which of two bowls placed behind the barrier contains the food. Then
the bowls are moved in opposite directions behind the barrier and the
task of the animal is to "extrapolate" from the motion of the bowls where
the food will reappear. Another variation of this experiment employs a
tunnel into which the moving food tray disappears. The behavior of the
animal is observed to see whether he goes to the other end of the tunnel
to await the food. Krushinsky has studied a wide variety of animals in
this situation and has shown that different species exhibit extrapolation
reflexes to markedly different degrees.[8]

While the research of Krushinsky proceeds almost directly from the
work of Pavlov, Krushinsky's emphasis on the fact that animals possess
the ability to determine certain cause-and-effect relations among stimuli
has led him to expand a largely neglected segment of Pavloviana. In this
respect the contributions of E. A. Asratian and I. S. Beritov represent
more substantial modifications to the often claimed universality of the
conditioned reflex. Asratian added a new dimension to the entire domain
with the introduction of his phasic-tonic distinction, while Beritov limited this domain to exclude the "psychoneural activity" governing reactions to place. However, the most promising contribution to the condi-

tioned reflex and the one which has already permanently changed the course of research in this area (as well as in other areas of psychology) was made when P. K. Anokhin introduced the concept of feedback. The concept of feedback provided the "fourth link" closing the classical Cartesian reflex arc and heralded the still very much alive cybernetic revolution in Russian psychophysiology.

Since 1930 the laboratory of P. K. Anokhin has been continuously studying the mechanisms of compensation for impaired functions.[9] The fact that the central nervous system obviously does compensate for impaired functions raised the following three questions for Anokhin: (1) Can the nervous system initiate the compensatory process without a signal from the periphery concerning the nature of the defect? (2) What physiological mechanism determines the direction of the resulting chain of compensatory adjustments? (3) On the basis of what information does the central nervous system determine the completion of the adaptational changes so as not to overreact? Since without a satisfactory answer to these three questions there could be no adequate theory for the compensation of functions, Anokhin carefully concentrated his research on these problems. The result was two far-reaching innovations for reflex theory in general: return afferentation and the "acceptor of action." [10]

Return afferentation refers to the afferent signals arising as a result of reflex activity in the periphery and directed back toward the central nervous system processes which conditioned the peripheral reaction in the first place. The concept is often used to explain the formation of coordinated responses where afferent impulses from the muscles play an important role in regulating the extent of muscular activity. Thus return afferentation is essentially the same as negative feedback. But any feedback system must include a comparator component to determine when the necessary action has been completed (see Anokhin's third question). The "acceptor of action" is just such a sanctioning device. It compares the return afferentation coming from a certain action with a previously established internal model or expectation of the results of that action. If these patterns of stimulation coincide, this sanctioning mechanism "accepts the effect" of the response; otherwise it rejects the effect, and further compensation or orienting behavior results. An entire series of experiments has been aimed at discovering the concrete neurophysiological mechanisms which provide a basis for this anticipatory apparatus.[11]

Anokhin has devised a convincing demonstration of the role of the feedback mechanism elaborated above in the regulation of respiratory reflexes. This particular physiological preparation stands as a tribute to the insight which Anokhin has gained from his experiments; for with it the experimenter himself, through the use of electronic devices, is able to become an integral link in a delicate closed neurological feedback loop. In Anokhin's experiment the command given by the higher respiratory center to the respiratory muscles to take in a specific quantity of air was changed en route by means of electronic instruments. Thus the lung received only a part of the necessary air, and the lung receptors signaled to the respiratory center that an insufficient quantity of air had been inhaled. This information on the actual result was clearly in disagreement with that predicted by the respiratory center. Therefore, the respiratory center immediately increased the number of impulses directed to the respiratory muscles. As a result the lungs inhaled far more air than was actually needed to compensate for the insufficiency in the previous breath. Consequently, the respiratory center, in sending a command to the periphery to inhale a specific quantity of air, simultaneously formed an apparatus for comparing the supposed result with the one received.[12]

This closed reflex crcuit with a feedback connection was being formulated in the laboratories of Anokhin as early as the 1930's. Although its initial conception came long before the appearance of Norbert Wiener's works on cybernetics, it was not until after the death of Stalin that the notions of return afferentation and "acceptor of action" were integrated into Soviet psychology. Indeed, the enthusiasm for cybernetics generated by the Western scientific community in the early 1950's acted as a catalyst for the cybernetic revolution that was to sweep the Soviet Union a few years later; for Soviet psychology had already been well primed to support such a revolution. Since the time of Sechenov and Pavlov, Russian psychophysiologists had carefully laid out an elaborate system of conditioned connections between stimuli and responses. The opportunities for shunting these conditioned connections with simple feedback links were bountiful.

A clear example of the profound influence of the cybernetic revolution is cited by N. A. Bernstein,[13] starting with the bitter struggle which he encountered in first proposing the principle of cyclic control (feedback) in the 1930's and 1940's. As a result his initial research on the construction of motor acts [14] bore more the character of an analytical decomposition of complicated movements than the construction of an isomorphic model to simulate their occurrence. The latter approach came to prevail in his works only after the cybernetic revolution, when such theorizing was met with great enthusiasm. In fact, Bernstein's latest block-diagram model of the self-regulating locomotor apparatus contains no less than six separate stages with multiple feedback connections between them. They include programmer, receptor, comparator, coder, regulator, and effector operations, making Bernstein's model a much more refined and flexible apparatus for the execution of complex coordinated movements than the Pavlovian composite of conditioned reflexes.[15]

As the cybernetic revolution progressed, it continued to enrich the conditioned reflex by adding more and more self-regulatory feedback links. At the same time the research of E. Sh. Ayrapetiants and his colleagues was drawing the conditioned reflex deeper and deeper into the internal milieu of the organism. These investigators were exploring the laws governing interoceptive conditioning, where either the conditioned stimulus or the unconditioned stimulus or both are delivered to the internal organs of the body. Strictly speaking, this work does not represent a departure from earlier Soviet psychological research, since it consists of an uninterrupted continuation of the prolific investigations of K. M. Bykov.[16] However, interoceptive conditioning is today a vigorously explored area of Russian psychophysiology and promises to yield important insights into what Razran has called the "observable unconscious." [17]

The typical methods employed in interoceptive conditioning involve the distension of internal organs by the use of fistulas or balloons filled with air or water whose pressure is varied. Often the balloons are irrigated with water of different temperatures to create thermal stimuli. A wide variety of experiments becomes possible with these techniques, and various internal organs can be made to condition one another. Ayrapetiants *et al.*[18] report one such experiment on patients with urinary-bladder fistulas which permitted the experimenter to control the distension of their bladders. Throughout the experiment simultaneous recordings were made of urinary secretions, respiratory changes, vascular constrictions, the galvanic skin response, and the verbal reports of the subjects as to the intensity of their "urinary" urges. (This simultaneous recording of several physiological changes in the course of a conditioning experiment is a salient feature of Russian psychophysiological research, and one that is not often encountered in its Western counterpart.) In addition the apparatus was so constructed that the subjects could monitor the degree of their bladder distension on conspicuous dials, converting these scale readings into conditioned stimuli. Then the dials were detached without the subjects' knowledge, and the readings were varied independently by the experimenter. Conditioning to the sham readings was readily effected. The patients began reporting intense urinary urges, accompanied by most of the associated physiological changes, whenever the dial readings were high, regardless of the actual amount of distension their bladders had sustained.[19]

Such experiments have resulted in a body of general laws of interoceptive conditioning. But, unlike exteroceptive stimulation, the continuum of interoceptive stimulation leads to largely unconscious responses. Most often subjects cannot verbalize the fact that one internal organ is conditioned by experimental manipulations occurring in another organ, but these visceral reflexes are the same ones which form the physiological basis for many emotional reactions. Thus the "observable unconscious" accessible through the quantitative methods of interoceptive conditioning bears considerable relevance to Freudian theory. No matter how far removed Freudian psychodynamics is from physiological conditioning, its eventual concrete validation will rest largely upon an expanded understanding of the laws of visceral actions. Furthermore, the relationship between interoceptive conditioning and Freudian theory is far closer than the often cited relationship between purely exteroceptive conditioning and Freudian theory, since the former does not suffer from two obvious shortcomings of the latter. Exteroceptive conditioning generally involves (1) largely conscious conditioned connections and (2) organismically inconsequential reactions.[20] Of course, the Russians do not view interoceptive conditioning as a possible validation of Freudian dynamics, and seldom even mention its relevance. Freudian theory is considered to be a "decadent" outgrowth of bourgeois society tinged with "idealistic" (as opposed to materialistic) philosophical connotations. For the same reason motivation rarely enters as a variable in Soviet research on conditioned reflexes and learning. The concept is referred to as Freudian and "idealistic" in origin.[21]

It has often been pointed out that in general the field of Soviet reflexology is far less concerned with problems of conceptualization than its Western learning-theory counterpart. The Russians are more interested in what reflexes *can be* conditioned or associated than in what *is* conditioned or associated, and as a result their research is often reported in a form not very far removed from the raw data. This condition is quite the opposite of that characterizing Western psychology, which in many branches may well be classed as being overloaded with theorizing.[22] However, in the above brief survey of present-day Soviet research on conditioned reflexes it should be evident that the Russians are moving away from their extreme reluctance to conceptualize. Although the major impetus for this departure stemmed from the recent cybernetic revolution and its associated abstract models, the theoretical offshoots of E. A. Asratian and I. S. Beritov have also contributed toward this trend. Unfortunately, space does not permit elaboration of further contributions made by A. V. Napalkov, P. S. Kupalov, L. G. Voronin, and others. Taken as a whole, however, these investigators have transformed the conditioned reflex into a viable and challenging area for modern research. While in its present state Soviet reflexology still reaches back to the principles of Pavlov for its theoretical roots, the direction of its further growth is no longer rigidly restricted by Pavlovian concepts.

Cognitive Processes

The study of cognitive processes in the Soviet Union rests heavily upon the philosophical tenets of Marx, Engels, and Lenin. The philosophy of dialectical materialism as developed by them argues for the existence of the real world, for the primacy of matter, and against any influences from idealism. Idealism is here defined as any sense in which ideas influence, define, or determine reality. Thus, with respect to psychology, the Marxist-Leninist position clearly rejects the theories of both Freud and Gestalt psychology on the grounds that they ascribe too much of a functional status to the role of ideas. Instead sensory information is considered to be completely adequate to create a reflection or image of reality. These images mirror the real world, according to Lenin, because they have been developed by constant interaction with the real world. The fact that man has achieved a high degree of mastery over nature is taken as proof of the validity of the images or copies formed in man's consciousness. In this sense consciousness is defined as the highest form of organized matter.[23]

The Marxist-Leninist materialist philosophy emphasizes that the images so vital to man's psychological manipulation of the environment are formed by constant and active interplay with the environment. Consciousness is not regarded as a purely passive awareness of environmental stimuli, as is often the case in Western philosophy and psychology. This emphasis on the active nature of cognitive processes has led to a considerable experimental interest in response-produced stimuli and feedback mechanisms. It is also reflected in the basic theoretical position of one of the most influential Soviet psychologists in this area, A. N. Leontiev. In the opinion of Leontiev,[24] the functional value of consciousness is that it enables an organism to respond not only to stimuli that are of immediate, vital significance to survival, but also to stimuli which may signal the imminent occurrence of other stimuli of survival value.[25]

To test this hypothesis, Leontiev conducted an experiment where an electric shock delivered to the hand was invariably preceded by a light shone on the palm. The subjects could not see the light and were not aware of the exact nature of the "influence" which they were told would stimulate the hand before the onset of the shock. Even though all sensation of heat had been eliminated, the subjects soon learned to remove their fingers before the onset of the shock whenever the light was shining on their palms. The subjects came to experience a variety of unusual sensations, described as "a little wind," "a trembling," or "a streaming sensation"; but none of them was aware of what it was that signaled him to remove his finger at a given moment. Thus Leontiev has succeeded in demonstrating that, when a light shone on the hand becomes the signal for an imminent event of biological significance, human subjects can develop a conscious awareness of the sensation. He explains this occurrence by the subject's awareness of a reflex that has been conditioned to the stimulus (possibly an orienting reflex) rather than an awareness of the stimulus light itself.[26] Indeed, this discovery resulted in a rash of scientific experiments in the Soviet Union on the phenomenon of dermo-optic perception, once it was discovered that certain individuals could discriminate colors and even read printed texts with their fingers.[27] This particular line of investigation has been largely abandoned in the last few years.

Another experiment, this time utilizing the auditory modality, demonstrates a second aspect of Leontiev's approach to perception: the motor-copy theory. This procedure began with the determination of the difference threshold for pitch in the classical manner, using pure tones. The thresholds determined in this way corresponded with previous data, and ranged from 5 to 135 musical cents (scale for pitch). Then the pure tones were converted into timbre-distorted tones (tdt's) by the addition of certain harmonics. Once this transformation had been made on the stimuli, the fine-grained pitch discrimination of many of the subjects deteriorated drastically, in some cases exceeding 1,200 musical cents. Furthermore, there was no correlation between the original pure-tone discrimination threshold and the new threshold for the tdt's. However, when the subjects were trained to vocalize (sing) each tdt before making the discrimination, the thresholds demonstrated a sharp decrease over those obtained without vocalization. When the subjects were subsequently instructed not to vocalize, the thresholds reverted to their high levels for tdt's.[28] Such data provide evidence of a close association between vocalization and tone discrimination in a case where the motor copy is generated in a modality (voice musculature) altogether separate from the one receiving the stimulation (auditory apparatus).

Much experimentation has also been conducted where the active process of perceiving and the actual perceptual apparatus are in the same modality. The most convincing evidence for the motor-copy theory accrued in this manner has been found with stabilized images.* In this case, instead of permitting an unpracticed motor response to become active and assist in perception, the method involves completely eliminating the complex, innately active process of visual scanning. The effect of the restriction of eye movements was explored most thoroughly by A. L. Yarbus,[29] using an extremely simple device. It is well known that no matter how carefully a subject attempts to fixate one small point in the visual field, micromovements of the eye will occur beyond his conscious control. The technique employed by Yarbus consisted of eliminating these micromovements by placing the object to be perceived on a contact lens which remained stationary on the eyeball. This method permitted absolutely no movement of the object relative to the retina of the eye. When subjects were presented with these objects attached to their eyeballs, all perception of the object whatsoever disappeared in one to three seconds. In other words, the completely stabilized eye was found to be blind. Thus eye movements were shown to be essential for vision, and the recording of eye movements during various perceptual tasks promised to yield certain insights into the mechanism behind visual perception.

Sechenov had long ago asserted that the hand teaches the eye. He based this statement on the observation that, early in both phylogenetic and ontogenetic development, the sense of touch often precedes or dominates the sense of vision in the exploration of the environment and the recognition of objects. Just as Yarbus used the technique of recording eye movements in an attempt to understand the mechanism of vision, so B. F. Lomov recorded the palpation movements of the hands and of the digits in an attempt to gain insight into the mechanism of haptic perception.[30] Lomov found both micro- and macromovements of the hands and digits to play an important role in haptic perception, just as similar types of movements had been found to be essential in visual perception. In addition his experiments showed how certain sensory information and subsequent hypotheses generated by the subjects could alter the course of palpatory exploration. The experimental results revealed that in the bimanual palpation of vertically symmetric objects the hands proceeded synchronously, whereas asymmetric objects were not so explored. Thus

---

* The original Soviet research on stabilized images was reported by A. L. Yarbus in 1956, about the same time as the discovery of similar phenomena in the West. See R. W. Ditchburn and D. H. Fender, "The Stabilized Retinal Image," *Optica Acta*, 2 (1955): 128.

symmetry proved to be one of the first qualities extracted in the active process of exploration.

Both the research of Yarbus on eye movements and the experiments of Lomov in haptic perception, related to some extent by Sechenov's observation that the hand teaches the eye, closely support Leontiev's general motor-copy theory. Although they do not confirm the motor-copy theory by demonstrating the effectiveness of direct imitation, as in the tone-discrimination experiments of Leontiev, they do corroborate the theory in other ways. For example, it can be shown in the above studies that both hand and eye movements closely follow figure contours in scanning and recognition tasks, creating response patterns strikingly similar to the objects being perceived. This evidence can be used to affirm the motor-copy theory of Leontiev, which can in turn be traced back through Lenin to Marx for its philosophical foundations. However, the modern expression of this theory in terms of concrete experimental operations and results is far more sophisticated than the philosophical conjectures made by early Soviet psychologists on the nature of man's reflective images of reality. In other words, the old Marxist philosophical tenets relating consciousness and reality have been translated by present-day Soviet psychologists into concrete operations accessible to experimentation and scientific investigation.[31]

The recent Soviet research on cognitive processes is also considerably more sophisticated in its generation and handling of quantitative data than that conducted before the death of Stalin. As a result of the cybernetic revolution, the mathematical language of stochastic models and information theory has taken its place alongside Marxist-Leninist rhetoric in the scientific literature. There is, after all, a strong philosophical affinity between modern cybernetics and Marxian dialectics: both are materialistic, both close the gap between the living and the nonliving, and both aim at optimization. The Russians, however, are not naïve in their adoption of these mathematical tools. A. N. Leontiev and Ye. P. Krinchik argue quite convincingly [32] against the application of information theory as a metric whenever the signals used vary with respect to "importance" to the organism (as opposed to probability of occurrence). They base this caution on experiments where they succeeded in making subjects respond with significantly lower reaction times to "emergency signals" than would be predicted on the basis of the informational content of the signal. V. D. Glezer, on the other hand, describes an experiment where the amount of time necessary to recognize drawings of objects was found to be directly proportional to the amount of information contained in the alphabet of drawings presented.[33] The data were collected by tachistoscopic techniques and showed a clearly defined visual channel capacity of 49 bits per second, regardless of the alphabet size, in strict accord with information-theory predictions. Besides being enriched by the mathematical rigor and elegance of these products of the cybernetic revolution, Soviet research on cognitive processes moved closer to the motor-copy theory of perception by the adoption of information-theory measures. Both of the above experiments essentially confirmed Hick's law [34] that the reaction time of an individual varies linearly with the amount of information in the stimulus whenever the signals are of equal "importance" to the individual. Thus more time is spent reacting to an infrequent signal than to a frequent signal, since the former is the least expected event and therefore conveys the most information. This added time may have been consumed in executing an internalized search process which was accessible for external measurement only at some earlier stage in the individual's development.

By a similar extension of the theory to cover internalized responses, even the complex process of speech perception can be subsumed under the motor-copy theory. Subjects are said to recognize speech when they are able to reproduce the meaningful content of continuously presented speech samples. L. A. Chistovich and colleagues [35] measured the time lag between presented speech sounds and the verbatim repetition (shadowing) of these sounds by their subjects. Continuous texts were presented to the subjects through earphones, and the subjects were instructed to shadow these speech samples. After the experiment was concluded it was found that the subjects grouped themselves into a bimodal distribution along the time-delay dimension. One group of subjects shadowed the texts with a 1-second average time lag, while another group was able to maintain an average delay of only 0.25 second. The first group (1 second) repeated the words with few errors and with good comprehension of the meaning of the passage. The second group (whose latency of 0.25 second was within the limits of a simple reaction time) generated more errors and demonstrated little comprehension. When the second (fast) group was instructed to repeat the texts "with understanding," the time lag increased to a level commensurate with that of the first (slow) group. Chistovich and colleagues present their results as support for a motor theory of speech perception, in which some kind of imitation of the articulatory responses necessary to produce speech sounds plays a role in their perception. In mature individuals, however, this process is much abbreviated and fully internalized.

Related to Chistovich's work on speech perception and the comprehension of meaning is the considerable body of Soviet research on semantic conditioning, only in this case an artificial response is established to speech sounds instead of an articulatory imitation. The basic technique employed in this field of research goes back to the experiments of A. G. Ivanov-Smolensky and N. I. Krasnogorsky in the 1930's. A conditioned reflex is established to a certain critical word, and the generalization of that response to other words closely related in meaning is subsequently measured. The recent work of A. R. Luria and O. S. Vinogradova [36] exemplifies how this technique can provide information on various levels of relatedness of meaning between semantic fields. The subjects in their experiment made involuntary defensive reflexes to the critical word followed by shock, as well as to other words related in meaning to that critical word but not reinforced by shock. To words more distantly related in meaning from the critical word no defensive reflex was elicited, but instead an orienting response resulted. By means of measuring the relative magnitude of these responses, objective quantitative data can be collected on the degree of semantic relatedness between words and concepts. The resulting generalization gradients form an objective indicator of higher cognitive processes and represent quantitative data on what Razran has called the "inferable conscious" in Soviet psychology.[37] However, the recent experiments in this area can be distinguished from their earlier counterparts by a more modern approach to the Pavlovian conditioning paradigm which forms their basis, e.g., by the inclusion of such a recent development as the orienting response.

No discussion of Soviet research in cognitive processes would be complete without mention of the independent Georgian school of psychological research that is actively continuing the tradition of its founder, D. N. Uznadze.[38] Today the most prominent spokesman for this school is A. S. Prangishvili. From his characterization of its theoretical position, it is obvious that the Georgian school is not influenced by either Pavlov or Marx and their associated theories.[39] However, its research is even more strongly oriented in one particular direction than that of its Russian counterparts in the areas of reflexology and cognitive processes. The entire Georgian school of psychology strictly adheres to the basic theoretical position of Uznadze concerning the universality of the "fixated set," which maintains that the mental set, and not the conditioned reflex or the motor copy, is the ultimate basic unit of human action.[40]

The prototypical experiment for the Georgian school of psychology is the Fechner weight illusion. If two balls of differing weights are repeatedly judged as to which is heavier, and then the two balls of different weight are replaced by two balls of equal weight, subjects will for the most part judge these now equal balls as being unequal in weight. The resulting illusion of inequality is regarded as a manifestation of the influence of a "fixated set." Uznadze characterized the above experiment in the following way: A certain psychological state, which can in no way be described as merely a physiological state, precedes the emergence of conscious psychological processes and acts as a "set" to determine their final outcome. Thus "set" is defined as a preparation for a certain kind of action resulting from (1) a need to act in a certain way (judge one ball as heavier) and (2) a situation for fulfilling that need (presentation of equal balls). In this sense the concept is similar to the Gestalt notion of "determining tendency." When such a set is established as a result of repeated presentation of the inducing circumstances, it is called a "fixated set." [41]

Some Georgian researchers have recognized the close relationship between the "fixated set" and the general problem of constancy in perception. As a result a number of experiments investigating concrete psychophysical phenomena were conducted under the auspices of this school. One such experiment involved the controlled elimination of secondary spatial cues in a size-judgment task. When a set was established for "perspectiveless" vision, the phenomenon of size constancy disappeared even in a more fully enriched environment of spatial cues.[42] But still other Georgian researchers, instead of recognizing specific applications, took the direction of expanding the concept of "fixated set" to embrace practically all spheres of psychology from social relations to personality traits. In fact, in its most generalized definition, for these investigators "set" is defined as the "mode of being" and the "essence of personality" at any given moment. Indeed, personality is considered to be nothing more than an aggregate of various sets.[43] It is not altogether surprising that the concept of set should have been expanded in this way, when one considers its position as a mediating link between stimulus and response, as well as its expression in terms of generalized needs and fulfilling circumstances. But there always remains the danger, with such expansion of psychological theories, that they soon lose their usefulness and become merely synonyms for the discipline itself. In Georgia, psychology is the fixated set, for better or for worse.

Regarding Soviet research on cognitive processes in general, the Western behaviorist observer may be quite dismayed by the widespread use of terms such as "mental images" and "copies of reality." Whereas, for the behaviorist at least, Skinner had eliminated the problem of consciousness from the realm of psychological research in the West, as is evident in the above review of the Soviet approach, the problem of consciousness still plays a focal role in research on cognitive processes in the Soviet Union. Soviet psychology never underwent a behaviorist revolution of the type wrought by Watson and Skinner, for the simple reason that there was no need for one. In the areas of learning and conditioned reflexes the theories of Sechenov and Pavlov had long ago provided Soviet investigators with an adequate, objective approach toward the study of behavior. As a result the Russians criticize Western behaviorism for going too far in abandoning the problem of consciousness altogether. Thus in the Soviet Union behaviorism is referred to as a form of "vulgar materialism" and viewed as being particularly naïve in pretending that the scientific problem of consciousness does not exist.[44] For Soviet research in cognitive processes the problem of consciousness has always existed and is still one of mental images of reality as stated by Lenin. Only today these images are expressed in terms of motor copies, measurable responses, and objective operations. This translation of the reflective mental images that occupied much of the armchair theorizing in the field before the death of Stalin into the repeatable operations and experiments behind Leontiev's contemporary motor-copy theory represents a significant advance in the study of cognitive processes in the Soviet Union. For now, regardless of his theoretical bias with respect to Marx and Lenin, the reader of the present Russian psychological literature on cognitive processes is confronted by a considerable body of empirical data that can and do stand by themselves. The earlier deductive trend from the teachings of Marx to a possible relevant experiment has been reversed by a basically inductive argument from experimental data to possible conclusions about Marxist philosophy.

Developmental Parameters

The Marxist-Leninist approach in philosophy places heavy emphasis on the social determinants of behavior. Although this emphasis did not find its expression in the development of a mature branch of social psychology in the Soviet Union, nevertheless the work of L. S. Vygotsky [45] quite amply stressed the role that the social environment plays in the development of the individual. Vygotsky pointed out that among the most valuable tools inherited by the individual from the social environment are those linguistic and conceptual devices that permit him to direct and regulate his own behavior. At the same time the Marxist-Leninist philosophical doctrine emphasizes the historical approach in the sciences. In psychology the historical approach is translated into the study of the evolution of behavior in phylogeny and ontogeny. With this dual philosophical concentration on social determinants and growth factors, it is not surprising that a vigorous program of research in developmental psychology was established, with Vygotsky's three most prominent students, A. N. Leontiev, A. R. Luria, and A. V. Zaporozhets, leading the way.

The work of A. R. Luria represents a synthesis of these two influences in Soviet developmental psychology. For many years Luria has studied the problem of the role played by language in the regulation of behavior and the gradual internalization of this guiding process. Furthermore, the results of his studies have been extremely fruitful, largely because of his adoption of a developmental approach in exploring the problem. His basic experiment in this area involved observing the response of children in bringing an extremely simple situation under the control of verbal instructions. Luria's young subjects were merely asked to squeeze a small rubber bulb or not to squeeze it. For a one-to-two-year-old child the utterance of any word by the experimenter readily served as a signal to initiate the squeezing response, but the child could not differentiate between the two types of instructions and squeezed the bulb every time. The child of two to three years was able to squeeze or refrain from squeezing on command, but the command had to be given before each trial. Instructions like "Squeeze only when the light is green" could not be consistently followed. In this case, the words uttered by the experimenter still retained their initiating stimulus aspect and could not be responded to for their meaningful content. In addition the children were observed to mimic the commands by saying them aloud before each trial. Only in the next stage of development (four to five years of age) could the meaningful content of the instructions play a role in regulating behavior. At this stage the child is able to organize his behavior in accord with generalized instructions, since the regulatory speech process has by then become fully internalized. However, if the task becomes too difficult, even these older children can be observed to utter the instructions aloud at critical instants. Extrapolating from these data, Luria suggests that the fully mature adult generates his own internalized verbal instructions in order to regulate his own behavior. In its final stage internalized speech becomes the basis for man's self-regulated form of behavior.[46]

In his extensive studies of local brain lesions [47] Luria found a confirmation of the regulatory role of speech as well as an indication of the neurophysiological substratum for this internalized process. In certain cases of frontal lobe brain lesions that did not yield the typical symptoms of aphasia, there did appear, nonetheless, a disruption of the ability of speech to regulate behavior. Thus the frontal lobe becomes the general physiological locus for this regulatory mechanism, although Luria's neurophysiological studies in general indicate that there is no strict localization of function in the brain. His diagrammatic scheme of brain processes includes only three general divisions (activating, information-processing, and programming systems), with a second level of organization cutting across these three sections. This second level of organization is called the "functional system." It represents an aggregate of various cortical areas that share in the accomplishment of some complex psychological function such as reading. From the example given it is obvious that this second level of brain organization, the functional system, possesses the interesting property that many of the functions upon which it is based are acquired instead of innate. In pointing out the acquired nature of functional systems, this recent work of Luria has established the earlier recognized socially inherited aspects of development on a more firm neurophysiological basis.

Whereas Luria investigated the gradual internalization of the regulatory role of language, another one of Vygotsky's students, A. V. Zaporozhets, concentrated on the development of voluntary movements from early childhood onward. His studies of human voluntary movements [48] show that such acts are composed of two parts: orientation and execution. In early childhood the uncoordinated nature of these opposing functions causes difficulty in the learning of voluntary motor acts. Experiments on children with distant manipulanda demonstrate the interference of orienting movements in the execution of certain responses. Later on more coordination is observed in the response, but the role of orienting and investigatory activity is still important in determining the topography and speed of formation of motor habits. Experiments on the tactile recognition of objects have shown the relative role of movements connected with the use of the object, with its passive tactile perception, and with its active tactile exploration. With increasing age (three to seven and a half years) the modal activity shifts from motor usage to active tactile exploration. Later on in ontogeny imitation plays an important part in the acquisition of motor skills, and still later speech begins to play a triggering role in their execution. These latter observations of Zaporozhets are related to Leontiev's motor-copy theory as well as to Luria's theory of internalized speech, representing a more detailed elaboration of the parameters affecting the response side of these theoretical formulations. In this way the pioneering studies of these three outstanding disciples of Vygotsky have mutually reinforced each other in expanding the Soviet frontiers of psychological research and theorizing on developmental parameters.

V. G. Ananiev has studied the development of space perception in children. The theoretical departure for his work [49] proceeds directly from the historical traditions of psychology in the Soviet Union. In the view of Ananiev, space perception is basically reflex in nature and develops according to the laws of conditioned reflex activity (Pavlov). As a prerequisite for this development there must first appear the stable discrimination of objects, i.e., of the material world (Marx). Then discriminations based on the relations between these objects lead to the development of space perception in children. This latter process is accomplished by the participation of various response systems and sensory modalities, e.g., the hand teaches the eye (Sechenov). By conducting experiments with young children, Ananiev discovered that visual space perception does in fact follow a developmental course similar to the one described above. From long-term studies of visual acuity, visual perimeter, and distance measurement by eye, Ananiev was able to construct a profile of this developmental course in children from three to fifteen years of age.

All three of the above investigators, Luria, Zaporozhets, and Ananiev, have been concerned with ontogenetic changes that occur in the individual, i.e., with changes in the individual's speech processes, motor activity, and visual perception with maturation. There is another Russian school of psychology that is concerned with the static factors influencing the psychological development of the individual. These static factors are expressed in terms of nervous system types, which form the constant background upon which the above dynamic relations of development are elaborated. They derive from the fundamental properties of the nervous system and are the basis for a well-articulated psychology of individual differences founded by B. M. Teplov. Teplov has modified the Pavlovian classification system for the various nervous system types in dogs to make it applicable to human psychology. Thus the type of an individual's nervous system becomes intimately associated with what has long been termed his temperament.[50]

According to Pavlov, there are four types of nervous system, which correspond to the four classical temperaments—choleric, sanguine, phlegmatic, and melancholy. These four types are realized in given individuals by a particular combination of the three basic properties of the nervous system: strength, balance, and mobility. For example, the phlegmatic (tranquil) individual is characterized as having a strong, balanced, and inert nervous system. In order to classify an individual, it was necessary to develop an experimental methodology for measuring the three basic properties of the nervous system. To take just one property as an example, the methodology adopted by Teplov defined nervous system strength in terms of (1) ability to support prolonged conditioned reflexes (resistance to "ultramaximal" inhibition), (2) insusceptibility to distractions (resistance to "external" inhibition), and (3) higher sensory thresholds.

The last characteristic leads to the conclusion that weak types are generally more sensitive. In a similar way the balance of the nervous system is measured in terms of the speed of formation and differentiation of conditioned reflexes, and the mobility of the nervous system is measured in terms of conditioned reversals. However, as might be expected, the profile of an individual's nervous system obtained in this way often does not represent a very clearly defined pattern. Thus in the past few years a keen interest has been generated in the methods of factor analysis [51] as a means of readjusting the defining parameters of Pavlov's nervous system properties. This and other mathematical tools promise to move the theoretical position of the Teplov school even further from the Pavlovian foundation to which it clung before the death of Stalin.

Related to these general theoretical studies of developmental parameters is the vast research area of applied child and educational psychology that has always flourished in the Soviet Union. Space does not permit elaboration of the contributions to this field made by P. Ia. Galperin, D. B. Elkonin, and others. However, the paths of the applied and theoretical branches of developmental psychology follow each other rather closely in the Soviet Union, even more so than in the West, where pragmatism has created a definite schism between theory and practice. Thus the changes that have taken place in the theoretical sphere since the death of Stalin are true of the applied branch of developmental psychology as well. In general, the Soviet approach to the study of developmental parameters has shifted its frame of reference from the impoverished notion of Pavlov's conditioned reflex to the enriched conception of Vygotsky's socially inherited skills.

Orienting Reactions

The orienting reaction stands as a full-grown branch of psychological investigation that is unique both to the Soviet Union and to the period after the death of Stalin. Although the orienting response was first described by Pavlov, Ye. N. Sokolov has elevated the concept to the status of a mature and independent research area. Its maturity is expressed in the quality and scope of its prolific output,[52] while its independence is asserted by its tendency to make numerous analogies to the theoretical system of Pavlov instead of constant identities with it.[53] The following survey of current research on the orienting response is presented in considerable detail in order to convey the flavor of this most important single development in Soviet psychology since the death of Stalin.

The orienting response, or OR, is not a single response, but a pattern of several simultaneous responses which yields a consistent and repeatable profile. There are five basic components to the OR: (1) motor components, which include the turning of the head and eyes or ears as well as a general increase in muscular tension; (2) autonomic components, which are reflected in changes in the galvanic skin response (GSR), vascular dilation or constriction, and changes in heart rate; (3) sensory components, which can be found in pupil dilation, lowering of sensory thresholds, and an improvement in temporal resolution; (4) EEG components, which consist of general activation and desychronization of the alpha rhythm; and (5) conditioned reflex components, which can be observed in changes in the dynamic relations of already established or forming conditioned connections. Whenever all of these components are simultaneously present in certain fixed relations to each other, there exists the possibility of measuring the OR.[54]

Certain interrelations between these components further define the OR pattern. In humans the dilation of the blood vessels in the forehead and their constriction in the digits is considered to be solely an OR. In the case of pupil dilation, to take another example, the situation is not so clearly delineated. Pupil dilation is almost always an OR to nonvisual stimuli, but only 20 percent of the time does it qualify as an OR for visual stimuli. The other 80 percent of the time represents inhibition by the local pupillary reflex. Furthermore, the motor components observed in the OR are distinct from other motor reflexes, and in the view of Razran should be termed "versive," since they exhibit neither approach nor avoidance qualities. Thus the OR pattern does not really "manage" the stimuli, as in the conditioned reflex, but merely reacts to their presence. Its reactions are more preparatory than consummatory and more preadaptive than adaptive.[55]

The OR is generally considered to be a response to "novelty." Novelty does not mean here that no previous stimulation of this type has been presented, but is only another way of saying that the OR will be evoked only for a limited number of presentations. In fact, all those reactions which are associated with the intensification of the receptive state of the organism may be ascribed to the system of the orienting response, providing that they arise in connection with the novelty of the stimulus. To test whether a given reaction is a response to novelty, it is not sufficient to observe whether the reaction dies with repeated presentation. The reaction must also be independent of the direction of the change in the stimulating agent whenever the OR is restored. For example, suppose that the OR has ceased to occur at the presentation of a certain intensity of tone; then a change to either a lower or a higher intensity should restore the OR.[56]

Lynn has pointed out [57] that sensitivity of the OR to such a variety of stimulus changes cannot be explained by a one-stage physiological model. A two-stage model involving memory traces and comparator operations is necessary. The model of OR activity proposed by Sokolov [58] contains the necessary features and conforms with present knowledge about anatomical connections in the brain. Briefly, the model operates as follows: A "neuronal model" of novel stimulus conditions is gradually formed in the cerebral cortex by repeated sensory stimulation. This same sensory input is also led by collateral nerve fibers to the reticular formation of the brain that produces the OR pattern. Once the "neuronal model" has been formed in the cortex, the stimulus conditions are no longer novel, since present sensory input now corresponds with past sensory experience. Consequently, the cortical modeling mechanism inhibits the input to the reticular formation, which in turn ceases to produce the OR. The neuronal model, therefore, would function as a selective filter. The characteristics of the filter could be defined by changing one parameter of the stimulus used for habituation and recording the magnitude of the OR that develops. The definition of all the filter characteristics would be a tedious task, however, since the neuronal model is a polyvalent model of the total stimulus, in which all or a considerable group of its properties are represented.[59]

The physiological mechanism for the OR must involve both cortical and subcortical regions, as supposed by Pavlov. Motor, GSR, and EEG changes are known to originate from the cortex, whereas vascular, oculomotor, respiratory, and pupillary changes are known to originate from subcortical areas. In stimulating twenty-eight cats and four apes with electrodes placed in various parts of the brain, N. I. Lagutina [60] obtained clearly defined OR patterns from both cortical and subcortical areas. Detailed examination of her data showed two kinds of OR reactions, (1) of general watchfulness and (2) of an exploratory type, emerging from electrical stimulation of a variety of specific brain structures. In addition O. S. Vinogradova, in her comprehensive review of the literature on the OR,[61] cites several studies where decortication has resulted in the loss of the orienting response mechanism. There remain a few physiological observations that cannot be handled by the model, but in general physiological evidence supports the Sokolov conception.[62]

Russian experimenters have also collected considerable data on phylogenetic and ontogenetic differences in the OR. The higher the organism is along the phylogenetic scale, the more pronounced will be the OR component reactions, especially the somatic ones. In addition, habituation of the OR becomes more rapid and the general flexibility of the OR mechanism is increased as more cortex is added.[63] Yet with respect to the effectiveness of stimuli that evoke the OR, differences between animals appear to be often a matter of ecological rather than purely phyletic factors. Other Russian investigators have explored some of these ecological factors.[64] The elimination of such species-specific differences in ontogenetic studies of the OR makes the data obtained in this area more readily comparable. Three major changes are reported in the OR as the organism matures: (1) autonomic components of the OR are present in the newborn organism, while motor components are not, but develop later; (2) instrumental learning is possible only after the motor components of the OR have appeared; (3) the OR is more resistant to habituation in young individuals (less cortical influence) than in older ones.[65]

With the advent of the cybernetic revolution, the salient characteristic of the OR as a detector of novelty led to the rapid development of OR analysis along the lines of information theory. Quantitatively the degree of novelty of a stimulus may be represented by the value of uncertainty associated with it, i.e., by the entropy which the appearance of the stimulus creates in the situation. At the moment in time when an accepted hypothesis or neuronal model ceases to coincide with the sensory input, the uncertainty of the situation temporarily increases. The OR is correspondingly stronger and of longer duration, the greater the initial uncertainty and the more difficult it is to eliminate it in the course of observing the signal. On the basis of Bayes' theorem, the subject successively ascertains the conditional probabilities of the various hypotheses after observations of the stimulus. The degree of uncertainty at each moment in time is equal to the entropy in the distribution of hypotheses. The OR appears when the uncertainty of the situation reaches a certain threshold value.[66]

A comparison of such a scheme with actual experiments confirms the inferences made above. Experiments show that the OR persists the most stably at moments that carry the most information, the degree of the OR being proportional to the anticipated information. In further experiments with the tactile recognition of letters, an active process of seeking out those points in the stimulus sequence that yielded the most information was observed. With knowledge of the system of presented configurations, it is possible to predict the most informative points at each step of palpation. Thus it is theoretically possible to calculate the most effective trajectories in the tactile recognition task. Experiments have shown good coincidence between such theoretically calculated trajectories and those obtained in the laboratory.[67]

Thus the notion of the orienting response has been expanded to include extended search tasks and more complicated abstract perceptual stimuli. In the motor feedback used in palpation the OR has moved exceedingly close to Anokhin's mechanism of "acceptor of action." Meanwhile, the ascertaining of expected information is contiguous with Krushinsky's notion of "extrapolation reflexes." Thus the OR, defined as a response to the abstract stimulus of novelty, and measured by an unbounded set of dependent variables, has broadened to subsume two other important theoretical approaches in Soviet psychology. The overlapping of these concepts produces some tempting inferences, but there still remains the danger that the concrete and useful meaning of the orienting response might be lost as it expands to embrace all sorts of other psychological phenomena. In a very functional sense, the orienting response stands as a sort of bridge between conditioned reflexes on the one hand and cognitive processes on the other. As long as it remains independently supported, the OR will retain its status as the most important single development in recent Soviet psychology.

Conclusion

This brief survey of Soviet research in experimental psychology has sought to illuminate certain trends in the recent growth of this discipline in the Soviet Union. In each of the four major research areas explored, the contemporary picture has been found to be quite different from the one characterizing that area before the death of Stalin. The conditioned reflex, previously the exclusive domain of the theories of Pavlov, has been both expanded and opposed in ways quite foreign to its founder. In the study of cognitive processes, the motor-copy theory of A. N. Leontiev has converted Marxist doctrine concerning images into the concrete, testable psychological argument of the peripheralist. With regard to the study of developmental parameters, the work of A. R. Luria is largely responsible for a shift of theoretical emphasis from the views of Pavlov to those of Vygotsky. Finally, the orienting reaction of Ye. N. Sokolov has emerged as a mature and independent field of investigation. These advances have substantially changed the character of Soviet psychological research since the death of Stalin: psychology in the Soviet Union is no longer synonymous with Pavlov and Marx.

Notes

1. A. Mintz, "Introduction to Contemporary Soviet Psychology," in *Some Views on Soviet Psychology*, ed. R. A. Bauer (Washington: American Psychological Association, 1962).

2. E. A. Asratian, "The Physiology of the Conditioned Reflex," in *Psychological Research in the U.S.S.R.* (in English) (Moscow: Izdatelstvo "Progress," 1966).

3. E. A. Asratian and P. V. Simonov, *Nadyozhnost Mozga* (Moscow: Izdatelstvo Akademii Nauk SSSR, 1962).

4. I. S. Beritov, *Nervnye Mekhanizmy Povedeniya Vysshikh Pozvonochnykh Zhivotnykh* (Moscow: Izdatelstvo Akademii Nauk SSSR, 1961).

5. N. E. Miller, C. Pfaffman, and P. Schlosberg, "Aspects of Psychophysiology in the U.S.S.R.," in *Some Views on Soviet Psychology*.

6. See Beritov, *Nervnye Mekhanizmy*.

7. L. V. Krushinsky, *Formirovanie Povedeniya Zhivotnykh v Norme i Patologii* (Moscow: MGU, 1960).

8. D. Bowden and M. Cole, "Glossary of Terms Frequently Encountered in Soviet Psychology," *Soviet Psychology and Psychiatry*, 4 (1966): 10–15.

9. P. K. Anokhin, *Vnytrennee Tormozhenic kak Problema Fiziologii* (Moscow: Medgiz, 1958).

10. P. K. Anokhin, "Special Features of the Afferent Apparatus of the Conditioned Reflex and Their Importance to Psychology," in *Psychological Research in the U.S.S.R.*

11. *Ibid.*

12. P. K. Anokhin, "Advances in Brain Research," in *Nauka i Chelovechestvo* (Moscow: Znanie, 1965).

13. N. A. Bernstein, "Some Problems on the Control of Motor Acts," in *Psychological Research in the U.S.S.R.*

14. N. A. Bernstein, *O Postroyenii Dvizheniya* (Moscow: Medgiz, 1947).

15. See Bernstein, "Some Problems on the Control of Motor Acts."

16. K. M. Bykov, *The Cerebral Cortex and the Internal Organs* (New York: Chemical Publishing Co., 1957).

17. G. Razran, "The Observable Unconscious and the Inferable Conscious in Current Soviet Psychophysiology," *Psychological Review*, 68 (1961): 81–147.

18. E. Sh. Ayrapetiants, L. V. Lobanova, and L. S. Cherkasova, "Materials on the Physiology of the Internal Analyzer in Man," *Trudy Inst. Fiziologii Pavlova*, 1 (1952): 3–20.

19. See Razran, "The Observable Unconscious and the Inferable Conscious."

20. *Ibid.*

21. See Miller, Pfaffmann, and Schlosberg, "Aspects of Psychophysiology."

22. See Razran, "The Observable Unconscious and the Inferable Conscious."

23. H. L. Pick, "Perception in Soviet Psychology," *Psychological Bulletin*, 62 (1964): 21–35.

24. A. N. Leontiev, *Problemy Razvitiya Psikhiki* (Moscow: Izdatelstvo Akademii Pedagogicheskikh Nauk RSFSR, 1959).

25. J. A. Gray, "Attention, Consciousness, and Voluntary Control of Behavior in Soviet Psychology: Philosophical Roots and Research Branches," in *Present-Day Russian Psychology*, ed. N. O'Connor (Oxford: Pergamon Press, 1966).

26. See Leontiev, *Problemy Razvitiya Psikhiki.*

27. G. Razran, "Dermo-optical Perception or Human Extraocular Color Sensitivity: A Clarification of Current Soviet Research and an Article in *Science*," *Soviet Psychology,* 5 (1966): 4–13.

28. Iu. B. Gippenreiter, *O Vospriyatii Vysoty Zvuka* (Moscow: Izdatelstvo Akademii Pedagogicheskikh Nauk RSFSR, 1960).

29. A. L. Yarbus, *Rol Dvizheniy Glaz v Protsesse Zreniya* (Moscow: Izdatelstvo "Nauka," 1965).

30. B. F. Lomov, "Manual Interaction in the Process of Tactile Perception," in *Psychological Research in the U.S.S.R.*

31. See Pick, "Perception in Soviet Psychology."

32. A. N. Leontiev and Ye. P. Krinchik, "Some Characteristics of Information Processing in Man," *Voprosy Psikhologii,* 85 (1962): 14–25.

33. V. D. Glezer, *Mekhanizmy Opoznaniya Zritelnikh Obrazov* (Moscow: Izdatelstvo Akademii Nauk SSSR, 1966).

34. W. E. Hick, "On the Rate of Gain of Information," *Quarterly Journal of Experimental Psychology,* 4 (1952): 11–26.

35. L. A. Chistovich, Iu. A. Klass, and R. O. Alekin, "On the Significance of Imitation for the Discrimination of Sound Sequences," *Voprosy Psikhologii,* 7 (1961): 173–82.

36. A. R. Luria and O. S. Vinogradova, "An Objective Investigation of the Dynamics of Semantic Systems," *British Journal of Psychology,* 50 (1959): 89–105.

37. See Razran, "The Observable Unconscious and the Inferable Conscious."

38. D. N. Uznadze, *Psikhologicheskie Issledovaniya* (Moscow: Izdatelstvo "Nauka," 1966).

39. A. S. Prangishvili and Z. I. Khodzhava, eds., *Eksperimentalnye Issledovaniya po Psikhologii Ustanovki* (Tbilisi: Izdatelstvo Akademii Nauk GSSR, 1958).

40. G. Razran, "Growth, Scope, and Direction of Current Soviet Psychology: The 1963 All-Union Congress," *American Psychologist,* 19 (1964): 432–39.

41. See Uznadze, *Psikhologicheskie Issledovaniya.*

42. R. G. Natadze, "On One Factor in Size Constancy," *Voprosy Psikhologii,* 6 (1960): 24–32.

43. See Miller, Pfaffman, and Schlosberg, "Aspects of Psychophysiology."

44. See Gray, "Attention, Consciousness, and Voluntary Control."

45. L. S. Vygotsky, *Thought and Language* (New York: John Wiley & Sons, 1962).

46. A. R. Luria, *The Role of Speech in the Regulation of Normal and Abnormal Behavior* (Oxford: Pergamon Press, 1961).

47. A. R. Luria, "Verbal Regulation of Behavior," in *The Central Nervous System and Behavior, Transactions of the Third Conference,* ed. M. A. B. Brazier (New York: Josiah Macy, Jr., Foundation, 1960).

48. A. V. Zaporozhets, *Razvitie Proizvolnykh Dvizheniy* (Moscow: Izdatelstvo Akademii Pedagogicheskikh Nauk RSFSR, 1960).

49. V. G. Ananiev and Ye. F. Rybalko, *Osobennosti Vospriyatiya Prostranstva y Detyey* (Moscow: Izdatelstvo "Enlightenment," 1964).

50. B. M. Teplov and V. D. Nebylitsyn, "A Study of the Basic Properties of the Nervous System and Their Significance for the Psychology of Individual Differences," *Voprosy Psikhologii,* 9 (1963): 38–46.

51. V. D. Nebylitsyn, *Osnovnye Svoystva Nervnoy Sistemy Cheloveka* (Moscow: Izdatelstvo "Enlightenment," 1966).

52. O. S. Vinogradova, *Orientirovochny Refleks i yevo Neyrofiziologicheskie*

Mekhanizmy (Moscow: Izdatelstvo Akademii Pedagogicheskikh Nauk RSFSR, 1961).

53. Ye. N. Sokolov, "The Orienting Reflex as a Regulator of Information," in *Psychological Research in the U.S.S.R.*

54. See Gray, "Attention, Consciousness, and Voluntary Control."

55. See Razran, "The Observable Unconscious and the Inferable Conscious."

56. Ye. N. Sokolov, "The Orienting Reflex as a Regulator of Information," in *Orientirovochny Refleks i Problemy Retseptsii v Norme i Patologii*, ed. Ye. N. Sokolov (Moscow: Izdatelstvo "Enlightenment," 1964).

57. R. Lynn, *Attention, Arousal and the Orienting Reaction* (Oxford: Pergamon Press, 1966).

58. See Sokolov, in *Orientirovochny Refleks i Problemy Retsepsii.*

59. Ye. N. Sokolov, *Perception and the Conditioned Reflex* (New York: Macmillan, 1963).

60. N. I. Lagutina, "On the Question of the Structure of Orienting Reflexes," in *The Orienting Reflex and Exploratory Behavior*, eds. L. G. Voronin *et al.* (Washington: American Institute of Biological Science, 1965).

61. See Vinogradova, *Orientirovochny Refleks.*

62. See Gray, "Attention, Consciousness, and Voluntary Control."

63. See Vinogradova, *Orientirovochny Refleks.*

64. See Razran, "The Observed Unconscious and the Inferable Conscious."

65. See Vinogradova, *Orientirovochny Refleks.*

66. See Sokolov, in *Orientirovochny Refleks i Problemy Retseptsii.*

67. See Sokolov, in *Psychological Research in the U.S.S.R.*

IX : Psychiatry

Soviet Psychiatry: Past, Present, and Future

Isidore Ziferstein, M.D.

Introduction: Extrascientific Barriers to Understanding

In 1950 the president of a U.S. publishing firm that was issuing a book on Soviet psychiatry found it necessary to write a special publisher's foreword with the following disclaimer: "Again it may be unnecessary, but desirable in order to dissipate any doubt, to declare flatly that our publication of this volume must not be taken to imply (contrary to fact) any admiration on our part for Soviet science, economy, or ideology." [1] Although the publisher wrote that the disclaimer "may be unnecessary, but desirable," the reverse was actually true. In truth, it was necessary for the well-being of his commercial enterprise, in view of the cold war and the prevalence of McCarthyism in 1950, for the publisher to disclaim any possible admiration for Soviet science. But such a disclaimer, though necessary, had the highly undesirable effect of producing

The research on which this article is based was aided by grants from the Foundations Fund for Research in Psychiatry, New Haven; the Louis M. Rabinowitz Foundation, New York; and the Postgraduate Center for Mental Health, New York.

tension in the reader and prejudicing him in relation to the subject matter before he had even begun to read the book.

Now, eighteen years later, the tensions of the cold war are still with us. And the disclaimer quoted above illustrates but one of the many extrascientific stresses and pressures which plague any effort to establish understanding between American and Soviet psychiatrists.

Another barrier to mutual understanding is illustrated by the fact that many Soviet psychiatrists would probably maintain that it is improper to include psychiatry in a symposium on the social sciences in the Soviet Union, alongside Soviet jurisprudence, philosophy, and education. They would insist that in the Soviet Union, with its scientific-materialist orientation, psychiatry is firmly based on physiology and medicine, and is therefore primarily a biological science. They might even protest that people who write about Soviet psychiatry in a symposium on social sciences demonstrate by that very act their fundamental noncomprehension of psychiatry as it has developed in the Soviet Union, and that such people are therefore totally incapable of interpreting Soviet psychiatry to their Western colleagues.

Still a third obstacle to mutual understanding is presented by the marked differences in tradition, ideology, and life experiences of American and Soviet psychiatrists, to say nothing of the language barrier. Over the years, the Russians have kept *au courant* with Western psychiatry. Most Soviet psychiatrists have a second language, usually German or English or French, and they read our psychiatric literaure. Their psychiatric writings, therefore, abound with criticisms of Western psychiatry, and especially psychoanalysis. One reads such statements as:

It should be noted, however, that success in the study of the brain as the substrate of psychic processes was hindered not only by the complexity of the subject and the difficulty in investigating it. Foreign bourgeois scientists, most of whom held reactionary idealistic views, opposed in every way the goal of scientific investigation of the activity of the brain as the substrate of psychic processes. In their struggle against materialism they, making a virtue of necessity, tried in one way or another to counterpose the "psychic" to the "physical" and to proclaim that psychological phenomena were independent of processes occurring in the brain.[2]

Or the following statement about psychoanalysis:

The teachings of Freud have been accepted as an ideological weapon of reaction, which strives to justify wars and the social depravities of the capitalist order.[3]

In contradistinction to the Soviet psychiatrists, who have stressed the importance of carrying on an "ideological struggle" against what they consider the false doctrines of Western psychiatry, American psychiatrists chose, until very recently, to ignore Soviet psychiatry almost entirely. This was not too difficult to do, especially since so few American psychiatrists read Russian. This ignoring was rationalized by the conviction that the Russians were so far behind in everything, including psychiatry, that it would be a waste of effort to learn their difficult language or to have their works translated.

To sum up: A basic obstacle to mutual understanding between American and Soviet behavioral scientists has been a "one-upmanship" struggle between them—a manifestation of the perversion of science by ideological, political, and cultural conflicts.

Two events have contributed to an improvement in this situation: the de-Stalinization of the Soviet Union following the death of Stalin, and the launching by the Russians of their first sputnik on October 4, 1957.

The first to respond to the latter event were, of course, the physical scientists, who were moved by admiration or apprehension, or both, of the suddenly no longer backward Russians, and wanted to learn more about how they accomplished their leap forward. This change in attitude gradually filtered into other disciplines, including the social sciences. With this new interest, a few Russian-speaking psychiatrists, and others with a smattering of Russian, began to visit Soviet psychiatric institutions. They returned and published brief reports, the tone of which is reminiscent at times of the writings of the early explorers about exotic lands and peoples.

I was one of these "explorers," visiting the Soviet Union briefly in 1959 and 1961, and writing impressionistic reports about these visits. These brief glimpses of Soviet psychiatry, while intriguing, did not yield sufficient information. It was clear that more prolonged and closer contact with Soviet psychiatrists and, if possible, direct observation of their work were necessary and desirable. In 1963–64, with the aid of grants from American foundations, I was able to spend fifteen months doing just this. What follows is based essentially on my firsthand observations during this period, supplemented by discussions with Russian, Czech, and Polish psychiatrists, reading of the Soviet psychiatric literature, and comparing notes with other American psychiatrists who have made their own observations.

Understanding the Soviet Psychiatrist

Of the fifteen months of my sojourn in the Soviet Union, I spent thirteen months working at the V. M. Bekhterev Psychoneurological Research Institute in Leningrad. There I sat daily in the treatment room with psychiatrists and patients, observing the actual process of psychiatric treatment. In the course of these observations, I learned at least as much about the personalities and attitudes of the Soviet psychiatrists whose work I observed as I did about the patients.

It became clear that, in addition to studying the theories on which Soviet psychiatry is founded and the various therapeutic modalities that are applied in clinical practice, I had to understand the personality and the attitudes of the Soviet psychiatrist, who is the essential mediator between theory and practice. To understand Soviet psychiatry, one must understand the upbringing of the Soviet psychiatrist, his social attitudes, his concepts about the influence of society on the emotional health of his patients, his view of his society as a therapeutic community, and finally, his ideas about his place in society and in the overall structure of Soviet medicine and psychiatry.

An important aspect of the Soviet psychiatrist's professional ego is his awareness of himself as a member of a collective. This awareness seems to be characteristic of the vast majority of Soviet citizens and is apparently the result of their collective upbringing from earliest childhood.

From birth, one might even say since before birth,* the Soviet child (the future psychiatrist) functions as a member of a group, of a collective. This orientation continues in the crèche, the kindergarten, the school, the organizations of Octobrists and Young Pioneers (organizations of schoolchildren for after-school activities) and the Komsomol (the Young Communist League).

In these institutions and organizations, the child and young adult becomes oriented very early in life to consider that his personal problems are also problems for the collective, and that, conversely, the problems of

---

* David and Vera Mace report: "Soviet mothers like to deliver their babies in the atmosphere of the collective. They would consider it almost a punishment to be banished to a private room" (*The Soviet Family* [Garden City, N.Y.: Doubleday & Co., 1963], p. 256).

the collective are very much his problems. If he has misbehaved, or if he is doing badly in his studies, it is not only a matter concerning himself, his teacher, and his parents, but a matter of concern to his classmates and to the organization of Young Pioneers.

If his parents are not getting along harmoniously and this is interfering with his studying, this will become the concern not only of his Pioneer group, but also of the trade-union organization and Communist party organization in the factory or office in which his parents work.

When he is a medical student, the future psychiatrist knows that he is receiving free a very expensive medical education, and is drawing a stipend into the bargain. He knows that society is providing this for him because society needs his talents and the contribution that he will make. This is but a special case of the general atmosphere that permeates the society, which expects that every able-bodied citizen, male or female, will make a contribution to society: that "he who works not, neither shall he eat."

After completing his medical training, the Soviet psychotherapist continues to function as a member of a collective. He is on the staff of an institution which, as he is aware, is part of a well-organized and coordinated network of therapeutic-prophylactic-educational-research establishments.

As a consequence of his collective upbringing and orientation, the Soviet psychiatrist has a strong conviction that the prophylactic and therapeutic measures he employs depend for their full effectiveness on the support he receives in his efforts from society. Soviet psychiatrists consider their society to be a therapeutic community. They feel that their society promotes mental health precisely because it is a collective cooperative society in which competitiveness and interpersonal tensions are diminished. They point in addition to such mental-health-promoting factors as the absence of unemployment, full opportunity for choosing a lifework that accords with the individual's inclinations and abilities (through the provision of free education and stipends for students in professional schools and universities), and the provision of material security in case of illness and old age. They point to "the broad network of crèches, kindergartens, boarding schools, and other institutions for children, which are accessible to all, [in which] medical workers in close contact with the pedagogical personnel carry out a broad program which promotes the development of a strong, stable personality and of correct relations to reality." [4] They point, among other things, to the consistent and organized programs their society provides to ensure the continuing mental health of elderly, retired citizens by involving them in community affairs and keeping them socially active and vigorous.

The point here is not whether, and to what degree, other societies make similar provisions. What is significant for our study is that the average Soviet psychiatrist looks upon these measures as part of his prophylactic-therapeutic armamentarium; and, conversely, he has a strong awareness of himself and his work as an integral part of the overall social effort.

As a result of his collective upbringing and his functioning throughout his lifetime as a member of one or more collectives, the Soviet psychiatrist has thoroughly assimilated and integrated into his personality the slogan *"Nikogda nie bit postoronnim"* ("Never be a bystander"). This means that in Soviet society everyone is expected to be, and he himself expects to be, his brother's keeper. If, in a given situation, one citizen has more knowledge than others, it is his responsibility to share his knowledge with those less well informed. If he sees someone behaving improperly, it is his obligation to correct and teach the erring citizen.

The Soviet psychiatrist carries over these attitudes, which stem from his collective upbringing and functioning, into the therapeutic relationship with his patients. Since the patient is obviously the citizen who has lost his way, and the psychiatrist is the expert, the latter naturally assumes the active role of helper, adviser, guide, and giver of support. As Professor Vladimir Miasishchev puts it, "It may be stated without exaggeration that the doctor becomes a teacher of life to the patient." [5]

The Soviet psychiatrist presents himself to the patient as a strong, benign, mature parental figure, to whom the patient can look with confidence for help and guidance. He does not have any of the apprehensions which trouble many psychiatrists in our country, that the patient may develop an unresolvable dependency on the doctor. In my discussions with Soviet psychiatrists, I asked them about the danger of unresolved transference. They assured me that this was not a problem, and that their follow-up studies showed that their patients were able to carry on independently in outside life after discharge from treatment. It may be that the parental attitude of the doctor is not a disturbing factor because the patient, like the doctor, falls naturally into his role in the therapeutic relationship as he would in any other life situation where he knew less than a fellow citizen. Furthermore, after the patient is discharged from treatment, he will have available many parental figures, should he need them, primarily in the form of his collective.

The Soviet psychiatrist, then, plays a very active role in treatment, diametrically opposite to the passive, purely interpretive role that is advocated by psychoanalysis. This activity is manifested in many ways. The psychiatrist may manipulate the patient's environment, his job, his occupation, his place of work, or his place of residence, if he considers these to be factors in the patient's illness. The doctor will not only advise a change of job or residence. He will personally (not through a social worker) contact the appropriate authorities—the factory manager or the housing committee—to see that the prescribed changes are carried out.

This was illustrated in a case I observed in which the patient was a young factory worker. In the course of therapy, the psychiatrist arrived at the conclusion that a major factor in the patient's neurosis was the unchallenging, unrewarding nature of his work. The therapist felt that the patient had the capacity to become an engineer, and that this would help him develop into a competent, fulfilled, and healthy person. On discharging the patient, the doctor wrote a prescription, addressed to the factory director, which required that the patient be enrolled in an engineering institute and that the factory pay his full salary during the entire period of his schooling. Such prescriptions are binding on the factory management.

In keeping with his position as the expert, as "the citizen who knows," the Soviet psychiatrist is "in charge" during the entire course of treatment. When conducting psychotherapy, the psychiatrist decides, after the first two or three exploratory sessions, what the patient's major problem areas are. He then discusses with the patient the goals of the treatment, and proceeds to direct and guide the content and form of each session, so as to deal systematically with each problem area in turn.

Because of his collective upbringing and his "brother's keeper" orientation, the Soviet psychiatrist involves himself much more actively and with much more emotional cathexis in his patients than the psychoanalysts I have observed in this country.*

The importance of active, emotionally cathected involvement by the psychiatrist has been enunciated as a major principle of Soviet psychotherapy by its leading theoreticians. G. A. Giliarovsky writes that psychiatric treatment "requires not only a kind, loving attitude toward the patient. It also requires active intervention in his life and the lives of the people around him. . . . The Soviet doctor is not an observer, but an active friend and servant of those who suffer." [6]

Another leading Soviet psychiatrist, Professor V. N. Miasishchev, director of research at the Bekhterev Institute, writes:

*Observations in this country were carried out as part of a research project, "A Study of the Psychotherapeutic Process." The research was carried out at the Institute for Psychiatric and Psychosomatic Research, Mt. Sinai Hospital, Los Angeles (director, Franz Alexander), and was supported by a grant from the Ford Foundation. (See Franz Alexander, "A Study of the Therapeutic Process," paper presented at the western divisional meeting of the American Psychiatric Association, Los Angeles, November 21, 1957; Hedda Bolgar, "Values in Therapy," in *Science and Psychoanalysis*, ed. Jules H. Masserman [New York: Grune & Stratton, 1960], vol. 3; Norman Levy, "An Investigation into the Nature of the Psychotherapeutic Process," in *ibid.* [1961], vol. 4.)

The relationship of the patient to the doctor is most important and decisive. This relationship becomes an effective force only when it acquires a positive emotional character. The authority of the doctor, the trust, esteem, and love of the patients for him, are not acquired at once, but gradually, as the doctor, by his skillful approach to the patient, helps him to gain an understanding of his life story, of the complicated, confused, ununderstood and misunderstood circumstances of his past and present.[7]

The Soviet psychiatrist believes that it is the doctor's responsibility to maintain a positive climate in the therapy—a climate in which the patient develops "trust, esteem, and love" for the doctor. If the climate is not positive, or if the patient develops negative feelings, this is considered to be the result of errors committed by the doctor. It is then the psychiatrist's responsibility to take active steps to gain or regain the patient's positive feelings.

The Soviet psychiatrist is therefore very active in giving the patient emotional support and building up the patient's self-esteem. The doctor does not hesitate to give the patient advice and guidance in his day-to-day problems. His efforts to reconstruct the unhealthy personality structure involve exploring its pathogenesis, but with the predominant emphasis on active reeducation, presenting to the patient those values and standards of behavior which are considered correct, realistic, and socially desirable.

Soviet psychiatrists are active themselves and they expect activity of their patients. The treatment received by patients at the Bekhterev Institute was active and vigorous, and was reminiscent of the "total push" program advocated in our country for the hospitalized mental patient. The patient's waking time was almost totally occupied with a variety of activities, and the mental illness was attacked on a variety of fronts simultaneously.

A central part of this total-push approach is work therapy. On the grounds of the Bekhterev Institute were a number of fully equipped factories in which several hundred patients were employed. About half were inpatients. The rest were outpatients living in the neighborhood of the institute. In these factories, trained foremen as well as psychiatrists supervised the patients in the production of such articles as furniture, clothing, fountain pens, and hammocks. These articles were sold under contract to retail stores, and the patients were paid for their work.

The hours that the patient spends in the hospital factory, engaged in productive work, are considered a crucial part of his treatment, and all patients who are physically able are required to work. The Bekhterev Institute is conducting intensive research on the applications and results of work therapy. One finding which has already emerged from this research is that epileptics engaged in work therapy demonstrated a significant decrease in frequency of seizures and a more rapid improvement in various disturbances of function when compared with a control group that was not so engaged.

Work therapy is considered by Soviet psychiatrists a major tool in their therapeutic armamentarium, just as their society looks upon work as a central element in the life of every person, male or female; and their Marxist ideology teaches that the evolution of man was made possible by the emergence of social labor, i.e., work that is carried out cooperatively and that is socially useful.

Soviet psychiatrists emphasize that work therapy helps to maintain the patient's contact with reality and to prevent emotional isolation and retreat from the real world; that doing socially useful work, and getting paid for it, helps restore and enhance the patient's self-esteem; and that work under the protected conditions of the therapeutic workshop helps prepare the patient for a return to normal life and work on the outside.

Some patients continue working in the protected hospital workshops after discharge until such time as they are ready to return to work under ordinary conditions. There are patients for whom the hospital workshop offers an opportunity for retraining in a new skill which suits them better and/or is more highly paid.

I recall a patient who was assigned to work in the electronics shop. During the three months of his hospitalization, he acquired considerable skill in assembling and repairing electronic devices used in medical research. When he was ready for discharge he asked and obtained permission to continue working in the electronics shop for several more months to increase his skill. He finally became proficient enough to obtain an interesting, highly skilled, and well-paid job in industry. In a follow-up interview, I noted that for this man there was no longer any stigma attached to psychiatric hospitalization. He told me that he boasted to his neighbors and friends about the high-status profession he had learned at the Bekhterev Institute.

Still another manifestation of the psychiatrist's immersion in the collective feeling is the emphasis on informality and on availability of the doctor. The patients whose treatment I observed were all hospitalized, and there were no preset appointments for psychotherapeutic sessions. Patients were seen at various times of the day, depending on the schedule of the other treatments and activities. Sessions were not limited to the fifty-minute psychoanalytic hour but varied quite informally in duration from a half hour to two hours or longer. I was interested to find, moreover, that this informality and easy availability of the therapist applied not only to the hospitalized patients, but also to former patients who occasionally wanted to see their former psychiatrist.

This was brought to my attention dramatically one day when I was observing a therapeutic session. The door suddenly opened and, without knocking, a man poked his head into the room. With no apology or preamble, he asked to see the doctor. I, the American observer, was the only one upset by this invasion. The doctor and the patient remained quite unperturbed. The doctor quietly advised the intruder that he would be able to see him in a half hour. I later learned that the intruder was a former patient. The doctor did not agree with my suggestion that the patient ought to have telephoned in advance for an appointment. He felt that it was an important part of the therapeutic relationship that the patient should know that the doctor was available whenever he was needed.

As is to be expected from one whose life is oriented toward the central role of the collective in the security system of the individual, in the satisfaction of his material and emotional needs, and in the furthering of his growth and development, the Soviet psychiatrist makes active and frequent use of the collective for therapeutic purposes. In the forefront of his awareness is a realization of his reciprocal interaction with his society: society employs his profesional skills for the benefit of the overall social enterprise, and he uses society, its regulations and institutions, to assist him in his professional work with the individual patient.

The psychiatrist has a large number of collectives available for his therapeutic purposes. He often calls upon the patient's collective and other social institutions, in addition to the family, to help in obtaining an anamnesis. He depends on members of the collective to visit the patient, to maintain contact with him, to help keep up his spirits, and to prevent isolation and withdrawal from reality. For example, in the case of the young worker referred to earlier, a delegation from his collective came to the hospital to take him to a holiday outing arranged by the factory trade-union organization. When the patient is discharged, the doctor may write to the trade-union organization, giving suggestions and instructions about attitudes toward the patient which will help promote recovery.

In the case of patients hospitalized at the Bekhterev Institute, I was able to observe how, consciously and unconsciously, the staff used the collective as a therapeutic instrument. The patient's time was almost totally occupied with a variety of activities involving constant interaction with fellow patients and the staff. The emphasis was always on the collective as an inspirational, encouraging, supportive, pressuring, corrective, and reality-testing medium.

The clinical conference at which patients were presented to the entire staff, including Professor Miasishchev, was also used consciously and actively by the staff as a therapeutic aid. It was impressed on the patient that at the conference he was privileged to have the benefit of the collective wisdom of the entire staff. The staff members interacted with the patient in a way that was clearly intended not only to clarify obscure points, but also to have a direct psychotherapeutic impact on the patient. And it usually did. Weekly ward rounds by the entire staff were similarly used to exert a collective therapeutic effect on the patients.

The Soviet psychiatrists' total involvement in the use of the collective and their inability to let anyone be a bystander was illustrated dramatically in their relationship to me. I had explained to the staff that my aim was to be a totally nonparticipant observer. But both the patients and the psychiatrists seemed to be constitutionally unable to let anyone be merely an observer. Verbally and nonverbally, patients and therapists seemed constantly to be saying to me, "Don't just sit there! Do something!"

Not infrequently during therapeutic sessions, either the therapist or the patient would turn to me with "Don't you think so, Isidor Samuilovich?" "What do *you* think, Isidor Samuilovich?" "How is this problem handled in your country?" I finally came to realize that, willy-nilly, I had become a participant member in a therapeutic *collectif-à-trois*, whose aim, like that of all collectives, was to increase the well-being of the individual and of the collective.

The Organization of Psychiatric Care in the Soviet Union

The omnipresence of the collective spirit is manifested in many ways. The lead headlines in the newspapers are always devoted to the latest achievements of the collective farmers in such places as the Krasnodarsk region who fulfilled 118 percent of their quota of grain sold to the government, or the miners of the Kuzbass who have already produced 120,000 tons of coal over their yearly quota. To the foreigner all this seems boring, but to the Soviet citizen it is of absorbing interest.

Similarly, a conversation with a Soviet psychiatrist quickly turns to a discussion of the organization of psychiatric care in the Soviet Union.

He is not a private practitioner. His professional past, present, and future are intimately connected with the collective of which he is a member. And he is very much aware of the place his institution occupies in the overall network of psychiatric establishments in the country, and of the contribution it is making to the overall goal of maintaining and improving the mental health of the people.

From my conversations with Soviet psychiatrists, I learned a great deal about their collectivized system of psychiatric care. My discussion of contemporary Soviet psychiatry would not be complete without at least a brief description of it.

The basic unit in the mental-health setup of the Soviet Union is the district psychiatric outpatient dispensary. Every city or region is divided into districts, each with its district dispensary, which is increasingly becoming the mental-health center for the district it serves. The dispensary not only treats psychiatric outpatients referred to it from the district's general medical polyclinic, from the factory medico-sanitary section, or by the school physicians. It also, and more importantly, concerns itself with the overall mental-health needs of its district, with special emphasis on psychoprophylaxis. Each dispensary psychiatrist is in effect the public-health officer of his subdistrict. In this capacity, he makes regular inspections of all industrial and mercantile establishments in his subdistrict. If he finds conditions that he considers hazardous, such as excessive noise or excessive speed of an assembly line, he has the power to order changes.

Two hours of the dispensary psychiatrist's five-and-a-half-hour working day are set aside for mental-health education. He goes to factories, housing projects, and "palaces of labor" to present lectures and lead discussions on mental health and mental hygiene, and to conduct individual and group consultations.

The staff of the district dispensary carries out surveys of the mental health of specific groups in the population. It investigates the impact of changes in the school curriculum on the mental health of children in the district, or the effect of automation on the mental health of workers in specific factories.

With the aid of these surveys, and by maintaining close contact with the general medical polyclinics and with the medical officers of factories, schools, and other establishments, the staff of the dispensary engages in early case finding. The success of this effort is greatly enhanced by the rigid requirement of annual medical examinations for all employees.

At the other end of the spectrum of psychiatric institutions is the psychiatric hospital, whose relative importance is diminishing because of the shift in emphasis to psychoprophylaxis, early case finding, and early outpatient treatment.

There are several noteworthy features of the Soviet psychiatric hospital. First is the relatively small number of hospitalized psychiatric patients—about 220,000 in the entire U.S.S.R. One reason is the still predominantly rural character of the Soviet Union, with its greater tolerance for the unhospitalized mental patient than is the case in urban populations. Another reason is that Soviet psychiatrists tend to discharge patients after relatively brief hospitalization, because they feel that prolonged hospitalization hinders ultimate recovery. If the discharged patient is not yet ready to care for himself, he will be referred to family care, with continuation of psychiatric treatment. Often the family to which the patient is sent will be his own, and the government pays the family a stipend for caring for the patient. (In this way, the mental illness of a member of the family may be a financial windfall, since the ill member continues to draw his regular salary, and the family is paid for caring for him.)

Another feature is the trend toward building hospitals of 300–400-bed capacity in the districts they serve, thus making them more accessible to the population. This makes it easier to visit hospitalized patients, and it also makes it possible for discharged patients to continue working in the sheltered workshops of the hospital until they are ready to return to their regular work in the community. Here also, as in the case of the dispensary, the emphasis is on close contact and interaction between the psychiatric facility and the community.

There are a number of intermediate links between the dispensary and the psychiatric hospital. One of these is the day hospital, which is intended for patients who require more intensive observation and treatment than can be given on an ambulatory basis, but who are well enough to go home each day after their daily course of treatment. An important feature of the day hospital is the therapeutic workshop, just as it is in the inpatient hospital and the outpatient dispensary.

There are also night hospitals for patients who are well enough to work outside, but who still need to live in a protected environment, or who have to return to the hospital after work for special treatments, or who cannot return home because of conflictual relationships.

Another intermediate link between dispensary and hospital is the sanatorium, which is intended for the short-term accommodation of patients with incipient forms of mental illness or for patients convalescing after a period of treatment in a psychiatric hospital. The regime in the sanatorium is more like that in a rest home than in a hospital, but the patient is still under medical observation and receives special care. Often the sanatoria are located in the countryside, and many of them are in the resort areas of the Crimea and the Caucasus.

When a patient is discharged from the hospital or from one of the intermediate institutions and is ready to return to the community, he is referred back to the dispensary of his district, where he may continue to be under the supervision of the psychiatrist and nurse for as long as two or three years. And so, again, the dispensary psychiatrist assumes his role of family psychiatrist to the people of his subdistrict, in addition to his other roles of public-health officer, mental-health educator, and general guardian of the mental health of the community.

The Three Theoretical Pillars of Soviet Psychiatry

We have seen how the Soviet psychiatrist and his clinical practices are products of the collective society in which he has been reared. They are also products of the traditions of the Russian people—traditions which, even in tsarist times, stressed the importance of cooperation within the collective of the ancient *mir*, or village cooperative agricultural commune. We shall find, similarly, that the theoretical foundations upon which Soviet psychiatric practice is based arise out of a complex interaction of Russian history, tradition, culture, ideology, and the daily life experience of the Soviet people.

Russian psychiatric thinking and practice developed rather independently of Western psychiatry. From the beginning, Russian psychiatry and psychotherapy maintained a close connection with medicine and physiology. The pioneers of Russian psychotherapy, Korsakov and Bekhterev, based their concepts on the work of the Russian physiologist Sechenov, the forerunner of Pavlov. Influenced by Sechenov's researches, Korsakov regarded mental acts as very complex reflexes and believed that derangements of the normal reflex activity of the brain underlie all mental disorders. Korsakov's classical research "On a Form of Mental Disease Combined with Degenerative Polyneuritis" [8] (Korsakov's syndrome) was undertaken as part of his efforts to confirm the theory that psychopathology could be shown to be related to lesions and malfunctions of the brain and the nervous system. Bekhterev's works "Foundations of Reflexology" [9] and "Collective Reflexology" [10] stressed, in addition, the importance of social and environmental factors in the causation and treatment of mental disorders. Bekhterev emphasized the necessity for active intervention in psychotherapy, including environmental manipulation and work therapy.

The first theoretical pillar of Russian psychiatry was the doctrine that all mental disorders are caused by derangements of the normal reflex activity of the brain. Based on the pronouncements of the physiologist I. M. Sechenov [11] and applied in psychiatric research by Korsakov, it was given a solid experimental foundation by the work of Pavlov and his pupils. Devoting many years of intensive work to the most painstaking and detailed study of a relatively simple reflex in dogs, the secretion of saliva in response to the presentation of food, or in response to stimuli which had established "a temporary nervous connection" with the stimulus of the presentation of food, Pavlov and his collaborators developed a complex theoretical structure, which attempts to account physiologically for all of the so-called psychological phenomena observed in animals and man. In his later years Pavlov devoted himself to applying the theoretical principles of his system to specific clinical psychiatric illnesses in man.

THE PATHOPHYSIOLOGY OF MENTAL DISORDERS

According to Pavlov, all psychic activity of animals and man is in fact the activity of the cerebral hemispheres and of the nearest underlying subcortex. The basic unit of this "psychic" activity is the neural reflex arc, involving three parts—(1) the receptors and afferent nerves, (2) the central nervous system, and (3) the efferent nerves and effectors—just as the neural reflex arc is the basic unit of all functioning of the nervous system. Pavlov writes:

This real activity of the hemispheres and of the neighboring subcortex, which ensures for the organism as a whole a normal adaptation in its complex relations with the external world, should rightly be considered and called *the higher nervous activity*, determining the external behavior of the animal (instead of the previously used term of "psychical"), thus distinguishing this activity from that of the other parts of the brain and spinal cord, which mainly control the reciprocal relations and integration of various parts of the organism. This latter activity should be termed *the lower nervous activity.*[12]

The activity of the cerebral hemispheres and neighboring cortex which "ensures the normal adaptation of the organism to the external world" is the elaboration and mediation of conditioned reflexes. The organism is born with a number of preformed reflexes, which Pavlov calls unconditioned. Complexes or chains of these unconditioned reflexes form what are known as instincts. Pavlov at one time divided the instincts into two groups: the sex reflexes or instincts, which serve to preserve the species, and the self-preservative instincts, which serve to safeguard the individual.*

The unconditioned reflexes serve to adapt the organism to those features of the environment which are constant. They constitute the primary adaptive equipment of the organism. The adaptation of the organism to the constantly changing aspects of the environment is accomplished by the superimposition of conditioned reflexes upon the unconditioned reflexes. Pavlov defines the conditioned reflex as "a temporary nervous connection between the innumerable agents of the environment and specific activities of the organism." [13] This means that the organism now reacts not only to the original stimuli that were effective at birth (the unconditioned stimuli), but also to the myriad environmental stimuli which have established temporary connections with the unconditioned stimuli. In this way, these conditioned stimuli act as signals, representing the original unconditioned stimuli; and the capacity of the organism to interact with the environment is vastly enriched and refined as these temporary connections are constantly changed and corrected in response to changes in the environment.

The degree of successful adaptation will depend on the exquisiteness with which the making and unmaking of these "temporary connections" —the conditioned reflexes—is attuned to the environment; that is, on the accuracy and speed with which the conditioned reflexes can change in response to minute changes in stimuli coming from the environment.

Mental illness is basically a breakdown in the responsiveness of the reflex activity to changes in external reality. Breakdowns may occur in various areas of conditioned reflex activity, giving rise to different symptom complexes.

In his later years Pavlov tried to establish correlations between the known nosological psychiatric entities and specific types of breakdown of the physiology of the higher nervous activity. He did this partly by analogy with some of his experimentally produced neuroses in dogs, but mostly by direct study of human patients at the Balinsky Psychiatric Hospital in Leningrad.[14]

For example, on the basis of studies at the Balinsky Hospital, Pavlov

---

* Note the similarity to Freud's early classification of instincts. Also analogous to Freud's formulations is Pavlov's statement that "The subcortex is the source of energy for all of the higher nervous activity, while the cortex plays the role of a regulator in relation to this blind force, exquisitely controlling and restraining it. . . . In the subcortical centers are preserved traces of unusually powerful stimulations of the past, and these traces make themselves known, as soon as there is a weakening of the inhibiting effect of the cerebral cortex on the subcortical centers" (*Fiziologiia i patologiia visshei nervoi deyatelnosti* [Leningrad and Moscow: Gosmedizdat, 1930], pp. 32–33). This is very much like Freud's conception of the relationship between the ego and the id.

and his collaborators arrived at the conclusion that the individual prone
to develop hysteria has a relatively weak cerebral cortex; that is, the
cells of the cortex are easily fatigued and therefore become subject to a
protective inhibition of their activity. In this situation, the subcortical
centers are relatively free from cortical control, and the patient may be
subject to violent affective discharges and primitive motor reactions,
which take the form of hysterical attacks or fits. The high inhibitability
of the cortex creates a favorable soil for the emergence of a deep state of
hypnosis and protracted torpor. On the other hand, the highly active
subcortex may establish isolated points of excitation in the cortex. Because of the state of inhibition in most of the cortex, these isolated points
of excitation are relatively free from cortical control. This explains the
increased suggestibility and autosuggestibility of patients suffering from
hysteria. The mechanism here is similar to the one that Pavlov postulated
for hypnotic and posthypnotic suggestion, where most of the cortex is
in a state of hypnotic inhibition and the hypnotist is able to have a strong,
direct influence on isolated cortical points of excitation.

Another characteristic of persons prone to hysteria is a relative weakness of the second signaling system. Pavlov referred to two systems of
signals which were effective in producing conditioned reflexes. The first
signal system consists of the direct sensations of objects in the environment, which, as Pavlov wrote, "are for us [and for animals] the primary
signals of reality, the concrete signals." The second signal system is constituted by "speech, chiefly the kinesthetic stimulations flowing into the
cortex from the speech organs, the signals of signals. They represent in
themselves abstractions of reality and permit of generalizations, which
indeed make up our added special human mentality, creating first a general human empiricism, finally science—the instruments of the higher
orientation of the human in the environment and toward himself." [15]
The relative weakness of the second signaling system may cause it to sink
into an inhibited state. As a result, the signals of the first system, with
their imagery and concreteness, come into play with full force, producing
vivid fantasies which distort the perception of reality, with fantasy and
daydreaming, leading at times to twilight states.

The question of the triggering mechanisms that will cause a hysteria-
prone person to decompensate and develop an overt hysteria was answered in part by studying the factors which produced neuroses in dogs
in the laboratory. Pavlov and his co-workers M. K. Petrova and V. V.
Rickman found that previously healthy dogs could be made neurotic
by a variety of noxious influences, either somatic or psychogenic. The
somatic influences included experimentally induced interferences with
glandular functions, as well as artificially induced infections and in-

toxications. The psychogenic influences brought to bear on the dogs included subjecting them simultaneously to several unusual and powerful stimuli, such as an overwhelmingly loud noise, a bizarre and threatening visual image, swinging the dog violently on a special platform, etc. Very significant was the production of experimental neuroses by subjecting the dogs to conflicting stimuli, such as requiring the animal to respond to painful electrical shocks not by the normal defensive unconditioned reflex, but by a conditioned response of licking the food platter; or by subjecting the dog to excessively delicate discriminations, such as responding in one way to a circle and in an opposite way to an ellipse. In the former case the neurotic breakdown would occur when the painfulness of the shocks exceeded a certain strength; in the latter case, when the ellipse came successively closer to looking like a circle. The resulting breakdowns resembled in many ways human neuroses and psychoses, and Pavlov and his co-workers considered them as rough and simplified models of mental illness in humans.

It is worth noting that Pavlov was well aware of the connection between this work and Freud's psychoanalytic investigations. In 1935 Pavlov was visited in his laboratory by Dr. Ralph W. Gerard, an American researcher.

They were discussing his work on conditioning and especially the production of experimental "neuroses" in dogs by presenting them with a task of discrimination which was too difficult. To Dr. Gerard's surprise, Pavlov said with a twinkle, "Do you know that I was led to try these experiments by reading some of Freud's work?" He then proceeded to speak of his indebtedness to Freud for stimulating his thoughts and his experiments into this productive channel, and added that he anticipated that deeper understanding of behavior would come from a fusion of the concepts of the conditional reflex and of psychoanalysis.[16]

Another nosological entity, obsessive-compulsive neurosis, was explained by analogy to a particular type of experimental neurosis produced in dogs. Pavlov writes:

With our pathogenic techniques, by which we make the entire cortex pathological, it is also possible to produce illness in a completely isolated region of the cortex. This is an extraordinarily important and highly impressive fact. Consider a dog with a series of different acoustic conditioned stimuli: beats of a metronome, a noise, a tone, a crackling sound, a gurgling sound, etc. It is not difficult to bring about a state in which only one of all these stimuli will be pathogenic, and will evoke a sharp deviation from the normal.[17]

This "sick point" may then be characterized by a state of "pathological inertness," which means that it is no longer possible by the usual methods to extinguish the conditioned reflexes related to stimulation of this area of the cortex, and such conditioned reflexes may then persist for years. Pavlov drew an analogy between the characteristics of such a "sick point" in his experimental animals (with its isolation from the rest of the cortex and excessive stability of its pathological reactions) and obsessive phenomena in humans, which are often isolated "pathological points" in an otherwise relatively unchanged mental activity. In his work with human patients Pavlov found that obsessive-compulsive individuals demonstrate, in addition, a marked predominance of the second signal system (the verbal, intellectual aspects of the personality) over the first signal system (the sensuous, concrete, emotional aspects).

Pavlov and his co-workers carried out similar investigations of manic-depressive psychosis, paranoia, neurasthenia, psychasthenia, catatonic schizophrenia, hebephrenic schizophrenia, delirium, etc. These investigations are being continued, and have had a significant impact on the treatment of mental illness in the Soviet Union. For example, the Soviet psychotherapist invariably employs, in addition to psychotherapy, various drugs, the use of which is determined by whether there is thought to be a predominance of excitation or inhibition; whether the nervous system is in need of protective inhibition; whether roborant or tonicizing substances are indicated, etc. The use of prolonged sleep therapy is explained, on the basis of Pavlov's teachings, as providing protective inhibition to nerve cells that have been traumatized by excessive stimulation. In my observations of psychotherapy, I found that Soviet psychotherapists avoided direct confrontation or interpretations of the patient's latent negative feelings or attitudes. Instead, the therapist would find a way to give the patient a countervailing positive suggestion. It was explained to me that, in accordance with Pavlov's findings, making a patient conscious of fears and other negative feelings has an antitherapeutic effect, since it reinforces the already existing unhealthy "dominant" or pattern that has been formed in the patient's higher nervous activity; and that such negative reinforcement is particularly strong when it comes from the authoritative person of the therapist.

DIALECTICAL AND HISTORICAL MATERIALISM

Professor Yevgeny Popov, a member of the Academy of Medical Sciences of the U.S.S.R., summed up the significance of Pavlov's work for psychiatry as follows:

Thus Pavlov's teaching is important for psychiatry primarily in that it has opened before us the possibility of physiological, strictly objective investigation of the most complex cerebral phenomena which were formerly considered accessible to analysis only from the subjective psychological point of view. At the same time his discoveries prove the correctness and fruitfulness of the materialist approach to the study of the psychic and confirm that "the psychical, the mind, etc., is the highest product of matter (i.e., the physical); it is a function of that particularly complex fragment of matter called the human brain." (V. I. Lenin, *Materialism and Empirio-Criticism*, Foreign Languages Publishing House, Moscow, 1952, p. 233.)[18]

This brings us to a consideration of the second theoretical pillar of Soviet psychiatry, the philosophical orientation of dialectical materialism. The Soviet psychiatrist is very much concerned with philosophical questions. He appears to be more knowledgeable in this area than the American psychiatrist, and he maintains that a correct philosophical orientation is crucial; that an incorrect philosophical foundation must lead to distortions in psychiatric theory and practice. He attributes much of what he considers erroneous in Western psychiatric theory and practice to false "idealist" philosophical underpinnings, or to lack of philosophical clarity.

The Soviet psychiatrists with whom I worked proudly pointed out that the Russian intellectual tradition is deeply grounded in materialist philosophy; that the leading Russian intellectuals, writers, scientists, philosophers, and progressive political thinkers had for many generations engaged in an uncompromising struggle for the philosophy of materialism against the obscurantism of the tsarist regime and its philosophically idealist state religion. And to this day *diamat* (dialectical materialism) is an important subject of study in all graduate schools in the country, including schools of medicine.

The Soviet psychiatrist is, as he believes all scientists should be, philosophically a materialist. He asserts that all mental phenomena are manifestations of the activity of highly organized matter. He "struggles against" the philosophic idealists, for whom mental processes are primary; who assert that we cannot be certain of the existence of the material world and can know with certainty only our perceptions of it and our ideas about it. The Soviet psychiatrist believes in the reality and primacy of matter. He states that man's consciousness is a reflection of the real, material world, and that this world would continue to exist even if there were no one to perceive it or be conscious of it.

For example, V. N. Miasishchev writes:

Without a scientific, materialist psychology, it is impossible to solve the problem of psychogenesis and psychotherapy. Modern Soviet psychology is developing on the foundation of the general theory of dialectical and historical materialism and on the foundation of the teachings of I. P. Pavlov. It takes as its point of departure the socio-historical and natural historical understanding of man. . . . Man is not only an object, but a subject, whose consciousness reflects reality and at the same time transforms it.[19]

Soviet psychiatrists attach great value to Pavlovian conditioned reflex theory precisely because they consider it the most fruitful approach to the study of man's psyche as a complex manifestation of the activity of highly organized matter—the brain.

In emphasizing the importance of the "socio-historical understanding of man," Soviet psychiatrists often accuse Western psychiatrists, especially psychoanalysts, of being one-sidedly preoccupied with the intrapsychic conflicts of the patient, to the exclusion of social and neurophysiological factors. The Soviet psychiatrist stresses that the social structure in which the individual is born and reared is crucial in determining the way in which his neurophysiological functioning develops. For this reason, environmental manipulation plays an important role in the Soviet psychiatrist's therapeutic approaches.

INTRAPSYCHIC CONFLICTS AND DYNAMIC PSYCHOTHERAPY

In addition to Pavlovian neurophysiology and Marxian dialectical materialism, Soviet psychiatry has a third basic theoretical aspect, the study of the intrapsychic conflicts and of the personality of the patient as crucial factors in his illness. This theoretical interest is, of course, closely related to the practice of what we would call dynamic (or uncovering) psychotherapy.

Western behavioral scientists are generally under the impression that dynamic psychotherapy is not practiced in the Soviet Union. Many even have the impression that dynamic psychotherapy is proscribed there. These beliefs are probably overdetermined. A major reason is the lack of communication between Western and Soviet behavioral scientists.

A second reason for Western belief that dynamic psychotherapy is not practiced or even tolerated in the Soviet Union is the well-known opposition, even hostility, of Soviet psychiatry to psychoanalysis as a theory of human personality and as a healing art.

A third reason is the fact that until recently very little could be found in the Russian neuropsychiatric journals about dynamic psychotherapy. Joseph Wortis' comprehensive study *Soviet Psychiatry*,[20] which was published in 1950, and Bruno Lustig's excellent surveys of Soviet psychiatry, published in 1955[21] and 1957,[22] leave the reader with the distinct impression that Russian psychiatrists employ somatic treatments almost exclusively, and that what little psychotherapy is practiced consists of hypnosis, suggestion, and similar techniques.

In the course of my three sojourns in the Soviet Union, I learned that dynamic psychotherapy is a living and growing entity there. I met psychotherapists who had practiced and taught this type of psychotherapy for many years. Many of them were familiar with Western writings on the subject.

That the interest in dynamic psychotherapy is growing is attested to by the appearance in recent years of such books as V. N. Miasishchev's *Personality and the Neuroses*,[23] a collection of articles that had been published between 1935 and 1960; *Problems of Psychotherapy of Functional Disorders in the Sexual Sphere in Medical Practice*, by Professor N. V. Ivanov, of Gorky; [24] contributions on "Psychotherapy Today" by A. D. Zurabashvili, of Tbilisi, and others; [25] *Problems of Psychotherapy*, edited by M. S. Lebedinsky, of Moscow; [26] *The Neuroses and Their Treatment*, by A. M. Sviadosh, of Karaganda, Kazakhstan; [27] *The Word as a Physiological and Therapeutic Factor*, by K. I. Platonov, of Kharkov; [28] and *Essays on Psychotherapy*, by M. S. Lebedinsky.[29]

The fact that the authors of these works are among the best-known and most highly regarded psychiatrists in the Soviet Union, and that they head institutes in such widely scattered places as Leningrad, Moscow, Gorky, Tbilisi (Georgia), Kharkov (Ukraine), and Karaganda (Kazakhstan), indicates that dynamic psychotherapy is not a localized, limited phenomenon in the Soviet Union.

Furthermore, F. V. Bassin, a leading Soviet theoretician, wrote an article in a volume issued in 1963 by the Institute of Philosophy of the Academy of Sciences of the U.S.S.R. in which, while criticizing psychoanalysis, he urges Soviet investigators to pay more attention to studies of the unconscious. He writes:

The study of the unconscious has for a long time not been given the attention which corresponds to the important role played by these peculiar manifestations of mental activity. This underestimation of the theory of unconscious psychic processes appears to have been an exaggerated, and therefore inadequate, reaction to the pseudoscientific character that was attached to the theory of "the Unconscious" by idealistic philosophy and by Freudism. As a result of this, the correct development of these important problems was held back for many years. Only now are we beginning to appreciate the damage caused to both theory and clinical practice by this unwarranted aloofness of dialectico-materialistically oriented investigators from the scientific examination of an important category of psychic and nervous processes.[30]

The interest in dynamic psychotherapy is not just a recent development. As early as 1937, V. N. Miasishchev and Y. K. Iakovleva published a paper in a leading psychoneurological journal about the psychogenesis of visceral disorders, in which they included a great many case histories, dating back over a period of many years, illustrating their technique of "pathogenetic psychotherapy." [31]

"Pathogenetic psychotherapy" was developed and taught at the Bekhterev Psychoneurological Research Institute in Leningrad by Vladimir Nikolayevich Miasishchev, a pupil of Bekhterev. In the later years of the Stalin regime, with the increase in repression, rigidity, and dogmatism, Miasishchev and the Bekhterev Institute were subjected to severe criticism, and even the threat of purge. Fortunately, psychiatry was spared until the famous "joint session of the two academies" (the Academy of Sciences of the U.S.S.R. and the Academy of Medical Sciences of the U.S.S.R.) of June–July, 1950, at which Soviet medicine and psychiatry were severely criticized for not applying the teachings of Pavlov rigidly enough to their disciplines.

In a recent book Professor Miasishchev alludes to this period as follows:

Branded as anti-Pavlovian fabrications were any criticisms of dogmatism or any proposals that all elements of the organism and the various levels of the nervous system be taken into consideration in studying the regulation of the activities of the organism, without one-sided biologizing and without underestimation of social conditions. The ruling orientation in the 1950's not only did not further the development of the physiology and pathophysiology of the nervous system, but it alienated and pushed aside realistically thinking theoreticians and clinicians from the ideas of nervism, and inflicted substantial damage to the development of a unified theory of medicine.[32]

Since Stalin died in 1953, and the process of "de-Stalinization" began almost immediately after Stalin's death, the onslaught on psychiatry was of relatively brief duration. Fairly soon voices began to be heard calling for a liberalization of attitudes. For example, Professor F. V. Bassin stated at a conference that scientific work had been adversely affected

by the general conditions created by the cult of Stalin's personality. This bred dogmatism in the social and natural sciences, an uncritical attitude toward scientific authorities, and the resort to meaningless quotations as a substitute for independent research. Instead of solving scientific problems in an atmosphere of free discussion among competent specialists, the declaration of theoretical postulates became more or less the rule.[33]

Professor Bassin deplored the neglect of psychology and the overemphasis on biology. He criticized the neglect of other approaches, such as cybernetics, information theory, and psychopharmacology, and stated:

The theory of the higher nervous activity should not be considered as the only possible method for the study of the functions of the higher regions of the nervous system. Other approaches to the problem must also be used. . . . Both method and theory should be developed not only through a variety of disciplines, but also on the basis of diversified positions and from the point of view of diverse trends.[34]

In a recent article, three leading Soviet theoreticians declare that

to "reduce" the manifestations of consciousness to their physiological foundations, whether we are dealing with psychopathology or psychology, is in principle unacceptable. The concept that physiological factors are *general* but not *specific* determinants of consciousness is made evident, for example, by all the data of contemporary psychopharmacology.[35]

And they conclude:

For all these reasons, it is out of the question to attribute an exhaustive explanatory role to the physiological factors in elucidating *all* the aspects of consciousness.[36]

Along with this liberalization of thought has come a greater understanding and tolerance for Western psychiatric works and a marked diminution in dogmatic criticism of them. For example, *Meditsinskii rabotnik* of May 25, 1962, reported that a high-level committee of psychiatrists

noted that name-calling and labeling in the past had unfortunately discouraged theoretical discussion, and that this must now be avoided at all costs. . . . One of the members, Dr. B. I. Smulevich, held that the attitude toward foreign scientists was incorrect. They were being portrayed either as reactionaries or as vulgarizers of science. They are, however, often honest scientists who are seeking correct answers. Since it would be difficult for them to suddenly think along materialist lines, a friendly, tactful attitude should be taken toward them, and their work should be analyzed and criticized with conscientious accuracy.

An indication that this new spirit still prevails is a recent review in the *S. S. Korsakov Journal of Neuropathology and Psychiatry* of the book by Redlich and Friedman, *The Theory and Practice of Psychiatry*. The reviewer writes:

The problems of the incidence, forms, clinical study, and treatment of drug addiction and alcoholism are given an interesting and, in connection with specific practical requirements, a more detailed exposition than in Soviet textbooks.

Although the approach of the authors to "the theory and practice of psychiatry," to the clinical study of psychic illnesses, their pathogenesis and treatment, is in many ways different from the positions of Soviet psychiatry, we believe that Soviet readers will with interest acquaint themselves with this serious and informative work. This book gives an objective and full presentation of the currents and views which prevail in contemporary American psychiatry, and is an example of an interpretation of psychic disorders which differs from ours, but which is integrated and consistent. The authors obviously have mastery over the entire many-sided experience of the scientific study of the psychoses, although this experience is subjected to a one-sided interpretation.[37]

This new, flexible orientation of Soviet theory has vindicated the various schools of dynamic psychotherapy in the Soviet Union, and has given impetus to their continuing development.

The basic approach of one of these schools, "pathogenetic psycho-therapy" (whose work I observed), is summed up by Professor Yekat-erina K. Iakovleva of the Bekhterev Institute as follows:

The pathophysiological mechanism of psychasthenia and obsessive-com-pulsive states is elucidated by the works of I. P. Pavlov and his school. However, the clinical investigation of these states, as of other neuro-psychiatric illnesses, *requires a knowledge not only of their pathophysio-logical basis, but also of the specific characteristics of the personality, its conscious relations, and other aspects of the psyche. Only by taking these into account can we understand the pathogenesis of the illness and work out a rational system of treatment.*

The basic method in treating these illnesses is psychotherapy, combined with somatotherapy. Experience shows that the most effective method of psychotherapy is deep or rational psychotherapy, a system which, in con-tradistinction to other authors (Dubois, Freud, and others), stems from an investigation of the real life history of the patient and his experiences, and has the aim of restructuring the interpersonal relations and helping the individual toward a constructive resolution of his life problems. [Emphasis added.] [38]

However, the flavor of Soviet dynamic psychotherapy can be com-municated best by presenting a complete case history, exactly as it was written by the therapist, Professor Iakovleva.

Case History

Patient C., a 24-year-old woman engineer, has been suffering for two years with a "phobia" of a bad odor emanating from her own person. Because of this fear she stopped work, stopped associating with people, and even stopped going out of the house, since she smelled everywhere an unpleasant odor which she ascribed to herself. During the years of illness she developed a habit of sniffing the air. As a result her sense of smell became extraordinarily acute.

The patient was unable to state the causes of her illness. She only noted that she first sensed the bad odor in a movie theater, but at that time she did not yet attribute it to herself. On the following day, in the auditorium of the institute, among her fellow students, she again smelled the odor, decided it emanated from herself, and immediately left. After that she began to observe herself intensely, stopped attending lectures, went to the institute only for examinations. After graduating with difficulty, she began to work, but soon had to quit because of the odor which followed her. No treatment helped, and because of suspicion of emotional illness, the patient was sent to Leningrad, to the Bekhterev Institute.

She was born into the family of a white-collar worker. Healthy child. No infections. No pathological heredity. Until the age of eight she was the only child; mother's entire attention was concentrated on her. She studied at public school and in a school of music. She had great success everywhere. The family considered her capable, gifted. On graduation from school she entered an industrial institute. During the siege of Leningrad, she was evacuated with her mother and younger brother to Omsk. She experienced many difficulties, including malnutrition. There were many tragic experiences—she lost her brother, who died of dysentery, and her father and younger sister, who had remained in occupied territory. However, she managed to cope with these difficulties, and continued her studies at the institute. At the age of twenty-two, while still in Omsk, she married a soldier. Her husband left for the front the day after the marriage. She took his departure very hard, and she cried a great deal when she was informed that he had been wounded. On his discharge from the hospital, the husband unexpectedly announced he would not return to her. This news shook the patient.

Objectively: The patient is somewhat asthenic, pale. No pathological findings in the internal organs and nervous system. Consciousness clear. Intellect good. Conduct completely adequate. Emotional reactions lively, but mood somewhat depressed because of her condition, which she finds hard to bear. The idea of the odor emanating from her is persistent, not yielding to correction at first; but her critical attitude toward it is preserved, although at times she experiences doubts and ambivalence toward her pathological idea.

In the hospital she kept herself isolated; avoided association with patients. She is rather tense, and constantly sniffs the air.

In view of the peculiarity of the patient's symptom, Professor I. K. Ziuzin proposed a series of experiments to investigate the acuteness of her sense of smell. It turned out to be amazingly acute, e.g., the patient distinguished the odor of spirits of camphor in a dilution of 1 to 50,000, and with some uncertainty in a dilution of 1 to 100,000. With closed eyes she could distinguish to whom a pair of gloves belonged, after having smelled the hands of various people, a feat that no one else could duplicate.

Worthy of attention also is the sharply slowed-up smell adaptation of the patient and the easy establishment of previously perceived odors under the influence of the stimulation of other sensory organs. Such a change in perception in the patient in connection with pathogenic conditions is interesting. If we conjecture that, according to anamnestic data, the patient's olfactory functions had in the past not been unusual, and if we associate with this the fact that since her illness she tensely sniffs the air, then we can appreciate the dependence of our functions upon our attitude toward them, and upon the mobilization of alerted attention (dependence on cortical influences).

For the understanding of the pathogenesis of the given illness, the first anamnestic information communicated by the patient was, naturally, insufficient. However, in psychotherapeutic conversations with the patient, directing her attention, we succeeded in obtaining essential additional information which clarified the genesis of the symptom. A detailed study of the conditions of her upbringing showed that despite their apparent normality, there really obtained a series of unfavorable influences which had considerable significance in the formation of the patient's relation to herself and to the surrounding reality. It became clear that after the birth of her younger sister, the patient, who until then had been the idol of the family, was quickly pushed into the background. The patient's mother, who was very unstable and emotional, displaced all of her attention to her second daughter from the moment of her birth. She openly began to value the younger daughter more highly than the older, frequently telling everyone that the younger was better, smarter, and prettier; and even, according to the patient, frequently calling the patient, in the presence of others, an idiot. The younger sister, as she grew up, gradually adopted the same attitude toward the patient.

It appears that this entire childhood period, about which the patient at the beginning had given no information, was full of unpleasant, degrading experiences for her because of the mother's attitude toward her. At the beginning, the mother, praising her and being ecstatic over her, developed in her a striving for distinction, toward a heightened self-evaluation; later, the mother began sharply to emphasize her shortcomings, and this made the little girl reserved and withdrawn. The patient recalls that early in life she was a happy, attractive little girl who loved noisy games, dances; later, she became serious. Deciding, in accordance with the mother's evaluation, that she was ugly, and therefore would never marry, the patient became completely absorbed in her studies. She became an outstanding student in the university, and this, according to the patient, completely compensated her, so that she considered herself, in spite of the series of hardships, quite healthy.

A serious psychic trauma, which served as the source of her breakdown, was produced by her marriage. She was married at age twenty-two, while in the evacuation, to a man whom she knew very little, but who at the beginning demonstrated great persistence in courting her. At first the patient did not want to marry because he was beneath her culturally, and her mother did not like him; but, feeling a powerful sexual attraction to him, she registered a marriage with him against her mother's wishes.

The first night of the marriage was, according to the patient's admission, a source of difficult, unpleasant experiences. Finding herself in the same room with her mother, she was very embarrassed by her presence; and so, in spite of her great sexual excitement, she was very reserved with her husband, avoiding his endearments and his attempts to approach her. The husband, irritated by her attitude and not understanding the reasons, made many coarse remarks to her, and, turning toward the wall, fell asleep. This deeply offended the patient. On the following day he left for the army. The patient changed markedly from that night on. Again there appeared her feeling of low self-esteem, which had previously been compensated by her successes at the institute. She felt herself pitiful, insignificant, "worse than the others." It oppressed her that her mother had witnessed her degradation. It was painful to hear her mother's recriminations about her thoughtless marriage. But along with these experiences of degradation, there increased steadily her awakened sexual attraction to her husband. During the two months after his departure, she was in a constant state of excitement—she waited for his letters, often went to the post office, cried a great deal. It became clear that it was precisely during this period that her sensation that she was producing an odor became manifest.

How did this symptom develop?

In order to determine this, it was necessary to clarify all of the preceding life situations and the patient's reactions to them, as well as to know the peculiarities of her personality. In conversations with the patient, there gradually emerged a series of facts which she had not previously communicated because, in her opinion, they had no relation to the illness. However, these facts helped us to achieve a deeper insight into the genesis of the symptom.

The patient perceived the odor for the first time in the movie theater, where it was stuffy, crowded, and where the air was indeed saturated with all kinds of odors. There, the patient related, she sat next to a young man, a neighbor in their apartment, who began to declare his love for her. She too, at the moment, felt a powerful attraction, which she was afraid to acknowledge, even to herself. On the following day, while she was sitting at table among her fellow students, the thought occurred to her that she could still be attractive to young men. At this point, she again became sexually excited, but then immediately there appeared the fear that she might give herself away. At this time she suddenly smelled an odor exactly the same as in the movie theater, which she now attributed to herself, and, feeling deeply ashamed, she left. We can conjecture that at this moment there developed in her a conditional connection between sexual excitement and the odor. On the following day she began to seat herself at a distance from everybody, to avoid association with her fellow students, because as soon as young men came near her, she experienced a certain agitation in her stomach, and she began to perceive that same odor. Because of her fear of this odor, which it seemed to her now emanated from her, she finally stopped attending the institute, and later left her work.

In conversations with the patient it was established that the events in the movie theater showed her the possibility for satisfying her sexual drive; the patient saw that she could be pleasing to a young man; but these events at the same time called forth a need to suppress her sexual feeling. In accordance with the moral standards that she set for herself, she considered it impossible to establish a liaison with another man while she was married. The development of this viewpoint, as was shown by a study of her concrete life story, was furthered by the authority of her father, who always severely criticized "moral looseness," and who even broke off his friendship with his best friend when he found out that the latter had left his family. As the patient later explained, her awakened sexual feelings were extremely unpleasant to her; she felt a revulsion against herself for having such an "animal instinct."

Further questioning clarified still another series of circumstances which explained why the patient developed specifically a phobia of odors. Alongside of what has already been presented, the patient communicated the following information about herself: Not long before her marriage, there lived with her family for two weeks a cousin, a very slovenly man, who importunately pressed her with his love. His overtures seemed to her "an animal excitement"; his bad odor was unpleasant to her, and elicited feelings of revulsion in her. In addition, her previous landlady had suffered from flatus, but continued to go out socially. In the patient's words, she was very embarrassed by the conduct of this woman. It seemed to her that with such a defect it was impossible to be among people.

All these conditions reinforced the pathological temporal connection, and strengthened her notion about the impossibility of being among people because of the unpleasant odor she gave forth. But her absenting herself from society, especially from the company of men, because of her fear that her odor would expose her sexual excitement, "like an animal's," naturally did not resolve the contradictions which had arisen. On the contrary, these contradictions kept growing stronger since, being a passionate woman, she had a great urge for male company, and she therefore had to make ever greater efforts to struggle against these strivings.

In this case history . . . we are presenting schematically those data about the development of the illness and the formation of the symptom which in reality became clear only gradually in the course of acquainting ourselves with the concrete life story of the patient.

At the beginning of the treatment with psychotherapy, she did not connect the symptoms of her illness with the circumstances enumerated above. Gradually, however, in connection with the ever greater uncovering of the sources of the development of the "sick point," she began to clarify and to understand the connection between her symptom and her experiences. The conflict between her sexual excitation and the striving to suppress it because of her moralistic attitudes then became clear. As she became aware of the connection between her symptom and her experiences, her pathological state began gradually to be eliminated. The patient began to associate with other patients, began to go into the "Red Corner," and even to participate in the evening amateur theatricals of the patients. She also stopped sniffing the air. Gradually the symptoms faded and finally completely disappeared. The patient was discharged in good condition.

Further observations showed that she continued well, associated with people, went back to work, and, significantly, her sense of smell, which had become acute during her illness, became normal. Two years after the therapy the patient remarried, gave birth normally, continues to work at her specialty, and there is no trace of her previous illness.

In conclusion, we can say that the precipitating factor in the development of the illness was the unsuccessful marriage, which turned out to be the source of a complicated inner conflict. In the development of the illness, there played a role, on the one hand, the patient's entire past life experience, the attitudes which she had toward herself and toward the questions of friendship, love, marriage, and morals; and on the other hand, the awakened powerful sexual drive. As a result of the conflict which developed, there was established an emotional overstrain which weakened her nervous activity. On the basis of such a weakened "prepared" foundation, the patient at this period developed a phobic symptom as a pathological conditioned reflex. The patient's lack of understanding of the essence of the conflict furthered the reinforcement of the developing symptom. Only the uncovering of the true causes of the illness in the process of psychotherapy, the elucidation, with the help of the doctor, of the connection of the phobic symptom with her complex experiences, helped the patient to become aware of the sources of her conflict, and rationally to evaluate the situation that had developed. Psychotherapy structured along these lines brought about the cure of the neurosis.[39]

Notes

1. Robert S. Gill, "Publisher's Foreword" to Joseph Wortis, *Soviet Psychiatry* (Baltimore: Williams & Wilkins Co., 1950), pp. vii–viii.

2. Yevgeny A. Popov, "Znachenie rabot I. P. Pavlova v oblasti psikhiatrii," in Ivan P. Pavlov, *Psikhopatologiia i psikhiatriia* (Moscow: Academy of Medical Sciences of the U.S.S.R., 1949), pp. 213–14.

3. A. M. Sviadosh, *Nevrozy i ich lechenie* (Moscow: Medgiz, 1959), p. 25.

4. Boris A. Lebedev, "Principles and Systems of Organization of Psychiatric Care in the Soviet Union" (in Russian) (in press).

5. Vladimir N. Miasishchev, *Lichnost i nevrozy* (Leningrad: Leningrad University Press, 1960), p. 379.

6. V. A. Giliarovsky, in Lydia Bogdanovich, *Zapisky psikhiatra* (Moscow: Medgiz, 1959), p. 5.

7. Miasishchev, *Lichnost i nevrozy*, p. 378.

8. Sergei S. Korsakov, *Kurs psikhiatrii*, 2nd ed. (Moscow, 1901).

9. Vladimir M. Bekhterev, *Obshchie osnovy refleksologii cheloveka* (Petrograd, 1917).

10. Bekhterev, *Kollektivnaia refleksologiia* (Petrograd, 1921).

11. Ivan M. Sechenov, "Refleksy golovnovo mozga," *Meditsinskii vestnik*, 1863, nos. 47–48.

12. Pavlov, "Fiziologiia visshei nervnoi deyatelnosti," in *Complete Works* (in Russian) (Moscow and Leningrad, 1951), vol. 3, bk. 2, pp. 219–34; paper read at the International Physiological Congress in Rome, September 2, 1932.

13. *Ibid.*

14. Akademiia Nauk SSSR, *Pavlovskie sredy* (Moscow and Leningrad, 1949), vols. 1–3.

15. Pavlov, *Conditioned Reflexes and Psychiatry* (New York: International Publishers, 1941), p. 93.

16. Lawrence S. Kubie, "Pavlov, Freud and Soviet Psychiatry," as quoted by Zigmond M. Lebensohn in *Pavlovian Conditioning and American Psychiatry*, Symposium no. 9, March, 1964 (New York: Group for the Advancement of Psychiatry, 1964), pp. 202–203.

17. Pavlov, *Eksperimentalnaia patologiia visshei nervnoi deyatelnosti* (Leningrad: Biomedgiz, 1935).

18. Popov, "Pavlov's Physiological Teaching and Psychiatry," in Pavlov, *Psychopathology and Psychiatry* (Moscow: Foreign Languages Publishing House, 1961), p. 422.

19. Miasishchev, "Nekotorye voprosy teorii psikhoterapii," in *Voprosy psikhoterapii*, ed. Mark S. Lebedinsky (Moscow: Medgiz, 1958), pp. 7–8.

20. Joseph Wortis, *Soviet Psychiatry* (Baltimore: Williams & Wilkins Co., 1950).

21. Bruno Lustig, *Die Sowjetische Psychiatrie*, Berichte des Osteuropa-Instituts an der Freien Universität Berlin (Berlin, 1955), vol. 17.

22. Lustig, *New Research in Soviet Psychiatry*, Medical Series of the Reports of the Osteuropa Institute of the Berlin Free University, no. 14 (Berlin, 1957). English translation in mimeographed form.

23. Miasishchev, *Lichnost i nervozy*.

24. Nikolai V. Ivanov, *Voprosy psikhoterapii funktzionalnich rasstroistv polovoi sferi vo vrachnebnoi praktike* (Moscow: Ministry of Health of the R.S.F.S.R., 1961).

25. A. D. Zurabashvili, "Psikhoterapiia sevodnia," *Aktualnye voprosy psikhiatrii i nevropatologii*, ed. G. V. Morozov (Moscow: Ministry of Health of the U.S.S.R., 1963).

26. Lebedinsky, ed., *Voprosy psikhoterapii*.

27. Sviadosh, *Nevrozy i ich lechenie*.

28. Konstantin I. Platonov, *The Word as a Physiological and Therapeutic Factor* (Moscow: Foreign Languages Publishing House, 1959).

29. Lebedinsky, *Ocherky psikhoterapii* (Moscow: Medgiz, 1959).

30. Filip V. Bassin, "Soznanie i 'bessoznatelnoie,'" in *Filosofskye voprosy fiziologii visshei nervnoi deyatelnosti i psikhologii* (Moscow: Izdatelstvo Akademii Nauk SSSR, 1963), pp. 425–26.

31. Vladimir N. Miasishchev and Yekaterina K. Iakovleva, "O psikhogennykh vistzeralnykh narushenniakh," *Sovetskaia psikhonevrologiia*, 13, no. 3: 17–28.

32. Miasishchev, "O razlitchnykh formakh sviazy psikhogennykh i somatogennykh narushenii kak aktualnoi problemi meditzini," in *Nevrozy i somaticheskie rasstroistva* (Leningrad, 1966), p. 3.

33. Bassin, in *Meditsinskii rabotnik,* June 12, 1962, as quoted in Wortis, "A 'Thaw' in Soviet Psychiatry?" *American Journal of Psychiatry,* 119, no. 6 (December, 1962): 586.

34. *Ibid.*

35. S. A. Sarkissov, F. V. Bassin, and V. M. Banshchikov, "Problème du rôle des conceptions neurophysiologiques en psychopathologie," *Revue de Médecine Psychosomatique,* 7, no. 1 (1965): 69–70.

36. *Ibid.*

37. E. Ya. Sternberg, review of F. C. Redlich and D. K. Freedman, *The Theory and Practice of Psychiatry, Zhurnal nevropatologii i psikhiatrii imeni S. S. Korsakova,* 67, no. 8 (August, 1967): 1262.

38. Iakovleva, *Patogenez i terapiia nevroza naviazchivikh sostoyanii i psikhastenii* (Leningrad: Bekhterev Psychoneurological Research Institute, 1958), pp. 135–37.

39. *Ibid.,* pp. 104–110.

X : Linguistics

Structural Linguistics in the Soviet Union

William R. Schmalstieg

In the recent history of Soviet linguistics a more epoch-making date than that of the death of Stalin was June 20, 1950, when Stalin himself dethroned the linguistic theories of Nikolai Iakovlevich Marr in an article in *Pravda*.[1] Political considerations, of course, had prepared the way for this switch in linguistic direction. Marr's theories presupposed that all languages were somehow related. But during World War II it had been necessary to promote the unity of the Slavic peoples.[2] For this reason, from the beginning of the war Slavic comparative linguistics had been rehabilitated, and existed side by side with Marrist linguistics until 1950. At about this time the Caucasian philologist A. Chikobava, having had an argument with some highly placed Marrist linguists, felt himself threatened by them and initiated an attack on Marrism with an article in the May 9 issue of *Pravda*.[3] This was followed by a spate of pro and con articles until the celebrated June 20 article by Stalin, after which those linguists who had supported Marrism recanted in letters to the editor of *Pravda*. Whatever one may think of Stalin as a dictator, his criticisms of Marrist linguistic theory contain a certain amount of

I wish to thank my colleagues Professor Thomas F. Magner and Professor Joseph Paternost for their helpful comments on this paper. I myself am solely responsible for its contents.

common sense. Consider the following quotation from Stalin: "N. Ia. Marr arrogantly dismissed any attempt to study groups [families] of languages as a manifestation of the theory of 'protolanguage.' It cannot be denied, however, that language kinship, for example, of such nations as the Slavs, is beyond dispute, that the study of the linguistic kinship of these nations could be of great benefit to linguistics in studying the laws of development of language." [4] Actually, of course, Stalin proposed nothing new in linguistics, but merely a return to the older well-established forms of linguistic thought of western Europe of the end of the nineteenth century. Cornelius H. van Schooneveld says that the adjective most appropriate to describe the official Soviet linguistic doctrine as formulated by Stalin in 1950 is "neogrammarian." [5] (*Webster's Third New International Dictionary* [p. 1516] defines a neogrammarian as "one of a school of philologists arising in Germany about 1875, advocating the more exact formulation of phonetic law and its more rigid application to linguistic phenomena, maintaining that phonetic laws admit no real exceptions, and recognizing analogy as a normal factor in linguistic change.")

After the overthrow of Marr, the periodical *Problems in Linguistics* (*Voprosy iazykoznaniia*) was established in 1952 as the chief organ of publication for the best articles of Soviet linguists, and indeed it has remained such until the present day. The lead article of the first issue, "The Tasks of Soviet Linguistics in the Light of the Works of J. V. Stalin and the Periodical 'Problems in Linguistics,'" begins with attacks on various Western linguists, who are censured for being structuralists. The chief fault of structural linguistics, according to the authors of this article, is that it is antihistorical, it separates thought from language and language from the history of the people.[6] Antihistoricalism is the banner of idealism of foreign linguistics. Thus, for example, the celebrated Danish linguist Louis Hjelmslev is reproached for affirming that the existence of the verb in the most varied languages allows us to suppose that the verb is a category which is characteristic of human languages in general. In addition to attacking linguists, the article assails Charles Morris, Rudolph Carnap, and Stuart Chase. These latter are charged with clever sophistry the goal of which is the separation of the content and logical meaning of concepts from the objective world. Having "destroyed" all the bourgeois Western linguists and philosophers, the authors proceed to demolish Marr and then get down to the tasks of Soviet linguistics. Soviet linguists should, the article insists, occupy themselves with all aspects of the study of Eastern languages, the stylistics of all languages, the alphabets of the non-Slavic population of the U.S.S.R., the psychology of child language learning, the writing of new textbooks on

linguistics that would be free of Marrist dogma, and the reformation of
the teaching of linguistics. Finally, all the aims of Soviet linguistics are
"subject to one main goal—to inculcate Marxism into the science of
language, to make Soviet linguistics worthy of the great Stalinist
epoch." [7]

The first volume of *Problems in Linguistics* contains articles such as
the following: "Elements of the Comparative-Historical Method in In-
dology"; "The Development of the Languages and Writing System of
the Peoples of the U.S.S.R."; "Linguistic Geography and the History
of the Russian Language"; "Concerning the Problem of Parts of Speech
in the Altaic Languages"; and so on.[8] The major defect of these articles
is an adherence to the "cult of personality": there is a clear overabun-
dance of references to Stalin. Otherwise we find solid, although in most
cases pedestrian and unimaginative, articles typical of traditional comparative-historical linguistics.

In spite of criticism of American descriptive linguistics, there was apparently some interest in it even in 1952. I refer to the article "A Criticism of Bourgeois Linguistics: Concerning the Method of Linguistic
Research of the American Structuralists," an article that in my opinion
contains some valid criticism of positivism in American linguistics.[9] But
the conclusion of this article reads:

> The research methods worked out by American structuralists cannot
> find an application in Soviet linguistics. A study of their works is necessary
> and important for the discovery of their essential characteristics, for
> the clarification of their antiscientific character, and as a means of guarding
> against mistakes. . . . In our science the perfected system of Marxist lin-
> guistics created by J. V. Stalin unshakably opposes all the sophistries and
> twists of contemporary bourgeois positivists.[10]

It is interesting to note that this same author, Olga S. Akhmanova, in her
review of *Current Trends in Linguistics* (see note 2), where she takes
offense at certain of the comments on Soviet linguistics, says:

> If regular scholarly exchange is our objective, we should begin by
> carefully eliminating from our writing all that may engender bitter feelings,
> offend, or occasion emotional discomfiture. It is true that, to the Soviet
> scientist, politics is a continuously present concern; the political life of a
> nation has a direct bearing on the development of science on its soil.[11]

It seems possible to me that Akhmanova's earlier characterization of the
work of American structuralist linguists as having an "antiscientific character" might have engendered bitterness or occasioned emotional discomfiture among them, if indeed it were taken seriously. The very title
of one of her articles, "The Glossematics of Louis Hjelmslev as a Mani-

festation of the Decadence of Contemporary Bourgeois Linguistics," might be expected to call forth at least a small degree of emotional discomfiture among the followers of this famous Danish structuralist.[12] But it is clearly unfair for me to compare Akhmanova's articles of the early fifties with those of 1965. One might even doubt the sincerity of the apparent anti-Western attitude of many Soviet scholars and ascribe their anti-Western statements to the exigencies of the survival code in Communist eastern Europe. In the past, failure to show evidence of the appropriate antibourgeois reflexes could well have led to disaster for a scholarly career. Thus Soviet scholars interested in Western linguistics at that time are worthy of praise for their courage in studying such a potentially dangerous topic rather than blame for their negative statements about it. Essentially such scholars have served to bring Western linguistic thought to the attention of the wider Soviet scholarly public.

The death of Stalin in March of 1953 had no immediate effect on Soviet linguistics. Thus in the last number of the 1954 issue of *Problems in Linguistics* there appeared an article entitled "Stalin—The Great Continuator of the Cause of Lenin." [13] This article was in honor of the seventy-fifth anniversary of the birth of Stalin on December 21, 1879. According to this brief laudatory statement, Stalin benefited linguistic science by defeating Marrism completely and by doing away with the mechanical approach to the separate formulas and conclusions of Marxism. "The works of J. V. Stalin are a model of creative development of the Marxist-Leninist theory. All his life and work are a shining example of self-sacrificing service to the people, the Communist party, and the socialist government." [14] The articles continue pretty much in the same vein as in previous issues. An interesting example for Americans is the article "E. Sapir and 'Ethnolinguistics': Concerning One of the Reactionary Conceptions in Contemporary American Linguistics." [15] In this article we read:

Ethnolinguistics had its origin in the study of the numerous Indian languages and was shaped in recent decades by racist ethnography and anthropology. The work of Sapir on questions of ethnography, his preoccupation with reactionary conceptions of ethnopsychology, and finally the transfer of "patterning" into the field of ethnographic investigations, where it received a purely racist use . . . all this helped to unify this linguistic trend with contemporary American ethnography and put a specific stamp on the later investigations of Sapir and his students.[16]

The article ends with the statement that ethnolinguistics is closely allied with general semantics, which is a typical product of the pseudoscience of the contemporary bourgeois world.

Khrushchev's speech denouncing Stalin at the 20th Congress of the Communist party had a very salutary effect on the development of Soviet linguistics. As a consequence of this speech and the subsequent dethronement of Stalin, an extremely important editorial entitled "Concerning Certain Current Tasks of Soviet Linguistics" was published in *Problems in Linguistics*.[17] This editorial criticizes many of the earlier articles that had appeared on its pages, and which reportedly contained mistaken evaluations of foreign linguists. Thus, for example, ". . . the great American linguist E. Sapir was accused, without foundation in fact, of propagating racism. But it is well known that Sapir stubbornly fought against anti-Semitism and all manifestations of racial discrimination in the U.S.A. and other capitalistic countries." [18] The editorial praises Sapir as an investigator of North American Indian languages and as one who frequently spoke out against the erroneous identification of race and language. Thus although Sapir's work may contain erroneous idealistic philosophical views, according to the editorial it does contain many valuable linguistic conclusions and generalizations made from a careful analysis of the facts of a large variety of languages from different families. There have been similar mistakes regarding the evaluation of other foreign linguists, but more importantly there are problems of Soviet linguistics that cannot be solved without using the experience of foreign linguists.

The crucial factor in this change of direction in linguistics was the sixth five-year plan, according to which special attention was to be directed at the production of electronic computers and devices for machine translation. The editorial notes that a requirement for the quickest possible creation of such devices is the solution of a number of purely linguistic problems, the most important of which is the reduction of the grammar of a language to a system of rules expressed by a definite code. The study of methods of structural linguistics and mathematical logic is necessary to attain this goal. The editorial is careful to say, however, that the fact that certain methods of structural analysis of language help in the creation and use of electronic translating machines should not be construed as a justification for the principles of structuralism. Nevertheless, the editorial concludes with a call for more articles that would show the respective merits and deficiencies of structural linguistics. It is with this editorial that Soviet linguistics began its present course, a course bringing it into increasing contact with the West and in fact almost internationalizing Soviet linguistic thought.

The editors of *Problems in Linguistics* did not issue their call for more articles on structural linguistics in vain, for in the very next issue

S. K. Shaumian published a study entitled "Concerning the Essence of Structural Linguistics." [19] This article contains a brief but well-balanced account of structural linguistics, which is traced back to De Saussure (1857–1913), who is said to have been the first to recognize that for the study of linguistics it is not the sounds and meaning of a language that are of primary importance, but rather the relationships between the sounds and meanings. This network of relationships is a system or a structure. According to Shaumian, N. S. Trubetskoi (1890–1938) clarified the concept of relationship by radically reworking the doctrine of the phoneme of the brilliant Polish-Russian linguist Baudouin de Courtenay (1845–1929). (The well-known fact that Trubetskoi was an émigré Russian prince who taught at the University of Vienna until his death is not mentioned in any of the Soviet accounts that I have seen.)

Shaumian says that the rapid development of structural linguistics began in 1929 when the Linguistic Circle of Prague, headed by N. S. Trubetskoi, published its first volume. Copenhagen became the second great center of structural linguistics, and the third center was the United States, where the representatives of the so-called descriptive linguistic school founded by Leonard Bloomfield joined the structuralists. Essentially there are three contemporary schools of structural linguistics: the Prague school, the Copenhagen school, and the American school.

The increasing interest in structuralism became clear with the publication of the 1957 volume of *Problems in Linguistics*, in which we find a multitude of articles with such titles as "A Discussion of Questions of Structuralism and Syntagmatic Theory"; "Structural Linguistics, Semantics, and Problems of Word Study"; "Toward an Evaluation of Structural Linguistics"; "What is Structuralism?"; "A Few Remarks about Structuralism"; etc.[20] It is noteworthy that the author of the last named article remarks that the great deterrent to the development of linguistics in the Soviet Union in the past was dogmatism, and that he hopes that in the future no single brand of structuralism will be declared dogma.

In 1958 there appeared an important article by O. S. Kulagina entitled "Concerning a Method of Defining the Parts of Speech on the Basis of Set Theory." [21] According to her Soviet colleague N. D. Andreev, this is virtually a refined version of distributional analysis.[22] Andreev adds that ". . . the set-theoretic approach is very interesting . . . but its possibilities are inherently limited." [23]

Bearing witness to the interest in mathematical linguistics was the conference on this subject at the University of Leningrad in 1959. Further evidence of this interest is seen in the fact that the presidium of the

Academy of Sciences passed a resolution on the development of structural and mathematical methods of linguistic research in 1960.[24]

In 1960 a series of volumes entitled *New Trends in Linguistics* was initiated under the general editorship of V. A. Zvegintsev.[25] The purpose of these volumes was to make available to the Soviet public Russian translations of important articles by foreign linguists. The first volume contains Russian translations of articles by Morris Swadesh on glottochronology and by Benjamin Lee Whorf on language and logic, and a Russian translation of Louis Hjelmslev's *Prolegomena to a Theory of Language*, along with translations of reviews of this book by André Martinet and Einar Haugen. The second volume, which appeared in 1962, is divided into three sections, one on semantics, one on phonemics, and a third devoted to transformational grammar. The first two parts have Russian translations of such articles as "Analysis of Meanings and Dictionary Making" by Eugene Nida, "Meaning and Linguistic Analysis" by Charles C. Fries, "Phonology in Relation to Phonetics" by Roman Jakobson and Morris Halle, etc. The third part contains complete Russian translations of Noam Chomsky's *Syntactic Structures,* Zellig Harris' "Co-occurrence and Transformation in Linguistic Structure," Dean S. Worth's "Transform Analysis of Russian Instrumental Constructions," and an original article by S. K. Shaumian, "The Theoretical Bases of Transformational Grammar." [26] Another interesting evaluative and informative book is *Basic Trends of Structuralism*, which contains articles by leading Soviet linguistics on the Prague school, glossematics, the London school, and American descriptive linguistics.[27] According to N. D. Arutiunova, author of the section on American descriptivist grammar, descriptive grammar tried to answer the question of how a sentence is made up of smaller units, but transformational grammar has a completely different goal: how to derive a given statement from another sentence or sentences.[28] Arutiunova goes on to say that the transformational model of a generative grammar is divided into two components, syntactic and phonological.[29] The syntactic component in turn consists of two subcomponents, the first of which contains the rules of classification and union of the elements of a sentence. The second subcomponent contains a selection of complex operations for the processing of the grammatical structure of sentences. With the help of these operations, simpler sentences can be transformed into more complicated syntactic structures. The phonological component contains a set of rules that turns the chains of symbols generated by the syntactic component into a real speech sequence. One must say that generative grammar seems to be as popular now in the Soviet Union as it is in the United States. Attention should also be called to the fact that *Problems in Linguistics* has published several original articles on transformational grammar by the well-known American specialist in the field Robert B. Lees.[30]

Probably the most brilliant of the young Soviet structuralists is S. K. Shaumian, who developed what he calls the "two-level approach" to linguistic analysis.[31] The two levels are respectively the "observational" and the "construct" level, both of which are necessary because certain antinomies develop otherwise. For example, take the two statements: (1) Phonemes are elements serving to differentiate linguistic units; and (2) Phonemes are acoustic elements. It follows from the first statement that phonemes can be transposed into other kinds of elements—for example, graphic (cf. the letters of a phonemic alphabet). The second statement, however, implies that phonemes cannot be transposed into letters. According to Shaumian, "To overcome this antinomy we must split the concept of the phoneme into the concept of the phoneme proper and the phonemoid." [32] Phonemes are on the "construct" level and phonemoids on the "observational" level. Commenting on this paper, Herbert Pilch asks why there should be just two rather than three or more levels of abstraction in linguistic theory.[33] Likewise Pilch doubts that phonemes (or phonemoids) are immediately observable objects. What we observe is more likely to be a physical continuum. Thus neither of Shaumian's levels, as he describes them, is really an observational level. In addition, the fact that phonemes are distinctive does not necessarily imply that all distinctive elements are phonemes.

In 1963 S. K. Shaumian and P. A. Soboleva authored the book *Applicational Generative Model and Transformational Calculus as Applied to the Russian Language*.[34] According to the authors:

> The model suggested features a single generative process based on a universal operation, termed application, which makes it possible to dispense with transformations. Therefore, in the applicational model transformations are no longer a means of generating phrases, but a means of establishing invariance relations between phrases obtained by application. Owing to the interaction of two matrices—the matrix of class generation and the matrix of application—it becomes possible within the framework of the applicational generative model to obtain transformations automatically as a result of definite calculus rules, while in all previously suggested models transformations are set down as an arbitrary list.[35]

Noam Chomsky, however, finds the theory "defective in crucial aspects," [36] and refers the reader to Barbara Hall's review of the book.[37] Hall, indeed, finds many shortcomings, among them the fact that although Shaumian and Soboleva assume the existence of four classes of stems—noun, verb, adjective, adverb—there is no mention as to how the membership of a stem in one class or another is to be determined. In addition, there is only one syntactic position in the simple sentence for both the adverb and the noun, so that nouns used adverbially in the accusative case are not distinguished from those nouns in the accusative case which are used as the direct object of the verb. Thus it is possible to generate both the correct Russian sentence *Ivan chital knigu i gazetu,* "Ivan was reading a book and a newspaper," as well as the incorrect sentence *Ivan chital knigu i chas,* "Ivan was reading a book and for an hour." According to Hall:

A second shortcoming of the proposed phrase structure is that because applicational rules are allowed to apply over and over, each of the major categories can be conjoined, with the sole exception of the head noun of the sentence. Such a restriction leads to a strange selection of generable conjunctions: it is possible to generate long strings of adjectives, each with its own string of modifying adverbs, modifying a noun; it is also possible to generate compound verb phrases and compound object nouns. But it is not possible to generate a compound sentence or a simple sentence with a compound subject. . . . The division thus produced is clearly arbitrary; it does not correspond to any linguistic facts, but is simply an unfortunate by-product of the formalism.[38]

In conclusion Hall says:

Perhaps the book would not be so disappointing if its introduction were not so full of great promises. It is necessary to work through a complicated tangle of mathematical notation to find out what the authors have to say about linguistics; the mathematics turns out to be more ornamental than functional, and once it is stripped away, the underlying linguistic ideas turn out to be of little value.[39]

Negative comments about Soviet versions of transformational or generative grammars do not all come from Western sources, and all Soviet linguists have not suddenly and uncritically taken up the banner of structuralism or transformational grammar. In the book *Theoretical Problems of Contemporary Soviet Linguistics*, V. V. Vinogradov, the chief editor of the authoritative *Academy Grammar of Russian*, quotes Shaumian as saying, "Language must be viewed as a cybernetic generative device, at the input of which are given the primary objects—classes of words—and the operations on these objects, and at the output of which are the expressions produced as a result of the given operations." [40] Vinogradov then objects, "Here, except for the terminology, everything is in general as old as the world; I have in mind the linguistic world, i.e., the world since the time when people began to use language." [41] Vinogradov then goes on to accuse Shaumian of violating the norms of the Russian language with his use of expressions equivalent to the English "at the input" and "at the output." In his article "Contemporary Linguistics and Structural Linguistics," the well-known authority on the history of Russian syntax and White Russian T. P. Lomtev writes, "Transformational operations can show identity or ambiguity of expression, but they cannot establish content, the essence of the meanings themselves . . . The claim of the representatives of transformational grammar to establish by formal means the essence of syntactic objects is without foundation." [42] Lomtev regrets that the belief in causality in language is losing ground, and that economy and simplicity, rather than correspondence with reality, are acquiring importance for the evaluation of a linguistic theory.[43] He feels that the question of the truth of linguistic theories is disappearing everywhere and that the principle of appropriateness is being propagated. According to Lomtev, these new incorrect, un-Marxist theses are now considered the latest word in science, and a criticism of these is felt to be a sign of backwardness. Lomtev laments that it has even become bad taste to talk about Marxism in linguistics.

Or consider the following quotation from the book *Paths of Development of Contemporary Linguistics:*

And although in all countries linguists evaluate Hjelmslev's theory quite soberly, rejecting it as unacceptable in the investigation of language, it is paradoxical that among us, in the Soviet Union, in the country of the Marxist materialistic world view, the theory has its active and zealous followers. It is painful and offensive that to this group of followers headed by S. K. Shaumian there belong young talented linguists (like Shaumian himself) who could quite effectively develop linguistic science in the right direction.[44]

In emphasizing the importance of Shaumian and other structuralists, I have ignored much of the work in syntax that has nothing to do with generative grammar. Dean S. Worth gives a great deal of bibliographical information about such articles, which he characterizes as having their value more in the "conscientious accumulation of material than in bold new attempts at classification." [45] Defending her compatriots, Olga S. Akhmanova remarks, however, that most Russian scholars will not wish or be able to discard a traditional approach concerned with the *facts* of modern Russian in favor of a militant structuralism that gives priority to relational and distributional criteria.[46]

I have virtually omitted all references to phonological studies, because there are no changes in direction which could be connected either with

Stalin's death or with the pronouncements of the 20th Congress. Morris Halle criticizes Soviet theories of phonology on the grounds that they do not include "simplicity, elegance and conceptual economy" among the criteria used for solutions to phonological problems.[47] According to Halle, since "the appeal to simplicity has been one of the most powerful tools in other areas of human knowledge, there is no reason why linguistics should not make use of it."[48] Replying to this criticism in her review, Akhmanova says that she would find it hard to accept descriptive elegance, simplicity and conceptual economy as the most powerful tools for the discovery of truths about language.[49] It is fairly clear from her comments on Worth and Halle that she belongs to the older school of Soviet linguists, among those who still believe that facts somehow force an interpretation. But there are others who realize that this is not the case. We can see, for instance, from Shaumian's article, "Processing of Information in Cognition and the Two-Level Theory of Structural Linguistics," that he well understands this older view to be wrong.[50] He quotes the following from Albert Einstein: "Physical concepts are free creations of the human mind, and are not, however it may seem, uniquely determined by the external world."[51] Shaumian proceeds to say that the same is true for all sciences, even linguistics; therefore linguistic concepts are free creations of the human mind.[52] They are not derived from observational data by means of statistical or other mechanical rules.

According to Robert Abernathy, there are three basic principles of division used in Soviet schematizations of language.[53] The first of these is the contrast between *structural* and *statistical* studies of language. The structural approach is probably important for machine translation research, whereas the statistical approach could be of value in the compilation of dictionaries. A second principle of division is between *analytic* and *synthetic* models or methods. An analytic model produces a kind of systematic description of the language, whereas a synthetic one produces the language (or at least sentences in the language) by some kind of automatic procedure. A third principle is the distinction between the *paradigmatic* and the *syntagmatic* relationships of words. Abernathy suggests that the preference for paradigmatic models is a result of native experience with a highly inflected language.[54] Abernathy's evaluation of Soviet mathematical linguistics is positive, although he suggests that probably the closeness of the tie between theory and applications (specifically machine translation) is more emphasized in the Soviet Union than elsewhere.

The first Soviet experiments in machine translation date back to 1955, and the first period of activity in this field may be characterized by an attempt to construct rules by which an electronic computer could effect translation between various languages.[55] After it was seen that this approach was probably fruitless, there began a second period characterized by more interest in linguistic research.

According to Harper, "recent machine translation research in the Soviet Union is proceeding along two main paths: a more detailed analysis of specific language phenomena and the construction of linguistic theory." [56] Nevertheless, Harper finds that many of the theoretical constructs presented in the current literature are of doubtful validity and even trivial.

One interesting difference between Soviet and American attempts at machine translation is the Soviet plan for an intermediary computer language. The reasoning behind this is that in the long run it will require less work to translate from each of the world's languages into and from the computer language than to construct separate programs for translation into and from every language in the world. This plan was criticized by Abernathy, who says that it seems likely that natural languages resemble each other more than they do computer languages.[57]

In this essay I have directed my attention mainly to the most recent trends in structural linguistics, since I thought that that would be of most interest to contemporary American readers. It should be emphasized, however, that a great deal of work is being done in the fields of the individual languages. A recent publication, *Fifty Years of Soviet Linguistics,* contains some thirty-five articles devoted to the recent history of various language families studied in the Soviet Union.[58] These articles deal with the well-studied Slavic, Germanic, Romance, and classical languages, as well as the more exotic Turkic, Japanese, Chinese, Semito-Hamitic, southeast Asian, African, and other language families. Considerable activity is to be found in all these fields.

In conclusion, then, one can say that since the 20th Party Congress Soviet linguistics has been characterized by a lively interest in various brands of structural linguistics, a relative freedom of expression, and a high quality of work that is acceptable on an international level. Russian translations of all important Western works on linguistics appear regularly. Some Russian linguists publish articles and reviews in Western publications and some Western linguists publish in Soviet periodicals. There is regular contact by correspondence and in person between Soviet and Western linguists. Barring any return to an outworn politically imposed mythology such as that of Marrism, there is every reason to expect a brilliant future for Soviet linguistics.

Notes

1. See John V. Murra, Robert M. Hankin, and Fred Holling, *The Soviet Linguistic Controversy* (New York: King's Crown Press, 1951), pp. 70–76. It is difficult to explain Marr's theories with any clarity or brevity, partly because the theories themselves are so self-contradictory and confused. But suffice it to say that Marr denied traditional formulations of comparative Indo-European linguistics and assumed that all languages stem from four basic elements, *sal, ber, yon,* and *rosh,* which he manipulated in an ad hoc fashion in order to establish all sorts of incredible etymologies. Marr's theories were as unacceptable to Western linguists as were those of Lysenko to Western geneticists. A good survey of Marrist thought is to be found in Lawrence L. Thomas, *The Linguistic Theories of N. Ja. Marr* (Berkeley and Los Angeles: University of California Press, 1957).

2. See Valentin Kiparsky, "Comparative and Historical Slavistics," in *Current Trends in Linguistics,* ed. Thomas E. Sebeok (The Hague: Mouton & Co., 1963), vol. 1. This volume is devoted to a description of various aspects of linguistics in the Soviet Union and other east European countries.

3. Murra, Hankin, and Holling, *Soviet Linguistic Controversy,* p. 9.

4. *Ibid.,* p. 76.

5. Cornelis H. van Schooneveld, "Morphemics," in *Current Trends,* p. 23.

6. Anon., "Zadachi sovetskogo iazykoznaniia v svete trudov J. V. Stalina i zhurnal 'Voprosy iazykoznaniia,'" *Voprosy iazykoznaniia,* 1 (January–February, 1952): 3–40. (Titles in Russian are translated into English in the body of the text.)

7. *Ibid.,* p. 40.

8. A. P. Baranikov, "Elementy sravnitel'no-istoricheskogo metoda v indologicheskoi lingvisticheskoi traditsii," *Voprosy iazykoznaniia,* 1 (March–April, 1952): 44–61; N. A. Baskakov, "Razvitie iazykov i pis'mennosti narodov SSR," *Voprosy iazykoznaniia,* 1 (May–June, 1952): 20–44; R. I. Avanesov, "Lingvisticheskaia geografiia i istoriia russkogo iazyka," *Voprosy iazykoznaniia,* 1 (November–December, 1952): 25–47; G. D. Sanzheev, "K probleme chastei rechi v Altaiskikh iazykakh," *Voprosy iazykoznaniia,* 1 (November–December, 1952): 84–102.

9. Olga S. Akhmanova, "Kritika burzhuaznogo iazykoznaniia: O metode lingvisticheskogo issledovaniia u amerikanskikh strukturalistov," *Voprosy iazykoznaniia,* 1 (September–October, 1952): 92–105.

10. *Ibid.,* p. 105.

11. Akhmanova, review of *Current Trends* (see n. 2) in *Word,* 21 (April, 1965): 180.

12. Akhmanova, "Glossematika Lui Elmsleva kak proiavlenie upadka sovremennogo burzhuaznogo iazykozaniia," *Voprosy iazykoznaniia,* 2 (May–June, 1953): 25–47.

13. Anon., "Stalin—velikii prodolzhatel' dela Lenina," *Voprosy iazykoznaniia,* 3 (November–December, 1954): 3–5.

14. *Ibid.,* p. 5.

15. M. M. Gukhman, "E. Sapir i 'etnograficheskaia lingvistika': Ob odnoi iz reaksionnykh kontsepstii v sovremennom amerikanskom iazykoznanii," *Voprosy iazykoznaniia,* 3 (January–February, 1954): 110–27.

16. *Ibid.,* p. 111.

17. Anon., "O nekotorykh aktualnykh zadachakh sovetskogo iazykoznaniia," *Voprosy iazykoznaniia,* 5 (July–August, 1956): 3–13.

18. *Ibid.,* p. 4.

19. S. K. Shaumian, "O sushchnosti strukturnoi lingvistiki," *Voprosy iazykoznaniia,* 5 (September–October, 1956): 38–54.

20. F. Mikush, "Obsuzhdenie voprosov strukturalizma i sintagmaticheskaia teoriia," *Voprosy iazykoznaniia,* 6 (January–February, 1957): 27–34; I. I. Revzin, "Strukturalnaia lingvistika, semantika i problemy izucheniia slova," *Voprosy iazykoznaniia,* 6 (March–April, 1957): 31–41; A. S. Melnichuk, "K otsenke lingvisticheskogo strukturalizma," *Voprosy iazykoznaniia,* 6 (November–December, 1957): 38–49; A. A. Reformatsky, "Chto takoe strukturalizm?" *Voprosy iazykoznaniia,* 6 (November-December, 1957): 25–37; M. I. Steblin-Kamensky, *"Nesol'ko* zamechanii o strukturalizme," *Voprosy iazykoznaniia,* 6 (January–February, 1957): 35–40.

21. O. S. Kulagina, "Ob odnom sposobe opredeleniia grammaticheskikh poniatii na baze teorii mnozhestv," *Problemy kibernetiki,* 1 (1958): 203–14.

22. N. D. Andreev, "Models as a Tool in the Development of Linguistic Theory," *Word,* 18 (April-August, 1962): 186–97.

23. *Ibid.,* p. 187.

24. See Robert Abernathy, "Soviet Mathematical Linguistics," in *Current Trends,* p. 113.

25. V. A. Zvegintsev, ed., *Novoe v lingvistike* (Moscow: Izdatelstvo Inostrannoi Literatury, 1960), vol. 1.

26. Shaumian, "Teoreticheskie osnovy transformatsionnoi grammatiki," in *Novoe v lingvistike* (1962), 2: 361–411.

27. M. M. Gukhman and V. N. Zhartseva, eds., *Osnovnie napravleniia strukturalizma* (Moscow: Izdatelstvo "Nauka," 1964).

28. *Ibid.,* p. 293.

29. *Ibid.,* p. 295.

30. Robert B. Lees, "What Are Transformations?" ("Chto takoe transformatsiia?"), *Voprosy iazykoznaniia,* 10 (May–June, 1961): 69–77; "On Reformulating Transformational Grammars" ("O pereformulirovanii transformatsionnykh grammatik"), *Voprosy iazykoznaniia,* 10 (November–December, 1961): 41–50.

31. Shaumian, "Concerning the Logical Basis of Linguistic Theory," in *Proceedings of the Ninth International Congress of Linguists,* ed. Horace G. Hunt (The Hague: Mouton & Co., 1964), pp. 155–60.

32. *Ibid.,* p. 156.

33. Herbert Pilch, discussion of Shaumian's paper "Concerning the Logical Basis of Linguistic Theory," in *ibid.,* p. 160.

34. S. K. Shaumian and P. A. Soboleva, *Applikativnaia porozhdaiushchaia model' i ischislenie transformatsii v russkom iazyke* (Moscow: Izdatelstvo Akademii Nauk SSSR, 1963).

35. *Ibid.,* p. 124 (quoted from the summary, which was in English in the original text).

36. Noam Chomsky, *Aspects of the Theory of Syntax* (Cambridge, Mass.: M.I.T. Press), p. 221.

37. Barbara Hall, review of Shaumian and Soboleva, *Applikativnaia porozhdaiushchaia model',* in *Language,* 40 (July–September, 1964): 397–410.

38. *Ibid.,* p. 403.

39. *Ibid.,* p. 410.

40. V. V. Vinogradov, *Teoreticheskie problemy sovremennogo sovetskogo iazykoznaniia* (Moscow: Izdatelstvo "Nauka," 1964), p. 4.

41. *Ibid.*

42. T. P. Lomtev, "Sovremennoe iazykoznanie i strukturnaia lingvistika," in *Teoreticheskie problemy,* p. 151.

43. *Ibid.*, p. 152.

44. T. A. Degtereva, *Puti razvitiia sovremennoi lingvistiki* (Moscow: Izdatelstvo "Mysl," 1964), 3: 82.

45. Dean S. Worth, "Syntax," *Current Trends*, p. 59.

46. Akhmanova, review of *Current Trends* in *Word*, 21 (April, 1965): 173.

47. Morris Halle, "Phonemics," in *Current Trends*, pp. 5–21.

48. *Ibid.*, p. 19.

49. Akhmanova, review of *Current Trends* in *Word*, p. 169.

50. Shaumian, "Preobrazovanie informatsii v protsesse poznaniia i dvukhstupenchataia teoriia strukturnoi lingvistiki," in *Problemy strukturnoi lingvistiki*, ed. Shaumian (Moscow: Izdatelstvo Akademii Nauk SSSR, 1962), pp. 5–12.

51. Albert Einstein and Leopold Infeld, *The Evolution of Physics* (New York: Simon & Schuster, 1938), p. 33.

52. Shaumian, "Preobrazovanie informatsii," p. 7.

53. Abernathy, "Soviet Mathematical Linguistics," pp. 113–32.

54. *Ibid.*, p. 119.

55. Kenneth E. Harper, "Machine Translation," in *Current Trends*, pp. 133–42.

56. *Ibid.*, p. 134.

57. Abernathy, "Soviet Mathematical Linguistics," pp. 120–21.

58. F. P. Filin, ed., *Sovetskoe iazykoznanie za 50 let* (Moscow: Izdatelstvo "Nauka," 1967).

XI : Anthropology

Current Soviet Ethnography: A Status Report

Stephen P. Dunn

Introduction

The Russian term *etnografiia* corresponds to what we understand by cultural and social anthropology, but does not properly include physical anthropology (although the chief Soviet professional journal, *Sovetskaia etnografiia*, does carry articles in this field). In view of the difference in usage and for the sake of economy, I will use the term "ethnography" in its Soviet sense throughout this paper. However, ethnography, as defined in the Soviet Union, includes some subsidiary fields with which, for various reasons, I will not be dealing. For instance, I will say nothing about archeology and prehistory, which have a distinct tradition and a rather different history from ethnography proper. Also, I will not discuss folklore studies in the literary sense (the comparative study of folk tales, songs, proverbs, epos, etc.), which is a broad and flourishing field in the Soviet Union and deserves separate treatment.

This investigation was supported in part by Research Grant No. RD-2607-G from the Vocational Rehabilitation Administration, Department of Health, Education and Welfare, Washington, D.C. 20201.

Soviet ethnography (cultural and social anthropology in the broad sense, including theoretical issues) possesses a historical tradition of a depth almost equal to that of its Western counterpart, although the field does not compare in size—that is, in the sheer number of persons and institutions involved—with what we have in the West. The forefather of Russian ethnography is generally considered to have been Afanasy Nikitin, a fifteenth-century merchant from Novgorod who made a trip to India and left a colorful and detailed account of his experiences entitled *A Journey Beyond the Three Seas*. With the expansion of the Russian state into the outlying areas of Siberia, central Asia, and later the Caucasus, the reports of military leaders, provincial governors, merchants, and scouts began to accumulate and formed the empirical foundation for later Russian ethnography. However, just as in the West, it was not until fairly late in the nineteenth century that ethnography became a field of learning in its own right, with academic appointments, journals, meetings, expeditions, and the other standard paraphernalia. Because of the relative isolation of Russia from the currents of western European thought up to that point, the field developed to some degree independently, and the relation of the various subdivisions within it differed—and to some degree still differs—from what we are accustomed to. For example, folklore studies, including particularly the study of popular festivals and rituals, are a central component of the Russian ethnographic tradition, rather than a more specialized branch. The study of material culture has been developed in great detail. On the other hand, what one might call "comparative sociology"—social anthropology in the modern British sense—is much less developed, despite certain significant contributions.

At the time of the 1917 Revolution, there was one chair of ethnography in the country, at Moscow University. This was held by D. N. Anuchin, a scholar who, in his energy and in the scope and variety of his researches, recalls Franz Boas. Anuchin worked in all the subfields of anthropology that existed in his time, including physical anthropology, and he trained an entire generation of scholars—those who are now the senior people in the field. Although definitely not a Marxist, he is looked up to by most Soviet ethnographers as a founding father, much as Boas is among us.

The newly established Soviet regime faced formidable problems in molding a wide variety of ethnic groups at various levels of social and economic development into a viable state. The demand for the professional skills of ethnographers far exceeded the supply. In this situation, it became necessary to train government and Communist party officials in the fundamentals of ethnography on an ad hoc basis, send them out into the borderlands, and later have them train their successors. This was the situation during most of the 1920's; there was very little time to bother about fine points of theory or ideological orthodoxy.

With the advent of Stalin to absolute power, the situation changed drastically. The prerevolutionary generation of ethnographers, except for those who were willing to go along with the new regime and make some pretense of conversion to Marxist orthodoxy, were removed from positions of influence, and in some cases imprisoned or executed. The empirical ethnographic studies that were carried out in the middle and late 1920's under the guidance of older ethnographers such as V. G. Bogoraz, V. I. Iiokhelson, and L. Ia. Shternberg [1] were brought to a halt. Many of the most talented and promising younger ethnographers left the field entirely, some to become historians (the line between the two disciplines in the Russian tradition has always been flexible and somewhat vague), others to become pure archeologists, and still others to quit academic life entirely for service in the government bureaucracy or in industry. Finally, some very gifted people worked during this period in rather menial capacities on the fringes of scholarship, as librarians, editors, curators, and so forth. The effects of this mass exodus are still being felt.[2] Even more serious than the loss of personnel from central institutions was the virtual dismantling of the rather extensive system of local museums and study groups around the country which had been built up since the Revolution and to some extent before it, and out of which many of the younger ethnographers had come.

Soviet ethnography during this period was reduced to the status of a historical subdiscipline, whose function was to provide examples and arguments from ancient and primitive life to support historical or more often ideological points. Empirical research was impossible (with a few peripheral exceptions, noted below). This did not mean, however, that ethnographic data did not appear during this period. Particularly in journals and books dealing with the Far North, and with the government's official campaign against religion, it may be possible to find valuable materials. I say *may* because many of these sources are not available in this country and have become rare even in the Soviet Union.[3] The formal training of ethnographers was not carried on during this period.

Considerable empirical research was done in such peripheral fields of ethnography as folklore studies [4] and prehistoric archeology. However, the theoretical contributions of these years, particularly in archeology, were compromised by the influence of the linguist and archeologist N. Ia. Marr,[5] as well as by a strong nationalistic bias, which prevented the recognition of any of the prehistoric cultures on Soviet territory as being of external origin. These contributions have been repudiated almost in toto by recent Soviet scholarship.

The rebirth of Soviet ethnography dates from 1946. That year was marked by the establishment of the Institute of Ethnography under the U.S.S.R. Academy of Sciences[6] as an organization for research and the training of specialists, and by the resumption of regular publication of *Sovetskaia etnografiia*, the main professional journal. This journal is officially considered to have been founded in 1926, but for the first twenty years of its existence publication was extremely irregular.

If one surveys the first six or seven years of the postwar series of *Sovetskaia etnografiia*, one finds that the emphasis is still heavily archeological and historical (including folklore in the broad sense). Except for the characteristically bitter anti-Western polemics of these years, the articles breathe a somewhat musty air reminiscent of the Frazer-Mac-Lennan era.

The new emphasis in Soviet ethnography on empirical study of the current social situation, the daily life of the collective-farm peasantry and (although this has hardly begun) the urban workers, becomes noticeable with the final repudiation of Marr in 1950–52 and after the death of Stalin in 1953. There were a number of cogent reasons for this change. First, it was an urgent political necessity to know with some precision what was happening in the countryside, and what the results of the epochal changes of the previous thirty years had been. In addition, the last survivors of the prerevolutionary generation were leaving the scene. The younger generation, who had not personally witnessed the Revolution and its consequences and were better educated, were less inclined than their fathers had been to accept passively the privations, both physical and moral, of the early Soviet period. Beginning about 1951, and gathering momentum until the present time, there has been a stream of publications dealing with the contemporary culture of the peoples of the Soviet Union in almost all its aspects. This reflects intense activity by expeditions sent out both by the Institute of Ethnography of the U.S.S.R. Academy of Sciences and by the provincial institutes. Despite certain geographical and thematic lacunae, it is possible to get a fairly accurate picture of the state of affairs in the countryside, particularly if one does not confine oneself to the ethnographic literature as such, but consults also the journals dealing with economics and local administration.

Let us discuss these data by large geographical areas and try to single out the most important features for each area.

The Far North and the Far East

This was traditionally an area inhabited by small hunting-and-gathering or reindeer-herding groups of very simple culture and social structure. At the time of the Revolution most of these groups were still in what is called in Marxist terminology the primitive-communal stage—i.e., before the appearance of classes, stable political structure, or any significant development of private property. During the 1920's and 1930's the government made considerable efforts to raise the cultural level of these peoples by supplying education, by developing the economy, and by superimposing the characteristic Soviet political structure over their extremely primitive communities. The basic motivation for these policies was the need to exploit the peculiar Arctic environment more effectively. Despite considerable material progress, the policies applied by the government to the native populations of the Far North now appear to have reached an impasse. The spread of education has produced a situation where the younger people are no longer satisfied with the traditional occupations of hunting, fishing, and reindeer herding. At the same time, full-scale industrialization under Arctic conditions demands a higher level of education and technical skill than the native peoples seem to possess at this time. Most of the work must accordingly be done by people sent in from outside, who are not acclimatized and suffer greatly from the sharp change in living conditions. All this has given rise to a rather intense debate among Soviet ethnographers and government officials over the direction in which and the pace at which development of these peoples should proceed. Many ethnographers, including some of those with the greatest experience in the area, fall into what might be called the camp of the traditionalists. They tend to hold (although with significant variations) that the traditional economy of the small northern peoples is the one best adapted to their peculiar geographical conditions, and that, accordingly, the traditional occupations should be developed and improved wherever possible, with the framework of the culture being left intact. The opposite view (which, since its partisans are for the most part not intellectuals, is not usually as clearly formulated) stresses the need to develop the Far North industrially in a much wider context, even at the risk of displacing permanently some of the smaller groups. The basic values of Soviet culture as it has developed (independently of the previous traditional culture of any of the Soviet peoples) would seem to favor the second alternative, and the same can be said of the course of history so far. After all, to what extent can a traditional hunting and reindeer-herding economy carried on with the aid of helicopters, tractors, radio communication, stainless-steel traps, and the like still be called traditional? The chief difficulty is one of priorities and investment and its distribution. The plans for the industrialization of the Far North now being seriously discussed have a rather science-fiction air about them: the use of atomic power to melt the permafrost, huge dams to alter the course of rivers, the building of entire cities under glass, and so forth. In principle, these things are quite feasible, but the investment required will be huge, and must be balanced off against other priorities. Meanwhile, the traditional economy is limping in many areas because of shortage of personnel and absence of the technology that would be required to counteract this shortage.[7]

Ethnographic material on the Far North and the Far East continues to appear in considerable abundance, considering the small numbers of the peoples involved. The tradition of ethnographic investigation of these areas is virtually unbroken since before the Revolution, and the problems involved in culture change here are set forth frankly and fully.[8]

Central Asia

Ethnographic investigation of the peoples of central Asia, including Kazakhstan, is also an old tradition in Russian and Soviet social science, though somewhat narrower than the study of the Far North, and subject to great ideological pressures. It was initiated during the last century by a group of Russian explorers, civil servants, and political exiles, and by a few scholars from the native nationalities such as the Kazakh Chokan Valikhanov.[9] Considerable material appeared in *Sovetskaia etnografiia* during the late 1920's and early 1930's, but this was mainly of a historical nature. Archaic customs concerned with totemism and the like were described in an attempt to shed light on earlier stages of social evolution, but little or no effort was made to describe the changes actually taking place at the time, or the direction in which culture change was proceeding. During the period of Stalin's and Marr's ascendancy, empirical research in this area was virtually halted, although some historical articles continued to appear. With the revival of interest in contemporary ethnography after World War II, there have been a series of "community studies" (as we would call them; actually, the unit usually studied is the collective farm) concerning the various central Asian peoples—Tadzhiks,[10] Kirgiz,[11] Uzbeks.[12] Unfortunately, because of the early date of most of these studies, they suffer from serious lacunae and persistent vagueness, particularly in dealing with economic matters. More detailed information on individual aspects of culture appeared later in *Sovetskaia etnografiia* and elsewhere.[13] Some monographs of the community-study type are now in preparation, according to latest reports. A collective work, *The Peoples of Central Asia and Kazakhstan*, has appeared,[14] and contains much useful information, but organizational flaws and the lack of detailed documentation—extensive bibliographies are given at the end, but references for particular points are not provided—make it rather difficult to use. It should be noted that the Soviet periodical literature on central Asian ethnography creates a special pitfall for the student, in that ethnographic articles are likely to emphasize groups that are atypical, economically or geographically, or phenomena that represent survivals of bygone stages of social evolution. This creates an exaggerated idea of the conservatism of central Asian society, which under present conditions is difficult to correct.[15]

The situation in central Asia does not lend itself to summarization as easily as does that in the Far North. Whereas in the latter case, one could say (with some oversimplification) that there was a choice between leaving the native culture basically undisturbed, on the one hand, and on the other—given the necessary investment—scrapping it entirely and substituting something else, the same thing does not hold true in central Asia. Here there was a considerable variety of natural environments and native cultures before the Revolution, and a large part of this variety persists. The northern part of the area was inhabited—except for settler populations of Slavic language and culture—by nomadic pastoralists. The tendency of such groups toward extreme cultural conservatism is well known in anthropology. The southern part, including fertile oases and river valleys, was occupied by peasant populations practicing irrigated agriculture, or in some cases dry farming. These people had rudimentary political institutions, and consequently, I would hypothesize, methods of absorbing alien influences without breaking the cultural mold entirely. The ethnographic data indicate that the central Asian peoples as a whole, in their major subdivisions of pastoral nomads (or former nomads) and sedentary farmers, retain a strong sense of ethnic identity,[16] and are markedly selective with regard to the cultural items offered them. I

would doubt whether, as some authorities contend, this can most usefully
be seen in terms of failed "Russification," [17] but certainly the convergence of all the national cultures into a single Soviet culture, foreseen by
Soviet theorists, lies far in the future as far as the central Asians are
concerned.

Slavic and Baltic Peoples

The Slavic peoples, as the largest ethnic group (taken together) in the
Soviet Union, and the dominant one in certain respects, occupy a special
position in Soviet ethnography. Culture change among them is described
in terms different from those applied to the Far North, central Asia, or
the Caucasus. In ethnographic and sociological material dealing with the
Russians, we are likely to hear more about "the erasure of the differences
between city and countryside" (which in effect means the urbanization
of the countryside) and less about specific cultural borrowings from
other peoples. It is also important to note that the nature of the ethnographic tradition itself, as applied to the Russians and Ukrainians, differs
from that relating to outlying peoples. The two major sources for the
ethnography of the Russian and Ukrainian peasantry as it developed during the nineteenth century were, on the one hand, the tradition of folklore studies (in the broad sense, including folk ceremonies and superstitions), and on the other, a tradition of empirical, social, and economic
investigation. This was usually done by people who were "on the side"
of the peasants, and consequently opposed, in various ways and to various
degrees, to the central government. In the first years after the Revolution, this tradition continued, because despite the change in form of government, wide differences of opinion were still possible among people
who considered themselves, in broad terms, Marxists. This tradition is
reflected in some of the works mentioned in note 1. During the Stalin
era, concrete and objective social investigations were, to say the least,
not encouraged, and it was only in the late 1950's that ethnographers
began to publish data on the Russian countryside in any quantity. It is
now possible to arrive at a reasonably complete and accurate picture of
the processes taking place among the Russian peasantry, and to a lesser
extent the Ukrainian.[18] However, the Western anthropologist working
in this field soon finds that he is called upon to consider many matters
which his formal training did not cover: the economics of farm-equip-

ment supply, variation in soils, crop structure, the lending policy of the
Soviet State Bank, wage norms for various cultural and service workers,
and the like. This is merely another way of saying that culture change in
the Russian countryside is largely a matter of investment, resource allocation, and supply. This is perhaps true both elsewhere in the Soviet
Union and in other parts of the world; but in the case of the Russian
peasantry, one is not distracted, as in many other areas of the Soviet
Union, by the presence of "exotic" culture patterns at marked variance
with the Western model.

At the same time, it should be noted that the economic and social organization of the Russian peasantry, particularly in the northern part of
the country, showed some peculiarities even before the Revolution, so
that models for peasant society derived from other parts of the world fit
only imperfectly, if at all. In many places the Russian peasantry was
partly or wholly industrialized [19] and highly mobile geographically; in
many ways, these people did not "behave like peasants." The effects of
these peculiar conditions are still felt in the fact that, for instance, many
people living on collective-farm land work elsewhere all or part of the
time.[20]

The Russian populations of Siberia present a number of problems distinct from any encountered elsewhere in the Soviet Union. This is due to
the fact that many of the Russian settlers were either exiled religious
dissidents or military colonists (cossacks), and some fell into both categories at once. Many of the Russian populations in Siberia (for example,
east of Lake Baikal, in what is now the Buriat A.S.S.R.) formed and still
form distinct ethnic groups with marked differences in costume, language, habits, and religion from other Russian-derived populations that
came from European Russia at a later date. These "Transbaikalians" were
Old Believers—adherents of one of the groups that split off from the
Russian Orthodox Church in the 1650's, at the time of the church reforms
of Patriarch Nikon. Before the Revolution and for some time afterward
they maintained a strong religious isolation; in some places, marriage to a
converted non-Russian native was considered less heinous than marriage
to a member of the Russian Orthodox Church. This isolation is now
breaking down, according to the ethnographic data, but the cultural
tradition is still very much alive. No large-scale community studies have
been done among this population since 1930, but a small expedition has
been active in the area for a number of years, and some scattered data
have been published recently.[21]

The non-Old-Believer populations in Siberia, known collectively as
Sibiriaky or *starozhily* (old settlers), are physically and sometimes culturally hybridized with the native non-Russians, and present still dif-

ferent problems. They have been handled rather gingerly by Soviet ethnographers. This may be because some of them belonged to dissident religious sects, and some have to one extent or another adopted the characteristics of the non-Russian native populations.[22] Actually, there is a close parallel between these Russian old settlers and the mountaineers of West Virginia and eastern Kentucky, who are ethnically distinct, but whom no one would think of considering anything but Anglo-Saxon in culture.

The tsarist practice of exiling dissident religious groups to the borderlands or of encouraging their settlement there has created enclaves not only in Siberia, but in other areas as well. During the nineteenth century several journalists and government officials wrote reports and sketches on these groups, and after a period of silence, ethnographic data on them have begun to appear again.[23]

A small but rather significant section of the Soviet ethnographic literature is that which deals with the Baltic peoples—Letts, Estonians, and Lithuanians. For historical and cultural reasons, these peoples form a special group within the Soviet population. They have been part of the Soviet Union for practical purposes only since World War II, and their original culture, unlike that of the Russians or any other people of the Soviet Union, belonged without question to the western European type. Both of these facts give the Baltic peoples an interest for the Western anthropologist which is out of proportion both to their numbers and to the amount of attention they have so far received. As far as I have been able to determine, the specifically Soviet features of social organization— the collective-farm system and the settlement pattern connected with it —have not "taken" particularly well in the Baltic area. Reading between the lines, one can deduce a strong resistance to what is interpreted as "Russification." In the Baltic area (as in the Soviet Union generally, but to an even greater degree) the influx of people from other parts of the country has been concentrated in the cities, which of course accentuates the difference in milieu between city and countryside, and the social conservatism of the latter.[24] This may account for some of the residual phenomena (as Soviet ethnographers consider them) which are so vividly documented in the Soviet literature on the area.[25]

The Caucasus

The Caucasus is an area presenting special problems and difficulties, both to the Soviet investigator and to the Western reporter. It includes a multiplicity of languages and ethnic groups, and a wide variety of natural habitats and types of social organization. The tradition of ethnographic investigation here is long and rich, but much of the relevant material is in the native languages (chiefly Georgian, Armenian, and Azerbaidzhani) and has not been translated or adequately summarized in Russian or in any western European language. References to material in the archives of the Institute of Ethnography and other institutions indicate that a great deal remains unpublished—a consequence of ideological and political difficulties of the Marr period. The tendency to publish in the native languages continues even now, and it is my impression that this is a manifestation of residual nationalism. The empirical data that have been published on the Caucasian peoples relating to the modern period and which are available to me—these deal chiefly with the north Caucasus— suggest a marked social conservatism in the area, which is the more striking because social organization here takes extreme and "exotic" forms. For example, among many people of the north Caucasus and Dagestan (the eastern slope of the Great Caucasus Range, adjoining the Caspian), there has been historically a strong development of the ritual avoidance of affines, coupled with widespread use of fosterage as a social device. Current data show that avoidance of affines persists in moderated form even among the educated classes, and practically unchanged among the collective-farm peasantry. While the fostering of children is no longer generally practiced, a peculiar form of fosterage continues to be part of the wedding ceremony: on the arrival of the bride and groom in the groom's village, they are housed separately in the homes of two unre- lated families, which thereafter enter into important ritual relationships with the families of the bride and groom and with each other. Until after World War II these relationships involved important material obligations, which have now lost some of their significance, presumably because the supply of consumer goods has improved. In general, the Caucasian cul- tures in all parts of the area show a strong ritualization of social life, which the new conditions have only diluted in certain respects, but not undermined or done away with.[26]

Conclusion

I have deliberately avoided saying anything about the situation in Soviet ethnographic theory, for two main reasons. First, during the past five years or so, the Soviet scholars themselves appear to have largely lost interest in the theoretical issues that were so hotly debated previously. This is to say, not that they have ceased to be Marxists, but rather that Marxism has become a *pro forma* matter and has ceased to determine rigidly the attitude of any given individual on any given topic. There is now no final authority to which appeal can be made, and which will settle the question permanently. The texts that are appealed to as authorities— chiefly the writings of Marx, Engels, and Lenin—are subject to differing interpretations, and these interpretations are not circumscribed by secondary authorities, as they were in the past. The Central Committee of the Communist party, which would be an ultimate authority, has been markedly circumspect in recent years in making pronouncements on ideological matters, and has proposed nothing new or startling. Also, in its last three congresses it has stressed the purely practical necessity of greater freedom of inquiry in social science. After all, if one is going to make over a society in a self-conscious way, it is vital to know the precise results of one's measures.

At the same time, Soviet ethnography has not as yet developed a body of theory independent of the Marxist canons to supplement or replace the postulates that have fallen into disuse. The new theoretical departures being made in Soviet social science fall primarily within the purview of sociology and constitute a selective and critical application of ideas adopted from Western sociology.

A word should be said about the attitude of Soviet ethnographers toward the work of their Western colleagues, and their familiarity with this work. *Sovetskaia etnografiia* regularly carries reviews of individual Western publications, and longer review articles dealing with particular fields and topics. These reviews are, by and large, well informed and show considerable sophistication. One can also find in *Sovetskaia etnografiia* regular articles dealing mainly with New World archeology, and showing good familiarity with the English-language sources. In general, it is fair to say that our Soviet colleagues know much more about us than we do about them. On a higher theoretical level, there are certain attitudes toward tendencies or schools of thought in Western anthropology which are traceable in all of Soviet writing on the subject. These can be briefly characterized as follows: (1) hostility toward anything that can be interpreted as "racist" (for Soviet purposes, this includes most explanations of human behavior which are based on heredity, and also those based on individual psychology); [27] (2) an insistence on the importance of history as a factor in determining the status of individual tribes and peoples at given points in time, and in limiting the applicability of any except the most general "laws of development"; [28] (3) a highly critical attitude, if not outright hostility, toward the concept of cultural relativism, since this concept is difficult to reconcile with an overall evolutionary scheme.[29] It is worth pointing out that each of these attitudes is shared by a number of Western ethnographers, who are not for this reason automatically classified as Marxists.[30]

In summary, I would note the following major characteristics of Soviet ethnography as a discipline: (1) increasing professionalization and technical sophistication; (2) a marked empirical slant, with little interest in broad theoretical issues; and (3) increasing candor in describing the objective situation in the Soviet Union, and decreasing influence of ideological or political restrictions.

Notes

1. V. G. Bogoraz, ed., *Starii i novii byt* (Leningrad, 1924); Bogoraz, ed., *Obnovlennaia derevnia* (Leningrad, 1925); Bogoraz, ed., *Evreiskoe mestechko v revoliutsii* (Moscow and Leningrad, 1926); Bogoraz, ed., *Trudy i byt v kolkhozakh* (Leningrad, 1931), vol. 1; M. Ia. Fenomenov, *Sovremennaia derevnia* (Moscow and Leningrad, 1925). This list is by no means complete, even for this period. For further references see L. P. Potapov, "Ethnographic Study of the Socialist Culture and Mode of the Peoples of the USSR," *Soviet Anthropology and Archeology*, 1, no. 3 (1962): 3–16; A. S. Bezhkovich *et al.*, *Khoziaistvo i byt russkikh krestian: Opredelitel* (Moscow, 1959), pp. 118–21; see also the literature cited in the series *Narody mira*, which contains volumes on the major ethnographic areas of the Soviet Union, such as Siberia, central Asia, the Caucasus, and European Russia, published by the Institute of Ethnography in Moscow.

2. See Potapov, "Ethnographic Study," p. 5, and "The Teaching of Social, Cultural, and Physical Anthropology in Secondary Schools and Higher Educational Institutions," *Sovetskaia etnografiia*, 1963, no. 1, trans. in *Soviet Anthropology and Archeology*, 2, no. 1 (1963): 3–7.

3. For citations to a mass of material from the 1920's and 1930's not otherwise

available, see M. A. Sergeev, *Nekapitelisticheskii put razvitiia malyk narodov severa* (Moscow and Leningrad, 1955). This is a valuable work and should certainly be translated.

4. For a summary of the discussions in folklore studies during this period, see V. E. Gusev, "Folklor (Istoriia termina i ego sovremennie znacheniia)," *Sovetskaia etnografiia*, 1966, no. 2, pp. 3–21. Generally speaking, there were and are two definitions of "folklore" current in the Soviet Union. The first and narrower makes it more or less equivalent to "folk literature." Those who held to this view formed a special unit under the Institute of Literature (Pushkin House). The second and broader definition includes folk rituals and ceremonies, and superstitions in the technical sense, and thus overlaps partially with the subject matter of cultural anthropology. The adherents of this second definition went over to the Institute of Ethnography of the U.S.S.R. Academy of Sciences when it was established, or to its provincial counterparts.

5. For a useful summary of Marr's career and theories, see Lawrence L. Thomas, *The Linguistic Theories of N. I. Marr*, University of California Publications in Linguistics, vol. 14 (Berkeley, 1957). The official critique of Marr that resulted in his posthumous repudiation is given in J. V. Stalin, *Marxism and Questions of Linguistics* (New York, 1951).

6. During the war, there was no Institute of Ethnography; before the war, it had been part of the State Academy of the History of Material Culture (GAIMK), which had been Marr's personal preserve, and which was engaged almost exclusively in archeological work.

7. For further details see Stephen P. Dunn and Ethel Dunn, "The Transformation of Economy and Culture in the Soviet North," *Arctic Anthropology*, 1, no. 2 (1963): 1–28; Ethel Dunn, "Educating the Small Peoples of the North: The Limits of Culture Change," *Arctic Anthropology* (in press).

8. See I. S. Gurvich, "Directions To Be Taken in the Further Reorganization of the Economy and Culture of the Peoples of the North," *Soviet Anthropology and Archeology*, 1, no. 2 (1962): 22–31; Z. P. Sokolova, "Certain Ethnic Processes among the Sel'kups, Khanty and Evenks of Tomsk Oblast," *Soviet Anthropology and Archeology*, 1, no. 2 (1962): 50–56; V. A. Tugolukov, "The Vitim-Olekma Evenki," *Soviet Anthropology and Archeology*, 2, no. 2 (1963): 15–40; V. I. Vasiliev, "The Forest Entsy (An Essay on Their History, Economy and Culture)," *Soviet Anthropology and Archeology*, 4, no. 3 (1965–66): 3–32; V. I. Vasiliev, Iu. B. Simchenko, and Z. P. Sokolova, "Problems of the Reconstruction of Daily Life among the Small Peoples of the Far North," *Soviet Anthropology and Archeology*, 5, no. 2 (1966): 11–21.

9. For information on Valikhanov and his views, see E. A. Masanov, "Vydaiushchiisia uchenyi kazakhskogo naroda Ch. Ch. Valikhanov," *Sovetskaia etnografiia*, 1965, no. 5, pp. 57–73.

10. N. N. Ershov *et al.*, *Kultura i byt tadzhikskogo kolkhoznogo krestianstva* (Moscow and Leningrad, 1954).

11. S. M. Abramzon *et al.*, *Byt kolkhoznikov kirgizskikh selenii Darkhan i Chichkan* (Moscow, 1958).

12. O. A. Sukhareva and M. A. Bikzhanova, *Proshloe i nastoiashchie seleniia Aikyran* (Tashkent, 1955).

13. See T. A. Zhdanko, "Mode of Life of Members of Fishing Co-operatives on the Islands of the South Aral," *Soviet Anthropology and Archeology*, 1, no. 2 (1962): 40–49; E. A. Masanov, "Some Results of Ethnographic Expeditions of 1959–1960 [in Kazakhstan]," *Soviet Anthropology and Archeology*, 1, no. 4 (1962): 57–62; Kh. Esbergenov, "On the Struggle against Survivals of Obsolete Customs and Rites (The Karakalpak 'As' Memorial Feast)," *Soviet Anthropology and Archeology*, 3, no. 1 (1964): 9–20; K. L. Zadykhina, "Ethnographic Data on the Mode of Life of the Uzbek Workers of Tashkent and Andizhan," *Soviet Sociology*,

1, no. 4 (1963): 10–19 and 2, no. 1 (1964): 36–47; Sh. B. Annaklychev, "A Contribution to the History of the Oil Workers of Nebit-Dag and Kum-Dag [Turkmen SSR]," *Soviet Sociology*, 3, no. 3 (1965): 12–40; 3, no. 4 (1965): 36–43; 4, no. 1 (1966): 3–18; 4, no. 2 (1966): 34–57; 4, no. 3 (1966): 16–31. For a discussion of these and other articles on the ethnography of central Asia, see Stephen P. Dunn and Ethel Dunn, "Soviet Regime and Native Culture in Central Asia and Kazakhstan: The Major Peoples," *Current Anthropology*, 8, no. 3 (1967): 147–208; pp. 184–206 contain extensive Soviet and Western commentary, with a rebuttal by the authors.

14. S. P. Tolstov *et al.*, eds., *Narody srednei Azii i Kazakhstana*, 2 vols. (Moscow, 1962–63).

15. See the Soviet comment in Dunn and Dunn, "Soviet Regime," pp. 191–92. As examples of the Soviet preoccupation with what they themselves regard as residual phenomena, one may cite the following: G. P. Snesarev, "O nekotorikh prichinakh sokhraneniia religiozno-bytovikh perezhitkov u uzbekov Khorezma," *Sovetskaia etnografiia*, 1957, no. 2, pp. 60–72; Snesarev, "Materialy o pervobytno-obshchinnikh perezhitkakh v obychaiakh i obriadakh uzbekov Khorezma," *Trudy khorezmskoi arkheologo-etnograficheskoi ekspeditsii*, 4 (1960): 134–45; Esbergenov, "Struggle against Survivals." These articles are among the most interesting to the Western observer in the whole Soviet ethnographic literature, and precisely because of their intrinsic interest they are likely to warp his estimate both of the Soviet ethnographic tradition and of the reality that it reflects.

16. This identity expresses itself, rather to the discomfiture of the regime, in religious terms. The central Asian, even when he is an atheist by conviction, is more than likely to consider himself a Moslem by virtue of his ethnic status and to perform various Moslem rituals (circumcision, various forms of funeral services) on the same basis; see S. Dorzhenov, "Musulmanin li ia?" *Nauka i religiia*, 1967, no. 4, pp. 50–52. This represents a traditional outlook and not merely (as some Western observers theorize) a reaction to Sovietization or Russification.

17. See Garé Le Compte, "Central Asia," *Ararat*, Autumn, 1965, pp. 57–61.

18. The available material on the Ukrainians in Russian is largely limited to material culture, and to folklore in the narrow literary sense. I have not attempted to cover material in Ukrainian for lack of both the requisite linguistic competence and the actual sources. The latter point is a continual irritant to the specialist in Soviet social science (except in fields like economics and "policy studies," which enjoy a high priority on this side). In fact, I would go so far as to say that there will be no really satisfactory international communication in the anthropological or sociological field until the exchange of materials becomes better organized than it shows signs of doing as yet.

19. The word "industrialized" is used here in the sense of production of goods or performance of services for cash, not necessarily in the sense of factory labor. This characteristic of the Russian peasantry in many places antedated the development of industry in the ordinary sense, and was due to poor soil and climate and relative overpopulation.

20. For more detailed discussion of these and related points, see Dunn and Dunn, *The Peasants of Central Russia* (New York, 1967).

21. See G. S. Maslova and L. M. Saburova, "An Ethnographic Study of the Russian Collective-Farm Peasantry of Eastern Siberia in 1957–59," *Soviet Anthropology and Archeology*, 1, no. 1 (1962): 19–27; G. I. Ilina, "Ob izuchenii sovremennogo byta 'semeiskikh,'" *Etnograficheskii sbornik* (Buriat Combined Research Institute, Siberian Division, U.S.S.R. Academy of Sciences), 1960, no. 1, pp. 108–22; G. I. Okhrimenko, "Rezba po derevu u semeiskikh," *Etnograficheskii sbornik*, 1961, no. 2, pp. 71–84; A. A. Lebedeva, "Nekotorye itogi izucheniia sem'i i semeinogo byta u russkikh Zabaikal'ia," *Etnograficheskii sbornik*, 1962, no. 3, pp. 27–37; Okhrimenko, "Russian Decorative House-Painting of the Transbaikal,"

Soviet Anthropology and Archeology, 6, no. 2 (1967): 38–51; Lebedeva, "Anket kak etnograficheskii istochnik (Po materialam sploshnogo podvornogo issledovaniia 1897 g. v. Zabaikal'e)," *Sovetskaia etnografiia*, 1967, no. 1, pp. 99–103.

22. See Gurvich, "Russian Old Settlers along the Kamchatka River Valley (A Contribution to the History and Ultimate Destiny of Isolated Groups of the Russian People in Siberia)," *Soviet Anthropology and Archeology*, 2, no. 3 (1963–64): 39–48; Saburova, "Nekotorye cherty obshchestvennogo i semeinogo byta russkogo naseleniia Priangariia v pervie gody sovetskoi vlasti (1919–1929)," *Sovetskaia etnografiia*, 1965, no. 2, pp. 28–39.

23. On the problems connected with the study of sectarian populations see Ethel Dunn, "Russian Sectarianism in New Soviet Marxist Scholarship," *Slavic Review*, 26 (1967): 128–40. Valuable data have been appearing since 1960 in annuals such as *Voprosy istorii religii i ateizma*, *Ezhegodnik muzeia istorii religii i ateizma*, and *Voprosy nauchnogo ateizma*, among others; often the sheer weight of generalization staggers even the most diligent researcher: an index of literature on questions of religion and atheism published in Russian in 1960 contained 1,300 items. It is true that the index was very broadly conceived (book reviews were also included), but ethnographic content was very high, and, unfortunately, this is largely unobtainable here. Much of this work, unless scrutinized microscopically, is repetitious, as if the mere assertion that religion is dying out would cause it to be so. Two noteworthy exceptions are: E. G. Zolotov, "Reaktsionnii kharakter molokanstva (po materialam sobrannym v 1959–1960 gg. v Gruzinskoi SSR)," *Ezhegodnik muzeia istorii religii i ateizma*, 6 (1962): 152–59; K. I. Kozlova, "Izmeneniia v religioznoi zhizni i deiatelnosti molokanskikh obshchin," *Voprosy nauchnogo ateizma*, 1966, no. 2, pp. 305–21. Kozlova's article is based on material collected on an ethnographic expedition sent out by Moscow State University in the summer of 1963–64 and is far and away the best in the collection.

24. It is worth noting that in the Baltic area, the ethnic difference between urban and rural population antedates the Soviet period. The cities were largely settled by merchants, bureaucrats, and minor nobility of German, Russian, or other origin.

25. See V. Ia. Kalits, "New Features in the Life of the Peasants of Kihnu Island," *Soviet Anthropology and Archeology*, 1, no. 1 (1962): 27–36; A. I. Vyshniauskaite, "Family Life of Lithuanian Collective Farmers," *Soviet Anthropology and Archeology*, 3, no. 4 (1965): 3–50; A. Daniliauskas, "A Contribution to the Study of the Culture and the Mode of Life of Lithuanian Workers," *Soviet Sociology*, 2, no. 1 (1963): 47–51; L. S. Efremova, A. A. Luts, and E. P. Chivkul, "Changes in Fishing Technology and in the Culture and Daily Life of the Fishermen of Soviet Latvia and Estonia," *Soviet Sociology*, 3, no. 2 (1964): 20–25, 38. These and other articles are discussed in Stephen P. Dunn, *Cultural Processes in the Baltic Area under Soviet Rule*, Institute of International Studies Research Series Monograph no. 11 (Berkeley, Calif., 1966).

26. The material in this paragraph derives mainly from the following: A. G. Autlev and L. I. Lavrov, eds., *Kultura i byt kolkhoznogo krestianstva adygeiskoi avtonomnoi oblasti* (Moscow and Leningrad, 1964); Ia. S. Smirnova, "Avoidance Customs among the Adygei and Their Disappearance during the Soviet Era," *Soviet Anthropology and Archeology*, 1, no. 2 (1962): 31–39; G. A. Sergeeva, "Field Work in Dagestan in 1959," *Soviet Anthropology and Archeology*, 1, no. 2 (1962): 57–63; Smirnova, "Some Religious Survivals among the Black Sea Adygei," *Soviet Anthropology and Archeology*, 3, no. 1 (1964): 3–8; M. A. Aglarov, "Forms of Marriage and Certain Features of Wedding Ceremonial among the 19th-Century Andii (Based on Field Data of 1959–1960)," *Soviet Anthropology and Archeology*, 3, no. 4 (1965): 51–59; Smirnova, "Novie cherty v adygeiskoi svadbe," *Sovetskaia etnografiia*, 1962, no. 5, pp. 30–40. It should be noted that my research in the Caucasian area is still in its first stages, and does not yet allow firm conclusions.

27. There are recent signs of a rather marked change in this regard; see I. S. Korolev, "Some Questions of Ethno-Psychological Studies Abroad," *Soviet Anthropology and Archeology*, 5, no. 2 (1966): 3–10. In this article Korolev admits (as Soviet writers have not done previously) the existence of national character, and the legitimacy of studying it in the context of cultural anthropology—although he has some valid reservations about the term "national character" itself. He criticizes severely, but in my opinion justifiably, most of what has been done along this line in the West.

28. This does not compromise the firm belief in social evolution, which is the birthright of every convinced Marxist. Rather, it is now recognized (as for a long time it was not) that the hypotheses of Marx and Engels were formulated at an extremely high level of abstraction, and hence leave room for all kinds of variations, and that great care must be taken in applying them to individual cases.

29. See the exchange on this topic between myself and S. N. Artanovski, a leading younger Soviet theoretical ethnographer, in *Sovetskaia etnografiia*, 1965, no. 6, pp. 76–91. This exchange was in the context of a discussion of *Sovremennaia amerikanskaia etnografiia*, ed. A. V. Efimov and Iu. P. Averkieva (Moscow, 1963). In my part of the exchange, I put forward a very narrow methodological definition of cultural relativism, which I thought would obviate this long-standing dispute between Marxist and non-Marxist scholars. In his reply, Artanovski denied that the problem of cultural relativism can be relegated to the methodological sphere. "Witchcraft among backward Australian tribes, or the Eskimo custom of killing one's aged parent—these are facts, for the description of which various working methods, having no content relating to world view, can be used. But the comparative evaluation of the social function of witchcraft in a preliterate society, on the one hand, and of the superstitious or psychopathological acts of single individuals in a contemporary highly developed society, on the other—this is a complex question which goes beyond the bounds of the most technically sophisticated ethnographic description; this is a problem of philosophico-ethical interpretation" (quoted from my mimeographed translation, p. 17). Thus my attempt to shift the ground of the argument would seem to have failed. However, Artanovski proceeds later: "Absolute norms of culture, applicable to all societies known to history, do not exist: all cultural norms and customs are historically determined and relative. But this relativity, from the point of view of the materialist dialectic, is not limitless; it does not signify the absence of general regularities of historical development" (*ibid.*, p. 18). I never contended that it did. To a non-Marxist, however, the idea of degrees of relativity will seem somewhat grotesque: something either is relative—i.e., dependent on something else—or it is not.

30. For an excellent summary of the theoretical bases of Soviet ethnography, see Alex Vucinich's comment in Dunn and Dunn, "Soviet Regime," pp. 202–203, and "Ethnography in the USSR," *Survey*, 55 (1965): 151–62.

XII : Sociology

International Contributions by Soviet Sociologists

Alex Simirenko

Current Status of Soviet Sociology

Recent publications of Soviet sociologists reveal their apparent wonderment at the popularity of their revived discipline. This is well illustrated by the pronouncements of Vladimir Aleksandrovich Yadov, a successful and prolific Soviet sociologist who at the age of thirty organized the first sociological laboratory in the country:

Many hopes rest on sociology. In the public's mind the sociologist's profession is associated with a scientific, objective, comprehensive approach to social problems. Of course, far from everything published under the heading "Sociological Notes" lies strictly within the limits of social problems by our economists, psychologists, demographers, and, incidentally, a large army of talented journalists who have a keen sense for the pulse of life. Why deprive social scientists of their own names and classify them all under the generic term "sociologist"? But such, evidently, are the trends of the time, which frequently turn out to be the whims of fashion. And sociology is becoming a fashionable science.[1]

The great popularity of sociology was also noted at the June, 1967, symposium of the Soviet Sociological Association, which took place in

Sukhumi. A. Yanov, reporting on the meeting for *Komsomolskaia pravda,* comments that sociology "has now become well nigh the most 'fashionable' in our country." [2]

Despite some of the continued difficulties faced by present-day Soviet sociology, its development in the past decade is a story of success.[3] Forgotten are the years between 1956 and 1964, when neither the public nor the party officials were quite sure of the meaning of or the need for sociology. Gone are the days when every Soviet sociologist writing on the subject was expected to proclaim his and other sociologists' loyalty to Marxism-Leninism and to provide simpleminded illustrations of the usefulness of sociological research to the country and the party. To be sure, these utterances are still being made on occasion, generally by obscure novices in the field, but they are rare. The time has come when scientists like Yadov are beginning to feel that the public and the officials are much too taken with the new science. They caution the Soviet public against the dangers of believing that all sociological research presents complete and impartial truth. They indicate that there is a difference between good and bad research, and that even in the best research, sociologists are getting at only an approximation of reality. In Yadov's words:

Yet, in my view, the merging of the field of sociology with the subject matter of adjacent sciences is not so dangerous at all: ultimately the experts themselves will determine who should study what. Danger threatens from another side: Is today's sociologist justifying the hopes that rest on him? Yes, his conclusions have been clothed in the strict form of impartial facts and have been covered with the halo of the most precise science—mathematics. Alas! At times this science-like form merely creates the semblance of scientific content.[4]

Soviet Sociologists Today

Soviet ability to relocate resources and personnel into endeavors deemed important by the party elite is best illustrated by the revival and development of sociology as a distinct discipline. As recently as 1963, George Fischer estimated that the number of practicing Soviet sociologists could be counted only in the dozens.[5] In contrast, the first national meetings of Soviet sociologists, which were held February 16–19, 1966, in Leningrad, were attended by 600 persons. The majority of attending sociologists reported in a questionnaire distributed during the conference that they had been doing work in sociology for at least three to four years—at that point, a lengthy career.[6] Publications on sociological subjects also reveal the rapid recent growth of the discipline. In the period from 1960 through 1965, the number of publications increased by 241.8 percent.[7]

The new discipline is being built up by men who by necessity have been educated in some field other than sociology. The greatest number of them, 27 percent, were originally trained as historians; 25 percent were trained as philosophers, 10 percent as economists, 3 percent as psychologists, and 30.5 percent in some other fields of the social sciences and humanities. The remaining 4.5 percent received their education in the technical fields.[8]

Today Soviet sociology is a complex profession that defies uniform characterization. It is primarily a research profession, which still depends upon other disciplines to train and educate its own cadres of new researchers. Professional training is largely received in the course of practical graduate experience, which is supplemented with a seminar or two in theory and methodology. These seminars are available only in a few educational institutions and are apparently still offered on an ad hoc basis. Consequently, very few Soviet sociologists are also teachers of sociology. This rare and honored role is exercised by V. A. Yadov, head of the sociological laboratory at Leningrad State University, who is also listed as lecturer in sociology at the university, and G. V. Osipov, present president of the Soviet Sociological Association, who is professor of sociology at Moscow State University.

Soviet sociologists are very much aware of the need for the establishment of an educational curriculum at least on the graduate, if not the undergraduate, level. A profession that has a thousand or more practitioners cannot be based on amateur self-education without becoming discredited in the eyes of officials and the public. According to Yadov:

> The level of training of many "professional" sociologists is, alas, very low at the moment. Numerous volunteer assistants to sociologists have no training at all. We have neither teaching aids on the methodology and techniques of empirical research nor specialization in sociological research in the humanities departments. The U.S.S.R. Ministry of Higher and Specialized Education obviously thinks sociology should continue to develop "on a volunteer basis." Otherwise it is difficult to explain why for the third year now the ministry is not reacting to persistent appeals to offer the appropriate specialties in at least three of the country's universities—Moscow, Leningrad and Novosibirsk, where there are trained cadres of specialists.

The Soviet sociologist bears a special responsibility for his conclusions and recommendations. He is responsible not to a private firm but to the people, to the state. Hasty conclusions obtained without reliable scientific foundation can do at least as much damage as speculative harebrained scheming. This must not be forgotten. It is time to train cadres of first-rate specialists who have mastered the most advanced social theories and an advanced research methodology that conforms to the present-day level of scientific knowledge.[9]

The Sukhumi meetings of the Soviet Sociological Association also emphasized the dangerous dilettantism of its sociologists, which at this point threatens the very survival of the discipline. The headline slogan of the meetings was the transition of sociology "from dilettantism to high professionalism." [10]

With persistent demands by sociologists it is likely that Soviet institutions of higher education will be providing training opportunities to the forthcoming generation of sociologists. In the meantime, however, sociologists are being trained in the many research centers scattered throughout the Soviet Union. Whereas seven years ago there were only two centers of sociological research (Leningrad and Moscow), today sociology is an established part of scientific institutions throughout the country. Of the 600 participants at the national meetings, 380 represented various cities. Major centers of sociological research are now established in Leningrad, Moscow, Novosibirsk, Sverdlovsk, Gorky, Kiev, and Minsk. Whereas five years ago the great majority of Soviet sociologists were Russian by nationality, today there are also many Ukrainian, Belorussian, Georgian, and other nationalities represented among them. It may be noted that the best sociologist is Jewish—I. S. Kon, a philosopher fluent in English, German, and French, whose theoretical writings are as good as any in the West.

During the past five years Soviet sociologists have been advocating the establishment of their own sociological journal, without success. Their official journal continues to be shared with philosophers: a monthly called *Problems of Philosophy* (*Voprosy filosofii*) also carries summaries of all the major articles on sociology in the English language.

Failure in the establishment of a journal is matched by the tardiness with which preparations are being made for the opening of an independent institute of concrete social research within the Academy of Sciences of the U.S.S.R. Soviet sociologists had privately reported that such an institute would definitely be established in the spring of 1966,[11] but in the summer of 1967 they were still fighting to bring it to reality.*

---

* As this book goes into print, *Isvestiia* (June 8, 1968) has announced the formation of such an institute. Private sources reveal that the director is to be Academician A. M. Rumyantsev and that definite plans are being made to publish a sociological journal.

Resistance encountered by sociologists in establishing sociological curricula in institutions of higher education and in the creation of a distinct
journal, as well as in the opening of a separate institute, is an indication
of a still powerful distrust and perhaps resentment of sociology on the
part of some representatives of long-established disciplines, particularly
philosophy and economics.[12] It is important to note, however, that resistance to sociology since the middle of the 1960's has no direct political
overtones. The major justifications offered for holding sociology back are
financial in character. These challenges to Soviet sociology are well illustrated in the report of the meeting of the presidium of the Soviet Sociological Association in June, 1967, following the Sukhumi symposium:

There is no scientific center. There are insufficient cadres. There is no
training of cadres. No journal. No textbook. No popular literature. No
this, no that.

There was a time when doubts existed: Are these really needed? No one
seems to have doubts on this score. At any rate, doubts have not been
voiced publicly. What is the trouble now? Formally, the basic conclusion
is that funds are lacking. There are no funds to open an Institute of
Sociology. No funds for journals. Let us economize. But is this the place
for economizing? And is it economical? Whatever the case might be, many
thousands of persons are engaged (or try to engage) in applied sociology.
They engage in it in an unskilled manner and with little result. Polling is
often conceived to be the be-all and end-all of sociology. Those who love
visual techniques can already calculate how many times the questionnaires
that have been filled out would go around the equator if placed end to end.
But what about results?

"Economizing" turns into wastefulness. In the long run it is not so important which line of the budget or which institution's budget covers
expenditures in sociology. These expenditures are not so great, and the
yield might be incomparably greater than at present.

Surely a sociology magazine does not require great outlays. We are
confident that if it were well managed it would promptly yield a direct
and immediate profit. We need hardly mention that it would undoubtedly
raise the scientific level of those who wish to become sociologists. Today
amateur sociologists are trying to learn from other countries' textbooks,
from translated monographs, from articles in foreign journals, from type-
written translations of lectures delivered in Polish educational institutions.
Because we do not have our own textbooks. Is this economizing too?
To think that it is possible to economize on the Institute of Sociology or
a sociological journal is approximately the same as thinking one economizes
on a milk pail by not milking the cow.[13]

Sociological Research Centers

Creation of an independent institute of concrete social research within the U.S.S.R. Academy of Sciences, if it is achieved, will signify the arrival of sociology as an equal science among other Soviet sciences. Such an institute would undoubtedly become the major research center in the country. In the meantime, the most prestigious and influential research organization remains the Institute of Philosophy at the U.S.S.R. Academy of Sciences. Its two divisions, the Division of Historical Materialism and the Division of Concrete Social Research, conduct empirical research. The Division of Historical Materialism, as the name implies, is more analytical in orientation, and its researchers are often assigned tasks of reviewing and criticizing Western sociological theory and research. Occasionally, however, the division does undertake empirical research, depending upon the initiative of its various branches outside Moscow. Thus, for example, its specialists in Kharkov are presently involved in a study of Kharkov workers. The division is headed by M. T. Yovchuk, a Belorussian.

The Division of Concrete Social Research, headed by G. V. Osipov, has performed the major task of building up sociology as a discipline in the Soviet Union during the past six years. It sponsors empirical research as well as most of the major publications in the area of sociology. The history-making two-volume symposium *Sociology in the U.S.S.R.* was prepared and published by this division in 1965. Its most impressive empirical study to date is that of the life and work of workers in the town of Gorky and the Gorky region, which has accumulated data on as many as 14,000 people. So far only partial results from this study have been made available.[14] Currently the Division of Concrete Social Research is collaborating with Polish sociologists in research on the problems of industrial sociology. With the creation of an independent institute, the Division of Concrete Social Research will probably transfer its functions there.

Most major Soviet universities now have laboratories for sociological research. The oldest and most prestigious of these are the Laboratory of Sociological Investigations at Leningrad University, the Laboratory for Research and Mathematical Economics with its Sociological Group at Novosibirsk University, and the Sociological Laboratory within the Department of Philosophy of Moscow University. Leningrad University also sponsors three other social science laboratories investigating social psychology, economics, and engineering psychology. Since 1963 the four Leningrad laboratories have coordinated their work. Most of the work of the university laboratories, whether in Novosibirsk or in Moscow, is primarily concerned with the study of industrial and occupational problems.

The oldest of these laboratories was established in 1959 at Leningrad University. Its researchers have conducted many studies dealing with worker productivity and morale. Currently the most interesting activity is a study of the relative prestige of occupations in the opinion of Soviet citizens.

The laboratory at Novosibirsk University has earned the reputation of conducting the best and most farsighted sociological research in the country. Its study of occupational choices and problems of secondary-school graduates has already established itself as a sociological classic. So far, only partial results of the study are available, but the data that are available place it at the front of all other such research.[15] A detailed discussion of this research follows in later pages.

The laboratory at Moscow University is not as active or as diversified in its research as those in Leningrad and Novosibirsk. Currently it is engaged in a three-year study of the workers in the tool and die industry of Moscow and its suburbs.

Other Soviet universities have also initiated sociological research in the past several years. At Ural University there are two departments conducting empirical research: the Department of Philosophy and the Department of Dialectical and Historical Materialism. The University of Kiev has established a Laboratory of Concrete Social Investigations attached to the Department of Dialectical and Historical Materialism. Needless to say, most of the university-centered sociological research is combined with the training of students in this area.

Perhaps the best-known center for sociological study is the Institute of Public Opinion, sponsored by the official daily of the Young Communist League, *Komsomolskaia pravda*. The institute gained attention with its survey of readers in 1961 inquiring into the values and mood of the new generation of Soviet man. The twelve-point questionnaire included such inquiries as "What do you think of your generation?" and "Do you have a goal in life?" For the first time since the 1920's, the reports of the study included both negative and positive responses, responses that reflected alienation and discontent among Soviet youth.[16] Since 1961 the institute has conducted a variety of other studies, many of them based on responses elicited from the readers of the newspaper. Some studies, however, such as a study of the nonworking hours of Soviet urban man, were based on personal interviews with a cross section of urban dwellers. A discussion of this study follows later in this chapter.[17]

A number of other organizations are also concerned with sociological research. The Academy of Social Sciences of the Central Committee of the Communist party has several departments that occasionally conduct empirical research. These are the Departments of Philosophy, Political Economy, and History of the U.S.S.R. Their research is conducted by students in the form of dissertations. An old and venerable institution, the N. N. Miklukho-Maklai Institute of Ethnography of the U.S.S.R. Academy of Sciences, conducts research on peasants and makes ethnographic studies of the life of various nationalities, as well as occasionally investigating the life of the former peasant population that has moved into cities. The Institute of Philosophy at the Academy of Sciences of Belorussia is concerned with studies similar to those conducted in the various laboratories. The Central Institute for the Scientific Investigation and Planning of Urban Development of the U.S.S.R. Department of Urban Development is primarily concerned with the study of urban problems and planning of Soviet cities. The Institute of Government and Law at the U.S.S.R. Academy of Sciences studies crime and delinquency.[18]

The quality of sociological research varies greatly, depending on the organization that sponsors it. The sociological product of the Academy of Social Sciences is likely to be inferior, because it is generally conducted by those who are apprentices in the field, and also because the academy itself is specifically entrusted with maintaining the ideological purity of Marxist doctrine. The best research today is done by experienced professional sociologists in Novosibirsk, Leningrad, and the Institute of Philosophy of the U.S.S.R. Academy of Sciences. The time has arrived when a Western scholar is faced with a difficult problem of selection and evaluation of Soviet sociological research, because it contains widely varying qualities of product.

Definition of Soviet Sociology

A definition of Soviet sociology in the mid-1960's is sufficiently broad to free it for the pursuit of purely theoretical studies as well as the relatively routine practical investigations facilitating rational economic planning and performance. The clearest definition to date has been given by G. V. Osipov:

Marxist sociology *is a science discovering laws on the formation, development, and change of socioeconomic structures. These laws appear in the forms of various concrete social (material as well as spiritual) manifestations, processes, and factors.* Not only are these factors products of human action which reflect more or less the objective possibilities and necessities of social development of a particular historical epoch, but they are also factors which actively influence the consciousness of people and therefore determine their social behavior and activity.

Sociology also studies the regularities of the developing social structure of society and the interrelationship of its parts. Its task is to explore the various elements of social structure (such as classes, nations, social institutions, social values, etc.) in their organic relations and interrelations, not only between the parts themselves, but also including the study of man's social relationships, which represent the object and subject of social interaction.

. . . [We believe that] the development of society is based upon material forces and is governed by objective laws. As in any natural process, these regularities are expressed through the chaos of accidental occurrences, the struggle of social forces, the antagonisms, conflict, and cooperation of classes, and the diverse forms of human activity. Man participates consciously and actively in this process, reflecting the naturally developing material life and influencing its form, character, and speed of development. But the historical movement on the whole is subordinated to objective regularities.[19]

Historical materialism still remains a thesis to which Soviet sociologists will continue to pledge their allegiance. It is, however, a very broad and general theory, which Soviet sociologists are pledged to amplify and clarify in many of its details. The task is indeed a very challenging one, and it is hoped that it will be carried on by the new discipline. At this point, most Soviet sociologists are ignoring theoretically relevant studies, and with the aid of survey research have plunged into the exploration of Soviet society.[20]

The Sukhumi meetings revealed considerable disagreement among Soviet sociologists as to the basic purpose of sociology. What seems to be happening is that the best trained and most experienced sociologists of the country are endorsing and soliciting support for pure research in addition to the theoretically relevant applied research. A larger segment of the profession, however, is only rudimentally acquainted with sociology, and ridicules the methodological consciousness of the elite. This majority demands support for an applied research giving quick results and demanding little methodological sophistication on the part of the researchers.[21]

Contributions of the New Soviet Sociologists

Although the denunciation of Stalin's historical role by Khrushchev occurred in February, 1956, the institutionalized bonds of Stalinism have continued to plague Soviet social science, including sociology. It was only in January, 1964, that an official and concerted effort was made to free social science from the Stalinist practices of rigid dogmatism, falsification, and distortion of historical records, and the demands on scholars to play the role of servile propagandists.[22] Very little time has elapsed since to permit Soviet sociologists to produce works in the new scholarly atmosphere. Most of the productive research, therefore, was initiated and largely carried out in the old period. Nevertheless, the more relaxed editorial policies of recent years have given some of this research an international value.

Four specific contributions have been selected for review in the present discussion. These studies are in the areas of political sociology, demography, sociology of education and social stratification, and sociology of leisure.

POLITICAL SOCIOLOGY

One of the direct consequences of the 1917 Revolution in the field of scholarship was the introduction of a series of historical studies investigating political movements and social ideas of the lower strata of society. Despite their earlier acceptance, the best of such studies began to appear in published form only in the last decade. For a political sociologist these studies constitute a tremendous wealth of data on the rise of social movements and the formation and destruction of ideologies.[23] The first attempt at a summary and a sociological generalization of some of these studies appeared in 1966, written by the venerable Academician S. G. Strumilin.[24]

Following a discussion of the social meaning of exploitation, Strumilin details the ways in which the Russian serfs struck back at their masters. In the outlying provinces of Russia the most popular form of resistance was simply escape. Thus, for example, the Stroganovs' Ural properties listed as many as 33,235 males (or 42 percent of all the serfs) missing and unaccounted for. Such escapes, however, were quite difficult in the central regions of Russia, and here the resistance of the serfs and workers took other forms: wildcat strikes, as well as milder forms of discontent while at work. In the decade of 1850 to 1860 alone, historians discovered 188 labor-management conflicts, with the total participation of 48,363 workers. The average number of workers participating in each incident was 257.

The decade immediately after the February 19, 1861, proclamation of the freeing of the serfs was a relatively calm one, perhaps accounted for by the rising hopes of the workers for further improvement in their life. When no further reforms were made, a drastic increase of conflicts followed. In the period between 1861 and 1868 there were only 68 recorded conflicts; the period of 1869–76 lists as many as 228 conflicts, an increase of 335 percent over the earlier period. From 1877 to 1884 the number of conflicts advanced to 280, or 412 percent in comparison with the earlier period.

Unfortunately, space does not permit even a cursory summary of pertinent data provided by Strumilin. In Strumilin's view, these data provide an explanation of why Russia, an agricultural land and one of the most culturally backward countries in Europe, was the first country to turn to socialism. The Russian proletariat was also several times weaker than the proletariat of Germany, England, or the United States, yet it emerged victorious only in Russia. Strumilin objects to the view that explains this phenomenon on the basis of Russia's backwardness itself, the view that this very backwardness caused the country's political order to topple under the weight of the imperialist war. In Strumilin's view, such an explanation may account, although not too well, for the occurrence of the February Revolution, but it is quite unacceptable with regard to the October Revolution.

In Strumilin's view, two major factors accounted for the difference between the Russian Empire and the other countries of Europe which led to the successful proletarian revolution in Russia and its failure elsewhere. The first factor is an economic one, reflecting a high concentration of Russia's industrial economy. The second factor is a political one—specifically, the tsarist regime with all its attributes.

The following table reflects the high degree of industrial concentration in industries of over 1,000 laborers. According to Strumilin, it should be kept in mind that the table underrepresents to a considerable degree the Russian figures by about one-third, since it includes only those industries that came under industrial inspection and excludes the large metallurgical and government-run factories.[25]

TABLE 1

Proportion of Laborers Concentrated in Large Industries
with Over 1,000 Workers

YEAR	GERMANY (%)	UNITED STATES (%)	EUROPEAN RUSSIA (%)
1895	(13.0)	......	(31.0)
1904	15.0	......	38.8
1907	......	17.9	39.2
1914	......	20.5	43.8

SOURCE: S. G. Strumilin, *Ocherki ekonomicheskoi istorii Rossii i SSSR* (Moscow: Izdatelstvo "Nauka," 1966).

Much more significant than the above figures is the prevalence in Russia of giant factories with over 5,000 workers each. In 1907 Germany had only 12 such factories with a total of 119,000 workers; in the same year St. Petersburg alone had 14 such factories with a total of 132,000 workers. Strumilin concludes that Russia was a country of giant factories and a well-developed system of industrial capitalism. In this respect it can by no means be regarded as backward in comparison with other industrial countries.

The revolutionary strike activity of the Russian workers centered almost exclusively in the giant factories. According to Strumilin's figures, strike activity is directly correlated with the size of the factory.[26] As a result, the number of participating workers in Russian strikes is considerably higher than in other countries in Europe. This is illustrated in Table 2, with the figures for Russia again being underrepresented by an estimated 30 percent.

TABLE 2

Yearly Number of Strikers
(In Thousands)

COUNTRY	PERIOD STUDIED	MINIMUM	MAXI-MUM	AVERAGE	PERCENT OF RUSSIA
Germany	1900–1913	40	397	154	34
France	1893–1911	46	438	167	37
United States	1893–1905	176	533	341	75
England *	1893–1915	87	1,463	369	81
Russia	1895–1916	25	2,863	453	100

* Figures include miners and transport workers.
SOURCE: S. G. Strumilin, *Ocherki ekonomicheskoi istorii Rossii i SSSR.*

The political situation in Russia was also of considerable causal importance for the creation of a revolutionary mood. In the West, the parliamentary system had offered workers an illusion of power and representation. It had fostered political apathy. Strikes were used for the improvement of economic conditions without calling into question the legality of the class structure as such. In Russia the situation was quite different. The workers had no such parliamentary illusions. It is not surprising, then, that the class struggle in Russia had taken on a considerably sharper and more determined character. Strumilin concludes that under these circumstances a proportionately small proletarian class with a highly developed revolutionary determination was capable of capturing power in Russia. As he says, "What is important, then, is not the quantity but the quality."

The events of the October Revolution are well accounted for by Strumilin's explanation. The Russian proletariat successfully and with little struggle captured the industrial cities at the outset of the Revolution. In contrast to the Communist success in China, where the peasants played a dominant role, Russian peasantry had to be subjugated with the force of arms. Some sociologists may perhaps want to take issue with either the figures presented by Academician Strumilin or his interpretation of the data.[27] No political sociologist, however, can ignore them.

POPULATION AND SOCIAL STRUCTURE

Demographic studies in the Soviet Union are in a predicament somewhat similar to the situation in political sociology. The best studies are in historical demography covering the prerevolutionary period of Russian history. Scholars in this area generally concentrate on providing the best possible demographic picture of the past and prefer to avoid making significant theoretical generalizations. Providing a picture of population composition and its changes in one large area of the world,[28] the work of Soviet historical demographers is indispensable to international sociology.

Academician Strumilin was again the first scholar to attempt any kind of generalization about the various demographic studies accumulated in the past half century. His work in this area was published first in 1958 and revised in 1963.[29] In his critical review of the ideas advanced by Malthus and Sadler, Strumilin ably counterposes the ideas of Marx. In Marx's formulation each specific historical mode of production has its own population laws. Some kind of abstract population laws apply only to plants and animals as long as man does not interfere. Such a formulation, according to Strumilin, does not deny the influence of purely biological factors that apply to man as an animal. Certainly a mother's age has a great deal to do with her ability to reproduce, just as do hunger and other related factors. Different societies, however, treat the biological factor differently. While it may be said that the reproductive capacities of women are related to age, marriage itself is a social and not a biological phenomenon. Such factors as the marriageable age of a girl and the proportion of married women are determined differently by different societies.

✻ Strumilin notes that Adam Smith was one of the first to notice the positive relationship between poverty and fertility and the inverse relationship among well-to-do women. Marx was familiar with Smith's comments on the subject and had himself formulated the following generalization while writing about workers in capitalist society: "It is true that not only the births and deaths, but also the absolute size of families are inversely proportionate to income; that is, to that totality of a family's resources which are commanded by the different categories of workers." [30] According to Strumilin, Marx emphasized that such a formulation cannot be expected to apply to either the tribal life of a preclass society or the Communist society of the future. Marx had limited himself to the examination of capitalist society.[31]

It is possible now, says Strumilin, to continue the investigation of population laws under the new conditions of Soviet society. Since Soviet society is still only in the first phase of development, and since it still redistributes material rewards according to the principle "to each according to his work," quite similar to that which had prevailed in capitalist times, what then is the law of population growth at this stage? His answer is that similar population principles apply to both the present Soviet society and the capitalist societies.[32] A 1934 survey of 10,000 mothers in families of factory workers revealed the inverse relationship between fertility and income, as is illustrated by the following table:

TABLE 3

Income and Fertility of Families of Factory Workers
(For Each 1,000 Women)

GROUPS ACCORDING TO INCOME	INCOME IN RUBLES PER PERSON	NUMBER OF BIRTHS
I	Under 45	226
II	45–75	192
III	Over 75	141

SOURCE: S. G. Strumilin, "O zakonomernostiakh vosproizvodstva naseleniia," in his *Izbrannye proizvedeniia* (Moscow: Izdatelstvo "Nauka," 1963), vol. 1.

Similar conclusions are reached on the fertility as well as infant mortality of the different occupational categories of factory personnel.[33]

TABLE 4

Social Category, Fertility, and Infant Mortality

SOCIAL CATEGORY	NUMBER OF BIRTHS *	NUMBER OF DEATHS †
Laborers	191	160
Office workers	124	143
Engineers and technical personnel	118	118

* Per 1,000 married population per year.
† Per 1,000 births up to one year of age.
SOURCE: Strumilin, "O zakonomernostiakh vosproizvodstva naseleniia."

On a different level of analysis, Strumilin directs attention to the problem of population as a factor in the development of society. He is especially concerned with the popular idea that the growth of population as such is a source of progress and change. Such arguments are generally based on the idea that when society reaches its maximum growth potential in a particular economic arrangement, its people have to seek out new and more productive solutions for their economic problems. One famous prerevolutionary sociologist to hold such ideas was Maxim M. Kovalevsky, who is quoted by Strumilin as having said: "Prolonged researches have led me to the conclusion that the major factor in all changes of economic structure is nothing else than population growth." [34]

According to Strumilin, such a hypothesis can be shown to be misleading by a simple comparison among countries. Thus, for example, the population of China in 1939 was four times that of the United States, but China remained a semifeudal country. The principles that are operating are quite the reverse of Kovalevsky's hypothesis: it is the mode of production and the economic structures that determine the population growth. Strumilin illustrates the operation of this principle with reference to the findings of several Soviet historical demographers.

Strumilin maintains that not only the growth of population but also its rate of growth are influenced by the different economic structures of societies. Thus during the classic period of serfdom in Russia (1742–96), the country's population growth was considerably higher than at the end of the feudal era. In the decade between 1850 and 1860, the whole of Russia's rate of growth was no higher than 6.5 per 1,000 population, while among the serfs the death rate was higher than the birth rate. From

1835 through 1858, the number of serfs in the European part of the Russian Empire had decreased from 22,888,000 persons to 21,164,000, that is, by 1,724,000 or 7.5 percent. The decrease was so staggering that even the tsarist minister of finance N. K. Bunge had to admit that the figures could not be explained by the transition of serfs into the domain of the government or their assumption of freedom.[35]

With the changeover from a feudal to a capitalist economic system in 1861, there was a sudden jump in Russia's population growth. In the first decade alone, 1861–71, the rate increased from 6.5 to 13.3 per 1,000 population. The figures for subsequent decades show Russia's population increasing until the peak was reached in 1900 at a rate of 17.4 for each 1,000 population. From 1900 to 1915 the population growth decreased.

TABLE 5

Population Growth in the Russian Empire

YEARS	NATURAL INCREASE (PER 1,000 PERSONS)	PERCENT CHANGE
1896–1900	17.4	100
1901–1905	16.7	96
1906–1910	16.3	94
1911–1915	10.5	60

SOURCE: Strumilin, "O zakonomernostiakh vosproizvodstva naseleniia," p. 125; figures based on A. G. Rashin, *Naselenie Rossii za 100 let* (Moscow, 1956).

The population increase that followed the abolition of serfdom and introduction of full-scale capitalism was primarily achieved by lowering the death rate. This was also the case in other countries of the West. According to Strumilin, hired labor was considerably more productive than the labor of the serfs.

The development of capitalism was accompanied by technical progress, a rise in the standard of living, and a rise in the general educational level of the population. Complex machinery had to be run by men of skill and training. All this produced an environment that reduced mortality. A. G. Rashin's demographic research [36] demonstrates that even a very small improvement in the literacy of Russian mothers had immediate consequences in lowered infant mortality and consequently the mortality of the whole population. Table 6 illustrates these trends with reference to the European part of the Russian Empire.

The problem of causal primacy of various social factors was not entirely resolved by the contributions of Academician Strumilin, but it had received considerable illumination. At the same time, Strumilin's insistence that present Soviet demographic trends are in many ways akin to those of capitalist countries represented an act of considerable courage and scholarly forthrightness. The most recent Soviet studies of current trends tend to corroborate Strumilin's generalization based on the 1934 data. This represents another important step taken by Soviet sociologists toward the reestablishment of sociology's scholarly rectitude.

TABLE 6

Growth in the European Part of Russia
(Per 1,000 Population)

YEARS	BIRTH RATE	MORTALITY	INCREASE
1861–1870	50.2	36.9	12.3
1871–1880	50.4	36.4	14.0
1881–1890	50.4	35.5	14.9
1891–1900	49.2	34.2	15.0
1901–1905	47.7	31.0	16.7
1906–1910	45.8	29.5	16.3
1911	45.0	27.4	17.6
1912	43.7	26.5	17.2
1913	43.1	27.4	15.7
1861–1914	48.9	34.0	14.9

SOURCE: Strumilin, "O zakonomernostiakh vosproizvodstva naseleniia," p. 125; figures based on Rashin, *Naselenie Rossii za 100 let.*

SOCIOLOGY OF EDUCATION AND SOCIAL STRATIFICATION

A study of vocational plans and occupational mobility of secondary-school graduates is the best-known empirical research conducted by the new Soviet sociologists.[37] Since it was performed by a dozen sociologists at Novosibirsk University, headed by Vladimir N. Shubkin, the study is generally referred to as the Novosibirsk study. It is impressive in its methodological sophistication, its sound scholarship, and especially its political daring. Without any doubt the study has paved the way for future objective exploration of Soviet society. Frank reporting of results of the study disproved the contention of a number of Western scholars that no such study could be performed by Soviet sociologists under the current regime.

The study, conducted with the acknowledged support of party officials, was intended to provide a series of factual details on the occupational problems of young people in Soviet society in order to facilitate more effective social planning for the future. Research was begun in 1962 with the construction of a questionnaire and its pretesting on 300 secondary-school seniors selected from both urban and rural schools. In the spring of 1963 the questionnaires were sent to all the secondary schools of the Novosibirsk region, and in addition to the 10 percent of the schools that did not offer a complete secondary education. School officials were requested to distribute them to all of the 4,427 members of the graduating class and to abstain from any kind of influence over the students' answers. The laboratory received back 2,940 completed questionnaires, or 66.4 percent of the graduating seniors. In the fall of 1963, additional questionnaires on postgraduate activity, whether work or study, were distributed to the people who had completed the previous questionnaires. Sixteen percent of the follow-up questionnaires were not completed. For a preliminary rapid processing of this information, 280 of the combined questionnaires were selected for statistical analysis. For the purposes of sampling, respondents were grouped into eight distinct categories: (1) males of the city of Novosibirsk, (2) females of the city of Novosibirsk, (3) males from medium-sized cities of the region, (4) females from medium-sized cities, (5) males from small towns, (6) females from small towns, (7) males from villages, and (8) females from villages. By taking every tenth questionnaire in each of the eight categories, the researchers obtained a sample of 103 males and 177 females.

The same mailing, with fairly similar results (3,000 returned questionnaires), was repeated in the spring of 1964 in order to study the reliability of the initial responses, as well as to ascertain the stability of the social processes under study. In the same year the Leningrad sociologists used the same questionnaire to study 7,000 seniors of the Leningrad region. In 1965 Soviet sociologists, in cooperation with sociologists in Poland, again collected similar information with the aid of a revised questionnaire obtained by a cooperative agreement of both parties. The exact number of questionnaires collected in the course of this investigation has not been made public as yet.

The initial reports of the study are extremely interesting and rich in the kind of data on Soviet society that were never available earlier. Only a cursory glimpse of the data can be provided in this review. One interesting finding, illustrating the new objectivity of the Soviet social sciences, pertains to the disparity between the vocational plans of secondary-school graduates and their execution of these plans.

In the further analysis of the problem it was revealed, among other

TABLE 7

Personal Plans of Graduates and Their Realization *

PLANS	MEN (%)	WOMEN (%)	BOTH (%)	ACTUALITY	MEN (%)	WOMEN (%)	BOTH (%)
Planned to work.....	8	8	8	Went to work...	26	35	32
Planned to work and continue part-time studies	7	14	12	Went to work and con-tinued part-time studies ...	2	3	3
Planned to study.....	85	78	80	Studied	48	41	44
Total	100	100	100	Total	100 †	100 †	100 †

* Results of complete 1963 mailing.
† Includes other responses in addition to the three categories tabulated.
SOURCE: V. N. Shubkin, "Molodezh vstupaet v zhizn," *Voprosy filosofii*, 19, no. 5 (May, 1965): 62.

things, that the ability to pursue further studies and occupational preparation had a high correlation with the family's social position. Shubkin
makes the following candid generalization of the data:

Thus, while we categorically oppose any broad interpretation of these
selective data, we do have grounds for affirming that the paths through
life taken by young people from various social groups today show significant
divergences. Of every 100 secondary-school graduates coming from families
of collective-farm members and state-farm workers, only 10 continued to
study after completion of secondary school and 90 went to work, while
of every 100 graduates coming from the families of urban non-manual
persons, 82 continued their studies and only 15 went to work.[38]

The study revealed that most seniors formulating their plans for the
future are trying to escape the undesirable social position of their
parents. Very few of the respondents wish to work either in the field of
agricultural production or in the service occupations. The great majority
desires work either in the field of industrial production or in the professions. Significantly, children of agricultural laborers seem to be well
aware that professional occupations are beyond their dreams.

The data below and others like them force the authors to conclude
that unless something is done soon to change the social meaning of agricultural and service occupations, Soviet society is likely to be faced with
a tremendous shortage of workers in these fields. Up till now, service
occupations and agricultural production have been glorified in the Soviet
press without any other objective attempt being made to improve the

TABLE 8

*Family's Social Position Related to Personal Plans
of Graduates and Their Realization**

	PLANS			ACTUALITY		
GROUPS TO WHICH PARENTS BELONG	WORK	WORK WITH STUDY	STUDY	WORK	WORK WITH STUDY	STUDY
Urban intelligentsia	2%	5%	93%	15%	3%	82%
Village intelligentsia	11	13	76	42	......	58
Workers in industry and construction	11	6	83	36	3	61
Workers in transport and communications	......	18	82	55	......	45
Agricultural workers	10	14	76	90	......	10
Service personnel	9	15	76	38	3	59
Other	12	3	50	63	12	25
Percent of total	7	10	83	37	2	61

* Results of the 10 percent sample selected from the responses of the 1963 secondary-school graduates.
SOURCE: V. N. Shubkin, "Molodezh vstupaet v zhizn."

lot of people filling these positions. Shubkin and his colleagues maintain that much more than this has to be done literally to save these occupations. Youth desires a different way of life, not simply better remuneration for its services. Young people desire comforts and cultural stimulation that are now offered only in cities. At the same time, they also desire occupations that will permit greater creativity and open a greater variety of opportunities for their talents.

The uneven opportunities to study beyond secondary education for the different social groupings of Soviet youth are social in character and have only a small relationship to the abilities of these young people. Comparing the average grades received by the seniors with the educational attainment of their mothers and fathers, one finds that ability is pretty well distributed among all groupings. This is as it should be if we assume that ability and intelligence are equally distributed among all men. It is to the credit of Soviet teachers that these figures reflect their distribution of rewards according to the students' performance rather than their social position in Soviet society.

TABLE 9

Social Position of Fathers and the Inclinations of Children

	DESIRED OCCUPATIONS OF CHILDREN				
FATHER'S OCCUPATION	INDUSTRIAL PRODUCTION & CON- STRUCTION	AGRI- CULTURAL PRODUCTION	SERVICE OCCU- PATIONS	PROFESSIONS	TOTAL %
Industrial production and construction	35%	....%	5%	60%	100%
Agricultural production	88	12	......	......	100
Service occupations	56	4	4	36	100
Professions	25	1	3	71	100

SOURCE: V. N. Shubkin *et al.*, "Kolichestvennye metody v sotsiologicheskikh issledovaniiakh problem trudoustroistva i vybora profesii," in *Kolichestvennye metody v sotsiologii*, ed. A. G. Agabegian, G. V. Osipov, and V. N. Shubkin (Moscow: Izdatelstvo "Nauka," 1966), p. 191.

TABLE 10

Relationship between the Education of Parents and the Grades of Secondary-School Seniors

	AVERAGE GRADE *	
EDUCATION OF PARENTS	ACCORDING TO FATHER'S EDUCATION	ACCORDING TO MOTHER'S EDUCATION
Lower than 4 grades	3.83	3.54
4–6 grades	3.74	3.60
7–9 grades	3.70	3.83
10 grades	3.92	3.76
Secondary specialized education	3.82	4.00
College education	3.96	3.95

* Based on a 5-point grading scale, with 5 as the top grade.
SOURCE: V. N. Shubkin *et al.*, "Kolichestvennye metody," p. 204.

The sociologists also failed to discover a significant difference between the material standard of living of students and their school performance. The figures show that it affects only the male students in the very lowest income bracket.

TABLE 11

Relationship between Income and School Performance of Seniors

INCOME IN RUBLES (FOR EACH MEMBER OF THE FAMILY)	AVERAGE GRADE *		
	ALL STUDENTS	MALES	FEMALES
Under 20	3.66	3.14	3.82
21–40	3.72	3.68	3.75
41–60	3.92	3.69	4.07
61–80	3.85	3.83	4.12
81–100	4.06	3.87	4.20
Above 100	3.97	3.96	4.00

* Based on a 5-point grading scale, with 5 as the top grade.
SOURCE: V. N. Shubkin *et al.*, "Kolichestvennye metody," p. 203.

It is impossible to summarize here all the salient points of the study. It includes much information pertaining to significant shifts in Soviet occupational life which is only indirectly related to the structure of Soviet social stratification. Soviet society has always afforded women easier access to the various professional occupations often reserved to males in Western societies. According to the present study, however, more and more women are choosing either humanitarian or biological disciplines for further study. The males, on the other hand, are almost uniformly opposed to entering these professions, and prefer to specialize in technical and physico-mathematical sciences. Soviet sociologists are puzzled by these changes and express a certain apprehension. In their words, "Whatever the causes of such phenomena, society is hardly to be served by the prospect of having all the engineers males, while doctors and teachers are females." [39]

Whatever else can be said about this study, Soviet sociologists have begun to concern themselves with the social problems facing their society in the most admirable way. While serving their society, they also produced a sociological study worthy of international attention.

SOCIOLOGY OF LEISURE

Another important survey of modern Soviet society is the study of leisure and its uses conducted by the Institute of Public Opinion under the auspices of the official Komsomol daily, *Komsomolskaia pravda*. The study, directed by B. A. Grushin and based on a carefully stratified sample of 2,730 interviews, is a frank exploration of the nonworking hours of Soviet urbanites.[40]

Stratified sampling categorized the Soviet urban population according to:

1. Economic and geographic distribution, to account for all Soviet cities and their different functions.

2. Size of city: under 10,000 population, 10,000–100,000, 100,000–500,000, above 500,000.

3. Occupation: laborer, technical professional personnel, professional employed outside industry, office worker, student, pensioner, housewife.

4. Sex.

5. Age: 16–24, 25–29, 30–39, 40–59, 60 and above.

6. Education.

7. Marital status.

8. Number of children under 16 years of age.

9. Living conditions: separate dwelling, separate apartment, part of an apartment, dormitory, no permanent housing.[41]

The study began in 1963 and took three years to reach the publication stage. In the first major report of the study, Grushin took considerable pains to establish the representativeness of the survey by comparing the population categories represented in the survey with the categories of the total Soviet urban population. As it stands, the study is the first Soviet survey to explore the whole of Soviet urban society.

One of the many findings of this study revealed that working hours vary from one occupational category to another. As in the United States, the higher the education and occupational status of the individual, the more hours he is likely to spend at his work. Nine hours and more of daily work are reported by 6.5 percent of laborers, 12.1 percent of clerical workers, 17.3 percent of technical professional personnel, and as much as 38.8 percent of the professionals employed outside factories.

The study of leisure by Soviet sociologists is always referred to as the study of nonworking time. They point out that nonworking time cannot be equated with leisure time, since much of it is spent in shopping, cooking, cleaning, and transportation to and from work, as well as in child care. Shopping, cooking, and washing alone take up to one hour for 7.7 percent of urbanites, between one and two hours for 29.4 percent, between two and three hours for 16.3 percent, and over three hours daily for 28 percent of urbanites. Although nontechnical professionals spend more hours at their work, many of their nonworking hours

TABLE 12

Actual Length of a Working Day
(Percent of All Respondents)

NUMBER OF HOURS	LABORERS	TECHNICAL PRO- FESSIONAL PERSONNEL	PRO- FESSIONALS OUTSIDE INDUSTRY	OFFICE WORKERS
Less than 6 hours	0.5%	......%	3.1%	1.0%
6 hours	3.4	4.7	11.6	3.4
7 hours	65.8	48.0	24.8	57.9
8 hours	22.5	25.9	21.7	22.2
9 or more hours	6.5	17.3	38.8	12.1
No answer	1.3	4.1	......	3.4
Total	100.0	100.0	100.0	100.0

SOURCE: B. A. Grushin, "Kak vy provodite svobodnoe vremia?" *Komsomolskaia pravda*, February 24, 1966, p. 3.

are spent in providing for the necessities of life, thus limiting their opportunities for the pursuit of leisure.

The categories of the Soviet population most deprived of free time are those of employed women and housewives, whose duties include preparing meals and standing in queues while shopping. Time spent on daily routines is also positively related to the size of cities: the larger the city, the longer it takes to perform the various chores. Free time is also related to age. Two hours or more daily are spent on household chores by 24.7 percent of persons under 25 years of age, by 44.9 percent of persons between the ages of 25 and 29, by 48.1 percent between the ages of 30 and 40, by 51.1 percent between the ages of 40 and 50, and by as many as 61.8 percent of persons 60 years old or older. It is the retired grandmothers and grandfathers who generally perform the functions of baby-sitters, housekeepers, and shoppers in the families of their working sons and daughters, and this fact is reflected in the figures of this survey.

Grushin concludes that the average worker has little if any time for leisure pursuits. If one spends from 8 to 9 hours a day on sleep and other physiological necessities, a minimum of 1 to 1½ hours on transportation and similar efforts associated with work, and a minimum of 3 to 4 hours on daily chores, which include 1 to 1½ hours on child care, the total hours spent are already between 13 and 14.

Despite the limited time at their disposal, Soviet citizens do pursue

TABLE 13

Time Spent on Daily Routine of Shopping, Cooking, and Cleaning *
(Percent of All Respondents)

NUMBER OF HOURS	TOTAL SAMPLE	MEN	WOMEN	LABORERS	TECHNICAL PROFESSIONAL PERSONNEL	PROFESSIONALS OUTSIDE INDUSTRY	OFFICE WORKERS	STUDENTS	PENSIONERS	HOUSEWIVES
None	13.9%	22.1%	6.5%	14.6%	14.1%	13.9%	12.4%	27.0%	11.1%	1.2%
Up to 1 hour	7.7	12.5	3.2	9.4	12.6	8.5	7.4	11.4	1.5	1.2
1–2 hours	29.4	35.1	24.3	34.5	33.0	37.9	30.9	49.3	10.0	3.8
2–3 hours	16.3	14.4	18.0	19.5	22.0	23.2	17.7	4.7	12.2	3.8
Over 3 hours	28.0	9.3	44.9	18.7	15.7	16.2	21.9	4.7	55.1	85.8
No answer	4.7	6.6	3.1	2.3	2.6	0.3	9.7	2.9	10.1	4.2
	100.0%	100.0%	100.0%	99.0%	100.0%	100.0%	100.0%	100.0%	100.0%	100.0%

* This table does not include time devoted to child care.
SOURCE: Grushin, "Kak vy provodite svobodnoe vremia?" *Komsomolskaia pravda*, February 24, 1966, p. 4.

leisure activities, generally on weekends and in the time snatched between and during various work activities and daily routines. Their
various leisure pursuits are detailed in the following valuable two tables.

TABLE 14

Selected Leisure Practices
(Percent of All Respondents)

POPULATION CATEGORIES	NEWSPAPER READING *	MAGAZINE READING †	BOOK READING ‡	RADIO LISTENING *	TELEVISION WATCHING †
Total	89.3%	72.3%	75.3%	78.9%	45.3%
Males	92.5	73.8	79.7	78.3	43.0
Females	86.5	71.0	71.2	79.5	47.5
Laborers	90.4	67.3	74.6	75.8	44.5
Technical professional personnel	94.4	91.2	86.5	76.3	54.2
Professionals outside industry	93.0	82.0	73.5	81.3	43.2
Office workers	92.2	86.1	75.5	78.5	39.0
Students	83.0	68.7	85.0	77.6	51.2
Pensioners	83.4	65.4	68.0	87.3	50.0
Housewives	78.7	56.3	73.0	83.2	45.4
Moscow	92.1	81.4	81.3	81.1	76.9
Cities, Type I (over 500,000 pop.)	91.8	75.0	80.2	71.0	79.4
Cities, Type II (100,000–500,000 pop.)	94.1	75.5	75.2	83.2	47.4
Cities, Type III (10,000–100,000 pop.)	83.6	68.1	72.6	81.3	24.7
Cities, Type IV (below 10,000 pop.)	91.2	65.8	67.0	82.9	17.6
Below secondary education	82.8	61.1	66.7	79.5	36.7
Secondary education	94.6	75.9	81.6	79.9	49.3
Higher education	94.7	90.5	82.5	74.5	55.0
16–24 years	91.1	76.2	88.9	83.6	47.6
25–29 years	98.4	89.2	86.7	89.7	46.6
30–39 years	78.2	63.0	66.6	66.7	42.1
40–59 years	75.5	59.1	58.9	70.6	42.8
60 years and older	81.1	65.7	60.9	85.5	49.4

* At least several times a week.
† At least several times a month.
‡ At least several times a year.

TABLE 14 (Continued)

Selected Leisure Practices
(Percent of All Respondents)

POPULATION CATEGORIES	ATTENDANCE AT MOVIES †	THEATER ATTEND- ANCE ‡	TOURIST TRAVEL AND OUTINGS OUTSIDE CITY ‡	STROLLING AND HIKING *	GAMES AND OTH ACTIVITI WITH CHILDRE?
Total	73.3%	42.2%	31.1%	44.7%	40.5%
Males	74.4	40.3	33.9	45.1	39.1
Females	72.3	43.9	28.5	44.3	41.8
Laborers	75.6	38.7	32.7	43.8	43.9
Technical professional personnel	80.2	61.9	44.7	43.2	38.5
Professionals outside industry	81.3	48.8	36.3	35.5	37.9
Office workers	72.1	44.4	32.6	37.5	45.4
Students	87.0	51.8	37.7	58.7	6.7
Pensioners	56.6	31.2	13.6	53.5	29.0
Housewives	67.1	41.4	26.7	43.5	66.6
Moscow	72.2	50.8	54.9	49.8	31.1
Cities, Type I (over 500,000 pop.)	64.4	61.5	39.2	49.7	44.0
Cities, Type II (100,000–500,000 pop.)	78.5	49.7	31.7	44.8	39.2
Cities, Type III (10,000–100,000 pop.)	76.3	29.6	28.2	46.4	38.2
Cities, Type IV (below 10,000 pop.)	68.8	11.1	19.8	21.2	45.2
Below secondary education	66.4	28.0	21.2	29.8	42.0
Secondary education	79.2	50.3	37.9	51.2	44.7
Higher education	72.4	56.2	36.6	39.1	40.5
16–24 years	84.1	49.9	42.6	54.5	21.7
25–29 years	92.5	46.5	38.1	45.9	52.3
30–39 years	61.9	37.8	31.1	34.0	64.3
40–59 years	52.7	37.8	22.6	33.5	41.4
60 years and older	56.3	29.7	13.0	56.9	47.1

* At least several times a week.
† At least several times a month.
‡ At least several times a year.
SOURCE: Grushin, "Kak vy provodite svobodnoe vremia?" *Komsomolskaia pravda*, February 25, 1966,

TABLE 15

Selected Leisure Practices
(Percent of All Respondents)

POPULATION CATEGORIES	TELEVISION WATCHING *	ATTENDING SYMPHONIC AND LITERARY CONCERTS †	ATTENDING OPEN-AIR CONCERTS †	VISITING GALLERIES AND MUSEUMS †
Total	37.5%	17.8%	36.6%	24.0%
Males	36.1	17.1	36.7	23.9
Females	38.7	18.6	36.3	24.0
Laborers	36.5	13.2	38.4	21.9
Technical professional personnel	48.7	36.0	37.7	32.9
Professionals outside industry	33.2	31.0	40.9	31.6
Office workers	31.6	17.5	43.5	22.0
Students	41.1	31.6	47.9	41.0
Pensioners	40.5	11.8	15.6	19.9
Housewives	42.2	14.0	30.6	15.9
Moscow	63.1	13.9	48.2	66.1
Cities, Type I (over 500,000 pop.)	68.1	26.0	36.8	31.5
Cities, Type II (100,000–500,000 pop.)	38.6	18.6	43.6	29.0
Cities, Type III (10,000–100,000 pop.)	19.4	12.5	34.7	11.1
Cities, Type IV (below 10,000 pop.)	12.9	7.6	24.1	10.6
Below secondary education	31.8	10.1	28.2	15.1
Secondary education	39.3	16.4	43.0	26.2
Higher education	46.4	35.4	37.0	31.4
16–24 years	39.7	25.4	54.6	26.6
25–29 years	35.0	19.3	46.6	21.9
30–39 years	36.7	14.5	29.2	14.8
40–59 years	38.2	12.9	22.8	16.0
60 years and older	38.5	11.3	13.4	17.5

* At least several times a week.
† At least several times a year.

TABLE 15 (Continued)

Selected Leisure Practices
(Percent of All Respondents)

POPULATION CATEGORIES	ATTENDING SPORTS EVENTS †	AN EVENING OF DANCING *	PARTICIPATING IN ARTISTIC CREATION †	PARTICIPATING IN SPORTS †
Total	31.9%	21.4%	14.0%	21.6%
Males	45.4	24.8	14.7	30.1
Females	19.7	18.2	13.4	13.9
Laborers	37.8	29.3	17.0	25.2
Technical professional personnel	47.0	14.1	9.2	22.7
Professionals outside industry	26.2	10.0	11.5	21.7
Office workers	35.3	19.4	14.3	17.3
Students	45.0	49.8	32.9	49.9
Pensioners	7.1	1.9	2.7	7.6
Housewives	15.2	7.0	5.6	8.9
Moscow	40.5	15.0	9.5	28.6
Cities, Type I (over 500,000 pop.)	33.2	17.7	15.7	23.8
Cities, Type II (100,000–500,000 pop.)	32.6	19.4	9.8	20.4
Cities, Type III (10,000–100,000 pop.)	34.6	27.9	16.6	22.9
Cities, Type IV (below 10,000 pop.)	15.8	14.1	12.3	12.3
Below secondary education	25.9	19.5	9.6	13.8
Secondary education	36.3	25.2	18.4	26.1
Higher education	31.5	11.0	20.2	20.7
16–24 years	40.4	51.5	27.3	40.7
25–29 years	35.4	25.7	16.7	22.4
30–39 years	28.1	6.6	10.7	13.9
40–59 years	21.9	2.2	3.7	11.7
60 years and older	5.6	2.1	3.8	7.8

* At least several times a month.
† At least several times a year.

TABLE 15 (Continued)

Selected Leisure Practices
(Percent of All Respondents)

POPULATION CATEGORIES	HOBBIES †	VISITING AND ENTERTAINING GUESTS *	VISITING RESTAURANTS, BARS, AND CAFÉS *
Total	25.6%	64.1%	13.7%
Males	42.0	60.8	23.3
Females	10.6	67.0	5.0
Laborers	27.6	68.5	18.9
Technical professional personnel	44.8	69.2	22.7
Professionals outside industry	28.6	44.8	8.5
Office workers	25.5	62.3	12.1
Students	26.9	53.0	11.4
Pensioners	17.8	62.3	6.4
Housewives	8.8	70.4	3.2
Moscow	33.1	55.8	16.8
Cities, Type I (over 500,000 pop.)	21.9	64.5	10.2
Cities, Type II (100,000–500,000 pop.)	30.5	64.8	13.6
Cities, Type III (10,000–100,000 pop.)	25.1	64.4	16.0
Cities, Type IV (below 10,000 pop.)	25.7	61.1	17.0
Below secondary education	22.1	66.4	13.7
Secondary education	26.1	69.1	14.8
Higher education	30.8	53.6	12.7
16–24 years	29.8	71.9	17.4
25–29 years	27.3	64.4	17.9
30–39 years	24.8	58.7	12.5
40–59 years	22.7	58.8	10.9
60 years and older	17.8	40.2	5.2

* At least several times a month.
† At least several times a year.
SOURCE: Grushin, "Kak vy provodite svobodnoe vremia?" *Komsomolskaia pravda*, February 25, 1966, p. 4.

The final practical conclusion and recommendation of the study are that it is more important at this point to shorten the time it takes to care for the necessities of life than to cut the working time of the population. It is estimated that at the present time shopping, cooking, and cleaning alone take 100 billion hours of work yearly, equaling one year of life for 12 million people. These are extremely sensitive and politically daring proposals. To decrease the time spent on the necessities of life, the government would have to give more consideration to the needs of the individual. Soviet sociologists are both expressing and scientifically validating the desires of Soviet citizens for more effective servicing of their needs. It is not surprising, then, that there should continue to be considerable distrust generated by influential individuals toward the work of sociologists.

Conclusion

The revival of Soviet sociology began ten years ago. Today there is no longer any question as to the survival of the new science under Soviet conditions. Nor is there any question as to the compatibility of sociology with Soviet Marxism, for Soviet social scientists have succeeded in making sociology an essential part of Marxist thought.

An important question that remains is what kind of science will Soviet sociology be? Will it be primarily an administrative arm for fact gathering and planning? Will it be capable of turning itself into a theoretical discipline satisfying intellectual curiosity? Will its practitioners be freed from taboos of the past to conduct research and evaluate their findings objectively?

None of these questions can be answered with any certainty at this time. However, in the light of the international contributions by Soviet sociologists during the short period since the revival of the new discipline, the future of Soviet sociology looks very promising.

Notes

1. V. A. Yadov, "Problems and Facts of Sociology: Responsibility," *Literaturnaia gazeta*, November 12, 1966, p. 2, trans. in *Current Digest of the Soviet Press*,

18, no. 48: 18. Translation from the *Current Digest of the Soviet Press*, published weekly at Columbia University by the Joint Committee on Slavic Studies, appointed by the American Council of Learned Societies and the Social Science Research Council. Copyright 1966, the Joint Committee on Slavic Studies. Reprinted by permission.

2. A. Yanov, "Time to Mature," *Komsomolskaia pravda*, June 2, 1967, p. 2, trans. in *Current Digest of the Soviet Press*, 19, no. 25: 16.

3. For a more detailed discussion of the revival of Soviet sociology, see Alex Simirenko, ed., *Soviet Sociology: Historical Antecedents and Current Appraisals* (Chicago: Quadrangle Books, Inc., 1966); George Fischer, *Science and Politics: The New Sociology in the Soviet Union* (Ithaca, N.Y.: Center for International Studies, Cornell University, 1964); Fischer, "Current Soviet Work in Sociology," *American Sociologist*, 1, no. 3 (May, 1966): 127–32; Elizabeth Ann Weinberg, "Soviet Sociology, 1960–1963," multilithed (Cambridge: Center for International Studies, Massachusetts Institute of Technology, October 1, 1964).

4. Yadov, "Problems and Facts of Sociology"; see n. 1.

5. Fischer, *Science and Politics*.

6. Ye. V. Belyaev, G. I. Saganenko, Iu. A. Dmitriev, S. I. Golod, "Vsesoyuzny simpozium sotsiologov," *Voprosy filosofii*, 20, no. 10: 156–65.

7. Anatoly A. Zvorykin, "A Structural Analysis of Publication in the Field of Social Studies in the Soviet Union, 1960–1965," *Social Research*, 33, no. 4 (Winter, 1966): 552–61.

8. Belyaev *et al.*, "Vsesoyuzny simpozium sotsiologov."

9. Yadov, "Problems and Facts of Sociology"; see n. 1.

10. See V. Mikhailov and V. Perevedentsev, "Great Expectations," *Literaturnaia gazeta*, no. 24 (June 14, 1967), p. 10, trans. in *Current Digest of the Soviet Press*, 19, no. 25: 18.

11. See Talcott Parsons, "The Editor's Column," *American Sociologist*, 1, no. 5 (November, 1966): 240.

12. See, for example, an attack on sociologists exploring economic problems by an economist, Academician L. Leontyev, in *Literaturnaia gazeta*, May 26, 1966. Attacks by philosophers are indicated by Mikhailov and Perevedentsev, "Great Expectations," p. 18.

13. Mikhailov and Perevedentsev, "Great Expectations," p. 19. Translation from the *Current Digest of the Soviet Press*, published weekly at Columbia University by the Joint Committee on Slavic Studies, appointed by the American Council of Learned Societies and the Social Science Research Council. Copyright 1967, the Joint Committee on Slavic Studies. Reprinted by permission.

14. *Sociology in the U.S.S.R.* contains research reports on the Gorky study. Ostensibly, several books are in preparation, but only one has been published so far. See G. V. Osipov, V. A. Tikhomirov, S. F. Frolov, and I. I. Chansli, eds., *Rabochii klass i teckhnicheskii progress* (Moscow: Izdatelstvo "Nauka," 1965).

15. See V. N. Shubkin, "Social Mobility and Choice of Occupation," in *Industry and Labour in the U.S.S.R.*, ed. G. V. Osipov (New York: Barnes & Noble, 1966), pp. 86–98. For an initial Western evaluation of the study, see Fischer, "Current Soviet Work in Sociology," p. 129, and Simirenko, *Soviet Sociology*, pp. 31–33.

16. B. A. Grushin and V. V. Chikin, *Ispoved pokeleniia* (Moscow: Komsomol, 1962).

17. See Grushin, "Kak vy provodite svobodnoe vremia?" *Komsomolskaia pravda*, February 24–26, 1966. For a more detailed discussion of studies conducted by the Institute of Public Opinion, see Grushin, "K probleme kachestvennoi reprezentatsii v vyborochnom oprose," in *Opyt i metodika konkretnykh sotsiologicheskikh issledovanii*, ed. G. E. Glezerman and V. G. Afanaseva (Moscow: Izdatelstvo "Mysl," 1965), pp. 61–107.

18. For a further discussion see "Sostoianie i khod sotsialnykh issledovanii v

strane," in N. V. Novikov, G. V. Osipov, and G. A. Slesarev, eds., *Sotsialnye issledovaniia* (Moscow: Izdatelstvo "Nauka," 1965), pp. 202–15.

19. Osipov, "Osnovnie cherty i osobennosti marksistkoi sotsiologii," in *Sotsiologiia v SSSR*, ed. Osipov (Moscow: Izdatelstvo "Mysl," 1966), pp. 42–43. (Osipov's italics; my translation. Another translation of the article is found in *Soviet Sociology*, 5, no. 1 [Summer, 1966]: 7–12).

20. See Fischer, "Current Soviet Work in Sociology"; Alex Simirenko and Stephen P. Dunn, "Survey Research in the U.S.S.R." (in process).

21. See Yanov, "Time to Mature," pp. 16–17.

22. See Simirenko, *Soviet Sociology*, pp. 25–29.

23. See, for example, the following recent titles: M. V. Nechkina *et al.*, eds., *Revolutsionnaia situatsiia v Rossii v 1859–1861 gg* (Moscow: Izdatelstvo "Nauka," 1965); N. V. Ustiugov *et al.*, eds., *Voprosy sotsialno-ekomincheskoi istorii i istochnikovedeniia perioda feodalizma v Rosii* (Moscow: Izdatelstvo Akademii Nauk SSSR, 1961); L. A. Kogan, *Krepostnye voldnodumtsy: XIX vek* (Moscow: Izdatelstvo "Nauka," 1966); Yu. Ya. Kogan, *Ocherki po istorii russkoi ateisticheskoi mysli XVIII v.* (Moscow: Izdatelstvo Akademii Nauk SSSR, 1962).

24. See S. G. Strumilin, "Zabastovki i revolutsiia: 1850–1917 gg," in Strumilin, *Ocherki ekonomicheskoi istorii Rossii i SSSR* (Moscow: Izdatelstvo "Nauka," 1966), pp. 459–76.

25. According to a study by N. V. Pogozhev, the proportion of laborers concentrated in large industries in 1902 increases from 31.5 percent to 47.6 percent if all industries are included in the inspection. See Pogozhev, *Uchet chislennosti i sostava rabochkikh v Rossii* (St. Petersburg, 1906), pp. 45, 59–60.

26. It may be noted that the riots, disturbances, and conflicts with the police in the American Negro ghettos of today can also be correlated with the concentration of slum dwellers in these neighborhoods.

27. Some Western historians have recognized for some time the significant relationship between high concentration of Russia's industry and the revolutionary sentiment of its workers. See, for example, E. H. Carr, "Historical Background of the Russian Revolution," in *Soviet Society: A Book of Readings,* ed. Alex Inkeles and Kent Geiger (Boston: Houghton Mifflin Co., 1961), p. 29.

28. For one such excellent recent study, see V. M. Kabuzan, *Narodonaselenie Rossii v XVIII–pervoi polovine XIX v.* (Moscow: Izdatelstvo Akademii Nauk SSSR, 1963).

29. Strumilin, "O zakonomernostiakh vosproizvodstva naseleniia," in his *Izbrannye proizvedeniia* (Moscow: Izdatelstvo "Nauka," 1963), 1: 116–30.

30. *Ibid.*, p. 118.

31. It can be noted that these ideas were later restated in a popular form by Arsène Dumont in his principle of social capillarity. See Arsène Dumont, *La Morale basée sur la démographie* (Paris: Sliecher Frères, 1901).

32. Strumilin, "O zakonomernostiakh vosproizvodstva naseleniia," p. 118.

32. *Ibid.*, p. 119. Analysis made by other Soviet demographers based on the 1959 census figures also corroborates Strumilin's thesis. See L. S. Demin, "O nekotorykh osobennostiakh dinamiki naseleniia v SSSR," *Voprosy filosofii*, 20, no. 11 (November, 1966): 127–35.

34. Similar assumptions of the importance of population growth to social change have been postulated again in the 1950's by David Riesman, Reuel Denney, and Nathan Glazer in their famous *The Lonely Crowd* (New Haven, Conn.: Yale University Press, 1950).

35. Strumilin's case could also be strengthened by pointing out that slaves also have a tendency not to reproduce themselves, and that similar factors were probably operating in the reproduction of serfs.

36. A. G. Rashin, *Naselenie Rossii za 100 let* (Moscow, 1956).

37. The results of the study are still being processed and only partial results have been made available. In addition to the citation in n. 15, see Shubkin,

"Nekotorye voprosy adaptatsii molodezhi k trudu," in *Sotsialnye issledovaniia*, ed. Novikov, Osipov, and Slesarev, pp. 118-30; Shubkin, "Molodezh vstupaet v zhizn," *Voprosy filosofii*, 19, no. 5 (May, 1965): 57-70, trans. in *Soviet Sociology*, 4, no. 3 (Winter, 1965): 3-15; and Shubkin *et al.*, "Kolichestvennye metody v sotsiologicheskikh issledovaniiakh problem trudoustroistva i vybora profesii," in *Kolichestvennye metody v sotsiologii*, ed. A. G. Agabegian, G. V. Osipov, and V. N. Shubkin (Moscow: Izdatelstvo "Nauka," 1966), pp. 168-231. The last article is intended as a methodological discussion, but it furnishes more data than any previous publication.

38. Shubkin, "Youth Enters Life," pp. 10-11.

39. Shubkin *et al.*, "Kolichestvennye metody," p. 187.

40. Grushin, "Kak vy provodite svobodnoe vremia?"

41. Grushin, "K probleme kachestvennoi reprezentatsii," pp. 81-82.

Index

A Note on the Authors

DONALD D. BARRY received his Ph.D. from Syracuse University in 1963. Since then, he has been teaching in the Department of Government at Lehigh University, where he is presently an associate professor. He has contributed articles to *Soviet Studies, Survey, Rutgers Law Review, International and Comparative Law Quarterly, The New York Times Magazine,* and the book *Cases in American National Government and Politics,* edited by Tresolini and Frost. At the present time he is editing a volume for Leiden University's "Law in Eastern Europe" series on governmental tort liabilities in the east European countries.

BOHDAN R. BOCIURKIW, a native of the Ukraine, received his B.A. and M.A. degrees from the University of Manitoba and his Ph.D. in political science from the University of Chicago. He has taught at the University of Alberta in Edmonton, Alberta, Canada, since 1956, and is now professor of political science. He is past president of the Canadian Association of Slavists and is presently a member of the executive council of the Canadian Political Science Association. He has published a number of papers on Soviet politics and church-state relations in the U.S.S.R. in Canadian, American, British, French, German, and Ukrainian journals and symposia.

URIE BRONFENBRENNER is a social psychologist at Cornell University. For the past several years he has been conducting cross-cultural studies of child rearing in a number of countries, including the U.S.S.R. He has visited the Soviet Union many times, twice for extended periods as visiting scientist at the Institute of Psychology in Moscow. His concerns extend beyond science to application. In connection with the latter interest, he is a member of the Planning Committee for Project Head Start and of the Social Science Advisory Board to the U.S. Arms Control Agency. Among his published works are several edited volumes and many articles and chapters.

STEPHEN P. DUNN received his Ph.D. in anthropology from Columbia University in 1959, writing his dissertation on the modern Jewish community in Rome. Since then he has been studying directed culture change in the Soviet Union. A considerable part of his work has been done in collaboration with his wife, Ethel Dunn, and they are both currently associated with the Center for Slavic Studies, University of California, Berkeley. In 1964 he attended the Seventh International Congress of Anthropological and Ethnological Sciences in Moscow with the aid of a grant from the Wenner-Gren Foundation for Anthropological Research. Among his many works on culture change in the Soviet Union are

Cultural Processes in the Baltic Area under Soviet Rule (1966) and *The Peasants of Central Russia* (with Ethel Dunn, 1967). One of his articles was also published in *Sovetskaia etnografiia*. Among his edited works is the English translation of *The Peoples of Siberia* (1964). He is currently editor of *Soviet Sociology* and *Soviet Anthropology and Archeology*.

EUGENE KAMENKA, born in 1928, took first-class honors in philosophy at the University of Sydney and received his Ph.D. in social philosophy at the Australian National University, Canberra. He has taught moral and political philosophy at the Universities of Sydney and Singapore and is now senior fellow in the history of ideas at the Institute of Advanced Studies of the Australian National University. In 1965–66 he worked as a visiting research worker in the faculty of philosophy at Moscow State University, and in 1968 he visited the United States as senior fellow at the Research Institute on Communist Affairs, Columbia University, New York.

Dr. Kamenka's doctoral thesis, *The Ethical Foundations of Marxism*, published in London and New York in 1962, has been translated into Japanese (Tokyo: Iwanami, 1965) and Hebrew (Tel Aviv: Ayanoth, 1967), and two other books, *The Philosophy of Ludwig Feuerbach* and *Marxist Ethics*, were published in London in 1968. Dr. Kamenka is now working on a book on contemporary Soviet philosophy, emphasizing its comparative professionalization and the resultant disintegration of a Marxist philosophical system.

Collected works such as the present volume trace their origins, in the Soviet field, to the special issue of the *American Sociological Review*, June, 1944, titled "Recent Social Trends in the Soviet Union." WILLIAM M. MANDEL was an invited contributor on that occasion as well as a consultant in its planning. That year also saw the appearance of his first book, *The Soviet Far East and Central Asia*, although he had published in scholarly journals since 1941. His latest book is *Russia Re-examined* (revised edition, 1967). In 1947, at the Hoover Institution, Stanford University, he was one of the first two individuals in the United States to be awarded postdoctoral fellowships in a Slavic studies program. He teaches sociology at San Francisco State College, translates quarterlies covering the spectrum of social science in the U.S.S.R., is an associate of *Current Anthropology*, and has been awarded honorary memberships in organizations in geography and sociology. His most recent publication is "Reflection on the Soviet System," in Hendel and Braham, *The USSR after 50 Years* (1967). Mr. Mandel has made four visits to the U.S.S.R. over a span of thirty-five years, including one stay of a year's duration.

Born in Chicago, Illinois, in 1927, Professor ARTHUR P. MENDEL received his Ph.D. in history at Harvard University in 1956. He has taught Russian history at Roosevelt College (Chicago), the University of Iowa, New York University, and the University of Michigan, where he has been on the faculty since 1962. His principal areas of interest are Russian intellectual history and general Russian history of the nineteenth and twentieth centuries. Besides his principal monograph, *Dilemmas of Progress in Tsarist Russia*, he has published articles in various scholarly journals and has edited several books of readings and memoirs, most recently the memoirs of Paul Miliukov and P. A. Annenkov. In 1960 and 1965 he spent brief periods of research in the Soviet Union. On his most recent visit, in 1965, he submitted a questionnaire in historiography to Soviet historians in connection with a study from which the present article also derives. The questionnaire and the replies were later published in *Voprosy istorii* and, in translation, *History and Theory*.

JOHN MOLINO received his B.A. from Columbia College in 1963 with a dual major in experimental psychology and Russian literature. He holds an M.A. in psychology from Columbia University (1965) and will soon receive his doctoral degree. At Columbia he has taught and conducted experimental research in psychology. His chapter is the result of one year of study as an exchange student at Moscow State University (1965–1966).

WILLIAM R. SCHMALSTIEG was granted his doctorate by the University of Pennsylvania and is now a professor of Slavic languages at Pennsylvania State University. He has contributed numerous articles in the field of Baltic and Slavic linguistics to professional journals here and abroad and is co-author of the recently published *Introduction to Modern Lithuanian*. He has served as secretary and chairman of the Slavic linguistics section of the Modern Language Association's annual program and is currently an associate editor of *General Linguistics* and head of the Slavic linguistics section of the Modern Language Association's bibliography committee.

HOWARD J. SHERMAN is an associate professor at the University of California, Riverside. He has taught at Wayne State University (Detroit), the California Institute of Technology, and the University of California at Berkeley. He holds a Ph.D. in economics from the University of California at Berkeley and a *juris doctorum* (Jur. D.) from the University of Chicago Law School. His published books include *Macrodynamic Economics, Elementary Aggregate Economics*, and *The Soviet Economy* (forthcoming).

ALEX SIMIRENKO is an associate professor at the University of Nevada, and received his Ph.D. in sociology from the University of Minnesota in 1961. He is author of *Pilgrims, Colonists, and Frontiersmen: An Ethnic Community in Transition* (1964), a study of a Russian community in Minneapolis, Minnesota. He is also editor of *Soviet Sociology: Historical Antecedents and Current Appraisals* (Quadrangle Books, 1966). At the present time he is writing a book on *Soviet Society*.

ISIDORE ZIFERSTEIN, M.D., has been engaged in the practice of psychiatry and psychoanalysis, and in research and teaching, for the past thirty years. He is a member of the faculty of the Southern California Psychoanalytic Institute and a research consultant of the Postgraduate Center for Mental Health, New York. Formerly he was associate clinical professor of psychiatry at the University of Southern California.

His major research interests are group psychotherapy, group dynamics, and transcultural psychiatry. He has published extensively on these areas of research. From 1955 until 1963 he was engaged in the research project "A Study of the Psychotherapeutic Process" at the Psychiatric and Psychosomatic Research Institute, Mount Sinai Hospital, Los Angeles (Franz Alexander, director). Then, for a period of fifteen months in 1963 and 1964, he made direct comparative observations of psychotherapy in the Soviet Union. His contribution to this volume is a result of his research in transcultural psychiatry.